# Oprah

ALSO BY KITTY KELLEY

*Jackie Oh!*
*Elizabeth Taylor: The Last Star*
*His Way: The Unauthorized Biography of Frank Sinatra*
*Nancy Reagan: The Unauthorized Biography*
*The Royals*
*The Family: The Real Story of the Bush Dynasty*

# Oprah

A BIOGRAPHY

# Kitty Kelley

THREE RIVERS PRESS
NEW YORK

Library of Congress Cataloging-in-Publication Data
is available upon request.

ISBN 978-0-307-39487-3
eISBN 978-0-307-71877-8

Printed in the United States of America

BOOK DESIGN BY BARBARA STURMAN
COVER DESIGN BY DAVID TRAN
AUTHOR PHOTO BY BLACKMORE

10 9 8 7 6 5 4 3 2 1

First Paperback Edition

AGAIN AND ALWAYS—

FOR MY HUSBAND, JOHN

# Contents

*Foreword*                                    xi

$O$ne                                          1
Two                                           19
Three                                         44
Four                                          59
Five                                          81
Six                                          100
Seven                                        120
Eight                                        135
Nine                                         150
Ten                                          173
Eleven                                       193
Twelve                                       224
Thirteen                                     242
Fourteen                                     262
Fifteen                                      285
Sixteen                                      316
Seventeen                                    348
Eighteen                                     373
Nineteen                                     403
Twenty                                       438

*Afterword*                                   473
*Some Oprah Credits, 1984–2009*               479
*Notes*                                       485
*Bibliography*                                545
*Acknowledgments*                             549
*Photograph Credits*                          555
*Index*                                       557

## AUTHOR'S NOTE

This is a revised and updated edition of the original book published in 2010. All additions to the text run throughout the book and have been set in **boldfaced** type.

# Foreword

I MET OPRAH WINFREY when I was on a book promotion tour in Baltimore in 1981, and she was cohosting WJZ's morning show, *People Are Talking*, with Richard Sher. We sat down before the show began, and as I recall, Richard did most of the talking, while Oprah seemed a bit standoffish, which I didn't understand until later. He interviewed me on the air and then joined Oprah on the set with a compliment about our lively exchange. Oprah shook her head with displeasure. "I don't approve of that kind of book," she said. "I have relatives she wrote a book about and they didn't like it at all."

I looked at the producer and asked what in the world she was talking about. I understood what she meant by "that kind of book"—an unauthorized biography written without the subject's cooperation or control—but I was perplexed by her reference to my having written a book about her relatives. The only biography I had written at the time was the life story of Jacqueline Kennedy Onassis *(Jackie Oh!)*, and my research had not turned up any Winfrey relatives in that family tree.

The producer looked slightly uncomfortable. "Well . . . Oprah is close to Maria Shriver, plus she's very much in awe of the Kennedys. . . . I guess she considers herself part of the family in a way and . . . she knows they were upset by your book because it was so revealing . . . and . . . well, that's why we decided to have Richard do your segment."

I jotted down the exchange on the back of my book-promotion schedule, just in case the publisher asked how things had gone in Baltimore. I had no idea that twenty-five years later Oprah Winfrey would be a supernova in our firmament, and I would devote four years to writing "that kind of book" about her.

For the last three decades I've chosen to write biographies of living icons without their cooperation and independent of their control. These people are not merely celebrities, but titans of society who have left their imprint on our culture. With each biography the challenge has been to answer the question John F. Kennedy posed when he said, "What makes journalism so fascinating and biography so interesting is the struggle to answer the question: 'What's he like?'" In writing about contemporary figures, I've found the unauthorized biography avoids the pureed truths of revisionist history—the pitfall of authorized biography. Without having to follow the dictates of the subject, the unauthorized biographer has a much better chance to penetrate the manufactured public image, which is crucial. For, to quote President Kennedy again, "The great enemy of the truth is very often not the lie—deliberate, contrived and dishonest—but the myth—persistent, persuasive and unrealistic."

Yet I've never felt completely comfortable with the term *unauthorized,* probably because it sounds slightly nefarious, almost as if it involves breaking and entering. Admittedly, biography is, by its very nature, an invasion of a life—an intimate examination by the biographer, who tries to burrow into the marrow of the bone to probe the unknown and reveal the unseen. Despite my discomfort with the term, I understand why the unauthorized biography raises the hackles of its subjects, for it means an independent presentation of their lives, irrespective of their demands and decrees. It is not bended-knee biography. It does not genuflect to fame or curtsy to celebrity, and powerful public figures, accustomed to deference, quite naturally resist the scrutiny that such a biography requires. Oprah Winfrey was no exception.

At first she seemed sanguine when Crown Publishers announced in December 2006 that I would be writing her biography. She was asked her reaction, and her publicist responded, "She is aware of the book but has no plans to contribute." Six months later Oprah told the New York *Daily News,* "I'm not cooperating with it, but if she wants to write a book, fine. This is America. I'm not discouraging it or encouraging it." Then, with a wink, she added, "And you know I can encourage."

By April 2008 she had changed her attitude. In a webcast with Eckhart Tolle, author of *A New Earth,* she said, "I live in a world where people write things that are not true all the time.

Somebody's working on a biography of me now, unauthorized. So I know it's going to be lots of things in there that are not true."

I immediately wrote to Oprah, saying the truth was as important to me as it was to her. I repeated my intention to be fair, honest, and accurate, and again asked for an interview. I had written to her before—first as a matter of courtesy, to say that I was working on the book and hoped to present her life with empathy and insight. I wrote several times later, asking for an interview, but did not receive a response. I should not have been surprised, considering Oprah had written her own autobiography years earlier but withdrew it before publication because she felt it had revealed too much. Still, I kept trying, but after several more unanswered letters, I remembered what John Updike said when he was stonewalled by baseball great Ted Williams: "Gods do not answer letters."

Midway into my research, I finally received a call from Oprah's publicist, Lisa Halliday, who said, "Ms. Winfrey has asked me to tell you she declines to be interviewed." By then I had learned from Chicago reporters that Oprah had stopped giving interviews and responded to the press mostly through publicists rather than directly. If reporters persisted, as Cheryl Reed did when she was editor of the editorial page of the *Chicago Sun-Times*, Oprah's publicists provided a list of prepared questions and canned answers. "[Oprah is] always asked the same questions," the publicist told Ms. Reed. "[This is] how Miss Winfrey prefers to respond."

I told Ms. Halliday that I needed to be accurate in what I wrote and asked if Ms. Winfrey would be willing to check facts. Ms. Halliday said, "If you have questions of fact, you can reach out to me." So I tried, but each time I called Harpo, Ms. Halliday was unavailable. In the end it was Oprah herself who turned out to be a major source of information.

In lieu of speaking to her directly and having to rely on fragmented memories, I decided to gather every interview she had given in the last twenty-five years to newspapers and magazines and on radio and television in the United States and the United Kingdom, including Canada and Australia. I filed each—and there were hundreds—by names, dates, and topics, for a total of 2,732 files. From this resource I was able to use Oprah's own words with surety. Laid out on a grid, the information from these interviews, plus the hundreds of interviews I did with her family, friends, classmates, and coworkers, provided a psychological profile that I could never have acquired in any other way. Gathering these interviews given over more than two decades took considerable time, but once assembled and catalogued, they were invaluable in providing her voice. Throughout this book I have been able to cite Oprah in her own words, expressing her thoughts and emotions in response to events in her life as they occurred. Sometimes her public reflections did not jibe with the private recollections of others, but even the truths she shaved, as well as those she shared, added dimension to her fascinating persona.

Being one of the most admired women in the world, Oprah Winfrey is adored by millions for her many good works. She is an exemplar of black achievement in a white society, an African American icon who broke the barriers of discrimination to achieve unparalleled success. In a world that worships wealth, she is idolized not simply because of her net worth (approximately $2.4 billion), but because she made her fortune herself, without benefit of marriage or inheritance. Within publishing she is heralded as a heroine for bringing the joys of reading to millions, enriching the lives of writers as well as readers.

Yet as much as Oprah is loved, she is also feared, which is not unusual among society's giants. In writing about Frank Sinatra years ago, I found many people afraid to talk about a man connected to organized crime for fear of losing their limbs, or even their lives. With Nancy Reagan and the Bush family dynasty, the fears were of losing presidential access or a federal job, plus getting clobbered with an IRS audit. With the British monarchy, it was the fear of losing royal approbation or a possible knighthood. Writing about Oprah exposed a different kind of fear.

**"I was afraid of Oprah for twenty years,"** said her first cousin Jo Baldwin. **"She's dangerous . . . she told me if I ever opened my mouth [about what I know] she'd sue my pants off. . . ."**

Baldwin, an ordained minister in Mississippi, was not afraid of physical reprisals, but she feared the personal and professional retributions that could come her way because of Oprah's vast power and immense wealth. Consequently, Reverend Jo, as she is called, refused to talk about her famous relative for the hardback version of this book, but since its publication in April 2010 she has received tenure as a university professor at Mississippi Valley State and no longer feels that Oprah can threaten her livelihood. So she stepped forward in the summer of 2010 to tell her stories.

As is true of many in Oprah's family, her negative feelings stem from resentment over the way she has been treated. The power of Oprah's vast wealth makes most of her relatives quake. They want to be part of the luxurious life that she offers on occasion (her lavish Christmas presents, her birthday checks, even her hand-me-downs), but they chafe at the way she has dismissed them since she became famous and know that she does not cherish them as family.

"Shortly after I received my PhD in 1985 from the University of Wisconsin-Milwaukee, Oprah asked me where I was going to work," said Jo Baldwin. "I said I would be applying for a position at *Ebony* magazine as a copy editor. Oprah said she did not like Linda Johnson Rice [owner of *Ebony*] and I should come to work for her instead. So I did.

"I was to work for her for three years, but she fired me without notice after two years.... I heard from someone later that she got rid of me because she got tired of me talking about Jesus all the time.... Whenever something significant happened I would read her verses and passages from the Bible to keep her grounded, but Oprah preferred the teachings of Shirley MacLaine's books, such as *Dancing in the Light* and *Out on a Limb*, which Oprah made me read but I didn't think much of."

Jo Baldwin became estranged from Oprah after working for her. "I believe she wanted to take away my family's respect by implying I was a loser because she had fired me. I also believe that Oprah financially harmed me by preventing my novel from getting published. Mainly, though, she wanted to shame

**and humiliate me for being a follower of Jesus, as if to say, 'What is He doing for you that's so great?' Oprah inflicts emotional wounds that could lead to physical illness if they aren't healed. My faith kept me from getting sick."**

Since 1995 Oprah has required all her employees at Harpo and later at *O, The Oprah Magazine,* to sign confidentiality agreements, swearing never to reveal anything about her, her business, her personal life, her friends, or her associates to anyone at any time. Almost everyone who enters her realm must sign these nondisclosure contracts, and the prospect of being sued for breaking them keeps many—but not all—people silent. Surprisingly, I discovered that Oprah is as frightened of the unvarnished truths from the lips of her former employees as they are of her potential lawsuits.

Aside from those chained to confidentiality agreements, there were others afraid to talk simply for fear of offending someone famous, much like those who admired the fabled emperor's new clothes. This, too, was not unusual, except among journalists, normally as brave as marines and supposedly immune to celebrity worship. Considering that Oprah is the gold standard for marketing, a certain amount of hesitancy is understandable on the part of anyone who wants to sell products on her show, including journalists who long to write books that she will bless. When I called Jonathan Van Meter to ask about the effusive cover story he had written on Oprah for *Vogue,* he said, "I just can't talk to you . . . yeah, maybe I am scared . . . it just wouldn't help me to help you." He admitted—reluctantly—that he had put "all the negative bits" from his *Vogue* research into a profile of Oprah he later published in *The Oxford American.* "Not much circulation there," he said nervously.

When I called Jura Koncius of *The Washington Post,* she said, "I knew Oprah before she was Oprah, when she wore an Afro. . . . Every year at Christmas she would send a limo to get me to come on her Baltimore show to talk about holiday gifts . . . but I don't want to discuss my experiences, and I certainly don't want to be included in your long list of acknowledgments." Duly noted, Ms. Koncius.

My researcher received an even more heated response from Erin Moriarty of CBS-TV, who had roomed with Oprah for a couple of months in Baltimore. Since then Ms. Moriarty has regaled friends with her tales of Oprah during that time, and after hearing all those stories from others, I requested an interview. Unwilling to go on the record, Ms. Moriarty was less than cordial when she learned that her Oprah stories had traveled so far and wide.

**I saw the full force of Oprah's power and influence upon publication in April 2010, when some in the mainstream media boycotted this book. Larry King barred me from his CNN talk show because he did not want to offend Oprah. Joy Behar also closed the door, as did Barbara Walters, who went on *The View* to denounce unauthorized biographies, particularly this one, as simply "trying to get dirt." Since she had not read the book, I sent her a copy with a letter expressing disappointment in her public denunciation. She never responded. At the time she was negotiating with ABC for *The View* to be syndicated in the 4 P.M. time slot of *The Oprah Winfrey Show* in 2011 when Oprah retired from broadcast television. ABC refused to syndicate Ms. Walters's show, which she acknowledged lost her millions of dollars.**

Biographies, whether authorized or unauthorized, could never be written without the help of journalists, which is why I reached out to so many. Their work provides the first draft of history and lays the foundation for future scholars and historians. So I am grateful for the generosity I received, especially in Chicago, where journalists have been covering Oprah for twenty-five years and know her well. I also appreciate those too frightened to help, because their fears underscored the effect that Oprah has had on much of the media.

Over the years the woman who appears so warm and embracing on television has become increasingly wary and mistrustful of those around her, and from the research I've done for this book, I can certainly understand why she says she sometimes feels like an ATM. When her former lover from Baltimore was called for an interview, he said, "I need a cut of the take to talk." I wrote to him saying that I do not pay for interviews because it casts a cloud on the information being imparted, making it potentially unreliable and suspect. Such a transaction destroys the trust the reader must have in the writer that the information being disclosed is fair, honest, and accurate, and not coerced in any way or influenced by money. The man responded by email saying he really had not asked to be paid to talk about Oprah, and had never been paid to talk about her in the past, a claim later disputed by a tabloid editor.

During the course of writing I also received a call from a Chicago attorney representing a client who claimed "to have the goods on Oprah" and wanted to sell me his information. I was curious enough to ask if his client, who had worked with her, had signed one of Oprah's binding confidentiality agreements. "No," said the lawyer. "He's free and clear." His client's asking price: $1 million. Again, I said I do not pay for information.

I ended this book feeling much the way I did when I started: full of admiration and respect for my subject, and with the hope that this unauthorized biography will be received in the same spirit, if not by Ms. Winfrey herself, then by those who have been inspired by her, particularly women. For I've tried to follow President Kennedy's true compass and penetrate the myth in order to answer the eternal question: What's she *really* like? In the process I found a remarkable woman, hugely complicated and contradictory. Sometimes generous, magnanimous, and deeply caring. Sometimes petty, small-minded, and self-centered. She has done an extraordinary amount of good and also backed products and ideas that are not only controversial but considered by many to be harmful. There is a warm side to Oprah and a side that can only be called as cold as ice. She is not a First Lady, an elected official, or even a movie star, but she is a unique American personage who has left an indelible mark on society, even as she has sought to change it. She has made the American dream come true—for herself and for many.

KITTY KELLEY
*March 2010*

www.KittyKelleyWriter.com

FREE SPEECH NOT ONLY LIVES,
IT ROCKS.

—Oprah Winfrey
February 26, 1998

# Oprah

# One

OPRAH WINFREY blew into Chicago from Baltimore in December 1983 when a dangerous cold wave plunged the Windy City temperatures to twenty-three degrees below zero.

She had arrived to host a local daytime talk show and, on January 2, 1984, introduced all 233 pounds of herself to the city by marching in her very own parade, arranged by WLS-TV. She wore one of her five fur coats, a Jheri curl, and what she called her "big mama earrings." Waving to people along State Street, she yelled, "Hi, I'm Oprah Winfrey. I'm the new host of *A.M. Chicago*. . . . Miss Negro on the air."

She was a big one-woman carnival full of yeow, whoopee, and hallelujah. "I thought WLS was crazy when I heard they had hired an African American woman to host the morning show in the most racially divided city in America for their audience of suburban, white stay-at-home moms," said Bill Zwecker of the *Chicago Sun-Times*. "Happily, I was wrong."

Chicago was in for a lollapalooza of a ride. During Oprah's first week, her local morning show trounced the nationally syndicated *Donahue* show in the ratings, and within a year Phil Donahue, the master of talk show television, was packing his bags for New York City. Oprah continued her ratings rout and, having forced him to change his locale, she now compelled him to change his time slot, so as not to compete with her. By then she was on the verge of becoming nationally syndicated herself, having received a $1 million signing bonus when *The Oprah Winfrey Show* was sold in 138 markets. During that first year she became such an immediate sensation that she appeared on *The Tonight Show,* won two local Emmys, and was poised to make her movie debut in *The Color Purple.* Her "discovery" for the role of Sofia in that film had brought her a Cinderella following, and would later reward her with Golden Globe and Oscar nominations for Best Supporting Actress.

"I was just like Lana Turner at the soda fountain, only a different color," Oprah joked, telling the story of how Quincy Jones, in Chicago on business, had seen her on television one morning and called Steven Spielberg to say he had found the perfect person to play Sofia. "She is so fine," said Jones. "Fat and feisty. Very feisty."

Oprah spent the summer of 1985 filming the movie, which she later recalled as the happiest time of her life. "*The Color Purple* was the first time I ever remember being in a family of people where I truly felt loved . . . when people genuinely see your soul and love your soul, when they love you for who you are and what you have to give."

By that time she felt she was on the cusp of the kind of success she had always dreamed of for herself. "I was destined for great things," she said. "I'm Diana Ross, and Tina Turner, and Maya Angelou." Brimming with confidence, she told Steven Spielberg he should put her name on theater marquees and her face on the film's posters. "I am probably the most popular person in Chicago," she said. When Spielberg demurred, saying it was not in her contract, she chided him for making a big mistake. "You wait. You'll see. I'm going national. I'm going to be huge."

Spielberg did not change his mind, and Oprah did not forget. When she became as "huge" as she had predicted, he became a weed in her garden of grudges. She recounted their conversation thirteen years later in a 1998 interview with *Vogue:* "I'm gonna be on TV and people are gonna, like, know me. And Steven said, 'Really?' And I said, 'You might want to put my name on the poster for the movie.' He said, 'No, can't do that. . . .' And I say: 'But I think I'm really gonna be kinda famous.' Which is my favorite I-told-you-so, Steven, you should've put my name on that poster!"

A week before the movie's premiere Oprah decided to do a show on rape, incest, and sexual molestation. When management balked, she said she was going to be seen on the big screen in a few days in a film about the subject, so why not explore it first for her local audience. The station agreed, reluctantly at first, and then ran announcements asking for volunteers to talk about their sexual abuse on the air.

This particular show became Oprah's signature program—a victim who triumphs over adversity—and the start of the Oprah Winfrey phenomenon. No one realized it at the time, but that show would elevate her to national prominence and eventually make her a champion for victims of sexual abuse. During that program, she introduced a new kind of television that plunged her viewers into two decades of muddy lows and starry highs. In the process, she became the world's first black female billionaire and a cultural icon of near-saintly status.

"I am the instrument of God," she said at various times along the way. "I am his messenger. . . . My show is my ministry."

Oprah's show on sexual abuse was promoted for days in advance to draw an audience interested in "Incest Victims." Except for her small staff, no one knew what she intended to do, other than present a titillating subject, which she had been doing since she started on WLS. No one had any idea that she was about to blur the long-standing line in television between discussion and confession, between interviewing and self-revelation. Between objectivity and a fuzzy area of fantasy and factual manipulation.

On Thursday, December 5, 1985, Oprah began her 9:00 A.M. show by introducing a young white woman she identified only as Laurie.

"One out of three women in this country have been sexually abused or molested," she told her audience before turning to her guest.

"Your father started out fondling you. When did it lead to something other than fondling?"

"I think around between nine and ten," said Laurie.

"What happened? Do you remember the first time your father had sexual intercourse with you? What did he say to you, how did he tell you, what did he tell you?"

There was not a sound from the audience of mostly white women.

"He just told me that he wanted to make me feel good," said Laurie.

"Where was your mother?"

"She had gone on a trip somewhere—she was out of town. She was gone for three weeks and I stayed with my father for those three weeks."

"So he came into your room . . . and he started fondling you. That has to be a pretty frightening thing when you're nine years old and your father has sexual intercourse with you."

Laurie nodded but said nothing.

"I know it's hard to tell—I really do. I know how hard it is. When he was finished, what did he—or during this act—well, first of all, wasn't it painful for you?"

Laurie squirmed a bit. "Um. He used to tell me that he was sorry and that he would never do it again. A lot of times after he would do something, he would kneel down and make me pray to the Lord that he wouldn't do it anymore."

Moments later Oprah waded into the audience and planted her microphone in front of a middle-aged white woman in glasses.

"I was sexually abused, too," the woman said. "Well, my life kind of started like Laurie's with the fondling and . . . It resulted in a child who's now—he's thirty years old right now, but sixteen years of his life he's been in a state institution [for autism]."

"Were you sexually abused by a member of your family?"

The woman choked up as she admitted being impregnated by her father.

"So this is your father's child?" said Oprah.

"Yes. It happened very frequently—as with Laurie also— practically every day when my mother would go to work. One of the most horrible experiences that I can remember."

As the woman broke down and struggled to regain control, Oprah flung her arm around her and then burst into tears herself, covering her eyes with her left hand. With the mic in her right hand, she signaled to the control room. She said later it was to stop the cameras, but they kept rolling as she sobbed into the woman's shoulder. "The same thing happened to me," she said. "The fact that I had all these unfortunate experiences permeates my life."

For the next few seconds Oprah appeared to be discovering for the first time that what she had experienced as a nine-year-old child was indeed rape, a defilement so unspeakable that she had never been able to put it into words until that very moment. Her audience felt as if they were watching the fissures of a soul split open as she admitted her shameful secret. Oprah revealed that she had been raped by her nineteen-year-old cousin when she was forced to share a bed with him in her mother's apartment. "He told me not to tell. Then he took me to the zoo and bought me an ice-cream cone." Later she said she was also sexually molested by her cousin's boyfriend and then her favorite uncle. "I was continually molested from the age of nine until I was fourteen."

Oprah's staggering personal confession made national news, and she was applauded by many for her honesty and forthrightness. But her family vehemently denied her accusations, and some people suggested that she was trying to get publicity for her movie role, since she had never discussed her abuse with *anyone* before her public revelation. "I was so offended [by that]," she said later. "There was something in *Parade* magazine, a question published not too long ago: 'Was Oprah Winfrey really sexually abused, or was that just hype for the Oscars?' Well, I thought, it amazes me that somebody would think that I'd do that as hype. But I suppose it has been done. I suppose."

She said the management of her station was upset by her "shocking" revelations, and even twenty-three years later, Dennis Swanson, former vice president and general manager of WLS-TV, would not discuss the matter. Long credited with hiring Oprah and bringing her to Chicago, he would not comment on his reactions to her first show about sexual abuse.

At the time, Swanson and his promotion manager, Tim Bennett, were elated by Oprah's spectacular ratings but stung by press criticism of her emphasis on sex shows, particularly the show she had done on pornography. The TV critic of the *Chicago Sun-Times,* P. J. Bednarski, had castigated them and the "corporate morality" of WLS for allowing Oprah to devote an hourlong show to hard-core sex. "Shame on them," he wrote, and then blasted Oprah for inviting three female porn stars to talk about male organs, male endurance, and male ejaculations.

> In the saddest portion [of the show] there was a discussion of what they called on the air—the graphic lovemaking "money shot." That got a lot of laughs.... The Ask-the-Porn Stars program, amazingly, carried not a minute of discussion in which Winfrey stated, asked, or even worried that these X-rated stars were, in fact, cheap hucksters, talentless, sleazy skin traders. She barely wondered if these films demeaned women. Instead, she asked, "Don't you get sore?"

"For someone with the natural talent of Winfrey, it was telling evidence she's got some growing up to do," Bednarski wrote, before adding that Oprah's porn show got a 30 percent share of the 9:00 A.M. Chicago audience, much larger than usual. "It also got mentioned all around town and got its own column right here." The column's headline: "When Nothing's Off Limits: Oprah Winfrey Profits from Porn Stars' Appeal."

Oprah understood the axiom of television: She who gets ratings rules. "My mandate is to win," she told reporters. During crucial "sweeps" weeks she insisted on "bang-bang, shoot-'em-up" shows, for which her producer, Debra DiMaio, led the eureka hunt, with Oprah weighing in with her own ideas. "I'd love to get a priest to talk about sex," she said. "I'd love to get one to say, 'Yes, I have a lover. I worship Jesus and her. Yes, I love her and her name is Carolyn.'"

In her race for ratings during Black History Month, Oprah booked members of the Ku Klux Klan in their white sheets and cone hoods. She also did a show featuring members of a nudist colony who sat onstage naked. Only their faces were shown on television, but the studio audience got a full frontal view, so management insisted the show be taped. "That will allow us to make sure nothing that's not supposed to be seen on TV will get on," said Debra DiMaio. Management also said that each member of the audience who arranged to attend had to be called and reminded that the guests would be nude. "No one was turned off," said DiMaio. "On the contrary, they were excited. I mean, what fun."

Oprah admitted to being nervous during the nudist show. "I pride myself in being real honest, but on that show I was really faking it. I had to act like it was a perfectly normal thing to be interviewing a bunch of naked people and not look. I wanted to look into the camera and say, 'My God! There are penises here!' But I couldn't. And that made me real nervous."

When she told her bosses she wanted to do "Women with Sexual Disorders" and interview a woman who had not had an orgasm once during her eighteen-year marriage, and then interview the male sex surrogate who gave her orgasm lessons, and then a young woman so sexually addicted that one night she had twenty-five men in her bed, the program director blanched.

"Management doesn't want problems, but they want ratings," Oprah said. "I told them I'll be decent and I was. They don't understand what women feel, and I do. Men think, for instance, that if you do a show about mastectomy, you can't show a breast. I say you have to show the breast."

The day after her sexual disorders show, the WLS switchboard lit up with irate callers, so Oprah asked her producer to come onstage and invited comments from her studio audience.

"Yesterday's show was gross," said one woman. "I don't know how else to describe it. Absolutely degrading."

"There are millions of women who never experience sexual pleasure," said Oprah. "We had six hundred and thirty-three calls from women yesterday after the show, on the computer. We made lots of women feel they are not alone."

"With so many quality subjects, why go to the bottom of the barrel?"

DiMaio fielded that question: "What's bottom of the barrel

for one person may not be for someone else. We feel good about shows in which we talk about problems, whether it's incest or agoraphobia or lack of orgasm."

Oprah stepped in. "It bothers me when we're accused of being sensational and exploitive. We are not. We are a caring group of people." A brief pause. "Sometimes we make mistakes."

Oprah might have been referring to one of her earlier shows, titled "Does Sexual Size Matter?" During a discussion about penis size, she had blurted out, "If you had your choice, you'd like to have a big one if you could. Bring a big one home to Mama!" You could almost hear the collective gasp of 2.95 million TV households in the Chicago market. When the local media had picked themselves off the floor, most were sputtering. P. J. Bednarski said that Oprah had "stretched the limits of taste," but Alan G. Artner wrote in the *Chicago Tribune* that Oprah was simply being natural in the way that many people are when "blindly and without guile their self-absorption leads them to play the jester."

Later Oprah promised reporters that when she went national she would not say the word *penis* without giving her audience fair warning. "Now I can say *penis* whenever I want. There. I just said it," she whooped. "Penis, penis, penis."

By then she had reporters dancing on strings. They loved her colorful copy and could not conjure adjectives fast enough to describe her. "Big, brassy, loud, aggressive, hyper, laughable, lovable, soulful, lowdown, earthy, raw, hungry," wrote Howard Rosenberg, TV critic for the *Los Angeles Times.* Another critic confessed, "I don't care if she's a mile wide and an inch deep, she's irresistible." *The Philadelphia Inquirer Magazine* dubbed her show the *National Enquirer* of the Air. "It raises the Lowest Common Denominator to new and lower depths. It's a yeasty mix of sleaze, freaks, pathos, tack, camp, hype, hugs, hollers, gush, fads and tease marinated in tears."

Her audience was intoxicated by her raunchy brew. Taping bumpers for an upcoming show, she was supposed to read, "Tuesday on *A.M. Chicago:* Couples who suffer from impotency." After flubbing the line twice, she said, "Next week on *A.M. Chicago:* Couples who can't get it up."

Discussing a new diet, she turned to her audience and said, "Oh, yeah. That's the one that makes your bowel movements smell better."

During the show on impotence, a solemn middle-aged man said that following his corrective surgery, his testicles had inflated to the size of basketballs. "Wait a minute," hollered Oprah. "How do you walk with testicles the size of basketballs?"

On another show she interviewed a woman who claimed to have been seduced by seven priests. "What did you do when the priest pulled his pants down?"

"Nothing," said the woman. "But then he took my hand." Oprah rolled her eyes, and her audience roared. They loved her irreverence, her inappropriate comments, and her outrageous questions.

"Why did you become a lesbian?" she asked one woman.

On another show, a sociologist described how having a roommate could lead to having a lesbian relationship, and Oprah emphatically announced, "Then I'm never getting a roommate."

During an interview with a department store official in charge of loss prevention, she asked, "What happens when you catch people stealing? Do they really lose body control? I mean, do they break down and wet themselves?"

Not even celebrities were spared. She questioned Brooke Shields: "Are you really a nice girl?" She asked Sally Field if Burt Reynolds wore his toupee in bed. She blasted Calvin Klein for his advertising. "I hate all those jeans ads. They all have tiny little butts in those ads." She queried Dudley Moore how a man as short as he was could sleep with women who were so tall. "Luckily," said the movie star, "most of the extra length seems to be in their legs." Indeed, she seemed preoccupied with short men in bed. While discussing an appearance by Christie Brinkley, who was soon to marry Billy Joel, Oprah said to her producers, "Who really cares about her acting career? I want to know about her relationship with Billy Joel . . . [and] what's it like making love with a short guy? Billy Joel is pretty short, isn't he?"

Oprah became so popular that WLS extended the morning show to an hour and renamed it in her honor. They also gave her a theme song titled "Everybody Loves Oprah," which declared, "She's mod, she's hip, she's really got a style."

Dennis Swanson tried to capitalize on her popularity by putting her on the news. "He wanted to experiment with her as an anchor because her talk show was such a hit," said Ed Kosowski, a former WLS producer. "She anchored the four P.M. news for a week. It didn't work. It was a risk for the station and a gamble for Oprah. Swanson took her off immediately. She just didn't have the journalistic chops. Absolutely no authority. She's great at the girly-girl stuff, but she just can't do news."

Undeterred, Swanson sent his $200,000-a-year talk show host to Ethiopia, with anchors Mary Ann Childers and Dick Johnson, to report on Chicago's project to ship grain to the African nation in the midst of its famine. A week before she left, Oprah had started a televised diet on Channel 7, to lose fifty pounds, having made a public bet with comedienne Joan Rivers on *The Tonight Show*. The timing seemed awkward to P. J. Bednarski, who commented on the image of an overfed correspondent interviewing victims of starvation. "Isn't it a problem sending a personality who confesses to such a love for food to a country where there is so little?" he asked.

Oprah agreed. "You're right. It's sick, isn't it?"

FOR A FEW DAYS after her sexual abuse show, she tried to placate management by not talking about rape and incest. But when she saw the show's ratings, the letters that poured in, the calls to the WLS switchboard, and the reactions of women on the street, she knew she had given voice to a taboo torment that many women had suffered. She had found an issue that resonated with her predominantly female audience, so she pushed for more shows on sexual abuse. In the process, she fostered an image of herself as anti-male, because so many of her shows presented men as pigs. However, she became a heroine to women and a champion for children.

With that show, and her confession of what she had endured as a child, Oprah became more than a talk show host who entertained by trolling the raw side of the street. As someone who had suffered and survived and shared her pain, she became an inspiration for victims who felt defeated by adversity.

She was not the first to give voice to the sordid defilement of child abuse. She had been preceded by writers such as Maya Angelou (*I Know Why the Caged Bird Sings*), Toni Morrison (*The Bluest Eye*), and Alice Walker (*The Color Purple*), but Oprah had the megaphone of television, and she used it to reach women shackled by the shame of what had been done to them as children. "What I think is that sexual abuse of children is more common than uncommon in this country," she said in 1986. "You get five women in one room, and you can get three of them to admit it." Her own confession, plus her subsequent shows exploring the devastation of sexual molestation, became the strongest force in society to help women begin to heal and recover their lives.

- "Incest Victims" (12/5/85)
- Serial killer John Wayne Gacy (2/11/86)
- "Men Who Rape and Treatment for Rapists" (9/23/86)
- "Sexual Abuse in Families" (11/10/86)
- The Lisa Steinberg death (2/87)
- "Men Who Have Been Raped" (11/87)
- Parents whose children have been hurt by babysitters (1988)
- Women who have borne children by their own fathers (1988)
- "I Want My Abused Kids Back" (1988)
- Rape and rape victims (11/7/88)
- "In Search of Missing Children" (8/14/89)
- "Rapists" (8/23/89)
- "Clergy Abuse" (9/14/89)
- "'She Asked for It' . . . The Rape Decision" (10/17/89)
- "Date Rape" (12/7/89)

- Truddi Chase, victim of multiple personality disorder, discusses her sexual abuse (8/10/90)
- How to protect yourself from abduction by a would-be rapist (1991)
- "Child Victims of Crime" (3/13/91)
- "Teaching Children How to Protect Themselves" (1993)
- Mothers who killed their children interviewed in prison (1993)
- Talk show effects on society, including abuse defense (2/22/94)
- "Teen Dating Violence" (8/12/94)
- "My Wife Was Raped" (10/10/94)
- "Married to a Molester" (5/23/95)
- "Children and Guns, Part I" (10/30/95)
- "Children and Guns, Part II" (10/30/95)
- "Domestic Violence Through the Eyes of a Child" (3/18/96)
- "Pedophiles" (5/31/96)
- "Women Abused During Pregnancy" (6/12/96)
- Follow-up to 1991 show on how to protect yourself from a rapist (1998)
- "Protect Yourself from Rape" (2/3/99)
- "Would You Know If Your Child Was Being Sexually Abused?" (3/25/99)
- "Abusive Teen Dating" (4/16/99)
- "The Husband with 24 Personalities" (6/17/99)
- "Little League Pedophiles" (9/24/99)
- "Kids Online: What Parents Need to Know" (10/1/99)
- "Tortured Children" (4/3/00)
- "Should Women Be Allowed to Abandon Their Babies?" (4/19/00)
- "Tortured Children Follow-up" (5/4/00)
- "Why Are These Child Killers Out of Prison?" (12/20/00)
- "A Child Called 'It' " (1/30/02)
- "Child Stalkers Online" (2/7/02)
- "What You Need to Know About Rape" (2/15/02)
- "Teen Dating Abuse" (2/28/02)
- "Sex Scandals in the Catholic Church" (3/28/02)

- "The Secret World of Child Molestation" (4/26/02)
- "Mothers Who Lose Control" (10/21/02)
- "Abductions: Children Who Got Away" (12/9/02)
- "Is There a Child Molester in Your Neighborhood?" (2/25/03)
- "Oprah Goes to Elizabeth Smart's Home" (10/27/03)
- "Confronting Family Secrets" (11/12/03)
- "In Prison for Having Teenage Sex" (2/26/04)
- "Kidnapped and Held Captive" (5/5/04)
- "Atrocities Against Children" (7/15/04)
- "This Show Could Change Your Life" (how to deter a rapist) (9/28/04)
- "I Shot My Molester" (10/1/04)
- "Sexually Abused Women Come Forward" (10/21/04)
- "The Day I Found Out My Husband Was a Child Molester" (5/11/05)
- "Molested by a Priest" (6/13/05)
- "When a Mother Secretly Thinks About Killing Her Children" (7/11/05)
- "When the One You Love Is a Pedophile" (8/2/05)
- "Captured by a Pedophile: The Shasta Groene Tragedy" (10/4/05)
- "The Oprah Show Captures Accused Child Molesters" (10/11/05)
- "Oprah Presents Another $100,000 Reward" (for capture of a child molester) (10/27/05)
- "Oprah's Latest Capture: From Boys' School Director to Most Wanted Pedophile" (1/17/06)
- "Oprah's Latest Capture: Hiding in Mexico, Turned in by a Friend" (3/7/06)
- "Ending the Cycle of Violence" (4/19/06)
- "The Child Rape Epidemic: Oprah One-on-One with the Youngest Victims" (4/20/06)
- "Female Teachers, Young Boys, Secret Sex at School" (4/27/06)
- "Teri Hatcher's Desperate Secret: *Desperate Housewives* Star Sexually Abused as Child" (5/2/06)

- "Ricky Martin on Children Being Sold into Sexual Slavery" (6/16/06)
- "What Pedophiles Don't Want You to Know" (9/28/06)
- "Why 15-year-old Jessica Coleman Killed Her Baby" (11/3/06)
- "Dad Kills Twins: The Truth About Depression" (11/14/06)
- "Miracle in Missouri: Shawn Hornbeck's Family's First Interview" (1/18/07)
- "The Little Boy Oprah Couldn't Forget" (child slavery in Ghana) (2/9/07)
- "Kidnapped as a Child: Why I Didn't Run" (2/21/07)
- "Beauty Queen Raped by Her Husband" (11/7/07)
- "A Suburban Mother's Nightmare Captured on Tape" (5/8 and 5/23/08)
- "Internet Predators: How Bad Is It?" (9/11/08)
- "Lured at 13: Held Captive as a Sex Slave" (4/15/09)
- "Released from Prison After Killing Her Father" (5/7/09)
- "Former Child Star Mackenzie Phillips' Stunning Revelations" (9/23/09)
- "Mackenzie and Chynna Phillips" (9/25/09)
- "Shattering the Secrecy of Incest: Mackenzie Phillips Follow-up" (10/16/09)

Some members of Oprah's family, who denied her own story of sexual abuse, accused her of presenting sensational shows on the subject simply for high ratings. She countered that their refusal to accept her story indicated their denial, their inability to face their own complicity in the matter, and the depth of shame all families endure because of sexual molestation.

As a champion for victims of child abuse, Oprah spoke to the Senate Judiciary Committee in 1991 to support mandatory sentencing of child abusers. "We have to demonstrate that we value our children enough to say that when you hurt a child, this is what happens to you. It's not negotiable." She hosted *Scared Silent: Exposing and Ending Child Abuse,* a 1992 documentary shown on PBS, NBC, CBS, and ABC, which became the most-watched documentary aired on national television to that date. In 1993 she initiated the National Child Protection Act, which established a database of convicted child abusers and became known as the Oprah Bill. Unfortunately, the legislation was not effective. The bill was supposed to provide information gathered from all states concerning sex offenders and violent felons to organizations working with children. Most states did not set up the procedures for the organizations to apply for background checks and, according to a June 2006 report by the U.S. Attorney General, the Oprah Bill did not have the intended impact of broadening background checks.

Years later she created Oprah's Child Predator Watch List at www.oprah.com, to help track down child sex offenders. In December 2005 there were ten men on the list, and fifteen months later five of them had been captured because Oprah had drawn attention to their cases. She offered to give a reward of $100,000 for information leading to the capture of any of the men on the list, and by September 2008 her company announced that nine of the men had been captured. In at least three cases Oprah paid out $100,000 to those who turned the men in.

Throughout the years she continued to do shows on sexual abuse. Some of those shows were gratuitous ("I Want My Abused Kids Back," "Call Girls and Madams," "Fathers Dating Their Daughters' Friends," "Women Who Turn to Lesbianism"), others were groundbreaking ("Sexual Abuse in Families," "Rape and Rape Victims," "How to Protect Yourself from Abduction by a Rapist"), but each show brought her closer to understanding what had happened to her.

Still, it took her a long time to comprehend the real destruction wreaked by child molestation. She learned that sexual abuse is a crime that continues its damage long after the predator is gone, sometimes leaving its survivors suffering from post-traumatic stress disorder many years later—but she did not think she was one of them. Initially, she asserted that she had sailed through her experience of rape completely unscathed. She was strong, sassy, confident. "It was not a horrible thing in my life," she said of her years of sexual abuse, adding that she let the fondling continue because she liked the attention. "And I think a lot of the confusion and guilt comes to the child because it does feel good. It really does."

Always more forthcoming with black publications, she admitted to *Ebony* in 1993, even as she testified before Congress that no child is responsible for being sexually abused, that she still felt in her case she must have done or said something provocative to encourage her molesters. "Only now am I letting go of that shame," she said.

In the days before she knew better, Oprah dismissed rape as sex, not violence. During her debut week in Chicago, the soap opera star Tony Geary was a guest. A woman in the audience asked about the *General Hospital* story line in which Geary's character commits rape. Oprah quipped, "Well, if you're going to get raped, you might as well be raped by Tony Geary."

It took many more shows for her to see the connection between the crime that had scarred her as a child and the ravages that followed—adolescent promiscuity, an unwanted pregnancy, abysmal relationships with men, gravitation to women, drug abuse, an obsessive need to control, and the compulsive eating that drove her weight up and down the scale for decades.

Rather than seek psychotherapy to deal with her wounds, she sought the salve of public confession on television, thinking that would be the best solution for herself and for others.

"A lot of me talking about myself has been as cathartic for me as it is for the guests on my show. I understand why they let a lot of it out, because once it's out there it doesn't hold you anymore. I mean, coming out and saying I was sexually abused did more for me than it did for anybody. I couldn't have done it any other way and still been me."

With that particular show she had identified herself as a victim, which gave her a platform of authority to address the issue, but she refused to be defeated by the abuse. As a result, she was rewarded with huge ratings, national attention, and waves of sympathy that inoculated her against criticism. Once she went public with her private shame, she wore it like a new hat, even adding to her official press biography that she was "a childhood victim of sexual abuse."

She began accepting invitations to speak at rape centers, address victims of incest, and raise money for children who had been molested. She testified before Congress, and got legislation proposed, passed, and signed into law by the president of the United States. Within a few months she felt safe enough to talk about her own rape in further detail.

"The guy was a cousin by marriage. I was nine and he was nineteen. Nobody else was home at the time. I didn't know what was happening. I'd never seen a man. I may not have even known that boys were different. I knew, though, that it was a bad thing, because it started with him rubbing me and feeling me. I remember it was painful. Afterwards, he took me to the zoo as payment for not telling anyone. I was still hurting and recall bleeding on the way there. That year I found out where babies came from and I lived in absolute horror that at any moment I was going to have a baby. For the entire fifth grade I got these stomach aches during which I would excuse myself to go to the bathroom so I could have the baby there and not tell anyone."

Many years later she talked about what had happened in her mother's house. "[T]he boyfriend of my mother's cousin . . . was a constant sexual molester of mine. And I just felt like this is what happens to you. I felt like I was marked, somehow. I thought it was my fault. . . . I thought I was the only person that had ever happened to, and it was very lonely and I knew in my spirit that it would not have been safe for me to tell. I felt in-stinctively that if I told I would be blamed, you know, because those were the days when people said, 'Well, you were fast any-way, you know?' Or else, like Pa says of Celie in Alice Walker's novel *The Color Purple*, 'She always did lie.'

"My abuser practically told everybody. He'd say, 'I'm in love with Oprah. I'm gonna marry her, she's smarter than all of you.' He would say it and we'd go off to places together. Everybody knew it. And they just chose to look the other way. They were in denial. And then there was this sick thing going on—my cousin who lived with us was also a battered woman. And I used to bargain with her boyfriend that he could have sex with me if he wouldn't beat her. I felt protective of her and I'd say, 'God, okay, I'll go with you if you promise not to beat Alice. And that's how it was. . . . It was just an ongoing, continuous thing. So much so that I started to think, you know, 'This is the way life is.' "

Oprah appeared to be so open with revelations about her intimacies on television that no one suspected she might be hiding secrets. Like comedians who cover their darkness with humor, she had learned to joke away her pain, and keep what hurt the most stuffed deep inside. She knew how to give just enough information to be amusing and to deflect further inquiry, which is one reason she insisted on taking control of her own public relations when her show went national. While she looked like she was telling the world everything about herself, she was actually keeping locked within more than she would share on television. She felt she needed to present herself as open, warm, and cozy on the air, and conceal the part of her that was cold, closed, and calculating. She was afraid she wouldn't be liked if people saw a more complex dimension to the winning persona she chose to present. "Pleasing people is what I do," she said. "I need to be liked . . . even by people I dislike."

Her personal victimization would shadow her shows for the next twenty years, influencing her choice of topics and guests, her book club selections, her charities, and even her relationships. She was forever trying to come to terms with what had happened in her mother's house. She used her sad childhood to try to help others as she tried to help herself, but without therapy, her struggle was never-ending, showing itself in a constant battle with weight—losing and gaining, bingeing and fasting. Her excessive need for control, plus the immense gratification she derived from being the center of attention, applause, and approval, had its roots in her adolescent sexual abuse. The need to climb out of that sordid hole would drive her toward unparalleled success, which brought the rich rewards of an extravagant lifestyle, a healing balm to growing up poor.

# $T$WO

THE LEGEND of Oprah Winfrey as a dirt-poor fatherless black child neglected by her teenage mother, who Oprah claimed carried her "in shame," took hold when Oprah began giving interviews in Chicago. "I never had a store-bought dress," she told reporters, "or a pair of shoes until I was six years old. . . . The only toy I had was a corn cob doll with toothpicks. . . ." She recalled her early years as lonely, with no one to play with except the pigs that she rode bareback around her grandmother's yard. "I had only the barnyard animals to talk to. . . . I read them Bible stories." The years with her welfare mother in Milwaukee were even worse. "We were so poor we couldn't afford a dog or cat, so I made pets out of two cockroaches. . . . I put them in a jar, and named them Melinda and Sandy."

She regaled her audiences with stories of having to carry water from the well, milk cows, and empty the slop jar—a childhood of cinders and ashes that was the stuff of fairy tales. Oprah morphed into Oprah-rella as she spun her tales about the switch-wielding grandmother and cane-thumping grandfather who raised her until she was six years old.

"Oh, the whuppins I got," she said. "The reason I wanted to be white was that I never saw little white kids get whippings," she told writer Lyn Tornabene. "I used to get them all the time from my grandmother. It's just part of Southern tradition—the way old people raised kids. You spill something, you get a whipping; you tell a story, you get a whipping. . . . My grandmother whipped me with switches. . . . She could beat me every day and never get tired."

Oprah played with race like a kitten batting a ball of yarn. "I was jes' a po' little ole' nappy-headed colored chile," she said of her birth, on January 29, 1954, in Mississippi, the most racist state in the nation. Rather than deal cards of recrimination, she spread her deck like a swansdown fan, teasing and titillating, as she slipped into dialect to talk about growing up in Kosciusko, Mississippi. "That place is so small you can spit and be out of town before your spit hits the ground," she said of the small community (population 6,700) where she was born in her grandmother's wooden shack beyond the county line.

"We were colored folks back then—that was before we all became Negroes—and colored folks lived outside the city limits with no running water. And y'all know what *that* means," she drawled. "Yes, ma'am," she said, rolling her big brown eyes. "A two-holer with nothin' but a Sears and Roebuck catalogue to wipe yo'self clean." She recalled her grandmother's outhouse with exaggerated shudders. "Oh, my sweet lord. The smell of that thang. . . . I was always afraid I was going to fall in."

Oprah said she prayed every night to have ringlet curls like Shirley Temple's. "I wanted my hair to bounce like hers instead of being oiled and braided into plaits with seventeen barrettes." She tried to reconfigure her nose, "trying to get it to turn up," by wearing a clothespin to bed every night. "Yes, I admit it," she told Barbara Walters. "I wanted to be white. Growing up in Mississippi [I thought that] white kids were loved more. They received more. Their parents were nicer to them. And so I wanted that kind of life."

Oprah's sister later dismissed the myth of grinding poverty. "Sure, we weren't rich," Patricia Lloyd told a reporter. "But Oprah exaggerated how bad we had it—I guess to get sympathy from her viewers and widen her audience. She never had cockroaches for pets. She always had a dog. She also had a white cat, an eel in an aquarium, and a parakeet called Bo-Peep that she tried to teach to talk."

Giving an interview to *Life* magazine in 1997, Oprah, then forty-three, broke down and sobbed over her miserable childhood, prompting the reporter to write: "Oprah was the least powerful of girls, born poor and illegitimate in the segregated South on a farm in Kosciusko, Mississippi. She spent her first six years there abandoned to her maternal grandmother."

Not everyone in her family agreed with the forlorn tone of that assessment. As her mother, Vernita Lee, put it when asked about her daughter's tendency toward self-dramatization, "Oprah toots it up a little." The family historian, Katharine Carr Esters, the cousin Oprah calls Aunt Katharine, was not so tolerant.

"All things considered, those six years with Hattie Mae were the best thing that could have happened to a baby girl born to poor kin," she said. "Oprah grew up as an only child with the full and undivided attention of every one of us—her grandparents, her aunts, uncles, and cousins, as well as her mother, who Oprah never mentions was with her every day for the first four and a half years of Oprah's life, until she went North to Milwaukee to find a better job. . . .

"Where Oprah got that nonsense about growing up in filth and roaches I have no idea. Aunt Hat kept a spotless house. . . . It was a wooden, six-room house with a large living room that had a fireplace and rocking chairs. There were three big windows with white Priscilla-style lace curtains. The dining room was filled with beautiful Chippendale furniture. And in Aunt Hat's bedroom she had this beautiful white bedspread across her bed that all the kids knew was off-limits for playing on."

At the age of seventy-nine, Katharine Carr Esters sat on the "Ladies Porch" of Seasonings Eatery in Kosciusko during the summer of 2007 with her good friend Jewette Battles and shared her recollections of Oprah's "growing-up years" in Mississippi.

"Now, you have to understand that I love Oprah, and I love all the good work she does for others, but I do not understand the lies that she tells. She's been doing it for years now," said Mrs. Esters.

"Well, her stories have a bitty bit of truth in them," said Mrs. Battles, "but I suppose that Oprah does embroider them beyond all recognition into stories that—"

"They are not stories," said the no-nonsense Mrs. Esters. "They are lies. Pure and simple. Lies . . . Oprah tells her viewers all the time that she and Elvis Presley's little girl, Lisa Marie, are cousins, and oh, Lord, that is a preposterous lie. . . . Yes, we have Presleys in our family, but they are no kin to Elvis, and Oprah knows that, but she likes to make out that she is a distant cousin of Elvis because that makes her more than she is."

Mrs. Esters is adamant about setting straight the family history. "Oprah wasn't raised on a pig farm. There was one pig. She didn't milk cows; there was only one cow. . . . Yes, they were poor—we all were—but Aunt Hat owned her own house, plus two acres of land and a few chickens, which made her better off than most folks in the Buffalo community. Hattie Mae did not beat Oprah every day of her life, and Oprah most certainly did not go without dolls and dresses. . . . Oh, I've talked to her about this over the years. I've confronted her and asked, 'Why do you tell such lies?' Oprah told me, 'That's what people want to hear. The truth is boring, Aunt Katharine. People don't want to be bored. They want stories with drama.'

"Oprah makes her first six years sound like the worst thing that ever befell a child born to folks just trying to survive. I was there for most of that time, and I can tell you she was spoiled and petted and indulged better than any little girl in these parts. . . . Every parent knows that a child's first six years lays the foundation for life, and those first six years down here with Hattie Mae gave Oprah the foundation for her self-confidence, her speaking ability, and her desire to succeed. What happened later in her adolescence—well, that was a different matter."

Mrs. Esters will not accept Oprah's colorful stories as merely fanciful. "She makes up stories to make more of herself, and that's not right. . . . She's not straight with the truth. Never has been. She claims that she didn't have as a little girl, but she did. You should've seen the clothes and dolls and toys and little books that Aunt Hat brought home for her. Hattie Mae was working for the Leonards then—they were the richest white people in Kosciusko—and they made sure that Oprah had everything their own little girls had. Now, it's true that the ribbons and ruffled pinafores and so forth were not brand-new; they were hand-me-downs from the Leonards, but they were still mighty fine. The Leonards owned the big department store in town, and their things were the best. Hattie Mae dressed Oprah like a little doll every Sunday and took her to the Buffalo Baptist Church, where she began saying her little pieces."

Aunt Katharine remembered Oprah as a precocious child, who walked and talked early. "She was always the center of attention because she was the only baby in the household. And she always wanted to have the spotlight. If adults were talking and she couldn't get their attention, she'd walk over and hit them to make them pay attention to her."

Vernita confirmed that her daughter was indulged by everyone, including her grandmother. "She [Hattie Mae] was strict, but Oprah got away with a lot of stuff that I never could, because she was the first grandchild. She was a sweet little girl but very bossy. She always wanted to be boss."

By the time she was three years old, Oprah was mesmerizing her grandmother's country congregation by reciting the story of Daniel in the lion's den. "I would just get up in front of her friends and start doing pieces I had memorized," Oprah once said. "Everywhere I went, I'd say, 'Do you want to hear me do something?'"

Oprah's grandmother Hattie Mae Presley was the grand-daughter of slaves. She raised six children while working as a cook for the sheriff of Kosciusko and keeping house for the Leonards, whom she called "good white folks." She was educated only as far as the third grade, and her husband, Earlist Lee (called Earless by the family), could not read or write his name. "But Aunt Hat certainly knew her Bible, and she taught those stories to Oprah. She also taught her the shape of letters, and then my father taught Oprah how to read, so by the time she was six years old she had learned enough to skip kindergarten and go right into the first grade," said Katharine Esters, the first person in her family to earn a college degree. "It took me twelve years of night school to get that diploma, but I finally did it. . . . I bought a thesaurus and read it like a novel."

Katharine's mother, Ida Presley Carr, named Vernita Lee's baby Orpah after the sister-in-law of Ruth in the Old Testament, but en route to the county courthouse to file the birth certificate, the midwife, Rebecca Presley, misspelled the biblical name, and Orpah became Oprah, never to be called anything else.

The birth certificate for Oprah Gail Lee contained another error, naming Vernon Winfrey as her father. "We found out years later that couldn't possibly have been true, but at the time, Bunny—that's what the family calls Vernita—named Vernon as the father because he was the last of the three men she said she had laid down with. And he accepted the responsibility. . . . He didn't realize the truth until years later, when he checked his service records and saw for sure he couldn't have given life to a baby born in January 1954. But by the time he found out the truth, Oprah had already called him Daddy."

Although Oprah came to appreciate her grandmother's work ethic, she recalled her years with Hattie Mae, whom she called "Mama," as miserable and unhappy. Still, before she died in 2007, Oprah's maternal aunt Susie Mae Peeler, who described Oprah as a sweet, smart youngster, said, "We all just adored her. We just worshipped her and everything. My mother, Hattie, gave Oprah everything she wanted her to have and everything Oprah wanted. And so we were poor people. But we got it for her. We dressed her real nice and everything. She went on and made something out of herself, too.

"Oprah claims she never had a store-bought dress, but she had more store-bought dresses than I had! She claimed she had no dolls, but she had lots of dolls—all kinds of dolls."

The closest Oprah came to revising her "no dolls" story was during her 2009 interview with Barbra Streisand, who said she had grown up so poor that she transformed a hot water bottle into her one and only doll. "Wow," said Oprah. "You were poorer than I was."

The black community began leaving Kosciusko in the 1950s when the town's biggest employer, the Apponaug Cotton Mill, closed. "Jobs became scarce and so a lot of us headed north to find work," said Mrs. Esters, describing what became the

largest population shift in American history, known as the
Great Migration. "During those years there wasn't an empty car
to be seen leaving town. We'd pack them full and drive to
Chicago and Detroit and Milwaukee in hopes of finding manu-
facturing jobs with better pay. All over the South, black grandmothers were raising their grandchildren because mothers and
fathers left for the North to get jobs and make money. There was
nothing to be had staying in the South. Cotton was not being
picked and folks wanted more than to be servants in the houses
where their kin had worked. Oprah's mother, who never finished
high school, worked as a domestic here, but she wanted something better for herself and her child, so I drove her to Milwaukee
[1958], where she lived with me until she got on her feet. . . . She's
lived there ever since, but I returned to Kosciusko in 1972."

Oprah's grandfather Earlist Lee died in 1959, when Oprah
was five years old. She recalls him only as a dark presence in her
life. "I feared him. . . . I remember him always throwing things at
me or trying to shoo me away with his cane." Hattie Mae, then
sixty and in ill health, could no longer care for her, so Oprah was
sent to live with her twenty-five-year-old mother, who by then
had given birth to another daughter, named Patricia Lee, born
June 3, 1959. Patricia's father was listed years later on her death
certificate as Frank Stricklen, although he and Vernita never
married. Vernita and her baby were living in a rooming house
run by the baby's godmother when Oprah arrived.

"Mrs. Miller [the landlady] didn't like me because of the
color of my skin," Oprah recalled. "Mrs. Miller was a light-
skinned black woman who did not like darker-skinned black
people. And my half sister [was] light-skinned, and she was
adored. It was not something that was ever said to me, but [it
was] absolutely understood that she is adored because she is
light-skinned and I am not."

Later, when she moved to Chicago, she expanded her views
on skin color, talking about Harold Washington, the city's first
African American mayor. "We're fudgies," she said, categorizing
her race by color, and revealing a leitmotiv that influenced her selection of male and female friends over the years. "There are

fudgies, gingerbreads and vanilla creams. Gingerbreads are the ones who, even though you know they're black, have all the features of whites. . . . Vanilla creams are those who could pass if they wanted to, and then there's folks like me and the Mayor. No mistakin' us for anything but fudgies."

Oprah's cousin, Jo Baldwin, remembered Oprah calling after reading Baldwin's novel *Louvenia, Belle's Girl*. "Oprah said, 'Hello. This is Louvenia calling.'

"I said, 'Oprah, is that you?'

"'This is Louvenia,' she said.

"I laughed. 'Oprah, you can't be Louvenia, because her character is based on how I look. But you can be Belle. She has the best lines anyway.'"

In Baldwin's novel Belle is Louvenia's dark-skinned, heavy-set mother, married to a light-skinned preacher's son, which accounts for her daughter's light tan skin.

"Hearing me say that she couldn't be Louvenia made Oprah real quiet . . . and unhappy."

Oprah maintained that because of her dark skin she had to sleep on the porch in the back of the rooming house, while her light-skinned sister slept with her mother in Vernita's bedroom. She said that discrimination made her feel ugly. "White people never made me feel less," she said years later. "Black people made me feel less. I felt less in that house with Mrs. Miller. I felt less because I was too dark and my hair was too kinky. . . . I felt like an outcast."

Katharine Esters responded sternly to Oprah's poignant memory. "This bothers me more than her corncob doll lies and her cockroach lies, because it plays into the damaging discrimination practiced by our own people," she said. "I'm a dark-skinned woman, Oprah's grandfather Earless was black enough to be painted by a brush, and Oprah is as dark as a preacher's prayer book, but when she says things like that she reminds me of my cousin Frank, who did not wish to be what he was and discriminated among his kin, preferring the lighter-skinned to the darker-skinned folks.

"Oprah slept on the porch in the back of the rooming house

only because Vernita had to take care of her baby and there was just one bedroom. That's it. Period. If Oprah was discriminated against because of her skin color, I'd tell you," said Mrs. Esters, a civil rights activist who worked for the Urban League in Milwaukee. "I believe in telling the truth—spiders, snakes, and all—because I believe some good can come from opening up dark secrets to the light. . . . Oprah puts too much stock on color. . . . I suppose that her wanting to be white makes her see things the way she does, but sleeping on the porch had nothing to do with her dark skin. The fact of the matter is that Oprah was no longer an only child when she came to Milwaukee. She was not the princess anymore or the center of everyone's attention. Her mother and the landlady fussed over the babies, not Oprah, and that was very hard for her."

Over the years Oprah's memories of growing up have become rife with disregard and discrimination. "The only photo I have of my grandmother she's holding a white child," she said at the age of fifty-one. Yet a published picture of Oprah's desk shows a photo of her grandmother with her arm draped lovingly around Oprah as a little girl, with no white child in sight. Yet Oprah recalled: "Every time she would ever talk about those white children there would be this sort of glow inside her. . . . No one ever glowed when they saw me."

Less than a year after Oprah moved to Milwaukee to be with her mother, Vernita had a third child, Jeffrey Lee, on December 14, 1960. His father was listed years later on his death certificate as Willie Wright, the man Vernita eventually hoped to marry but never did. After Jeffrey's birth she moved into the small apartment of her cousin Alice Cooper, and lived for a while on welfare. Taking care of three children became so difficult that Vernita sent Oprah to live with Vernon Winfrey in Nashville. "Vernita's lifestyle was not ideal at that time," said Katharine Esters, who claimed Vernita spent her welfare money on clothes and cosmetics, "so sending Oprah away was a blessing for her."

"That was the beginning of shuttling her back and forth between my house in Nashville and her mother's house in Milwaukee," said Vernon Winfrey many years later. "It was a mistake. King Solomon taught long ago that you can't divide a child."

Vernon, who married Zelma Myers in 1958, lived in a little brick house on Owens Street in East Nashville and worked for Vanderbilt University as a janitor. At that time, he still believed he was Oprah's father.

"So we welcomed Oprah and gave her a proper home with structure—schooling, regular visits to the library, a little bit of television, playtime, and church every single Sunday. I'd drive us to the Baptist church in my old 1950 Mercury and cover the seats to keep the lint off our clothes."

At church Oprah grabbed center stage. "She's never been a backseat person," Vernon said. "She always loved the limelight. One time she was a little louder than I wanted, and I told her, 'Honey, people see you when you're quiet, and they see you when you're loud. Nine times out of ten, you're better thought of when you're quiet.' I toned her down a little."

During the spring of 2008, Vernon Winfrey, then seventy-five and still working in the Nashville barbershop he'd opened in 1964, reflected wistfully on his daughter when she was seven and played in the backyard of his house. "I'd watch from the window as she and her little friends Lilly and Betty Jean played imaginary games. Those three would amuse themselves for hours, sitting in child-size chairs, which I placed in the speckled shade of our maple tree. . . . I still have those chairs, by the way. . . . From what I observed then, Lilly and Betty Jean didn't enjoy playing school as much as Oprah did. I think that's because she was always the teacher, always scolding her little playmates as she scrawled invisible lessons on a make-believe blackboard. Lilly and Betty Jean would sit attentively at imaginary desks, hoping against hope that Oprah didn't call their names during spelling bees. Can't say I much blamed them, because if they misspelled a word, there was trouble. Oprah would get her little switch, which was not at all imaginary, and spank the palms of their hands."

Oprah had learned from her grandmother how to punish.

"One day I confronted her," said Vernon. " 'Why don't you let your friends play the teacher sometimes?'

"She looked at me with the sweetest expression, all cute, and bewildered about how I could ask such a silly thing. 'Why, Daddy,' she informed me, 'Lilly and Betty Jean can't teach till they learn how to read.' "

Vernon related this incident almost exactly as it appeared in the 2007 book proposal he submitted to publishers. Working with the writer Craig Marberry, he had produced several sample chapters of an autobiography that he titled *Things Unspoken*.

"I wanted to write a book about my life—my mother and my father and their nine children and how we all came up in the South." As a black man born in Mississippi in 1933, Vernon faced challenges that he said his daughter would never know. "Oprah talks about Martin Luther King, and she can recite all his speeches, but she doesn't know anything about the struggle. I lived it. Oprah just got in on the fly up.... She reaped the harvest Dr. King sowed.... I can go back seventy years in that struggle, and I want to write about it.... I know that Oprah's a part of my life, of course, and I did right by her, but Oprah is not all of my life, and I don't have to tell her everything I do. I'm not her boy. I'm a grown man and I can do what I want as long as I stay at the side of the Lord. So, no, I didn't tell Oprah about my book beforehand."

During a public appearance in New York City in 2007, Oprah was stunned when a reporter asked about her father's plans to write a book. "That's impossible," she said. "I can assure you it's not true.... The last person in the world to be doing a book about me is Vernon Winfrey. The last person."

Vernon smiled wryly at Oprah's reaction. "She doesn't understand that my book is not all about her, but that's what she and that girlfriend of hers thinks.... When Oprah called me the next day she was just as mad as you please. She said, 'Daddy, are you really writing a book?' I told her yes. She was upset because she said she now looked like a liar to the reporters. She said I made her look like a fool.

"I said, 'Oprah, I'm entitled to tell my story, aren't I?'

"'Yes, Daddy, but it would have been nice if you had told me about it first.'

"Then Gayle King called me. 'Mr. Winfrey, how dare you do a book,' she said. 'No one cares about you. No one wants to read about you. The only reason anyone on earth would be interested in what you have to say is because of Oprah.' She called me here at the barbershop. I was standing right over there." He pointed to the gray phone on the wall. "I said to Gayle, 'Call my wife. She knows more about it than I do,' and I hung up on her.

"Gayle is nothing but a street heifer. . . . I've never been talked to like that, so disrespectful, in my life. I told Oprah later the only reason I didn't cuss Gayle out right then and there and call her the word that begins with *B* and sounds like *witch* was because I was cutting a preacher's hair and didn't want to talk ugly in front of him. But I told Oprah I would have nothing more to do with Gayle King ever again.

"Oprah said, 'The people who care about me are watching out for me and protecting me.'

"I said, 'When we had our troubles when you were a teenager, I left everyone else out of it, and that's how it should be between you and me now.'"

A proud man, Vernon Winfrey chafed under the yoke of his daughter's control, and they did not speak again for quite some time. "That all happened in May of 2007," he said. "I was very upset, and I had a stroke a few months later. Took me three months of physical therapy to recover, and I've finally calmed down now, but I still feel the same way about that dirt hog Gayle. She called me back after she spoke to Oprah, but even then she did not apologize. She said she did not think she had been disrespectful to me, but she was not the recipient of her words. I was. And in her words she told me I was not worth anything and that my life counted for nothing."

After Oprah's public objection to his book proposal, Oprah's father said that several potential publishers had backed off. "They now want her permission before they will proceed. . . ." He shook his head at the fear his daughter had instilled. "I've put the book aside for the time being because my cowriter is out of the country, but I intend to finish it ... despite what Oprah says. . . .

"It disappoints me that she has changed so much over the years. She's become too close to that woman Gayle, and she no longer believes in Jesus Christ as her savior. That's just not how I raised her."

If Oprah had seen her father's sixty-two-page book proposal, she would have realized that it was, as he said, as much about his life as the sixth of nine children born to Elmore and Ella Winfrey as it was about raising Oprah. What would concern her, though, was what he wrote about her "secrets, dark secrets. Some I didn't discover till she was a grown woman, till it was too late." He also expressed regret for having to be stern and hard on her during her teenage years and for not expressing his love as effectively as his discipline.

Still, he continued to disapprove of the "dark secrets" he discovered about the little girl he had raised. "She may be admired by the world, but I know the truth. So does God and so does Oprah. Two of us remain ashamed." He pointed to the sign behind his barber chair as if he were sending his daughter a message: "Live So the Preacher Won't Have to Tell Lies at Your Funeral."

The television set in Winfrey's Barber Shop is no longer tuned to Oprah's show at 4:00 P.M. on weekdays the way it once was, but one of her early publicity photos, unsigned, remains taped to the mirror behind Vernon's chair, next to a photograph of his Yorkshire terrier, Fluff. When it was noted that the photo of Fluff gets pride of place over Oprah's photo, Vernon smiled slyly. "So it does," he said. "I just love that little dog."

Vernon's role as Oprah's revered father came to an end in the summer of 1963, when he drove her to Milwaukee to spend a few weeks with her mother. "I never saw that sweet little girl again," he said. "The innocent child that I knew in Nashville disappeared forever when I left her with her mother. I shed tears that day because I knew I was leaving her in a bad environment that was no place for a young child, but there was nothing I could do about it."

Oprah agreed at the end of the summer to stay with Vernita because her mother said she was going to get married and wanted to have a real family. Besides, Oprah's life with "Daddy" and "Mama Zelma" in Nashville had been a bit too regimented, with only an hour of television a day, and never on Sundays. Vernita promised Oprah all the television she wanted in Milwaukee, and, ironically, it was that little bribe that led to a life-changing moment for her daughter.

"I stopped wanting to be white when I was ten years old and saw Diana Ross and The Supremes perform on *The Ed Sullivan Show*," Oprah said. "I was watching television on the linoleum floor in my mother's apartment [on a Sunday night]. . . . I'll never forget it. . . . It was the first time I had ever seen a colored person wearing diamonds that I knew were real. . . . I wanted to be Diana Ross. . . . I had to be Diana Ross."

The phones had started ringing in the inner cities of Detroit, Chicago, Cleveland, Philadelphia, and Milwaukee a few days before Christmas 1964: The Supremes were going to be on *The Ed Sullivan Show*, then the premier showcase for talent in America.

"Colored girls" on prime-time television were like Yankees in Atlanta—enough to give Southerners the vapors and sponsors the bends. But Ed Sullivan, who had an integrationist booking policy, was not to be deterred. He had introduced Elvis Presley to television audiences in 1956, and had launched the Beatles in America earlier in 1964. He was determined to present what he called "three colored gifts" from Motown who had produced three number one hits that year. His decision came five months after President Lyndon Johnson signed the Civil Rights Act, which put the federal government squarely behind the drive for racial equality in the country. Now Ed Sullivan was going to change the national mind-set.

Up to that point blacks had seen themselves portrayed on television primarily as scheming scalawags (*Amos and Andy*), wire-haired scamps (Buckwheat in *Little Rascals* and *Our Gang*), or "yes, ma'am" maids and "no, sir" chauffeurs. To see themselves presented with beauty and grace and elegance would be revolutionary, and to be applauded by whites was almost unimaginable.

The Supremes appeared fourteen times on *The Ed Sullivan Show* between 1964 and 1969, but the impact of their first appearance, on December 27, 1964, cannot be overstated. It was a clarifying moment for the country as both ends of the racial spectrum came together to be entranced and entertained by three exquisite young women singing "Come See About Me."

"Many felt pride seeing The Supremes [that evening]," recalled Diahann Carroll, the first African American woman to star in her own television series (*Julia*, 1968–1971). "Young people will have to understand, that period of dreams and civil rights taught all of us in entertainment how to find our stepping-stones. It taught us how to pull others up in a manner that was beneficial to all people."

As someone who started dreaming that night, Oprah never forgot how she felt watching The Supremes. "In those days, anytime you saw a black person on television, it was so rare that everybody called everybody else, saying: 'Colored people are on.' You'd miss the performance because by the time you called everyone, the act was over. I remember saying, 'What? A colored woman can look like that?' Another electrifying moment was seeing Sidney Poitier. I was watching the Academy Awards [in 1964] and Sidney Poitier won for *Lilies of the Field*. That was the first time I ever saw a black man get out of a limousine instead of driving one. . . . I remember thinking, 'If a colored man could do that, I wonder what I can do.' He opened the door for me."

Symbolically, cymbals clashed, drums rolled, and trumpets blew throughout black America that year. It was a new beginning for people of color to see their own portrayed with style and sophistication on television. Motown Music had invested thousands of dollars grooming The Supremes for mainstream stardom—charm school, makeup lessons, splendid wigs, beaded gowns, sparkling jewelry—and the investment paid off. Among the thousands of black children watching *Ed Sullivan* that evening were a six-year-old boy and a ten-year-old girl, both hypnotized by the dazzling style of the lithe lead singer. Each child would grow up to become a reflection of the glamour they saw in her that night. Michael Jackson in Gary, Indiana, and Oprah Winfrey in Milwaukee, Wisconsin, wanted nothing more in life than to be Diana Ross. She became their polestar.

The same year that The Supremes electrified America on television, Congress passed the Economic Opportunity Act as part of the nation's "War on Poverty." The legislation was later criticized for inefficiency and waste, but many blacks benefited, especially through the Head Start program for preschool children and the Upward Bound Program for high-school students. One of those kissed by the affirmative action of Upward Bound was Oprah, then a student at Lincoln Middle School, which was considered "the melting pot" of Milwaukee. The program director, Eugene H. Abrams, had noticed her in the school cafeteria reading a book, and recommended her as one of six black students—three girls, three boys—to integrate Nicolet High School in the wealthy country club suburb of Glendale.

Years later Oprah said that she had been given "a scholarship" to the privileged school, and was the only one in her class selected for that honor. "I was in a situation where I was the only black kid, and I mean the only one, in a school of two thousand upper-middle-class suburban Jewish kids. I would take the bus in the morning to school with the maids who worked in their homes. I had to transfer three times."

Being one of "the bus kids," as the other students called them, Oprah was noticed. "She stood out from the crowd," said Irene Hoe, one of five Asian students at Nicolet and a senior when Oprah was a freshman. "She did not live in the predominantly affluent, mostly white suburban neighborhoods of Milwaukee, which fed their children to our high school. . . . Back in those politically incorrect days . . . it might have been said that she did not 'belong.'"

No one recognized that displacement more acutely than Oprah, who suddenly saw how poor she was next to wealthy girls who wore different sweater sets every day of the week and had allowances for pizza, records, and milk shakes after school.

"For the first time I understood that there was another side," she said. "All of a sudden the ghetto didn't look so good anymore.

"In 1968 it was real hip to know a black person, so I was very popular. The kids would all bring me back to their houses, pull out their Pearl Bailey albums, bring out their maid from the back and say, 'Oprah, do you know Mabel?' They figured all blacks knew each other. It was real strange and real tough."

Mothers encouraged their daughters to invite "Opie" home after school. "Like I was a toy," she said. "They'd all sit around talking about Sammy Davis, Jr., like I knew him."

Oprah wanted to have money like the other kids, but her mother, working two jobs at the time, had none to spare. So Oprah began stealing from Vernita. "I started having some real problems," she said later. "I guess you could call me troubled—to put it mildly."

Her sister, Patricia, remembered Oprah stealing $200 from their mother, which was an entire week's pay. Another time she stole one of her mother's rings and pawned it. "Oprah said she'd taken the ring to have it cleaned. But Mom found the pawn ticket in a pillowcase and made Oprah get the ring back."

Her relatives recall Oprah as an out-of-control teenager who would do anything for money. At one point she wanted to get rid of her "ugly butterfly bifocals." She asked her mother to buy her a new pair of octagonal glasses like the kids at Nicolet wore. Vernita said she could not afford the expense. Oprah was determined to get the new glasses.

"I staged a robbery, broke my glasses and pretended I was unconscious and feigned amnesia. I stayed home from school one day and stomped the glasses on the floor into a million pieces. I pulled down the curtains, knocked over the lamps, and cut my left cheek enough to draw blood. I called the police, laid myself down on the floor, and waited for them to arrive."

Then, exactly as she had seen on an episode of *Marcus Welby, M.D.*, she feigned amnesia. She showed the police a bump on her head but said she did not remember what had happened. The police called her mother, but Oprah pretended not to recognize Vernita, who was shaken until the police mentioned that the only thing broken during the robbery was a pair of glasses.

"Oprah was always a big actress," said her sister. "She had a wild imagination."

After becoming sexually promiscuous, Oprah devised another way to make money. "She invited men over during the day while my mother was working," said Patricia. "Her boyfriends were all much older than her, about 19 or in their early 20s. Whenever a guy arrived at our door, Oprah would give Popsicles to me and our younger brother Jeffrey and say, 'You two go out on the porch and play now.' Oprah then would go inside with her boyfriend. . . . I didn't find out what Oprah was doing until I was older and she showed me how she did 'The Horse'—which is what she called the sex act."

It took Patricia many years to realize that Oprah was selling "The Horse"—trading sexual favors for money. Patricia's awareness of this information and willingness to turn it over to the media eventually led to a rift between the two sisters that would never fully heal, and in 1993 it would lead to one of Oprah's more momentous decisions when dealing with the publication of her autobiography.

Oprah has admitted to promiscuity during her adolescent years, saying she ran the streets and had sex with any man who would have her because she wanted attention. She also said that she was continually molested by the men in her mother's house. "I was 36-23-36 at age thirteen, which created a few problems. I was not allowed to talk to boys and they were everywhere. . . . This happens in a lot of families where there's a single parent and the mother runs the family: there are boyfriends going in and out of the house and daughters particularly see this. Mothers say, 'Don't let some man do this. You keep your dress down! You do what I say!' When what the child sees is entirely different from what the mother is saying. I had that when I was a kid. 'Do as I say, not what I do.' But that doesn't work. Doesn't work."

Her family saw only a promiscuous teenager who threw herself at men, which is why they did not believe her when she finally told them about being sexually molested. They could not see her as a victim.

"I don't believe a bit of it," said her "aunt" Katharine many years later. "Oprah was a wild child running the streets of Milwaukee in those days, and not accepting discipline from her mother. She shames herself and her family to now suggest otherwise." Mrs. Esters pointed to the timing of Oprah's revelation of sexual abuse and suggested that she simply wanted publicity when she was taking her show national. "That story helped launch Oprah and make her what she is today," she said. "I don't hold with telling lies, but in this case I forgive Oprah because she has done so much for other people. Maybe this was the only way for a poor child to succeed and become rich. Now she does her good works to make her amends. . . . No one in the family believes her stories [of sexual abuse] but now that she's so rich and powerful everyone is afraid to contradict her. I'm not afraid because I'm not financially dependent on Oprah. . . . Her audiences may believe her stories. Her family does not. . . . Let's leave it at that."

For Oprah, like other victims of sexual abuse, the burden of not being believed weighs as heavily as the shame of being molested. Most families cannot or will not face the defilement caused by a loved one or by their own complicity—intentional or unintentional—in the violation of a child they did not protect. Sadly, like her relatives, Oprah blamed herself, even as she was counseling others not to accept condemnation. "All the years that I convinced myself I was healed, I wasn't. I still carried the shame and I unconsciously blamed myself for those men's acts. Something deep within me felt I must have been a bad little girl for those men to have abused me."

When school let out in the summer of 1968, Oprah went to Nashville to visit Vernon and Zelma, and was driven there by her favorite uncle, Trenton Winfrey, her father's closest brother. During the drive Trenton asked her if she had been dating boys.

"I said, 'Yeah, but it's really hard because all the boys want to do is French kiss.' And immediately after the conversation about French kissing, he asked me to pull over to the side and take off my panties. . . . All those years I thought that if I hadn't brought up the subject of French kissing, he wouldn't have done that, because he was my favorite uncle."

Oprah complained to her father and stepmother about her uncle, but they did not believe her then, and Trenton denied her story. Years later Vernon still seemed conflicted. "I know she feels that I didn't handle it well," he said, "[but] Trent was my closest brother. We were torn."

When Oprah returned to Milwaukee, she ran away from home and stayed on the streets for a week. "Mom was frantic and called all her friends looking for her," said her sister. "Mom didn't know if she was dead or alive."

Oprah joked about the incident years later as she recalled hustling Aretha Franklin, who was appearing in Milwaukee. When she saw the singer sitting in a limousine, Oprah threw herself into another drama. "I rushed up to her, started crying, said I was an abandoned child and needed money to return to Ohio. I liked the sound of Ohio. She gave me $100." Oprah, then fourteen years old, claims she went to a nearby hotel, took a room by herself, and spent the money drinking wine and ordering room service. Then she called the pastor of her mother's church and begged him to help her get back home.

"After I ran out of money I told the late Reverend Tully everything that was going on in my house and how bad I felt. So he took me back to my house and gave my mother a lecture, which really pleased me."

Her sister was ecstatic to see her, but Vernita was furious. After the pastor left, she picked up a small chair to beat Oprah, who, according to Patricia, "was crying and cowering. I was screaming and begging Mom, 'Please don't kill Oprah!'" Vernita finally put the chair down, but she insisted Oprah accompany her to the juvenile detention center.

"I remember going to the interview process where they treat you like you're already a known convict and thinking to myself, 'How in the world is this happening to me?' I was four-teen and I knew that I was a smart person; I knew I wasn't a bad person, and I remember thinking, 'How did this happen? How did I get here?'"

Vernita was told she would have to wait two weeks before Oprah could be processed. "I can't wait two weeks," said her mother.

"She wanted me out of the house that minute," said Oprah.

Back in the apartment, Vernita called Vernon in Nashville and told him he had to take over, but by then Vernon had realized he was not Oprah's birth father. Nine months before Oprah's birth in January 1954 he was in the service.

Knowing that Vernon and Zelma were unable to have children, Katharine Carr Esters called and urged Vernon to take Oprah. "I knew he wasn't her father but I told him, 'Claim her as your own. You and Zelma want a child, and Oprah needs help. Her mother can't handle her.' . . . I told him everything that Oprah had done, and he finally agreed to take her, but under strict conditions of discipline that she no longer go back and forth to Vernita and that he would be in charge. Vernita agreed. . . . We were all there when Oprah left—her mother, her sister and brother and all of her cousins."

Patricia recalled her sister in tears at having to leave Milwaukee. "Oprah didn't want to go. She was crying and hugged me before she got into Vernon's car."

Reserved by temperament, Vernon had been shocked by the stories of Oprah's behavior, which he later described as "Oprah making herself available to men." Once inside his house on Arrington Street he sat her down at the kitchen table and laid down the law. He told her that he would rather see her dead and floating faceup in the Cumberland River than have her bring disgrace and shame on his family.

"No more halter tops, no more short shorts, and no more heavy eye makeup . . . You'll start dressing like a proper young lady."

"Okay, Pops," said Oprah, who now referred to Mama Zelma as "Peach."

Vernon nearly erupted. He wrote in his book proposal that Oprah's response smacked of disrespect. "I felt like my daughter dusted her shoes with my white hankie and stuffed it back in my pocket. There was something snide behind the new names . . . something ill-mannered."

He laid down more rules that Oprah was to follow: curfews, chores, homework. "She didn't have to like them; she just had to obey them. 'If you run away, stay away.' That's what I told her. You have to behave, behave as if you want to make something of yourself. . . . That means no association with boys. . . . And," he added, "I'm still Daddy. I'll always be Daddy. My wife says you can call her Peach. That's her business. But don't call me Pops!"

"Okay, Daddy," said Oprah, who came to see her ramrod father as an unbending martinet. "He used to tell me, 'Listen, girl, if I say a mosquito can pull a wagon, don't ask me no questions. Just hitch him up.'" Recalling her father for Toronto's *Star-week,* she said, "I hated him and my stepmother, Zelma, as I was growing up."

Vernon and Zelma started to transform Oprah into a "proper young lady," and she hated that, too. "Every morning of my life my step-mother would check me out to make sure I'd picked out the right socks, that everything matched," she told *TV Guide.* "When I weighed 70 pounds I had to wear a girdle and a slip every day. God forbid somebody should see through your skirt! What are they going to see? The outline of your leg, that's all!"

Vernon saw his daughter as a wild runaway horse that had been let loose for five years. "When it came to discipline, hard was the only way I knew," he said. Years later he wished he had parented with a little patience and more humor. "My own daddy could wring a hoot from the mourners' bench," Vernon said, "[but] Oprah had a way of keeping my blood up. If I pulled east, she'd tug west. If I pointed north, she was hell-bent on south. She wasn't an unpleasant child. In fact, her company was a great joy to me. But she did have a problem with directions."

In addition to doing household chores, Oprah was put to work in the small grocery store that Vernon operated next to his barbershop, where he posted a sign: "Attention Teenagers: If

You Are Tired of Being Hassled by Unreasonable Parents, Now Is the Time for Action. Leave Home and Pay Your Own Way While You Still Know Everything." Selling penny candy after school to poor neighborhood kids was a far cry from having milk and cookies served on silver trays by black maids in the homes of Nicolet students. "I hated working in that store," Oprah said, "hated every minute of it."

In the fall of 1968 she started school as a sophomore at East Nashville High, in the first class to officially integrate the school. "We were lily-white up to that point," said Larry Carpenter, class of 1971, "but we were under court order that year to admit black students, and it was the best thing that ever happened to the school, and to the country, for that matter."

As part of the seventy–thirty black minority, Oprah went unnoticed for most of her first year at East, unlike her arrival at Nicolet. She attended class every day but sat quietly in the back, a peculiar departure for someone who always sat up front and antagonized other students by knowing every answer and constantly waving her hand to ingratiate herself with the teachers.

"I could walk into any classroom and I was always the smartest kid in the class. . . . I was raised to believe that the lighter your skin, the better you were. I wasn't light-skinned, so I decided to be the best and the smartest."

When she brought home her first report card from East, Vernon was irate. "Troubled teen or not, I wasn't having any of that. My expectations of her were a mountain most high. I told her, 'If you were a C student, you could bring me C's. You are not a C student! Hear me?'

" 'Yes, Daddy.'

" 'If you bring me any more C's, I'm going to place heavy burdens on you. . . . Heavy burdens.' "

He explained that "heavy burdens" were biblical weights for a daughter he saw drifting aimlessly in 1968, who had announced that she wanted to be a hippie.

"She was only fourteen, but I didn't care if she were forty. No child of mine was going to stick wildflowers in her hair and light that Hindu incense—or light any other nonsense. Oh, no.

Not in my house! Maybe it was a costume thing. Maybe the tie-dyed dashikis and bell-bottom pants enchanted her, the sandals and beaded necklaces. Maybe the hippie life looked fun, fashionable. But I knew better. A life of drugs and sexual freedom would bring all her promise to ruin."

The hippie phase passed, but Oprah continued to drift. "I talked to her about her studies," said Vernon. " 'What happened to you, Oprah? You used to love school. You used to love to lead the class.' "

He recalled her sad response: "School was fun when I was little. Things are different now."

That year, during the winter, Oprah began wearing her heavy coat in the house and complaining of being cold. When her legs and ankles swelled over her shoes and her belly looked distended, her stepmother took her to a doctor, who told Oprah what she already knew. She was pregnant.

"Having to go home and tell my father was the hardest thing I ever did," Oprah said later. "I wanted to kill myself." She admitted she had spent half her time in denial and the other half trying to hurt herself to lose the baby. After her pregnancy she told her father what his brother Trent had done to her, and that he could be the baby's father. "Everybody in the family sort of shoved it under a rock," Oprah told *Ebony*'s Laura Randolph. "Because I had already been involved in sexual promiscuity they thought if anything happened, it had to be my fault and because I couldn't definitely say that he was the father of the child, the issue became 'Is he the father?' not the abuse. . . . I wasn't the kind of kid who would persist in telling until someone believes you. I didn't think enough of myself to keep telling."

For Vernon, having a daughter with a child out of wedlock was considered so shameful that he and his wife considered getting Oprah an abortion or sending her away to have the baby and then putting it up for adoption. "We thought about it all and then I just decided whenever it comes I'll just have me a grandson or granddaughter."

The stress of having to tell her father and stepmother that she was pregnant sent Oprah into labor in her seventh month.

On the evening of February 8, 1969, a few days after her fifteenth birthday, she gave birth to a baby boy in Hubbard Hospital at the all-black Meharry Medical College. Her name
appears on the birth certificate as Orpah Gail Lee, not Oprah
Winfrey. She named her little boy Vincent Miquelle Lee.

"He was premature and born very ill," recalled Vernon.
"They kept him in an incubator because he was having such a
tough time." Oprah, who stayed in the hospital only two days,
said she was psychologically disconnected from herself and
never saw her child. The baby died one month and eight days
after he was born, and his body was given to Meharry Medical
College.

"I don't know what happened after the baby died," said Vernon. "I don't know what they did with the body—whether they
used it in experiments or what. We tried to keep the fact of the
baby quiet, even within the family. There was no funeral, no
death notice."

Vernon did call Vernita, who came to Nashville to be with
Oprah for a week, but few others knew what had happened.
"Oprah never talked about her lost baby," said her sister, Patricia.
"It was a deep family secret that was almost never discussed
within the family." In 1990, Patricia, in desperate need of drug
money, sold the secret to the tabloids for $19,000.

When Vernon told Oprah her baby had died, he said, "This is
your second chance. We were prepared, Zelma and I, to take this
baby and let you continue your schooling, but God has chosen to
take this baby and so I think God is giving you a second chance,
and if I were you, I would use it." They never said another word
about the tragedy. "We didn't talk about it then," Vernon said in
2008. "We don't discuss it now."

# $T$hree

SPRINTING FORWARD, Oprah blocked out her pregnancy, confident that no one would ever find out. "I went back to school and not a soul knew. Nobody," she told the historian Henry Louis Gates, Jr., in 2007. "Otherwise, I would not have had this life that I've had."

Whether or not that belief is correct, Oprah made the clear choice that secrecy was her salvation, and she closed her past even to her closest friends. "I dated Oprah for two and a half years in high school," said Anthony Otey. "That's why I [was later] so stunned to learn that the girl I thought I knew so well had actually had a baby before I even met her. How was she able to suppress it?

"We never had sex, not even on prom night. We agreed when we first started dating as fifteen-year-olds in our old neighborhood in Nashville that we would never go all the way. It was a matter of our Christian upbringing and our determination to make something of ourselves as adults.

"In all the time we dated, she never mentioned a single word about any of this to me. She never spoke about her past. Oprah never talked about her mother, and she never told me that she had a brother and a sister."

Her teachers, too, were dumbfounded. "I taught her every day at school and traveled with her through the state and around the country to speech tournaments," said Andrea Haynes, "and I had no idea of her travail. When I heard that she had had a baby I felt very sorry that she had come from such a sad place.... I can assure you that Oprah did not emit any symptoms of an emotionally disturbed child when I knew her."

Luvenia Harrison Butler, her best friend in those days, was not surprised. She recalled Oprah as great fun but very secretive. "She had so many secrets, dark secrets. I didn't know what they were but [I knew] there were reasons Vernon was so strict, and believe me, he was strict. Even in girl talk Oprah was guarded.... I know she seems to be so open with her audiences, but that's just because she's a good actress.... I'm not saying she needs to tell everybody everything, but she's the one who says she's so open and honest and truthful about her life. Fact is, she only shares her personal stuff when forced to.... For instance, she admitted her drug use on the air only when someone was set to tell all in an article, and her pregnancy only when her sister outed her."

Oprah recalled that pregnancy as "the shaming, most embarrassing, horrible thing" of her young life. She illustrated the disgrace with a story about a girl in her senior class who was barred from graduation because she had become pregnant. "[T]here was this big brouhaha whether she would even be allowed to ... walk with the rest of the graduating class. And the decision was no, she could not walk with the rest of the class. So my entire life would have been different [if anyone had known I had had a baby]. Entirely different."

Her classmates do not recall the story that Oprah tells. "I never heard about anyone being pregnant and not allowed to graduate," said Larry Carpenter, the East alumni representative for the class of 1971. "We were a big class, about three hundred, but that's something that would've been known."

"Not so," said Cynthia Connor Shelton. "I was in Oprah's class at East, and I had a friend who was seven months pregnant our senior year and she graduated with us.... Certainly there was a social stigma attached to unwed pregnancy, but not enough to deny a girl graduation."

Whether or not a pregnant student was barred from walking with the class at East Nashville High, Oprah's story reflects her own fear about her situation, which she knew could have drastically altered the life she wanted. So she wrapped herself in secrecy as a protective coating. For a churchgoing child there were Ten Commandments to live by, but no stone tablets about how to bury the past. Whether her pregnancy was the result of sexual molestation or promiscuity, it was something she felt she needed to hide.

The power of her denial through the years became evident when she entered the Miss Black Nashville contest in 1972 and signed an affidavit swearing she had "never conceived a child." During a 1986 *Oprah* show on racism, a white man said to her, "You [black people] took over Chicago. . . . In twenty years, Chicago became eighty percent black . . . so you have to be breeding." Oprah said, "I haven't bred one person." And in 1994 when she hosted a show titled "Is There Life After High School?" she asked a panel of five former classmates from East to relate the most humiliating moment from their high-school years. Each gave an example of adolescent mortification, which made Oprah laugh. "I did not have any embarrassing moments in high school," she said. "Nothing humiliating."

After the pregnancy Vernon had tightened the reins on his "wild runaway horse" and led her back to the stable, where, slightly tamed but still spirited, she started her run for the roses. "I became the high-school state champion in speaking and winning drama contests, trying to prove myself, prove that I was a good girl," she said.

A week after giving birth, and almost a month before her baby died, Oprah pulled on her knee-highs, ribboned her hair into two ponytails, and returned to East Nashville High, where she began to reinvent herself. Gone was the sullen student with swollen ankles crouched in the back row wearing a baggy sweater. In her place was a bright-eyed, energetic sophomore with relentless confidence who demanded to be recognized beyond the confines of her school and her church.

Andrea Haynes, who taught Oprah speech, drama, and English at East, recalled their meeting in the spring of 1969. "I still remember her bounding into my classroom, saying, 'Are you Miss Haynes? Well, I'm Oprah Gail Winfrey.'" She later announced that she was going to be an actress—"a movie star." She did not say she *wanted* to be a star; she declared firmly she was *going* to be a star. "I've got to change my name," she told Ms. Haynes. "Nobody has a name like Oprah. I could go as Gail. I've already told my family to call me Gail."

The teacher immediately saw a student with marquee ambitions. "You stick with Oprah," she said. "It's a unique name and you have a unique talent."

On her own, Oprah started making a name for herself in the black churches around Nashville after Ms. Haynes introduced her to readings from *God's Trombones: Eight Negro Sermons in Verse,* by James Weldon Johnson. "I used to do them for churches all over the city," said Oprah. "You sort of get known for that."

Gary Holt, the former student body president of East, remembered her performing at the Eastland Baptist Church on Gallatin Road. "She did a reading from a Negro spiritual in which she was the Preacher; she delivered a sermon with that great big voice of hers, and she was wonderful."

Those performances earned Oprah a trip to Los Angeles to speak to other church groups. During that time, she toured Hollywood's Walk of Fame in front of Grauman's Chinese Theatre, which further fired her fantasies. "When she came back, she said, 'Daddy, I got down on my knees there and ran my hand along all those stars on the street and I said to myself, *One day, I'm going to put my own star among these stars,*'" said Vernon. "That was the foreshadowing I had that she would one day be famous."

Oprah did not hide her ambitions. In junior high in Milwaukee, when she filled out one of those "Where Will I Be in Twenty Years?" forms, she checked "Famous." She said, "I always knew I'd do great things in my life. I just didn't know what."

"She knew what she wanted very early in life," said Anthony Otey. "She said she wanted to be a movie star and she was willing to put aside a lot of things."

"She was driven, even back then," said Gary Holt, who considered Oprah, an only child who was always well dressed, to be one of the more privileged in their class. Ironically, at East High she looked like one of the students she used to envy at

Nicolet. "You've got to understand that East was lower, lower, lower middle class," he said. "Most of us—black and white—were poor kids whose parents, if they worked at all, had blue-collar jobs. Vernon Winfrey had his own business—being a barber is a good cash business—and he also owned his own house. So he was definitely middle class to us."

Having had a lifetime of "bad jobs, low-paying jobs," Vernon emphasized to Oprah the need for getting an education. "She complained sometimes about other children dressing better than she dressed," he said. "And I said to her, 'You get something here'"—he tapped his head—"'and you can dress like you want to in days to come.'"

At school Oprah joined the National Forensic League and worked closely with Ms. Haynes on dramatic interpretations to prepare for competitions. The goal was to win the Tennessee State Forensic Tournament and qualify for the nationals. By her junior year she was the school's best entry.

Again enacting the role of the Preacher, who tells the story of the Apocalypse from *God's Trombones*, she won the first-place dramatics trophy on March 21, 1970. "It's like winning an Academy Award," she told her school newspaper. "I prayed before I competed and said, 'Now, God, you just help me tell them about this [The Judgment Day]. They need to know about the Judgment. So help me tell them." Then, as she had seen Oscar winners do on television, she said, "I want to thank God, Miss Haynes, and Lana [Lott], also Paula Stewart for telling me she wouldn't speak to me anymore if I didn't win." After winning at the state level, Oprah went to the nationals in Overland, Kansas, but she was eliminated before the quarterfinals.

That same year she was one of twelve finalists sponsored by the Black Elks Club of Nashville, a service organization formally known as the Improved Benevolent Protective Order of Elks of the World.

"I can't remember what I said but my topic [for the two-and-a-half-minute speech] was 'The Negro, The Constitution, and The United States.' I delivered it in front of 10,000 people in Philadelphia and I felt really comfortable up there. I had always worried whether my slip was hanging down whenever I got up to speak but in front of 10,000 people you realize nobody can see if it's hanging down. You can't get scared when it's a sea of people everywhere you look."

Oprah won the competition at the Seventy-first Grand Lodge Convention, which honored Mayor Charles Evers of Fayette, Mississippi, with its highest award. The mayor was the older brother of Medgar Evers, the civil rights worker murdered in 1963 by a white supremacist.

While the Black Elks were meeting in Philadelphia, the white Elks met in San Francisco and voted to keep their "whites only" membership requirement. They maintained that God did not make a single black man acceptable to their "brotherhood." At the time, a spokesman for the white Elks said their discussion, barred to the press, had been "amicable" and "in the spirit of brotherly love."

The next year, Oprah competed in the Tennessee State Forensic Tournament, again won first place, and went to the 1971 nationals at Stanford University in Palo Alto, California. "I don't recall any other black student at the nationals that year," said Andrea Haynes, "and there certainly weren't any among the finalists. Oprah was the only one. She performed and won almost every single day of that week, ending up in the top five."

During a five-hour break between presentations, Oprah went shopping in San Francisco and bought a silk scarf for her teacher, who recalled the incident with delight. "She was so impressed that she had paid fifteen dollars for that scarf, and so impressed that she had bought it at Saks Fifth Avenue." The scarf was a splurge for a seventeen-year-old girl from Nashville, Tennessee, who, in 1971, spent seventy-two cents for two pieces of Minnie Pearl fried chicken.

Losing the national tournament disappointed Oprah, who had presented a stirring reading from Margaret Walker's novel, *Jubilee,* the black version of *Gone With the Wind,* in which a female slave named Vyry is doused with urine by the slave master's wife, who is jealous of her mother. Vyry is later whipped to a bloody pulp while trying to escape.

"In retrospect, it was a bold selection, putting the slave experience in the faces of whites, but Oprah, who was not an activist in any way, captured the humanity of the character and presented her without anger or bitterness," said Ms. Haynes.

Dressed in a long cotton skirt and an old shawl, and with a white knit hairnet covering her long black hair, Oprah delivered her oration to her classmates before the state tournament.

"I will never forget the force of energy when she walked to the front of the room, already in character, her eyes sweeping across the room, making eye contact with as many of her fellow students as possible," recalled classmate Sylvia Watts Blann more than thirty-five years later. "Without much ado, she launched into a powerful performance, relating the first-person story of a female slave as she was examined, [offered but not sold] on the block, eventually tied to a post and whipped for having too much spirit and had salt rubbed into her wounds.

"I wasn't the only one that morning with tears in my eyes as the class was transported back one hundred and ten years to a horrifying time when white people presumed to own black people in this very nation—in this very state. I have always been struck with the way she, rather than lashing out in personal anger, chose to mirror back to us the legacy of this crime against humanity. Over the years, as Oprah went about building her career in public life, I thought back many times on the heart-wrenching reality conveyed by her performance. We knew she was special even back then."

While the Civil Rights Act had mandated integration in public schools and public facilities, the social line separating blacks and whites remained firmly in place in Nashville in 1970. "We were all friends during the day, but you didn't do anything with them [the black kids] after school," said Larry Carpenter. "Oprah tried to socialize with whites and she was chastised for it. The black kids felt she dealt with the other race too much."

"That's when I was first called an Oreo [black on the outside, white on the inside]," Oprah recalled. "I crossed the lines and sat with the whites in cafeteria. . . . In high school I was the teacher's pet, which created other problems. I never spoke in di-

alect—I'm not sure why, perhaps I was ashamed—and I was attacked for 'talking proper like white folks,' for selling out."

As a teenager, Oprah was embarrassed by the images of
Africans she saw on television and in films. "I was ashamed if
anybody asked, 'You from Africa?' in the school. I didn't want
anybody to talk about it. And if it was ever discussed in any classroom I was in, it was always about the Pygmies and the . . . prim-
itive and barbarian behavior of Africans. . . . I remember, like,
wanting to get over that period really quickly. The bare-breasted
*National Geographic* pictures? I was embarrassed by all of it."

Being in the minority, the black students at East strength-
ened their numbers by voting in a bloc, especially for student
body offices and superlatives, the prized designations of Most
Popular, Most Handsome, Most Talented, Most Likely to Succeed, Most Bashful, etc. They banded together, nominated one
person, and voted only for that person, while the white students,
with several nominees, inevitably split their vote, which usually
enabled the black candidate to win. "That's why my getting
elected student body president was considered such an upset," recalled Gary Holt. "I was one of two whites running against one
black, and I couldn't have won without black support."

At the same time, Oprah was the only black student running
for vice president. Her campaign picture carried the slogan
"Put a Little Color in Your Life. Vote for the Grand Ole
Oprah." She held her birthday party in the school gymnasium,
and promised better food in the cafeteria and a live band (half-
black, half-white) at the prom instead of records. She, too, was
elected because she pulled black as well as white votes. She also
won one of the coveted superlatives because, according to Cynthia Connor Shelton, she was bold enough to nominate herself.
"That speaks to her self-confidence and her determination to be
recognized," said her classmate. Many years later a member of
the black nominating group confirmed that Oprah had indeed
nominated herself Most Popular Girl, and had won because of
the all-black bloc vote.

Vernon Winfrey was not impressed by her victory. "Any
dog in the street can be popular," he said. "Who was voted

Most Likely to Succeed?" He had not encouraged Oprah to run for Miss East Nashville High or Miss Wool, and he was unsympathetic when she lost both contests. He didn't care that she wasn't homecoming queen, tulip queen, prom queen, or even a cheerleader. He was disappointed that she was not in the National Achievement Scholarship Program for Outstanding Negro Students, because he wanted her to graduate as valedictorian, but he settled for the good grades that put her into the National Honor Society. Tapping her on the head, he said, "Get something up there that no one can take away from you."

From the beginning he and Zelma insisted she go to the library once a week, choose a book, and write a book report for them, which exposed Oprah to the lives of Sojourner Truth, Harriet Tubman, and Fannie Lou Hamer, and to the poetry of Langston Hughes and Maya Angelou. "Not only did I have homework from school, but homework at home," said Oprah. "Plus, I was only allowed an hour a day to watch television, and that hour was always before *Leave It to Beaver* came on! I hated that."

She complained bitterly and constantly about her father's strictness. "Vernon was a tough old bird," said Gary Holt, "and he made sure he knew where she was every minute of the day. . . . There was not much socializing between the races in those days, but if it had been acceptable, Oprah and I might have gotten together. . . . We were great friends and shared the same strong Christian beliefs—then."

Oprah wrote in Holt's yearbook:

> You have showed me more by your actions, by the way you live from day to day, that there is truly only One Way, Jesus Christ! And that without Him taking control, without Him running the whole show, life is just an endless go-round with no meaning.

"Interracial dating was really not tolerated when we were in high school," Holt said, "but Oprah wanted to pull a fast one on Vernon. So she invited me to her house and made him think I was her date. Vernon was stunned when he opened the door and saw me standing there. He was cordial but obviously concerned about a white boy calling on his daughter. It was like *Guess Who's Coming to Dinner* and I was Sidney Poitier. Oprah made him sweat for a while; then she started laughing and told him we were working on plans for the prom."

Oprah and her black friends teased their white speech teacher in the same way. "If we were in a department store or a restaurant, they would yell at me from across the room: 'Hey, Mama. Come on over here.' Then they'd roar with laughter when all the white people turned and saw that I was their mama." Ms. Haynes frequently drove her forensic students to tournaments in the state in her little red Mustang. Once, to get an early-morning start, she suggested Oprah spend the night and share a bedroom with her younger sister, who was visiting. "My sister was coming out of the shower and Oprah was talking on the phone to one of her friends: 'Yeah, she's in the shower right now,' she said. 'You know how these white girls love to wash their hair. All the time washing their hair.' "

The struggle for civil rights had hit Nashville hard in the 1960s, with boycotts, sit-ins, protests, demonstrations, and marches—all part of the racial turbulence rumbling across the South in those years. By the time Oprah was in high school, affirmative action was taking hold to give blacks, so long denied, a lift toward equal opportunity.

As the first black student body officer at East, and someone known in all the black churches of Nashville, Oprah was selected as one of the delegates to the 1971 White House Conference on Children and Youth. The director, Stephen Hess, had promised "an honest cross-section of American youth . . . not just . . . white middle-class student activists." He said the fourteen-to-twenty-four-year age group would reflect the demographics of the country. In the end, minorities, who comprised 30 percent of the delegates, were intentionally overrepresented, so as not to smack of tokenism. In later years Oprah would say she was "the only student selected from my state," but her slight exaggeration does not diminish the honor.

She attended the conference in Estes Park, Colorado, with one thousand delegates, most of whom were clean, crew cut–wearing Christians. James S. Kunen, author of *The Straw-berry Statement*, also attended. "I didn't think they could find this many straight kids in America," he said. As traditional as the young delegates looked, their recommendations from the conference were anything but conventional.

For five hours in one session, some of the crew cuts sat in the front rows openly smoking pot as their drug task force made its report on legalizing marijuana. The conference attendees denounced the invasion of Cambodia, opposed the war in Vietnam, supported a withdrawal of U.S. troops by year's end, and asked for an end to the draft. They proposed a guaranteed income of $6,500 for a family of four, stipulated that one quarter of the national budget be allocated for education, condemned slavery and its evil legacy as "the country's darkest blemish," and asked President Richard Nixon to proclaim racism "the cancer of American society."

Despite the antiestablishment resolutions of her delegation, Oprah did not return home a political activist. Quite the contrary. "The only march she ever took part in," said her boyfriend Anthony Otey, "was the March of Dimes."

That march led Oprah to WVOL, the black radio station in Nashville, to look for sponsorship. "She explained that she walked so many miles and I would have to pay for the number of miles she walked," said John Heidelberg, one of the disc jockeys, who later became president and owner of the station. "I said, 'Sure, I'll do it.'"

A few weeks later Oprah returned to collect the money. "I admired her voice," he recalled. "She was very articulate. Her grammar was good. . . . I'm from outside the boondocks of Mississippi. The concept and image that people get of blacks living in the South can sometimes be very negative. . . . [When I heard Oprah] I thought, 'Hey, here's a young lady who can go places.'"

He asked if she would be willing to make a tape. He took her into the newsroom, ripped some copy off the wire, and listened to her read in a rich, deep, clear voice without a drawl or dialect. He promised to give the tape to the station manager.

"[For years] it was hard for women to get into radio," he

said. But when the FCC required radio stations to begin affirmative action programs, things began to change. "Station managers hired them because they needed a minority. They felt like, 'Well, we've got to protect our license, so we'll hire some females.' . . . We were a training ground for a lot of young blacks who otherwise wouldn't have had a chance to make it in radio."

Heidelberg soon convinced WVOL management to take a chance on the seventeen-year-old and give her on-the-job training. "Oprah knew she had something on the ball," he said. "She didn't feel intimidated or threatened by anything. Nothing bothered her."

"She was aggressive," said Dana Davidson, who worked at WVOL with Oprah. "She knew where she was going."

Shortly after Oprah started working part-time, the station manager's house burned down, and the fire department responded so quickly that the manager decided the radio station would participate in the upcoming Miss Fire Prevention contest. Each year several Nashville businesses selected a candidate, usually a white teenage girl with red hair, to represent them in the contest. WVOL, whose call sign derives from Tennessee being known as the Volunteer State, volunteered Oprah. "I was the Negro surprise of the day," she said.

"Miss Fire Prevention was a big deal back then," said Nancy Solinski, who held the title in 1970. "It was not a beauty contest. The prize was based on your ability to speak, your poise, and your presentation, because your main responsibility was to go around to school assemblies and talk about the importance of obeying fire safety rules. Up to 1971, all the winners had been white. But that year Oprah was one of fifteen contestants. She was the only black, but she never blinked because she had it all and she knew it. She was absolutely color-blind to herself. The judges were all white old men, and when she walked out to present her piece you could almost see them thinking, 'What does she think she's doing here?' "

The judges asked the contestants what they wanted to do with their lives. Oprah said, "I believe in truth and I want to perpetuate truth. So I want to be a journalist like Barbara Walters."

Next they asked what the contestants would do if given a million dollars. Most said they would give it to charity, help the poor, or buy their parents a new house. Not Oprah.

"Lord, you just watch me," she said, lifting her eyes to Heaven. "If I had a million dollars, I would be a spendin' fool. I'm not quite sure what I would spend it on, but I would spend, spend, spend. Just be a spendin' fool."

"Everybody laughed," said Nancy Solinski, "and I was pleased, although frankly surprised, that she won. I put the crown on her head, so grateful that the judges had gotten over their own prejudices. It was time."

John Heidelberg had accompanied Oprah to the event. "The crowd was just overwhelmed with her, and you could see that she was just loving every minute of it." He remembered how thrilled she was to have newspaper photographers rushing to take her picture. " 'Here I am,' she'd yell. Oprah loved the camera. 'Where's the camera? Here I am. Come see me.' She loved the limelight." He laughed as he recalled her reactions. "[She thought,] 'This is great. Hey, I love this! This is going places!' "

A few weeks after riding atop a parade float as Miss Fire Prevention, Oprah walked with the class of 1971 to receive her diploma and graduate. Fifteen years later, East Nashville High School graduated its last class and became East Literature Magnet School. Even with the school doors closed, many from the class wanted to stay connected, but Oprah never looked back.

"Not even to contribute a brick," said Larry Carpenter at the East Alumni House as he walked up the path paved with legacy bricks carrying the names of former students and the years in which they graduated. The bricks, which cost fifty dollars, finance scholarships for poor children in Nashville. As of 2008, there was no brick in the name of the school's most famous graduate. "I have written to Oprah many times in hopes that she might want to contribute to our scholarship fund, but I've never received a reply."

The president of the East Nashville High Alumni Association, Patsy Rainey Cline, also tried to solicit Oprah's support for the school's scholarship program, but to no avail. "She has not shown any interest in any activity of the school since she left Nashville.... She seems so interested in underprivileged children and different nationalities of black children, and that situation certainly is prevalent at East High, but ..."

Considering the millions of dollars Oprah would later give to charity, Larry Carpenter and Patsy Rainey Cline cannot be faulted for thinking her exclusion of East High is deliberate. Luvenia Harrison Butler felt Oprah ignored her high school in Nashville because of painful memories. "It's all part of her secretive past," she said.

Yet when the class of '71 decided to have a reunion in 1994, they again contacted Oprah, and this time she responded by saying that she'd like to have the reunion on her television show. "We spent weeks getting all the names and addresses of everyone for her producers," Luvenia said. "It was a lot of work, but we thought it was a great way to bring everyone together. Unfortunately, it didn't quite happen that way."

The promised reunion for the class resulted in a show more focused on the host than on her classmates. Oprah invited only a few to appear, plus her favorite teacher, Andrea Haynes. "I felt taken advantage of—used, really—when I got to Chicago and realized that the show wasn't going to be the reunion that was promised," recalled Gary Holt.

When Oprah introduced the former student body president as a computer science teacher, she said, "I thought you'd be president of a company or something." When he related his story about getting "the wooden paddle" his senior year for having left the grounds during school hours, she was astounded. "How could you be paddled? You were the student body president."

"Rules are rules, Oprah," he said. "For everyone."

Before taping the show he had seen her in the hall surrounded by her coterie of hairstylists, makeup men, and producers. "I gave her a big hug and said, 'Hon, why are you doing all of this?' She said, 'Because I want to bring the truth to the world.'" He handed her his 1971 yearbook, which she had first signed when they were seniors. Next to that entry, which said, in part, "I want you to know that in a very special way—I love you," she now wrote: "Gary—22 years later God is still King! Thank you for what you've done and continue to do to live well! Oprah." He didn't know what she meant. "Possibly, it's just a safe statement that she or her staff has coined for the general public."

During one segment of that show, Oprah introduced a man who had written a book about the difficulty of fulfilling high-school achievements. He said, "To be a high-school hero is the biggest thing in life. It's hard to equal that kind of esteem later on."

Aside from a cardiac surgeon, Andre Churchwell, who graduated from East in 1971, Oprah seemed to be the only one sitting onstage who had exceeded the promise of high-school potential. At the end of the show, she asked her classmates how they looked back on their high-school years. Each responded with warmth and sentiment, saying those years were a valuable proving ground, and a time when they felt they had been a family.

Oprah looked amused. Standing in her own spotlight, finally thin and glamorous at the age of forty, she was anything but nostalgic. "Boy, I didn't feel it was a family," she said. "I felt like it was just a phase. I moved on."

# $F$our

I LOVED THE girl that Oprah was back then," said Luvenia Harrison Butler. "She was Ope or Opie, and I was Luv or Veenie. . . . We met in high school and were close until she left town. We used to crack each other up doing Geraldine." Luvenia laughed as she recalled the comedian Flip Wilson's cross-dressing impersonation of a sassy female he called Geraldine. Each week on his variety show he sashayed across the stage in a tight Pucci dress, high heels, and a long black wig as a babe brassy enough to scare a bear. From 1970 to 1974, Geraldine was adored by television audiences, black and white.

"Oprah and I imitated Geraldine all the time," Luvenia said as she paged through her 1971 high-school yearbook thirty-seven years after graduation. She smiled at what Oprah had written:

> Hey, Luv—You are one of the nicest nuts I've ever known. Your friendship means and has meant so much to me. I'll always remember . . . "A pea's a pea, a bean's a bean, who you think you playin' with—Geraldine!" You'll go a long way and be ultra successful. Good luck! Remember me.

Over lunch in 2008, Luvenia shook her head with amusement. "Remember her? Lord in Heaven, who can forget her? She's announcing herself to the world every time you turn around."

The effects of the Sears Roebuck Charm School that Oprah attended in Milwaukee show in her yearbook pictures. Sitting with the honor society, she is the only girl who crossed her arms in an *X* on her lap, the perfect way to deflect camera focus from the stomach. Standing with the student body president, she tilted her head up, another charm-school trick to elongate a double chin. With the National Forensic League, she stood in the classic model pose, one foot in front of the other.

"Look at her head shot," said Luvenia, pointing to the picture of Oprah in dangly earrings with peace symbols. "See how dark she is there? Big wide nose and all. Now [over three decades later] she's different. She looks like she has bleached her skin and maybe had some kind of surgery. . . . The real Oprah is Sofia in *The Color Purple*. That's the real Oprah. Not the Photoshopped glamazon on the covers of her magazine who looks so light-skinned."

As an African American, Luvenia understands the tyranny of color among blacks. "Because Oprah is so dark she felt discrimination within our own community. . . . That's why she's always been attracted to high yella men. She needs to have a successful light-skinned man by her side to feel secure. In Nashville, it was Bill 'Bubba' Taylor, the mortician. When she left here she set her cap for Ed Bradley, the light-skinned correspondent for *60 Minutes*. She got sidetracked in Baltimore by some light-skinned disc jockey. Then Stedman. Obama. Even Gayle. They're all high yella."

Oprah's fixation with light skin is borne out by a famous psychological experiment cited in *Brown v. Board of Education* in which black children offered dolls of differing skin tones overwhelmingly chose to play with the white dolls. When asked to identify the "nice" doll, they chose the white one; when asked to select the "bad" doll, they pointed to the black one. "We interpreted it to mean that the Negro child accepts as early as six, seven, or eight the negative stereotypes about his own group," testified Kenneth Clark, one of the psychologists conducting the experiment.

Oprah admitted that color discrimination dominated her

life for many years, even dictating the college she selected. She said she enrolled at Tennessee State University, a historically black college in Nashville, rather than the private, more prestigious Fisk University because she didn't want to compete with light-skinned girls. In those days Fisk was known for "the paper bag test." Supposedly, applicants were required to attach photographs to their admission forms, and anyone darker than a brown paper bag was rejected.

"Oprah did not really want to go to college," said her high-school speech teacher, Andrea Haynes. "She had a paying job at the black radio station and was setting her sights on television, but Vernon insisted she get a college education. So she kept her radio job and enrolled at TSU, which, in my opinion, was really the lesser educational institution in Nashville." But TSU, which charged $318 a year for tuition compared to $1,750 a year at Fisk, was all Vernon Winfrey could afford. People have since written that Oprah won a scholarship to study speech and drama at TSU, but the school offered no records of such a scholarship, and Vernon dismissed the suggestion when he stood in his barbershop, proudly declaring, "This place put Oprah through college."

In 1971, Fisk was considered the black Harvard, the university for elites of color. Tennessee State University was for the sons and daughters of the black working class. This distinction was not lost on Oprah, who told *Interview* magazine, "I went to [TSU but] there was another black college in town where all the vanilla creams went. I thought it was a better school but I wouldn't go just because I didn't want to have to compete with the vanilla creams because they always got all the guys."

Oprah later told *People* magazine that she "hated, hated, hated" her college. "Now I bristle when somebody comes up and says they went to Tennessee State with me. Everybody was angry for four years. It was an all-black college, and it was in to be angry. Whenever there was any conversation on race, I was on the other side, maybe because I never felt the kind of repression other black people are exposed to. I think I was called 'nigger' once, when I was in fifth grade." She said her aversion to TSU stemmed from black activism on campus, and as she told Mike Wallace on *60 Minutes,* she was "not a dashiki-wearing kind of woman."

When she realized that the ruling class in America hailed from the Ivy League she was even more embarrassed about TSU. During her 2008 webcast with Eckhart Tolle she said she did not like to be identified by where she went to college. "[It] . . . annoys me [when] people will say, 'What school did you go to?' That's immediately to say whether or not you're in the[ir] category." She probably found the question irritating because she felt diminished by her college credentials.

Understandably, Oprah engendered bitterness among some TSU classmates, who dismissed her comments about the school as complete fabrications by someone trying to ingratiate herself with a white audience. "TSU was not like what Oprah said it was—maybe it was in the early sixties, but not when we were there," said Barbara Wright, who, like Oprah, was from the class of '75. "I came from the North because I wanted to go to a historically black college. We all wore Afro puffs in those days, like Angela Davis, but we were not marching in the streets." Known for her raised fist and struggle for black liberation, Davis, a former UCLA philosophy professor, made international news in 1970 when her gun was linked to the murder of a white judge in a courtroom battle that killed four people. She fled the jurisdiction but was arrested, detained, and harassed. After awaiting trial for twenty-two months, she was finally exonerated by an all-white jury in one of the most famous trials in U.S. history.

"We were real traditional kids who wanted the college experience of being away from home, living on campus, and joining a sorority," said Barbara Wright. "Oprah was not a part of our college life at all, probably because she was grown beyond her years, as we all found out later. How are you going to be friends with those who haven't experienced such? Also, Oprah was a townie who did not live on campus and did not get asked to join a sorority. Whenever she was around, she was hanging out at Fisk."

Oprah was drawn to Fisk like a hummingbird to sugar water. "She would go there every chance she got," said Sheryl

Harris Atkinson, another TSU classmate. "We took a speech and communication class together as freshmen. Speech was her major; mine was education, but the class was a required course for both of us. There were fifteen in the class, and Oprah sat right next to me. 'You seem really sweet and so I'm going to help you become a better communicator,' she said. She mentored me in that class. We were peers, but she decided that I was her student, probably because I was the opposite of her. I'm not verbally aggressive or assertive. She would follow me around. 'I'm behind you,' she'd yell in the hall or on the stairs. 'I'm following you.' She was determined to be my friend. I was considered a pretty girl back then, and that's why she wanted to befriend me. She knew I had been recruited by American Airlines, which was a big deal at that time. They were going to use me in their advertising commercials. So Oprah figured, 'I'm going to get close to her.' It was a 'pretty girl' thing. Nothing to do with any accomplishment or my personality. Just how I looked."

For all her rampaging self-confidence, Oprah later admitted that her self-image was frayed around the edges. "I remember that every single month, on the day *Seventeen* magazine came out, I'd wait by the newsstand for the delivery truck. They'd throw a stack of magazines off, and I'd be there to buy the first copy and read all the beauty tips. I mean, my god, the idea of being a pretty girl! I thought if I could just be pretty, my life would be fine. So I'd look at the models and at every makeup trick there was and I'd try them all. I even ironed my hair. Here I was, a negro girl who had no business ironing anything but her shirt, and I was ironing my hair."

**Oprah's first cousin, Jo Baldwin, a vice president at Harpo, Inc., from 1986 to 1988, remembered how upset Oprah was when Jo attracted the attention of Bryant Gumbel, and Arthur Ashe stopped his limousine on Madison Avenue to ask her name. "Oprah said, 'I get tired of men looking at you all the time. . . . I would give half my fortune to look like you.'" More than twenty years later, Jo Baldwin laughed as she recalled her response. "I told her she was a fool."**

Oprah admitted to the actress Charlize Theron that she

grew up "idolizing beautiful girls." She said, "I'd think, 'What would it be like to look like that?'" When she met Diane Sawyer she seemed besotted by the beautiful blond cohost of *Good Morning America*, who, like Oprah, was a Southern beauty queen, crowned America's Junior Miss in 1963.

Some employees at ABC-TV noticed the affectionate relationship between the two women, and winked as if to say, "Guess who's got a crush on Diane?" They recalled the giggly late-night phone calls, their excited plans for future joint programs, the hugs, and Oprah's lavish gifts—the gigantic sprays of orchids that arrived after every one of Diane's big exclusives, the expensive Kieselstein-Cord handbag, the one-carat diamond toe ring.

"There was a whisper in the workplace," said Bonnie Goldstein, a former producer for *ABC News*.

"I don't even know how [our friendship] happened," Oprah told *InStyle* magazine in 1998. "We used to sit around the table and say, 'You know who is the coolest person? That Diane Sawyer.' Then out of the clear darn blue sky Diane called and invited me to Martha's Vineyard. We had so much fun. Fun, fun, fun."

Another beautiful woman Oprah befriended after she became famous was Julia Roberts, the star of *Pretty Woman*, who appeared on her talk show ten times and described Oprah in 2004 as her "best friend." Intrigued by the actress's luscious good looks, Oprah asked, "Does the pretty thing ever get to ya? . . . I'm wondering. I was having this discussion with my girlfriend the other day. I said, 'It's a really great thing we were never, like, pretty women, because now we don't have to worry about losing that.'" The actress said: "You can't really complain about being in a movie called *Pretty Woman* when you're the woman." Oprah nodded in agreement and smiled adoringly.

In college she seemed to collect pretty people. "She had her eye on my boyfriend at Fisk and was always asking me questions about him," said Sheryl Atkinson. "He looked a lot like Stedman—what we call a pretty boy, high yella—light-skinned with European features and a caramel complexion. . . . Oprah was quite aggressive in her pursuit of him. I remember lying on my bed in the dorm one Sunday night listening to her on WVOL. I heard her dedicate a song to him. I couldn't believe it. I wasn't mad, because I knew he wasn't interested in her, but I was amazed at how forward she was. But she was like that in class, too. The professors didn't like her because she would debate with them and tell them they were wrong. They might say something and Oprah would come back and rebuke them. She would take over the class. Very bossy."

Not all TSU professors felt that way. Dr. W. D. Cox remembered Oprah as an outstanding student. "I knew her from age sixteen to about twenty-one. I taught her in stage lighting, scenery, and the history of the theater. She was a very likeable student, carried a full load, and took responsibility seriously." He recalled taking his class to Chicago in 1972 for a speech project and "enjoy[ing] a little foolishness" at Oprah's expense.

"During our stay [in the city] a girl was reported raped on the second floor. I told a lie on Oprah. If Oprah had known about the rape, she'd have shouted, 'Yoo-hoo. I'm up here!' Oprah didn't take too kindly to that joke. She was quite provoked."

Dr. Cox regretted making fun of Oprah's aggressiveness when he learned of her history of sexual molestation. "I was astonished," he said. "Her father and stepmother were the strength behind her. [Vernon's] attitude was strict, and he was the best thing that ever happened to her."

In her sophomore year Oprah joined the Tennessee State Players Guild to play the role of Coretta Scott King in a drama titled *The Tragedy of Martin Luther King, Jr.* Headlining the review in *The Meter,* the TSU newspaper was brutal: "Martin Luther King Murdered Twice." The drama critic was unsparing:

> Oprah Winfrey, playing Coretta King, somewhat disappointed me. Oprah, newscaster for a local radio station, shows versatility in her radio broadcasts on WVOL. She however failed to do this on stage and fluctuated very little during the play.

Years later Oprah attributed her unpopularity in college to envy. "My classmates were so jealous of me because I had a paying job. I remember taking my little $115 paycheck, and at the time I was trying to appease them. Anytime anybody needed any money I was always offering, 'Oh, you need ten dollars?' or taking them out for pizza, ordering pizza for the class, things like that. That whole 'disease to please.' That's where it was the worst for me, I think, because I had wanted to be accepted by them and could not be."

Her classmates did not recognize her behavior as insecurity. "She acted as if she knew she was going to be someone and stick it to all of us later on," said Sheryl Atkinson. "She walked down the hallway with her head up in the air and swishing from side to side as if to say, 'I'm the best thing walkin'.' When people saw her coming, they avoided her. She had the kind of confidence that said, 'I don't care that you don't like me—I'm going to be someone big and you'll be sorry.' She did become someone very big, but I'm not sorry. I applaud her, and I commend her on the good works she's done. I just wish she weren't so bitter about our school. But that springs from stuff deep inside Oprah, from secrets that are too dark and deep to look at. . . . People struggle with that kind of stuff their entire lives. . . . Maybe her dark stuff was connected to her father's strictness. I know she disliked him intensely when we were in school."

Later in life Oprah publicly thanked Vernon for saving her. "Without his direction, I'd have wound up pregnant and another statistic." But that gratitude was a long time coming. When she turned eighteen, she broke away from his strict control and moved out of his house.

"I had to help her, because Vernon was so pissed off he wouldn't lift a finger," said Luvenia Harrison Butler. "We moved her into an apartment on Cane Ridge Road in Hickory Hollow." In later years, Oprah maintained that she continued living under her father's roof and the whip of his midnight curfews until she left Nashville at the age of twenty-two. "I don't know why she'd say something like that—maybe to put forward the image of a good little girl. . . . Whatever the reason, it's probably connected to those damn secrets of hers. . . . That's why she makes everyone who works for her sign those confidentiality agreements that forbid them from ever breathing a word about their personal or professional experiences with her. I guess it's her way of keeping control over what people find out about her. . . . It's kind of sad."

Soon after Oprah moved into her own apartment she called upon Gordon El Greco Brown, a local promoter who had purchased the franchise for Miss Black Nashville and Miss Black Tennessee in 1972. "Her stepmother, Miss Zelma, had first brought her to meet me for Miss Fire Prevention. . . . When she started at TSU she enrolled in my modeling school near campus. She waltzed in one day and announced, 'Hi. I'm going to be a big star someday. Where do I sign up, baby?' She was only 17 and not beautiful. But I could tell she had something. She was very poised and had a great speaking voice."

The deep timbre of Oprah's voice never failed to impress. In high school her rich vocal range was compared to that of the American contralto Marian Anderson. For a teenager, Oprah's commanding voice was always a revelation.

"Miss Black Nashville was the first time there had ever been a beauty pageant for black girls. In the past it was white girls only," said El Greco Brown. "Oprah [saw] that contest as a stepping stone for the big career she so desperately wanted. . . . I had to practically beg everyone else to participate because there was no cash incentive. No scholarship. No record deal. No Hollywood contract. Just a title, a sash and a bouquet."

Oprah filled out the pageant application, stating her height: 5'6½"; weight: 135 lbs.; measurements: 36–25–37; shoe size: 8–8½. She listed her hobbies: swimming and people; her talent: dramatic interpretation; and her parents: Mr. and Mrs. Vernon Winfrey, with no mention of her mother, Vernita Lee, in Milwaukee. For "Why are you entering the Miss Black America beauty pageant?" she wrote, "I would like to try to instill a sense of individual (black) pride within our people. Self-dignity." She stated that she had "never been married, annulled, divorced or separated," and had "never conceived a child."

The night of March 10, 1972, there was not an empty seat at the Black Elks lodge on Jefferson Street. "I had managed to get fifteen contestants, and they were judged on beauty in evening gown and swimsuit competitions, plus talent," said El Greco Brown. "Oprah gave an average showing in the [beauty] competitions but when her talent turn came she did a dramatic reading and sang—and she knocked the audience off their feet. She was so good; it moved her into the top five.

"There was only one girl who out-excelled Oprah in talent. Her name was Maude Mobley and she later worked as a backup singer at the Grand Ole Opry. Not only was Maude talented, she had a beautiful figure and scored top marks in the swimsuit and evening gown competitions. Everyone picked her as the winner as soon as her foot hit the stage."

The six judges tabulated their scores and the winners were announced from last to first: "I couldn't believe it when [the MC] read out the name of the fourth runner-up: Maude Mobley. He continued to read the winners, pausing briefly before he called out: 'The winner, and the first Miss Black Nashville, is Oprah Gail Winfrey.' "

Recalling a collective gasp of shock from the audience, the promoter said he was besieged by people who claimed the contest had been fixed. "I was confused myself. So I gathered up all the judges' scorecards and tallied up the votes. I couldn't believe what I discovered: the number four runner-up and the winner's scores had been switched. I'm convinced the scoring switch was an error. The judges were honest men and women."

The promoter said he went to the Winfreys' house the next day to explain the mix-up. "I asked Oprah if she would consider giving the crown to . . . the rightful winner. Oprah stood up and said angrily, 'No, it's mine! My name was called and I am Miss Black Nashville.'

"I tried to reason with her. 'How would you feel if you had been in Maude's shoes?'

" 'I don't care,' she said."

The next week Oprah's picture appeared in the Nashville newspapers as the winner. Her photograph, with a press release mentioning Patrice Patton as the first runner-up, was sent to black newspapers across the country. There was no mention of Maude Mobley.

"Everyone at TSU talked about the Miss Black Nashville contest," said Sheryl Atkinson. "We discussed it among ourselves, because Oprah seemed least likely to win. She certainly wasn't the prettiest, but I'm sure she was the most vocal."

"I think she got it because she was well known from her radio show," said Barbara Wright. "She couldn't have gotten it any other way."

The confusion over tabulating the scores did not become public until Oprah became famous. Then Gordon El Greco Brown wanted to publish a book of photographs. "I had hundreds of pictures of Oprah from those pageants and wrote her to say that I'd like to publish something. Her lawyer Jeff Jacobs wrote me back and said they'd like to see all the pictures. When I saw that he was a lawyer, I said I'd come to Chicago with my lawyer so we could make a deal. But Jacobs said no, I couldn't bring a lawyer. I had to meet with him and Oprah alone. They flew me to Chicago, put me up in a hotel, and sent a limousine to bring me to the Harpo studios. Oprah met me, hugged me, and was my best friend. Then she handed me off to her lawyer, who really roughed me up.

"'We just want to see what you've got,' said Jacobs. So I showed him all my pictures. I said I had spent three years promoting Oprah [for free] and would now like to do a book.

"Jacobs said, 'No book. No job. No nothing. We'll put some money on the table and the pictures stay with us. Take it or leave it.' I said I wanted to keep my pictures. Jacobs said, 'So leave, but we don't want to see those pictures all over the place.' When I left Harpo, they canceled the limo to the airport, and I had to flag a cab."

Feeling spurned, the promoter sold his story and some of his photos to the *National Enquirer*, which ran the headline "Oprah Stole Beauty Contest Crown!" Her publicist denied the story: "Oprah was never told of any alleged problems with any pageants she was in at any time."

Maude Mobley, described in the 1992 story as the "rightful pageant winner," sounded fearful. "Oprah's a rich and powerful woman. I would rather not talk about this. It might anger her."

Maude's mother was not so cautious. "I knew something wasn't right when they called out Oprah as the winner," she said twenty years after the pageant. "After I talked to Maude, I was so angry that I wrote to everybody I could think of to get the situation righted. But no one was interested. It's true that Oprah stole that crown."

Another version of the switched-votes story surfaced when Patrice Patton, the first runner-up for Miss Black Nashville, noticed Gordon El Greco Brown's tabloid story when she was grocery shopping. "I already knew that the scores had been switched, and that Oprah had not won," she said in 2008, "but I don't believe what Gordon is quoted as saying in that story. . . . I don't believe for one minute that Oprah knew about the switch or that Gordon ever confronted her. I was told by the pageant coordinator that Gordon was the one who switched the votes on Miss Black Nashville. The pageant coordinator said she had confronted him at the time, and when he didn't step forward to correct the situation, she quit. I ran into her a few years later and she told me the truth: that I had actually won Miss Black Nashville and Oprah had been the runner-up. I never said anything, because it was five years after the fact and I would've looked like a sore loser. Besides, I liked Oprah. She was good folks. . . .

"She had a following in Nashville at the time, from all the publicity she got being the first black girl to be Miss Fire Prevention, plus she had her own radio show. It's my opinion that if Oprah hadn't been declared the winner of Miss Black Nashville, Gordon wouldn't have been able to sell tickets to the Miss Black Tennessee pageant. So he made her the winner. . . .

"After the pageant coordinator quit, Gordon gave me the job and we traveled all over Tennessee just trying to get girls to participate. Even then we only got a few. A few days before the pageant, Gordon moved out of his house in Nashville and we moved in so I could get everyone ready to make the rounds of radio stations and churches and department stores. Oprah drove some of us in her father's pickup truck. . . . I still remember how determined she was to get into shape for competition. She wanted to be a certain size, so she had started dieting. . . . She was the first black person I ever saw to eat yogurt. We just didn't eat yogurt in those days. But she did and she lost a bunch of weight."

Oprah said she was as surprised as anyone to be crowned Miss Black Tennessee. "I didn't expect to win, nor did anybody else expect me to, because there were all these vanillas and here I was a fudge child. And Lord, were they upset, and I was upset for them, really, I was. I said, 'Beats me, girls. I'm as shocked as you are. I don't know how I won, either.'"

As Miss Black Tennessee, Oprah flew to California in August 1972 to compete for the crown of Miss Black America. For the talent portion of the pageant, she sang "Sometimes I Feel Like a Motherless Child," a spiritual dating back to slavery. Her chaperone, Dr. Janet Burch, a Nashville psychologist, recalled for the writer Robert Waldron how focused Oprah was on becoming successful. "I have never seen anybody who wanted to do well as much as Oprah did. She used to talk about things, like how one day she was going to be very, very, very wealthy. The thought always precedes the happening. If you really think you're going to be very wealthy, and very popular, and prominent, and you sincerely believe it, it's going to happen. You see, some people say it, but they don't really believe it. She believed it. People say, 'I'd like to be wealthy.' Oprah said, 'I'm *going* to be wealthy.'"

Oprah did not win, place, or show in the race for Miss Black America. "As district pageant organizer I had access to those final tallies and ascertained that she came in number 34 out of 36 contestants—almost flat bottom," recalled El Greco Brown. Oprah dismissed her loss by blaming the winner. "The girl from California won because she stripped," she said. Yet the *New York Times* coverage makes no mention of the beautiful California singer who won as having performed a striptease.

During the week, Oprah, who had been sponsored by her radio station, told Dr. Burch that she was going "to be a big TV personality." After the pageant, she returned to Nashville ready to raise her game.

"Our general manager got a call from WVOL that they had a girl who wanted to get into broadcasting," said Chris Clark, the former anchor, producer, and news director of WLAC, later WTVF-TV. "So I was told that I had to interview her."

The station had already hired Bill Perkins, the first black face on Nashville television, now deceased, and Ruth Ann Leach, the first woman, who said, "I was the first female fanny to sit on the news desk next to the anchor during a newscast. This was back when NewsChannel 5 was trying desperately to meet its FCC obligation to diversify the on-air talent. So there was Bill Perkins and me. Everyone else on the air was white and male."

Oprah said she had been pursued by the CBS affiliate for the on-air position, but Clark remembers that WVOL pushed for her hiring, and Joseph Davis, a cameraman, formerly with WDCN-TV, the public education channel, concurred. "There was a small group of young black people in Nashville that the NAACP got behind to place in positions above entry level—in middle management and on-camera," Davis said. "Oprah was part of that group to come out of WVOL." In 2008 he produced a photograph of the group taken on the set at WDCN, when they appeared to discuss "Blacks and Their Role in the Media." "Out of the ten people in this picture, Oprah is the only one who did not get sidetracked by marriage or children. She never let life interfere with her ambition to get to the top."

Chris Clark was sensitive to the demands for diversity at that time. "I felt we needed to look like the face of Nashville, which was then 80 percent white and 20 percent black. We had a brave mayor [Clifton Beverly Briley] who said that segregation was over and we had to move toward integration. . . . I was responsive to this because when I was coming up in television in the 1960s, it was a white-bread world—no room for blacks, women, Jews, or Greeks like me. My real name is Christopher Botsaris, but I had to change it to get a job on the air. By the time I got to WLAC, Nashville had been through the really rough civil rights battles, but we still needed to show that we were committed to integration.

"As far as I'm concerned, Oprah was not a token. Yeah, she

was black and we needed a black face, and she was a woman, so I guess that helped. But she was a no-brainer for me," he said. "She was drop-dead gorgeous, very well spoken, and known in town from being Miss Black Nashville and Little Miss Spark Plug or whatever she was [Miss Fire Prevention]. So I made her a reporter—we didn't have correspondents in those days. I sent her out with a Bell and Howell camera to cover city hall. I didn't find out until later that she didn't know what the hell she was doing."

Years later Oprah admitted she had lied on her job application and during her job interview about her experience, but she walked into her first assignment with great determination. "I announced to everybody there, 'This is my first day on the job, and I don't know anything. Please help me because I have told the news director at Channel 5 that I know what I'm doing. Pleeeeze help me.' And they did. And from that point on all those councilmen became my friends."

Chris Clark, who retired in 2007, does not claim a medal for hiring Oprah, but he does acknowledge "getting the fisheye from management. . . . You have to remember it was a very racially tense time in Nashville, and she was the first black woman on television." He admitted that the front office was not enthusiastic. "I could make the decision because, as anchor, I was also director and producer of news, but they made it quite clear that if Oprah didn't work out—if the audience did not accept her—it would be on me."

Others recall the hire as very courageous. "No question," said Patty Outlaw, who did traffic ads for the station. "It was a big risk for Chris."

"He went out on a limb when he brought Oprah in," said Jimmy Norton, who worked in production, "especially when he promoted her to coanchor. . . . There was grumbling in the back of the newsroom. . . . It bothered some to see Oprah on the air doing news, but you have to remember what Nashville was like in those days. . . . The *N* word was still being used freely."

Ruth Ann Leach recalled her first encounter with the word when Oprah started doing the news. "I accompanied a family member to a pleasant suburban home. . . . I sat with the . . . wife. She greeted me warmly and told me she used to enjoy watching me on television.

" 'What do you mean "used to"?' I asked.

" 'Well, I cain't watch your station anymore, now that you have a nigger reading the news.' "

Oprah herself got walloped with the hateful word when she went on assignment in a segregated area of Nashville. She introduced herself to a shop owner and extended her hand.

"We don't shake hands with niggers down here," he said.

She shot back, "I'll bet the niggers are glad."

At TSU her classmates considered her television job nothing but a big wet kiss from the affirmative action fairy. They dismissed her as a "two-fer," a mere token, and she agreed. "No way did I deserve the job," she said later. "I was a classic token, but I sure was one happy token."

"She was so excited to be on television," recalled the makeup artist Joyce Daniel Hill. "I was with the Joe Colter Agency and had been hired by the station to teach the news team to do makeup and get supplies for them every month. We were just getting used to color cameras in those days and had only a few shades of pancake makeup available. . . . I blended a special shade for Oprah. . . . She's considerably lighter now than she was thirty-four years ago. I have no idea why. Maybe it's just better makeup artists or some kind of skin bleaching. . . . She took me with her to cover the *Ebony* fashion fair because we both loved clothes. . . . She was a joy to work with."

Hired at $150 a week, Oprah made her television debut in Nashville in January 1974. By the following year she had received several awards as the city's first black female on television. She was named National Executive Woman of the Year by the National Association of Women Executives. The Middle Tennessee Business Association named her Outstanding Businesswoman of the Year, and she won the Negro Business and Professional Women's Club award as Woman of the Year in 1975. "She was terrific," said Chris Clark, "although she wasn't a great reporter. Couldn't write. Never could." In fact, she had so much trouble writing she caused the station to go black for two minutes of a five-minute cut-in one morning because she had not finished typing. "Chris should have fired me that day," Oprah said.

Instead, Clark concentrated on her other gifts. "She was wonderful with people," he recalled. "And that was her downfall as a journalist, because she could not be detached. She'd be sent to cover a fire, come back to the station, and work the phones trying to get help for the burnt-out family instead of writing the story for the evening news."

Easy and casual at work, Oprah kicked off her shoes and padded around the newsroom in bare feet. "She was as country as cornbread in those days," said one former coworker.

"I think people expected her to be a 'yes, sir, no, sir' type, you know—very grateful—but she wasn't that way at all," said Jimmy Norton. "She was driven. I saw it shortly after she started, when we were doing a public service spot for Black History Week. The producer was not very good, so Oprah stepped in and completely took over. She shoved the producer aside, told the cameraman what to do, and directed the segment herself. That was an eye-opener for me. This girl knew what she wanted and was willing to do whatever she had to do to accomplish her goals."

Patty Outlaw agreed. "She was real confident for her young self—ambitious, yes, but not a backstabber. I liked her a lot. . . . I saw her every day in those years, because I worked on the floor above the newsroom. It was just nuts working at that station. Drugs, drugs, drugs all the time—drugs all over the place. They were even selling 'windowpanes' [LSD] in the hall." Drugs were so prevalent that the news staff gave Vic Mason, Oprah's coanchor, a coke spoon as a gift. "Chris and I looked the other way," said Jimmy Norton, who confirmed that station management removed a vending machine once they discovered it had been rigged to dispense marijuana. Years later Oprah indicated that her own drug use started in Nashville, with cocaine, and continued during her years in Baltimore and later in Chicago.

"I remember raving on the elevator about a guy I was dating, and Oprah listened to me carry on for two floors. As she got off, she said, 'Ooooh, girl. He sounds like Jesus' brother,'" said Patty Outlaw. "In those days Oprah and I talked about boys, diets, and makeup. That's all we cared about then. . . . Funny, isn't it, but she's still talking about the same things on her show three decades later."

"She was a little heavy then, but nothing like now," Patty said in 2008. "I had started taking ballet and mentioned my lessons to Jimmy Norton. 'Ballet must be big,' he said. 'Oprah did a little story during the newscast last night. She did it in her tutu or, in her case, her four-four. . . .' Oprah lived on junk food then, and nobody got between her and her Ding Dongs."

Harry Chapman, who coanchored the weekend news with Oprah, recalled her fondness for Chicken Shack chicken. "They used cayenne pepper and Tabasco sauce—hottest chicken I ever put in my mouth. We'd have that on weekends, in between newscasts."

As the thirtieth-largest television market, Nashville was a training ground for many young broadcasters. "It was a very exciting time to be in TV," said Elaine Ganick, former news anchor for the NBC affiliate, WSMV, and later a correspondent for *Entertainment Tonight*. "I started out about the same time as Oprah; Pat Sajak was a weatherman; and John Tesh, our news anchor, hit the big time in New York before his ten years with *Entertainment Tonight*."

Tesh, the tall (six foot six), handsome, blond anchorman for WSMV, once described his Nashville days and nights with Pat Sajak, Dan Miller, and Oprah: "We were all single, ran in a pack, and got into a lot of trouble acting like jerks." Some time after he became the news anchor for WCBS-TV in New York City, Tesh told a woman he dated seriously that when he was in Nashville he had lived with Oprah for a short time, at her apartment in Hickory Hollow. "He said one night he looked down and saw his white body next to her black body and couldn't take it anymore. He walked out in the middle of the night. . . . He told me he later felt very guilty about it." The social pressure then, in Nashville,

Tennessee, concerning an interracial couple was extreme. **In 2010, Tesh publicly confirmed his affair with Oprah.**

Toasting her talk show's tenth anniversary in 1996, she invited her former lover to appear with his *ET* cohost Mary Hart, and reminded him of what she called their "one date—strictly two friends having dinner." More than three decades later some people who worked with them in Nashville found their intimate relationship hard to believe. "[I would've thought] Oprah would've been leery about dating a white person . . . interracial dating was not acceptable then," said Jimmy Norton. "After all, we were just ninety miles south of Pulaski, home of the Ku Klux Klan."

Patty Outlaw acknowledged that the coupling of a black woman and a white man was considered "pretty scandalous" at the time, but she remembered a snowy evening when the station put a lot of people up for the night at a Ramada Inn. "I think if you asked Oprah and Vic Mason about that night they might have some fond recollections of each other."

In 1975, Oprah, who was coanchoring the weeknight news, was recruited by WSB in Atlanta. "It was time for a black anchor on weekday TV," said former news director Kenneth Tiven. "She came down and was terrific. I remember having her home to dinner. . . . She had even then an extraordinary sense of self-confidence, an eerie comprehension of what was expected of her as an upwardly mobile black woman and budding television star. However, I suddenly bolted Atlanta for Philadelphia KYW as news director, and she said, 'Without you I am not coming.'"

Chris Clark recalled Oprah coming to him with the WSB job offer. "I talked her out of it because she wasn't ready and we didn't want to lose her. We were just starting field anchoring and I thought she'd be great. So I gave her a five-thousand-dollar raise, and she stayed with us—for a while. Then, a year or so later, she got an offer from Baltimore's WJZ-TV. Again, management told me to talk her out of leaving. So I called her in. 'Oprah, management has told me to talk you out of leaving. Have I tried to talk you out of it? Good. Now I think you should take the job. You're ready.'"

Baltimore was a much larger television market, and the job paid $40,000 a year, but Oprah did not leap at the opportunity to coanchor the news on WJZ. "I hated Baltimore when I first went there," she told WDCN's Gail Choice in her "Farewell to Nashville" interview. "But I took the free trip they offered and looked at the Westinghouse-owned station, which I loved. They own[ed] five other stations, and they said, 'We have big plans for you.' They wanted me to sign a five-year contract but I said no. 'I'll be too old in five years to do what I want to do.' So I negotiated it down to three years." Oprah, then twenty-one, said she envisioned herself going from coanchoring the news in Baltimore to transferring to the more glamorous ABC affiliate in San Francisco and finally to becoming "the black Barbara Walters. . . . If she can make $1 million a year, I figure we can make $500,000," Oprah told her black interviewer.

"I hate to leave but it's just about necessary for me to do what I want to do later, and that's to anchor in one of the top 10 markets." Oprah said she would not have considered moving to Baltimore if WJZ had not been the number one station in its market.

Gail Choice appeared wide-eyed with wonder at her colleague's strategic vision, and, dripping with admiration, she commended Oprah on her good fortune. "I was lucky, lucky, lucky . . . in the right place at the right time," said Oprah. Years later she would say it was all a part of God's plan for her.

When she signed her three-year contract with WJZ and prepared to move to Baltimore, she asked her father for a loan until she started getting paid in her new job. "Vernon Winfrey was a good customer of mine at the Third National Bank in East Nashville," said Janet Wassom. "He took out papers and cosigned with Oprah for a loan to pay her expenses for relocating. . . . He was known in the black community as someone people went to for help, and he helped those who helped themselves. Didn't believe in handouts. Made everyone pay him back, and I'm sure he did the same with Oprah."

Oprah repaid her father many times over in the years to come, with luxury cars, fine clothes, gold watches, immense houses, and exotic vacations. She even offered to retire him for life. "She calls this place a crummy old dump," he said in 2008 of his dilapidated barbershop on Vernon Winfrey Avenue. Yet, even at the age of seventy-five and following a stroke, the man who believed in a hand up ignored his daughter's offer of a handout.

"I hated to see Oprah leave Nashville, but I wanted to give her a great send-off," said Luvenia Harrison Butler, "so I threw a big going-away party—made all the arrangements for invitations, food, drinks, and music. I had it at the Gazebo apartments off Thompson Lane, and strange as this may sound, she never even thanked me for it. She left town and basically never came back, except when she returned to promote *The Color Purple*. . . . That was the last I saw of Oprah before all those Arnold Schwarzenegger types took over her life and she got all Maria Shrivered up. She divorced herself from Nashville. Probably because it was too painful for her to come back because we knew her when, or else because we're just too down-country for her now."

Oprah's friend, who became president of the League of Women Voters in Nashville, did not try to conceal her disappointment over the lost friendship. "I don't think Oprah knows how much we admire her for all she's done, especially for the little girls in South Africa."

Perhaps for Oprah the price of surviving was to forget, and the down payment on dreams as big as hers meant dropping a guillotine on the past. She did return to Nashville in 2004, for the fiftieth anniversary of WTVF-TV, and appeared on television to congratulate NewsChannel 5, but she did not come back three years later for Chris Clark's retirement party. "We were all there," said one former coworker. "Jimmy Norton cut short a church mission in New Orleans to be on hand, and Ruth Ann Leach flew in from New York City. Even the governor was there, but Oprah didn't show."

Her absence surprised many. "We have always been a family

at the station, and Chris was on the air there for forty years, probably a record for any anchorman in the country, which is why his retirement party was a big deal," said Jimmy Norton. "So I think everyone expected Oprah would be there. After all, Chris had given her her big break. . . . But thirty years had passed and . . . well . . . Oprah has changed. . . . She's not the same sweet nineteen-year-old kid we used to know. . . . She did invite Chris to her big splashy fiftieth birthday party earlier that same year, and sent a plane for him and all, so maybe she felt she had done enough for him, I don't know. . . . I won't say she *wouldn't* come to his retirement party. I'll just say she *didn't* come."

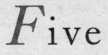

# $F$ive

COUNTEE CULLEN, a leading poet of the Harlem Renaissance, wrote "Incident," his most famous poem, about what happened to him as a child:

> Once riding in old Baltimore
> Heart-filled, head-filled with glee.
> I saw a Baltimorean
> Keep looking straight at me.
>
> Now I was eight and very small,
> And he was no whit bigger,
> And so I smiled, but he poked out
> His tongue and called me "nigger."
>
> I saw the whole of Baltimore
> From May until December;
> Of all the things that happened there
> That's all that I remember.

Baltimore had changed since that poem was published in 1925, but even with a 55 percent black population, its attempts at integration were often hesitant and halting. Situated north of the Confederacy, south of the Mason-Dixon Line, and in the shadow of Washington, D.C., the city produced world-renowned figures such as Edgar Allan Poe, Emily Post, Upton Sinclair, H. L. Mencken, Babe Ruth, Cab Calloway, Billie Holiday, and Thurgood Marshall. By the time Oprah Winfrey arrived in the Bicentennial summer of 1976, Baltimore was known as "Charm City," after a gimmick to lure tourists with charm bracelets. The ad campaign was launched ten days into a garbage strike that was exacerbated by a 110-degree heat wave that baked the city in a gagging stench and triggered riots requiring the deployment of state troopers in gas masks.

"It took me a year to become charmed by Baltimore," Oprah said, unimpressed by the city's historic row houses. "I didn't understand why they were all stuck together.... [And] the first time I saw the downtown area I got so depressed that I called my daddy in Nashville and burst into tears. In Nashville you had a yard, even if you didn't have a porch. But the houses on Pennsylvania Avenue [in Baltimore] had neither. I picked Columbia for the grass and trees."

A lovely verdant suburb, Columbia, Maryland, was designed in 1967 to look like a village spread across fourteen thousand acres and to eliminate subdivisions as well as segregation by race, religion, and income. The neighborhoods contained single-family homes, town houses, condominiums, and apartments like the one Oprah rented. The street names came from famous works of art and literature: Hobbit's Glen, from J.R.R. Tolkien; Running Brook, from the poetry of Robert Frost; and Clemens Crossing, from Mark Twain. Oprah lived on Windstream Drive near Bryant Woods, where the street names came from the poetry of William Cullen Bryant.

After driving her to Baltimore and helping her unpack, her Nashville boyfriend, William "Bubba" Taylor, was ready to return home. "We agreed she had to make the move and I had to stay," he said many years later. "It was too small a TV market for her in Nashville, and I had many things to keep me here, such as my family's funeral home."

The couple had been dating semi-seriously since Oprah had gotten Taylor a job at WVOL radio. "I hired Billy just to keep Oprah's sanity," recalled Clarence Kilcrease, the station manager. "She kept pushing me to do it. She was gaga over him." They had met at the Progressive Baptist Church when

Taylor, a twenty-seven-year-old Vietnam vet, was attending John A. Gupton Mortuary College.

"She was just nineteen but she was driven even back then," Taylor said. "She'd tell me: 'Someday, I'm going to be famous!' You could see that she meant it." So he was not surprised to see Oprah on *60 Minutes* a decade later, but he was floored by her melodramatic recollection of their parting in Baltimore.

"Lord, I wanted him," Oprah told Mike Wallace. "I threw his keys down the toilet, stood in front of the door and threatened to jump off the balcony if he didn't stay. I was on my knees begging him, 'Please don't go, please don't go.'"

Bubba Taylor chuckled, knowing he had not been the man who had sparked those theatrics. "When she took me to the airport for my flight back to Nashville, her eyes glistened and she squeezed my hand before kissing me goodbye. We promised to stay in touch, of course, but I guess we both knew it was over." Oprah later fell in love with a married disc jockey in Baltimore who would bring her to her knees, and it was her desperation over losing him that she recounted on *60 Minutes,* to illustrate how far she had traveled from her doormat days. Some might consider that recollection an example of what Oprah's "aunt" Katharine Esters called another one of "Oprah's lies," while others would accept her tendency to rearrange the truth as her way of telling a good, if inconsistent, story. Or perhaps the only way Oprah can deal with a painful truth is by attributing it to a situation that doesn't hurt (Bubba) rather than to one that still pains (the Baltimore disc jockey).

In the 1970s, local news became a real moneymaker for television, especially in Baltimore, where Jerry Turner anchored on WJZ-TV every night, and consistently outdrew Walter Cronkite, then the Brahmin of broadcasting.

"You cannot overstate the stature of Jerry Turner in this town at that time," said WJZ's weatherman, Bob Turk. "He simply had no peers."

The former general manager of WJZ concurred. "Jerry Turner was as superb an anchor as you could find anywhere in the business," said William F. Baker. "He was appealing, authoritative, and, most importantly, he was adored by the Baltimore community. Absolutely worshipped. He was the reason WJZ ranked number one in the market for years, and as you know, news is the jewel of the crown in television, and determines how a station fares in terms of money and prestige."

In 1976 the station decided to go to an hour news format, which was too much for one person to anchor. So they announced they were launching an "intensive search" for a coanchor to share Turner's throne. This was tantamount to a trumpet throughout the kingdom: the forty-six-year-old prince is looking for a princess to wear the glass slipper. (The assumption then was that since Turner was a white male, his coanchor had to be a black female.) Seven months later the so-called search team announced they had found their princess. They paid her $40,000 a year ($150,816.87 in 2009 dollars).

"I was news director at WJZ and I hired Oprah after seeing a demo tape that she had sent," Gary Elion said in 2007. "It was very impressive; she had a compelling delivery, and we hired her on the basis of that tape."

The newsroom was aghast. "It did not matter that Oprah Winfrey from Nashville, Tennessee, knew nothing about Baltimore, or that she was twenty-two years old, or that she had almost no reporting experience," recalled Michael Olesker, a former print journalist who became WJZ's on-air essayist. "For television news Oprah was perfect. . . . Why? Because in television news, journalism has always been considered optional."

At the time there were only a few black women on television in Baltimore, despite the city's large black population. Maria Broom, a dancer with little experience in journalism, had been hired by WJZ to be the consumer reporter before Oprah arrived. "I was black, and I had a nice bush," said Broom, who achieved national recognition in the (2000–2008) HBO hit series *The Wire*. "It was a time of big Afros. I was a picture of the modern black woman. So it was like a movie. They said, 'We're going to make you a star,' and then they did. . . . I was what they gave the black people."

Sue Simmons had arrived in 1974 to work at WBAL. She stayed two years before moving to Washington, D.C., and then to New York City, where she has anchored the news at WNBC for more than two decades. Upon leaving Baltimore, a reporter asked what her strengths were. Simmons replied, "I'm pretty and I can read."

In 1976, for any woman—black, white, yellow, or brown—to share the throne of Jerry Turner was to receive a crown never before bestowed.

"Getting that . . . news coanchor job at twenty-two was such a big deal," Oprah said many years later. "It felt like the biggest deal in the world at the time."

When it was announced that a young black woman from Nashville had been anointed, even Baltimore's major television critic was taken aback. "That they have this much confidence in a new face for Baltimore is interesting," Bill Carter wrote in *The Baltimore Sun*. "It must be considered a risk anytime the news is handled by anyone other than Turner at Channel 13.

"But if Winfrey can be established as a popular news person, the station will have a big leg up when it finally does get its act together and puts the full hour news on the air."

WJZ immediately began working with Mayor William D. Schaefer's office to develop a series of feature stories about Baltimore neighborhoods that Oprah could present each night during the forty-five-day City Fair between July and September.

"It's good P.R. for me," she told reporters, admitting she did no research or reporting for the series. She simply showed up at a different neighborhood each day with a camera crew to interview whomever had been selected by the community association. "It was a great way of introducing me to the city. I probably know more about the neighborhoods now than anybody else at the station."

Her comment irked some in the newsroom, particularly Al Sanders, a black reporter who had effectively anchored the news in Turner's absence and expected to be considered as his coanchor. "For up to three years before we went to the hour format, there had been talk that if a coanchor situation were to come along I would be considered," he said. "When it did come along, no one at the station was considered. Someone was brought in from the outside."

Still, the deck was stacked against Oprah. "Even before she hit town, WJZ ran a childish series of promotional spots, asking, 'Do you know what an Oprah is?' " recalled Michael Olesker.

" 'Ofrey?' the people in the commercial would answer.

" 'Oprah? What's an Oprah?'

"In hindsight no one could imagine CBS introducing its anchor years earlier by asking, 'Do you know what a Cronkite is?' The spots demeaned Oprah and the entire notion of news anchors as serious figures."

Oprah saw the promotion as anticlimactic. "The whole thing backfired," she said. "People were expecting The Second Coming and all they got was me."

Oprah made her debut on August 16, 1976, but all the hoorahs went to Jerry Turner. "He has managed to become a co-anchor without losing any of his impressive prestige and class," wrote television critic Bill Carter. "More and more he drives home the point that he is head and shoulders above anyone else as a local newsman, maybe above most of the local newsmen in any market in the country. Which brings up the question of why he was ever given any anchor help at all."

Oprah was saluted for "flawless" news reading and accorded "some style," but not much. "It is a subdued kind of style that might be easily forgettable. . . . This is not to demean her on-camera abilities, which are considerable. But . . . Oprah's personality is not as strong as some of the other Channel 13 people or else it has not really come through yet. . . . [S]he is not in any way arresting—at least not yet."

Within weeks it became clear that the chemistry between Oprah and her silver-haired, silver-tongued coanchor was toxic. He saw himself as the reincarnation of Edward R. Murrow, and to him she looked like an imposter who had no right to serve the sacred host of television news to the community of Baltimore. He was astounded that she allowed others to write her copy and then went on the air without reading it ahead of time. This was incomprehensible to a man who revered writing and always came to the office early to compose his newscast. He was appalled by the arch manner she assumed on the air, which she later mocked herself as her condescending lady-to-the-manor-born tone of voice, saying she thought that was how an anchorwoman was supposed to sound. Turner was flabbergasted when Oprah read the word *Canada* from the teleprompter as "Ca-NAY-da" three times in one newscast. She later mispronounced *Barbados* as "Barb-a-DOZE." She read a report about a vote in absentia in California as if "Inabsentia" were a town near San Francisco. A few nights later she characterized someone as having "a blaze attitude," not knowing how to pronounce *blasé.* Then she began editorializing on the news, breaking in at one point to say, "Wow, that's terrible." Ratings tanked.

For Turner, though, the capper came when Oprah, twenty-four years his junior, turned to him on the air and quipped, "You're old enough to be my father." That ripped it, and unbeknownst to Oprah, her days were numbered.

"From the start I knew it wouldn't work out," said Bob Turk. "Oprah was just too inexperienced and limited in her knowledge of world affairs, especially geography, to be placed in [the] position . . . of anchoring with the dean of Baltimore news."

When the dean became displeased, Oprah got dumped, and all the king's horses and all the king's men could not put her back together again. On April Fool's Day 1977, eight months into her reign, Oprah lost her crown. Toppled from the most prestigious position at the station, anchoring the news, she was tossed into television's scut bucket, to do early-morning cut-ins. The consensus around the station was that while she may have been a power pitcher in Nashville, she couldn't get the ball over the plate in Baltimore. A minor leaguer who would never make the majors, Oprah became the baseball goat, shunned by fans and blamed by the team for failure.

Years later she and her best friend, Gayle King, a WJZ production assistant at the time, recalled what happened:

OPRAH: [T]hey decided it wasn't working because the
anchorman—

GAYLE: Didn't like you.

OPRAH: But I didn't know it. I was so naive. The day
they decided that they were going to take me off the 6
o'clock news, I said to Gayle—

GAYLE: I'm just typing at my desk. She goes, "Get in the
bathroom now."

OPRAH: We'd always meet in the bathroom. We were
like, "Oh, my God. Do you think Jerry Turner knows?"
Of course, Jerry Turner was the main anchor who was
kicking my ass out, but we didn't know that. Jerry was
like, "Babe, I don't even know what happened, Babe."
You know, "Sorry, Babe."

GAYLE: I was stunned.

OPRAH: It's like your life is over.

Al Sanders was immediately promoted to coanchor, and
left no doubt that he had been sent in to clean up the mess. "I've
been in this business seventeen years," he said, drawing a stark
contrast to Oprah's lack of experience. "Whenever you replace
anybody on a job and people think that things weren't quite
right before, there is pressure. But I'm comfortable."

He and Jerry Turner swiftly resurrected the ratings and
then dominated the landscape for the next decade. "They were
the best local news team in America," said William F. Baker.
Until their deaths—Turner died of esophageal cancer in 1987,
Sanders of lung cancer in 1995—WJZ reigned as the number
one station in Baltimore.

At the time of Oprah's severe demotion, the station tried to
counter the obvious. "We can't account for what people will
think," said the general manager, Steve Kimatian. "But we believe this is an opportunity for her to develop herself, to work
more on her own. When people see how Oprah does in the as-
signments she is given they will be convinced that the profile we
have of Oprah is a high one."

Translation: Oprah was a goner.

For someone who had given herself three years to become television's black Barbara Walters and anchor the news in a top ten market at a network-owned station, or else to take Joan Lunden's place as the cohost of *Good Morning America,* Oprah had been brought low. The self-confidence that had hurtled her upward seeped away like a big hot-air balloon dropping from the sky. She was no longer a star. While her contract guaranteed twenty-five more months of pay, she had no standing at the station. Yet she couldn't quit, because she needed the money. Promotion to a news job in a larger market was out of the question, and to go to a smaller market would dash all of her exalted dreams. For the first time in her life she had no upward options to dodge the fireball of failure rolling her way. Her father and her friends advised her to stay put and hold on. After all, they said, she was still in television in a large market, and getting paid. So Oprah picked up the only mop and pail available. In addition to doing the local cut-ins for *Good Morning America,* she became "weekend features reporter," which, as she said, was the lowest position on the newsroom food chain.

"I did mindless, inane, stupid stories and I hated every minute of it," she said, "but thought even while I was doing it, 'Well, it doesn't make any sense to quit because everyone else thinks this is such a great job.'"

No longer a show horse, she trudged into work at six every morning and stayed all day, taking every dreary assignment thrown at her. She covered a cockatoo's birthday party at the zoo, did live shots of elephants when the circus came to town, and chased fire engines. She also took guff when she interviewed the organizer of the Mr. Black Baltimore contest.

"In the newsroom she was asked, 'Did you go for the Miss Black America title?'" recalled Michael Olesker. "If she boasted about it, she had no sense of nuance. If she joked, she understood she was in a business where everyone had an ego."

Oprah rose to the occasion. "Yeah, honey," she said, patting her rear end, "but I've got the black woman's behind. It's a disease God inflicted on the black women of America."

Open and cheerful, she was eager to please and desperate to

be liked. "I'm the kind of person who can get along with anyone," she said. "I have a fear of being disliked, even by people I dislike." She made friends with everyone at the station and treated her camera crews well. "In those days when we used film, a film editor could make or break a reporter who was on a tight deadline," said Gary Elion. "They always busted their backs to help Oprah because she was so nice to them. Some people would try to get their way by being tough and nasty and aggressive. Oprah was just the opposite. . . . She made it a point to get along."

Most important, she hid her resentment toward Jerry Turner and Al Sanders. That bitterness she confided only to her closest female friends, Gayle King and Maria Broom, who understood the difficulty of dealing with male divas. Oprah's animus surfaced only after both men had died. She was nowhere to be seen among the thousand mourners who thronged Jerry Turner's funeral in 1987, nor was she among those who came to Baltimore to say goodbye to Al Sanders eight years later.

Her demotion, while hellish at the time, proved to be her crucible, forcing her to develop the formula she needed for future success. She learned that flaming ambition combined with grinding hard work and enduring stamina would reap rich rewards. "I've kept a diary since I was 15," she said, "and I remember writing in the diary . . . 'I wonder if I'll ever be able to master this so-called success!' I was always frustrated with myself, thinking I wasn't doing enough. I just had to achieve."

In addition to working overtime on her job at WJZ, she joined the Association of Black Media Workers and gave speeches throughout the city about women in broadcasting. She became active in her church as a member of Bethel A.M.E., and began mentoring young girls, speaking at schools all over the city. She espoused the goals of the Rev. Jesse Jackson, who had impressed her the first time she heard him speak, in 1969. "He lit a fire in me that changed the way I saw life. . . . He said, 'Excellence is the best deterrent to racism. Therefore be excellent,' and 'If you can conceive it and believe it, you can achieve it.' That was what I lived by." As a teenager she made a poster out of construction paper with Jackson's words and taped it to her mirror, where it stayed until she left Nashville. In Baltimore she helped organize a fund-raising rally for Jackson's Operation PUSH (People United to Serve Humanity) at the Civic Center.

She attended Sunday services every week, always sitting in the center of the second row of the sixteen-hundred-seat church, and became a beloved fixture in the black community through her speaking engagements as well as her political support of local politicians such as Kurt Schmoke and Kweisi Mfume.

"Oprah learned about the city's power structure, who was important and what made them powerful," recalled Gary Elion. "She learned the names and faces, where the bones were buried, everything about the power structure, and she learned to use that information to her benefit in gathering the news. She became a force in the city very quickly, because she knew how the city worked. She was very bright, and I knew she was going to go far. She wasn't terribly partisan—at least she never talked about it with me—but she was highly astute politically. She seemed to have a natural instinct for it and used it to her advantage."

Oprah increased her visibility in Baltimore through Bethel A.M.E. as much as through her job on television. "I met her . . . through her church," said Dr. Bernice Johnson Reagon, founder of the female a cappella group Sweet Honey in the Rock. "I was contacted to work collaboratively with her on a project that they would then present. I interviewed Oprah and created a script from that interview, [plus] poetry and song by Sweet Honey. The centerpiece was an excerpt she performed from *Jubilee* by Margaret [Walker] Alexander. . . . We premiered ["To Make a Poet Black and Beautiful and Bid Her Sing"] at Morgan State in Baltimore, and performed in Nashville and in New York City."

"Oprah wanted to be an actress more than anything else," said Jane McClary, a former producer at WJZ.

"She used to put on this one-woman show [with] which, through poetry and dramatic reading, she reenacted black history," recalled WJZ's Richard Sher. "And she was fabulous. She played to standing ovations."

Bill Baker also remembered Oprah's "little recitals . . . she always invited me and I always made a point of going. . . . She became notable in the black community."

Years later Oprah's impact on black women in Baltimore became the subject of an academic book by Johns Hopkins University sociology professor Katrina Bell McDonald, titled *Embracing Sisterhood.* "These women marvel at Oprah's staying power—her ability to have survived some of the most difficult struggles black women face and to have won the envy of a world that typically finds little regard for black women."

Long after she left Baltimore, several women recalled her traumatic breakup with Lloyd Kramer, a Jewish reporter who worked for WBAL-TV. Even in the late 1970s, interracial relationships were rare in Baltimore. At the time Oprah was involved with Kramer, a local (white) radio personality viciously joked that "Omar Sharif is dating Aunt Jemima."

"But that didn't faze them," said Maria Broom. "She really loved him. They were so close. I thought they might get married and have children. . . . [When] Oprah's confidence was wrecked, that's when Lloyd really helped her. . . . It was a deep and caring relationship."

One of Kramer's closest friends at the time recalled first meeting Oprah. "Lloyd called me from Baltimore, said he was coming to New York with his new girlfriend and could they stay with me," said the editor and writer Peter Gethers. "I said, 'Sure,' and asked him about her. Lloyd, being Lloyd, hemmed and hawed a bit, then said that she was black and that his parents were really upset that he was dating a black woman. He told me her name was Oprah—which led to a few laughs, because it was not your normal white girlfriend name—and that she was an on-air reporter at a rival station in Baltimore. So a week or two later, Lloyd and Oprah came to New York and stayed with me in my fifth-floor walk-up, West Village, somewhat cockroach-infested apartment. I didn't have a spare bedroom, or even a spare bed, so they both slept on a pillow couch—which wasn't really a couch, just a bunch of pillows arranged to be in the shape of a couch—on the living room floor. They spent the weekend, and we had a lot of laughs, hanging out with a few other friends who Lloyd didn't get to see regularly, having moved to Baltimore."

The relationship floundered when Kramer left Baltimore for a job at WCBS in New York City and met actress Adrienne Meltzer, whom he married in 1982. "Oprah suffered quietly even though her heart was breaking," said Maria Broom. "She was hurting, but she moved on with her life." She also remained grateful and stayed friends with Kramer, later making him a TV director of note. She told Chicago journalist Judy Markey, "Lloyd was wonderful. He stuck with me through the whole demoralizing [Baltimore] experience. That man was the most fun romance I ever had."

When Oprah joined Bethel A.M.E. in 1976, she arrived with the biblical precepts of a young country girl who had been called "Preacher Woman" by her classmates. A deeply religious Christian who quoted Genesis and Leviticus, she believed that homosexuality was wrong. She was ashamed of her gay brother, Jeffrey, and a year before he died of AIDS she told him he would not go to Heaven because he was a homosexual. In the next seven years she would travel far from the doctrinaire concepts of her Baptist childhood. "I was raised to not question God. It's a sin," she said. "[But] I started to think for myself . . . and that's when I really started, in my mid-twenties, my own journey towards my spirituality, my spiritual self."

The journey began when her pastor, Rev. John Richard Bryant, gave a sermon about God being a jealous God. "I was just sitting there thinking for the first time after being raised Baptist . . . church, church, church, Sunday, Sunday, Sunday . . . I thought, 'Now why would God, who is omnipotent, who has everything, who was able to create me and raise the sun every morning, why would that God be jealous of anything that I have to say? Or be threatened by a question that I would have to ask?' "

Even bolstered by religion, she found her public humiliation taking its toll, physically and emotionally. "Reporters leaving the building would find her sitting in her car weeping, unable to summon energy to start the engine," said Michael Olesker.

"The stress was so bad that her hair started falling out," recalled Jane McClary. "She said later that she had had a bad perm, but it was definitely stress."

Oprah consoled herself with food, eating around the clock. "I still have the check I wrote to my first diet doctor—Baltimore 1977," she said years later. "I was 23 years old, 148 pounds, a size 8, and I thought I was fat. The doctor put me on a 1,200 calorie regimen, and in less than two weeks I had lost ten pounds. . . . Two months later, I'd regained 12. Thus began the cycle of discontent, the struggle with my body. With myself."

The stories that Oprah and others tell of her battle with food are sometimes comical, but more often sad. "I first met her at Overeaters Anonymous," said Hilda Ford, the former secretary of human resources for the state of Maryland. "We became close friends, despite our thirty-year age difference. . . . We were both heavy black women who were outsiders to Baltimore at the time. . . . We attended OA meetings, worked out at the gym together, and then went to Oprah's favorite deli in Cross Keys and—can you believe it?—we gorged on fried chicken."

People from WJZ recall a party thrown by Pat Wheeler, one of WBAL's producers. "At the end of the evening Pat was ushering everyone out, but she couldn't get Oprah to leave because there was a huge platter of salmon on the dining room table that hadn't been touched," said a reporter. "Oprah, an enormous eater, wouldn't go until she devoured the whole thing. It was quite an amazing display of gluttony." Oprah freely admitted to compulsive eating. She said her addiction to chocolate chip cookies frequently led her out of her apartment at night in boots and a coat on top of her pajamas for trips to the bakery. Most people understood that her eating was a substitute for something else. "I would hear stories about how she would have binges of eating when she was lonely," said Bill Carter.

"After her string of successes, Oprah was 'devastated' by [her] demotion," Gerri Kobren wrote in *The Baltimore Sun*. "She feared her career was grinding to a halt, and thought briefly about leaving town. Her hair fell out, leaving great bald patches; she had to keep her head wrapped in scarves while working."

Later, in the first flush of national success, Oprah would put an entirely different spin on losing her hair. Rather than admit to ravaged nerves, she blamed the assistant news director at WJZ, claiming he had sent her to New York City for a makeover after telling her, " 'Your hair is too thick, your eyes are too far apart, your nose is too wide, your chin is too long and you need to do something about it.' " She said they wanted to perform plastic surgery on her. In her confabulated tales, delivered with gusto to gullible feature writers and adoring audiences, she said the assistant news director came to her one day to announce, "We're having problems with the way you look. We're going to send you to New York. They have people there who can help you." She claimed she was sent to "a very chi chi poo poo lah dee dah salon. The kind that serves you wine, so that when you leave it does not matter what you look like. So . . . I said, 'Do you all know how to do black hair?' And the response was, 'Oui, madame, we do black hair, we do red hair, we do blonde hair and we do your hair.' So this French man put a French perm on my black hair. And I was the kind of woman at the time—this was 1977—that I sat there and let this French perm burn through my cerebral cortex rather than tell this man, 'It's hurting.' . . . He left this perm on my head to the point when I got up out of the chair, the only thing holding my hair follicles in were scabs."

More amusing than accurate, her exaggerated yarn about getting her head fried until she was "as bald as a billiard ball" was all part of a buoyant performance that took her audiences on a happy ride, but something her "aunt" Katharine Esters might have called another one of "Oprah's lies." Truth to tell, she had gone to a high-end beauty salon in Manhattan, but she had not been sent by the station. "We didn't have the budget for that sort of thing," said the news producer Larry Singer.

"I have no recollection of her being sent to New York City to have her hair redone by a French hairdresser," said the news director Gary Elion. "I don't know where that [story] came from."

Being hell-bent on cosmetic self-improvement, Oprah had taken herself to New York City, but in her mythology of the makeover supposedly mandated by dunderheaded male management, she wailed, "They wanted to make me a Puerto Rican. . . . They wanted me to bleach my skin, change my nose." At this point in her speeches she usually took a swipe at the news director who had hired and fired her. She claimed he had also wanted her to change her name. Sometimes she said he wanted her to call herself Suzie. Putting a hand on her hip, she would grin and ask her audience, "Do I look like a Suzie to you?" Other times she said he wanted her to be called Cathy.

The only reporter who ever questioned Oprah on her fabulist tales was the television critic for *The Baltimore Sun*, Bill Carter, later with *The New York Times*. After interviewing her in 1986, when she insisted that Gary Elion had wanted her to change her name, Carter called the former news director, then a practicing lawyer.

"I'm flattered that Oprah even remembers me," Elion said ten years after leaving the station, "but I never asked anyone to change her name, except my wife when I asked her to marry me." Remaining gracious as Oprah pounded away at him in interviews and speeches, Elion simply resigned himself to Winston Churchill's observation that a lie flies halfway around the world before the truth puts its pants on.

In the spring of 1977, William F. Baker arrived to become general manager of WJZ, and was soon promoted to president of Westinghouse Television and Group W Satellite Communications. "We all called him Dr. Baker because he had a PhD," said Jane McClary, who had been hired by Baker in Cleveland. "I got my job right out of college because my brother-in-law was press secretary to Senator John Glenn of Ohio. Bill Baker was so smart that way. He hired Arleen Weiner, whose husband was a big-time lawyer in Baltimore, and he also hired Maria Shriver. He saw the advantage of hiring people with those kind of connections. . . . Maria wanted to be on the air, but she was too heavy and unattractive then, so Dr. Baker put her in as an associate producer on the *Evening Exchange*."

Having created *Morning Exchange* in Cleveland, Ohio, the highest-rated local morning program in the country and the template for ABC's *Good Morning America,* Baker's mandate was to do the same in Baltimore.

"Daytime television was then an untapped audience of stay-at-home moms, who were completely underestimated," he said. "All they had were soap operas and game shows. I wanted to give them something more, and after my wife and I had gone to a few parties and gotten to know people at the station, she suggested I consider Oprah. 'You want to do another *Morning Exchange* here, and you need a female cohost. I think you should look at Oprah. She wears her heart on her sleeve. Talks all the time, and relates well to people. I think she'd do well for you.'"

By then Oprah had worked herself back into news and was anchoring weekdays at noon. She wasn't permanent and she wasn't prime time, but she was back in the game. The last thing she wanted to do was to start Dialing for Dollars on a daytime talk show.

"Oh, please, no," she begged Baker when told that he was buying the popular franchise, and that her new job as cohost of *People Are Talking* would include giving the Dialing for Dollars password at the start of the program; at the end of the hour she would randomly select a phone number from a bowl of phone numbers previously submitted by viewers. If the selected viewer was watching the show and answered the phone with the correct password, he or she would win money. If the phone was not answered, the money would be added to the jackpot for the next day's call. It was a forty-five-second device producers used to keep viewers tuned in.

Suddenly cockatoos, circus elephants, and fire engines looked substantive. "The truth is that Oprah was on her way out," Baker said many years later. "She was simply serving out her contract until she could be let go. . . . I knew she couldn't read a [news] script very well, but that's not using the medium to its fullest potential, and it's not what I had in mind for a morning talk show. I needed someone good at ad-libbing, interested in people, who could handle viewer call-ins and all manner of guests. I thought Oprah would be good at fluff, too, so I suggested her to the program director, Alan Frank, and he recommended we pair her with Richard Sher, a solid news guy who had been at the station since 1975."

Frank said, "If we do this show right, it should have a white guy and a black woman. It crosses all lines then."

Baker agreed. "Then came the hard part," he said. "I had to talk Oprah into it."

Even at the end of her rope, she would have preferred being let go to doing daytime television. "She really wanted to be a news person," Baker said. "She knew that news was all that mattered in television at the time. She saw daytime as a real come-down, a failure. She started crying. 'Please don't do this to me,' she begged. 'It's the lowest of the low.' I told her, 'If you can become a success in daytime, Oprah, I promise that you can have a more profound effect on Baltimore than you can as a news anchor.' What I was offering her was a real job and, quite frankly, she had no other option."

Rather than play his take-it-or-leave-it card, Baker promised to help. "I told her I'd open my Rolodex. 'I'll do the booking, if need be,' I said. 'I'll make the calls. I'll oversee the producers. I'll be there every step of the way, because I've got my career riding on this morning talk show as much as you do. We'll make it a success together.'"

What Bill Baker told Oprah he also told reporters. "This show will be the ultimate refinement of every morning talk show that has ever been presented. . . . Housewives are bright, intelligent people. They are deep-thinking people." He promised to give them shows of substance, which he defined at the time as dealing with Valium abuse, special diets, male sexuality, fashion, and cooking. "*People Are Talking* will be the biggest studio morning show this city—or any city—has ever done." He also wanted to create a talk show to compete with *The Phil Donahue Show,* which was getting astounding ratings all over the country, including in Baltimore.

Baker promised Oprah a big production budget, a raise in salary, an elaborate new set, a sophisticated telephone hookup, wardrobe consultants, and lighting and makeup specialists, plus the booking office of Westinghouse, which he said would ensure better guests because they would be offered the opportunity of appearing on all five Westinghouse stations around the country.

"Oprah finally agreed to do it," Baker recalled years later, "but she left my office with tears in her eyes."

# $S$ix

$R$ICHARD SHER cringed as he recalled the August 14, 1978, debut of *People Are Talking*. "I still remember the headline in *The Baltimore Sun*," he said decades later: "'A Breath of Hot Stale Air.'"

Television critics shredded the new morning talk show. They blasted Bill Baker for promising intelligent fare for stay-at-home moms and then delivering a "mindless" show about soap operas. They blasted Richard Sher for hogging airtime with an ego that "swallow[ed] up the co-host, the guests and most of the furniture." They slammed the producers for a herky-jerky pace: "*People Are Talking* sputtered into life yesterday like some sort of souped-up car with a rookie driver who had never used a clutch before."

Only Oprah escaped the damning reviews. She was commended for a "well polished" smile and handling the Dialing for Dollars segment "with unusual grace, giving this tacky little gimmick about as much class as is possible." Still, Bill Carter issued a warning in *The Baltimore Sun*: "A long run at this and Oprah's image as a news reporter is not going to be helped."

Oprah continued anchoring the news at noon, but she was no longer driven to become "the black Barbara Walters." She had been so nervous the day before her talk show debut that she ate three Payday candy bars and five chocolate chip cookies the size of pancakes. But after interviewing two actors from her favorite soap opera, *All My Children*, she said she felt like she had finally

found her place in television. She loved the talk show format—
"I used to watch *Donahue* to figure out how to do it"—and she
could hardly wait for the next show to interview men who had
had plastic surgery to look like Elvis Presley. Obsessed with the
concept of fame as a reflection of greatness, and having worshipped Diana Ross since she was ten years old, Oprah saw
*People Are Talking* as a gateway to celebrities, even lunatic Elvis
wannabes.

"She used to come into the makeup room like a little girl and
sit down on a stool while I was being made up and ask questions
about people she was interested in," said Dick Maurice, the entertainment editor of the *Las Vegas Sun* and a frequent guest.
"She had this quest for information about stars."

After the debut show, Oprah was the only one to walk off
the set giddy with delight. "We live," she yelled as she grabbed a
glass of champagne and hugged Richard Sher, who was reeling
with misgivings. The producers were also a little shaky, but
Oprah was soaring. "I came off the air, and I knew that was
what I was supposed to do. . . . This is it. This is what I was born
to do. . . . It just felt like breathing. It was the most natural
process for me."

Within a week, *The Baltimore Sun* agreed. "Oprah is rapidly
proving that she was an excellent selection for a morning talk
show host," wrote Bill Carter. "She simply looks very good in the
morning talk format. She is low key but bright and attractive,
and that combination works well over a morning cup of coffee."

"It took us two or three years to jell," said Richard Sher, the
dominant partner to Oprah's second banana. "My Afro was as
big as hers." Quick and witty, Sher had been selected because he
resembled Phil Donahue and might appeal to Donahue's female audience, which Sher never disputed, even given a chance.
"He was the talent," joked Oprah. "Just ask him." As a Southern
black woman who shrank from confrontation and described
herself as a "people pleaser," she accommodated her cocky cohost, and gave his ego a wide berth. She had learned from her
bruising debacle with Jerry Turner and was determined to
make this partnership work.

"We were very close," recalled Sher. "I'll never work with anyone again like that. We knew what each other was thinking. . . . I once took her to the hospital because she had chest pains and she put me down as next of kin. She had her own pretzel and potato chip drawer in our house. She'd jog up, we'd hear the door open, and the drawer open and we'd know Ope was there. She was real close to my wife, Annabelle, and the kids. She used to call me her best girlfriend."

"He taught me how to be Jewish," said Oprah. "He also taught me to swear."

"Oprah and Richard had a very close relationship," said Barbara Hamm, an associate producer for *People Are Talking*. "They were like brother and sister, although they had creative disagreements about what guests should be on the show and the line of questioning." She preferred movie stars, rock stars, and soap opera stars; he wanted government officials and corporate moguls. She asked questions that made him squirm.

"Oprah liked to have fun," Hamm said, "get the audience into the show. Richard wasn't so sure. He didn't want to lose control. During one show she got the audience literally dancing in the aisles. It was wild and it worked."

Unlike her cohost, Oprah was not overly concerned about her professional image. Nor was she afraid to ask naive questions and look silly, even undignified, on occasion. She exercised with manic fitness guru Richard Simmons, danced with ethnic dancers, and interviewed a prostitute who had killed a client. She also decorated cakes, basted turkeys, and bobbed for apples. When Richard Sher entered into a ponderous discussion about television journalism with Frank Reynolds, the network anchor for ABC-TV, Oprah sat on the couch listening quietly.

"Her cohost was asking all these serious, boring questions," recalled Kelly Craig, a nineteen-year-old college student who later became a reporter on WTVJ in Miami. "When it was Oprah's turn, she asked, 'So what does Frank Reynolds eat for dinner?'" The young woman was impressed by Oprah's off-the-wall query because she felt this was what the audience really

wanted to know. Craig decided if she ever got the chance to interview celebrities, she'd ask questions like Oprah's.

"Oprah had to be taught how to ask those questions," recalled Jane McClary, "and you have to give the producer Sherry
Burns credit for training Oprah to be Oprah. . . . I can remember
Sherry screaming and yelling and swearing at Oprah day after
day. 'Oprah, what the hell were you thinking? What was in your
head? Why didn't you ask that obvious question? You should always ask the first thing that comes to mind. Just say it. Say it. Say
it. Put your gut out there, girl. Don't be afraid.' Just do it.' "

One morning *People Are Talking* booked conjoined twins as
guests, thirty-two-year-old women attached at the tops of their
heads. They talked about going through life sharing everything.
Oprah was intrigued. "When one of you has to go to the bathroom at night, does the other one have to go with her?" she
asked. Richard Sher nearly fell off his perch.

Oprah soon saw herself as the audience's back-fence neighbor. "I was dishing the dirt and meddling in other folks' business
which is what I do best. My acting came in handy. In acting you
lose your personality in favor of the character you're playing but
you use it to provide energy for your character. The same way on
[a talk show]. I . . . use it to concentrate on bringing the most out
of my guests."

She certainly did that with the poultry mogul Frank Perdue.
"He was a difficult guest, almost surly," recalled Barbara
Hamm. "Toward the end of the show, Oprah asked if it bothered
him when people said he looked like a chicken. He took offense
and asked if she minded people saying she looked like a baboon.
Oprah couldn't believe . . . that he would make such a racist remark. Her chicken comment may have been a little rude, but to
come back with that . . . We cut to a commercial. Oprah took it
graciously and let it go. It was a stunning moment."

Years later, when she became overly concerned about her
public image and did not want to be seen as a victim of racism,
Oprah denied the exchange had ever taken place. "Frank Perdue did not call me a baboon," she told *Vibe* magazine in 1997,

dismissing the story as an urban myth. Those at WJZ who saw the show, such as Barbara Hamm and Marty Bass, could not explain her denial. Bob Leffler, a public relations executive in Baltimore, said, "I forget now whether Frank Perdue called her a gorilla or a monkey or a baboon. But it was some kind of primate. . . . I saw the show and have never forgotten it." The incident was not covered in the Baltimore papers, and few tapes of *People Are Talking* exist. "We used two-inch tapes then," said Bill Baker. "They were very expensive, so we reused them and recorded over [everything]."

WJZ's essayist, Mike Olesker, mentioned the Frank Perdue show in his book about television news, but the most indelible show was the one on which Oprah and Richard interviewed the famous fashion model Beverly Johnson.

"I like handsome, sexy men," she said.

"What's your ideal first date?" Oprah asked.

"To be taken to a nice restaurant and to be wined and dined. And then have the man take me home . . ."

"Yes?"

"And give me an enema," she said.

Richard Sher immediately broke for a commercial. "He and Oprah hooted about the remark for years," said Olesker. "But at that moment, it was another reminder for Sher: Could he talk to fashion models in the morning, risking diarrheic confessions, and maintain credibility in the evening [reporting the news]?"

Even in retirement, Sher was unapologetic about the tabloid-like shows that he and Oprah did on *People Are Talking*. "When sex got big, we did shows on the man with the micropenis. We did the thirty-minute orgasm. We did a lot of the tough topics—the transsexual mother with brittle bone disease."

One of their most exploitive shows became meaningful to Oprah and altered her way of thinking. The guest was a transsexual quadriplegic whose boyfriend's sperm was inserted into her sister. The quadriplegic became the biological aunt/uncle and also adopted the child. The show was criticized when it aired, but afterward Oprah happened to see the child with the transsexual quadriplegic.

"It was just a moving thing," she said. "I thought, 'This child will grow up with more love than most children.' Before, I was one of those people who thought all homosexuals or anything like that were going to burn in hell because the Scriptures said it."

At the time, Oprah's strong Baptist beliefs were being tested because of her intimate involvement with Tim Watts, a married man with a young son and no intention of leaving his wife, Donna.

"He was her first real love," said Oprah's sister, Patricia Lee Lloyd.

"Oh, God," said Barbara Hamm, remembering when Oprah was so depressed over Tim Watts's breaking up with her that she could not get out of bed for three days.

Arleen Weiner, the producer of *People Are Talking*, recalled "the many, many tearful phone calls at one, two, three, four in the morning."

The women on the production staff were sympathetic and did all they could to help Oprah, who was so obsessed with the six-foot-six disc jockey that she once ran after him in her nightgown and threw herself on the hood of his car to try to make him stay with her. Another time she blocked the front door of her apartment, screaming, "Don't go, don't leave," and then threw his keys down the toilet. This was the story she later told Mike Wallace on *60 Minutes*, attributing it to her more benign relationship with Bubba Taylor.

After Watts walked out on her at 3:00 A.M., she called her best friend, Gayle King, who she knew had been in a similar situation. "For her it wasn't throwing keys, it was checking the odometer," Oprah said of King. "We both have done equally crazy things. I was on the hood, but Gayle was on the bumper. So because she has been there and lived in that place, she never judged me. But she was always there to listen and support me."

The men on staff were not so tolerant of Oprah's hysterics. More than two decades after working with her, Dave Gosey, the director of *People Are Talking*, could not say one kind word about her. "My mother told me if you can't say something nice about someone, say nothing at all. So I have nothing at all to say about Oprah Winfrey."

Her volcanic affair with Tim Watts started in 1979 and crested and cratered for five years, even after she left Baltimore and moved to Chicago. "Those years were the worst of my life," she said. "I had bad man troubles." Being in love with a married man meant snatched hours, empty weekends, and lonely holidays that left her feeling desperate and forlorn.

"Poor thing. She had to spend Thanksgiving with us one year [1980] because she had no place else to go," said Michael Fox, whose parents, Jim and Roberta Fox, were close to Richard and Annabelle Sher. "We didn't know her until the Shers brought her to our house. . . . I sat next to her at dinner. She ate so much food that night I couldn't believe it. I've never seen a human being eat as much as Oprah did. . . . Paul Yates [WJZ's general manager] told me about her affair with Tim Watts and how miserable she was."

Oprah did not mind being seen in public with a married man, but when she found out that he was also having an affair with a pretty young blonde, she said she felt "devastated" about being "two-timed."

"My affair with Tim started in 1980 [in the midst of his with Oprah]," said Judy Lee Colteryahn, the daughter of Lloyd Colteryahn, a former football star from the University of Maryland who played for the Baltimore Colts. "Tim always said that Oprah couldn't know about us because it would ruin his business opportunities [with her]. . . . He led me to believe that he was only seeing her to get a job at Channel 13. . . . He did get a weekly Sunday show there for a while. . . . So I didn't pay much attention at first, but then my friends started seeing Tim and Oprah having dinner at The Rusty Scupper when he was supposed to be with me. . . . He played basketball for the station on Friday nights, so one night I walked into the gym [unexpectedly] just as they were finishing up a game. I saw Tim walk over to the bleachers with his cowboy boots and hand them to Oprah. He leaned over, whispered in her ear, and she started walking out with his boots. Then he saw me. 'What are you doing here?

Oprah's father, Vernon Winfrey, whispering to the author, Kitty Kelley, during their interview in Vernon's barbershop in Nashville, Tennessee, on April 22, 2008.

Katharine Carr Esters, Oprah's cousin, whom she calls "Aunt Katharine," stands with the author outside Seasonings Eatery in Kosciusko, Mississippi, on July 30, 2007.

Hattie Mae Presley Lee (4/15/1900–2/27/63), Oprah's maternal grandmother, who raised her in Kosciusko until she was six years old when she moved to Milwaukee to live with her mother, Vernita Lee.

Oprah at the age of twelve, standing next to her sister, Patricia (6/3/59–2/19/03), seven years old, and her brother, Jeffrey (12/14/60–12/22/89), six years old, outside her Aunt Katharine's house on West Center Street in Milwaukee.

Oprah as a junior at East Nashville High School, April 1970, after winning first place in the State Forensic Tournament. "It's like winning an Academy Award," she told the student newspaper.

## Oprah Heads For Forensic Nationals

As knots mounted in the stomachs and the hands were wringing with wet anticipation Oprah Winfrey's name was called and through tears approached her destination to receive her first place Dramatics trophy in the State Forensic Tournament on March 21, 1970.

"It's like winning an Academy Award", exclaimed Oprah upon winning the opportunity to represent Tennessee in Dramatic competition in the National Tournament to be held in Kansas in June of this year.

"I prayed before I competed

and said, Now God, You just help me tell them about (The Judgment Day). They need to know about the Judgment. So help me tell them," added Oprah.

"I want to thank God, Mrs. Haynes and Lana. Also, Paula Stewart for telling me she wouldn't speak to me anymore if I didn't win."

And the East Forensic team would like to thank Oprah for taking the time to represent them and winning the honor. Good-luck in the nationals Oprah!

**OPRAH WINFREY** is keeping her fingers crossed for luck in the upcoming Forensic Nationals.

Oprah represented Tennessee in dramatic competition in the National Tournament with a reading from *God's Trombones* by James Weldon Johnson.

Oprah as Student Body Vice President, East High School, Nashville, Tennessee. *Left to right:* Gary Holt, Student Body President; Oprah.

Oprah wearing peace symbol earrings in her graduation picture for the yearbook, Class of 1971, East Nashville High School.

The contestants for Miss Black Nashville in June 1972. *Left to right:* Maude Mobley; unknown; Patrice Patton-Price; and the winner Oprah Winfrey, who became Miss Black Tennessee and competed for Miss Black America. "The girl from California won because she stripped," said Oprah, although *The New York Times* made no mention of the beautiful California singer who won as having performed a striptease.

On Oprah's application for Miss Black Nashville, she signed herself as Oprah Gail Winfrey and stated that she had "never conceived a child," although she had given birth to a little boy she named Vincent Miquelle Lee on February 8, 1969. The baby died March 16, 1969.

APPLICATION FOR "MISS BLACK ___NASHVILLE___ OF THE MISS BLACK AMERICA BEAUTY PAGEANT, INC.
(indicate CITY or STATE pageant)

_____ _____ _____
Sponsored By                        Address                          Date

(Fill out in duplicate)
THE FOLLOWING MUST ACCOMPANY THIS APPLICATION:   1. Recent photograph of yourself
                                                 2. Photostat of your Birth Certificate
                                                 3. Photostat of your High School Diploma

NAME ___WINFREY___ ___OPRAH___ ___GAIL___ DATE OF BIRTH 1 29/ 54
(Please Print)   Last        First        Middle

ADDRESS (Current) ___332 ARRINGTON STREET___

CITY ___NASHVILLE___ STATE ___TENNESSEE___ ZIP CODE 37207 PHONE 228-0540

HOME ADDRESS _332 Arington Street Nashville Tenn 37207_
                              City              State       Zip Code

HOME PHONE _228-0540_ PARENTS' NAMES _Mr. and Mrs. Vernon Winfrey_

MEASUREMENTS: HEIGHT _5'6½"_ WEIGHT _135_ BUST _36_ WAIST _25_ HIPS _37_ DRESS _11-12_
SHOES _8-8½_ GLOVES _7_

EDUCATION: HIGH SCHOOL _____ YR. OF GRAD. _June 1971_

COLLEGE _Tennessee State University_ NO. OF YRS. ATTENDED _____

OTHER SCHOOLING _____

OCCUPATION AT PRESENT (work, school, etc.) _Student (freshman) WVOL Newscaster_

TYPE OF TALENT YOU WILL PERFORM (Specify nature of your 3 minute routine) _Dramatic Interpretation_

Are you contracted to any personal manager or agent? Yes___ No _X_ If so, what are the terms of such contract? _____

MUSIC OR PROPS REQUIRED FOR ROUTINE _NONE_

OTHER TALENTS _____ HOBBIES OR INTERESTS _Swimming + People_

WRITE A BRIEF STATEMENT ON WHY YOU ARE ENTERING THE MISS BLACK AMERICA BEAUTY PAGEANT:
_I would like to try to instill a sense of individual (black) pride within our people. Self-dignity_

I am a High School graduate; I am between the ages of 18 and 25 or I will become 18 prior to the final MBA Pageant; I am SINGLE and have NEVER BEEN MARRIED, ANNULLED, DIVORCED or SEPARATED and HAVE NEVER CONCEIVED A CHILD.

I understand that when I attach my signature to the foot hereof (or if I am under the legal age of 21, and my parents or legal guardians attach their signatures with mine to the foot hereof), I am contracted and committed to abide by the rules of the Miss Black America Beauty Pageant, Inc., and I have made all true statements on this application blank. In the event I am adjudged Miss Black America in the final competition, I will make myself available for one (1) year to The Miss Black America Beauty Pageant for personal appearances, speaking engagements, etc., and any and all commitments made on my behalf by the Miss Black America Beauty Pageant. If I am a student, I will forego my education for one (1) year. I understand that I will fall under the exclusive personal management of the Miss Black America Beauty Pageant.

If the foregoing represents your understanding, and/or your parents' or guardians' understanding, please indicate by signing in the space designated below, whereupon this will become a binding application and agreement between you and MBA Beauty Pageant, Inc.

_____                          _Oprah Gail Winfrey_
Parents' or Guardians' Signature if applicant under 21         Applicant's Signature

_____
Date

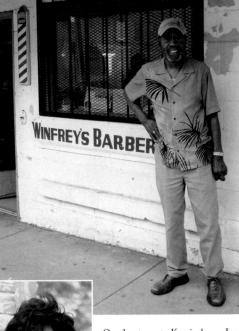

Oprah's father, Vernon Winfrey, seventy-five, standing in front of his barbershop, in Nashville, Tennessee, on April 22, 2008.

Oprah returns to Kosciusko on June 4, 1988, for Oprah Winfrey Day. "This is a real homecoming," she told the 300 people standing on a small portion of dirt road that had been named in her honor. "It is a deeply humbling experience to come back to the place where it all started."

Oprah's mother, Vernita Lee, fifty-three, as she appeared on Oprah Winfrey Day in Kosciusko, Mississippi, where she and Oprah were born in Vernita's parents' home outside the county line. Vernita, who moved to Milwaukee in 1958 during the Great Black Migration, had three children but never married.

Following a bet made with Joan Rivers on *The Tonight Show* on January 29, 1985, to lose fifteen pounds in six weeks, Oprah has her "last food fling" with her lover at the time, Randolph Cook.

Oprah standing at the top of Mt. Cuchama in 1980 at Rancho La Puerta in Tecate, Mexico. She began visiting spas at crucial points in her life to get her weight under control. She was at the Heartland Health and Fitness retreat in Gilman, Illinois, in 1985 when she got the call that she had been chosen for the role of Sophia in *The Color Purple*. "If you lose a pound, you'll lose the role," said the casting director. Oprah left immediately.

Roger King (left), chairman of the board of King World, and
Joseph Ahern (right), former general manager of WLS-TV, join
Oprah at a news conference in Chicago on July 24, 1985, to
announce the nationwide syndication of *The Oprah Winfrey Show*.
Oprah received a $1 million signing bonus and immediately called
her father to announce, "Daddy, I'm a millionaire."

Radio disc jockey Tim Watts and Oprah in Baltimore in 2007, thirty years after their tumultuous love affair. "He was her first real love," said Oprah's sister, Patricia, in 1990.

Photocopy of Stedman S. Graham, Jr., from the Fort Worth, Texas, police department. He started as a police academy trainee on January 6, 1975, and graduated three months later as a police officer. He later worked in the Bureau of Prisons.

Stedman S. Graham with President George H. W. Bush at a GOP fundraiser in Chicago, on September 26, 1990. Bush is holding a football he signed for the charitable organization Graham founded, Athletes Against Drugs: "A.A.D. Thanks and Best Wishes."

Oprah with her best friend, Gayle King. The two met in Baltimore at WJZ-TV during the 1970s. Oprah is godmother to both of King's children.

You need to go home right now. Right now. I'll be over later.' That's when my jealousy of Oprah started. . . . Then I found her credit cards in his pockets. . . . She really took good care of him. . . . He was always broke. . . . But he returned the favor later by keeping his mouth shut."

When Oprah became famous the tabloids pursued Watts and offered to pay him for the story of their love affair, including details of their drug use. "He called Oprah, said he didn't want to talk but he was strapped for cash," said Judy Colteryahn. "He said, 'Look at it from my point of view. I don't want to talk to these people, but I sure could use some money. I've got kids, I've got bills, but I am a friend to you. . . . What can we work out?' That's what he told me.

"That Christmas [1989] Gayle King delivered a gift-wrapped box to Tim in Baltimore, and Tim called me down on the Eastern Shore, where I was staying with my parents. He said, 'Oprah came through. Big-time. She really came through. Fifty thousand dollars, cash. Get your butt back here. We're going out for New Year's Eve.'

"Naturally I drove right back to Baltimore. Like Oprah, I was always available for Tim. Like her, I was always hanging out the window waiting for him to drive up in his blue Datsun. But . . . she was smarter than me. She only wasted five years of her life on him. I wasted more. . . . I did not intend to fall in love with a black man. . . . Tim is very light-skinned, so I told my friends that he was mulatto. . . . I nearly fainted the first time I saw a picture of Stedman Graham, because he looked exactly like Tim: tall—six-foot-five or six-foot-six—handsome, with a mustache, and very light-skinned. I thought, 'Wow. Oprah has found a replica for Tim in Stedman.'"

That New Year's Eve, Oprah's gift of $50,000 in cash financed her former lover's trip to Atlantic City with Judy Colteryahn. "Tim got a limousine and we had a big fancy hotel and front-row seats in Remo, a black jazz club. . . . At the time I thought he was a great guy for not selling Oprah out, especially on drugs, which we did all the time in those days. . . . Now that I'm older I realize how much power Oprah had and what she could have done [to him]. So they probably both had nooses around each other's necks.

"I asked [him] what he could say [to the tabloids] that would make Oprah pay him fifty thousand dollars in hush money not to talk. . . . That was big money then [$50,000 in 1989 equals $86,506.85 in 2009]. . . . I was wondering what he knew about her. . . . He said she did not want him to talk about her brother being gay [Jeffrey Lee died of AIDS December 22, 1989]. It's no big deal to have a brother who is homosexual, but apparently it was to Oprah. . . . Tim also said he knew about some lesbian affairs or whatever. . . . But that's all he said, and we never went into it."

Oprah never revealed Tim Watts by name as the man who had brought her so low in those years. Over the next two decades she referred to him on television as a "jerk," frequently telling her audience of the debasements she had endured because of him. "I was in love; it was an obsession," she said. "I was one of those sick women who believed that life was nothing without a man. . . . The more he rejected me, the more I wanted him. I felt depleted, powerless. . . . There's nothing worse than rejection. It's worse than death. I would wish sometimes for the guy to die because at least I could go to the grave and visit. . . . I have been down on the floor on my knees crying so hard, my eyes were swollen . . . then it came to me. I realized there was no difference between me and an abused woman, who has to go to a shelter—except that I could stay home."

African American women understand in their bones the slave mentality that leads sisters like Oprah to give their all to a man in complete subordination. One friend explained Oprah's obsession with Tim Watts and his rejection of her by citing Toni Morrison's novel *A Mercy,* in which a freed black man rejects a slave woman for not owning herself and for being a slave to her desire for him. Oprah tried to fight her own slave mentality but acknowledged through the years that she struggled not to surrender. "There's always a teeny, tiny little conflict that says, 'Maybe you already have enough. Why do you keep pushing?' That comes from lack of self-esteem, from what I consider to be a slavery mentality." Three years later she was still fighting it. "Every year I ask God for something. Last year it was love. This year it's going to be freedom . . . from everything that's kept me in bondage."

Oprah was still raw from being rejected by Watts when she told *Cosmopolitan* magazine in 1986, "If I start to talk about it, I'll weep on the floor. But I tell you, I will never travel that road again. The next time somebody tells me he's no good for me, I'm gonna believe him. I'm not going to say to myself, 'Well, maybe I'm too pushy, or maybe I don't talk enough about him, or maybe, maybe, maybe. I'm not racing home to meet him there and then not hear from him until midnight. Uh, uh. Too painful."

Even when she was supposedly happy in a committed relationship with Stedman Graham, she continued to refer to her doormat days with Tim Watts. In 1994 she told *Entertainment Weekly* that she was reading her journal from that time and was chagrined by her pathetic musings: " 'Maybe if I was rich enough or famous enough or was witty, clever, wise enough, I could be enough for you. . . .' This is a guy I used to take the seeds out of the watermelon for so he wouldn't have to spit!"

Twenty years after the affair she was still talking about him, unable to put the past to rest. In 2005 she told Tina Turner, "I just ran across a letter I wrote in my 20s, when I was in an emotionally abusive relationship. I'd written 12 pages to one of the great jerks of all time. I wanted to burn the letter. I want no record of the fact that I was ever so pitiful." In 2006 she told London's *Daily Mail,* "I will never be in a position where I love someone else more than myself, where I give over my power to someone else. I will never be in a position where I get in my car and follow them to see if they are going where they said they were going. And I'll never be in a position where I'm looking in someone's pocket or their wallet, or checking who they are on the phone with. And I will never be in the position where, if they lie to me more than once, I don't end that relationship."

During her affair with Watts, Oprah was living well in Baltimore, making $100,000 a year. She described herself then as young, attractive, and still slim. "I had so much going for me, but I still thought I was nothing without a man." She had moved into a pretty two-bedroom apartment in Cross Keys and bought a BMW. "I still remember one day we were hanging out and she transferred five thousand dollars from her savings account to her checking account just for the thrill of being able to do it," said Barbara Hamm.

Professionally, Oprah's star was shining. She and Richard Sher had become the toast of Baltimore as their show began outdrawing Phil Donahue's in the local ratings. They were so successful that their producers decided to go for syndication, which for Oprah rang the bells of big money and national recognition. It was the main reason she stayed at WJZ after her close friends Maria Shriver and Gayle King moved on to bigger markets.

Oprah and Richard shared the same agent, Ron Shapiro ("That's Sha-pie-row," the lawyer instructed), and she insisted he write into her new contract that if she wasn't working on a syndicated show, she could leave the station at the end of two years (1983) instead of three. So confident was everyone of syndication success that they signed off on the clause without objection.

In March 1981, the staff of *People Are Talking* went to New York City for the annual NATPE (National Association of Television Program Executives) convention, where syndication deals are made. They rented a suite in the New York Hilton decked out with signs that read: "The Show That Beats *Donahue*." Richard and Oprah held court with programming executives from around the country and sold the show in Rockford, Illinois; Minneapolis, Minnesota; and Sacramento, California, with potential deals in Milwaukee, Wisconsin; Bangor, Maine; Santa Rosa, California; and Casper, Wyoming. Unfortunately, none of the prospective buyers was a number one station offering a good time slot, but the producers still remained encouraged.

In anticipation of national exposure, Arleen Weiner hired an image consultant to help Oprah achieve a more sophisticated look. Up to that point she had been shopping at funky little stores such as The Bead Experience. "We were close to WJZ, a one-size-fits-all kind of store with gauzy, flowy tunics and caftans and palazzo pants," said Susan Rome, who was sixteen years old when she helped Oprah. "I tried to get her away from always buying fat-lady clothes in dark colors because she really wasn't fat—just a bit chunky and thick—but she was very uncomfortable with her size."

When the paid image consultant arrived, she met Oprah at her apartment and tore through her closet. "I was hired to give her an easier, more comfortable fit, and a look that was more stylish but would still play in Peoria," said Ellen Lightman. "There was a little trepidation on her part in the beginning, which is only natural for someone who has been directed to update her style and improve her image. . . . We retired all her beiges and camels, got her into jewel tones and clothes that fit better and were more flattering to her full figure."

The show also began booking more celebrities, for a broader appeal, which gave Oprah the chance to meet and interview Muhammad Ali, Maya Angelou, Pearl Bailey, Dick Cavett, Uri Geller, Jesse Jackson, Erica Jong, Ted Koppel, Barry Levinson, and Arnold Schwarzenegger. *People Are Talking* also became a major stop for authors on book promotion tours. "I remember being interviewed by Oprah the day after Ronald Reagan was elected president," said the writer Paul Dickson. "During a commercial break she talked about how awful Reagan was going to be for the country. She was very upset. 'This man will not be good for my people,' she said." But she said nothing on air because she was prohibited by contract from publicly expressing any political opinions.

Within six months it became clear to the producers that syndication was not going to happen. At its peak, the show was aired by only seventeen stations. Despite Oprah's great warmth on air, *People Are Talking* was simply too parochial to go national.

"The general manager after me was Art Kern, and he sold the show to half a dozen stations, but there was resistance within Westinghouse," said William F. Baker, by then chairman of Group W. "The guy in Hollywood below me did not think Oprah would make it as a talk show host. . . . I told Baltimore we were not to lose Oprah because she was a massive asset, but Baltimore was our smallest station and so the one I paid least attention to."

On Monday, September 7, 1981, the dreaded headline appeared in the TV and Radio section of *The Baltimore Sun:* " 'People Are Talking' Flops as Syndicated Show." Richard Sher was disappointed, but Oprah was devastated. This was her second big public failure in Baltimore. That evening she had another row with Tim Watts and he walked out on her, slamming the door on her hand.

"The problem with you, baby doll, is you think you're special," he said. As Oprah recalled, she was on the floor crying: " 'I'm not, please. I don't think I'm special. I don't, please come back.' Then, as I went to pick myself up, I caught a glimpse of myself in the mirror and I saw an image of my mother and I remembered her screaming one night when her boyfriend had left her. And I remembered my cousin, Alice, saying, 'It's all right. He's coming back.' That same cousin was in an abusive relationship. Her boyfriend had knocked her down the stairs and broken her leg and arms, and she still took him back. I saw myself through their eyes in that mirror. I always said I would not be a battered woman. I would not be screaming for some man. And when I heard myself saying, 'Come back. I don't think I'm special,' I'd become that. I got myself up, washed my face and said, 'That is it.' "

At 8:30 P.M. on September 8, 1981, she wrote a note to Gayle King, saying that personally and professionally her life did not seem worth living. "I'm so depressed, I want to die," she wrote. She told Gayle where to find her will and her insurance policies. "I even told her to water my plants," Oprah said later. She told the writer Barbara Grizzuti Harrison that she had not considered the ways and means to accomplish her death. "I didn't even have the courage to end the relationship," she said. Years later Gayle returned the note to Oprah, who said, "I see it now as a cry of self-pity. I never would have had the courage to do it." She told her audience: "The whole idea that you're going to kill yourself and they're all going to be mourning—that's not really the reality. I realized that if he even came to my funeral he would go on with the other girl and on with his life and still be happy."

The one-two punch of losing syndication, plus the love of her life, seemed unbearable at the time. Her friends were concerned enough to keep a quiet suicide watch, and one gently suggested that she seek psychotherapy, but Oprah refused. "I was so adamant about being my own person that I wouldn't go for counseling," she said. Her only solace was her star status in Baltimore. "She was known and loved throughout the city," said WJZ's former executive producer Eileen Solomon. "In that era Baltimore was still pretty much a town that saw itself in the shadow of Washington, D.C., with more of a blue-collar sensibility." And Oprah was its queen.

"She was a very big deal here," said Bob Leffler, "and we're a sports town, where the biggest celebrities are baseball and football stars. . . . I remember seeing Oprah at Ron Shapiro's spring party, where everyone ignored legendary Orioles like Eddie Murray and Jim Palmer and flocked to her. . . . Now that's saying something for Baltimore."

As a testament to Oprah's popularity, she was chosen by the students at Goucher, a prestigious women's college in Maryland, to deliver the commencement address in 1981, a huge honor for a twenty-seven-year-old woman, only five years older than most of the graduates. She spoke to them about her dreams as a little girl growing up in Mississippi and wanting what they had—the chance to go to a fine school, to graduate, and to begin life with the full expectation that all her dreams would come true. "When I became old enough or wise enough to know I couldn't be just like you, I wanted to be Diana Ross, or just be somebody's Supreme." Finally, she said she realized that wasn't going to be possible, either, so she learned to accept the numerators that set her apart—sex, race, education, talent, economics, family background. She said that even with all the differences that separated her from them, the Goucher graduates, they were more alike than unalike in their struggle to be good human beings. She said the struggle was harder for them as women, powerless in a man's world.

As if advising herself, she urged the graduates to nurture themselves. "Because unlike our mothers, we know that by the time we are middle-aged we have more than a fifty percent chance of never being married, divorced, widowed, or separated. So there's no denying the obvious. We have to take care of ourselves."

Her experience as an emotionally abused woman seemed to inform her speech. "I found myself one black woman rendered powerless. Being preyed upon by other people who were not only unreasonable, but just unfair. Powerless because I kept trying to be liked by people who didn't even like themselves. Powerless! Because I believed the world was one big popularity contest that I had to win or accept failure as a woman—as a human being."

Having grown up watching *The Donna Reed Show,* Oprah gently pricked the fantasy balloon of girls like herself who imagined themselves growing up, becoming Donna Reed, and living happily ever after as wives and mothers. She told them not to believe that Mr. Right was the answer to their prayers. She recited a Carolyn Rodgers poem about lonely women who are powerless because they judge their self-worth by the kind of man they attract. She spoke of the inequities facing women in the marketplace, making less money than men in the same jobs. Having experienced a secret and unwanted pregnancy, she chided the men who made policies that denied women the right to choose what to do with their own bodies. She did not use the word *abortion,* but she said those same men were denying women equality, rendering them powerless. Her wealthy white audience cheered when she repeated the words of slaves: "Ain't nobody free til we all is free." She recited Maya Angelou's poem "Phenomenal Woman," and concluded with the proud words of Sojourner Truth: "Everywhere I go people wants to talk to me about this women's rights. I tells them just like I'm telling you now. It seems to me if one woman, Eve, was able to turn this world upside down all by herself, then all of us womens in here together ought to be able to turn it right side up! And now that we's askin' to do it, y'all mens better let us." The ovation was long and loud and deserved. While Oprah would deliver many more commencement addresses over the years, none would be as heartfelt as that first one at Goucher College.

Around this time Oprah and Judy Colteryahn had to deal with the news of their lover getting his wife, Donna, pregnant and having a second son. Later, Tim Watts would have another child with a woman not his wife. Court records indicate that he had two children out of wedlock, plus two children with Donna, who eventually divorced him. "When his daughter was born on Oprah's birthday [January 29], Tim told me that Oprah took it as a sign she had been forgiven by God," said Judy Colteryahn. She had had to terminate a pregnancy and assumed that Oprah did as well. "She became the child's honorary godmother, and when her dog had puppies, she flew Tim and the little girl to New York City to give them a puppy. Tim showed me the pictures of all of them standing outside the Waldorf-Astoria hotel."

In spite of her previous resolve, Oprah resumed her rocky relationship with Watts in 1981, but this time she tried to protect herself with a workload that would leave less time to think about him. "I remember waiting for phone calls and being afraid to run the bathwater because I wouldn't hear the phone," she said. Still, she woke up on her twenty-eighth birthday and wept for hours because she had no one with whom to share her life. From 1982 to 1983 she appeared on the air three times a day. "She did the early-morning news, the hour talk show, and then the noon news," said Eileen Solomon. "That's an incredible amount of work every day, but she did it, and she won all her time slots against the competition."

By 1983, Oprah had to decide whether to renew her contract with WJZ and stay a big star in a small sky, or try to find another job. She was torn, especially after Debra DiMaio, one of her favorite producers, left for Chicago. When Oprah was poised to sign a new contract, DiMaio called and begged her to hold off. She said a great job was opening up because Robb Weller was leaving *A.M. Chicago.* "For God's sakes, don't sign yet." DiMaio urged her to send a tape and résumé to WLS, and on Labor Day, Oprah flew to Chicago for a formal interview.

Beforehand, she sat in her hotel room and watched the show. "I'd never seen it before," she said, adding that she was not impressed. "They baked cookies and gave you the latest in mascara techniques." When she went for her interview, she told WLS management their show was no good. "Too frivolous! I'm best at combinations: A sexual surrogate one day, Donny and Marie Osmond the next day. Then the Klan."

The general manager, Dennis Swanson, had already made up his mind about hiring Oprah, but just to make sure he auditioned her by setting up an interview with a group of sexually impotent men; then he told her to reminisce on camera about her deprived childhood and her time as a teenage runaway. "Her astute merger of prurience and uplift proved irresistible," wrote Peter Conrad in *The Observer.* Offered the job on the spot, she jumped at it. "The country's third market! My own show!"

Dennis Swanson was also dizzy with delight. "He was like a kid in a candy store," recalled Wayne S. Kabak, then vice president of the talent agency ICM. "I had traveled to Chicago to visit a client I represented named Candace Hasey, who hosted WLS's morning show. I stopped by to visit Swanson, her boss, who told me he had some bad news. He was going to fire Candy because he had found an extraordinarily talented replacement, who he thought would become a huge star. Notwithstanding that I was sitting in his office feeling rather downtrodden about Candy's fate, Dennis was so excited about his discovery that he insisted on showing me the tape of the woman who was replacing my client. He put the tape in the machine showing Oprah in Baltimore and, in a flash, I knew he was right. If any executive should have reaped the huge rewards of Oprah when she finally hit syndication, it was Dennis, who sadly did not because the laws at the time prevented companies that owned networks from syndicating shows. Since ABC owned WLS, syndication rights were dealt to King World which made hundreds of millions, if not more, from Oprah."

After her audition, she returned to Baltimore and called Ron Shapiro to negotiate her new contract. WJZ tried to keep her with inducements of a bigger salary (WLS was offering $200,000 a year), a company car, and a new apartment. "No one wanted her to go," said Eileen Solomon, "and some tried to pressure her by saying she'd never make it on her own in Chicago."

Bill Baker, then the chairman of Group W, called. "Oprah, you can't leave WJZ," he said. "Baltimore is your home. You're the leading lady of the city. You must stay." But Oprah had made her decision. Baker said he saw to it that Paul Yates, the general manager, was fired for letting her go.

Bill Carter felt that Oprah would succeed in Chicago, but he acknowledged that others did not. "There was an undercurrent of feeling here that this woman was not all that special," he said. "I guess because people are used to turning on their television sets and seeing nothing but attractive women, sexy or whatever. They really didn't see that substance in her. I think there's an element of racism in that. Oprah is a very black-looking black woman. . . . There were expectations that she would flop in Chicago."

Seeing he was losing her, Paul Yates would not release her until her contract expired at the end of the year. Then he played rough. "There's no way you can make it in Chicago up against Donahue," he said. "It's his home base. You're walking into a land mine and you can't even see it. You're committing career suicide. You're going to fail." Yates, an African American, said Chicago was a racist city that had not been entirely welcoming to its first black mayor, Harold Washington, and certainly wouldn't be welcoming to her. But Oprah had already factored race into her decision.

"I made a deliberate choice about where to go," she said. "Los Angeles? I'm black and female and they don't work in LA. Orientals and Hispanics are their minorities. New York? I don't like New York, period. Washington? There are thirteen women to every man in D.C. Forget it. I have enough problems." Chicago, the third-largest television market in the country, seemed ideal. "It's a big little town, sort of cosmopolitan country. The energy is different than Baltimore. It's more like New York, but you're not overwhelmed like in New York."

Having decided to make the move, she now had to wait four months to finish her contract in Baltimore before starting her new job. "I thought the [Chicago] show might not survive without a host for that long. I started eating. First I ate to celebrate getting the job, then [I ate] out of insecurity. If I failed in Chicago, I could say it was because I was fat." By the time she got to Chicago she had gained forty pounds.

"I was hired to take Oprah's place as coanchor of *People Are Talking*," said Beverly Burke, a television news reporter from North Carolina, "and it was a huge adjustment for me. But Oprah was great. She took me to lunch at the deli in Cross Keys and told me how the show worked. She talked candidly about Richard Sher, said he was Mr. Television—always on—and would totally dominate the show but that he was very good at what he does and quite professional. . . . If it weren't for Oprah, I wouldn't have gotten that job. If not for her success, they would've been looking for a white coanchor. . . .

"Still it was a huge adjustment for me. But I didn't feel I had to be Oprah. . . . She had never been an in-the-trenches reporter, which was more my style. Oprah was flash. She was criticized for showing up to do a news story wearing a fur coat."

In the weeks before she left, Richard Sher teased Oprah on the air. "She's leaving us behind and she'll forget all about us in no time. . . . Remember where you got your start." Beverly Burke saw an edge to his teasing. "She was leaving him behind and everybody knew it." But unlike others at the station, Sher encouraged Oprah. "I thought [the move] would be great for her," he said years later. "I knew she would become as big a star as she has become." As a going-away present, Oprah gave him a gold Rolex watch, on the back of which she had engraved, "Ope, 1978–1983."

The decision to leave Baltimore was the most important of Oprah's life, and she never forgot who encouraged her and who tried to hold her back. She remained close to Richard Sher, spoke at his synagogue, and even attended his sixtieth-birthday party. Publicly, she said she would be forever grateful to Bill Baker for giving her the start, but inexplicably, she never spoke to him again, despite his illustrious rise in broadcasting to become president of WNET public television in New York. Upon his retirement in 2007 he was celebrated with a magazine of tributes from networks and esteemed television colleagues: Bill Moyers, Charlie Rose, Joan Ganz Cooney, Newton Minow, and Bob Wright. But there was no tribute from Oprah Winfrey. She never spoke to Paul Yates again, either, but when Skip Ball, an engineer at WJZ, was dying, she flew to Baltimore to spend time with him in the hospital.

In December 1983 the station threw her a farewell party at Café des Artistes in Baltimore, which her mother, Vernita Lee, attended with Oprah's brother, Jeffrey. All of WJZ's on-air stars showed up—Jerry Turner, Al Sanders, Bob Turk, Don Scott, Marty Bass, and Richard Sher. Paul Yates presented her with a Cuisinart, a photo album of her days at the station, a basketful of her favorite ballpoint pens, and a twenty-five-inch Sony Trinitron television, but the gift that brought her to tears was the life-size Oprah doll wearing a copy of her favorite dress, made by Jorge Gonzalez, the station's makeup artist and graphic designer.

In her farewell speech, Oprah thanked everyone and praised Baltimore as the place where she grew up and became a woman. She then called Beverly Burke to the stage, gave her a warm introduction, and wagged her finger at the crowd, telling them to be nice to her.

Days later she packed up her five coats from Mano Swartz Furs and headed for Chicago, while Tim Watts quietly left town for Los Angeles to try to become a stand-up comic. For the next five months they planned to see each other on weekends, with Oprah flying back and forth to the West Coast. So leaving Baltimore was not as wrenching as she had anticipated. In fact, the future looked bright. Arleen Weiner drove her to the airport and kissed her goodbye, shouting down the terminal, "I hope you make it, hon. . . . I hope you make it."

# Seven

U NLEASHED AND uninhibited, Oprah chewed up the talk show competition. Chicago television viewers had never seen an overweight black female host before, and they were knocked breathless by the tornado that whirled into their homes every morning, shaking the rafters and jostling the furniture. Accustomed as they were to the cerebral style of Phil Donahue, the raunchy antics of Oprah Winfrey were a jolt, especially when she charged into the no-go zone of tabloid sex. "She receives higher ratings with controversial shows on male impotence, women who mother their men, and guys who roll over after doing it," observed the *Chicago Tribune*'s "INC." column, "while Donahue tries to combat her with right-wing spokesmen and computer crimes."

"I usually don't do homework," said Oprah. "I really have learned that for me and my style of interviewing, the less preparation I do, the better because what everybody is now calling Oprah's success is me being spontaneous and that's all it is." The *Chicago Sun-Times*'s Richard Roeper disagreed. He said her success was due "largely to loud, self-centered and often cheesy programming."

In your face and up your nose, Oprah left her audiences (and eventually Donahue's) gasping and begging for more. "The difference between Donahue and me is *me*," she said. "He's more intellectual in his approach. I appeal to the heart and relate personally to my audiences. I think it's pretentious to think you can go into a lot of depth on a subject in only an hour." Never plagued by self-inflicted doubts, Oprah appeared supremely confident, especially after Donahue moved from Chicago to New York City. The only signs of her internal combustion were nail-biting and nonstop eating. Otherwise, she seemed unintimidated by the talk show king. "We're stomping him in the ratings, you know, and suddenly he's gone [left town]. It was maaaahvelous."

Publicly she flicked Donahue a modicum of respect ("He listens"), but privately she complained that for the six months they were both in Chicago he did not contact her. "He never called just to say 'Hi Ope, welcome to town.'" She never forgot the slight.

Everyone else called, though, including Eppie Lederer, aka Ann Landers, the city's most famous resident. Oprah sent her a $1,000 jeweled Judith Leiber bag to say thank you, and invited the advice columnist to be a frequent guest on her show. The welcome call that paid pure gold came from Dori Wilson, a former model who owned her own public relations firm. "As a black woman I wanted to reach out and help Oprah feel good about our city. So I invited her to lunch. . . . She was the most driven person I ever met. Wanted to go straight to the top. . . . I rifled my Rolodex for her and helped with publicity here and there, pitching stories to various publications. . . . We became good friends for several years. Then, well, I guess you could say she dropped me."

During their first lunch, in 1984, Oprah asked Dori to recommend a lawyer/agent, and Dori called her friend Jeffrey D. Jacobs. ("The *D* is for *dependable*," Jacobs told clients.) "Jeff was then with Foos, Meyers and Jacobs and represented a lot of talent in Chicago, including Harry Caray [broadcaster for the Chicago Cubs] and the boxer James 'Quick' Tillis."

In Jacobs, Oprah found a Moses to lead her to the Promised Land. It was like Sears meeting Roebuck. Over the next eighteen years Winfrey and Jacobs built the House of Oprah, but then, just as Sears dropped Roebuck, Winfrey jettisoned Jacobs. Their friendship fractured over professional jealousies, and Oprah decided to reign over her own kingdom—one monarch, not two. She no longer wanted a partner, especially a hard-charger like Jacobs, whom she once described as "a piranha, which is what I need." By 2002 she was ready to be her own piranha. Following their acrimonious split, the lawyer was able to walk away from Harpo having earned approximately $100 million, with Oprah worth $988 million. "One of the reasons she is so financially successful," said Jacobs before their split, "is that we understand it's not just how much you make, but how much you keep."

*Fortune* magazine described Jeff Jacobs as "the little known power behind the media queen's throne"; others called him "Oprah's brain." As her consigliere for almost two decades, he handled every aspect of her business, becoming her lawyer, agent, manager, financial advisor, promoter, protector, and confidant. Keeping it further in the family, Jacobs's wife, Jennifer Aubrey, became Oprah's dresser, until *TV Guide* gave her its "Worst Dressed" award. Then Aubrey was jettisoned.

Within months of their meeting in 1984, Oprah became a full-time job for Jeff Jacobs, and by 1986 he had left his law firm to become her in-house counsel. He negotiated her contracts, supervised her staff, and oversaw production of her show. He also managed her endorsement opportunities, her speaking engagements, and her charitable contributions. He foresaw the future market for branding and pushed her to establish Harpo, Inc. (*Oprah* spelled backward); she was so grateful that she gave him 10 percent of the company and made him president. Having refused to hire an agent, a manager, or an attorney—"I don't get why anyone would want to pay 40 percent of their earnings in commissions and retainers"—she felt she got full value from Jeff Jacobs. "If something were to happen to him, I don't know what I would do," she said. "I don't know."

Oprah's cousin, Jo Baldwin, recalled Jacobs as a negotiating machine. "He was brilliant at making deals for her—that's what gave him his adrenaline. He once took Oprah from making $11 million in one week to making $33 million—in one week. . . . Yet she came to me and said she was going to fire Jeff.

Stedman told Oprah to let him go because he put his name on the door without asking her permission. I told Oprah that I had sat on the plane with Jeff and heard his visions for her and the empire he wanted to build in her name. I told her if she had a brain in her head she'd go to Jeff and tell him his name on the door was too small. Make those letters bigger. All that she has was Jeff's doing, and pushing him out like she did . . . well, that showed what Oprah was."

Oprah became an immediate sensation in Chicago, leaving in her wake nothing but breathless admirers. Cabbies honked, bus drivers waved, and pedestrians hugged her. People on the street ran into restaurants just to watch her eat. "These are the glory days, I'll tell you," she told the writer Lyn Tornabene. "I walk down the street and everyone is saying, 'Opry, how ya doin'?' 'Hey, Okra, how ya doin'?'" She even surprised herself with her success. "I've always done well," she said, "but I didn't expect it to happen this fast. I even did well in Nashville. People would call and say, 'You're all right for a black girl.' The callers meant well."

Oprah enjoyed playing with the subject of race. "'I say, Mabel, is that girl colored?' 'Why, ah believe she is,'" she would say, imitating an imagined viewer first tuning in to her show. "When I give a speech, the little old ladies say, 'What'd she say?' 'She said she used to be colored?'" Depending on which publication she was talking to, she either emphasized or dismissed her struggle as a black woman in broadcasting. She told African American magazines she found it tough to watch white newspeople advance ahead of her, although none ever had. "There was another obstacle," Oprah said, voicing her deepest insecurity. "I was too black-looking. A lot of producers and directors were looking for light skin, tiny noses, small lips. It was a heartache for me and a source of anger as well." To white reporters she claimed she never experienced discrimination. "Even when I was growing up on a farm in Mississippi I believed I would do great things. Everybody was talking about racism, but I always believed I was as good as everybody else. It never occurred to me that I was less than all the little white kids." She told *Cosmopolitan:* "Truth is I've never felt prevented from doing anything because I was either black or a woman."

Oprah identified herself as a woman first and then as a black woman, but certainly not as a black spokeswoman. "Whenever I hear the words 'community organization' or 'task force,' I know I'm in deep trouble. People feel you have to lead a Civil Rights movement every day of your life, that you have to be a spokeswoman and represent the race. I understand what they're talking about, but [I] don't have to do it, don't have to do what other people want [me] to do. Blackness is something I just am. I'm black. I'm a woman. I wear a size 10 shoe. It's all the same to me."

Yet she understood the commercial advantage of being a woman of color. "There aren't a lot of black women in the Chicago media," she said. "When I came on the air here it was like you could hear TVs clicking all over the city." She entertained her audiences with stories about being "a little nappy-headed colored chile," and gave them just enough shuffle and jive to feel hip. More important, though, she brought a heartwarming black presence into white suburban homes that lacked diversity. Debra DiMaio said the station manager was delighted he had managed to find someone who wasn't an "Angela Davis type who'd picket the station with a gun in her hair."

Oprah became the first black woman to successfully host her own daytime talk show on national television, although Della Reese had hosted a daytime variety show from 1969 to 1970. Oprah arrived at a time when African Americans were finally triumphing on the air: Bryant Gumbel reigned over the number one–rated network morning program, *The Today Show,* and Bill Cosby dominated prime time with *The Cosby Show,* the country's most watched television program. As a black female, Oprah benefited from affirmative action, but she also brought immense talent to her place at the table.

Much too shrewd to leave success to serendipity, she became the grand marshal of her own parade. She courted the Chicago media, befriended columnists, and burbled to reporters, granting every interview requested. She even gave full access to a waiter who wanted to write about her. "I had never done a one-on-one interview before I met Oprah," said waiter-turned-writer Robert Waldron. "I first called to do a piece for *Us* magazine, and was given four days of interviews, but then the piece was killed by the owner, Jann Wenner. Alice McGee, who handled Oprah's fan mail then, wanted me to place it elsewhere, so she helped me get the article on the cover of *The Star* [tabloid]. Oprah was delighted. Then I went back and proposed writing her biography. I nearly fainted when she said yes." The book, titled *Oprah!*, was published in 1987.

"Oh, those were the good old days," said Robert Feder, former television critic of the *Chicago Sun-Times*. "Oprah was a reporter's dream then . . . open, accessible, genial, and extremely cooperative. . . . I could always get her on the phone. . . . She'd call and leave me voice messages. . . . We'd lunch once a week in her office, where she'd pad around in bare feet or prop her cowboy boots up on her messy desk." At the start of each television season she sat down with Feder for a Q&A session about her plans and projects. For years he kept on his office wall a framed photo of the two of them that she had signed: "Hey, what a team! Oprah." Feder, her biggest cheerleader for a decade, removed the photo in 1994, the year many Chicago reporters call "The Dawn of the Diva."

Upon her arrival in town, Oprah saturated the media with so many items about herself and her thighs and her eating binges and her nights without a man that by the end of 1985, Clarence Petersen of the *Chicago Tribune* pronounced her "the city's most over-celebrated celebrity." Even Feder wrote, "Cool it on any more stories about Oprah Winfrey—until she wins an Oscar." But reporters could not get enough of Oprah, who was as enthralled with herself as they were. During an interview with *The Philadelphia Inquirer Magazine* she gushed like a geyser:

I'm very strong . . . very strong. I know there is nothing you or anybody can tell me that I don't already know. I have this inner spirit that directs and guides me. . . . I'll tell you what being interviewed has done for me. It's the therapy I never had. . . . I'm always growing. Now I've learned to acknowledge and accept the fact that I'm a kind person. I really like me, I really do. I'd like to know me, if I weren't me. And me knowing that is the most important thing.

The writer ended her profile by saying: "Thank you, Oprah. Now, please, hush up."

But Oprah didn't, couldn't, wouldn't hush up. Instinctively she knew that talking, talking, talking kept people from probing, probing, probing. The more she seemed to reveal about herself, the more she could hide, and still appear to be open and forthcoming. Her stories—the ones she chose to tell—were winning and farm fresh, which always left audiences rooting for her success.

"My greatest gift is my ability to talk," she told the writer Bill Zehme, "and to be myself at all times, no matter what. I am as comfortable in front of the camera with a million people watching me as I am sitting here talking to you. I have the ability to be perfectly vulnerable at all times."

Most of the media welcomed her self-promotion. What they may have branded as arrogant in someone else, they accepted as authentic in Oprah. She was allowed to play in the same league as baseball great Dizzy Dean, who said, "If you done it, it ain't braggin'." Shining her own star paid off so well that when she went national in 1986, she demanded control of her own public relations so she could continue shaping that image.

As the local host of *The Oprah Winfrey Show,* she received her first national publicity in *Newsweek,* when she dethroned Phil Donahue in the ratings. She was thrilled to get a full page in the national newsmagazine, but she resented being described as "nearly two hundred pounds of Mississippi-bred black womanhood, brassy, earthy, street smart and soulful."

"I did not like it," she told the writer Robert Waldron. "I don't like the term 'street smart.' I think it's a term that gets put off on black people a lot. Rather than say intelligent, it's easier to say we're street smart and that kind of explains a lot of things. 'Oh, well, she made it because she's street smart.' Well, I am the least of the street smarts. I've never lived on the streets. I don't know anything about it. I never was a hustling kid. I mean, I had my days of delinquency. But I was never like a hustling kid, or street-wise. I wouldn't last ten minutes on the streets."

Despite her defensiveness, she admitted that the *Newsweek* article "opened a lot of doors for me," including the ultimate in celebrity beatification: an invitation to appear on *The Tonight Show.*

"They said if I appeared with [substitute host] Joan Rivers, I could come back and appear with Johnny Carson. I said, 'Nooo problem.'"

The warden of the Cook County Jail was so taken with Oprah that he allowed inmates to stay up past their regular cur-few to watch her that night.

Jeff Jacobs, who accompanied Oprah and her staff to LA, told her to tape a couple of shows to promote ABC's miniseries *Hollywood Wives.* This would ingratiate her with the network that owned and operated WLS, bring a little glamour to her local audience, and promote her appearance on television's pre-mier late-night show. So with her camera crew in tow, Oprah lunched at Ma Maison and strolled the shops of Rodeo Drive with Angie Dickinson, Mary Crosby, and author Jackie Collins, sister of movie star Joan Collins.

The night before, she met her friend Maria Shriver and then-fiancé Arnold Schwarzenegger for dinner. "We sat in a restaurant booth and Arnold played Joan Rivers. He kept pumping me. 'Why are you successful?' 'Why did you gain weight?'"

At the time, Joan Rivers was famous for skewering Elizabeth Taylor with fat jokes: "She's got more chins than the Hong Kong phone book. . . ." "Her bumper sticker says, 'Honk if you have groceries.'" "The three biggest boobs in Virginia are John Warner [husband number six] and Elizabeth Taylor." So it was inevitable that the subject of Oprah's weight would come up during her seven-minute appearance on *The Tonight Show.*

Standing behind the curtain on January 29, 1985, Oprah listened to Joan Rivers's introduction: "I'm so anxious to meet her. They talk about her as streetwise, brassy, and soulful. Please help me welcome—Miss Oprah Winfrey."

Oprah felt put down. "I thought, 'Uh oh . . . She's read too much about this street-wise . . . Negro woman.' I mean when you hear that you think I'm gonna come out with a chicken and a watermelon wearing a bandanna around my head."

Oprah walked out in a royal blue suede dress dripping with strands of sequins and split up the front to reveal white hose and an $800 pair of blue suede shoes sparkling with rhinestones. In the fashion of the day, her hair was teased and sprayed to a lacquered hardness. Her eyes were painted purple and red, and her red lips were outlined in purple to complement the dress, which she said had been custom-made in Chicago by someone named Towana. Her earrings dripped with dangling rhinestones. She looked like she had come straight from a lounge act, without time to change at the truck stop.

Joan asked about her childhood, and Oprah spun her stories of "whuppins" and "pet cockroaches" before the conversation turned to dieting.

"How did you gain weight?" said Joan.

"I ate," said Oprah.

"You're a pretty girl and single. Lose it."

Oprah said later she wanted to slap the comedienne. "But . . . I'm on national television for the first time. . . . Then Joan Rivers, who is this small, made a bet with me to lose weight. I said okay. I'm on national television. What else am I going to say?"

Rivers said she would lose five pounds if Oprah lost fifteen. They shook hands and agreed to meet back on the show in six weeks to see who had won.

Oprah returned to Chicago the next day and made a reservation for her "final feast" at Papa Milano. She invited her staff to join her. "They are my family," she said. "We eat almost every meal together." She alerted the media to cover the revel, which Debbi DiMaio said started at 7:30 A.M. with grilled cheese sandwiches. Then came breakfast at the Pancake House. "I ordered real pancakes, potato pancakes, and an omelet," said Oprah. "When they brought the pancakes out, they said, 'We made these reluctantly because we want you to win your bet with Joan. Don't eat them all.' Then for lunch I had my last super-duper order of French fries. So I had my favorite food—pota-toes—twice."

The dinner menu consisted of pizza, pasta e fagioli, garlic bread, sweet peppers, ravioli, salad, cannoli, cookies, and spumoni. The next day a picture appeared in the *Chicago Tribune* of Oprah feeding a slice of pizza to her then-boyfriend Randy Cook, a tall, light-skinned African American man with a mustache.

"I was Stedman before Stedman," Cook said many years later. "I lived with Oprah in her apartment from January through May 1985."

Their five-month affair became a torment for Oprah years later, when Cook decided to go public with their relationship and write a book. By that time Oprah was living with Stedman Graham, who ran Athletes Against Drugs. Cook's book proposal was titled *The Wizard of O: The Truth Behind the Curtain: My Life with Oprah Winfrey.* His chapters included:

- Oprah Introduces Me to Smoking Cocaine
- Oprah: Drugs, Sex, Out of Control
- Oprah and Gayle

He described how Oprah introduced him to drugs and freebased her own crack cocaine in her twenty-fourth-floor condo. He wrote graphically that they became "carnally driven monsters" and indulged in "animalistic sex." He said Oprah regularly gave him her bank card to withdraw money to buy their drugs. She was the financier; he was the supplier. He claimed he became addicted because of Oprah, and his life spiraled out of control. When he bottomed out, he lost his job, declared bankruptcy, and finally got into a twelve-step recovery program. "One of the steps requires me to make amends," he wrote. "For me this means reaching out to Oprah. I go to her studio to talk but Oprah completely denies my existence."

Rejected and angry, Cook decided to write a tell-all. He sent his proposal to publishers, but no one wanted to publish a book about a beloved American icon cooking up crack cocaine and smoking herself sky-high. So Cook contacted Diane Dimond, the investigative reporter for *Hard Copy*, a tabloid news television show devoted to celebrity exposés that ran in syndication for ten years.

"In my experience with *Hard Copy*, which was owned by Paramount Pictures, there wasn't anyone we couldn't cover," said Diane Dimond. "I did stories on Michael Jackson and Heidi Fleiss [the Hollywood Madam, who went to prison], and she had the names of all my bosses in her little black book. I covered O. J. Simpson and I broke the William Kennedy Smith rape case, so no one seemed off-limits. But I found out fast that Oprah Winfrey was definitely the one untouchable when Linda Bell Blue, my producer . . . got a call from none other than Jonathan Dolgen, head of Paramount, who screamed and yelled until Linda promised to call me off. . . . She told me that we could not be seen as attacking one of the most successful black women in America. . . . I had talked to Cook and his lawyer several times . . . but at that point I had to drop the story."

Cook told *The Star* that Oprah was using her influence to stop him from telling his story. Oprah denied the charge and called him "a liar" and "a drug addict" who could not be trusted or believed. Further, Cook alleged, she said he would be very sorry if he told his story to anyone else. He backed off, eventually relapsed into drugs, and finally reentered recovery.

By then Oprah had learned that someone else claiming to have done drugs with her in Baltimore had also sold a story to the *National Enquirer*, and while the story had not been published, she felt threatened that soon her drug past would be splashed all over the tabloids. "We did have a story in the works entitled 'I Was Oprah's Drug Dealer,' but it got killed at the last minute," recalled the *Enquirer*'s senior editor. "As I recall, he came to us and we paid him, after he passed a lie detector test."

"I interviewed the guy in Baltimore who claimed he was Oprah's boyfriend when she worked at the local station," said the writer Jerry Oppenheimer. "He did coke with her and, as I recall, he had also sold drugs for a living when he was involved with her. He had photographs of the two of them together—that was always a *National Enquirer* requirement, that and passing a lie detector test—and I felt he was credible . . . a street guy but pretty articulate and very nice, very likeable."

Like most celebrities, Oprah came to despise the tabloids. Early in her career she had cooperated with them on stories about herself, even provided personal photographs, and paid someone to plant "do-good" stories about her donations to charities. But once she became famous, she reviled the grocery store weeklies as "verbal pornography" and railed against their coverage of her. She fired employees who leaked information to them and instituted a company rule that no one was allowed to say her name outside of the office. In public they were instructed to refer to her as "Mary," so that conversations overheard in restaurants or bars would not become tabloid fodder. They also were forbidden to take candid pictures of her. She became obsessed with the coverage of her weight in the tabloids, and their unflattering photos frequently brought her to tears.

"I once put a reporter on twenty-four-hour coverage of Oprah on vacation at Necker Island with Stedman," said a former assignment editor for the *National Enquirer*. "When Stedman went out to play golf, Oprah called room service and ordered two pecan pies. Our reporter helped the waiter with delivery. Oprah answered the door. No one else was in the room with her. An hour later she called room service to pick up the empty tins outside her door, which our guy photographed. . . . Of all the stories we did on Oprah and her weight over the years, that one stands out in my mind because of what it told me about the kind of obesity bingeing she did in secret when no one was around."

Her dearest friends pleaded with Oprah to ignore the tabloids: "They are not you," said Maya Angelou. "You are not in those stories." But Oprah knew that her audience was the tabloids' audience: they shared the same demographics. The women who watched her show every day shopped for groceries every week, and they saw the sensational stories each time they approached the cash register. Oprah assumed that most people were like her and believed what they read.

Having been sold out to the tabloids by money-hungry relatives and friends in the past, she now decided to take control. Meeting with her staff at the end of 1994, she discussed presenting a show on drug abuse so that she could allude (generally, with no specifics) to her own drug experience. The show would feature mothers, because women look more sympathetic than men do talking about dealing with their addictions. The hour would be taped—not live—so the show could be edited, if necessary. By then Oprah's ratings had fallen off by 13 percent in the last two seasons, but she remained high in public esteem, and some on her staff worried about the possible backlash from such an admission. But she felt she had no choice.

The show, taped on January 11, 1995, was heavily promoted. During the taping, Oprah broke down and made her tearful admission: "I did your drug," she told a mother who was talking about her addiction to crack cocaine. "It's my life's great big secret that has always been held over my head." Beyond that she offered no specifics as to where, when, or with whom she had done drugs, but her public admission now insulated her from anyone from her past stepping forward.

Oprah's revelation made national news, and her spokeswoman, Deborah Johns, told reporters that it was "totally spontaneous." Tim Bennett, president of Harpo Productions, concurred. "[P]urely spontaneous," he said. "From her heart, from Oprah." But Chicago columnists Bill Zwecker and Robert Feder, with sources deep inside Harpo, knew better; they reported that Oprah's admission was a premeditated ploy to boost her ratings and came about because unnamed others had threatened to reveal her secret themselves.

"Nothing is spontaneous with Oprah," said a former employee in 2007. "It may seem spontaneous, but it's all as carefully choreographed as Kabuki. She's fabulous on television—no one's better—but nothing is left to chance. . . . She's like Ronald Reagan. In Hollywood he was considered a B actor, not one of the greats. Not even close. But he was a magnificent communicator on television, with just enough acting ability to appear sincere. Oprah is the same way. She knows how to cry on cue.

She once told me that every tear is worth half a ratings point, and she can cry on a dime." The former employee noted that Oprah's biggest revelations came during or right before sweeps weeks (February, May, July, and November). "Ratings are everything to Oprah."

Whether her drug-use admission was designed to fuel her ratings or to defuse the tabloids, Oprah had been able to reveal her secret in a soft and sympathetic setting, and felt a great weight lifted. "I no longer have to worry about that now," she said. "I understand the shame. I understand the guilt. I understand the secrecy."

Following Oprah's public drug admission, Randy Cook filed a $20 million lawsuit against her for slander and emotional distress, but she was racked and ready. "I will fight this suit until I am bankrupt before I give even a penny to this liar," she was quoted as saying. In court documents, she later denied making the "liar" statement. By then Cook, with no visible means of employment, looked like a desperate man trying to feed off a former relationship with a famous woman who was now worth millions. His lawsuit was dismissed by the U.S. District Court of Illinois, but he appealed, and the U.S. Seventh Circuit reinstated several counts of his complaint. After two years of legal skirmishes, Oprah was forced to respond to his interrogatories. In her answers, she finally admitted what she had so long denied: that she and Cook had had sexual relations, and that she and Cook had used cocaine on a regular and consistent basis.

Cook won the right to a jury trial, but before a date could be set, he dismissed his suit "at the behest of [my] dying mother." He said his family and friends begged him not to go to court against Oprah Winfrey, but as late as 2007 he was still looking to be paid for his story of the five-month affair he had had more than two decades earlier, and he was still trying—unsuccessfully—to peddle his tell-all book. He claimed that he and Oprah were addicts when they lived together in 1985, but he did not know how she got off drugs. "On a few occasions, Oprah and I would be up all night getting high. Gayle King was set to arrive at the condo those same mornings. . . . We would clean up all the evidence and act like nothing happened moments before Gayle walked through the door. It wasn't until Oprah and I broke up that Gayle found out [about the drugs]. But when she did, she intervened and very well could have been the one who got Oprah off drugs for good," he said. "The last time I saw Oprah was in 1985 before she left to film *The Color Purple.*"

# $E$ight

AN IMMUTABLE bond exists among black women born in the South and rocked in the arms of grandmothers who wore Sunday church hats, swayed to spirituals, and instilled reverence for "the ancestors." When these women meet as strangers they embrace as sisters because they are connected to the soil of country roads in Arkansas, bayous in Louisiana, backwoods in Georgia, and swamps of Mississippi. They know each other before they are introduced.

"It was that connection to the goodness and strength of southern women that bound me to Oprah," recalled Alice Walker, the Pulitzer Prize–winning author of *The Color Purple*. "I wrote the role of Sofia based on my mother and gave Quincy Jones [producer] and Steven Spielberg [director] a picture of her when she was Oprah's age. So when Quincy saw Oprah on television he was looking at my mother. . . . When I met Oprah, I, too, saw my mother. That's the root of my affection for her, and despite the distance she's put between us since we made the film in 1985, I still feel grateful to her. She arrived to carry the spirit of my mother and she did it really, really well."

Oprah credited her self-confidence to her Southern roots. "I'm very blessed because I was raised in the South in Nashville and Mississippi," she said. "The whole Southern upbringing left me feeling I can do anything. It didn't do to me what it does to a lot of people. I never in my life felt oppressed."

Almost all the women who worked on *The Color Purple* had

some connection to the South, and that sensibility of sister-hood contributed to what Alice Walker called the "holy experi-ence" of making the movie. Before she sold the film rights, she insisted that the producer and director commit themselves to a diverse cast and crew. "I got it in writing that at least fifty percent of those hired had to be black, female or other minority," she said. "It was a happy set because we all came together in a blessed way to tell the story."

The director, Steven Spielberg, did not want a cast of un-knowns for what he called his first serious film. After signing Whoopi Goldberg, then unknown, for the lead of Celie, he hoped to sign Tina Turner for the singing role of Shug Avery. He planned to eliminate the lesbianism in the novel and film only one sweet kiss between Celie and Shug, but he wanted Whoopi Goldberg to feel comfortable. "If I'm going to kiss a woman, please let it be Tina," Whoopi said. Turner was also the first choice of the writer, the producer, and the casting director. As-suming she was on board, Quincy Jones scheduled her meeting with the director, but, as he said later, she flipped on him.

"I wouldn't do a black picture if I was dying," Turner said. "It took me twenty years to get out of that black shit and I ain't going back."

Jones said he was so shocked he couldn't open his mouth. "But I certainly understood her feelings about not wanting to play an abused woman." He knew about the years of beatings she had endured from her former husband. So the role went to the actress Margaret Avery, who performed brilliantly and received an Academy Award nomination for Best Supporting Actress. But Tina's rejection left the cast with no known stars and a soupçon of bile. "She turns down *The Color Purple* and she does *Mad Max: Be-yond Thunderdome*. All the while saying that she's seeking credi-bility as an actress," said Whoopi Goldberg. "Give me a break."

Quincy Jones wrote in his autobiography that Tina Turner's reaction reflected the attitude of Hollywood at the time. "Nobody wanted to make a black movie," he said, explaining the resistance he had to overcome to get the film made in 1985. Statistics backed him up. During that summer's release of teenage films, there had not been one black female face on-screen. So Jones decided to pursue the popular mainstream director of *E.T.: The Extra-Terrestrial,* whose magic made millions believe in the humanity of a wrinkled rubber alien who looked like Elmer Fudd. The producer then had to convince Alice Walker that Steven Spielberg was the right person to make her book into a major motion picture. Reluctant at first, Walker finally came around. "I guess if he can make people believe in Martians, he can do the same for our folks," she said.

Decades after writing the novel that brought her wealth, acclaim, and international recognition, Alice Walker maintained that *The Color Purple* was a gift given to her to give to others. Her lack of ego about writing the saga of a poor country girl's life of physical and sexual abuse by men elevated the process of filming for everyone. "We all wanted to make Alice proud," said Margaret Avery.

Oprah said that being chosen for the role of Sofia was the single happiest day of her life, and filming the movie was "the only time I ever felt part of a family surrounded by unconditional love." She recalled the experience with near-worshipful awe. "It was a spiritual evolvement for me," she said. "I learned to love people doing that film."

She forged strong friendships on the set, but few survived the passage of time. She fell out with Whoopi Goldberg, who would later compare her to Lonesome Rhodes, the power-hungry monster in *A Face in the Crowd*; she tangled with Akosua Busia, who also appeared with her in *Native Son* and wrote the first screenplay for *Beloved,* the movie Oprah felt would make her a film legend. She pulled away from Alice Walker and offended Steven Spielberg, but she held tight to Quincy Jones. "I love him more than any human being in the world," she once said. Revered for his musical genius, "Q," as his friends call him, opened his influential Hollywood circle to Oprah and made her part of his celebrity world. She once sent him a T-shirt that read: "Oprah Loves Me Unconditionally. I Can Never Fuck Up."

Later she would say that it was divine destiny that she got the role of Sofia in *The Color Purple.* "I wasn't really, really,

really surprised," she said. "It's exactly what was supposed to happen. To me."

Whether from God or good luck, her casting could definitely be credited to her girth. In the spring of 1985 she had gone to a fat farm to try to lose weight and win the bet she had made with Joan Rivers on *The Tonight Show*. While pounding the track, she received a call from the casting director, Reuben Cannon, who warned, "If you lose one pound, you lose the part." She immediately packed her bags and hightailed it to the nearest Dairy Queen.

At that point, the thirty-one-year-old talk show host was riding a comet of local fame across Chicago: "I could practically do no wrong," she said. She knew that a major role in a Steven Spielberg film could throw her star into the stratosphere. "I wanted that role more than anything I've ever wanted in my life," she said. When she found out she was in the running, she begged her lawyer not to negotiate too hard. "He was pushing, pushing, pushing. I said, 'Jeff, I'd do it for nothing—please, please don't ask for any *money* money.' He said, 'You're not doing it for free.'" Quincy Jones and Steven Spielberg had already accepted scale ($84,000 apiece), and so had the rest of the cast ($35,000 apiece). "It was a labor of love for everyone," said Oprah.

She auditioned on April Fool's Day of 1985, with Willard Pugh, who was to play her husband, Harpo, in the film. "After we were through, Steven said he'd like to see us upstairs in his office," she said. "He then told us he wanted us for the roles. I went nuts. I jumped on Steven's sofa, knocking over his NASA space shuttle model in the process, and that was nothin'—Willard passed out."

The director had occasion to recall that moment twenty years later, when his friend Tom Cruise, promoting Spielberg's *War of the Worlds,* jumped on Oprah's couch to demonstrate his love for Katie Holmes, soon to be his wife. There had been rumors in the tabloids about Cruise possibly being homosexual, and Oprah seemed to fan that speculation by telling reporters she was not convinced of the star's heterosexual enthusiasm. "I just didn't buy it," she said. "Didn't buy it." Following Cruise's appearance on her show, the phrase "jump the couch," meaning "strange or frenetic behavior," jumped into *A Historical Dictionary of American Slang*. Spielberg was upset by the criticism his friend received and publicly defended him. "Working with Tom is one of the greatest gifts I've ever been given by this business," he said. He did not mention the time Oprah had exhibited similar exuberance by jumping on his couch in 1985, but by 2005, their twenty-year friendship had frayed. Months after the Cruise couch-jumping, Spielberg stayed away from the Broadway premiere of Oprah's production of *The Color Purple—The Musical*, and she ignored the presentation of his lifetime achievement award at the Chicago Film Festival.

In the beginning, Oprah had been in awe of Steven Spielberg. "He's the most wonderful human being I've ever met," she told reporters in 1985, adding that everyone in the cast and crew was "awed out of our brains" to be working for him. "Oh, dear Gawd," she drawled, "I cans believe we is workin' for Mr. Steven." When she saw Spielberg's Amblin Entertainment empire, she elevated him to godlike status. He was the movie mogul she aspired to be. "That's when I wanted my own production company," she said. Until then, Harpo, Inc., was simply the corporate entity she needed for tax purposes—to answer her fan mail—but after seeing Spielberg's operation, she and Jeff Jacobs set about making Oprah the first black woman to own her own studio.

She claimed that as the only non-actor in the cast she was terrified during filming, but her costars laughed at the suggestion that she was intimidated by anybody or anything. Akosua Busia and Margaret Avery jokingly imitated her husky voice to mock her so-called fears: " 'I'm so terrified. Look out, everybody, here I come, and I'm scared out of my wits.' "

Oprah later criticized the casting of people of different skin tones as family. "[That] was one of the things that bothered me about *The Color Purple*." On the set she did not hesitate to tell the director he was making some of her scenes look too slapsticky. He barred her from watching the dailies. In one memorable scene, where her character wallops the white mayor of the town,

Oprah admitted she was not acting. Her response was real and visceral. "Steven had told the white actors to call me 'nigger,' but he didn't tell me what he was going to do. 'You big fat nigger bitch,' they said. . . . Nobody had ever called me that, or anything close to it, and I didn't need to be a method actor to react. . . . I was so shaken and angry that I . . . really decked the mayor." Her character pays with years in jail for assaulting a white man. She emerges broken, empty, and blind in one eye to become a maid for the mayor's wife. "I'm not a subservient person," said Oprah, "so playing that part of Sofia was hard for me."

Spielberg was so impressed by Oprah's talent for improvisation that he enlarged her part during filming, and drew a magnificent performance out of her that, sadly, she never equaled in subsequent films. But in *The Color Purple* she was superb. "Unforgettable," said the *Los Angeles Times*. "A brazen delight," said *Newsweek*. "Outstanding," agreed *The Washington Post*. Critics predicted her nomination for a Golden Globe and an Oscar as Best Supporting Actress. The only lackluster review came from her father: "I think I'd put Whoopi Goldberg first, Margaret Avery second, and maybe Oprah was third," said Vernon Winfrey.

In the middle of filming, Oprah flew to Chicago to sign contracts with King World to syndicate *The Oprah Winfrey Show* in the fall of 1986. At the press conference afterward she told reporters, "I'm thrilled at the prospect of beating Phil [Donahue] throughout the country." With more than one hundred stations committed to carrying her show, she received a $1 million signing bonus. She called her father, then a councilman in Nashville. "Daddy, I'm a millionaire," she shouted. "I'm a millionaire." She returned to North Carolina and told Steven Spielberg that he should reconsider putting her name on the movie's posters, which he did not.

"I think that hurt Oprah deeply," said Alice Walker, "and may have been the reason why she took over the theater marquee for the musical of *The Color Purple* twenty years later." The theater marquee did indeed read, "Oprah Winfrey Presents *The Color Purple*."

Being a part of the film changed Oprah's life forever. The

confluence of her Oscar nomination with the syndication of her talk show produced a perfect storm for star-making, and Jeff Jacobs, in conjunction with King World, mounted what Quincy Jones described as "an unprecedented promotional blitz that started her on the path to where she is now." Oprah began a round of radio, television, newspaper, and magazine interviews that lasted for months, making her name known from the cornfields of Kansas to the penthouses of Manhattan. She was profiled by *Cosmopolitan*, *Woman's Day*, *Elle*, *Interview*, *Newsweek*, *Ebony*, *The Wall Street Journal*, and *People*. She was interviewed on *The Merv Griffin Show*, *Good Morning America*, a *Barbara Walters Special*, *60 Minutes* with Mike Wallace, and *The Tonight Show with Johnny Carson*. She also appeared on *Late Night with David Letterman*, and hosted *Saturday Night Live*. "Seldom before in the history of the Motion Picture Academy of Arts and Sciences has one Academy Award nominee received so much publicity," wrote Lou Cedrone in the Baltimore *Evening Sun*. "Since the day she won the nomination, it has almost been impossible to pick up a newspaper, a magazine or a trade publication without coming face to face with the Winfrey image and attendant stories."

Oprah's movie debut had launched her beyond the realm of daytime television, and she could not help but enjoy her elevated status. TV critics who had characterized her as a big, brassy, tabloid talker now treated her with a newfound respect. She was no longer relegated to the entertainment sections of their newspapers; her picture now appeared on the front pages with glowing tributes. She became a full-fledged household name as she crisscrossed the country promoting herself, her movie, and her talk show. She readily acknowledged her new fame—"Ain't I something, child?"—but she refused to act as though she had been blessed by good luck.

"I had sense enough to know that the movie was something very special," she told Luther Young of *The Baltimore Sun*, "and I expected it to do everything it has done for me."

"Yes, I'm coming into my own," she told Ann Kolson of *The Philadelphia Inquirer*, "and it's a great feeling to know [I'm] not even there yet." Nonplussed, the reporter wrote, "The world has been good to this big, noisy, hip-shakin' mama who began life poor on a Mississippi farm."

When Jeff Strickler of the Minneapolis *StarTribune* suggested she was an "overnight sensation," Oprah let him have it. "I resent that," she said. "I take objection to people saying that because no one gets anywhere overnight. I am where I am just as you are where you are: because of everything you have done up to this moment."

Writing for *TV Guide,* R. C. Smith was struck by her immense self-confidence. "She claims to have believed, always, that for her anything was possible because she was just that good." When asked if she was going to give up her talk show, Oprah said, "I intend to do and have it all. I want to have a movie career, a television career, a talk show career. So I will do movies for television and movies for the big screen and I will have my talk show. I will have a wonderful life. I will continue to be fulfilled doing all of those things, because no one can tell me how to live my life. I believe in my own possibilities, so I can do whatever I feel I'm capable of doing, and I feel I can do it all."

What looked arrogant in print sounded only slightly less so in person, as Oprah's rich voice and commanding size transfixed listeners while she communicated the kind of self-assuredness only a fool would question. Yet when she leavened self-importance with self-deprecation, she was winning and wonderful.

In the days leading up to Oscar night, she joked with her audiences about having to lose weight and find a gown to camouflage "a behind as big as a boat." At a public appearance in Baltimore she showed up in a $10,000 full-length fox coat dyed purple and a purple sequined gown showing massive cleavage. "I'm dieting now. Can't you tell?" she joked. "Thinner thighs by Oscar night. Thinner thighs by Oscar night. That's what I keep telling myself."

Despite mixed reviews, *The Color Purple* received eleven Academy Award nominations, including one for Whoopi Goldberg as Best Actress, and two for Oprah and Margaret

Avery as Best Supporting Actress, but nothing for Spielberg as Best Director. This caused considerable comment because no director of a movie with that many nominations had ever been ignored. On top of that insult was an angry backlash from the black community, which threatened to doom the film's commercial success. The Coalition Against Black Exploitation boycotted *The Color Purple* because of its depiction of black men, and the uproar of rancorous debate prompted picket lines at the premieres in New York, Los Angeles, and Chicago. Steven Spielberg was denounced for turning a complex novel into patty-cake and purple flowers. Quincy Jones was slammed for selecting a white director to tell a black story, and Alice Walker was blasted for portraying black men as beasts to white audiences.

Few movies up to that time had caused such rabid racial reactions. Columnists and radio talk shows focused on the controversy, historical black colleges sponsored forums and seminars, and black churches across the country filled with passionate debate. The biggest outcry came from African American men who felt defiled by the film.

"It is very dangerous," said Leroy Clark, a law professor at Catholic University. "The men [in the film] are raping, committing incest, speaking harshly, separating people from their families. . . . It reinforces the notion of black men as beasts."

The cast rushed to the film's defense, including Oprah, whose excellent performance was untouched by the public vitriol. "This movie is not trying to represent the history of black people in this country any more than *The Godfather* was trying to represent the history of Italian Americans," she said.

"*The Color Purple* in no way identifies itself as the story of all black men," said Danny Glover, one of its male stars. "This is just this woman's story."

After receiving the Golden Globe for Best Actress, Whoopi Goldberg dismissed the protesters as "pissy."

The respected film critic Roger Ebert declared *The Color Purple* the best film of 1985, but when he viewed it again twenty years later, even he admitted "that the movie is single-minded in its conviction that African-American women are strong, brave, true and will endure, but African-American men are weak, cruel or comic caricatures." Still, he found humanity in the story of how Celie endures and finally finds hope.

Oscar night arrived, but without thinner thighs for Oprah. In fact, she said it took four people laying her on the floor to pull her dress on her, and at the end of the evening they had to scissor it off. "It was the worst night of my life. . . . I sat in that gown all night and I couldn't breathe. I was afraid the seams were gonna bust." When Lionel Richie appeared on her talk show later, he said she had looked nervous at the Oscars. "I'm telling you, there aren't many black faces at the Oscars," she said. "So when you walk through the door, everybody looks around to see. 'Is it Lionel Richie? No. It's not Brenda Richie. Who is it? It's some black girl in a tight dress,' is what they say. And that's why I was so uncomfortable. I thought, 'Oh, God! Lionel Richie is gonna see me in this dress!' It was the tightest dress known to womankind. It was a horrible night."

Oprah lost Best Supporting Actress to Anjelica Huston (*Prizzi's Honor*) and in one of the most stunning shutouts in the Academy's history *The Color Purple* did not win one of its eleven nominations, while *Out of Africa* won seven awards, including Best Picture. "I could not go through the night pretending that it was OK that *Color Purple* did not win an Oscar," Oprah said. "I was pissed and I was stunned."

Whoopi Goldberg blamed the Hollywood NAACP. "They killed the chances for me, Oprah, Margaret Avery, Quincy, everybody—I truly believe that. And blacks in Hollywood paid a price for years to come. Because after all the hell that was raised, the studios didn't want to do any more black movies for fear of the picket lines and boycotts."

The movie's loss did not dampen Oprah's intention to become a great star. "When you mention great actresses, you'll have to say my name: 'Meryl . . . Oprah,' 'Hepburn . . . Oprah.' That's what I want. What I am is an actress. I don't get paid for acting. But I was born to act." She continued her publicity blitz long after the movie's run, and piled up reams of reverential press in time for the September 1986 launch of her talk show. Her laudatory media coverage hit its first speed bump when Tina Brown, then editor of *Vanity Fair,* assigned Chicago writer Bill Zehme to profile Oprah. He accompanied her on her rounds of the good and the great, and described how, "with unabashed lustfulness," she pawed through the possessions of rich Chicagoans and poked in their closets, counting their shoes.

"She was like a little kid running around my apartment just oohing and aahing," said Rockefeller heiress Abra Prentice Anderson Wilkin. Chicago socialite Sugar Rautbord, who had profiled Oprah for *Interview,* Andy Warhol's monthly magazine, said, "There's a wonderful hunger about her. Some people yearn to be free. Oprah yearns to be rich."

Oprah did not hide her acquisitiveness from Zehme, who wrote that within the first hour of their meeting she had told him she was a millionaire. "'I knew I'd be a millionaire by the time I turned 32,' she said . . . again and again. . . . By the second hour she had added, puffing up with purpose, 'I certainly intend to be the richest black woman in America. I intend to be a mogul.'" Zehme captured Oprah's obsession with money but lacked the sensitivity to note that for a descendant of slaves, money would mean freedom from servitude forever.

She told him about her many fur coats ("I say minks were born to die!") and her immense income ("Money just falls off me, I mean it falls off!"). She opened the doors to her new $800,000 lakefront condominium, a marbled palace with a dripping crystal chandelier in the dressing room and ornate gold swans on the bathtub spigots, and led him into her bedroom, with its panoramic view of the city.

"She is sprawled lumpily across her bed at this point and I sit on its lower edge," he wrote as Oprah continued her me-me-me monologue: "'I transcend race, really. I believe that I have a higher calling. What I do goes beyond the realm of everyday parameters. I am profoundly effective. The response I get on the street—I mean Joan Lunden [former host of *Good Morning America*] doesn't get that and I know it. I know people really really love me, love me, love me. A bonding of the human spirit takes place. Being able to lift a whole consciousness—that's what I do.'"

Describing her as "an economy size glamour puss" and a "hyperkinetic amalgam of Mae West, Reverend Ike, Richard Simmons and Hulk Hogan," Zehme mentions her trademark "big mama earrings" and the way "she will name-drop unashamedly—the most frequent is 'Steven,' her director in *The Color Purple.*"

What the writer found most curious about Oprah was her conquest of the Kennedy compound at Hyannisport through her friendship with Maria Shriver, whom she had met in Baltimore. Oprah was asked to recite the Elizabeth Barrett Browning poem "How Do I Love Thee?" at Shriver's 1986 wedding to Arnold Schwarzenegger, and she told Zehme the only other speakers at the April ceremony were the bride's parents and her uncle Senator Ted Kennedy. Afterward, Oprah said she played charades at Ethel Kennedy's house and had several intimate chats with Jacqueline Kennedy Onassis.

"We talked life and perms and spirituality," Oprah said. "I was moved by her." She also mentioned that she had sent $650 replicas of a leather sailing jacket she had worn that weekend to Eunice Shriver and Ethel Kennedy because both had admired it. "I love that family," she said.

Years later few wedding guests recalled Oprah's poetry recitation as vividly as they remembered Arnold Schwarzenegger's endorsement of Kurt Waldheim, the president of Austria, who had been exposed for participating in Nazi war crimes during World War II. During the wedding reception Schwarzenegger strolled the broad expanse of lawn at Hyannisport carrying a large papier-mâché statue of himself in lederhosen and his bride in a dirndl. "I want you all to see the wedding present we have just received from my good friend Kurt Waldheim," Schwarzenegger told the crowd of judges, priests, and politicians. "My friends don't want me to mention Kurt's name, because of all the recent Nazi stuff . . . but I love him and Maria does too, and so thank you, Kurt." Waldheim could not attend the wedding because he had been officially declared persona non grata by the United States.

When Bill Zehme submitted his profile to *Vanity Fair*

about the "capaciously built, black and extremely noisy Oprah Winfrey" with "her great lippy smile," Tina Brown killed the piece, "not wishing to stir racial teacup tempests," said someone directly involved in the editorial decision. She paid Zehme in full and encouraged him to publish elsewhere. The piece appeared in the December 1986 issue of *Spy* magazine.

If the profile wasn't sexist, or even racist, in tone, it was certainly elitist. Zehme seemed to filet Oprah for being fat, famous, and full of herself, something he may have accepted from a fat, famous, full-of-himself white man. Undone by her own messianic pronouncements, she rallied with good humor and fired off a note, saying, "Dear Bill, I forgive you. Oprah." Zehme sent her flowers to make amends, but she never responded. He should not have been surprised, having written about "disapproving hostesses who carp that Oprah never RSVPs and surmise that she has no notion of thank-you note etiquette." In later years, when Oprah became omnipotent, Zehme tried to distance himself from the profile and even omitted it from a collection of his published writings. But it did him little good as far as Oprah was concerned. She never spoke to him again.

Years later, when Tina Brown left *Vanity Fair* to become editor of *The New Yorker*, she decided again to assign an in-depth profile on Oprah. She called the writer Erica Jong. "Tina knew that I knew Oprah—we had met in the sauna bath at Rancho La Puerta years and years before, and talked about how difficult men were. She invited me to come on her show in Baltimore, which I did. . . . She was so warm and sweet then."

Now Oprah was wary. She felt slammed by a cover story in *The New York Times Magazine*, titled "The Importance of Being Oprah," by Barbara Grizzuti Harrison. While Zehme's arrow had grazed the good ship *Oprah*, Harrison's was a torpedo to the hull. Not only did the writer declare Oprah's candor to be more apparent than real, but she also branded Oprah's New Age pronouncements nonsensical and her self-interest extreme. Further, she asserted that Oprah's message—"you can be born poor and black and female and make it to the top"—was a fraudulent sop to her white audience:

In a racist society, the majority needs and seeks, from time to time, proof that they are loved by the minority whom they have so long been accustomed to oppress, to fear exaggeratedly, or to disdain. They need that love, and they need to love in return, in order to believe that they are good. Oprah Winfrey—a one-person demilitarized zone—has served that purpose.

Most damning was the writer's assessment of Oprah's dangerous influence on the millions of her viewers "who lonely and uninstructed draw sustenance from her, from the flickering presence in their living rooms they call a friend." Obviously Barbara Grizzuti Harrison did not believe that false comfort is better than no comfort at all.

As a media darling accustomed to ribbons of praise, Oprah was irate. It wasn't just the writer's bite or her disdain for what she called Oprah's "superficial quality," it was also the prestigious placement of the profile. Getting shredded in a satirical magazine like *Spy* was one thing, but to be dissected on the cover of the country's most important Sunday magazine was intolerable.

"Oprah was furious about that article," said Erica Jong, "and she told me she did not want anyone writing about her, especially a white woman for a white publication. 'I don't need a honky magazine to canonize me,' she said. I assured her I would not be writing about her negatively, but she did not trust Tina Brown.

" 'What if she tells you to put in barbs? Will you be able to resist?' She said she'd pray on it and call me back, which she did, but in the end I was not able to give her the editorial control that she demanded."

Later, when Tina Brown left *The New Yorker* and started *Talk* magazine, she again wanted to profile Oprah. Sitting with several art directors to discuss possible covers, Tina said, "Oprah has really gotten full of herself. . . . Who the hell does she think she is? Let's do Oprah Pope-rah." The artists whipped up a mock cover of Oprah's black face half-covered with the white ceremonial miter of the Pontiff. "We couldn't put her whole face on the cover because we had to leave room for a big fat halo," said one of the artists. But the profile never got written because by then Oprah had stopped giving interviews.

After *Talk* folded, Brown wrote a book about Diana, the Princess of Wales, but could not get booked on *The Oprah Winfrey Show*. When she started her news site, *The Daily Beast*, she again took a poke at Oprah, for getting hoodwinked in 2008 by a Holocaust memoir that Oprah had recommended on her show but that had turned out not to be a true story. "You have to wonder why the big fat budget of that show doesn't at least extend to a fact checker," Brown wrote. In 2009 she dismissed Oprah as a "juggernaut business franchise" whose "authenticity can't help transmuting into something manufactured." She wrote that Oprah had become a brand, no longer a person. "[She] might as well have a little R in a circle next to [her] name."

Later in 2009, Brown's *Daily Beast* devoted a web page to "Oprah's Bad Press," with links to stories about a poet's $1.2 trillion lawsuit against Oprah for plagiarism; the lawsuit of a flight attendant on Oprah's plane who claimed she was wrongfully fired by Oprah; two deaths at a spiritual retreat led "by [an] Oprah-approved author"; the sex scandal at Oprah's school in South Africa; and Oprah's "ill advice," saying "she's not a doctor but plays one on TV."

Like Inspector Javert chasing Jean Valjean in *Les Misérables*, Tina Brown seemed more than a little preoccupied with Oprah, but when asked to discuss the matter, Brown avoided further controversy by responding through her assistant, who said, "Tina has never been a big student of Oprah and has no time to spend answering questions about her."

By then Oprah Winfrey was in total control of her public image. She had become exactly what she wanted—a gigantic mogul. She had her own media empire: her own television network, her own radio show, her own website, her own daily talk show, and her own magazine, whose every cover featured . . . her.

# Nine

AFTER THE seedling years of 1984–1986, Oprah burst into full bloom. She flowered as a national success at the age of thirty-two, and money rained down on her in torrents. *Variety* reported she would earn more than $31 million in 1987, making her television's highest-paid talk show host, topping even Johnny Carson, who made $20 million on *The Tonight Show*. As Miss Fire Prevention, Oprah had vowed to become "a spending fool" if she ever saw $1 million, and now she sprang with all fours. "I have allotted myself personally only to spend one million dollars this year," she said. "That's how much I'm giving myself to play with."

She began by buying herself a Mercedes and a Jaguar, and then she lavished mink coats on everyone—her mentor Maya Angelou; her cousins Jo Baldwin and Alice Cooper; and her female staff, who were accustomed to her extravagance. The year they had been denied Christmas bonuses by WLS station bosses, she had stepped in, giving each $10,000 in cash stuffed inside rolls of toilet paper. She also gave her producer, Debbie DiMaio, a fox jacket as a "thank you for getting me the talk show." Now she gave DiMaio a six-carat diamond bracelet. ("Brilliance deserves brilliance," Oprah wrote on the card.) She gave the only male on her staff, Billy Rizzo, the keys to a Volkswagen Rabbit convertible. She sent two producers to Switzerland on vacation, paid for the wedding of another, and took them all on a shopping spree in New York, where she turned them loose in three stores—an hour at a time—with orders to buy anything they wanted. "I get the biggest kick out of buying great presents," she said, listing her largesse for reporters. "That's why I'm a great friend to have. Once I gave my best friend [Gayle King] and her husband [William Bumpus] an all-expenses-paid trip to Europe for two weeks in all first-class hotels—and money to spend. But my best present to date was when I gave her a nanny to care for her two babies." Gayle recalled the day Oprah visited her and her husband in Connecticut, arriving in a stretch limo. "She was wearing one of her five fur coats, probably a $25,000 number, and white tennis shoes with rhinestones on them and a red sweat shirt that said, 'Husbands Can Be Temporary but Best Friends Last Forever.'" The story that she gave Gayle a check for $1,250,000 for Christmas so they could both be millionaires is also part of the Oprah legend. Years later she bought Gayle a house in Greenwich, Connecticut, for $3.6 million.

She made sure the media knew that Phil Donahue offered congratulations when she won Daytime Emmy Awards in 1987 for Best Talk Show and for Best Talk Show Host. "He kissed me," said Oprah. "Yep. That's right, Phil kissed me." She was so grateful for his public acknowledgment that she sent him twenty bottles of Louis Roederer Cristal Champagne to mark the twentieth anniversary of his talk show, pointing out to reporters that Cristal sold for eighty dollars a bottle.

She bought her father a new set of tires and a large television set for his barbershop, so he could watch her show, because he'd said that was all he wanted. She later bought him and his wife, Zelma, a new twelve-room house in Brentwood, Tennessee. "I called him and said, 'Dad, I'm a millionaire! I want to send you and your friends to any place in the world you want to go.' He said, 'All I want is some new tires for my truck.' I was so upset." Her mother, Vernita Lee, was another matter.

"I retired her, bought her a house, bought her a car and pay her double the salary that she made all of her life," Oprah told the *Chicago Sun-Times*. "So now she has no bills to pay and nothing to do all day. And you know what she said to me?

'Well, I'll try to make it.' Can you believe that? I said, 'You're going to *try* to make it? See if you can, Mom.' Then just the other day, she called me up to say, 'I need a new coat.' So I said, 'Go to Marshall Field's and get you one.' She says, 'I don't need a Marshall Field's coat. I need a fur coat.' So I said, 'Nobody *needs* a fur coat, Mother. Nobody *needs* one.' Well, I did buy her a mink coat. So now she has a fur coat, a new car, a new house, no bills and double her salary. And she's gonna *try* to make it."

But that, apparently, was not enough for Vernita. "Oprah told me that her mother stole her personal checkbook, wrote twenty thousand dollars in checks to herself, and thought nothing of it," said the designer Nancy Stoddart, who became close to Oprah in the 1980s. "I met Oprah and Stedman when I was with [the musician, composer, and producer] Nile Rodgers at La Samanna in St. Martin. Oprah and I immediately bonded when I held forth over dinner one night about the Theory of Relativity, which had nothing to do with Einstein and everything to do with greedy relatives who jump out of the woodwork to grab your money when you become rich. That's when Oprah began telling me about her mother and how greedy and grasping she was. . . . She really didn't like her mother at all.

"She said Vernita felt totally entitled. . . . She was just a greedy greenback. . . . But she got the big-time bucks because Oprah probably knew she would make her life a living hell if she didn't [by selling stories to the tabloids]."

As generous as Oprah was to her mother—one Mother's Day she arrived with a gift-wrapped box containing $100,000 in cash—she was still bitter toward Vernita for "giving me away," and she ricocheted from resentment to gratitude over those motherless years. She understood that the lack of her mother's unconditional love drove her to develop skills to get praise from others, but she also saw that she tried to fill her motherless hole with food as a substitute for love and comfort and security. It would be many years before she reckoned with the depth of her psychological damage.

"If [my mother] hadn't given me up, I would be in deep trouble now," she said. "I would have been barefoot and pregnant, had at least three kids by the time I was 20. No doubt about it. I would have been part of that whole ghetto mentality that's waiting for somebody to do something for them."

She was quite clear about what she thought of Vernita. "I don't feel I owe anybody anything but my mother feels I do. . . . She says, 'There are dues to pay.' I barely knew her [when I was little]. . . . That's why it's so hard now. My mother wants this whole wonderful relationship. She has another daughter and a son. And everyone now wants this close family relationship. . . . They want to pretend as though our past did not happen."

Oprah occasionally derided her mother on the air, once telling her audience that Vernita had borrowed her BMW two years before and hadn't returned it. She told *Life* magazine her mother cursed her as a child for being a bookworm, saying, "You think you're better than the other kids." She told Tina Turner her mother did not want her. "[I]t affected my self-esteem for years," said Oprah. "It's unnatural to not be wanted by your mother. That takes some overcoming." She told BET's Ed Gordon that she was hesitant to have children because of the poor mothering she'd received. "I would be afraid that I would make a lot of the mistakes that were made with me."

**Yet Vernita Lee defended herself as a mother. "I am a good mom," she said. "I know I am a good mom. When my children were small, I took care of them. I dressed them very nice and I took them to Sunday school and they went to church every Sunday. And we did things together, as hard as times was for us. It was hard. But we made it."**

The strained relationship between Oprah and her mother became obvious to everyone who watched them on Oprah's 1987 Mother's Day show. "I could not hug her," Oprah said later. "Oprah Winfrey who hugs everyone could not hug her own mother. But we have never hugged, we have never said, 'I love you.'" By then Oprah had emotionally erased Vernita as her mother, relegating her to the horde of grabby relatives she said always had their hands out. "I think that Maya Angelou was my mother in another life," Oprah said. "I love her deeply. Something is there between us. So fallopian tubes and ovaries do not a mother make."

Eventually Oprah created a new family for herself, one that she felt she deserved and could claim with pride. In place of her welfare mother with three illegitimate children, she selected the celebrated poet and author, an autodidact with no formal education beyond high school, who claimed the title of Dr. Angelou because of her many honorary degrees. Oprah carried Maya's monthly itinerary in her purse at all times so she could reach her morning, noon, and night. Quincy Jones stepped into the role of beloved uncle. "I truly learned how to love as a result of this man," Oprah said. "It's the first time I came to terms with, 'Yes, I love this man, and it has nothing to do with wanting to go to bed with him or be romantically involved. I unconditionally love him and . . .' I would slap the living shit out of somebody who said anything bad about Quincy." Gayle King was the adoring sister Oprah had substituted for the drug-addicted Patricia Lee, and John Travolta seemed to replace her brother, Jeffrey Lee, who died of AIDS. Even Vernon Winfrey was supplanted. Once Oprah met Sidney Poitier, she bound him to her like a kind and loving father. "I call Sidney every Sunday and . . . we talk about life, we talk about reincarnation, we talk about the cosmos, we talk about the stars, we talk about the planets, we talk about energy. We talk about everything."

**In 2010, to celebrate the tenth anniversary of her magazine, Oprah sat with fans to answer their questions and again talked about the love she felt she had never received from her mother and father. "I'm in awe of people who felt their parents' love every day of their lives," she said. "They start out in the world with a full cup. The rest of us go through life trying to fill ours."**

Oprah continued to see her natural family on occasion, gave them money when they asked ("Gobs of it," she said), and then fumed on the air about being treated like an ATM. Her sister, Patricia, felt that Oprah preferred giving money to her family instead of giving them her time and attention. "At times Oprah acts like she's embarrassed by her family," said Patricia. "She acts ashamed of her own mother, probably because Mom doesn't always pronounce things correctly and doesn't have a good education." Patricia said that Oprah gave their mother a $50,000

Mercedes but would not give Vernita her home phone number. "If Mom wants to get in touch with Oprah, she has to call the studio like any fan and leave a message for Oprah to call her. In a real emergency, Mom would have to call Oprah's secretary."

For Father's Day one year, Oprah gave Vernon a new Mercedes. "The 600 Mercedes," she told a reporter for publication. "The $130,000 600 Mercedes, black on black, fully loaded Mercedes. Had Roosevelt [her makeup artist] drive it down there. A couple days passed and I hadn't heard from my dad. So I called and said, 'Did the car get there?' He goes, 'Yes, it did and I sure do appreciate that.' I said, 'Do you think you could've called and said, "I received the brand new 600 Mercedes"? You think you could show a little excitement?'"

Her blood family knew they did not have Oprah's heart like the celebrity family she had reinvented for herself, and they resented their secondary position in her affections, but they knew their lack of acclaim could not enhance the image she wanted to present.

"We're just country folk," said her cousin Katharine Carr Esters, whom Oprah continued to embrace as "Aunt Katharine." "She needs more for herself than what we have. . . . Oprah doesn't see her real family much. Harpo is her family. She told me so. . . . I don't like Gayle much, but Oprah does and that's fine. I just think Gayle is too much into Gayle."

Oprah made it clear to all her relatives that "Gayle is the most important person in the world to me," and, as she told *TV Guide,* she gave them the steel-toed boot when they criticized Gayle. As she related to the writer: "It was my birthday party and all these family members were gathered in my house, and Gayle walked out of the room. And this distant relative says, 'What's sheee doing here? She's not family.' Well, I hit the ceiling. My hair stood up on my head. I had a screaming, raging, maniacal fit. I told them all—and I don't care who they were—my family, my mother—that they could get out of my house now and never set foot in it again. . . . My friends *are* my family."

Oprah frequently mentioned on her show how disgusted

she was with all the beggars in her life. "I'm hearing from so many people now who want me to give them money, or lend them money. I say, 'I'll give you the shirt off my back, as long as you don't ask me for it.'"

On the heels of her multimillions came thirty-five-year-old Stedman Sardar Graham, the man she had been telling audiences was walking ("slowly, very slowly") from Africa to be her Mr. Right. "He's coming, I just know it," she said, "and when he finally shows up, please God make him tall."

Graham, a prison guard by day and a part-time model by night, was handsome and light-skinned. "He's terrific," said Oprah. "Six feet six of terrific." A little too terrific for her protective staff, who wondered why such a gorgeous man would be attracted to their overweight boss.

"I remember they were very worried about why Stedman was dating her," said Nancy Stoddart. "When we went skiing together, Oprah was so fat that she had to buy her ski clothes in the men's department."

Oprah acknowledged her employees' concern. "They figured if he looked like that, he had to be either a jerk or want something," she said. "He was so handsome—oooh, what a body—so I figured the same thing. If he's calling me . . . there's something wrong with him I should know about." She turned him down the first few times he asked her out. "I thought he was kind of dorky because everyone said what a nice guy he was [and] I'm used to being mistreated. I'm not used to a nice guy who's gonna treat me well."

When she finally did accept a date, Stedman arrived with roses and paid for dinner. After several more dates people assumed he was after her money. "They say, 'She's this fat girl and he's this hot-looking guy, what else could there be?' [But] that invalidates me as a person," said Oprah. "Even though I understand, because when he first asked me out, that's exactly what I thought. But Stedman's spirit is so totally the opposite of somebody who's out to get something material from the relationship."

She told *Ladies' Home Journal,* "The rumors are classic jealousy. One of the reasons they persist is that Stedman's so good-looking, and I'm not the kind of woman you'd expect him to have. I'm over-weight, I'm not fair skinned and I'm not white. So you would think a guy who looks like that would be with Diahann Carroll or Jayne Kennedy or some willowy blonde."

Still Stedman became a national punch line and the butt of cruel jokes. During a break in taping the NAACP Image Awards, the comic Sinbad was entertaining the audience when he spotted Oprah and Stedman returning to their seats. "Look at Stedman, following Oprah's purse around," he jabbed. "I'm surprised he's not carrying it for her!" Stedman wasn't even safe among his friends. The former ABC-TV anchor Max Robinson teased, "She'll eat you out of house and home, brother. It's a good thing she owns them."

In later years some saw Stedman as more drone than predator. Debra Pickett, who wrote a "Lunch With" column for the *Chicago Sun-Times*, pronounced him the "biggest disappointment of the year." She wrote, "Graham, who is impossibly good-looking but incredibly dull, broke my heart by demonstrating that his life partner, Oprah, must be at least as shallow as the rest of us, since she clearly didn't fall for his conversational skills." New York *Daily News* columnists George Rush and Joanna Molloy were equally disappointed to find no humor behind the handsome façade. They reported that when Stedman accompanied Oprah to the Essence Awards at Radio City Music Hall, he was the only one not laughing at Bill Cosby's teasing from the stage.

"Stedman—is that a real name?" Cosby said, looking at the couple sitting in the front row. "I thought it's something he'd tell you at a party. 'I'm a steady man.'"

Oprah and the rest of the audience roared with laughter, but Stedman leveled a blank stare at Cosby. Afterward the comedian took Oprah aside backstage.

"What's the matter with him? Usually when people make fun of you, you laugh and go ha, ha, ha," Cosby told Oprah. "But he just stared into space."

The next night Joanna Molloy asked Stedman why he'd gotten so upset. "He was very grouchy. He said, 'It's my name, don't wear it out.' I instantly thought, 'Oh, no. You are not bright enough to be Ms. Oprah Winfrey's partner.'"

The actress E. Faye Butler knew Stedman from his modeling days. "We'd call him to model Johnson Products because he was handsome, but he was an awful model, so we'd make him stand still and have others move around him. . . . He was nice enough but boring as hell. . . . So boring . . . I remember he liked little petite light-skinned girls with straight hair, so I was surprised when he went with Oprah."

"He's a very somber person," said Nancy Stoddart, "almost like he has a childhood wound. I remember him telling me once, 'I used to be a really, really good basketball player, but my dad never came to a single one of my games.' It's the story of a child still hurting over a neglectful parent who never paid him any attention."

Whether or not Stedman was drawn to Oprah's money, he was definitely attracted to her brimming self-confidence and the easy way she moved to take her place in the world. "She absolutely transcends race," he said. In contrast, his view of the world had been strapped by racism, as he had grown up in the all-black township of Whitesboro, New Jersey (population six hundred), and attended an all-black grade school. "If you are an African American in this country, you are a victim of perception," he said. "You don't have as much value as someone else, and when you walk into corporate America, your image is lessened. I never imagined that I could be equal to white folks." Oprah never imagined she could be anything less.

"For 30 plus years I believed I was limited because of the color of my skin," Stedman said. "I [eventually] learned it's not about race but what it's really about is the powerful against the powerless. What matters is power, control, and economics." On this he and Oprah were in full agreement. "They both share the same pull-yourself-up-by-the-bootstraps philosophy," said Fran Johns, a close Chicago friend of Stedman's.

After graduating from college in 1974, Stedman hoped to be drafted for the NBA, like his roommate Harvey Catchings. When he was rejected, he joined the Fort Worth Police Department. He married Glenda Ann Brown that same year, and their daughter, Wendy, was born seven months later. Stedman then joined the army for three and a half years and was stationed in Germany, where he says he played armed service basketball. He returned to the states and began working in the prison system in Englewood, Colorado. He and his wife separated in 1981, and in 1983 he moved with his girlfriend, Robin Robinson, to Chicago, when she was hired by WBBM-TV. Stedman transferred to the Metropolitan Correction Center and founded Athletes Against Drugs in 1985. He began dating Oprah then and quit the Bureau of Prisons in 1987, when he met Robert J. Brown, founder of B&C Associates in High Point, North Carolina.

"Stedman always had something to prove," said Brown, who invited Stedman to accompany him on a trip to the Ivory Coast, where he was working with the government to attract business investors. Brown later hired Stedman as vice president of business development, which Stedman admitted was a glorified title for "trainee." Brown, an African American, alienated many blacks with his stand against economic sanctions to force South Africa to abandon apartheid, but he became President Reagan's choice to be U.S. ambassador to South Africa. However, he quickly withdrew his name after investigators began scrutinizing his business relationships with the former government of Nigeria and his union-busting activities. None of this concerned Stedman.

"[Brown's] in public relations and he's a multimillionaire," he said. "He was a special assistant to President Nixon. He's basically my mentor. Because of him I got to travel around the world and escort Mandela's children down to South Africa when he was released from prison and have breakfast with Nelson Mandela. I got to visit the White House and meet the president [George Herbert Walker Bush]. All this opened my eyes . . . [to] what I had been looking for."

Brown's courtship of the Mandelas stirred controversy in 1988, when he announced he had secured world rights to the family's name. Mandela supporters saw this as exploitation, but

Brown claimed he had contracted to protect the use of the name. From prison, Nelson Mandela renounced Brown's claim, but Winnie Mandela seemed eager to work with him. With Stedman in tow, Brown mentioned the former's relationship with the richest television star in America, and soon Oprah began funding hot lunches for seniors in Alexandra, a poor black township outside of Johannesburg, where people lived in tin shacks without water, electricity, or sewage disposal. "We wanted to focus attention on the plight of Alexandra," Brown told reporters. "This is one of the poorest and most ignored parts of the country." Newspapers carried photographs of Brown's two employees, Stedman Graham and Armstrong Williams, distributing hot meals. They later brought a television set to Alexandra and showed tapes of Oprah's talk show so the two hundred impoverished senior citizens could see their bene- factor; photos of this event also appeared in the press heralding Oprah's generosity and Brown's goodwill.

Winnie Mandela sent Oprah a note, which she framed and hung in her Chicago condominium: "Oprah, You must keep alive! Your mission is sacramental!! A nation loves you." Soon Winnie and Oprah were on the phone and Oprah was making arrangements to rent a Gulfstream jet to take the Mandela daughters skiing. Once known as "the Mother of the Revolu- tion," Winnie Mandela was later reviled by antiapartheid leaders when her bodyguards were convicted of abducting four teenage boys and killing one of them by slitting his throat. She, too, was convicted of kidnapping, and given a suspended sentence of six years in prison.

The mission of mercy in Alexandra showed Stedman and Williams how Brown operated on the international stage, part- nering with Oprah's money and garnering goodwill for her as well as for himself. They learned how publicizing good deeds works to good advantage. The two men later became business partners and formed the Graham Williams Group, a public re- lations company that Stedman used to promote his self- empowerment books. He made GWG sound as if it fogged mirrors. "The corporation helps people to become all that they can be," he told one reporter. "[It] maximizes resources and helps small firms become large corporations and large corporations become multi-corporations."

When asked to explain what he meant by this, his business partner shrugged. "Stedman and I have been close for a long time," Armstrong Williams said in 2008. "But I've had my problems with Oprah over the years so now I just deal with him." Williams removed from his house the two photos Oprah had inscribed to him ("Armstrong—My buddy, Oprah" and "Armstrong, You did great on the show! Thank you for doing it. Oprah") and packed them with the papers he donated to the University of South Carolina.

Oprah began pulling away from her friendship with Williams soon after the journalist David Brock wrote in his book *Blinded by the Right* that Williams had made a homosexual advance toward him. Williams was later sued by a male associate for sexual harassment but settled the case out of court. Oprah completely distanced herself when it became public that Williams, by then a conservative commentator, had been secretly paid $240,000 by the George W. Bush administration to promote the controversial No Child Left Behind Act. The media criticized Williams for unethical behavior and possibly illegal use of taxpayer money. His newspaper syndicate dropped his column, he lost his syndicated television show, and after a yearlong investigation he was asked to return $34,000 to the U.S. Department of Education in overpayment.

What Oprah did not know was that by then Armstrong Williams was also on the payroll of the tabloids, regularly feeding information to the *National Enquirer, The Star,* and the *Globe* for exclusives on Oprah. "We had a direct pipeline into her office and knew every move she was making, because she and Stedman exchanged their schedules every two weeks and Armstrong gave us copies," said a former tabloid editor. "So we knew where they were going and what they were doing, which is why our photographers got the intimate photos we published, especially during their vacations together."

Inadvertently, Oprah had initiated the double-dealing by

hiring Armstrong to be her conduit to the tabloids—to feed them stories about her good works. "I can assure you that Oprah definitely knew Armstrong was working with us for her, but she didn't know he was also working for us, and dishing her," said a senior tabloid editor involved with the relationship. "Oprah became so obsessed by our coverage that she had Jeff Jacobs call us to start a dialogue. We did not reach out to her. She reached out to us, to try to get some sort of control on what we were doing. We talked to Jacobs and agreed to give him a comment call within forty-eight hours of publication on any Oprah story. He told us there were hot-button issues, especially about her weight, but he wasn't crazed on the subject like she was. . . . Jacobs never dished Oprah, but Armstrong did and he was a great source for us for a long, long time. . . . He even put me on the phone with Stedman at one point and we solidified a relationship with him as well."

Stedman moved to North Carolina in 1988 to work with B&C Associates' Bob Brown, once a police officer like him, and he easily assumed Brown's conservative politics. "I can tell you Stedman is a Republican through and through," said Armstrong Williams. "Oprah is influenced by Hollywood politics. She can't help it. It's just the way she is. Stedman isn't. He's a very conservative dude."

Oprah admitted her political differences with Stedman when she was asked whether she would have an abortion if she discovered in pregnancy that her child might be born without arms and legs. "Yes, oh yes," she said. "I know that will stir a lot of folks up but I am real clear on this. I want my child to come into the world with every possible opportunity that nature can give him. Of course once the child is born you deal with what nature has given you but if I knew ahead of time that my child would be handicapped, I would definitely want an abortion. Stedman, however, does not agree with me at all. It would be a BIG DISCUSSION. It's terrifying when you think about it, to love somebody that you disagree with on such a pivotal issue."

As a couple, Oprah and Stedman were melded by their devotion to the gospel of self-help. Both upwardly mobile, they read everything on self-improvement, from *Creative Visualization* and *Psycho-cybernetics* to *The Nature of Personal Reality* and *The Road Less Traveled*. They shared similar religious beliefs—Oprah claimed they knelt every night to say their prayers before bed—and for eight years they attended the Rev. Jeremiah Wright's Trinity United Church in Chicago. Both had suffered from the insidious demarcations of color within their own culture: Oprah feeling she was too dark, and Stedman envied for being too light. Stedman's father, a housepainter, and his mother, a housekeeper, were first cousins, according to Carlton Jones, Stedman's third cousin, who said Stedman's parents had married each other to preserve the light skin that ran in the family.

"There's a lot of intermarriage in our family," Jones said. He later sold a sensational story about Stedman to a tabloid but was accused of lying for the money. "I'm related to Stedman through my mother's side of the family. She was a Spaulding. The Spauldings, Grahams, Mores, and Boyds from these parts were all light-skinned people. And they've been marrying each other for over a hundred years.

"We've produced folks who look as white as any white man—even with Caucasian features. But we've also produced retarded kids—and they marry, too. That's why there's so many retarded people in our family tree. First and second cousins got married to each other because they've got this skin thing."

Stedman said that being called "whitey" forced him to prove himself in his small black community. In addition, he had to cope with the social stigma heaped on the family by the learning disabilities of his two younger brothers, James and Darras. "Back then they were called retarded, though now they are described as developmentally disabled," he said. "Today there are many support groups and programs to help families deal with mental disabilities, but we didn't have access to those years ago." He refuted Carlton Jones's claim that his parents were first cousins, which could have contributed to the mental disabilities of his brothers. Stedman said his proof could be found in a family history titled *A Story of the Descendants of Benjamin Spaulding*.

His cousin Carlton said that while Stedman was growing up his parents would not let him bring black friends home. "His father would tell him, 'I don't want you bringing those black bastards into my house!' and he meant it. Stedman never brought his wife or his daughter home for the same reason." It took him several years to bring Oprah to Whitesboro, but she took him to Nashville to meet her father soon after they started dating.

At that point Stedman was still trying to cope with people shoving him aside to get Oprah's autograph and interrupting their restaurant meals to hug her. He couldn't understand why she tolerated the intrusions or how she derived any pleasure from the attention of rude strangers. In Nashville he sat slumped in Vernon's barbershop while people from the neighborhood flocked to see her, touch her, photograph her, and even sing to her. He wondered out loud if she had the ability to differentiate between people who were meaningful and those who just wanted to be around a celebrity. "Who's here after all these people are gone?" he asked. "Who really cares about her? I don't think she really understands, or maybe she understands and hasn't let that understanding affect her. But Oprah has been through so much, a tough childhood, a broken family, that it's kind of hard to say this is something she shouldn't enjoy."

Oprah and Stedman eventually became life partners, but even after living together for more than two decades they have not married. "You know I say all the time, 'Stedman, if we had married we wouldn't be together,'" she told Jann Carl of *ET.* "And he says, 'For sure. For sure we wouldn't.' [Ours] is not a traditional relationship, and marriage is a traditional institution, and certain expectations come with marriage. The truth is he has a life . . . he has his work . . . and I have mine, and it just wouldn't work."

Her father agreed. "Forget about a wedding," he said in 2008. "It will never happen. . . . She won't ever marry Stedman because . . . she's all for herself and not about to give up anything for anyone. . . . She's content with who she is. With Oprah it's root hog or die poor." Vernon Winfrey, then seventy-five and still working in his barbershop, explained that hogs must root for food or die of starvation, implying that Oprah needed to root for riches more than she needed to nourish a relationship. She seemed to confirm her father's assessment when she pronounced herself in favor of prenuptial agreements. "[They] imply you're not stupid," she said. "If somebody ever even tried to tell me they wanted to come and take half of everything I had— Oh, Oh, Oh, Oh—the thought!" She also told *TV Guide*, "Marriage to me means offering—sacrificing—yourself to the relationship. To become one with the relationship. I'm not capable of doing that right now."

"Not now, not ever," said Vernon, shaking his head. "My wife, Zelma, died in 1996, and a few years later, when I started seeing the woman [Barbara Williams] who became my second wife, Oprah called me. 'Are you in love?' she asked.

" 'Can you fall in love more than once?' I asked her.

" 'Yeah,' she said.

" 'No, you can't,' I told her. 'But my daddy used to say, "You can marry in like and then grow fonder. It's either that or you'll wander and go yonder." So I'm in like.'

"Oprah said, 'Daddy, I guess I'm like you. I'm in like, too. Not in love.'

" 'So we can have a double wedding then?' Oprah said no."

When she first started dating Stedman she burbled to her audiences about her new boyfriend, "Steddie"—how handsome he was, how romantic, how they might eventually marry, even have children. "I guess I'll spoil any baby Stedman and I have," she mused. "I already spoil his daughter, Wendy. I say to her and her friends, 'Okay, I'll give you a big shopping spree. You can have one hour at the store to buy whatever you want.' "

She talked to reporters about her "ticking clock." "Some days I really want a girl because you can dress her up and she'd be so cute—she'd be like me. Then I think I'd want to have a boy because I'd like to name him Canaan. Canaan Graham is such a strong name."

Years later she came closer to her own truth in a televised interview for *A&E Biography* in which she said, "I truly feel that what I went through at fourteen was a sign that children were not supposed to be part of the equation for me. I have conceived, I have given birth—and it didn't work out for me. I'm comfortable with the decision to move on."

Oprah said she surprised her best friend when she admitted she never really wanted children. "I said, 'No, never.' Even in seventh grade Gayle knew she wanted twins. She says, 'If I hadn't gotten married, I would have had a child. I would have felt like my life is not complete without a child.' I don't feel that at all."

Having announced their engagement on television in 1992 and posed for *People,* Oprah later regretted talking so much about her relationship with Stedman. "Someone once told me, 'Every time you mention his name, the perception is you're doing it because you're longing for something you cannot have.' And it never occurred to me that that's how it was being perceived. . . . But if I hadn't [talked about him] then everybody would be asking, 'Who's the Mystery Man?' 'Is she a lesbian?' "

Years later people did begin to wonder. Some dismissed Oprah's relationship with Stedman as a convenience for both, whispering about their sexuality and suggesting that each was helping the other hide same-sex preferences, especially Oprah, who was seen in public with Gayle King far more often than she was seen with Stedman. All three of them denied that they were homosexual, and so did their close friends, but the rumors persisted, particularly in Hollywood, where Oprah befriended a few glamorous female stars known as lipstick lesbians.

Soon she and Gayle and Stedman became fodder for comedians. Kathy Griffin, who won an Emmy in 2008 for her reality show, regaled a largely gay audience at DAR Constitution Hall in Washington, D.C., by asking why Oprah had taken Gayle to the Emmys that year. "Can't she go down in the basement and unleash Stedman? Just for one night?" The audience roared. "Oh, c'mon," Griffin said. "You know I'm supportive of Oprah and her boyfriend, Gayle."

On David Steinberg's television show Robin Williams imitated Secretary of State Condoleezza Rice talking to Oprah on the phone. Williams crossed his legs, daintily pointed his toes, and put his hand to his ear. "Oh, dear. You say Stedman is wearing your clothes again? Not good. Not good at all." The audience laughed at the send-up of Oprah's partner as a cross-dresser.

By then the couple was almost inured to public derision. They felt they had faced the worst when *News Extra*, a Canadian tabloid, published a story titled "New Oprah Shocker! Fiancé Stedman Had Gay Sex with Cousin." "That was the most difficult time for me," Oprah told Laura Randolph of *Ebony*, sobbing as she recounted the story of Stedman's gay cousin saying he had slept with Stedman at a local motel in Whitesboro, New Jersey. She said the rumor about Stedman's sexuality "hurt him, hurt him bad," and she blamed herself. "If I were lean and pretty, nobody would ever say that. What people were really saying is why would a straight, good-looking guy be with her?"

Oprah had brought the tabloid home to show Stedman. "He was so brave," she said, "and I have never loved him more. He taught me so much during that period. When I handed it to him, he looked at it and said, 'This is not my life. I don't have anything to do with this. God obviously has something he wants me to learn.' Now I'm standing in the middle of the floor and I'm crying, I'm hysterical, and you know what he started doing? He started looking in the closet and talking about resoling his shoes. And I'm, like, resoling your shoes! I have never seen greater manhood in my life."

Within days Oprah and Stedman filed a $300 million lawsuit against the tabloid for defamation, invasion of privacy, and intended infliction of emotional distress. Their attorney told reporters that Carlton Jones had sold his story nine months earlier to a U.S. tabloid but the tabloid had not published it because Oprah's attorneys convinced them the story was not true. Now, the attorney said, Jones said he had lied to the tabloid for money. *News Extra* chose not to answer the complaint. "I believe the publishers decided that they weren't going to defend that action," said the editor. Thirty-five days later, U.S. District Judge Marvin E. Aspen entered a default judgment against the Montreal-based tabloid, which had vacated its offices and gone out of business. Oprah and Stedman felt vindicated by the next day's headlines: "Oprah Winfrey Wins Suit by Default."

Stedman still had to steel himself against the derision of being tagged "Mr. Oprah," "The Little Mister," or, as the *National Review* put it, "the terminally affianced Stedman Graham, Miss Adelaide to Oprah's Nathan Detroit." In the early days he occasionally lashed out when he was referred to as "Oprah's boyfriend," but seven years into the relationship, Oprah told him to get over it. "It's the thing that bothers him most," she said, "but I told him if he dies, if he leaves, if he ends up owning Chicago, people are still going to say, 'That's Oprah Winfrey's boyfriend.'"

Stedman continued chafing at the description. "There's no respect in it," he said. "Although there is credibility in being able to hang with one of the most powerful women in the world, no one respects you for that." Respect was paramount to this proud man, who was working in a prison when he first met Oprah. During the day he wore the starched blue uniform of a corrections employee whose job was to pat down prisoners; at night he slipped into tasseled loafers, drove a Mercedes, and lived what he later called "a false life."

Through the pretty broadcaster Robin Robinson, Stedman had been given entrée into the gold coast of Chicago's black society, which included media stars like Oprah, athletes like Michael Jordan, and publishing mogul Linda Johnson Rice, whose family owned *Ebony* and *Jet*. Within this elite circle were Ivy League doctors, lawyers, bankers, and professors, who had achieved the kind of success Stedman never dreamed possible for himself. While he looked like he could belong to the crowd of accomplished professionals—all smooth, smart, and stylish—he knew his degree from the tiny Baptist college Hardin-Simmons in Abilene, Texas, gave him few bragging rights alongside graduates of Harvard.

Flying at that high altitude was transformative for Stedman, and soon he saw that body-searching felons was not going to give him the life he wanted. Prison guards did not get to socialize with Michael Jordan. As a high-school and college basketball star, Stedman wanted nothing more than to play for the

NBA, and not being selected had been the biggest disappointment of his life. So when Michael Jordan started doing commercials and needed a stand-in, Stedman leaped, eager to be a part—any part—of Jordan's world. He idolized the Chicago Bulls forward, not simply for his dazzling athleticism but for turning his success on the court into a lucrative business.

Wanting to associate himself with professional athletes, Stedman devised his plan for the nonprofit organization called Athletes Against Drugs. He enlisted Michael Jordan's endorsement to get other athletes to join and sign vague statements that they were "drug-free and . . . positive role models for today's youth." The wording of his first mission statement was equally vague: "Educate children to live a better lifestyle." He then refined it to "Educate youth to make healthy life decisions." He envisioned arranging public appearances for big-name athletes at sporting events and tournaments, to be underwritten by corporate sponsors, which would enable him to look like he was doing well by doing good while associating with big-time athletes. "Don't call Stedman a jock sniffer," warned Armstrong Williams. "He hates that image."

To start AAD, Stedman sold his Mercedes and cashed in his retirement fund from the corrections system, and used the little he had accumulated from his first job as a police officer in Fort Worth, Texas, followed by three years in the army. Even without an income or a business plan, he finally felt he had a sense of purpose and a little status. He continued runway modeling to pay expenses after resigning from the Bureau of Prisons, where he claimed to have been "on track to one day become a warden in the federal corrections system."

The tax returns for AAD indicate the organization collects an average of $275,000 a year, most of which is raised from an annual celebrity golf tournament. Contributors to AAD pay for the annual dinner gala that allows Stedman to sit at the head table with professional athletes. Being chairman of Athletes Against Drugs certainly gives him a grand title, but no longer a salary. Sometime before 2002, he had to lend his organization more than $200,000 to keep it afloat. How AAD distributes funds "to educate youth to make healthy life decisions" is not specified.

Oprah, who did not publicly admit her drug use until 1995, told Stedman about it early in their relationship. "I was concerned about how it would affect him, but he knew from the start it was one of the secrets I was having trouble dealing with and he encouraged me not to let it be a big fear," she said. "He's never taken a single drug and doesn't drink alcohol."

Stedman was intent on improving his lot, but if he needed goading, Oprah certainly provided it when she was asked if she cared what a man did for a living. She did not hesitate.

"I do care about whether or not he's a ditch digger. I know that sounds elitist. But I have such great aspirations for myself in life—to really fulfill my human potential—that I just don't understand people who don't aspire to do or be anything."

Oprah's ambitions were gargantuan, and her craving for recognition almost insatiable. Without an Off button, her engine churned constantly as she jammed her days and nights with nonstop activity. "My schedule is very hectic, but it's exactly the kind of life I've always wanted," she said. "I've always said I wanted to be so busy that I wouldn't have time to breathe."

Every morning after doing her talk show, at least in the early years, she spent time with her audiences—shaking hands, posing for pictures, signing autographs. She met with her producers to discuss the next day's show, and she scrutinized the overnight ratings. She pushed forward with plans to build her $10 million studio ("I've got to move on from millionaire to mogul"); she pursued movie roles ("I'm going to be a great, great actress"); she purchased book rights to produce her own films, the first being the biography of Madame C. J. Walker, who developed cosmetics for black women that were sold door-to-door, making her the first self-made female millionaire in America. Oprah explored developing her own clothing line for "the more substantial woman," because she couldn't find designer clothes to fit her. When she did find something she loved, her dresser had to buy two outfits in the largest size available and have them sewn together, which was costly and time-consuming. She met with Chicago's Lettuce Entertain You Enterprises to discuss opening a restaurant. She agreed to be a partner but would not allow her name to be used, because if it failed, she did not want to be blamed. She wanted to establish an institute for women as "an extension of what we try to do for an hour on the show . . . I don't know what to call it other than a center for self-improvement." She worked with Maya Angelou to write a one-woman show for her to take to Broadway, and she discussed writing her autobiography. Oprah knew 1987 was her time, as blacks stepped to the forefront in politics (Jesse Jackson), movies (Eddie Murphy), music (Whitney Houston), network news (Bryant Gumbel), and prime-time television (Bill Cosby).

Hell-bent on becoming a presence in prime time herself, Oprah wanted to star in her own sitcom, like Bill Cosby. "I will produce it and sell it to the network," she said, "and it will be a raging success." Having proved her genius on television, she considered herself a natural for a comedy about what goes on behind the scenes of a television talk show based in Chicago. She sold the idea for *Chicago Grapevine* and spent weeks in 1987 flying back and forth to Los Angeles to work on the pilot, but in the end Brandon Stoddard, president of ABC Entertainment, was unimpressed. He pronounced the concept "misguided," said the Oprah character was not depicted successfully as "outspoken and realistic," and canceled the thirteen-week series. Oprah did not see the cancellation as a failure, or even a setback. It was simply another step in her mystical evolution.

After filling her days, she booked her nights and weekends with photo shoots, interviews, speeches, and public appearances. "Even doing the number one talk show isn't enough— it's like breathing to me—I need something else to do," she said. She wanted Stedman to accompany her everywhere, as if to show him off and perhaps prove she could attract a delicious-looking man.

A year into their relationship they got walloped with the first of many tabloid "exclusives," this one claiming that Stedman had called off their wedding. Oprah, who had never learned to ignore the grocery store press, flew into a smackdown and denounced the story on her show and to every reporter within range.

"It's outrageous," she told Bill Carter of *The Baltimore Sun*. "We were going to sue," until the paper promised a retraction. "This story said I was jilted, and crying my heart out, thinking of taking a leave of absence from the show. I was shattered and bitter. And that wedding dress I was waiting to lose weight to get into. It was the worst thing I've ever [read]. I can't remember feeling that bad. Because people believed it and because of the kind of image not only that I created, but that I also believe in: Women being responsible for themselves. And so being portrayed as falling apart because I'd been jilted by some man, that was just too much. It was even worse than the wedding dress stuff."

Oprah told the reporter that she had called Jackie Onassis for consolation. "She had called me earlier about possibly doing a book," Oprah said, "and she told me I can't control [what] other people [write]."

The conversation with Jacqueline Kennedy Onassis was duly noted in Carter's story. "There still seems to be a side of Oprah that wants you to know all the amazing people her fame has brought her in touch with," he wrote. "She is one of the most impressive name-droppers in the U.S.A.:

The call to Jackie O. The show with Eddie (as in Murphy). The dinner in New York at a table next to Cal (as in Klein). The movie rights deal with Quincy (as in Jones)."

Yet Oprah hastened to assure the writer that despite all her newfound riches and fame and celebrity friends, she was just as plain and ordinary as the people who watched her show and loved her with such intensity. "I really do still think I'm just like everybody else," she said. "I'm just me."

# *T*en

W HEN OPRAH made the cover of *People* magazine on January 12, 1987, she reached the summit of cynosure status. It was her first of twelve *People* covers in twenty years, putting her in a league with Princess Diana (fifty-two covers), Julia Roberts (twenty-one covers), Michael Jackson (eighteen covers), and Elizabeth Taylor (fourteen covers). Being crowned by the celebrity chronicle made her an instant pop culture icon, and she was ecstatic. Those around her were not so pleased.

She rankled her family by talking in the article about the sexual abuse she'd suffered as a youngster, something they continued to deny. She upset child abuse victims by saying she'd found the attention pleasurable and that a lot of confusion and guilt over sexual molestation comes because "it does feel good." She insulted her overweight sisters by saying, "Women, always black women, 300 to 400 pounds, waddle up to me, rolling down the street and say, 'You know, people are always confusin' me for you.' I know when they're coming. I say, 'Here comes another one who thinks she looks like me.'" She alienated her alma mater by her "hated, hated, hated" line, referring to Tennessee State and her references about her unease when approached by anyone from her college days.

In response to her cutting comments, her family dummied up; child abuse victims fell silent; overweight black women held their tongues; and Tennessee State University rolled over, paws up, and invited her to be their commencement speaker. It was the first glimpse of the empress's new clothes. As Oprah said years later, "In this society . . . nobody listens to you unless you have some bling, some money, some clout, some access." Having acquired all of that and more, she now exerted a dizzying kind of power that compelled many people to be silent, even to genuflect, in the face of insult.

The invitation from TSU was a heavy load of bricks for some to carry. Nashville attorney Renard A. Hirsch, Sr., wrote a letter to the editor of *The Tennessean,* the city's largest newspaper, saying he had attended school with Oprah and did not recall the anger that she claimed was rampant there. Other TSU students were also riled. Greg Carr, president of the student government, said Oprah "talked about TSU like a dog." Roderick McDavis (Class of '86) wrote a letter to the editor of *The Meter,* the student newspaper, saying, "Some of us worked too damn hard at TSU to have a 'drop out' degrade and discredit our school." Lacking three credit hours, Oprah had never graduated from TSU.

*The Meter*'s editor, Jerry Ingram, acknowledged the negative reactions Oprah had stirred. "Some people were shocked. . . . If she said that in *People,* they wonder what she will say at commencement."

A few students who felt Oprah was trying to ingratiate herself to white audiences with comments about "angry" blacks predicted hisses and boos when she arrived on campus. The outrage at TSU arose not simply because a black woman had demeaned a historically black college and put students on the defensive, but because it was the most famous black woman in the country reviling them in a national magazine that circulated to twenty million people. Oprah's words were particularly wounding because TSU, beset by inadequate facilities and poor programs at the time, was undergoing a court-mandated plan to eradicate the pernicious effects of segregation that would not be completed for another nine years.

Interestingly, the university did not offer Oprah an honorary degree, which is customary for a commencement speaker. Instead, they proffered a plaque "in recognition of excellence in television and films." In return, Oprah asked for the college degree she had been denied in 1975. TSU agreed to give her a diploma and to graduate her with the class of 1987, if she wrote a paper to fulfill her requirements. (Apparently she did, although the university would not confirm the fact and neither would Oprah.)

Graduation day, May 2, 1987, was a dream come true for Vernon Winfrey, who finally had someone in the family with a college degree. "Even though I've gone on and done a few things in life," Oprah teased in her speech, "every time I called home, my father would say, 'When are you going to get that degree? You're not going to amount to anything without that degree. . . .' So this is a special day for my dad." She waved her diploma at Vernon, who beamed from the front row.

Oprah arrived in Nashville like a movie star. She told reporters she had flown in on a chartered jet with her entourage and was met at the airport by two gray limousines. She walked onto campus in bright yellow patent leather high heels to match the bright yellow sash on her black graduation gown. She charmed the audience with her speech—a mixture of high religious fervor and rollicking good humor. She mitigated the sting of her *People* comments by announcing plans to fund ten scholarships in her father's name. Three months later, when she wrote the first check ($50,000), she asked the university to fly someone to Chicago to pick it up and pose with her for photographs, which she released to the Associated Press. "This donation is certainly historical for us because we haven't had this kind of support in the past," said Dr. Calvin O. Atchison, executive director of the TSU Foundation, acknowledging that Oprah's donation was the largest the university had ever received.

For the next eight years she committed herself to funding the scholarships, which covered everything—room, board, books, and tuition, plus a spending allowance. She selected the scholarship winners from a list of incoming students and made sure each knew of the requirement to maintain a B average. When a couple of them let their grades slip, she wrote to them: "I understand that the first year is really difficult and there were a lot of adjustments to be made. I believe in you. We all made an agreement that it would be a three-point average, not a 2.483 and I know you want to uphold your end of the agreement, because I intend to uphold mine."

Her good intentions crashed in 1995 when one of the scholarship students alleged sexual harassment by Vernon Winfrey after seeking his help for additional funds. "I needed the money to take a summer microbiology class," said Pamela D. Kennedy. "Mr. Winfrey [was] a family friend and asked me to meet him at his barbershop. I expected it to be a short meeting."

After twenty-five minutes, she said, Vernon, sixty-two, excused himself to go to the bathroom. She claimed that when he returned he exposed himself and made an obscene gesture before grabbing her, kissing her, and begging her to touch him. " 'I'm doing you a favor,' he said. 'You need to do me a favor. Tomorrow's my birthday and you could really make an old man happy. Come on, honey.'

"At that moment, I knew I had been set up," she said. "He purposely had me come down to the shop when it was closed so we would be alone. Other girls might fall for his act, but I wouldn't think of prostituting myself. I told him, 'How dare you! I don't care if you are Oprah's father and can help me. I refuse to have sex with you.' " She said she ran from the barbershop and Vernon chased her down the street, trying to make amends. " 'Honey, I hope this doesn't ruin our friendship,' " he said.

That same day, January 30, 1995, the twenty-eight-year-old student filed a complaint with Nashville police against Vernon, a former member of the Metro Council. The crime of indecent exposure carried a fine of up to $2,500 and a jail sentence of several months. Vernon denied the charge. "I regret the day I ever let this girl set foot in my barbershop," he said. "Obviously she has dollar signs in her eyes."

When the sex scandal hit the press, Oprah was silent for a day or so. Then she issued a statement, standing foursquare behind her father. "He is one of the most honorable men I know," she said. "In his professional and personal life he has always tried to do what is right and help people."

When the police began investigating her father, she sent

lawyers to Nashville to help him. His accuser passed a lie detector test, which was made public, but weeks later prosecutors determined there was not sufficient evidence to prove the case beyond a reasonable doubt and dropped the charges against Vernon, in large part because Ms. Kennedy's lawyer, Frank Thompson-McLeod, had solicited a bribe, saying the charges would disappear if Vernon paid a certain amount of money. The attorney was arrested and lost his license to practice. Ms. Kennedy was not charged. "Greed is the only reason I can conclude that he did this," said the circuit court judge after sentencing the lawyer to thirty days in jail.

"I knew, knowing God as I do, that that would happen," Oprah said, "but I kept asking, 'Why has this happened and what am I supposed to learn from it?'" The answer, she believed, was what she had been telling her father: that her wealth and fame were so immense that people would try to use him to get to her. "My father still doesn't know who I am," she told *Ebony,* saying Vernon did not grasp the enormity of her celebrity. "So I think something had to happen for him to see he can't continue to be Mr. Friendly-Friendly." She said she felt guilty "because if he didn't have me for a daughter that could not have happened to him." But more than guilt was her fear of what the allegation might do to him. "I was really worried about him for a while, because I thought it was going to break his spirit."

The snakebite of the sex scandal marked the end of Oprah's involvement with TSU and the Vernon Winfrey scholarships. "They tried everything to reconnect, but she would not come back to Nashville," said Brooks Parker, former aide to Governor Donald K. Sundquist. "I suggested that the city's mayor and the governor send her an invitation saying they were going to give her a special award voted by the state legislature as the Most Outstanding Tennessean, or something like that. . . . It was planned as a citywide celebration, to take place on the campus of TSU. . . . I asked Chris Clark, her first boss, to write her a letter, which he did, and it was a great letter. Then I wrote to her, saying, 'The state and city are set to pay dignified homage to you.' But she never responded."

After sending his letter, Chris Clark, who knows how to dance both sides of the ballroom, called Oprah's assistant and told her to tell Oprah to ignore what he had written. "I said I wrote the damn letter because I had to and she shouldn't pay any attention to it. She didn't have to come home. No one else was going to get that award. It was just a publicity gimmick to get her to come to Nashville and be associated with TSU." So Oprah declined the governor's award.

She rarely returned to the city after that, except on occasion, to visit her father. "When she does come I send my adopted son [Thomas Walker] to pick her up at the airport in his police car," said Vernon. "He's with the Davidson County Sheriff's Office." Even on those unannounced visits, when they go out to eat catfish, Oprah is pestered for money. "We went to the cafeteria," said Vernon's second wife, Barbara, "and some lady slipped her a note asking for fifty thousand dollars." Oprah ignored most requests from the city's civic leaders for help on local projects. "No one in Nashville can get through to her," said Paul Moore of the William Morris Agency. "Not even Tipper Gore."

**Oprah's negative attitude toward Nashville seemed most obvious when the city was flooded with torrential rains in May 2010, causing ten deaths and flood damage estimated at $1.5 billion. Earlier she had mobilized her Angel Network to donate $1 million to Haiti after the earthquake in January 2010, but she did next to nothing four months later to help the people of Nashville. She did invite Dolly Parton to be on her show to solicit funds, but she did not provide a page on Oprah.com with links to make donations. Nor did she tweet or blog on her website about the need for money and assistance. For some, that slight must have felt like a slap.**

When she was funding scholarships at TSU, she became a benefactor of Morehouse College, a private men's school in Atlanta, Georgia, and the alma mater of Martin Luther King, Jr. "I did that because I care about black men, I really do," she said. "The last two movies I have been in [*The Color Purple* and *Native Son*] have not been great portrayals of black men, but I have great black men in my life, both my father and Stedman."

After receiving an honorary doctorate from Morehouse in 1988, she established the Oprah Winfrey Endowed Scholarship Fund, to which she donated $7 million. "My dream was—when I first started making money—to pass it on and I wanted to put 100 men through Morehouse," she said in 2004. "Right now we're at 250 and I want to make it a thousand." She felt she reaped far more goodwill from the men of Morehouse than she ever did from TSU.

Over the years, Oprah became a prized commencement speaker at colleges and universities, including Wesleyan, Stanford, Howard, Meharry, Wellesley, and Duke. In each speech, she cited her personal connection to the school through a friend or a relative, and she shared her beliefs about achieving greatness through service. She always invoked the glories of God and the need to give praise. Then, at some point, she frequently descended from the lofty to the low.

When her niece Chrishaunda La'ttice Lee graduated from Wesleyan in 1998, Oprah spent part of her ten-minute speech talking about "peeing." "All I can remember ten years later is Oprah talking about herself going to the bathroom," said a member of the class of '98. "Very uncommencement-like."

At the Stanford graduation of Gayle King's daughter, Kirby Bumpus, in 2008, Oprah quoted Martin Luther King, Jr., who said, "Not everyone can be famous." Then she added, "Everybody today seems to want to be famous. But fame is a trip. People follow you to the bathroom, listen to you pee. It's just— Try to pee quietly. It doesn't matter. They come out and say, 'Ohmigod, it's you. You peed.' That's the fame trip so I don't know if you want that."

A country girl with bathroom humor, Oprah liked to shock the prissy by announcing at every turn she had "to pee" or "go wee willie winkle." Over the years she softened her rough edges and learned company manners. She mastered thank-you note etiquette and the art of the hostess gift, instructing her audiences never to arrive at someone's home empty-handed. "Bring soaps—really good soaps," she once advised. She thumped gum chewers and smokers, and always tipped well. She sent lavish bouquets for special occasions and never forgot her friends' birthdays. She once spent $4 million to rent the yacht *Seabourn Pride* for a week's cruise for two hundred guests to celebrate Maya Angelou's seventieth birthday. But for all her social niceties, Oprah still lapsed into potty talk on occasion, and the occasions were often public ones that were supposed to be uplifting.

Some people found these restroom riffs to be funny and a part of her basic, earthy appeal, perhaps attributable to her outhouse years in Kosciusko and having had to empty the slop jar. Others found her comments coarse, jarring, and inappropriate.

To a paying audience at the Kennedy Center for the Nation's Capital Distinguished Speakers Series, Oprah shared her moments in a bathroom stall at O'Hare Airport. She gave similar information to six thousand people gathered for the American Women's Economic Development Corporation in New York City. In between inspiring quotes from Sojourner Truth and Edna St. Vincent Millay, she told the thunderous crowd, "I can't even pee straight, you see, because everywhere I go, people in the bathroom want me to sign their toilet paper."

Her compulsion to talk about bodily functions once gave her best friend pause when she heard that Oprah had shared with her national television audience the graphic details of watching Gayle give birth to her second child. "She said I pooped all over the table during the birth," Gayle recalled during a Q&A session with Oprah. "People literally stopped me on the street after that one."

"You know in retrospect I might have thought a little more before saying that," said Oprah. "But I was talking about pregnancy, what actually happens, and that's one of the things people never tell you. Gayle goes, 'Well listen . . .'"

"[I told her the] next time you're talking about shitting on a table, keep my name out of it," said Gayle. "I was a news anchor [WSBF-TV in Hartford, Connecticut] by then. 'I'm Gayle King. Eyewitness News.' And I'd get people saying: 'Yes, I saw you on the news. I didn't know you pooped all over.'"

During a speech at a fund-raising luncheon for the Holocaust Memorial Museum, Oprah showed a film clip of her visit to

Auschwitz (May 24, 2006) with Elie Wiesel. That show had been advertised on a jarring billboard over Sunset Boulevard in Los Angeles, showing Oprah, with a dazzling smile, next to the words "OPRAH GOES TO AUSCHWITZ. Wednesday 3 P.M." This drew barbed comments on the Internet:

"This is actually part of a series where Oprah tours historic atrocity sites:

'Oprah Goes Beach Blanket Bosnia on Thursday!'

'Hey Ho Hiroshima! Oprah learns the difference between sushi and sashimi—oh, and a little something about radiation poisoning on Friday!'"

Unfortunately, the interview Oprah conducted with Elie Wiesel on that trip was, in the estimation of frontpagemag .com, "vapid." She sounded inane as she walked the icy grounds of the death camp. "Wow," she said. "Unbelievable . . . wow . . . wow . . . unbelievable . . ."

Granted, the sight of ovens used to dispose of human beings challenges description, but as she interviewed Wiesel, Oprah began to sound like Little Miss Echo:

WIESEL: There were three to a bunk.
OPRAH: Three to a bunk . . .
WIESEL: Straw.
OPRAH: Straw . . .
WIESEL: There were trees.
OPRAH: There were trees.
WIESEL: But we didn't look at them.
OPRAH: But you didn't look at them.

She frequently repeats what her guests say as if she is a Berlitz translator.

Oprah later sold DVDs of her trip with Wiesel at The Oprah Store across the street from her studio, for thirty dollars apiece, prompting one critic to call it "Holocash."

During her speech at the Holocaust Memorial Museum, she talked about the devastation of concentration camps and then, inexplicably, segued into how hard it was to be famous and go to the bathroom in public. She said she had used the restroom earlier in the day and the person in the next stall had said, "You pee like a horse." After that, Oprah told the crowd, who had come to donate money in remembrance of the six million Jews who'd perished in death camps, that she had decided from now on to put lots of paper in the toilet to dampen the sound of her peeing. Robert Feder wrote in the *Chicago Sun-Times* that it was "one of the most outrageous utterances" of the year.

"I don't know what possesses Oprah to talk like that at the most inappropriate times," said Jewette Battles, who helped arrange Oprah's 1988 visit to Kosciusko. "She did something similar when she came back here to dedicate the Oprah Winfrey Road. . . . The whole town turned out to celebrate her on Oprah Winfrey Day and the mayor gave her a key to the city. It was a very big deal. . . . She's the biggest thing to come out of Mississippi since Elvis Presley. So when she got up on the stage of the Attala County Coliseum everyone was cheering, so happy she was there and so proud of her. . . . At first she made the crowd laugh and . . . then all of a sudden she started performing a piece about a slave girl and the plantation mistress who made her drink urine. . . . I don't know where the urine thing came from—if it was something from the book *Jubilee* or what—but people were shocked into absolute silence. . . . I did not understand Oprah's purpose except to say, 'Look at me now. I'm on top. . . .' And if that's what it was, who's to blame her? It's hard to be black and poor in America, but I wondered later if she didn't do that performance to throw up slavery to us as a part of Mississippi's awful past. . . . Even though she's five generations removed from slavery and was much too young to be mistreated when she was here as a child. . . . Besides, things have changed in Mississippi over the years. . . . We have overcome. . . . There's no sense in rubbing our noses in it now."

There are signs in the airport in Jackson, one and a half hours north of Kosciusko, that announce, "No Blacks. No Whites. Just the Blues," and the T-shirts on sale inform visitors "Yes, We Wear Shoes Down Here. Sometimes Even Cleats."

On her visit home on June 4, 1988, Oprah wore a bright turquoise silk dress from The Forgotten Woman, a label for large sizes. She was accompanied by her mother; her father and stepmother; Stedman; her personal secretary, Beverly Coleman; her attorney, Jeff Jacobs; her hairdresser, Andre Walker; her makeup man, Roosevelt Cartwright; three cameramen; and a producer. She planned to make her visit into a show about stars who return to their roots.

"This is a real homecoming," she told the three hundred people standing on a small portion of dirt road that had been named in her honor. "It is a deeply humbling experience to come back to the place where it all started. No one ever goes very far in life without remembering where they came from."

Her grandmother's small wooden shack had long ago been chopped down for firewood, and the outhouse had disappeared into decades of underbrush. There was no trace of the pretty blue hydrangeas that Hattie Mae had grown or the cow she kept to give the family milk. Only the small plot of land remained, which her children had inherited. They had debated opening a gift shop for people who wanted to see where Oprah Winfrey had grown up, but with it being three miles outside the city limits of Kosciusko, there wasn't enough tourism to support the idea. Instead, they erected a sign on the property:

> **• FIRST HOME SITE OF OPRAH WINFREY •**
>
> On January 29, 1954, Oprah Winfrey was born in a wood frame house located on this site. She resided here as a child before moving to Milwaukee at age 6. Within walking distance is the church where she made her first appearance in an Easter citation.
>
> She grew in the information/entertainment industry to become the world's foremost TV talk show host with a daily audience in the millions. At the same time she never forgot or overlooked her heritage and has been a regular support of folks back home as well as a role model to much of America.

With photographers trailing her and cameramen on either side, Oprah made her way to the church where her family had placed another sign: "Oprah Winfrey Faced First Audience Here."

"The church was my life," she recalled. "Baptist Training Union. Every black child in the world who grew up in the church knows about BTU. You did Sunday School, you did the morning service, which started at 11 and didn't end until 2:30, you had dinner on the ground in front of the church, and then you'd go back in for the 4 o'clock service. It was forever, oh, it was forever. It was how you spent your life."

She walked across the parched grass and into the humble cemetery next to the church, where five generations of her maternal ancestors lay buried. With Vernon on one side and Vernita on the other, she looked like she was flanked by Jack Sprat, who ate no fat, and his wife, who ate no lean. (Vernon would later say, "Oprah is definitely her mother's daughter in that respect. The women in her family are all heavy, very heavy.") They all bowed their heads for a few moments in front of two raised blocks of stone the size of shoe boxes on a sliver of granite:

| HATTIE MAE | EARLEST LEE |
|---|---|
| APRIL 15, 1900 | JUNE 16, 1883 |
| FEBRUARY 27, 1963 | DECEMBER 29, 1959 |

There are far more impressive grave sites than the ones for Oprah's grandparents, but as Katharine Carr Esters explained, it was what Hattie Mae's children could afford from the Davidson Marble and Granite Works in Kosciusko. "Poor black folks save their whole lives to buy these tombstones," she said. The name of Oprah's grandfather Earlist is misspelled on the gravestone. "Suzie Mae [his daughter and Oprah's aunt] spelled it the way she knew," said Mrs. Esters. "He didn't read or write, so he wouldn't have been much help."

The cemetery, a small field of scrubby grass filled with granite stones the size of For Sale signs, is sprinkled with a few pyramid towers and a couple of large crosses banked by plastic flowers, but most of the markers are modest. One is particularly joyful: a model of a coffin with an aluminum cover that reads, "Gone Fishing in Crystal Clear Water."

Oprah paid homage to her grandmother on that visit. "It was not in any words she said, it was just the way she lived. She instilled in me that I could do whatever I wanted to do, that I could be whatever I wanted to be, that I could go wherever I wanted to go." This was for the hometown folks. For other audiences she told a different story about her grandmother washing clothes in a boiling cauldron and telling Oprah to pay attention so that when she grew up she could get herself "some good white folks to work for." Oprah always ended that story by saying she knew at the age of four she would never take in wash like her grandmother: "I just wish she had lived long enough to see that I did grow up and I've now got some good white folks working for me."

That evening the family and several community leaders met with Oprah at Katharine Esters's home to discuss what Oprah could do to fulfill the sign's declaration that she supported the "folks back home." Her secretary took notes on the various suggestions, and Oprah promised to get back to them with her decision. Ten years later she returned to Kosciusko to dedicate a $30,000 Habitat for Humanity house that she had financed through Oprah's Angel Network. Ordinarily, she built Habitat houses in towns where television stations carried her talk show, but she made an exception for Kosciusko, and the town showed its appreciation. The front-page headline of *The Star-Herald* (circulation: 5,200) trumpeted, "Kosciusko Prepares for Oprah's Visit." One old-timer observed, "We haven't had that kind of a headline since Allied forces landed in Normandy."

The day before Oprah was to be photographed handing over the house keys to the lucky family, she visited the home and saw that it was empty. She called a nearby Eddie Bauer store and told them to furnish it overnight, from curtains and couches to towels and dishes. She also had every closet filled with clothes in the right size for each family member. Some estimated it cost more to furnish the house than to build it. Oprah laughed. "I couldn't give them an empty house," she said.

Most of the town was on its knees in gratitude, but Katharine Carr Esters, who spent years badgering the city to bring running water to the nearby black community, pushed Oprah to do more, especially for the poor children of Kosciusko. "That's when the seed was planted for the $5 million Oprah Winfrey Boys and Girls Club, which Oprah opened in 2006," she said. "It took eight years to complete but . . . the Boys and Girls Club has done more good than anything this community has ever seen. Teenage pregnancy has dropped, juvenile crime has decreased, and vandalism has almost disappeared because of the programs offered. In addition, the club has provided jobs for people. So Oprah did a wonderful thing for the people here, and praise God that she did. . . . But . . ."

Mrs. Esters cannot help but add a clear-eyed caveat about her cousin's philanthropy. "She does a lot of good things for people with her money, but it's easy when you have that much and you need tax deductions and all. And Oprah doesn't bang a nail for Habitat unless her cameras are running. Yes, she should get publicity for all her good works, and she certainly makes sure that she does. She never misses an opportunity, especially to make money. She does not come home to visit. She only comes home to do a show. She's been here all of three times in the last twenty years, and each time was to do a show. It's all business with Oprah. In 1988 she filmed the visit to Oprah Winfrey Road for one of her shows. In 1998 she dedicated a Habitat house at the same time her film *Beloved* was opening at our local theater, so she promoted her movie by giving a speech before every showing. In 2006 she had her cameras here again, to film the opening of the Oprah Winfrey Boys and Girls Club. . . . Nothing is wasted with that girl."

Worried that her friend, the straight-shooting Mrs. Esters, might have taken too deadly an aim, Jewette Battles interjected. "Oprah has her faults and frailties, just like the rest of us, but she does do good work. It's just that she presents her generosity as the whole of herself and her character, and that's not quite accurate." Both women had occasions over the years to see Oprah in various incarnations. The one they liked best was Oprah the philanthropist. The one they liked least was Oprah the self-promoter. "She will give money, but only if it's on her terms or her idea," said

Mrs. Battles. "Every move is calculated to further her brand and lift her image, which is why she does good works."

During one of her visits to Kosciusko, Oprah had a late-night talk with her "aunt" Katharine and broke down in sobs, begging to know the name of her real father.

"She put her head on my shoulder and cried and cried," recalled Mrs. Esters. " 'I know it's not Vernon,' she said to me. 'There is nothing of Vernon in me. I know that and you know that. . . . You know the whole story; you were there. So, please, Aunt Katharine, tell me who my real father is.' "

"I just couldn't do it," said Mrs. Esters many years later. "I told her it was her mother's place to tell her, not mine.

" 'My mother says it's Vernon,' Oprah said."

Katharine Carr Esters raised her eyes as she related the story, torn between wanting Oprah to know the truth and disapproving of Oprah's mother for not telling her. "I guess Bunny—that's what the family calls Vernita—doesn't want to get into it all at this stage, but I feel her daughter has a right to know if she wants to know. I just don't have the right to tell her."*

**Shortly after this book was published in April 2010, Mrs. Esters was questioned by reporters about her intimate revelations. Apparently feeling pressure, she claimed she had been "tricked" into divulging her true feelings about Oprah and the lies she told about growing up poor in Mississippi. Mrs. Esters also denied that she had revealed the true identity of Oprah's biological father, although she also had shared the same information with one of her closest friends. Hearing her mother's denial, her daughter Jo Baldwin told her son, Conrad, who lives with Mrs. Esters, to call Oprah to tell her that his grandmother had not revealed the name of Oprah's father to the author. "Conrad said he couldn't make that call to Oprah," said**

---

*On July 30, 2007, Mrs. Esters told the author the name and family background of Oprah's real father on the condition that the information not be published until Vernita Lee tells her daughter the entire story. "And you'll know when that happens because Oprah will probably have a show on Finding Your Real Father. As I said, the girl wastes nothing."

Jo Baldwin in an interview three months after publication of this book. "I asked him why not. He said, 'Because I heard her say it.'"

The issue of Oprah's real father stirred publicity, prompting at least one man to publicly declare paternity, which in turn prompted a response from Oprah when she was in New York to present an award to Gayle King.

"Last week was a rough week for Gayle when a so-called biography came out," Oprah told a luncheon crowd at the Waldorf-Astoria. "Every day she's getting herself more and more worked up about all of my new daddies that are now showing up. New daddies who are saying, 'Hello, daughter, call me. I need a new roof.' Well, this too shall pass."

Vernita Lee sidestepped the issue of Oprah's real father in a 2010 interview with *N'Digo*, a free weekly in Chicago. "The thing about Vernon is not Oprah's father, I hear it and I don't hear it," she said. "They can say whatever. I know who I am and I don't let that bother me. It will blow over or they will stop talking about it."

During three days of on-the-record interviews with Mrs. Esters, she had said she understood why Vernita Lee was not inclined to rock her well-heeled boat late in life and admit that someone other than Vernon Winfrey was Oprah's real father, especially since Oprah had never demanded a DNA test. Vernon had admitted he had not sired Oprah, but he took great pride in knowing that he had given her something better than blood.

"Oprah has taken very good care of her mother, who now buys five-hundred-dollar hats and has drivers who have drivers and helpers and cooks and all, but the story of Oprah and Vernita is sad and complicated," said Mrs. Esters. "Oprah does not love her mother at all.... She gives her a great deal financially but she does not give her the respect and affection a daughter should, and that bothers me. Vernita did the best she could with Oprah, who was a willful, runaway child.... Her mother has had to bury two of her three children over the years, and I can tell you that when a parent loses a child it can bring you to your knees. I know. I had to bury my son." She gestured to the painting of a young man hanging over her bed. "So Oprah should be more forgiving of her mother. . . . Even when she has had Bunny on her show she won't let her talk, because Bunny speaks colored dialect. . . . She's not as educated as Oprah would like."

Oprah had moved so far beyond the life of her grandmother's farm that there was nothing left for her in Kosciusko. After one of her visits she told a luncheon audience, "I was recently back in my hometown . . . and some of the people that I grew up with are still sitting on the same porch, doing the same thing. It's like time stopped and continues to stand still in parts of Mississippi. There's not a day that I'm not on my knees thanking God that I was one of the blessed ones to be able to leave that place and do something with my life."

Yet there was something she needed from the past, which she said she finally found in a $1 million mansion on a sprawling 160-acre estate in Rolling Prairie, Indiana. Having invented a family she could love, she now decided to invent her ideal home, with rolling hills, meadows of purple flowers, stables, a heated dog kennel, twelve bedrooms, a heliport, nine palomino horses, ten golden retrievers, three herds of black-faced sheep, one eight-room guesthouse, a log cabin, a pool, tennis courts, and pretty blue hydrangeas.

"I've never loved a place the way I love my farm," she said. "I grew up in the country, which is probably why I'm so attached to the land. I love it. I love the lay of the land. I love walking the land. And I love knowing that it's my land. . . . When I'm pulling into the gate and my dog comes running out to meet me because he knows the sound of the truck, I'm the happiest I've ever been. I walk in the woods. I do Tai Chi Ch'uan by the pond. I grow my own collards."

"The landscaping alone for that farm was a four-year project and cost nine million dollars," said the landscape architect James van Sweden of Oehme, van Sweden and Associates. "I met with Oprah every three weeks for four years to discuss the design. We had a wonderful time bricking the parking area, erecting limestone walls, laying flagstone walkways, grassing the pond, moving the tennis court and the swimming pool. I built her an eighty-five-foot-long pool, but the poor thing could not use it because she was at her heaviest then—she was hugely heavy—and the paparazzi were always buzzing the farm in helicopters and hiding across the lane with cameras that could catch a perfect picture from three thousand feet away. There was no way she could go into her pool without having her three-hundred-pound self splattered all over the tabloids. We also built a twelve-hundred-square-foot pool house so she could hold meetings. She was totally involved in the project from start to finish, and spent three to four hours with me at every meeting. Then I would spend weeks at the farm. . . .

"I remember when I first walked into her Indiana living room and saw those overstuffed couches and plump tufted chairs and what looked like one million pillows strewn everywhere. That's her decorator Anthony Browne's idea of 'Country English,' which poor Oprah bought into totally. She liked puffy things. Big puffy things. . . . Browne put fringe and ruche and piping and ruffles and cording on everything." The internationally acclaimed van Sweden is known for sleek, uncluttered design. "All of Oprah's servants are white, but her walls are black. She's got paintings of black shepherds and black farmers and black angels—all very tacky, but that, too, might've been Anthony Browne's fault for steering her to junky art. The color, though, Oprah insisted on. She said, 'I'm not going to have counts and countesses on my walls. Just black folks.'

"After our first lunch at the farm we walked outside and she told me I had to transform her meadows into *The Color Purple*. She insisted that she be able to see purple flowers from every angle of her bedroom. She couldn't understand why I couldn't plant that meadow (forty acres) as fast as Steven Spielberg did for the movie. 'It only took him three weeks,' she said. I tried to explain that was Hollywood and he'd done it with mirrors and lenses. I spent days in her bedroom designing plans from every window, so that by the time I was finished I knew every inch of that room, inside the closets and out, which is why I can tell you that there were no men's clothes in any of Oprah's closets and no trace of Stedman anywhere. Maybe she put him in the log cabin she built, which she called 'The Love Nest,' but I can tell you that Oprah sleeps alone in her bedroom and keeps a Bible next to her bed with loads of books.

"I designed a circle in the parking lot for her wedding, because I'd heard her talk on her show about eventually wanting to get married. I didn't tell her this at the time, but I had it in mind for her. Then I met Stedman and knew there wouldn't ever be a wedding. He's simply a fixture in her life. Window dressing. A way for a single, childless woman to appear normal to her married audience of women with husbands and children. Stedman is a nice man. I remember his beautiful, elegant, long fingers. He was handsome, too, but he's nothing more than an attractive escort. I never saw any warmth or affection between them—any at all during the four years I worked with Oprah. I never saw touching or hugging or kissing between them ever. They didn't even hold hands. But Oprah wants to come across as normal to her audience, so she needs to have Stedman around so she can refer to him. . . . She talked about Gayle far more than she ever did Stedman, but I don't think that she and Gayle are a lesbian couple. They're just very good friends. . . . Oprah keeps Stedman around because she wants her audience to accept her as a normal woman with a man in her life, but from what I saw during those four years I can tell you there's nothing there with Stedman. Nothing at all."

Months after van Sweden had planted the last purple flower on Oprah's Rolling Prairie farm, she and Stedman and Gayle were spending a fall weekend together. Gayle had arrived from Connecticut and was in the kitchen when Oprah went outside to greet Stedman, who was arriving from Chicago. She later related their brief conversation.

"I want you to marry me," he said.

"Is this the proposal?" asked Oprah.

"I think it's time."

"Oh, that's really great."

She walked into the kitchen a bit breathless. "You are not going to believe this," she whispered to Gayle. "Stedman just proposed." They planned to be married on September 8 of the following year, because that was the date of Vernon's wedding to Zelma. Oprah called Oscar de la Renta to design her wedding dress. She and Stedman announced their engagement in an interview with Gayle on television—or rather, Oprah made the announcement, which she said upset Stedman. Days later, on November 23, 1992, during the ratings sweeps, they were on the cover of *People,* next to a blaring headline: "OPRAH'S ENGAGED!"

Months before, in what was hyped as their first joint interview, Oprah and Stedman appeared on *Inside Edition* and complained to Nancy Glass that too much publicity threatened their relationship. "We've been through a lot of stress," Stedman said. "Not having any privacy when you go out." Apparently, neither saw the irony in going on national television to bemoan the public attention they attracted.

After six years, Stedman had officially progressed from boyfriend to fiancé. A decade later he would be politely described as Oprah's life partner, which is how he has remained for years and years—a perpetual escort, a roommate, and an occasional traveling companion.

# $E$leven

OPRAH'S REIGN as America's number one talk show host for more than two decades divides into the early years of 1984–1994 and the years that followed. For viewers, the first ten years marked Oprah sleaze, the second ten years, Oprah spirituality, or what Ann Landers told Oprah was her "touchy-feely crap." Within the television industry the demarcation is defined by the rise and fall of Oprah's former executive producer Debra DiMaio.

"She is the mother of us all," Oprah said in 1986 when she introduced the hard-charging executive producer to her national audience. "I owe everything to her."

DiMaio smiled and nodded in agreement. "Everything," she said, knowing that DiMaio's audition tape had landed Oprah the job in Chicago that led to her national syndication. "I feel very destined to have met her," DiMaio said later. "I have pretty much unconditional love for her."

DiMaio was the one to whom Oprah confided her fears of being assassinated. It was also DiMaio who received her late-night calls to go to Wendy's for sour cream potatoes, and even if she got the call at midnight, DiMaio would throw on a coat; hail a cab waving a twenty-dollar bill, and rush to get to her boss for a late-night binge. The two young women developed a symbiotic relationship that enabled each to complement the other. DiMaio, tough and controlled, was unafraid of confrontation. Oprah, more emotionally needy, wanted to please everyone and be liked. Together they made a perfect pair. In later years the staff would accuse Oprah of playing good cop to Debra's bad cop, a characterization Oprah did not like. But she could not deny that she allowed DiMaio to do all her dirty work (hiring, firing, correcting, criticizing) so she could reign as the beloved monarch. From the recollections of former employees, most of whom were terrified of DiMaio, Debra flew like an F22 fighter jet and treated everyone else as if they were Sopwith Camels. The daughter of a Marine colonel, DiMaio took charge and tolerated little nonsense from anyone, including, on occasion, Oprah. If the talk show host acted less than engaged on the air, Debra would break for a commercial and kick her into shape. During one show she told Oprah to stop showing her boredom. "You're an Oscar-nominated actress," she said. "Go out there and act like a talk show host." They never really clashed because they were both driven by ratings and the desire to dethrone Phil Donahue.

In the early days Oprah referred to her small staff—six women and one man—as "my girls." She sounded like the actress Maggie Smith in *The Prime of Miss Jean Brodie*, who described her starry-eyed pupils as "my gels." Oprah said of her staff: "These are my closest personal friends."

"We're each other's family," said associate producer Bill Rizzo, who frequently urged reporters to be kind to Oprah in their stories.

"We'll be out to dinner and will vow that by this time next month we'll be back with men," said Christine Tardio. "Then the next month rolls around and we're still together."

"We all band together like a family since we don't have anyone else," said Ellen Rakieten. "I talk to Oprah every night on the phone. She says I'm her soul mate."

All single and in their twenties, the "girls" worked fourteen-hour days, ate all their meals together, shopped together, and spent weekends together. They all worshipped Oprah. "I'd take a bullet for her," said Mary Kay Clinton.

"The hardest part of my job, in addition to the terribly long hours, is the reading I have to be continually doing," said Dianne

Hudson, the only African American on staff then. "We all read the tabs, like *The Star,* the *Globe,* and the *Enquirer.*"

Alice McGee, who started as an intern at WLS and became a publicist for Harpo and later a producer, worried about people kissing Oprah instead of just hugging her. "We gotta watch that," she said.

The "girls" were so devoted to Oprah in those days that they were afraid they sounded like Moonies when they talked about her. Some people referred to them as "the Oprah-ettes."

**"I was hired as Oprah's speechwriter," said her cousin Jo Baldwin. "I was also hired to tell her what not to say, but on those occasions I never said it in front of anyone. I always pulled her aside. Like when she ragged on welfare mothers on her show and said, 'Why are you having all these children?' I said, 'Don't say that, Oprah. Just look at your own mother.' Oprah hired me to be honest with her and I was, but I never gave her criticism in front of anyone—ever." But even in private, Oprah did not appreciate her cousin's assessments, and two years into a three-year contract, she fired her without notice.**

When Oprah took over ownership and production of her nationally syndicated show in 1988, she became CEO of Harpo Productions and started signing their checks. "Everybody tells me that you cannot have true friendships with people whose salaries you control," she said. "But I just don't think that's true in my case. Because they were my friends before I signed their paychecks. We sort of all grew up together with this show."

Within six years that loving family of best friends was split by discord and death. They buried Bill Rizzo, who died of AIDS in 1990, and four years later Debra DiMaio, "the mother of us all," was forced to resign following a staff coup in which she was branded as tyrannical. "Either she goes or we go," the producers told Oprah. So Oprah paid DiMaio $3.8 million [$5.5 million in 2009 dollars] to resign in exchange for signing a confidentiality agreement that she would "never speak or publish or in any way reveal" details about her personal or professional relationship with Oprah. More staff resignations followed. One employee sued Oprah for $200,000 in severance pay, and another said that "working for her was like working in a snake pit." Oprah settled the lawsuit out of court—quickly and quietly. With the forced resignation of Debra DiMaio in 1994, Oprah decided to back away from the trough of trash television.

"That's when she started getting into celebrities and New Age gurus," said Andy Behrman, a publicist who had worked closely with the show. "Before that it was heaven for me, because I could book anyone on Oprah, absolutely anyone."

The publicist's claim seemed preposterous given the numerous books, articles, and websites (28,100 by 2009) dedicated to getting on *The Oprah Winfrey Show,* but even Oprah admitted having to do on-air promotions to get guests in the early days and to drag audiences off the street. "Now getting a ticket to the show is like winning the lottery," said a staffer in 2005. By then Oprah's production company was receiving thousands of phone calls each week requesting tickets to the show.

"In the early years her show was easy to book because she and her little girls' club didn't know what the hell they were doing," said Behrman. "They were all young with hay behind their ears—unsophisticated small-town, small-time girls just trying to find husbands. . . . Don't forget that Oprah's first national show [September 9, 1986] was entitled 'How to Marry the Man of Your Choice,' which should tell you something."

Reminded that the "girls" were producing a number one–rated television talk show in syndication, the publicist maintained that "Oprah's sorority" merely slapped together local shows for national consumption on a daily basis. "For the most part her early years were devoted to tabloid sex trash that got huge ratings," he said, "and shows about getting a man and keeping a man, and, of course, losing weight, because that's all she and her little cult really cared about. Unlike Phil Donahue, they didn't know anything about current affairs, politics, or the larger world around them, and they didn't care."

A survey conducted by the Harvard Business School of topics covered in the first six years Oprah went national showed that she concentrated primarily on victims: rape victims, families of kidnapping victims, victims of physical and emotional abuse, teenage victims of alcoholism, female victims of workaholism, obsessive love, and childhood wounds. She also covered therapy for husbands, wives, and mistresses; infidelity among traveling businessmen; and the worlds of UFOs, tarot cards, channelers, and other psychic phenomena.

"Oprah's shows back then, and even now," said Andy Behrman in 2009, "are all about Oprah and her issues. . . . Back then it was all victims all the time, plus boys, clothes, and diets. Now that Oprah is going through menopause her show has become a way station for middle-aged women with PMS. It's all about health and hormones. When I was in my *Oprah*-booking prime I worked with Ellen Rakieten, who I'd talk to almost every day. I became her go-to guy in New York City, which was another planet for those girls. And Los Angeles? Forget it. That was an alternative universe. Most of them had never even been to Europe. They thought they'd hit the big time when they moved to Chicago and started shopping at Marshall Field. They loved to shop, but they were dull gray dumplings with no sense of style. Their idea of chic was an Ann Taylor dress, a little Echo scarf, black patent leather heels, and some plastic button earrings. Pathetic. They couldn't stay on diets, so they started going to spas. . . . Oh, the stories of Oprah and the girls at the fat farm . . . That's how I got all my diet-book clients on the show. I threw them Suzy Prudden and Blair Sabol—God, Oprah loved Blair because she was so smart and funny. She must've booked her three or four times. I even got the late Dr. Stuart Berger on *Oprah* to talk about dieting and—God help us—he weighed 350 pounds at the time. No matter who my client was, I simply pegged my pitches to Oprah's obsessions with getting a man or buying clothes or losing weight. Sometimes I had to stretch, but it always worked. . . . Most of my clients got on one, two, and three times, especially my plastic surgeons, diet doctors, and shrinks, some of whom were out-and-out frauds. Once I got them on *Oprah,* I could always book them on *Sally Jessy Raphael,* who picked up all of Oprah's crumbs."

Tall, handsome, and devilishly clever, the publicist said he became a regular booker for Oprah's show for several years.

"With the exception of Debbie DiMaio, who cracked a mean whip, those girls didn't know what was good and what was bad, which made it easy for me. I even booked my best female friend on the show, to talk about the pick-up lines guys use to get girls. I did that just to prove to her I could get anyone on *Oprah*. I was so close in those days that I was invited to Ellen Rakieten's wedding, where I stood with Oprah and Stedman and Rosie, the chef. Boy, was that a lifetime ago. . . .

"Early on, Ellen told me the sorority was worried about some guy dating Oprah for her money, and so I immediately suggested doing a show on gold diggers.

" 'Oh, that's great,' Ellen said. 'But how do we do it?'

" 'You get a guy like my client, who has written a book on neuro-linguistic programming, and he'll be able to tell you who is after money and who isn't based on scientific research. . . . I'll give you the questions Oprah can ask him and then she can take some prescreened questions from her audience, which I'll send to you. Then you get a panel and blah, blah, blah.' By the end of the conversation I had laid out the entire show for her.

"Now, of course, there's no science to determine whether or not someone is a gold digger, but I had to get my client on a national show, because I didn't want to drag him around on a fourteen-city book promotion tour. Who needs *Good Morning Cincinnati* and *Hello Peoria* when you can do *The Oprah Winfrey Show*?"

That gold-digging show was not an unqualified success for the author, who recalled the experience as "terrifying, not terrific." "I had written a book entitled *Instant Rapport* on neuro-linguistic programming, which had to do with how you verbally influence people," recalled Michael Brooks. "I was given the whole show—one hour with just me and Oprah—to talk about 'Secret Admirers,' which is how they spun the subject to dumb it down for her audience. I wasn't in any position to object, as this was my first national show.

"The Oprah that I met back in the 1980s was vastly different from the Oprah you see on television today. Back then, she was very dark-skinned—Sidney Poitier dark—and now she's very light-skinned. I know that makeup and lighting can do a lot, but I think she might've had some kind of skin bleaching . . . like Michael Jackson.

"The audience was interested in my subject—to a point—but when I lost them, I lost Oprah. She'd jump over to their side and belittle me if I made a dumb point. If I made a good point and the audience clapped, she'd jump back to my side. It was unnerving."

Even after an hour on *Oprah,* his book did not become a bestseller. "It did well, but it didn't make the list," he said.

"You had to get your book up to Oprah's breasts to become a bestseller," said the writer Blair Sabol. "Our publicist's rule was if she holds it in her lap, you'd make the list in two weeks. If she holds it at her waist, you'd be on in a week. If she clutches it to her bosom, you're headed for number one. So, naturally, we all aimed for Oprah's boobs."

In the early days, guests were allowed to sit and talk to Oprah as she was being made up before the show. "I was mesmerized by her hair and makeup guys," said Sabol. "They were nothing short of miracle workers, because Oprah without hair and makeup is a pretty scary sight. But once her prep people do their magic she becomes super glam. . . . They narrow her nose and thin her lips with three different liners. They shade her large round cheeks, contour her chin with some kind of glowing stuff, and apply double-decker eyelashes that cost five hundred dollars apiece . . . and her hair. Well, I can't even begin to describe the wonders they perform with her hair.

"Those guys—Reggie and Roosevelt and Andre—have been with her from the beginning, and she takes them everywhere she goes. I would, too. In fact, I'd ditch Stedman and Gayle before I ever let those prep guys go."

Perhaps because of Oprah's need for daily makeovers, she was susceptible to guests who were attractive and natural. With her arresting good looks and witty repartee, Blair Sabol was easy to book. "She was not like Marianne Williamson, who always wanted to take over the show from Oprah," said Behrman. "Blair was lively enough to keep it going and entertain Oprah. . . . I booked her for a show on 'Being a Bitch,' in which she appeared with Queen Latifah, and she was very funny. When I got Blair on with her book, *The Body of America,* in 1987, Richard Simmons got his panties in a knot because Blair had written that Simmons found 'a way to reduce fitness to a Vegas stand-up comic routine.' She put down the national obsession with diet and exercise, and was way ahead of the curve on that one."

After several sit-downs with Oprah before, during, and after her shows, Blair Sabol came to see the difference between the on-camera persona and the off-air presence. "Oprah gives it all to the camera, so there's very little left over. In person she's shut down, aloof, a bit stand-offish. She likes to laugh, but she's not really funny. I liked her because she was a girl's girl. Seeing her on television, though, you think she's warm and affectionate, but that's the persona. There's a sheet of ice between the person and the persona." The author Paxton Quigley also found Oprah cold off-camera. "I went on her show with my pro-gun book, *Not an Easy Target,* but her producers said I couldn't mention guns because Oprah is against guns. I was only allowed to talk about self-defense for women, so that's what I did. . . . I was surprised that I did not like Oprah at all. She only came to life when the camera was on; otherwise, she ignored me. That kind of treatment makes you feel so diminished. You realize that she's using you, but then that's why you're there—it's a mutual using, but I think guests expect her to be like the warm and cozy Oprah they see on the air. She isn't—at all."

Oprah's executive producer from her *People Are Talking* years in Baltimore explained the difference between Oprah on- and off-camera as an element of performance. "I'd say this about most on-air talent," said Eileen Solomon, now a professor of broadcast journalism at Webster University in St. Louis. "They save their best stuff for the camera, and that's how it was with Oprah. Off the air she was much quieter. Pleasant and perfectly collegial, but in no way effusive."

Occasionally the audience gets a glimpse of the two different Oprahs, which can be unsettling for those who expect a warm, huggy presence off-camera. "I attended a makeover show several years ago, and during the commercial break the charming Oprah became charmless," recalled Peggy Furth, a former Kellogg executive and now co-owner of the Chalk Hill Vineyards in California. "Oprah did not enjoy those of us in the audience in any way, until the camera went back on. Then she was terrific. Engaging and funny, *but* only on-camera."

Most viewers found the chemistry between Oprah and her guests to favor women over men, especially those with an issue she shared. "Because she was obsessed with losing weight, I booked Suzy Prudden, with her book *MetaFitness*, which was some kind of mumbo jumbo about using your mind to change your body through guided imagery and hypnosis," said Behrman. "Oprah fell for that one hook, line, and sinker. . . . Suzy had already done Oprah a few times in Baltimore, with *People Are Talking*, and then *A.M. Chicago*, so she wasn't such a tough sell for the national show."

Suzy Prudden's appearance on *Oprah* was so successful that one of the tabloids offered her a weekly column, in which she was promoted as "Oprah's diet guru."

"I became persona non grata after that," Prudden said years later. "Oprah was furious at me, and rightfully so, although I wasn't responsible for advertising myself that way. . . . I apologized and apologized, but it did no good. She never spoke to me again. . . . It was a horrible experience. . . . At first I was highly regarded by Oprah, and then I was dirt. . . . It wasn't that she said anything or screamed and yelled. . . . It was that the door once open to me was closed and it never opened again. . . . It was one of the worst experiences in my life."

The publicist, too, fell out of favor, which he attributed to "my troubles with the law" (a felony conviction for defrauding an art dealer). After serving five months in prison and five months house arrest, Behrman went back into public relations but was no longer able to book clients on Oprah's show. "I can't even get through to a secretary of the secretary of the secretary," he said with a laugh. "But it was a good run while it lasted."

The closing of Oprah's door wounded others who found

themselves suddenly banned without explanation. Mark Mathabane, who wrote *Kaffir Boy*, appeared on her show in 1987 to discuss his memoir about growing up in South Africa under the
barbaric system of apartheid. Oprah told reporters she had
found the book in paperback. "It went from the sale table to
Number 5 on *The New York Times* best-seller list, and I know it
was because of being on my show that the book made the list,"
she said. Moved by his story, she befriended the young man, flew
his family from South Africa the following year for a reunion on
her show, and even accompanied him to the airport to meet them
with a film crew. As she said, her support made Mathabane's
book a bestseller in paperback for thirteen weeks, reaching as
high as number three. She invited the author and his wife to parties, optioned the film rights to his book, and announced that
*Kaffir Boy* would be one of Harpo's first film productions. "She is
the most compassionate human being I've ever met," said
Mathabane. Then the door suddenly closed without explanation
or avenue for apology. Oprah did not renew her option for *Kaffir
Boy*, and she never spoke to the writer again.

"I remember very strongly the sense of hurt and confusion
his wife exuded," said a New York editor after meeting Mark
Mathabane and his wife, Gail Ernsberger. "She understood
that they had done something to offend Oprah, but it was relatively minor. I can't remember if it was asking for a book blurb or
talking to a magazine. What Gail seemed so blindsided by was
that someone who had been so helpful, so involved with her
husband's life, could suddenly cut him off without a word of explanation."

Oprah does not slam her door in fury, but rather with chill-
ing resolve. Even those who have tried to help her have been shut
out. When Eppie Lederer, the renowned advice columnist
known as Ann Landers, heard some distressing stories about
Stedman's sexual preferences that made Oprah look foolish, she
called her in confidence. Eppie had befriended Oprah when
she first arrived in Chicago and appeared on her show many
times, occasionally at the last minute to fill in for no-show
guests. Oprah lavished her with luxurious gifts, but once Eppie

told her the stories about her boyfriend, Oprah closed the door. "That was the end of the cashmere bathrobes and Judith Leiber bags at Christmas," said Lederer's daughter Margo Howard. Decades later, when Lederer died, her daughter published a book of letters from her famous mother, but Oprah refused to have Margo on the show to promote it. "I couldn't understand it, because Mother was a beloved figure, especially in Chicago, and her audience was Oprah's audience, but Oprah just wasn't going to do it because she, apparently, was still mad. A grudge unto the next generation."

Orlando Patterson, the distinguished John Cowles Professor of Sociology at Harvard, also ran afoul of Oprah after writing an op-ed in *The New York Times* criticizing her production of *There Are No Children Here* for ABC television as a "tendentious, dishonest dramatization of Alex Kotlowitz's book." Professor Patterson upbraided Oprah for distorting the real-life account of ghetto life in Chicago and perpetuating "the black establishment's dogma of victimization." Oprah stopped speaking to him.

The photographer Victor Skrebneski experienced a similar shutout and told friends he had no idea why. After seeing Oprah around town at various parties, he finally asked, "Why did our professional relationship end?" She shot him a look and hissed, "Black lipstick. You are the one who told me to wear black lipstick."

The photographer had been brought to Oprah by Sugar Rautbord, part of Chicago's social set, who was doing a Q&A with her for Andy Warhol's *Interview* magazine. "Andy kept asking me, 'Why is she so big? Why isn't she beautiful?' So I decided she had to be photographed like a star, and that's what Victor did. . . . Oprah posed for the picture but later told me she didn't like it. 'I am not a diva,' she said. 'I am everywoman. I should not look grander than other people.' She always took umbrage with that photograph. . . .

"I've done Oprah's show eleven times," said Sugar Rautbord. "I knew her before she became Oprah and moved up in the world. . . . She has a great quality of moving on and moving up. . . . Even back when she was local in Chicago I saw her great ambition and I was in awe. . . . She figured out early that the only way to have a successful career and make money—big money— was to delete husbands and children and carpools from life's agenda. None of those problems touch Oprah in the golden sphere in which she lives. Yet she still addresses our issues of husbands and children and carpools as if they were her issues, as if she really is Everywoman. . . . It's quite amazing."

Oprah preferred presenting herself to her audience as one of them, and adopted Whitney Houston's hit "I'm Every Woman" as the theme song for her show. She understood the importance of maintaining an appealing public image, which is why she insisted on controlling her own public relations, including all photographs of herself. "*Controlling* is the operative word with Oprah," said Myrna Blyth, the former editor of *Ladies' Home Journal.* "I think we were the first traditional women's magazine to put her on the cover, and we had her on many times. One time she insisted on choosing her own photographer, which is not unusual. A lot of celebrities do that, but after the shoot, Oprah did not like the picture. So she asked for another shoot by another photographer, whom she also chose. That is unusual, but we agreed, even though it was very expensive with the second photographer, but we wanted to please her. . . . She bought up all the first photographer's negatives so he couldn't publish them elsewhere. She does that with all her pictures, which is why you see so very few photos of Oprah that she doesn't want you to see, except in the tabloids."

Oprah told *Ladies' Home Journal* that she insisted on having total control over every aspect of her professional life. "It's tough to have a relationship with someone like me," she said. "And the older I get, the tougher I am. . . . Because I control so many things in my life, I have to work at not being controlling when I'm spending time with Stedman." She said that whenever they drive somewhere, she always dictates the route, sure that she knows the best way. One time she was so insistent that Stedman take a certain shortcut that he finally gave in, even though he knew the street was blocked. "When I realized that I had been a real jerk and that he had allowed me to be a jerk, I said, 'Why didn't you just tell me that you knew the street was blocked?' He said, 'It's easier for me to just drive down the street and turn around than to try to explain that to you, because you would be convinced that it wasn't blocked.' That's when I realized, God, I'm really bad."

Oprah's need for control also extended to her father, who frequently chafed under her yoke. "Oprah is all about control," said freelance writer Roger Hitts. "I used to talk to her stepmom, Zelma, a lot, but Oprah shut that down. She told all her relatives, 'You are not important. They only want to talk to you to get to me.' I went to Zelma's funeral [November 7, 1996] and Oprah gave the eulogy and took over everything. . . . She did the same when Vernon remarried four years later [June 16, 2000]. At the wedding, which Oprah paid for, Vernon was talkative and approachable—until she arrived. Then she took charge, telling him what he could and couldn't do. She wouldn't let him talk to anyone. She completely controlled the situation. The wedding was run on her clock. She was late, but nothing could start until she got there. Then her minders took control of everything, including the relatives. . . .

"I caught up with Vernon afterward. He was still talkative but dour, which had to do with Oprah. He is a pretty prideful guy, but he has had to do a lot of giving with her. She tells him what he can and cannot do all the time. She dictates his life. That's the relationship, and it grates on him."

Oprah had no control over what happened when she agreed to host the winners of the *Ladies' Home Journal* celebrity look-alike contest. "It never occurred to us to specify the sex of the applicants," said Myrna Blyth, "and we didn't expect to get an Oprah look-alike, but we got one who looked exactly like her. Only after we announced the winner [Jecquin Stitt], who beat out four thousand other contestants, did we find out that the Oprah look-alike was a man. . . . But we had to give him the award because of political correctness."

At the time of the contest, Stitt, who later underwent sex reassignment surgery to become a woman, was known as a transvestite in Flint, Michigan, where he worked as an account clerk for the Water Department. "I was a flaming queen [then]," Stitt said, "but the torch was turned way down at work."

The prize for the look-alike winners (Oprah, Madonna, Barbara Bush, Whoopi Goldberg, Carol Burnett, Janet Jackson, Cher, Liza Minnelli, and Joan Collins) was a trip to New York City, a makeover by John Frieda, makeup by Alfonso Noe, a photo shoot for the magazine by celebrity photographer Francesco Scavullo, and an appearance on *The Oprah Winfrey Show*.

"I have to say Oprah handled it very well, because she didn't make a big deal of it," said Blyth. "When he came out to meet her on the show, she said, 'If I had a wig, I'd take it off to you.' If she had reacted differently, it could have blown up into a big story, but she handled it so that it just went away quietly after the show. She and her people are very savvy, very smart. They protect her and do a great job."

The transvestite Oprah felt that, in protecting the real Oprah, her staff had trampled on him. He said he was denied the promised makeover and his photo in *Ladies' Home Journal*. While the other look-alikes were attended to in the Harpo prep room, he was ignored, although he had been promised that Oprah's hairdresser, Andre Walker, would make sure he looked like Oprah. He had also been promised that he would be on for half the show, and while the other look-alikes each got three minutes on air, he was not brought on until the very end, when Oprah was doing the sign-off. When the program aired during sweeps, the credits ran over his appearance. He sued *Ladies' Home Journal* for breach of contract, and the magazine paid him a settlement. He later said his treatment by Harpo was "ugly," but he got revenge a few days later when Joan Rivers decided to do a mock bridal shower for Oprah on her new talk show and invited the transvestite to appear in a Vera Wang wedding gown flanked by look-alikes for Madonna and Cher. After that show, Oprah closed the door on Joan Rivers and never spoke to the comedienne again, even after appearing with her three times on *The Tonight Show* early in her career.

Oprah and her producers turned themselves inside out for shows during sweeps, because the ratings then determined how much the show could charge for license fees and advertising rates. Higher ratings meant more money, so sweeps shows tended to be highly controversial, to increase viewership, and Oprah awarded $10,100 bonuses to her producers if their sweeps programs achieved at least a 10.1 rating, as measured by Nielsen. For the February 1987 sweeps, she presented a show that shot her ratings through the roof. She took her cameras into the town of Cumming, in all-white Forsyth County, Georgia, which had received negative publicity when members of the Ku Klux Klan threw bricks at civil rights workers celebrating Martin Luther King, Jr.'s birthday. A week after the brick-throwing incident, the Rev. Hosea Williams organized a march of twenty thousand people into Forsyth County in one of the biggest civil rights demonstrations since the 1960s. They, too, were attacked with rocks and stones and shouts of "Nigger, go home."

With the attention of the world upon her, Oprah ventured into the all-white community and excluded any participation on the show by civil rights representatives. "We're here simply to ask why this community has not allowed black people to live here since 1912," she said, "and we felt that the people of Cumming are in the best position to answer that question."

Rev. Hosea Williams protested the exclusion of civil rights representatives. He said he had been misled by Oprah's producers into believing that blacks would have an opportunity to express their views. Consequently, he said he and his demonstrators would march with signs that read, "Like Forsyth, *The Oprah Winfrey Show* Turns All White." The protesters were arrested at the restaurant where Oprah was broadcasting, charged with unlawful assembly, and thrown into jail. Oprah's cameras showed the police handcuffing them. Afterward she said she was "very, very sorry" about the arrest. "I have nothing but respect for Rev. Hosea Williams."

Her producers had selected one hundred of the county's thirty-eight thousand citizens to be on-camera, representing a range of opinion: some felt blacks deserved equality; others did not.

"Tell me," said Oprah, "where did the people come from who were shouting, 'Nigger go home'?"

Frank Shirley, head of the Committee to Keep Forsyth White, said, "This was the largest white people's protest against communism and race mixing in the last thirty years.... Many of [those marchers] are outright communists and homosexuals...."

"You're not just anti-black," Oprah said, "you're also anti-gay, too."

"I'm opposed to communism, race mixing, and low morals, and homosexuals are of low morals, in my opinion."

Oprah asked another town resident, "What's the difference between a 'black person' and a 'nigger' for you?" She was told, "Blacks stayed at home during the civil rights march. Niggers are the ones that marched. . . . A nigger is one like Hosea Williams. He wants to come up here and cause trouble."

Oprah listened to a liberal businesswoman talk about "us" and "them."

"I like the way you speak of 'them,' " Oprah said. "It's like black people are from Mars or something." Becoming exasperated, she asked, "Does everyone in this town never even come in contact with black people? Do you not even watch *The Cosby Show*?"

Oprah's show from Forsyth County received national press coverage, blockbuster ratings, and a tip of the rabbit ears from TV critics. "For sheer audacity and sweeps smarts," wrote Howard Rosenberg in the *Los Angeles Times,* "nothing has topped black Oprah Winfrey's venture into an area whose white-might ugliness has recently attracted global media attention." The *Chicago Sun-Times* applauded her for keeping her dignity and composure as she stood among some of the nation's most notorious racists. "So it seems Winfrey accomplished precisely what she had set out to do," wrote Robert Feder. "She served up an hour of sensational television about an explosive issue while generating tons of publicity."

After doing the show in Forsyth County on a Monday,

Oprah returned to Chicago and devoted the rest of her week to drag queens, women murderers, religious fundamentalists, and sexy clothes. Each week, TV critics received an Oprah advisory about her upcoming shows. "Here are my top 10 favorites from recent weeks," wrote Jeff Jarvis of *People,* never a big Oprah fan:

1. Hairdresser Horror Stories
2. Housewife Prostitutes
3. Men Who Can't Be Intimate
4. Men Who Fight Over Women
5. Man-Stealing Relatives
6. Polygamy
7. Unforgivable Acts Between Couples
8. Sexy Dressing
9. Get Rich and Quit Work
10. Women Who Are Allergic to Their Husbands

During the November 1987 sweeps, Oprah headed for Williamson, West Virginia, a town on the Kentucky border that was in the clutches of AIDS hysteria. A young man with the disease had come home to die. He went swimming in the public pool, and the mayor ordered it closed for a week of "scrubbing" after hearing rumors that the young AIDS victim had purposely cut himself to infect others. The town went on a witch hunt. The young man, who died nine years later, appeared on Oprah's show and faced his accusers, who spat out fear, ignorance, and homophobia.

"God gave him AIDS for a reason," said one. "It's His way of saying, 'What you're doing is no good.'"

Another said, "You want us to hug him, to let him babysit our kids. We can't handle that. I'm not afraid of this man. I am repulsed by the man's lifestyle. I am repulsed by his disease. I am repulsed by him."

Oprah let everyone speak before she made her own observation. "I hear this is a God-fearing community. Is that right?" she asked. The crowd clapped and cheered to signal affirmation.

"So where is your Christian love and understanding?"

Again, she received rave reviews and rocketing ratings. Several months later, the *National Enquirer* reported that her brother, Jeffrey Lee, was dying of AIDS and had given an interview saying he felt abandoned by Oprah. "She's virtually disowned me," he said. "She's made it clear that AIDS or not, I'm on my own. . . . Her attitude is, 'It's your own fault. It serves you right.' Oprah believes that every gay is going to get AIDS eventually. . . . I don't think homosexuality as such offends Oprah. What really upset her was my lifestyle—partying, running around, not holding down a job. Oprah told me, 'You need to get God in your life. You really need Jesus.'" Perhaps this was a step forward for Oprah, considering that she first told her brother that as a homosexual he would never go to Heaven.

Three days before Christmas 1989, Jeffrey Lee died in Milwaukee, with only his mother and his lover at his side. Two weeks later Oprah issued a statement: "For the last two years my brother had been living with AIDS. My family, like thousands of others throughout the world, grieves not just for the death of one young man but for the many unfulfilled dreams and accomplishments that society has been denied because of AIDS."

In the hope of generating more bombshell ratings for the February '88 sweeps, Oprah booked her first big celebrity interview with the woman once described as the most beautiful in the world. Elizabeth Taylor, then fifty-six, had lost forty pounds, divorced her sixth husband, and written a book titled *Elizabeth Takes Off.* She launched its publication with Oprah, who flew her staff to Los Angeles to tape the show at the Hotel Bel-Air, without a studio audience.

"[It] was a very high-pressure situation," recalled the former Harpo photographer Paul Natkin. "I was told before we left Chicago that I would be allowed to shoot ten photographs and I would have approximately two minutes to do that. . . . As soon as I clicked the shutter the tenth time [Taylor's publicist] reached over, put her hand in front of the camera, and said, 'Sorry. That's it. We're done.'"

The photos show the slim and lovely star sparkling with glamour. In contrast, the talk show host looks like an electric dandelion, with a teased hairdo of scrambled ringlets sticking out of her head as if she'd stuck her finger in a socket. The interview was equally disastrous. Oprah could not cajole anything out of the Hollywood diva, and La Liz dismissed the electric dandelion as "cheeky" when she asked her about her romances with Malcolm Forbes and George Hamilton. "None of your business," Taylor snapped. She was so terse and unresponsive to questions that Oprah tried a little humor. "You're so revealing—you just tell everything! I declare you've got to stop talking so much, Ms. Taylor!"

Not in the least amused, the movie star looked at Oprah with icy hauteur.

"It was the worst interview of my life," Oprah said years later. "It's still painful to watch."

At the time, Oprah looked like an overfed, overdressed country girl overawed by a Hollywood legend, who could not have acted haughtier had she been handed a script. When the actress appeared on *Donahue* two weeks later, she opened up like a flower to the sun, and critics agreed that Oprah was just not ready to do celebrity interviews, something her executive producer had previously acknowledged. "We like to stay away from celebrity-oriented shows," said Debra DiMaio. "Oprah does better with controversial shows, with guests that have some kind of passion and emotion and a story to tell. . . . We call them true-life stories. . . . We always kid her, but Oprah has had such an incredible life that no matter what topic we do, it's usually something that happened to her in some way or another."

Still chasing fireworks for February sweeps, Oprah returned to Chicago and waded into a confrontation with white supremacist skinheads that made her tussle with Elizabeth Taylor look like a taffy pull. Security at the station had been increased for the show, requiring everyone to pass through a metal detector to make sure no weapons were smuggled into the studio. Racist comments and profane threats were spewed with abandon. At one point Oprah placed her hand on the arm of one of the skinheads, who yelled, "Don't touch me." Another called her "a monkey."

"You think . . . because I'm black [I'm] a monkey?"

"It's a proven fact," said the skinhead.

After the break, Oprah told her audience that "Mr. Monkey Comment" had been asked to leave. She admitted later that halfway through the show she regretted doing it. "In terms of racist hatred it's the worst thing I've ever done. I have never in my life felt so consumed by evil. Any one of those kids would have taken great pride in slashing my throat. And I know it. . . . They have no concept of what life is about, so they don't care about going to jail for killing a black person or a Jewish person."

The critic for the *Chicago Sun-Times* wrote, "So does all this soul-searching mean Oprah will finally quit subjecting herself to such indignities for the sake of ratings? Don't bet on it."

Booking bigots, self-proclaimed porn addicts, and witches as guests gave Oprah, then thirty-four, soaring ratings over fifty-two-year-old Phil Donahue, whose talk show the writer David Halberstam once described as "the most important graduate school in America," informing millions about changes in society and modern mores. For over twenty years Donahue had treated his female audience like intelligent women, and had reigned as the number one talk show host in the country. Having paved the way for a competitor who was now tromping him, he, too, began dipping into tabloid sleaze. "I don't want to die a hero," he said, explaining why he cross-dressed as a woman to do a show on transvestites. He later acknowledged that as a white male, he lacked Oprah's ability to get cozy with a female audience about finding a good man, a foolproof diet, or a bra that fit. While Oprah was besting Donahue at every turn, *The Wall Street Journal* reported on critics who called her show "Nuts 'n' Sluts" and "Freak of the Week." Her executive producer defended the tabloid programs, saying when viewers complained about a show on sex, it was only after they'd watched every minute of it. When she was asked about a show on child murderers, Debra DiMaio asked for clarification: "Are you talking about kids who kill kids, or kids who kill their parents?" Oprah had done shows on both.

She said she would never do another show with white supremacists, but she resented being criticized for doing tabloid television. "It bleeps me off when you guys write as if I do shows about how to dress your parakeet," Oprah told one critic. "I was uncomfortable doing 'Women Who Have Obnoxious Husbands,' but I turned down [televangelists] Jim and Tammy Faye Bakker. Won't talk to them. And I won't do 'Is Elvis Alive?'"

During the May sweeps of 1988, she stunned everyone when she chose to air a show on teenage boys who'd died of autoerotic asphyxia, a sexual practice that sometimes involves tying a noose around the neck during masturbation. By then she was not just competing against Phil Donahue, but also contending with the talk shows of Sally Jessy Raphael, Geraldo Rivera, Morton Downey, Jr., and Regis Philbin and Kathie Lee Gifford, with Joan Rivers, Jenny Jones, Jerry Springer, Maury Povich, Ricki Lake, and Montel Williams waiting in the wings. The pressure to top previous sweeps ratings and trounce the competition led Oprah to present a controversial show featuring the parents of two young boys who had accidentally strangled themselves as a result of the extreme sexual practice.

Dr. Harvey Resnik, a clinical psychiatrist, also appeared on the show. As former chief of the National Institute of Mental Health's Center for Studies of Suicide Prevention, he had published a paper on erotized repetitive sex hangings in which men bind their necks, or cover their heads in a plastic bag pulled tight with a drawstring, and achieve an intense high through masturbation while reducing the supply of oxygen to the brain. "When oxygen is depleted, more carbon dioxide is retained, causing an altered state of consciousness. The result is a light-headed giddiness known as a head rush, something that skin divers and pilots who lose oxygen also report. This altered state can affect the sexual pleasure center of the brain. The risk is that with diminished blood flow, the person passes out, slumps forward, and completely obstructs the airway, which results in death from asphyxiation. The behavior is well known to medical examiners."

As a consultant to survivors of victims of autoerotic asphyxia, Dr. Resnik understood the shame attached to that particular kind of death. "Just as with other problems we have in mental health, we know that self-help groups and the ability to share grief and to share information is quite helpful," he said.

The day before the show aired, Oprah's executive producer, Debra DiMaio, called Dr. Park Dietz, a forensic psychiatrist, criminologist, and professor of biobehavioral sciences at the UCLA School of Medicine. He warned her about broadcasting such a graphic subject. "I had a heated discussion with the producer. I argued that television is not a suitable medium for discussing this subject, because the risk of people imitating it is too high," he said. "I told her that if the show were aired, it would foreseeably result in one or more deaths." Dr. Dietz added that if anyone sued Oprah for reckless and negligent conduct, he would testify to a jury that he had warned the producer against airing the show. Oprah later said she had "meditated" on the matter and concluded that they should proceed. Months later DiMaio regretted the decision. "It was a dangerous thing to do," she said. "You never want to give that one kid the idea to go ahead and try it."

At the time, Dr. Resnik said the producer agreed to issue a parental warning before the show to restrict TV access to children. "Still, I don't think she or Oprah was prepared for such a powerful subject," he said, "but I applaud them for having the courage to bring the issue to the public."

That afternoon, May 11, 1988, after watching the show, thirty-eight-year-old John Holm retreated to the garage of his father's house in Thousand Oaks, California. When his father returned home hours later from an Elks meeting he could not find his son. "The television was still on Channel 7—the channel he'd watched *Oprah* on," said Robert Holm. "The garage lights were on, but the door was locked from the inside. I banged on the door, but there was no answer. I had to break in. That's when I found his body. It was horrible. I thought John had killed himself. But when the rescue squad came, one of the workers said he knew how my son had died because he'd seen the *Oprah* show that afternoon. I blame the *Oprah* show for my boy's death. I lost my son and my best friend in the world."

Mr. Holm hired a lawyer to investigate suing Oprah. "Her

show led to John's death—and I will never forgive her for that," he said. In the end he decided not to put his wife through the pain of a lawsuit. "He was our only son and a beautiful person. We can't bring him back."

Publicly, Oprah defended her show. "What I got afterward were responses from grieving parents: 'Thank you for explaining to us what happened to our boy.' They felt a lot better knowing, they said. Before, they had been torturing themselves that they were to blame." Privately, she worried about the possibility of having to defend a wrongful-death suit.

"I got a call after the show from her producer, saying parents might sue and asking if I would serve as a witness for Oprah," recalled Dr. Resnik. "I said I would because I believe that having information about such risky behavior is better than not having any information at all."

Oprah was accused of triggering another death when she hosted a show called "Bad Influence Friends," featuring a marriage therapist, an engaged couple having difficulties with their relationship, and a twenty-eight-year-old electronics technician branded by the engaged man's fiancée as the cause of the couple's problems. The engaged woman said that "Mike," her fiancé's best friend, was an ex–drug user and a big drinker who flirted with other women even though he was married. The camera zoomed in on Mike with the words *Bad Influence* under his face. Oprah told the audience, "Mike is married, but it doesn't stop him from being Tom's bad influence and keeping him out late—drinking and dancing and a little flirting, which Mike believes is all harmless fun." Mike said he enjoyed going out with his friends without his wife. Oprah looked at her predominantly female audience, who hissed and booed. One angry woman called him a "major nightmare," and the audience applauded. A shouting match erupted when Oprah asked Mike why he'd gotten married.

"Because I like the security. I like to come home. I like to have someone there."

Thoroughly incensed, one woman shouted, "You can't have both worlds, Mike."

"Yes, I can," he shot back.

"No, you can't."

Less than two weeks later, Mike's father found him hanging from a ceiling fan in his Northlake, Illinois, home. "I know in my heart that Oprah's show killed my son," said Michael LaCalamita, Sr. "I believe he killed himself because he couldn't take the humiliation [of how he came across] and the pressure [of the comments from friends and strangers after the show].... Oprah didn't give him a chance to defend himself. She kept egging him on and on. When the crowd stopped getting at him, she would start another round of attack. It wasn't fair. Oprah's a TV star and he's just a young kid. He didn't know what he was getting into."

The marriage therapist on the show, Dr. Donna Rankin, an associate professor at Loyola University in Chicago, told a writer she was surprised that Oprah had even aired the show. "From the things Mike was saying it was clear that he had severe emotional problems," she said. "Obviously, he needed help."

The only public statement Oprah made about the suicide came through her publicist, Colleen Raleigh: "Only Mike LaCalamita or perhaps a psychiatrist would know why he took his own life. Our deepest sympathies are extended to his family and friends."

Despite growing criticism over her tabloid programming, Oprah said her shows "just give people a voyeuristic look at other people's lives. It's not to shock." Still, she continued to demand what she called "bang, bang, shoot-'em-up shows," especially during sweeps, but when she did a highly controversial show on devil worship, she almost shot herself in the foot.

Broadcast on May 1, 1989, the show was titled "Mexican Satanic Cult Murders," and during one segment Oprah presented a woman under the pseudonym of "Rachel" who was undergoing long-term psychiatric treatment for multiple personality disorder.

"As a child my next guest was also used in worshipping the devil, participated in human sacrifice rituals and cannibalism," Oprah told her audience. "She is currently in extensive therapy, suffers from multiple personality disorder, meaning she's blocked out many of the terrifying and painful memories of her childhood. Meet 'Rachel,' who is also in disguise to protect her identity."

"Rachel" said she had witnessed the ritual sacrifice of children and had been a victim of ritualistic abuse. "I was born into a family that believes in this."

"And this is a—does everyone else think it's a nice Jewish family?" asked Oprah, introducing "Rachel's" religion. "From the outside you appear to be a nice Jewish girl. . . . And you are all worshipping the devil inside the home?"

"Right," said the disturbed "Rachel." "There's other Jewish families across the country. It's not just my own family."

"Really? And so who knows about it? Lots of people now."

"I talked to a police detective in the Chicago area. . . ."

"So when you were brought up in this kind of evilness did you just think it was normal?"

"Rachel" said she had blocked out a lot of the memories, but she remembered enough to say "there would be rituals in which babies would be sacrificed." She later added, "Not all Jewish people sacrifice babies. . . . It's not a typical thing."

"I think we all know that," said Oprah.

"I just want to point that out."

"This is the first time I heard of any Jewish people sacrificing babies, but anyway—so you witnessed the sacrifice?" said Oprah.

"Right. When I was very young I was forced to participate in that, and . . . I had to sacrifice an infant."

The phones at Harpo started jangling with hundreds of irate callers objecting to Oprah's blithe acceptance of "Rachel's" claims about Jews practicing devil worship. Television stations across the country—New York, Los Angeles, Houston, Cleveland, Washington, D.C.—were inundated with furious calls. Within hours, Jewish groups rose up in condemnation, and Oprah's show became a national news story. "We have grave concern about both the lack of judgment and the insensitive manipulation of this woman, who is clearly mentally ill, in a manner which can only inflame the basest prejudices of ignorant people," Rabbi David Saperstein of the Religious Action Center of Reformed Judaism told *The New York Times.*

Arthur J. Kropp, president of People for the American Way, a leading civil liberties organization, met with his board of directors in Washington, D.C. "There's been a lot of concern about so-called trash television," he said after reviewing the transcript of Oprah's show. "She was the one who introduced the religion. I don't think she introduced it to convey any correlation between the woman's Jewishness and what she saw, but nevertheless Oprah did do it and that was careless."

This wasn't the first bad publicity Oprah had ever received, but it was brutal because she was being criticized for offending sensibilities of race and religion, which she had always appeared to champion. It was an especially sorry position for a woman who had put herself forward as a "poor little ole nappy-headed colored chile" from the lynching state of Mississippi as a not-so-subtle reminder of the viciousness of bigotry. She now felt misunderstood by her accusers, but she also recognized that her career was in jeopardy.

"We are aware that the show has struck a nerve," said Jeff Jacobs, then COO of Harpo Productions. He pointed out to the press that Oprah had said on the air that "Rachel" was one particular person talking about her particular situation. "And she was identified at the top of the show as being mentally disturbed," he added, not commenting on why such a person would be allowed on the show in the first place. Recognizing the danger of a national boycott of *The Oprah Winfrey Show* and the potential loss of sponsors, which could spell financial ruin for everyone, Jacobs quickly offered to meet with Jewish leaders in Chicago to try to salvage the situation, but neither he nor Oprah offered a public apology. When reporters called, Jacobs said Oprah was "traveling" and "unavailable for comment."

The night after hosting her devil-worship show, she appeared on *The David Letterman Show* in Chicago and was unnerved by the comedian's quirky manner. The interview was awkward throughout, especially when someone in the crowd yelled, "Rip her, Dave." Letterman grinned his gleeful gap-toothed grin and said nothing. Years later he said, "I think she resented the fact that I didn't rise to the occasion and, you know, beat up on the guy. Which I probably should have, but I was completely out of control and didn't know what I was doing." A couple of nights later, Letterman, doing his show from the Chicago Theater, told his audience that he felt ill because he had eaten four clams at Oprah's restaurant, The Eccentric. That ripped it. Oprah closed the door on David Letterman and did not speak to him again for sixteen years.

Feeling battered by the bruising she was taking in the nation's press over her devil-worship show, Oprah remained close to her condominium at Water Tower Place when she wasn't working. Serendipitously, she happened to meet Harriet Brady (née Bookey), another resident, in the lobby. Mrs. Brady, then seventy-two, was well known in Chicago's Jewish community as a philanthropist. She approached Oprah to introduce herself, and then said kindly, "I think I can help you."

Within hours she was on the phone to her good friend Abraham Lincoln Marovitz, a federal judge whose contacts extended into every segment of society. He agreed to help, and for the next week Judge Marovitz and Mrs. Brady worked on Oprah's behalf to assemble a group of representatives from the region's Jewish community to meet at Harriet Brady's condominium to try to quell the raging controversy.

Oprah arrived at the meeting on May 9, 1989, with Debra DiMaio and two Jewish members of her senior staff, Jeffrey Jacobs and Ellen Rakieten. They sat down with Michael Kotzin, director of the Jewish Community Relations Council of Metropolitan Chicago; Jonathan Levine, midwest director of the American Jewish Committee; Barry Morrison, director of the Greater Chicago/Wisconsin Regional Office of the Anti-Defamation League of B'nai B'rith; Rabbi Herman Schaalman, president of the Chicago Board of Rabbis; Maynard Wishner, president of the Jewish Federation of Metropolitan Chicago; Judge Marovitz; and Mrs. Brady.

Oprah was sufficiently contrite and vowed never again to broadcast a show on devil worship. She agreed to reach out to

B'nai B'rith, which fights anti-Semitism and racism, whenever her show focused on those subjects, and she promised to exercise better judgment in selecting guests. The two sides came together over the next three days to work out two statements to be delivered to the press, which had been covering the story nearly every day. Oprah and her executive producer said, "We recognize that *The Oprah Winfrey Show* on May 1 could have contributed to the perpetuation and historical misconceptions and canards about Jews, and we regret that any harm may have been done. We are aware of community and group sensibilities and will make every effort to ensure that our program will reflect that concern."

Speaking on behalf of the Jewish community leaders, ADL representative Barry Morrison said, "We were all satisfied that Oprah Winfrey and her staff did not intend to offend anyone and that Oprah was genuinely sorry for any offense or misunderstanding. During the meeting, constructive recommendations were made and there was an extensive exchange of information which led to a greater understanding of Jewish perspective on the part of Oprah and her staff."

Not everyone was pleased with the outcome. "It's an inadequate response to the harm that may have been done on that broadcast," said Phil Baum, associate executive director of the American Jewish Congress. "It's not our sensitivities she ought to be concerned about. It's a question of the integrity of her show. This apology cannot possibly reach anything like the people [7,680,000 homes, according to the A.C. Nielsen Company] who were exposed to these statements."

Oprah refused to make an apology on her show or publicly comment on the program or the statements, but privately she embraced her two major defenders and kept Mrs. Brady and Judge Marovitz close to her for the rest of their lives. Both were invited to all her parties, and because of them she became more involved in Jewish causes.

When Judge Marovitz died in 2001 at the age of ninety-five, the elite of Chicago assembled in his courtroom on the twenty-fifth floor of the Dirksen Federal Building to remember him as, in Mayor Richard Daley's words, "a true friend and wonderful human being." Covering the memorial for the *Chicago Sun-Times,* Neil Steinberg was surprised to see Oprah in the crowd. "Every man would like a woman of mystery at his memorial," he wrote, "and it was fitting that Winfrey filled that role at Marovitz's service."

"I love him," Oprah said. "He was beyond wonderful. He was one of my inspirations. He was a dear friend to me when I most needed him."

"And what exactly did Marovitz do for you?" Steinberg asked.

Winfrey smiled, sphinxlike: "I'm not saying."

Two years later, when Harriet Brady, then eighty-six, was dying in the hospital, Oprah visited her often, and later attended her funeral. They, too, had become close over the years, and it was a relationship Oprah valued because Harriet Brady, wealthy in her own right and socially established, wanted nothing from her. "Oprah feels so ripped off by everyone that she appreciates people who, as she says, 'don't bleed me,'" said Bill Zwecker, the newspaper columnist and television commentator who had been covering the talk show host since she moved to Chicago.

Shortly after making her peace with Jewish America, Oprah was hit with a nasty blind item by Ann Gerber in the *Chicago Sun-Times* (May 14, 1989):

> Can it be true that the lover of one of our richest women was found in bed with her hairdresser when she returned early from a trip abroad? The battle that ensued brought her screaming out on to Lake Shore Drive, shocking her staid neighbors.

Although Oprah did not live on Lake Shore Drive, she knew she was the target of the gossip columnist, and she was irate. "She was angrier than I've ever seen her," recalled Patricia Lee Lloyd.

Three days later, on May 17, 1989, Ann Gerber responded to the calls she had received from Oprah's staff with another item, this time naming names:

Rumors that TV talk show star Oprah Winfrey and the hunk Stedman Graham had a major rift (one version has Oprah shooting him) just aren't true, friends insist.

The media flew into a frenzy, calling Chicago police and area hospitals to try to confirm the story, with no success. Oprah issued an emotional denial on her show (May 19, 1989):

> I have chosen to speak up because this rumor has become so widespread and so vulgar that I just wanted to go on record and let you know that it is not true. There is absolutely no truth whatsoever to any part of it.

She didn't say what the vulgar rumor was, so most of her audience was confused and did not understand why she was so upset. This triggered even more curiosity, proving, as Shakespeare wrote, that "Rumor is a pipe / that the blunt monster with uncounted heads / can play upon."

Oprah had recently hired a new publicist who had moved to Chicago that week to work for her, but in the furor over the rumor, she fired him while he was looking for an apartment to assume his new job. He later confided that he left Chicago grateful to put distance between himself and Oprah, who "seemed so completely surrounded by evil."

Bill Zwecker recalled that time as turbulent. "Oprah admitted to me that she had made a huge mistake by going on her national television show to denounce the rumor," he said. "By doing that she opened Pandora's box and allowed the tabloids to invade her privacy. She said it was a monumental error on her part, but she could not pull back, and Ann got fired over the incident. . . . The day the blind item ran, I saw Oprah at a women's charity event, and café society was falling all over her. A week later, when Ann was fired, the same café society was blaming Oprah for getting poor little Annie Gerber fired. I wrote a column about the hypocrisy of it all. Kiss kiss one week; diss diss the next." Later Zwecker received a note from Oprah:

> Bill—I shall never forget that when other people were kicking me in the teeth with that rumor you did the kindest thing. You

lifted me up. Seeing you the other night with your dad reminded me of what a gracious thing you did. Again I thank you.

Oprah's angry denial of the rumor did not receive much coverage until May 22, 1989, when the *Chicago Tribune*'s revered columnist Mike Royko defended her right to be outraged and quoted the irresponsible gossip columnist as saying, "It is a vicious rumor but I wanted to run the item even though there was no way I could verify the rumor." When Ann Gerber was fired the next day, she held a press conference "to clear my name." She said, "I think I was fired because the *Sun-Times* feared Oprah." Considering Oprah's immense influence in the city, most people accepted the statement as obvious, although Kenneth Towers, editor of the *Chicago Sun-Times,* denied receiving any pressure from Oprah or her attorney, Jeff Jacobs.

Recalling the trauma later, Oprah said, "I have been hurt and disappointed by things that people have said and tried to do to me, but through it all, even in my moments of great pain—this rumor being the biggest of it—I had the blessed assurance that I am God's child. . . . And nobody else's. That is really the source of my strength, my power. It is the source of all my success.

"The thing that got me through this rumor was the Bible verse Isaiah 54:17, which I have always believed. That is, 'No weapon that is formed against thee shall prosper; and every tongue that shall rise against thee in judgment thou shalt condemn.' And this I know, no matter how difficult things may get, this I know."

# $T$welve

O NCE OPRAH became a millionaire, she announced that she was going to become "the richest black woman in the world." At the time, she publicly restricted herself to her race, as if a black woman could not dream of becoming the richest woman in the world, but that might have been in keeping with her efforts then to be seen as "everywoman," not to appear, in her words, "uppity," or "to look grander than anyone else." As she told Fred Griffith, the host of Cleveland's *Morning Exchange,* in 1987, she always knew she would be successful, but she tried to sound modest. "Because [otherwise] people say, 'Look at the cocky Negro.'"

To the contrary, people seemed genuinely delighted by Oprah's success and inspired by her gospel: "If I can do it, you can do it." She sparked the imagination, especially of women twenty-five to fifty-four years old, television's most precious demographic. She was heralded for personifying the American Dream with all its honeyed promises of equal opportunity. Yet she told the writer Barbara Grizzuti Harrison she felt hurt by "negativity from black women," obviously forgetting that in 1988 she had told Barbara Walters on national television that as a little girl she had always wanted to be white. "[I]t's the kind of thing that I hesitate to say because when you say it, all the black groups call and say, 'How dare you say it?' But yes, I did [want to be white]."

Understandably some black women felt bruised, but Oprah

did not see why. She asked former television correspondent Janet Langhart Cohen if she, too, had the same problem. "Did you have black women calling you up and telling you you weren't black enough and asking why you don't have more blacks on the show?"

"Oh, don't tell me you're having that problem?"

"Oh, yeah," said Oprah. "I've had it in Chicago for two years. It's a small segment. Once it spreads, though, it becomes an issue. I mean, like on black radio stations—it's like the nighttime discussion. They call in and ask: 'Is Oprah Winfrey black enough?'"

"It's just plain jealousy," said Janet Langhart Cohen.

"That's what it is," said Oprah. "The hardest thing to come to terms with has been the jealousy."

Most of Oprah's worshipful audiences (predominantly white women) enjoyed her enthusiasm over her new riches and relished her reports of shopping and buying and spending, although on the air she carefully confined herself to girlish confessions about not having to buy panty hose at Walgreens anymore rather than discussing her more extravagant purchases, such as the $470,000 she spent at one furniture auction. "She paid two hundred forty thousand dollars for a little Shaker chest of drawers, and it's in her kitchen now," said her decorator Anthony Browne. "Why did she buy it? Because her idol is Bill Cosby [who collects Shaker furniture]. Everything he does, she has to do."

What many people missed in Oprah's rags-to-riches story was the towering ambition that motored her. Her drive was insatiable. Fueled by long days of hard work, she never stopped barreling forward—always reaching, stretching, extending. A self-propelled whirlwind of industry, she slept only four or five hours a night and rarely relaxed. During one week in 1988, she flew to Mobile, Alabama, to give a speech, then to Nashville, to give another speech. She returned to Chicago to tape back-to-back shows, flew to Cleveland for another speaking engagement, and then flew to Greensboro, North Carolina, to meet Stedman for dinner. She left the next morning for New York to accept an award, flew back to Nashville for a charity baseball game with Stedman, and returned to Chicago the next day. She pushed herself constantly, and she pushed everyone around her, which was probably necessary to achieve her kind of stratospheric success.

After filming *The Color Purple* she announced her plan to pursue a movie career in addition to her talk show. "I want it all. . . . I intend to be a great actress," she told *Ladies' Home Journal.* "A great actress."

Having undergone tortuous negotiations with WLS to get her the time off to make her first movie, Jeff Jacobs proposed she take ownership of her talk show so that she, and not WLS, could set her schedule for future films. The station had balked at giving her twelve weeks off, and she had threatened to quit if they didn't. So Jacobs forfeited all of her paid vacation and sick leave to get her the time, and the station agreed to bring in guest hosts and show reruns until she returned. At that point he told Oprah she had to think about producing her own show and building her own studio so she would have complete control of her professional life. "He allowed me to see that not even the sky was the limit," she said.

When she received a Golden Globe nomination for Best Supporting Actress, followed by the Academy Award nomination in 1986, she was unstoppable. "I've got to act," she told *Good Housekeeping.* "I'm a good interviewer largely because I taught myself how. But I was *born* to act." She told Larry King on CNN that she was at her "out of my mind happiest" when performing. "I hear people say this about having children. When their babies just come out of the womb and stuff, but I have those moments when I am acting."

She said she intended to make at least one film a year. In March 1988 she started her second movie, costarring with Geraldine Page, Elizabeth McGovern, and Matt Dillon in *Native Son,* based on the Richard Wright novel about a black man's murderous rage. Oprah was cast as the mother who begs for mercy from the parents of the white girl her son has murdered. Her performance failed to impress critics. "She weighs in with an overload of bathos," Julie Salamon wrote in *The Wall*

*Street Journal.* Hal Erickson, in the online database AMG (All-Movie Guide), concurred: "Oprah's excessive histrionics pale in comparison to her brilliant, well-modulated performance in *The Color Purple*." Vincent Canby wrote in *The New York Times* that "the film only seems dated when the performers, especially Oprah Winfrey, play for sentiment."

*Native Son* flopped at the box office and was pulled two weeks after release, but Oprah rose above the withering reviews. "I should do a comedy," she told the *Chicago Tribune*. When she was offered the role of the Manhattan cleaning lady in the film version of Truman Capote's short story "A Day's Work," she decided she was becoming typecast as the heavyset, woebegone woman with a gray bun on her head and support hose rolled down her legs. She told the writer Robert Waldron she was offended by those who accused her of playing only Aunt Jemima characters. "At first I would be very kind," she said. "Now I just want to slap them!" She told *AdWeek*, "I would like to do a character that has some sexuality. Like Dinah Washington, who was a great black singer who had seven different husbands and used to sexually exhaust her men." Oprah didn't want to play only black women who had problems. "It's important for me to tell our stories, but I refuse to be limited to just that."

Hearing her declarations about becoming a movie star, many assumed that King World would lose *The Oprah Winfrey Show*, its third-biggest moneymaker after *Wheel of Fortune* and *Jeopardy!*, but the distributor was not worried. "Oprah is very ambitious," said the chief financial officer, Jeffrey Epstein. "She wants to act in movies and TV shows, [but] there are not many great parts for black women. So she needs to produce shows herself, which cost a lot of money, and the best way to finance all that is to stick with her daytime job." Oprah had recently paid Toni Morrison $1 million for the rights to film her Pulitzer Prize–winning novel, *Beloved*. "I didn't even try to negotiate. . . . I just said, 'Name your price,' and I paid it." She believed she had made a $1 million investment in putting her name in lights.

Except for rock stars, movie stars, professional athletes, and Wall Street marauders, few people make more money than a syndicated television talk show host with a number one–rated show carried in two hundred U.S. cities and sixty-four international markets. In her first year of syndication, Oprah made $31 million; in her second year she made $37 million; three years later, she made $55 million and landed in *Forbes* as the ninth-highest-paid entertainer in the world. The talk show was the major source of her wealth, and she had no intention of ever giving it up. "It's my bosom, my root, and my foundation," she said. "Without it, nothing else could happen." Nor did she consider moving from Chicago to pursue films. While most of the acting jobs were in New York and Los Angeles, Oprah knew her show could not thrive in either city.

"I think that in the Midwest you can have people who are surprised by some of the experiences that are exhibited on our show," she told Fred Griffith. "If you have someone on my show who says, 'My father was dating a duck for many years,' in the Midwest people say, 'Oh, God, his father was dating a duck!' In New York they say, 'Oh, my cousin was dating a duck, too.'" Referring to the impressionable studio audiences she could assemble from the area that writer Calvin Trillin once described as a milieu in which "culture did not hang heavily in the air," Oprah told *Electronic Media,* "People can still be shocked here."

Her executive producer elaborated. "Our audience definitely takes on the personality of the city," said Debra DiMaio. "They reflect Midwestern values. They are outgoing. And nothing against Los Angeles or New York—their lifestyle is more human."

"It's true that Oprah couldn't do her show anyplace else," said Cheryl L. Reed, former editor of the editorial page of the *Chicago Sun-Times.* "People are too sophisticated and cynical in New York and Los Angeles, but Chicago is perfect for her kind of television."

The city was grateful to Oprah for staying because she brought international acclaim to Chicago and drew hordes of tourists, filling hotels and restaurants with those who attended her shows every year. They are such a draw that the Chicago Office of Tourism added a special listing of "talk show ticket information" to the brochure it mails out to prospective visitors. Oprah also annually contributes hundreds of thousands of dollars to local organizations, including a children's hospital, educational programs, schools, shelters, and literacy programs. In addition, she's given generously to various museums and arts organizations across the city, including the Shedd Aquarium, the Chicago Academy for the Arts, the Children's Museum in Oak Lawn, and the DuSable Museum of African American History.

A review of Oprah's tax returns for all her charities, plus statements she has made to the press, indicate that from 1987 through 2009 she contributed more than $30 million to various Chicago organizations. Some of these funds came from viewers' contributions to Oprah's Angel Network—money that Oprah collected from others and donated in her name.

By August 1988, Jeff Jacobs had completed negotiating the deal with Capital Cities/ABC to give Oprah total control of her weekday show. In addition, he hammered out a new contract with King World to renew her contract for five years, through 1993, and all seven Capital Cities/ABC stations agreed to carry her through that time. In addition, ABC gave her three network specials. Industry analysts estimated the deals to be worth more than $500 million for Oprah and King World. Twenty years later, they estimated that *The Oprah Winfrey Show* made $150 million a year, of which Oprah kept $100 million. In contrast, Ellen DeGeneres, another popular talk show host with high ratings, made $25 million a year, an impressive amount, but one quarter of what Oprah made. The considerable difference is because Oprah owns and produces her show, although she also benefits from having more profitable time slots, when TV viewership is greater. Oprah's show runs at 4:00 P.M. in all cities (except Chicago, where it runs at 9:00 A.M.) and leads in to the news, which makes it more valuable to a station than Ellen's show, which airs in the morning.

After the ownership news was announced in 1988, Oprah sat down with Robert Feder of the *Chicago Sun-Times*:

"I had been looking at pictures of Rosa Parks and Leontyne Price," she said, "and I believe I am the resurrection of a lot of my ancestors. I am the resurrected life for them. I am living the dream. Please, please quote me correctly, 'cause I don't want people thinkin' I'm Jesus. . . .

"All my life, I have done dramatic interpretations of black women. Harriet Tubman, Sojourner Truth, Fannie Lou Hamer are all a part of me. I've always felt that my life is their life fulfilled, that they are bridges that I crossed over on. They never dreamed it could be this good. I still feel that they're all with me, going, 'Go, girl. Go for it.' "

A week later the *Sun-Times* columnist Daniel Ruth was still sputtering. Declaring that Oprah's ego had gone on "a Falstaffian, gluttonous binge," he wrote, "Don't worry, Oprah. Just because you can turn pap into cash, you needn't fret too much about comparisons to Christ. . . . I have a hard time believing Sojourner Truth spent a lot of time wrestling with subjects like 'Victims of Freeloaders' (Oprah show: July 5, 1988), 'Soap Opera Stars and Their Fans' (Oprah show: June 29, 1988) or 'Dressing Sexy' (Oprah show: July 28, 1988)." To be fair, Ruth gave Oprah credit for covering a few substantial subjects, such as "Race Relations" (August 4, 1988), the controversy over the film *The Last Temptation of Christ* (August 16, 1988), and a debate on AIDS (July 15, 1988). But then he lambasted her: "Please, dearest Oprah, don't presume to place yourself in a class with genuine intellects, leaders, and such pioneering black women as Sojourner Truth, Harriet Tubman, Fannie Lou Hamer, Leontyne Price, and especially Rosa Parks, who earned their rightful acclaim through commitment, quality, and courage."

Once Oprah owned her own show, Jeff Jacobs began looking for a production studio, and within months he found a $4 million property (one hundred thousand square feet) on the Near West Side of the city, then a run-down area of scabby storefronts and vacant lots. Realizing that downtown Chicago could expand only in that direction, he advised Oprah to make the investment. He told her it would be her field of dreams. If she built it, they would come. She could produce her talk show there, as well as make movies for herself and others. "It's security," he said. "It's control of our destiny." He told reporters, "Harpo will be the studio be-

tween the coasts and enable Oprah to do whatever it is she wants
to do, economically and under her own control." Jacobs and King
World put up 20 percent of the purchase price, giving Oprah
80 percent ownership. She became chairman of Harpo Productions, Inc., and Jacobs became president and chief operating officer.

This acquisition made her the first African American
woman to own her own film studio, and only the third woman in
history to do so (the first two were Mary Pickford and Lucille
Ball). However, Oprah was the only one to do it completely on
her own, without a husband, although she did have the shrewd
counsel of her lawyer/agent, who encouraged her to bet on herself. "Don't be talent for hire," Jacobs said. "Own yourself.
Don't take a salary. Take a piece of the action." At that point in
her life Oprah described Jeff Jacobs as "a gift" and kept his
photo in a sterling-silver frame on her desk, next to pictures of
Bill Cosby, Quincy Jones, Stedman, and Gayle. "Jeff released
me from slave mentality," she said. "He helped me to see that I
really could have control."

Control was vital to Oprah, perhaps because of her terribly
vulnerable childhood in Milwaukee, but Jacobs still had to
push her into the concept of ownership. He assured her that
her companies need never go public, so she would not have to
contend with scrutiny, which she detested. Nor would she have
to answer to a board of directors, or trustees, or oversight com-
mittees. "My vision of control [then] was not having people
tell me what to do," she said. "[Until then] I was still thinking
like a slave. I was thinking like talent. You have to go to
another level of things to say, 'I want to own it.'" Fortuitously
for Jacobs, her wants outweighed her reservations.

He described his job as Oprah's counselor. "I present research, options, and opinions to her. We discuss them, and then
she makes the decisions. I work for her and with her, and because
of that, we've built an organization where she knows exactly
what's going on at all times. She signs the checks, she makes the
decisions. I protect her and look at things from a legal as well as
business standpoint, but she understands this organization
from top to bottom."

Before their acrimonious split in 2002, Jeff Jacobs helped Oprah build her media empire, which included:

**Harpo Productions, Inc.**
SUBSIDIARIES: Harpo Interactive, Harpo Music Publishing, Harpo Sounds Music Publishing, Oprah Music Publishing, Harpo Sounds
CREDITS INCLUDE: *No One Dies Alone* (1988); *The Oprah Winfrey Show* (1988–present); *Just Between Friends* (1989); *The Women of Brewster Place* (1989); *Brewster Place* (1990); *In the Name of Self-Esteem* (1990); ABC Afterschool Specials (1992–1993): *Girlfriend, I Hate the Way I Look, Shades of a Single Protein,* and *Surviving a Break Up; Nine* (1992); *Oprah Behind the Scenes* (1992); *Overexposed* (1992); *Michael Jackson Talks . . . to Oprah* (1993); *There Are No Children Here* (1993); *David and Lisa* (1998); *Tuesdays with Morrie* (1999); *Oprah Goes Online* (2000); *Use Your Life* (2001); *Oprah After the Show* (2002); *Dr. Phil* (2002–2005); *Oprah Winfrey Legends Ball* (2006); *Rachael Ray* (2006–present); *Building a Dream* (2007); *Oprah Winfrey Oscar Special* (2007); *Oprah's Big Give* (2008); *Dr. Oz* (2009–present)

**Harpo, Inc.**
Does administrative and some publicity chores and owns the trademarks OPRAH, *The Oprah Winfrey Show, Make the Connection,* Oprah's Book Club, Use Your Life, Oprah's Favorite Things, Wildest Dreams with Oprah, Oprah Boutique, The Oprah Store, oprah.com, Oprah's Big Give, The Big Give, Give Big or Go Home, Expert Minutes, Oprah & Friends, Oprah Radio, and Live Your Best Life, as well as the Oprah signature and "O" design.
In January 2008, Harpo, Inc., entered into a partnership with Discovery to create the Oprah Winfrey Network, a cable channel that is expected to go on the air in 2011.

**Harpo Entertainment Group**
Administrative umbrella encompassing Harpo Productions, Inc., Harpo Studios, Inc., and Harpo Films, Inc.

**Harpo Studios, Inc.**
Production studios for *The Oprah Winfrey Show* at 1058 West
  Washington Street; other production facilities, and busi-
  nesses offices, at 110 N. Carpenter Street

**Harpo Films, Inc.**
CREDITS INCLUDE: *Before Women Had Wings* (1997); *Beloved*
  (1998); *The Wedding* (1998); *Amy and Isabelle* (2001);
  *Their Eyes Were Watching God* (2005); *For One More Day*
  (2007); *The Great Debaters* (2007)
In 2008, Harpo Films made a three-year deal to provide
  programming for HBO.

In January 2009 Harpo Films announced a deal to film *The
Story of Edgar Sawtelle* in partnership with Tom Hanks's Playtone.
In February 2009, Oprah announced that she would support
the distribution of Sundance Film Festival award winner *Push:
Based on the Novel by Sapphire*, later called *Precious*, by releasing it
through Harpo Films.

**Harpo Print LLC**
CREDITS: *O, The Oprah Magazine*, and the now defunct *O at
  Home*, in partnership with Hearst
Owns the trademark *O, The Oprah Magazine*.

**Harpo Radio Inc.**
CREDITS: Programming for the Oprah Radio Network for
  Sirius XM

**Harpo Video Inc.**
CREDIT: *Make the Connection*

**OW Licensing Co.**
Holder of the rights of publicity of Oprah Winfrey.

**Oprah's Studio Merchandise Inc.**
Runs the Oprah Store and the Harpo gym and owns a
  $780,000 condo in Acorn Loftominiums, purchased in
  2006.

In addition to purchasing the property for Harpo Studios, Oprah and her partners invested another $16 million in renovating, extending, and equipping the production studio. They worked with architects, engineers, and designers for eighteen months. "Never in a lifetime, never did I imagine it would be this much work," she said later. "I still would have gone along with it. The reality is that it's work and *money*. I'm really not as overwhelmed by the financial responsibility as some people might be. . . . I went in knowing it would cost a lot of money."

Oprah invested fully—emotionally and financially—in creating a studio that would reflect the image she wanted to present to the world. She did the same with all the homes she built. After purchasing one hundred acres in Telluride, Colorado, she hired the renowned firm of Robert A. M. Stern, dean of the Yale School of Architecture.

"First meeting we showed her something natural to the surroundings—alpine timbers and logs," said one of the architects. "She dismissed it entirely. 'I want something that when people drive up they will say WOW.' So we went back to the drawing boards and gave her Tara on a ski slope with marble and white columns and sweeping verandas. When she came back and saw the plans, she said, 'I wanted a house that would make people say WOW. Not Holy shit!'" The house was never built.

Oprah wanted her Harpo Studios to become the major production center in the Midwest, with state-of-the-art facilities for television, commercials, and film production. "With cost factors being less here than in Hollywood, we hope to keep existing production and attract new production to Chicago, which will create new jobs and other economic benefits," she said. "It is a joy for me to be able to invest in the city whose people have been so supportive of my work."

Harpo's opulent facility covers one entire square block and contains three soundstages; office suites; conference rooms; control rooms; production and editing rooms; a screening room with a popcorn machine; a private dining room with an in-house chef; a gymnasium stocked with Nautilus bicycles, treadmills, and ellipticals; a beauty salon with hairdressers, makeup artists, and manicurists; plus a staff cafeteria. Oprah said she wanted "to create an environment so stimulating and comfortable that people will love coming to work." However, as one woman noted, Oprah did not build a day-care center for the children of her employees "because at Harpo it's full steam ahead for Oprah and only for Oprah, and of course, for her dogs."

She said she considered her cocker spaniels Sophie and Solomon to be her children, and allowed them to roam freely through the hallways of Harpo. "They are allowed to prowl through the offices," said a former employee. "Solomon wears a cone around his neck. Poor thing was walking into walls, always banging himself." Oprah occasionally included her dogs on her show. Once she teased an upcoming segment (May 2005) by announcing, "Stedman and I have a daughter. She has issues and I think it's my fault." The "daughter" was their dog Sophie.

Reflecting Oprah's fear of assassination, her studio is a fortress. In addition to the phalanx of security guards who pass a wand over the studio audiences at the entrance, checking all purses and packages, there is a private code that Harpo employees must punch into a computer at each steel door to be admitted. All guests must be scheduled and present identification. There is no access for visitors.

Harpo contains three different green rooms, two for ordinary guests—"We need two because sometimes we have to keep guests separated before they go on the air," said one employee. Ordinary guests get served fruit, muffins, and water. The VIP green room—for celebrity guests such as John Travolta, Tom Cruise, and Julia Roberts—has its own private side door leading into a lush area of soft leather chairs, a large television, fabulous foods, and a private bathroom filled with Molton Brown products. "The difference between the ordinary green rooms and the VIP green room is the difference between the Marriott and the Ritz," said a woman who has spent time in both.

In addition, Harpo also contains warehouse space the length of five football fields packed with Oprah's fan art, done and sent by viewers: crochet doilies of Oprah, oil paintings of Oprah as an angel or a Madonna, ceramic figurines of Oprah, rhinestone replicas of Oprah as queen of the world, watercolors of Oprah eating mashed potatoes (her favorite food), oil paintings of Stedman and Oprah on a wedding cake. "It was funny, interesting, quirky," said an art director who toured the space with Oprah. "I told her, 'This is really very touching.' She said, 'Well, yes and no. Most of them came with invoices.'"

Eventually Harpo would consist of six buildings, and her real estate corporation would purchase an additional building nearby for the Oprah Store, a 5,500-square-foot emporium that opened in 2008 to sell Oprah merchandise to Oprah fans, with all proceeds going to Oprah's Angel Network and the Oprah Winfrey Leadership Academy Foundation. Almost everything in the store is marked, stitched, embossed, or imprinted with an *O*. During the Christmas holidays the store sells a snow globe of *The Oprah Winfrey Show* that contains eighty-eight *O*s, including snowmen made of *O*s. Year-round there are *O* pajamas, *O* candles, *O* metallic purses, *O* canvas bags, *O* caps, *O* mugs, *O* place mats, even grocery bags marked "gr*O*ceries." In one corner of the store is "Oprah's Closet," which contains Oprah's hand-me-downs, ranging in size from ten to eighteen. Each item, including her used Prada skirt ($400) and Ferré boots ($300), contains a tag: "Harpo Inc. hereby certifies that the item to which this tag is attached is a genuine garment from the closet of Oprah Winfrey." The Oprah Store also sells chartreuse boxes of little Oprah note cards containing Oprah's inspirational sayings:

- *The work of your life is to discover your purpose and get on with the business of living it.*
- *Every day brings a chance for you to draw in a breath, kick off your shoes and step out and dance.*
- *What you do today creates every tomorrow.*
- *Everything you do and say shows the world who you really are. Live your truth.*
- *Live your own dreams.*
- *The joy of living well is the greatest reward.*
- *The only courage you need is the courage to follow your passion.*
- *The love you give = the love you get.*

After Harpo was built, the Near West Side of Chicago became gentrified. Developers moved into the area to build apartments and condominiums, thanks in large part to the substantial investment of Oprah in her production studio.

During the time she was building Harpo, Oprah flew to Los Angeles to film *The Women of Brewster Place*, based on the novel by Gloria Naylor about seven black women who bond to overcome the ghetto setbacks life has dealt them. "This will be the best miniseries any television network has done to date," Oprah told reporters. "Do you hear me? The best. You can quote me on that."

This was her first starring role and her first movie as executive producer. "After *The Color Purple* I wanted to prove my acting wasn't a fluke," she said. She chose Naylor's book of broken dreams, betrayal, and bitterness because she felt it made a statement about surviving with dignity in a world that tries to strip you of it. But all three networks turned the project down. "They said it was too womanish," said Oprah, who finally exercised her clout with ABC by flying to Los Angeles to meet directly with Brandon Stoddard, president of network entertainment. "Basically I got it on the air," she said later. "My participation convinced ABC to do it."

She then helped assemble the cast, including Cicely Tyson, Robin Givens, Jackée Harry, Lynn Whitfield, Lonette McKee, Olivia Cole, and Paula Kelly. "This is the first time [in my memory] that television has ever presented a drama dealing with the lives of black women," said the casting director, Reuben Cannon, a close friend of Oprah's.

The Gloria Naylor novel, like *The Color Purple* by Alice Walker, had been criticized for its treatment of black men, so Oprah softened some of the male characters to make them less menacing, but she refused a request from the NAACP to review the script. "I just don't think you can allow yourself to be controlled," she said. "[Besides] I'm insulted. I am more conscious of my legacy as a black person than anybody. I realize I didn't get here by myself, that I've crossed over on the backs of black people whose names made the history books, and a whole lot of them who did not. I have a responsibility not only as a black woman but as a human being to do good work. I am just as concerned about the images of black men as anybody, but there are black men who abuse their families, and there are white men who do it too, and brown men. It's just a fact of life; I deal with it every day. So I refuse to be controlled by other people's ideas and ideals of what I should do."

While changing some of the male characters in the book, she left intact the lesbian relationship, honoring the novelist's intent to represent the diversity of black women, from their skin color to their religious, political, and sexual preferences.

Oprah worked eighteen-hour days for six weeks to complete the film. As executive producer, she was the first one on the set every morning. "I made sure I knew everybody's name, so there was no one thinking I was Miss Mightier-Than-Thou."

*The Women of Brewster Place* was scheduled to air on Sunday and Monday evenings, March 19 and 20, 1989, and Oprah agreed to do national promotion for ABC beforehand, including a press conference for television critics. Jeff Jacobs stressed to reporters the importance of Oprah doing good work, whether or not it was commercially viable. "*The Women of Brewster Place* hasn't aired yet," he said. "When it does, we'll find out if people respond to it and give it a good number. But whether they do or they don't, it was an important book, an important film. It needed to get made. If we make money, great. And if we don't, well, there are other reasons to do projects besides making money."

Oprah turned to the reporters. "You want to know where I'll be Sunday night? You'll find me on my knees in front of the TV—praying for the Nielsens." While Jacobs indicated a commitment to the worth of the project, Oprah's commitment was to the ratings, and she was not disappointed. *The Women of Brewster Place* was the most watched two-part movie since NBC's *Fatal Vision* in 1984. Oprah's triumph averaged a 24.0 rating and a 37 share, according to A. C. Nielsen Co. figures, with one ratings point representing 904,000 households. On

Sunday her miniseries beat both *The Wizard of Oz* on CBS and NBC's airing of *Return of the Jedi*.

The reviews were mixed, but none surprised Oprah more than the one in the *Chicago Sun-Times* by Daniel Ruth, who had criticized her in the past but now praised her as "a woman of considerable talent—especially as a dramatic actress. Throughout . . . she exerts an energy that carries this production from beginning to end. It's a first-rate characterization."

Oprah wrote him a note, saying that she never thought she'd get a positive review out of him. He replied that he never thought she'd do anything to deserve one. "So," he said many years later, "we were even."

Now with her star power greatly enhanced, Oprah persuaded ABC to give her a weekly series in prime time based on the film. Her only caveat was that the show could not air on Thursday nights. "I will not be put in a situation where I'm up against Cosby," she said, referring to *The Cosby Show*, one of the most popular shows on television then. To appease critics who felt *The Women of Brewster Place* bashed black men, Oprah agreed to add some sympathetic male characters and simply call the series *Brewster Place*. The network threw its full support behind her and her new show. "We are delighted to have Oprah Winfrey join our prime-time schedule in this series," said Robert Iger, the new president of ABC entertainment. "The success of the mini-series last season and the ongoing popularity of her daily program are testament to Oprah's universal appeal."

*Brewster Place* began airing in May 1990, but drew such poor ratings that ABC canceled it after eleven episodes. The failed venture cost Oprah $10 million and left Harpo's facilities largely unused and unprofitable. Having once again lost a shot at prime-time television, she retreated to her farm in Indiana. She later told *Essence* magazine that she had failed because the noise of her ambition had drowned out "the voice of God."

"I thought I could make [the series] all right because I wanted it to be all right. . . . But I wasn't ready for it. My mistake was that I didn't listen to the voice. Me! The one who always preaches 'Listen to the voice,' 'Be guided by the voice,' 'Take direction from the voice,' by which I mean the voice of God within me. . . . The voice was speaking loud and clear and I didn't take heed."

Oprah could not comprehend that the failure of *Brewster Place* might have been in its conception, or the script, or maybe even the acting. She had said over and over again, "God is with me. That's why I always succeed. . . . I am God-centered."

She did not believe that bad things could happen to good people. Nor did she accept the anarchy of fate or wicked chaos, even bad luck. She totally dismissed good luck as having any part in her success. "Luck is a matter of preparation," she said. "I am highly attuned to my divine self." She believed that everything was dictated by holy design; including the 157 miracles she told viewers she had experienced. She told Nobel Peace Prize winner Elie Wiesel that his surviving the Holocaust was a miracle, but he disagreed. "If a miracle of God to spare me, why? There were people much better than me. . . . No, it was an accident," he said. Oprah looked at him incredulously.

Having credited her "triumphal" life to God's plan for her success, she now accepted her *Brewster Place* setback as another message from on high. "I truly understand that there is a lesson in everything that happens to us," she said. "So I tried not to spend my time asking, 'Why did this happen to me?' but trying to figure out why I had chosen [to do the series]. That's the answer you need. It's always a question of accepting responsibility for your choices. Anytime you look outside yourself for answers, you're looking in the wrong place."

In analyzing Oprah's beliefs for *The New York Times Magazine,* Barbara Grizzuti Harrison had written that her "knotty contradictions" and simplistic truths often collided with each other but were perfect for sound-bite television: "They make up in pith what they lack in profundity." The writer later admitted she could not bear to watch Oprah's show. "You'll forgive me, but it's white trailer trash. It debases language, it debases emotion. It provides everyone with glib psychological formulas. [These people] go around talking like a fortune cookie. And I think she is in very large part responsible for that." The writer Gretchen Reynolds agreed, if not quite so harshly. "[S]he is a true adherent . . . of the squishiest sort of self-help dogma. She believes you can 'get to know yourself by facing your fears.'"

Yet Oprah's little homilies touched her audiences and reflected their own spiritual quest. As she evolved from a child of Old Testament preachers into a New Age theorist who loosely defined God as a vague force of the universe, she gave her viewers what she called "a spiritual reawakening," so that they could all, in her words, "live your best life." That phrase became such an Oprah mantra that she had the four words trademarked by Harpo, Inc., as her own. She led Live Your Best Life seminars across the country, charging as much as $185 per person, and attracted thousands of women. She passed out Live Your Best Life journals and encouraged everyone to write their aspirations in order to realize them. She distributed Live Your Best Life gift bags filled with scented candles and tea bags. She preached like an old-fashioned Baptist minister, but her Live Your Best Life sermons did not contain fire and brimstone. Instead, she offered huggy, feel-good messages about "living in the present moment" and "following your dream" and "listening to the voice," which, she promised, would lead you to "live your best life." And to the hordes of paying participants who wrote down every word she said in their Live Your Best Life notebooks, there was no better proof of this than Oprah herself.

# *T*hirteen

D URING THE summer of 1988, Oprah heard a voice that led to the biggest change in her life and gave her the highest ratings of her career. It was the voice of Stedman Graham, who Oprah said had been sent to her by God after she had formally prayed on her knees.

Over dinner one night she asked if her size ever bothered him. He paused—a little too long. Then he said: "It has been something of an adjustment." Oprah looked at him in disbelief.

"At first I figured, 'Oh, great. I get to be somebody's personal growth experience.' But then I started to realize that, my God, he's been feeling that all this time [two years] and it took him this long to ever tell me about it."

On July 7, 1988, shortly after that conversation, Oprah started a protein-sparing fast, drinking a medical concoction of powder and water five times a day, plus sixty-four ounces of noncaloric liquids, and taking vitamin pills, but eating absolutely no solid food. Six weeks into the strenuous diet, she and Stedman were on vacation in Hawaii and Oprah started eating. "I felt terrible because I'd been so controlled up to that point. So Stedman said, 'Why don't you just decide you're going to eat on vacation and not make yourself crazy? When you go home, you can start the diet again.'

" 'How about if I had just one cheeseburger and got it out of my system?'

" 'Are you crazy?' "

Oprah became maniacal about that one cheeseburger. She waited for Stedman to go to his golf lesson and opened all the windows in the hotel room. Then she called room service and ordered the cheeseburger—with bacon and avocado. Minutes later she raced to the phone and called Gayle King to tell her what she had done. Gayle understood the binge because her husband, William Bumpus, had been on the same fasting diet and lost seventy-five pounds in twelve weeks. Oprah went back on her fast and jogged every day with Stedman. By the time she returned to Chicago in the fall she had dropped forty pounds.

The transformation of her five-six frame was startling. Her audiences could not believe their eyes. She promised she would reveal her secret as soon as she lost more weight. Viewers tuned in every day just to see what she looked like. By October she had dropped another fifteen pounds. Still, she would not say how she was shrinking every week. Finally she announced that she would share her secret during November sweeps, on a show titled "Diet Dreams Come True."

The buildup to this show seemed to galvanize the country. Everyone wanted to know how Oprah, who once said she didn't keep a handgun because she would shoot off her thighs, had finally managed to lose weight without joining the NRA. The Associated Press dispatched a photographer to Chicago, and newspaper editors around the country sent reporters to cover the "Diet Dreams" show. While acknowledging that Oprah's amazing weight loss had grabbed the nation's attention, the Knight Ridder correspondent groused that it was only "the most important social development since Michael Jackson's last nose job." Embarrassed to be covering Oprah's diet revelation, he added, "Did she find the cure for cancer? Did she eliminate the specter of AIDS? Did she reduce the national deficit?"

The day of the much-ballyhooed show, November 15, 1988, Oprah sashayed onto her soundstage in a big bright red coat. "This is a very, very personal show," she said. Then, like an exuberant stripper, she ripped off the red coat to reveal half of her former self. "As of this morning I have lost sixty-seven pounds," she said, justifiably proud of her new figure, which was tucked into a pair of size-ten Calvin Klein jeans that had been hanging in her closet since 1981. She twirled around the stage to show off her new body in a cinched belt with a silver buckle, a tight black turtleneck, and spike-heeled boots. The audience cheered her wildly, waving the little yellow pom-poms they had been given for just that purpose.

Oprah held up a package of Optifast powder, which she said she mixed with water in an Optifast cup and drank five times a day. This gave her four hundred calories of nutrition without solid food on a fast that supposedly spared the body's loss of protein. Before she had ended her first segment, Optifast operators were bombarded. A company spokesman reported one million attempts to get through to the toll-free number after Oprah mentioned the brand name seven times. "I'm sure a lot of people think I own stock in Optifast," she said. "I don't."

After a commercial break, she returned pulling a little red wagon loaded with sixty-seven pounds of greasy white animal fat. Bending down, she tried to lift the bag of blubber. "Is this gross or what? It's amazing to me I can't lift it, but I used to carry it around every day."

Then she became very serious. "This has been the most difficult thing I've done in my life. . . . It is my greatest accomplishment." She then made her personal diary public, reading entries she had made after talking with an Optifast counselor about why she wanted to lose weight. "What is the bigger issue here? Self-esteem. For me, it is getting control of my life. I realize this fat is just a blocker. It is like having mud on my wings. It keeps me from flying. It is a barrier to better things. It has been a way of staying comfortable with other people. My fat puts them at ease. Makes them feel less threatened. Makes me insecure. So I dream of walking into a room one day where this fat is not the issue. And that will happen this year because the bigger issue for me is making myself the best that I can be."

The next segment of the show featured a congratulatory call from Stedman in High Point, North Carolina, to say how proud he was of her. At that time he was working for his mentor, Bob Brown, and seeing Oprah only on weekends. "I hate it," she told reporters then. "It's going to last another year. Then he says he's going to move back to Chicago." Her regular viewers knew who Stedman was, although they had yet to see him. She was saving that introduction for a February sweeps show titled "How Fame Affects a Relationship." Stedman's phone call of congratulations was followed by a video clip from Shirley MacLaine, whom the audience knew to be Oprah's movie-star guide to all things paranormal.

The "fat wagon" show became the most watched show of Oprah's career, with her highest overnight rating ever in sixteen of Nielsen's major markets, meaning that 44 percent of the daytime television audience watched. "These are unbelievable numbers," said Stephen W. Palley, COO of King World. "Those people who didn't see the show certainly heard about it." Oprah's eye-popping weight loss riveted the nation's media for days after the show, as nutritionists and doctors and commentators debated the merits of protein-sparing fasts, with everyone wagering on how long Oprah would keep the weight off.

Lost in the hullabaloo of headlines from coast to coast was the ill-timed salute of *Ms.* magazine (November 1988) to Oprah as one of six women to receive its 1988 Woman of the Year Award:

"In a society where fat is taboo, she made it in a medium that worships thin and celebrates a bland, white-bread prettiness of body and personality. . . . But Winfrey made fat sexy, elegant—damned near gorgeous—with her drop dead wardrobe, easy body language, and cheerful sensuality."

Oprah wanted no part of the tribute to her weight. "I never was happy when I was fat," she said. "And I'll never be fat again. Never." She became irritated with people who asked if she would maintain her new size. "Asking me if I'll keep the weight off is like asking, 'Will you ever be in a relationship again where you allow yourself to be emotionally battered?'" she said. "I've been there—and I don't intend to go back." She said her romance with Stedman would keep her highly motivated. "I feel so much sexier. . . . We're just sexy, sexy, sexy now. My weight loss has just absolutely changed our relationship."

In a stand-up routine, Rosie O'Donnell said she was sick of hearing about Stedman. "Now that Oprah's thin, she talks about Stedman all the time. Every five minutes it's Stedman this and Stedman that. If she mentions Stedman one more time, I'm gonna fly to Chicago and force-feed her Twinkies through an IV tube."

Oprah vowed never to blimp up again because she was afraid of the grocery store press. "I have fear of tabloids because of the stories they would print." But the pressure became intense, and the press began piling on. For the next year she was subjected to a national Amber Alert on her food intake, not simply from the tabloids but from the mainstream media, which also hounded her. Within weeks of unveiling her new starvation size, she was caught in a gluttonous feast by the syndicated gossip columnist Liz Smith, who wrote in the New York *Daily News:*

> Is our darling Oprah Winfrey becoming "The Phantom of the Oprah" we used to know—that is, just a shell of her former self? . . . Well, not to worry . . . Last Saturday she dined at Le Cirque in New York, consuming not only fettuccini with wild mushrooms, but a braised snapper. Then, on Sunday, she was with a party of six at New York's Sign of the Dove and ordered poached eggs on a brioche with Hollandaise sauce. After that, Oprah decided the lunches of her companions were inadequate and ordered a chicken for the table, consuming almost half of it herself. Then Oprah moved on to Serendipity for a 20-ounce frozen hot chocolate with whipped cream.

The next week, *People* reported Oprah was eating goat-cheese pizza at Spago in Hollywood. Then *Vanity Fair* weighed in: "Oprah Winfrey seems to be fleshing out a pair of larger than size 8 jeans," adding, "Forget the Optifast—we prefer the grand old Oprah." In its "Conventional Wisdom Watch" column, *Newsweek* said, "Oprah Winfrey—built terrific studio but working overtime at the dinner table again." The unkindest cut came in August 1989, when *TV Guide* decided that Oprah's body was not good enough to illustrate its cover story on her: "Oprah!

The Richest Woman on TV? How She Amassed Her $250 Million Fortune." So the magazine put her face on Ann-Margret's dazzling figure, sitting atop a pile of money. The editor said it was not *TV Guide*'s policy to misrepresent, but he couldn't see why anyone should complain. "After all, Oprah looks great, Bob Mackie got his gown on the front of the nation's largest-circulation magazine, and Ann-Margret made the cover—most of her, anyway."

Oprah did not need the media to keep a death watch on her diet. She knew she was in trouble just days after she dragged her little red wagon across the stage. In her journal she wrote:

November 29, 1988: I've been eating out of control. I've got to bring it to an end. I can't get used to being thin.

December 13, 1988: I came home and ate as much cereal as I could hold. I eat junk all day.

December 26, 1988: There's a party in Aspen, I don't want to go. I've gained five more pounds.

January 7, 1989: I'm out of control. Start out my day trying to fast. By noon I was frustrated and hungry just thinking about the agony of it all. I ate three bowls of raisin bran. Left the house and bought some caramel and cheese corn, came back at 3:00 staring at food in the cabinets. And now I want some fries with lots of salt. I'm out of control.

For a few weeks after her "Diet Dreams" show, she savored the delicious sensation of buying beautiful clothes in designer boutiques, no longer having to shop at The Forgotten Woman or buy the two largest sizes of a dress at Marshall Field and have them sewn together to fit her. She indulged in shopping from the couture collections of Christian Dior, Chanel, and Yves Saint Laurent. She posed for Richard Avedon in a black silk bodysuit for a national ad as one of Revlon's most unforgettable women. "I loved doing the Revlon shoot," she said. "It changed the way I felt about me. I never imagined myself as beautiful. But that ad made me feel beautiful. So for that reason alone it was worth shooting just to feel that." She felt so good about her new thin self that she gave away all her fat clothes, donating them to the homeless. "It didn't solve their problem," she said, "but they're sure lookin' good." She felt that after four months of starvation she had finally conquered her weight problem. So she stopped the Optifast group counseling and discontinued the supervised maintenance program.

Within a year she gained back seventeen of the sixty-seven pounds she had lost. "It's a battle I'm still fighting every waking minute of my life," she told her audience, most of whom nodded in sympathetic agreement. At that point, according to the National Center for Health Statistics, 27 percent of American women and 24 percent of American men were considered to be overweight, bordering on obese. Oprah showed a video of herself chugging up a mountain at a high-priced spa, struggling to burn off calories. She looked defeated as she pleaded with viewers to leave her alone if they saw her shoveling down mashed potatoes. "I've decided I'm not going to go through life depriving myself of things that make me feel good."

A year later she wrote one of her saddest journal entries:

I cried in my office with Debra [DiMaio]. . . . I cried for my poor miserable self having gotten to this state. Scale said 203 this morning. Controlled—just controlled by it . . . By the end of the day . . . feeling diminished, less of a person, guilty, ugly . . . I really am fat again.

During the November sweeps of 1990, Oprah acknowledged the nightmare of her "Diet Dreams" with a show titled "The Pain of Regain": she had gained back all of the sixty-seven pounds, plus more. She would not say how much she weighed, but she later confided it was more than Mike Tyson, boxing's heavyweight champion. "I will never diet again," she said. "I certainly will never fast again."

From her fan mail, Oprah knew her audiences adored her, so she was surprised when most said they preferred the original fat

Oprah to the new "lite" version. They said when she was heavy she was more approachable; she laughed easily and hugged everyone. The thin Oprah seemed pinched and strained, as if the effort to diet had sapped her of her cheerfulness. Viewers let her know that they were much more comfortable with hefty Oprah than sylph Oprah, who, they felt, acted a little smug and a trifle self-satisfied. Her bulk had reassured people that looks were superficial, only skin-deep. Now they realized that she never really believed that. Years later she admitted as much. "I do know what it's like to live inside of a body that's twice your size. . . . I know that anybody who's there would want it to be different. Even people who say they've made peace with it. You reach a point where you fight it, fight it, fight it, and then you say you don't want to fight it anymore. . . .

"I can tell you this, even being a famous person, that people treat you so differently when you're fat than when you're thin. It is discrimination that nobody ever talks about."

As much as Oprah disliked her heavy self, she, too, seemed more at ease with her corpulence than she did without it. "I always felt safer and more protected when I was heavy," she said, "although I didn't really know what I was trying to protect, any more than I knew what I was afraid of." It seemed that the same limitless ambition that had rocketed her to the top of her career had set her appestat: while gaining weight worked to her professional advantage, making her what *Essence* described as "the quintessential mammy figure," her huge size made her absolutely miserable as a person. *Ebony* suggested that her "touchy-feely" manner toward her predominantly white audiences "is reminiscent of the stereotypical Southern Mammy." *People* described her as "the powerful mommy figure," which she did not accept. "A woman told me recently, 'I used to think you were more compassionate when you were fat because you were like a mother to me. And now you're this sex thing,'" recalled Oprah. "I said, 'Is it something I said, something I did? Because I never felt like I was your mother.'"

Some black comedians were mean-spirited, particularly Keenan and Damon Wayans on *In Living Color*, the comedy show they developed for the Fox Network. In one spoof titled "Oprah on Eating," the comedians' sister Kim Wayans imitated Oprah doing an interview: she began eating ferociously until she blew up like a balloon and exploded potato chips all over her audience. Abiola Sinclair pronounced the skit "vicious" in the *New York Amsterdam News:* "Sensible and genuine Black people never were overly concerned about Oprah's weight. What was of more concern to many of us was her feeling the need to wear funny colored [green] contact lenses, seemingly indicative of some sort of racial dissatisfaction. At her heaviest Oprah never was a slob, and always looked good. In our opinion . . . a little weight on her looks better than that unnatural skin and bones body, with that big round head sitting on it. She could be a size 14 and still be fit. The key word is fit."

Oprah probably felt more discrimination for being fat than she ever did for being black. The African American community was far more accepting of large-scale women than the white stick world, which prized anorexics as straight as a fork tine.

As a black woman who broke the tape in her sprint to success, Oprah was universally applauded and rewarded for her professional triumph, but as a fat woman, she felt excluded from the fork-tine world, and the exclusion was painful. "People take you more seriously [when you're thin]," Oprah said. "You're more validated as a human being. . . ." "I hate myself fat. . . . It's made me terribly uncomfortable with men." "I don't believe fat people who say they're happy. They're not. I don't care what they say."

Over her career she would win seven Daytime Emmys for Outstanding Talk Show Host, nine Daytime Emmys for Outstanding Talk Show, seven NAACP Image awards, Broadcaster of the Year from the International Radio and Television Society, the George Foster Peabody Individual Achievement Award, a Lifetime Achievement Award from the Academy of Television Arts and Sciences, and the Golden Laurel Award from the Producers Guild of America. Yet, sadly, she felt her greatest accomplishment in life was losing sixty-seven pounds, and her biggest failure was regaining it.

"I remember [before she went on that fast] being at Oprah's show in Washington, D.C., when I was the research director for WUSA-TV," said Candy Miles-Crocker, a beautiful black woman. "Oprah wore a bright yellow knit suit and she must've weighed close to 275 pounds then. She was huge, and that knit skirt clung to her like the wrapper on a sausage. It was also slit up the front so that when she sat down the slit spread, as did her fat . . . and . . . oh, dear . . . it was horrible. I felt awful for her. She knew what was happening, so during the break she went off to the side and turned the skirt so the split wouldn't be in the front. Watching her try to maneuver that skirt over her thunderously fat thighs was like watching a ship try to dock in a slip for a rowboat."

Oprah's weight hung like a harness around her neck, but as beleaguered as she felt, she did not completely give up. She continued going to health spas, where she eventually met Rosie Daley, who became her chef, and later, Bob Greene, who became her trainer. Together, they managed to alter her lifestyle and her size in time for her fortieth birthday, but even then it was not easy.

"Before Rosie arrived, Mrs. Eddins [Oprah's honorary godmother from Nashville] did all the cooking, and every lunch was fried chicken, potato salad, heaping bowls of macaroni and cheese with freshly baked pies for dessert—and Oprah ate it all," recalled her landscape architect James van Sweden. "Rosie introduced her to fresh fruits and vegetables, but it took Oprah a while to make friends with food that wasn't fried or sauced." Oprah said herself that Rosie worked with her for two years before she ever lost a pound.

During the time she was regaining her weight in 1990, she was sledgehammered by her sister, who told the tabloids the long-held family secret of Oprah's pregnancy at the age of fourteen and of the baby boy she had given birth to. This tell-all came after Oprah had discontinued her sister's $1,200-a-month allowance because she was using it to buy drugs, so Patricia Lee Lloyd went to the *National Enquirer,* which paid her $19,000 to reveal details about Oprah's so-called "wild and promiscuous early years," when she sneaked older men into the house and did "The Horse" while her mother was at work.

"She said that's what she used to do," Patricia Lee Lloyd told the tabloid, "and I realized that all those afternoons she was making out with her men."

Oprah was so humiliated by her sister's revelations that she took to her bed for three days. "I thought my whole life was over," she said later. "The world's going to hate me. They're all going to say, 'What a shameful, wicked woman. What a little whore.' But Stedman . . . got me through it. He helped me to be brave about it. . . . I cried and cried. I remember him coming into the bedroom that Sunday afternoon, the room darkened from the closed curtains. Standing before me, looking like he, too, had shed tears, he handed me the tabloid and said, 'I'm so sorry. You don't deserve this.'" Stedman helped her see that what had happened to her happens to many, but he said that as one of God's special children, she would survive and thrive and be able to help others do the same. "Stedman thinks I'm one of those chosen people," Oprah said. "You know, hand-picked by the universe to do great things."

A week later she got slammed with the second installment of her "shameful secret past," in which her sister popped all the bubbles Oprah had blown about her poverty-stricken childhood. Patricia also revealed the "lies Oprah told that made Mom cry," and the stories Oprah had never told, about how she "pawned Mom's ring, stole her money and ran away from home."

Suddenly the mythology Oprah had created for herself started to unravel. "She told a hundred reporters about her pet cockroach, Sandy," recalled the novelist Jacquelyn Mitchard, then a columnist for the *Milwaukee Journal*. "She told me the Sandy story, too . . . back when she was only an upstart young television host giving Phil Donahue a headache. . . . Even back then, there was a drivenness about her that seemed not fully explained even by her towering ambition. She was an enigma, a high-flying solo pilot full of rehearsed one-liners but uncomfortable with too much introspection. And as any therapist can tell you, the people who run hardest usually are trying to outrun something, almost always something that was not their fault, almost always something in the past." In a sympathetic column titled "Maybe We Know Now What Makes Oprah Run," Mitchard wrote that if Oprah could embrace the truth of her life she would be able "to caution young girls in tough places to avoid early pregnancy." Interestingly, Mitchard's novel *The Deep End of the Ocean* became the first choice for the book club Oprah started six years later, but Oprah "fortunately" did not make the connection between the columnist and the novelist.

Pressed by her sister's tabloid revelations, Oprah issued a public statement: "It is true that when I was 14 years old I became pregnant. The baby was born prematurely and died shortly after birth. I had hoped this matter could stay private until I was fully able to deal with my own deep emotions and feelings. It saddens me deeply that a publication would pay large sums of money to a drug-dependent, deeply disturbed individual and then publish her remarks. My heart goes out to my half sister." Oprah later told reporters that she had paid for her sister's drug treatment at the Hazelden clinic. "[I told her] I'm going to spend whatever it costs. But if you blow it, you can die a junkie on the street. And I mean that with all my heart." Oprah did not speak to Patricia for two years after her tabloid revelations, but she generously paid for the education of her sister's two daughters, Alisha and Chrishaunda.

"[That article] was the most painful thing that has ever happened to me. The hurt, the feeling of betrayal was as bad as it gets," said Oprah. "But I kept reminding myself to look for the lesson—and all of a sudden something clicked for the first time. I connected my own sexual promiscuity as a teenager with the sexual abuse I had suffered as a child. Strange as it may seem, I had never seen the connection between the two before. It took that terrible article in the tabloids to make me realize I was still carrying that guilt around with me. I know that there are other lessons for me to learn, but the first one was that I was not responsible for the abuse and that I had to get rid of the shame I was carrying."

Finally, Oprah invited her sister to her farm in Indiana to try to make amends. "We spent the whole weekend talking," Patricia said later. "Oprah let me have it. She said I was a letdown, she was disappointed in me and I hadn't turned out the way she'd hoped. I had no degree, no career, no nothing."

A few years later Oprah again cut off all communication with her sister. "I told her in the last conversation we had that we don't share the same moral code, so there's no reason to pretend in 'sisterhood,'" she told reporters. "I bought her a home and provided her with hundreds of thousands of dollars to get set up, but she said she didn't need to work." Oprah disagreed—strongly. "I think people need to [work]."

Patricia continued to bounce in and out of rehab until 2003 when, at the age of forty-two, she died of an accidental drug overdose. "I had just put her through rehab [again]," Oprah told reporters, "and what happens is, if you've been used to taking a certain amount of a drug and then you go back to taking that same amount after you've been off it for a bit, it's too much."

Oprah had expected to be shunned after her sister's tabloid revelations. "I imagined that every person on the street was going to point their finger at me and scream, 'Pregnant at fourteen, you wicked girl. . . .' No one said a word, though—not strangers, not even people I knew. I was shocked. Nobody treated me differently."

It's impossible to estimate how many women Oprah helped with the story of her out-of-wedlock pregnancy, but she must have been a beacon to those who had endured similar sadness and shame. Because of her reach and visibility, her words carried weight with her audiences, who saw her as a woman of courage and determination. Having refused to be defeated by her searing childhood, she inspired hope, and women everywhere could look at the success she had made of her life and believe in a similar salvation for themselves. In sharing her own shame, Oprah inevitably touched thousands and helped them release their guilt by showing them they were not alone. In that sense her show became the healing ministry she had always claimed it to be.

The public humiliation she endured during this time

seemed to lead to a more empathetic Oprah, one who showed a new sensitivity to the exploitation of some of her "conflict" programs. "The day I felt clearly the worst I've ever felt on television was in 1989, when we were still live and we had the wife, the girlfriend, and the husband, and on the air the husband [unexpectedly] announced to the wife the girlfriend was pregnant. And the expression on her face . . . I looked at her and felt horrible for myself and felt horrible for her. So I turned to her and said, 'I'm really sorry you had to be put in this position and you had to hear this on television. This never should have happened.'" Still, Oprah would continue her "conflict" programming for another five years of rocketing ratings.

Months earlier, the Pulitzer Prize–winning television critic Tom Shales had sounded the first knell against the "talk rot" infecting airwaves and polluting the atmosphere. "Hours and hours are frittered away on shock, schlock and folly," he wrote in *The Washington Post*. Consumer advocate Ralph Nader singled out *The Oprah Winfrey Show* as the number one polluter. "They get all their ideas from the *National Enquirer*," Nader said. As an example of the shows Shales said Oprah was spoon-feeding "boob tube boobs," he cited a few weeks of her topics: subservient women, paternity fights, infidelity, man-hunting, threesomes, wife beaters, and shopaholics.

Even Erma Bombeck took a soft swipe at Oprah in her syndicated column. "I find myself grabbing for the listing every day to see what will come up next," she wrote. "Recently Oprah had a panel of men who thought their aunts were their mothers. Where do they find these people? Do individuals with unusual circumstances write the producers of the show and say: 'Hey, if you ever do something on spaceship babies trying to find their mother, I'm living in Chicago and would love to talk about it'? Or does a call go out for 'Women Who Raise Their Husbands as an Only Child,' encouraging them to submit résumés?" The beloved humorist may have thought she was poking gentle fun, but Oprah's producers do maintain a huge computerized retrieval system from on-air solicitations, plus the two to four thousand letters they receive every week, many of which run to several pages of intimate revelations. There are also several separate databases for potential interviewees, guests, and experts on every subject imaginable. Erma Bombeck did not live long enough to see Oprah's show of April 3, 2008, in which Oprah interviewed a transgender man who became pregnant so he and his wife could raise a child. He explained that he had taken male hormones, had his breasts removed, and legally changed his gender to male, but he decided not to have his female reproductive organs removed. He subsequently gave birth to a girl. That show provided Oprah with a 45 percent ratings increase over the previous week of shows.

Normally, she shrugged off her critics by citing her huge ratings; only occasionally did she admit to being "galled" by their criticism. "My answer to those who say [my] show is exploitative is that life is exploitative, sensational, bizarre, filled with trash and weird things. Television is where these subjects should be discussed." After all, she added, she didn't do bigots, racists, and sadomasochists anymore. "And I'll never do devil-worship again," she said. It would take her a few more years to acknowledge her embarrassing contributions to trash television. At the time, she maintained that her tabloid shows were educational.

But it wasn't all squalor all the time on *The Oprah Winfrey Show*. Though never as substantive as Donahue, she still presented a few serious subjects in the late 1980s and early 1990s, including the escalating crisis in American education and declining literacy among the young. (She promoted that show by looking into the camera and asking, "How dumb are we?") She explored drunk driving in a show with offenders and victims who had been catastrophically injured by intoxicated motorists. Later she said if she had a twenty-year-old son who got drunk, got in a car, and killed a pedestrian, she would testify against him in court. "I would put his ass in jail. I would say 'I love you, but your ass is going to jail.' I haven't even lost anybody in this way, but the soft laws on this make me crazy. I think when someone is a drunk driver, he should hang. And since I don't believe in capital punishment, that means you just hang him till he turns blue, then revive him for a while, and then put him back up to hang some more. Then you tie a knot around his privates. . . . I have no tolerance on this issue."

She was one of the first to examine sexual abuse of children by the clergy, and she told the story of AIDS in several different shows, including one about whether networks should run commercials advertising the use of a certain brand of condom as protection against AIDS. Despite those in her audience vehemently opposed to such advertising, Oprah announced that she was handing out free samples of "safe-sex kits" that included condoms. She even ventured into public service with shows such as "What to Do in an Emergency," demonstrating artificial respiration and the Heimlich maneuver. She raised more than $1 million in credit-card donations for Hurricane Hugo victims during a show from Charleston, South Carolina. "This is the quickest response from individuals that we have ever seen in a fund-raising effort," said James Krueger of the Red Cross.

"The subjects for discussion change over the years," she said in 1989. "It used to be better sex and the perfect orgasm. Then it was diet. The trend for the nineties is family and nurturing." To that end she presented shows such as "How to Have a Happy Step Family," "The Family Dinner Experiment," "In Search of Missing Children," and "How to Find Loved Ones," in which she showed viewers how to track down long-lost relatives.

Her most effective shows continued to be those that touched her own life and explored the personal issues she was coping with at the time, including her continual struggle with weight, the damage of sexual molestation, and the ravages of racism. She took her audience inside the life of an obese person by introducing twenty-five-year-old Stacey Halprin, who weighed 550 pounds the first time she was on the show. Stacey returned after losing 300 pounds following gastric bypass surgery and came back again after losing another 60 pounds to get an Oprah makeover, which also became one of the show's most popular staples.

In her 1989 show titled "Date Rape," Oprah said, "I know it will have liberated a lot of women who have been raped and never called it that. A major survey showed that eighty-seven percent of high-school boys believe they have the right to force a woman to have sex if they have spent money on a date—and forty-seven percent of girls agreed. It's amazing to me that women buy into that attitude."

On Martin Luther King, Jr.'s birthday in 1992 she announced that she would present shows throughout the year devoted to "Racism in America":

- "Racism in the Neighborhood"
- "I Hate Your Interracial Relationship"
- "Japanese Americans: The New Racism"
- "Are We All Racist?"
- "The Rodney King Verdict I and II"
- "My Parent Is a Racist"
- "An Experiment in Racism"
- "Too Little, Too Late: Native Americans Speak Out"
- "I Refuse to Date My Own Race"
- "Unsolved Hate Crimes"
- "White Men Who Fear Black Men"

She took her cameras to South Central Los Angeles in the wake of the riots that followed the acquittal of the white police officers who had beaten Rodney King, an African American. Bloody chaos erupted after the 1992 verdict, with the violent deaths of fifty-four people in one of the most deadly riots in U.S. history. South LA ignited into an inferno of 4,000 fires damaging 1,100 buildings, causing 2,382 injuries, and resulting in 13,212 arrests. That evening, television viewers watched in horror as Reginald Denny, a white man, was dragged from his truck and beaten by a black mob. President George Herbert Walker Bush finally sent in federal troops to restore order.

With the best of intentions, Oprah assembled a multiracial audience of whites, Asians, blacks, and Hispanics for her first taping in Los Angeles, but she ended up with a show of shrill militants, which prompted Howard Rosenberg to write in the *Los Angeles Times* that she was "overmatched in this withering onslaught of anger and outrage, watching helplessly as her studio full of warring multicultural guests screamed sound bites at each other." One black woman justified the riots by saying, "We had to do something to get Oprah into LA to get people talking." Rosenberg nearly despaired. "If this is talking," he wrote, "bring back shouting."

Despite the critics, Oprah maintained her position as the country's number one talk show host among a growing field of competitors. Her program's popularity and the intense loyalty of her female viewers made her the most influential voice in daytime television, and her made-for-television movies and specials had extended her audience, but she still wanted to engrave her presence in prime time. So, for her next network special, she and her executive producer, Debra DiMaio, cast their lines for a prize catch and managed to reel in Michael Jackson, the self-styled "King of Pop, Rock, and Soul," who was then the subject of international curiosity. He had not done a live interview in fourteen years, but because it was Oprah offering ninety minutes of prime-time television, and possibly because his record sales had dropped along with his popularity, he agreed to sit down with her at his Neverland ranch in Santa Ynez, California. Oprah promised not to ask him if he was gay, but she said she wanted to give him a chance to address the bizarre rumors about him bleaching his skin, sleeping in a hyperbaric chamber, and having serial plastic surgeries.

In addition, she asked:

- "Were your brothers jealous of you when you started getting all the attention?"
- "Did your father beat you?"
- "Are you a virgin?"
- "Why do you always grab your crotch?"
- "Do you go out, do you date?"
- "Who do you date?"
- "Have you ever been in love? We'd like to know whether or not there is a possibility that you are going to marry one day and have children."

Sixteen years later, after Michael Jackson died in 2009, Oprah played part of that interview. She said that she did not believe him when he told her that he had had only two plastic surgeries. She also seemed dubious about his claim of vitiligo, the disorder that he said bleached his skin.

During the interview, the smoke detectors went off at Neverland and the screeching noise forced Oprah to break for an unplanned commercial. Later, Diane Dimond, one of Jackson's biographers, speculated that Jackson had planned the interruption to disrupt Oprah's personal questions. Bob Jones, Jackson's publicist from 1987 to 2002, who had coined the term "King of Pop," recalled the interruption as a way for Jackson to bring on Elizabeth Taylor as a surprise.

"He had Liz there to trump Oprah's questions, and also because he knew that Liz would add to the ratings. . . . Liz should've been there, considering all the jewels Michael gave her over the years. That was a very expensive friendship, let me tell you."

Taylor told Oprah—who irritated the star by continuing to call her Liz instead of Elizabeth—that Michael was "the least weird man I have ever known," in addition to being "highly intelligent, shrewd, intuitive, understanding, sympathetic, generous." Years later Oprah said she did not think their friendship weird because they shared the same experiences of being child stars with abusive fathers.

During his 1993 interview, Michael Jackson looked "Off the Wall," Oprah wasn't "Bad," and it never got "Dangerous," but for ninety million viewers in the United States and one hundred million around the world, the interview was a pop culture "Thriller." Jackson defended his preoccupation with children as compensation for his lost childhood and the urge to surround himself with unconditional love. "I find a thing I never had through them," he said. Ten years later he would give an interview to British TV that led to his prosecution for child molestation, but he was found not guilty on all charges. He admitted to Oprah that he had a lifelong crush on Diana Ross, whom he seemed to resemble, and he claimed to be in love with Brooke Shields.

"Michael just BS'd Oprah about not being gay," said Bob Jones, who was on the set during the interview. "Michael was a much bigger star than Oprah at that time—he was once the biggest black performer in the world—but that interview served both of them quite well. The one person Michael really wanted to be associated with was not Oprah but Princess Diana, and we did everything possible to get him an introduction, but the princess would not return his calls. . . . Finally we did the Prince's Trust [a charity event] and Michael met her, at Wembley Stadium in London, but she didn't say much to him beyond hello."

Oprah's special on Michael Jackson was the highest-rated non–Super Bowl entertainment event in almost a decade, exceeding everyone's expectations, including those of sponsors. ABC reported that the show was one of the most watched entertainment programs in television history, and the fourth-highest-ranked entertainment show since 1960, behind only the finale of *M*A*S*H* (February 1983), the "Who Shot J.R.?" episode of *Dallas* (November 1980), and *The Day After* (November 1983). *Time* said, "Part grand Oprah, part soap Oprah, the Winfrey show was at the very least great TV: live, reckless, emotionally naked." *Life* concurred: "Oprah delivered the goods and accomplished the near-impossible: She brought Peter Pan down to earth." At last Oprah had won her place in prime time. "My finest hour in television," she said.

# *F*ourteen

F OR MANY years, the American Booksellers Association held its annual convention over the Memorial Day weekend, and in 1993, ABA, as it was called then, was a bacchanal. More than twenty-five thousand retailers, publishers, agents, and authors flew to Miami for four days and nights of buying, selling, and celebrating at splashy parties with author-celebrities such as William Styron, Maya Angelou, and Ken Follett, as well as celebrity authors such as Ann-Margret, Rush Limbaugh, and Dr. Ruth. But no one attracted more attention or applause than thirty-nine-year-old Oprah Winfrey, who was poised to publish her autobiography, which was expected to be the biggest-selling book in publishing history.

She was lionized by her publisher on Saturday evening of that weekend, at one of the most elaborate and expensive parties Alfred A. Knopf, the most prestigious publishing company in the book business, had ever thrown for an author. The exterior of Miami's International Palace was lit in purple as an homage to Oprah's favorite color and her first movie. Within the skyscraper, tables groaned with platters of shrimp the size of iPods for the eighteen hundred guests who swarmed around silver chafing dishes brimming with pasta, haunches of prime rib, and strips of sizzling sirloin. Tuxedoed waiters raced back and forth with trays of crystal flutes bubbling with champagne for booksellers more accustomed to cheap wine in paper cups.

Wearing a bright aqua suit, a once-again-thin Oprah arrived

on Stedman's arm and was introduced by the chairman of the board of Random House, Inc. She charmed everyone by saying she was so excited about her book that she wished she could get on *The Oprah Winfrey Show* to promote it. Although she had not yet started Oprah's Book Club, everyone knew what she could do for books she liked. Just two weeks earlier, she had taken her cameras to Iowa to do a segment on *The Bridges of Madison County*. The weeper was already a bestseller, but Oprah's show triggered an additional demand for 350,000 copies.

So it was understandable that as the featured speaker at the book and author breakfast the next morning, she would be received like Cleopatra on her barge for all of Rome to honor. The crowd was wall-to-wall and the applause was deafening as she approached the microphone. She began by saying that she thought everyone should sit down and write a book about themselves. "You can save yourself a huge therapy bill," she said. "For me, working on this book the past year and a half has been like ten years of therapy. I've learned so much about myself." She heaped praise on her collaborator, Joan Barthel, and quickly assured everyone that she had not written a celebrity kiss-and-tell. "I haven't done that much anyway, and besides, the people I did it with, you don't know 'em, so . . . you don't have to worry about that," she said to peals of laughter.

Turning on all of her telegenic charm, Oprah dazzled the booksellers with her often-told anecdotes—which, to those who had never seen her show, seemed fresh and spontaneous. She talked about growing up as "a poor little ole nappy-headed colored chile" who wanted to be Diana Ross "or just somebody supreme"; how she had to hide in a closet with a flashlight to read because her family made fun of her for being "an old bookworm" and accused her of "trying to be more than everybody else" because she loved books. She talked about her weight, how her bosses in Baltimore tried to make her over, and how she ended up bald. "You know you've got a struggle on your hands when you're black and fat and bald in America, *and* you're a woman on television," she said. Rocking with hilarity, the crowd clapped until their hands hurt.

"It doesn't matter how victimized any of us have been, we're all responsible for our lives," Oprah said. "This is a book about taking responsibility for the victories in your own life. Mine has been a wondrous amazing life. I grew up with feelings of not being loved, and that's why I feel so blessed to speak to 20 million viewers everyday who write . . . to tell me that they love me." She said she was going to bring people into bookstores who had never before been in them, words that fell on the assembled booksellers like manna from heaven. The idea of an adoring audience of twenty million potential book buyers made them giddy with anticipation. She concluded by adding high purpose to potential profit: "My goal is to uplift, encourage and empower people," she said. "I make no bones about wanting to really make a difference in the world, and I hope *Oprah: An Autobiography* will do just that."

Dizzy with delight, the booksellers jumped up to give her a standing ovation, shaking the coffee cups with reverberations from their applause. Here was an author who was going to lift every bookstore in the country and sprinkle gold dust on an entire industry. Publication was set for September 20, 1993; Knopf had announced a staggeringly large first printing of 750,000 copies; the Doubleday Book Club and the Literary Guild planned a direct mailing to five million homes; and, best of all, Oprah had promised to visit a different city every week in a thirty-city promotional tour from the fall of 1993 through the spring of 1994. Robert Wietrak, the director of merchandising for Barnes & Noble, was beside himself. "This will be the biggest book we've ever sold," he said.

Hearing the tsunami of praise pouring out of ABA, where Oprah had generated waves of rapture, reporters began calling Knopf, wanting to know more about her book. On June 9, 1993, fifteen weeks before publication, Erroll McDonald, Oprah's editor, told *The New York Times,* "Given that the media feeds off Oprah to a great degree, we don't want people to cannibalize the book before it comes out." He need not have worried.

Six days later Oprah called her publisher. "This is the hardest call I've ever had to make . . . but . . . I have to withdraw my book. . . . We can't publish now. . . . I have to postpone it."

After several anguished calls back and forth, the publisher pleading for Oprah to change her mind and Oprah apologizing profusely, at one point even offering to repay Knopf for the ABA party in her honor, she officially canceled publication with a statement that crushed booksellers: "I am in the heart of the learning curve. I feel there are important discoveries yet to be made."

The next day's headlines reflected the scale of the story that became national news:

"Oprah's Book Delay Leaves World Guessing" (*USA Today*)

"Rumors Still Swirl as Oprah Stays Silent" (*Los Angeles Sentinel*)

"More Lessons to Learn Before Oprah Tells All" (*New York Times*)

"Oprah Pulls Plug on Autobiography" (*Newsday*)

"Oprah Wanted Book to Be More Than Recitation" (*Chicago Sun-Times*)

Not surprisingly, the tabloid *Star* was the most explicit: "Why Oprah's Banning Her Sexy Tell-All Book."

Legally, Oprah could back away from her commitment to Knopf because she had not signed a standard contract, simply a nonbinding letter of agreement saying she would forgo an advance against royalties, but that she and the publisher would split all profits fifty-fifty. Customarily, authors receive an advance, and when the advance is earned out by book sales, they receive a percentage of the price of each book sold as a royalty. Oprah's copublishing arrangement with Knopf was extraordinary, and considering the early orders, was guaranteed to be phenomenally profitable for both author and publisher. The people at Knopf, where the book was now being called *Noprah*, tried to put the best face on what industry analysts estimated to be a $20 million loss.

"She felt she needed to put in more work," Erroll McDonald told reporters. "I think that the book, as it is, is very powerful and revealing, but I'm not its author."

The head of Knopf's public relations and publicity department, William T. Loverd, tried to soft-pedal the knockout punch. "She felt this was not the best job she could do," he said. "There was not enough of her in it. The book is only postponed."

Arlene Friedman, editor in chief of Doubleday Book Club, said, "We felt it was the book that every woman would want to read."

"The book is extremely strong and honest," said Sonny Mehta, the president and editor in chief of Knopf. "[But] it is her book, and we will of course abide by her wishes. We look forward to resuming work on the project when she is ready." And that, as Yiddish comics say, would be a year from Shavuos, the Jewish holiday that never comes.

Oprah's publicist was besieged by calls from reporters about the sudden cancellation, and she danced as fast as she could trying to interpret for them "the heart of the learning curve."

"Oprah felt it was premature [to publish] because she has a lot of positive things going on in her life right now that she would want to include in the book, like her marriage to Stedman and her recent weight loss from working out," said Colleen Raleigh. She explained that since Oprah's engagement she had been working with her chef and her trainer to try to lose eighty-five pounds by her fortieth birthday, and she was making excellent progress, but that didn't carry weight with reporters, who pushed for the real reason Oprah had canceled her book, asking if it was because of Stedman.

"No, no . . . Their relationship had nothing to do with it," said Raleigh. "It couldn't be stronger."

Despite Raleigh's best efforts, every news story on the book's cancellation carried the suggestion that Oprah's fiancé was aghast at what she had written about her past sex life, and pointed out that the couple had been officially engaged for seven months but still had not set a wedding date. Erroll McDonald tried to dismiss the idea that Oprah had derailed her book because of Stedman's objections. "That suggests that Oprah is at the mercy of what others say," he said, "that she's not capable of making up her own mind." But even he did not know what had really happened.

More confusing were the conflicting stories Oprah told about whether or not she and Stedman had ever set a wedding date. In October 1993 she told *Ebony:*

> We had decided it was going to be this fall. I had made an appointment with Oscar de la Renta. I was going to consult with the almanac on what week the leaves would be the best color and all that stuff. And then this whole book thing erupted. So we're going to resume talking about it, I guess.

The next month (November 1993), she told *Chicago* magazine:

> We are still getting married. But we did not set a date. Never. Let me say it again: We . . . did . . . not . . . set . . . a date. So how can we put it off? That was a notion concocted out of thin air by the press. It has nothing to do with the truth of Stedman and me. . . . But we will do it [get married]. Does that answer your question? This impression that we've broken up and gotten back together and broken up again, it is absolutely, categorically not true. Not true. It's a media-created story. Let me say again, it is not true . . . we have never broken up. Not once.

That same month (November 1993) a writer from *McCall's* interviewed her and noticed the books sitting on her desk: Martha Stewart's *Weddings,* Eleanor Munro's *Wedding Readings,* and a paperback titled *Wedding Planner.* Yet Oprah said, "I have never set a date for the wedding. It's because of the tabloids that there's a public perception the wedding has been on and off. I am in no hurry to get married. I dislike this notion of a desperate woman who wants to get married."

Four months later (February 1994) she told *Ladies' Home Journal:*

> There was a time in my life when I needed marriage to validate myself. But now I'm very content with what my relationship gives me. . . . I'm very sorry I ever mentioned Stedman's name to

the press. This whole wedding thing might not be such a big issue, if I had never mentioned it.

Then in *Vogue* (October 1998) she said:

We were supposed to get married September 8, 1993. Because that was my father's wedding day. My book, the big autobiography thing, was supposed to come out on September 12 and Stedman said, "All of that's gonna get confused. You can't do both at the same time. So we should postpone the wedding." So I said, "OK, fine. We'll postpone it." And I will tell you, it has never been discussed again. It is not even an issue. The relationship works.

Perhaps her most telling comment was to the *Daily Mail* (February 2006):

He proposed about ten years ago, so I called a little gathering of a few friends and I was trembling. Gayle said, "That's just cold feet." I said, "This is not just cold feet; it's two feet in an ice bucket." At the time we'd been together almost a decade. We'd chosen the date and my autobiography was supposed to be coming out two days after the wedding. Stedman said he did not approve of the book because telling the truth about my life would embarrass my family, and why would I want to do that?

While Stedman was aware of Oprah's traumatic childhood and the sexual molestation she had endured, her teenage pregnancy, her promiscuity, her disastrous affair with the married man in Baltimore, and even her past drug use, he was not prepared for the jolt of seeing it all laid out so starkly on the page. He objected to her naming the men in her family who had sexually abused her, and he was especially disturbed by the harsh way she had written about her mother.

For years Oprah had been telling viewers and interviewers that her mother had abandoned her shortly after she was born. "I was not wanted," she had said. "I was born in shame." Only after her collaborator, Joan Barthel, did some preliminary research did Oprah realize that her mother had been with her in Kosciusko for the first four and a half years of her life before leaving her in the care of her own mother, Hattie Mae Lee, to go "up North" to find a better-paying job. Yet in her autobiography, Oprah blamed her mother for the sexual molestation that befell her after she moved to Milwaukee, and Stedman objected. "Your mother doesn't need to read that she was not there for you," he said.

Oprah had also named all her sexual abusers, including her favorite uncle, Trenton Winfrey, who was still alive. In addition, Oprah felt her father had let her down when she tried to tell him what his brother had done to her during the summer of 1968. "I was in a rage about my abusers," she said. "I went into complete detail of the whole rape scene. How lonely that feels when you're ten [sic] years old and you're somebody's play thing. . . . I was not responsible. No child is. Those men abused me, a baby. And there is nothing more despicable."

She also wrote about her pregnancy at the age of fourteen. "Where I spent half the time in denial and half trying to hurt myself to lose the child."

Stedman felt that such private matters should be discussed within the family and not on the pages of a book for everyone to read. He later flew to Nashville to talk to Vernon Winfrey, who called his daughter and then came to her Indiana farm to say he was sorry about how he had reacted to her story of rape.

"I know she feels that I didn't handle it well [when she first told us]," Vernon said. "But Trent [who died in 1997] was my closest brother. We were torn." Vernon later admitted that Trent was probably the father of Oprah's baby.

Oprah recalled the conversation with her father at the farm as unsatisfactory. He had said, " 'Were you raped? Did he rape you?' What he was saying was, 'Were you forced against your will? Did you actively participate?' That's when I said, 'You don't get it. When you're 13 [sic] years old and in the car and it's happening, it is rape.' "

Oprah had also written about her drug use and smoking crack with her married lover in Baltimore. "I thought he was more open and more loving with me [when we were doing drugs]. I had heard about Richard Pryor freebasing but when it was offered to me, I didn't know that that's what it was." This was a brave admission on Oprah's part. She later went public about her drug use because, as she said, "There are some people who knew it was in the book and had been threatening to go to the press. So because I am a public person more and more shame became attached to the secret."

She admitted her foray into smoking crack in the comfortable setting of her own show in 1995, while tearfully empathizing with two recovering female addicts. "I did your drug," she told a woman who was addicted to crack cocaine, and those four little words made headlines. The British journalist Ginny Dougary found Oprah's confession oddly so-what-ish. "Sensational revelation, including the host's own, is the show's stock in trade," she wrote. "[But this was] unshocking after all the fuss in the press because Oprah never specified the precise nature of her drug use." Dougary asked her if she was a cocaine addict. "No, I was not addicted," Oprah said. Years later Randy Cook, her live-in drug partner for five months in 1985, disputed her statement.

Oprah acknowledged that her fiancé, understandably, was not enthusiastic about what she had written. "He didn't say anything was too explicit or shouldn't be said. He said it wasn't powerful enough." She felt her book lacked "clarity" and "introspection," and Stedman, a devotee of self-help and how-to books, said that it lacked "inspiration." He wanted her book to be more than an autobiography. "My experiences were meant to empower people," she said, "and make sense of life."

Yet Stedman's objections to the tone and content of her book were not the sole justifications for the cancellation. In a private conversation with a man who had received a telephone call from Oprah, she said, "The reason I pulled my book was because Maya Angelou came to me after the big ABA announcement and said, 'Is there anything in that book that is exaggerated? Is there anything that is not true in that book?' I said, 'Well, yeah, some things are written to read well. You know that. Some things are, you know . . .'

"No, baby, I don't know," said Maya. "I only know that you cannot have one exaggerated story, one untruth, one embroidered recollection. You cannot. If you do, take that book back. Do not publish it."

Angelou understood her friend's tendency to embellish for effect, perhaps pad a story for a laugh or a little sympathy. Angelou, who loved Oprah like a daughter, did not want her to be publicly humiliated by the media, which she said would peck her to death if they found manufactured anecdotes.

Interestingly, one of the publishers who read the manuscript, but whose company did not acquire it, was more concerned about Oprah's hard truths than her soft lies, particularly what she wrote about being a prostitute—the first time she had ever used that word to describe her adolescent promiscuity.

"I told her at the time she didn't need to tell people about that," said the publisher. "It was not necessary for everyone to know she had been a prostitute. Besides, I knew that she'd see it in print and pull back, which is exactly what she did. I've published enough celebrity memoirs to know what can happen between the initial excitement of selling their story and then actually publishing it. Once they see the seamy stuff down on the page that they left behind in their crawl to the top, they pull back. They either delete it or rewrite it. . . . It's called revisionist history."

The story of Oprah's days as an adolescent prostitute had been partially disclosed by her sister in the *National Enquirer* in 1990, but the tabloid revelation was ignored by the mainstream media, so those who did not read the grocery store press had no idea about Oprah's sordid past beyond what she chose to share on her show. For her now to admit in her autobiography that she had once been a prostitute—that was the hard truth; the unvarnished version of what her sister had described as Oprah making money by sneaking men into the house to do "The Horse"—was guaranteed to be headline-making news. Such an admission would be particularly difficult for her father, who still could not bring himself to use the word *prostitute* to describe his teenage daughter. To this day he cannot face that truth. Instead, he characterizes that troubled period of Oprah's life as one of her "dark secrets."

Oprah was so concerned about Angelou's warning that she summoned her and six other equally close friends to her farm in Indiana for the weekend after ABA. She gave all seven, including Stedman and Gayle, copies of the manuscript and asked for their honest assessment of whether she should go forward with publication. To a person, each recommended she cancel. During that weekend she was made to see that some people might not react kindly to finding out that what she had always called her "adolescent sexual promiscuity" was actually prostitution. Having been sexually abused as a child, she had garnered great sympathy from her audiences, who saw her as a victim of vicious predators and someone who had gone on to do great things to help other victims. Why mar that now? Why put forward something that could obliterate all the goodwill she had accumulated? Viewers might not be prepared to accept their heroine as a former hooker, or overlook the gulf between adolescent promiscuity and selling yourself for money. No one wanted Oprah to chip away at the pedestal on which she stood. "Why give them a club?" was the general reaction of those who wanted to protect her. She had constructed a revered public image as someone who had triumphed over racism, poverty, and sexual abuse, and to now admit to something like this might diminish all that. Her enemies would pounce, her fans could feel betrayed, and her sponsors might withdraw. It was simply too big a risk.

In the past Oprah controlled the release of information about herself, except for her sister's tabloid revelations about her teenage pregnancy. Her sister had alluded to her prostitution, but even in that case Oprah had issued a carefully worded statement about her pregnancy and been allowed to retreat into silence without being subjected to the probing questions of reporters. She would not be given the luxury of that kind of control on a thirty-city book promotional tour during which she could be asked the kinds of questions she frequently asked of others, especially young women, who had sold themselves for money.

A reading of a few of Oprah's past shows indicates how she attempted to explore the subject of the world's oldest profession, prostitution:

- "Profiling Prostitutes" (11/6/86)
- "Call Girls and Madams" (10/29/87)
- "Housewife Prostitutes" (9/5/88)
- "Suburban Teens: The New Prostitutes" (9/25/88)
- "Who Really Goes to Prostitutes?" (10/31/96)
- "Living a Secret Life" (9/21/04)
- "Children Being Sold into Sexual Slavery" (11/2/05)
- "Inside the Lives of Young Prostitutes" (5/8/06)
- "Inside the Notorious Bunny Ranch Brothel" (4/29/09)

Oprah wanted to play a prostitute on-screen after hearing Gloria Steinem's true story about a woman who had been jailed for prostitution and wondered why her pimps and her customers weren't in jail with her. The woman went to the prison library for law books, and upon her release continued studying until she finished high school, attended college at night, and finally became a lawyer. "I'm definitely going to do a lusty romantic role," said Oprah, "based on that true story. . . . I'll get to be a hooker and have a pimp. Can't wait for that."

After reading Endesha Ida Mae Holland's autobiographical script about her childhood as a prostitute and her eventual involvement in the civil rights movement, Oprah joined four other women in 1991 to finance a production of *From the Mississippi Delta* at New York's Circle in the Square Theatre.

Years later she returned to the subject of prostitution in one of her *After the Show* segments, which she taped for the Oxygen network. She interviewed the writer Jeannette Angell, who received a master's degree from the Yale Divinity School and later wrote a book titled *Callgirl*, chronicling her three years as a prostitute. The book is blunt and unapologetic about what she did to pay for her education. "It's really the ideal college job," Angell told the *Yale Daily News.* "I hate to say this but it's true. It's the perfect way to get through school because you have a minimum of time commitment for a maximum of money."

Oprah was less than hospitable to Angell, and from her facial expressions and cold tone of voice, she appeared to look down on her. "Boy, was your high school shocked," Oprah said. "Did you feel bad . . . did you feel high about it? Is it like a blind date? I'm just curious how do you do that? Do you get more [money] for . . . um . . . other things? Is there at least a pretense? . . . Do you have a conversation first?"

The writer soldiered through the segment and tried to laugh off what was a contentious examination by America's most beloved talk show host. When asked how she felt about getting fricasseed by Oprah Winfrey on national television after being promised a supportive environment in which to tell her story, Jeannette Angell responded by email: "Unfortunately, I am contractually prohibited from speaking or writing about my experience with anyone at Harpo. The company has far more and far better attorneys than I can afford. You may find that this is true of many people—even people who were with me, but not actually on the show, were obliged to sign contracts. With hindsight that should have raised a red flag right there. I wish I had seen it then."

Oprah reconsidered going public with her youthful tiptoe into prostitution, and after listening to her closest friends, she decided to cancel publication of her memoir. She later said it was the smartest thing she ever did, and from her point of view, she was absolutely right, although the writer Gretchen Reynolds said she "called down upon herself the worst publicity of her career." That characterization seemed a bit overblown for the relatively mild press reaction to Oprah's announcement, but it certainly captured Oprah's own excessive descriptions of her personal experiences, which were always "the most devastating," "the most difficult," "the worst," "the most painful," "the most awful."

Yet, while she always seemed to reach for the superlative to describe her feelings as a victim, she felt her book lacked the emotional insight to make it resonate with readers. She was unable to convey the beguiling contradictions that made her so fascinating, particularly the intriguing composition of a deeply secretive woman whose universal appeal sprang from her openness and her supposed spontaneity. It's part of the human condition to have two selves in the same psyche, but Oprah felt she could not chance exposing her dark self and possibly diminish the luminosity of her bright self.

She also worried that canceling the book would make "all the people at Knopf hate me," so the following year she gave the publisher her chef's book of low-fat recipes and wrote the foreword for *In the Kitchen with Rosie*. Oprah's newly slimmed body was the book's best advertisement, but she also invited Rosie onto the show on the day of publication. As a result, the book sold more than a million copies within the first three weeks. A year later it was in its thirty-sixth printing, with 5.9 million copies sold.

"I told Knopf, 'I think this is going to be big.' They were only printing about 400,000 copies," said Oprah. "I called Sonny Mehta and said, 'I don't think that's going to be enough.' He said, 'Oprah, you don't understand. We've done Julia Child, all the great cookbooks, and I'm telling you, 400,000 is an extraordinary amount for a cookbook. It's unheard of.' And I go, 'OK. You don't know what you're dealing with here.' I had been dieting ten years straight on TV. People saw this book as the answer.... It [became] the fastest selling book in the history of publishing. I can't resist an I-Told-You-So. That's really a character flaw. Wooo, I can't resist. Kinda live for that moment when an I-Told-You-So has to come up. So when you couldn't find the book in the stores, and there were waiting lists everywhere, I couldn't resist calling up Sonny Mehta, who's operating presses 24 hours a day, and saying, 'Sonny, I recall telling you . . .' And he said . . . 'Never in the history of publishing have we seen anything like it. Never. It's a phenomenon. No one could have predicted it.' [I said,] 'I tried to tell you.' "

With her own book canceled and her wedding now on hold, Oprah said she needed a grand Hollywood party to celebrate her fortieth birthday on January 29, 1994. She turned the planning over to Debra DiMaio, a maniac for detail, with only one request: that the weekend include a slumber party. This childhood ritual had been a surprise gift for her birthday the year before. "We even had her favorite Dr. Denton's footie pajamas waiting for her," recalled Gayle King. "As a kid, she never had sleepovers. She never even had a bicycle."

Gayle, on the other hand, grew up with all the comforts of an upper-middle-class family, including a maid and a swimming pool. The eldest of four daughters, she lived with her parents in California before moving to Chevy Chase, Maryland. She had met Oprah in Baltimore, after graduating from the University of Maryland. Pursuing her television career, Gayle moved to Kansas City, Missouri, where she became the local anchor. There she met William G. Bumpus, a policeman. They moved to Hartford, Connecticut, and married in 1982. Oprah was the reluctant maid of honor.

She admitted years later that she was sad at her best friend's wedding. "I just didn't think it was going to work out," she told Gayle in a joint interview in 2006. "You know how you go to weddings and they're full of joy. . . . I didn't feel that at yours. . . . It just felt it was kind of pitiful. I never told you because it wasn't my place to say that. . . . Maybe I couldn't feel the joy because I was feeling like our friendship was going to change. But it didn't."

That was unfortunate for Gayle's husband. "I knew them well in the early days [1985–1990]," said Oprah's good friend Nancy Stoddart. "Nile and I took ski weekends with Oprah and Stedman, and spent country weekends with Gayle and Billy. He was a cop then . . . and there was no way he could [provide for Gayle the way Oprah could]. He was pretty resentful of the effect that Oprah's fame was having on their relationship. . . . Billy later went to Yale Law School, became a lawyer, and is now assistant attorney general for the state of Connecticut. . . . He's done great stuff for himself. . . . At the time, he wanted to provide his family with a new house, but Oprah came in and bought Gayle a one-million-dollar home, which in those days was huge—just huge."

Gayle divorced Bumpus in 1992 because, as she said, "he cheated," and Oprah encouraged her to leave him rather than forgive his extramarital affair. "I've been to five therapists," Gayle said, "and nobody's been better than Oprah in terms of [my] marriage/life counseling." Bill Bumpus told a reporter in 1992 that he blamed Oprah for the breakup. "She didn't mean to hurt us, it wasn't malicious, but she ruined our marriage with her generosity and her insistence on taking up so much of Gayle's time. There probably are lots of husbands who complain about their wives watching *Oprah*, but at least they can turn off the television set. They don't have Oprah calling at all hours of the day and night. They don't have her buying their wives expensive presents. They don't have her giving their families things they can't afford. . . ." In the divorce, Bumpus paid one dollar and signed over to Gayle ownership of the million-dollar house Oprah had purchased.

By the time of Oprah's fortieth birthday, Gayle had been divorced two years. She continued to live and work as an anchorwoman in Connecticut, in order to share with her ex-husband custody of their two children. Oprah flew her back and forth to Chicago so they could spend more time together. Gayle described those trips as episodes from *Lifestyles of the Rich and Famous*. "The limo picks you up and everything is taken care of. You can literally go [to see Oprah] with five dollars in your pockets and return with $4.99—because you spent a penny for some gum."

For the celebration of her fortieth, Oprah had emailed her staff, which always fêted her birthdays, that no gifts were expected and none would be accepted. But for the special party in California, "40 for Oprah's 40th," as the engraved invitations read, she relented and said guests could bring a copy of their favorite book for her library.

"All year Oprah's been looking forward to turning forty," said Debra DiMaio. "For her it is part of a very positive milestone."

At a cost of $130,000, she flew everyone, including Stedman, Gayle, Maya Angelou, select members of her staff, her private photographer, and her five bodyguards, to Los Angeles on a private jet and gave them all $1,000-a-night suites at the Hotel Bel-Air. The celebration began with a dinner Friday evening at L'Orangerie that, according to press reports, cost more than $15,000. In a long white gown, Oprah, escorted by Stedman, greeted guests, including Steven Spielberg, Tina Turner, Julius "Dr. J" Irving, Quincy Jones and Nastassja Kinski, Maria Shriver and Arnold Schwarzenegger, and Sidney Poitier and his wife, Joanna. Oprah's photographer took pictures of everyone with Oprah, got them developed, placed them in sterling-silver frames, and gift-wrapped them by the end of the evening so that she could give each guest a memento of the dinner, just like Queen Elizabeth II does for guests at state dinners.

The next day, Debra arranged for a fleet of black stretch limousines to chauffeur everyone to lunch at The Ivy, to Montana Avenue in Santa Monica for a shopping spree, and then to the home of Maria Shriver and Arnold Schwarzenegger for a tea party. That night, leaving spouses and partners behind, the women headed for Oprah's bungalow for a slumber party.

During that evening they brainstormed about what they could do to extend Oprah's spiritual reach. Each believed that Oprah was a blessed disciple, a special messenger sent from God to do good. Maya Angelou later put the feeling into words: "In a queer way . . . she holds a spiritual position not unlike Norman Vincent Peale once did. Each culture and each time has its . . . moral mountains that we looked up to. . . . These are people, who, to lesser or greater degrees, are really the lights, the pinnacles of what is right and kind and true and good and moral. Well . . . she's sort of that."

Sipping Cristal champagne (Oprah's favorite), and led by her spiritual guru Marianne Williamson, self-described as "the bitch for God," the women decided that Oprah should contact the Pope, and together the two of them could lead the world in a weekend of prayer. No one voiced the slightest concern that an American talk show host might appear slightly brazen to be calling the Vatican to arrange a global pray-in with His Holiness. The papal weekend never took place, but such was Oprah's power at the time that national leaders—U.S. senators, presidential candidates, First Ladies—clamored to be on her show. Being in a position to pick and choose her guests, she no longer granted access to just any important personage. When it was suggested that she should interview Mother Teresa, the nun who ministered to the poor of Calcutta, Oprah vetoed the idea. "I don't think she's much of a talker," she said. "That would be a long hour on television."

The all-female slumber party ended with a group prayer led

by Marianne Williamson, and Oprah left determined to present more spiritual and less sensational shows in the future. "I've been guilty of doing trash TV and not even thinking it was trash," she told *Entertainment Weekly*. She later made a mea culpa to *TV Guide* and resolved to elevate her shows. Her timing was perfect. Within a year, William Bennett, who wrote the bestselling *The Book of Virtues*, joined forces with Senator Joseph Lieberman (D-Conn.) to denounce daytime television talk shows and the companies that produced them. Bennett, who was contemplating a presidential run in 1996, exempted Oprah and Phil Donahue because he had been on their shows to promote his books, but he castigated the hosts, owners, guests, advertisers, and viewers of Jerry Springer, Sally Jessy Raphael, Ricki Lake, Jenny Jones, Montel Williams, and Geraldo Rivera, saying they all must share the blame for the televised "rot" that "degrades human personality." A few years later Bennett, satirized as "The Virtues Czar," was publicly exposed as a compulsive gambler, and he apologized for blowing $8 million in Las Vegas, but his rant on rot had been effective. Procter & Gamble, the nation's biggest daytime television advertiser, announced its decision to pull $15 million to $20 million in advertising from four daytime talk shows, and Sears, Roebuck and Co. did the same, citing "offensive content" as the reason.

Flying back to Chicago after her birthday celebration, Oprah felt she had launched her forty-first year in great style. Finally in shape thanks to Bob Greene and his twice-daily workouts, she announced she was starting to train for the Marine Corps Marathon in October. Having pared herself down to a trim size eight, she again decided she would never need her "fat" wardrobe, so she staged a benefit sale of nine hundred dresses, plus hundreds of pants, blouses, and jackets, at the Hyatt Regency in Chicago for two thousand of the fifty thousand viewers who sent in postcards for tickets. She reserved fifteen special outfits to sell at a silent auction, including the purple sequined dress she had worn to the premiere of *The Color Purple* in 1985. She raised $150,000, which she donated to Chicago's Hull House and to FamiliesFirst in Sacramento, California.

The day before the *The Oprah Winfrey Show* was to go on summer hiatus in 1994, her senior producers presented her with their ultimatum: Either the "dictatorial" Debra DiMaio goes or we go. Having lost a dozen producers and associate producers over the last two years, Oprah could not afford any more staff upheaval. So she called in her executive producer, who was also vice president of Harpo, one of her oldest friends, and her closest professional colleague, and allowed her to resign. DiMaio signed a lifetime confidentiality agreement that she would never speak or write about her association with Oprah, and she walked out of Harpo with a check for $3.8 million. Oprah was now without the hard nose and soft shoulder of the woman who had functioned as her alter ego for the past ten years. Within the industry the unexplained departure of DiMaio, who had launched Oprah into national syndication and kept her at number one, resounded like thunder. Her successor, Dianne Hudson, pledged to keep the show "out of the talk-show gutter." Oprah immediately closed the studio, dispatched her staff, and disappeared on vacation, where she was "not available" for media calls, all of which fell again to Colleen Raleigh, her publicist.

In losing DiMaio, Oprah had lost her executive producer, chief of staff, party planner, confidante, nanny, and buffer against Jeff Jacobs. As a consequence, she became even more dependent on her personal assistant, Beverly Coleman, who soon caved under the strain and resigned two months later, saying she was "totally burned out." Oprah offered her $1 million to stay, but Beverly said she could no longer take the twenty-four-hour workdays.

Then, in September, Colleen Raleigh gave notice, and a few weeks later she sued Oprah for breach of contract, claiming she had been promised $200,000 in severance pay, $17,500 in back pay, and $6,000 in vacation pay. "As a public relations professional with a reputation as a reliable and honest source, she was no longer able, in good conscience, to foster the image of Oprah Winfrey, *The Oprah Winfrey Show,* and Harpo as happy and harmonious and humane," said Raleigh's lawyer. "She was continually placed in the position of trying to hide the truth about the disorganized management of Harpo" and about Oprah's "tumultuous partner-ship" with her company's chief operating officer, Jeffrey Jacobs. "Colleen devoted eight years of her life to Ms. Winfrey, but could no longer work in an environment of dishonesty and chaos."

Infuriated at being publicly embarrassed, Oprah told re-porters she would fight Raleigh's suit to the bitter end. "There will be no settlement," she said. Her lawyers tried to get the lawsuit dismissed, but managed only to require Raleigh's lawyer to file amended complaints. This continued for months, until Oprah was hit with interrogatories requiring her to respond under oath to questions about her turbulent relationship with Jeffrey Jacobs and all the work she had made Colleen Raleigh do for Stedman Graham to promote him and his business with the Graham Williams Group and Athletes Against Drugs, and to help him promote his clients the American Double-Dutch League World Invitational Championship and the Volvo Tennis Tournament. After four more months of court pleadings, Oprah saw that it was in her best interest (and Stedman's) to pay off her former employee and bind Colleen Raleigh for life with a confi-dentiality agreement that prevented her from ever talking or writing about her or Harpo. So, on March 29, 1996, Oprah set-tled the Raleigh lawsuit and put into place even more binding lifetime confidentiality agreements so that her employees— past, present, and future—could never talk or write about her. Now they were forbidden to take any candid photos of her, and banned from using cameras, camera phones, and tape recorders at work. These agreements were not simply for Harpo employ-ees but for everyone within her realm—guests on her show, do-mestic workers, caterers, security guards, pilots, dog walkers, chauffeurs, upholsterers, the little man in Washington, D.C., who waxed her eyebrows, the physician in Maryland who gave her Botox shots, and the head of the Oprah Winfrey Leadership Academy in South Africa. When asked about her gag rule over her universe, Oprah said, "It's all about trust," not realizing it was all about her distrust.

She expected her friends to abide by her dictates on not photographing her without her permission, and most did, with the exception of Henry Louis Gates, Jr., known as "Skip," who could not resist the temptation to sneak snapshots of her on his cell phone. "He likes to come into the faculty room and show us the pictures he's secretly taken of Oprah without her knowledge," said a professor at Harvard University.

Professionally, 1994 was the worst year of Oprah's life. She had driven her staff to exhaustion, and when her senior producers threatened to walk out because they no longer could endure the demands of Debra DiMaio for bigger and better ratings, she had to allow her dear friend to resign. By that point Oprah believed she had evolved beyond what Debra could deliver into a more exalted realm than a mere talk show host. She saw herself as a God-inspired missionary with a divine message to deliver. She no longer wanted to lead the trash pack. Instead, she sought the kind of respect that does not come from tabloid programming. With the exodus of DiMaio, Oprah decided to raise her show out of the gutter. She had read a report in *The Journal of Popular Culture* written by Vicki Abt, professor of sociology at Penn State, titled "The Shameless World of Phil, Sally, and Oprah." Now encouraged by her senior producers, she decided to chase her glory with a softer focus.

Professor Abt was surprised by Oprah's sudden about-face, but not filled with admiration. "I'm glad she has changed, but it's ten years and $350 million later. I think a lot of what these people do is self-serving. They do the dirty deed and then they cry mea culpa."

The year ended with a sucker punch when the December 1994 issue of *Redbook* hit the stands. The article, titled "Christmas at Oprah's," by former Harpo producer Dan Santow, looked like a frothy recollection of how Harpo employees honored their boss at Christmas and how she generously reciprocated. In between the lines was a searing X-ray of wretched excess and unimaginable extravagance in the workplace. Most damning was the fawning obeisance to the multi-millionaire boss and the slavish time and attention spent purchasing and presenting her gifts. This office ritual later evolved into the annual holiday show called "Oprah's Favorite Things," in which sponsors donated thousands of dollars' worth of merchandise that Oprah selected throughout the year as one of her favorite things (e.g., HDTV refrigerators, diamond necklaces, Black-Berrys, digital video cameras, flat-screen televisions) and then gave to her audience, complete with a list of retail prices.

Prior to that time, Debra DiMaio had organized the yearly Christmas luncheon, which lasted eleven hours so that Oprah and her senior producers could exchange presents. "The actual presentation of the gift at this luncheon was [extremely] important," recalled Santow, who was new to the staff and could not believe that Oprah really cared about how a gift was wrapped.

"She notices everything," he was told. The year before, Debra had given Oprah an antique porcelain tea set, and she had hand-stamped the tissue wrapping paper with little cups and saucers.

"I bet she didn't even notice," someone said.

"I bet she did," said DiMaio, picking up the phone. "Oprah, I'm here in my office with all of the producers. . . . We're just curious, but do you remember the tea service I gave you last year?"

"The one with the hand-stamped tissue paper?"

Santow started sweating.

A month before the 1993 Christmas luncheon producers had received an email from DiMaio asking them to answer a survey for Oprah:

1. List your hat, sweater, shoe, dress, glove and shirt size.
2. List five really expensive gift items I would cry with delight if I received.
3. Here is where you can purchase them: list stores, addresses and 800 numbers.
4. List five things that would make me very happy to receive as a gift.
5. List five possible gifts that you could buy and I would harbor no resentment toward you throughout the year.
6. Here are five gifts I would hate.
7. Here are five stores you should avoid buying me anything at.

The day of the luncheon Oprah began the gift-giving by handing her personal assistant, Beverly Coleman, a small box. Inside was a brochure of a Jeep Cherokee, and outside a horn was blaring. Then everyone heard Oprah's theme song, "I'm Every Woman." The producers ran to the window and saw the shiny black Jeep Grand Cherokee awaiting Beverly from the boss who saw herself as Everywoman. Her other stupendous gifts to her producers included: a Bang & Olufsen stereo system, a set of luggage with $10,000 worth of travel gift certificates, diamond earrings, and a truckload of antique furniture. She gave her executive producer a year's certificate for once-a-month dinners with friends in different cities around the world—Montreal, Paris, London—all expenses paid.

"When you work for one of the richest and most famous entertainers in America," said the *Redbook* subtitle, "two questions rule your holiday season: What will you give her? And what will you get?" The article hit Harpo like a wrecking ball. Yet, as one former employee said, "It wasn't a complete takedown. . . . I remember on Santow's list of 'Five Things That Would Make Me Very Happy to Receive as a Gift,' he had written 'Anything by Modigliani.' He saw Oprah a couple days later and she asked him if Modigliani was a local artist. I know he felt embarrassed for her that she didn't know who Modigliani was, and if he'd put that into the article he might have made her look really foolish."

Dan Santow retained the distinction of being one of the last employees to get over the fence without signing a lifetime confidentiality agreement, and the only one to put his hand in the cage to write about working for Oprah. His article dropped the hammer on all of Harpo, binding each and every future employee to a lifetime of silence about their employer. He also put an end to the annual rite of the producers' Christmas luncheon.

# $F$ifteen

JUST WHEN Oprah decided to yank her show out of the trough of trash television, she lost one million viewers. But so did all the other talk show hosts. None of them—not Donahue, Geraldo, Jenny Jones, Ricki Lake, Sally Jessy Raphael, Jerry Springer—could compete with O. J. Simpson and the most notorious murder in American history. On June 17, 1994, they were all run over by a white Bronco leading police on a sixty-mile chase across the freeways of Los Angeles with cameras whirring overhead as helicopters followed the sport utility vehicle until it finally stopped at Simpson's Tudor mansion in Brentwood. There he was immediately arrested, charged, and jailed for the slashing murders of his ex-wife Nicole Brown Simpson and her friend Ron Goldman.

For the next sixteen months every lurid detail of the vicious crime was disseminated and debated on television as the country became fixated on all things O. J. Court TV shows were created to analyze the crime, the suspect, the victims and their families, the prosecutors, the defense team, and the judge, who welcomed cameras to his courtroom, where the trial was televised live. Reporters such as ABC's Terry Moran, MSNBC's Dan Abrams, and Greta Van Susteren of Fox News became celebrities simply for covering the O. J. Simpson trial, and twentieth-century Americans sat in front of their television sets like Romans once gathered in the Colosseum to watch lions devour Christians and gladiators battle for their lives.

People who did not know their next-door neighbors came to know everyone associated with Orenthal James Simpson: his bumptious houseguest, Kato Kaelin; the 911 operator who took the call from Nicole in 1989 as O. J. was beating her; the criminal defense attorney Johnnie ("If it doesn't fit, you must acquit") Cochran; the prosecutors, Marcia Clark and Christopher Darden; the celebrity-loving judge, Lance Ito; and the disgraced LAPD detective Mark Fuhrman, whose racial epithet and Fifth Amendment evasions greatly swayed the jury. As Eric Zorn wrote in the *Chicago Tribune:* "The O. J. Simpson trial became the most tabloid friendly story since Elvis died on the toilet."

Until that night in June 1994, Simpson had reigned as the golden boy of American sports, who, upon retirement from football, never stopped hearing the cheers. The former Heisman Trophy winner, who for most of his career played for the Buffalo Bills, extended his fame as the high-flying star who galloped through airports in a series of television commercials for Hertz rent-a-car. He appeared in films such as *The Towering Inferno* and *The Naked Gun,* and worked with stars such as Paul Newman, Fred Astaire, Faye Dunaway, and Sophia Loren. He played golf at the most exclusive country clubs and received hefty honorariums just for showing up at Hollywood benefits to smile and shake hands. A black man embraced by white America, O. J. Simpson had it all—money, position, national recognition, and universal respect—until the night his ex-wife was found butchered alongside the waiter who had stopped by her house to return the sunglasses she had left at the Mezzaluna Trattoria earlier in the evening.

When the trial began in January 1995, Oprah saw her ratings tank. "I can look at the numbers and say, 'Was Kato on the stand? Who was on the stand?' Like yesterday, our numbers shot up a point and a half from what they've averaged for the past couple weeks because there was no court." Tim Bennett, the new president of Harpo Productions, defended her dip in the ratings. "While these are not the most outstanding numbers we've ever had, they're leading our nearest competitor by close to

100 percent. What other genre in all of television—comedies in prime time, network newscasts, late-night talk shows—can claim that?" He conceded the impact of the trial coverage "to the tune of 15 percent almost on a daily basis."

During the court's first day off in April 1995, Oprah leaped to recoup some of that lost percentage by booking four network trial commentators, plus the writer Dominick Dunne, who had been given a prize seat in the judge's courtroom because he was covering the trial for *Vanity Fair*. As soon as Oprah's audience had a chance to speak, they quickly established themselves as passionately in support of O. J. Simpson, and for the next six months they and the rest of the country wrangled about whether he could or would or should be found guilty. The debate went on behind the scenes at Harpo as well, and Oprah decided to do a show on October 3, 1995, following the verdict. When it was announced that O. J. was found not guilty, she appeared visibly shocked. Most of the black members of her audience shrieked and clapped and danced around, while some of the white members sat in stunned, disbelieving silence. The trial had splintered the country on race. Polls showed that 72 percent of white Americans believed O. J. was guilty, while 71 percent of black Americans believed he was innocent. Although privately Oprah had predicted the outcome, publicly she stood with white America. Ten years later polls recorded a shift, with only 40 percent of black Americans believing O. J. innocent, which brought black opinions closer to those of whites.

"For a long time after that, people wrote in asking what I was really thinking when they read the Not Guilty verdict," Oprah said. "So here it is: I was completely shocked. I couldn't believe that verdict. As a journalist, I was trying to keep some sense of balance in the midst of my own very strong opinions, but it was difficult to do that day." It was surprising to hear Oprah identify herself as a journalist, trying to keep "strong opinions" at bay. Rather, she was a shrewd talk show host not wanting to alienate members of her audience who believed O. J. should have been found not guilty.

A former Harpo employee remembers that before the verdict, those in the control room predicted O. J. would be convicted, but Oprah disagreed. "You don't know my people," she said of the predominantly black jury, understanding that Mark Fuhrman's racist comments would deny him any credibility among African American jurors. Publicly she said there was a perception among black people that almost all white people feel the way Fuhrman did. In a column for the *Nashville Banner*, Oprah's friend and former coworker at WTVF-TV, Ruth Ann Leach, focused on Oprah's belief that "most white people harbor deep hatred of black people." Pointing out that "Oprah's entire career has been nurtured, supported and made possible mainly by white people," Leach wrote, "This woman knows full well that she is worshipped by millions of white Americans. If she still feels that most whites hate most blacks, what must the less privileged people of color feel? Whites claim to be baffled by the polls that show African Americans believe O. J. Simpson did not do the crimes. How could anyone dismiss every drop of blood, every strand of fiber? Easily. Black people—not limited to the ladies and gentlemen of the jury—simply did not believe anything the racist cops and their racist support teams produced as evidence."

For two days after the verdict, Oprah dedicated her shows to "O. J. Simpson: The Aftermath." The tabloids reported that she had been promised his first broadcast interview, which she rushed to deny. "I will never interview O. J. Simpson," she declared. Days later she welcomed the TV star Loni Anderson, ex-wife of Burt Reynolds, who Anderson said had thrown her into furniture and smashed her head against the wall of their Hollywood home. Oprah looked shocked.

"I've had it with men who beat up women," she said. Turning to her audience, she announced she was banning all wife-beaters from her show. She again recited the humiliation of her married lover walking out on her in Baltimore and slamming the door on her hand. "I remember falling to the floor and crying. I remember being down on that floor and saying, 'Who am I really?' From that time on I made the decision that I was going to take charge of myself."

From the beginning of her career Oprah had established herself as America's girlfriend. She was the beloved sister-woman who knew the sorority secrets, some of which she divined from how-to books such as Sarah Ban Breathnach's *Simple Abundance*, an advice book for women. To her viewers, Oprah was the neighbor lady down the street who poured coffee for the wives after their husbands lunch-pailed to work. She was the misery madam who soothed and comforted and occasionally scolded. She was the town crier warning against pedophiles, wife-beaters, and all manner of abusers, and as such, she became a champion for women, especially downtrodden women who had been done wrong by men.

"If I could just get Black women connected to this whole abuse issue," she told Laura Randolph of *Ebony*. "I hear it all the time from Black women who say, 'Well, he slapped me around a few times, but he doesn't really beat me.' We are so accustomed to being treated badly that we don't even know that love is supposed to really feel good." She used her own life as an example of how her female viewers could shake free from the loser men in their lives and reclaim their self-esteem. "If I can do it," preached America's first black female billionaire, "you can do it."

While Oprah refused to interview O. J. Simpson, she did interview those around him, including Harvard professor Alan Dershowitz, who had been hired as O. J.'s appeals lawyer. He had written a novel, *The Advocate's Devil*, focused on a Harvard lawyer who thinks his client, a professional athlete, might be guilty of a felony, and the dilemma the lawyer faces in representing him. When Warner Books could not book Dershowitz on Oprah, he called the producers himself and insisted they do a show titled "How to Defend a Criminal."

"He actually bulldozed his way onto the show," said a former Warner Books publicist, "but then he got blindsided because they also booked Ron Goldman's family. Dershowitz was annoyed and kept mentioning his book over and over again. So much so that Oprah turned to her audience and made fun of him, saying, 'What's the name of the book again?' They all chorused the title. He was definitely overdoing it. . . . And if you and your book don't get the love treatment on her show, you lose." Dershowitz's book sank without a trace.

The most controversial O. J. shows Oprah did were her February 20 and 24, 1997, interviews with Mark Fuhrman, who swore in court that he had never used the word *nigger*. Tape recordings and witnesses proved he had lied, and Oprah pressed him on it.

"What do you mean there are no right or wrong answers? What about the truth?" she said. "Do you think you are a racist?"

Fuhrman said no.

"Why not? If you could use those words, why not? Do you believe you can use the *N* word and not be a racist?"

Even as she made clear her disgust with the detective, she was criticized in black newspapers for having had him on the show in the first place, especially during Black History Month. *The Chicago Defender* quoted former Illinois appellate court judge Eugene Pincham as saying it was "a slap in the face" to the country's African American community. Oprah admitted that her interview with Fuhrman provoked more viewer response than any other topic in the history of her show. She later interviewed the prosecutors, Marcia Clark and Christopher Darden, when they published their books about losing the case, and she especially empathized with Darden. "He felt that that trial—133 days—was a total waste of his life and time," Oprah said.

As she started her new season in September 1997, Oprah's producers suggested she interview Paula Barbieri, the *Playboy* model who had written a book about her relationship with O. J. Simpson. "When I heard that I said: 'Let me tell you this: OJ is over. I'm not going to go into another season discussing what should have already been over two years ago,'" Oprah reiterated to the *Chicago Sun-Times*. "'Paula Barbieri is not going to run my life. You hear me? It ain't gonna be Paula Barbieri.' I said, 'I didn't come twelve years of doing this show to start off a new season doing Paula Barbieri.'"

Someone suggested that Oprah's indignation might have been tinged by losing exclusivity to Larry King, Diane Sawyer, and Matt Lauer, all of whom had lined up to interview Barbieri. Richard Roeper, who had interviewed her two days before, accused Oprah of utter hypocrisy.

"Barbieri has accepted Jesus Christ as her savior and has abandoned Hollywood for a life of church work," he wrote in the *Chicago Sun-Times*. "Shouldn't Oprah be hugging her on camera and whispering, 'You go, girl!' as the tears flow?"

Weeks after the Barbieri brouhaha, Oprah decided to do a show titled "What's Black Enough?" During the two-and-a-half-hour taping on September 30, 1997, members of her audience criticized her for coddling white viewers and for having Mark Fuhrman on during Black History Month. She had scheduled the air date for October 8, 1997, but she canceled the show, possibly because she did not want to be publicly vilified and seen as the focus of so much racial dissension.

Reverberations from the O. J. Simpson trial continued for years. Following his acquittal in the criminal trial, he was later found liable in a civil trial for the wrongful deaths, and the families of Nicole Brown Simpson and Ron Goldman were awarded $33.5 million in damages, which the Goldmans sought to collect at every turn. A decade later, Simpson signed a $3.5 million contract with ReganBooks to write *If I Did It*, purportedly a novel about how he might have committed the murders. The victims' families protested, and the public outrage prompted Rupert Murdoch to cancel the contract and pulp the book (four hundred thousand copies). Fred Goldman, who had initially opposed publication, gained the rights to the book under the civil court judgment against Simpson and arranged to republish with a cover that reduced the *If* to the size of an insect so that the title appeared to read, *I Did It: Confessions of the Killer*, by O. J. Simpson. Goldman commissioned a new introduction and added an afterword by Dominick Dunne. The book was published in 2007, and once again Oprah waded into the muck.

During her opening show of 2007 she announced yet another show on O. J. Simpson, saying she had invited the Goldmans and Denise Brown, Nicole's sister, to discuss the confessional novel with the former prosecutors Marcia Clark and Christopher Darden. But Denise Brown was so angry at the Goldmans for proceeding with the book that she refused to appear with them and canceled her appearance. She finally agreed to tape a separate segment in which she could urge people to boycott the book.

Oprah opened that show (September 13, 2007) with Fred Goldman and his daughter, Kim, sitting onstage. "This is a moral and ethical dilemma for me," she said. "We sell books on this show. We promote books, but I think this book is despicable. . . . I'm all for it being published, because I don't believe in censorship, but I personally wouldn't want to be in a position to encourage people to buy this book."

Immediately thrown on the defensive, Kim Goldman responded, "It's either him or us." Oprah bored into the Goldmans on how much money they would make from the publication.

"Seventeen cents per book? That's all? What kind of a publishing deal is that? Seventeen cents?" Oprah said. "Does that ease your pain?" She returned to the money again and again.

"Do you consider the proceeds from the book blood money?"

The victim's sixty-six-year-old father said there wasn't that much money involved.

"If you're only going to get seventeen cents, who gets the rest of it?" said a skeptical Oprah.

"We have a judgment," said Fred Goldman, "the only form of justice that we were able to attain through the civil court. And that piece of paper is meaningless unless we pursue that judgment. We took away the opportunity from him [Simpson] to earn additional money, and that money is the only form of justice."

Oprah looked disgusted and disapproving. "We as a country have been able to move on," she said. "I would hope you would [be able to move on and] get peace."

Riled, Kim Goldman snapped, "It's insulting to assume we would ever get peace."

"I did not mean to be insulting," said Oprah. "Thank you for honoring your commitment to be here." She quickly moved to a commercial and then introduced Denise Brown.

"I will not be reading this book," Oprah told her. "My producers have read it and tell me that Nicole is depicted as a drug addict and slut and deserves the description." Denise Brown said the book was "evil" and publication was "morally wrong." At the end of the hour, Oprah looked like she had clean hands: she had said she wouldn't read the book, and she wouldn't recommend the book. Still, she allowed the principals to come on her show and give her huge ratings, while pushing O. J. Simpson's confessional novel to number two on *The New York Times* bestseller list.

**To celebrate the tenth anniversary of *O* magazine in May 2010, Oprah had herself photographed with ten fans for an article titled online as "The Ultimate *O* Interview: Oprah Answers All Your Questions." One fan asked, "After interviewing so many people, are there any . . . who . . . you still want to talk to?" Oprah said she still wanted to interview O. J. Simpson's daughter, Sydney Simpson.**

When Oprah started her book club in 1996 she gave all of her authors "the love treatment," and her enthusiastic endorsements sent their books charging up *The New York Times* bestseller list, a button-busting experience for any writer. Oprah's Book Club became a national sensation that enshrined her as a cultural icon while energizing publishers, enriching authors, and enlightening viewers. Yet when Alice McGee had first suggested in a memo that Oprah do a book club on the air, she did not think it would work. She worried about the ratings. "We'll get horrible numbers," she said. "We'll bomb. . . . Over the years we've tried to do fiction and always died in the ratings." But after Oprah received a gold medal from the National Book Foundation and an Honor from the Association of American Publishers, was named Person of the Year by the Literary Market Place, dubbed by *Newsweek* as the most important person in the world of books and media, and lauded as a "Library Lion" of the New York Public Library, she framed McGee's memo and hung it on her office wall.

At the time, book clubs were springing up all over the country and many booksellers ran author readings and study groups out of their stores. Oprah responded to the existing popularity of these groups and seized the zeitgeist. "She gets no credit for invention," joked *TV Guide* critic Jeff Jarvis, "but she certainly knows how to steal wisely."

She began her book club, as she did so many of her shows, with herself. Having gone from XXXL sweats to slinky spandex after losing almost eighty-five pounds in 1993, she felt she had turned her life around. She finally had accepted daily exercise as her metabolic savior, and she now wanted to convert her sedentary viewers. So she decided her May sweeps period would be an entire month of "Get Movin' with Oprah: Spring Training 1995." This set the stage for the fitness book she wanted to write with her trainer, which preceded her book club.

"We had this big discussion about what [that month of spring training] would do in the numbers and what about people who really didn't want to lose weight," she said. "And then we decided O. J. was on anyway so we could do what we wanted." By that time Oprah could do almost anything she wanted and stay at number one. She would soon win a Daytime Emmy for the fifth consecutive year as Best Talk Show Host, and would make her first appearance on the *Forbes* annual list of the four hundred richest Americans, with a net worth then of $340 million. *Life* magazine dubbed her "America's most powerful woman," and *Time* named her one of "The Most Influential People of the Century." As the dramatist Jean Anouilh once said, "Every man thinks God is on his side. The rich and powerful know he is."

Taking note of her monthlong workout, *The Onion,* a parody newspaper, ran a front-page headline announcing, "Oprah Secedes from U.S., Forms Independent Nation of Cheesecake-Eating Housewives." The tongue-in-cheek story reported that the newly formed republic of "Ugogirl" would be recognized by the UN as a sovereign nation with attitude and sass.

From the time she started losing weight with Bob Greene in 1993, Oprah talked about writing a book with him, and he began jotting down notes. When she determined the time was right, they found a writer and signed with Hyperion to coauthor *Make the Connection: Ten Steps to a Better Body—and a Better Life*. Oprah wrote the introduction and the front piece for every chapter, sharing photos of herself at her fattest and fittest, as well as poignant entries from her journals about how her weight had consumed her life.

She whipped up frenzied excitement about the book when Hyperion sponsored a breakfast with her and her trainer in Soldier Field stadium during the 1996 ABA convention in Chicago, which was followed by a mile-long power walk to McCormick Place, the convention center. "I can't tell you what I ate that morning, who shared my table or what I wore that day," wrote Renee A. James in the Allentown *Morning Call*. "But I do remember this very clearly: Oprah Winfrey was incredible. She looked great; she sounded approachable. As she spoke to the assembled masses, she came across as your very best girlfriend. Every woman in the crowd felt like Oprah was connecting specifically with her. We shared the same struggles, including the never-ending weight loss battle, despite the fact that Oprah was (back then) a millionaire with a hit television show and more money than the rest of us would see in several lifetimes. It didn't faze us that she was an international celebrity. She was just like us. She sounded exactly like each one of us when we talked to our girlfriends. Oprah would fit right in if she wandered into one of our get-together lunches. The whole experience was powerful. The connection she made that day with a couple thousand women was about much more than losing weight."

Sadly, James changed her mind about Oprah twelve years later. "Could it have something to do with the difference between the superstar billionaire we see in 2008 and the girlfriend I saw walking around, talking to people on Soldier Field in 1996? Somehow, Oprah is starting to feel a bit too 'empowered,' just a little too 'enlightened' for the rest of us. To me, this feels like the friend who got a little too impressed with herself and became just a little too good for the rest of us. Makes you sort of mad; but you still miss her."

Watching Oprah and her trainer in the summer of 1996

leading all those women huffing and puffing across parking lots, up highway overpasses, and along the lakefront convinced booksellers to place heavy orders for *Make the Connection,* which had a first printing of two million copies. On publication day Oprah dedicated her show to her book with Bob Greene, and she also posed for a cover story in *People:* "Oprah Buff: After Four Years with a New Fitness Philosophy Oprah Is Happy at Last." Within a month, *Make the Connection* was at the top of every bestseller list in the country.

Oprah was so convinced she would never gain weight again that she spent the next several months making a motivational home video titled *Oprah: Make the Connection* in which she talked about having conquered her weight problem. "The sixty-minute tape is less an instructional guide on getting in shape than it is an Oprah-fest," said the *Chicago Sun-Times.* "We see Oprah boxing on the beach with Greene. Oprah in a field of flowers with a puppy. Oprah in her dressing room. Oprah dancing. Oprah sitting around the dinner table with her buddies. Oprah finishing the marathon. We see fat Oprah. We see fit Oprah."

We also see generous Oprah, who announced that all proceeds from the video would go to A Better Chance, a Boston-based program that provides inner-city students with good grades the opportunity to attend the nation's best college preparatory schools.

Days after launching her own book, Oprah launched her book club to feature works of adult contemporary fiction. She made a few exceptions for her friends when she chose Maya Angelou's nonfiction book *The Heart of a Woman* and Bill Cosby's *Little Bill* children's stories. When she started featuring nonfiction in 2005, she rejected her "aunt" Katharine's memoir, *Jay Bird Creek,* because, according to Mrs. Esters, Oprah said her book was "too trite and mediocre. No drama or excitement."

"I self-published the book, and Oprah said she could not consider it for her show unless it was published by a publisher like Random House, Inc. . . . She also said her viewers would not like it." Mrs. Esters had written about growing up in the Jim

Crow South and her fight for civil rights. "My book was too lit-tle for Oprah to bother with."

Inexplicably, Oprah ignored the two women whose con-temporary fiction had given her an entrée into acting. Alice Walker, who wrote *The Color Purple*, and Gloria Naylor, who wrote *The Women of Brewster Place*, were never selected for Oprah's Book Club for any of their subsequent works. Particu-larly puzzling was the distance Oprah put between herself and Alice Walker, because *The Color Purple* had been such a signifi-cant part of Oprah's success, expanding and, in many ways, making her career. Her homage to the movie could be seen in the "Color Purple" meadow she created at her Indiana farm. Yet she never invited Alice Walker to see the landscaped hymn of praise to her novel.

"I love Oprah and I admire her and I think she's a gift to the planet," Walker said in 2008, "but she's put a huge remove be-tween us that I don't understand. . . . Maybe my views are just too out there for her."

Equally inexplicable was what looked like Oprah's total usurping of the novel when it became a musical and opened on Broadway in 2005. The marquee blared: "Oprah Winfrey Pre-sents *The Color Purple*." Only in the smallest print in the pro-grams and in the full-page ads that ran in newspapers were the words "Based upon the novel written by Alice Walker."

"Perhaps in claiming *The Color Purple* in this way she was healing a wound she had acquired when Steven [Spielberg] re-fused to put her name on the marquee for the movie," Walker suggested. "I know that hurt Oprah very deeply, and I think that she was trying to get back at him and gain some ground that she felt was lost. So she took over the whole thing, the whole marquee, without really thinking about me, or about whether it was fair. . . . It was not particularly graceful on her part or Scott's [Scott Sanders, the producer] part. I don't know how they could do it, but since they did, I expect that they will live with it. You know I can."

Neither Alice Walker nor Gloria Naylor could explain being omitted from Oprah's Book Club, which from 1996 until she temporarily discontinued it in 2002 concentrated on fiction by living authors, mostly female. She would announce her pick and then give viewers a month to read it. In the interim, her producers filmed the author at home, and over dinner with Oprah and a few fans discussing the book, scenes that were later woven into the show that was done about the book. Her first book club choice was *The Deep End of the Ocean,* by Jacquelyn Mitchard, a story about a mother whose child is kidnapped. Mitchard's publicity director at Viking Penguin remembered Oprah calling her to say, "We're gonna create the biggest book club in the world," which was no exaggeration since *The Oprah Winfrey Show* was then broadcast in 130 countries. Oprah knew enough from previous book promotions to warn the publicist to print thousands of extra copies and then to get out of the way of the stampede. Mitchard's book, which had a first run of sixty-eight thousand copies, sold more than four million copies after being chosen by Oprah's Book Club.

"I want to get the country reading," said Oprah, who recognized her power as a cultural force. For the next six years she chose books that mirrored her own interests, which some critics called "middle brow," "sentimental," and "commercial." Mostly she chose sad stories written by women about women who survived misery and pain to find redemption. They were women like her, who triumphed over sexual abuse, careless mothering, racism, poverty, unrequited love, weak men, unwanted pregnancy, drugs, even obesity. "Reading is like everything else," Oprah said. "You're drawn to people who are like yourself."

Oprah may have seen herself in Wally Lamb's debut novel, *She's Come Undone,* about an obese teenager overcoming rape and self-hatred, which became a 1997 book club choice. Twelve years later she joined forces with Tyler Perry to coproduce *Precious,* a film about an obese, pregnant Harlem teenage mother who overcomes rape, illiteracy, and an evil mother to make a new life for herself. The film was based on the novel *Push,* by Sapphire. For the most part, Oprah's book club choices featured women who had been raped, molested, or murdered by men who committed adultery or acted abusively toward their families.

In several of the novels, the men were threatening and the women nurturing. The *New York Times* literary critic Tom Shone said, "The Oprah list offers us that rather ominous thing: not a world without pity, but a world composed of nothing but."

## 1996–2002

1. *The Deep End of the Ocean,* by Jacquelyn Mitchard
2. *Song of Solomon,* by Toni Morrison
3. *The Book of Ruth,* by Jane Hamilton
4. *She's Come Undone,* by Wally Lamb
5. *Stones from the River,* by Ursula Hegi
6. *The Rapture of Canaan,* by Sheri Reynolds
7. *The Heart of a Woman,* by Maya Angelou
8. *Songs in Ordinary Time,* by Mary McGarry Morris
9. *A Lesson Before Dying,* by Ernest J. Gaines
10. *Ellen Foster,* by Kaye Gibbons
11. *A Virtuous Woman,* by Kaye Gibbons
12. *The Meanest Thing to Say,* by Bill Cosby
13. *The Treasure Hunt,* by Bill Cosby
14. *The Best Way to Play,* by Bill Cosby
15. *Paradise,* by Toni Morrison
16. *Here on Earth,* by Alice Hoffman
17. *Black and Blue,* by Anna Quindlen
18. *Breath, Eyes, Memory,* by Edwidge Danticat
19. *I Know This Much Is True,* by Wally Lamb
20. *What Looks Like Crazy on an Ordinary Day,* by Pearl Cleage
21. *Midwives,* by Chris Bohjalian
22. *Where the Heart Is,* by Billie Letts
23. *Jewel,* by Bret Lott
24. *The Reader,* by Bernhard Schlink
25. *The Pilot's Wife,* by Anita Shreve
26. *White Oleander,* by Janet Fitch
27. *Mother of Pearl,* by Melinda Haynes
28. *Tara Road,* by Maeve Binchy
29. *River, Cross My Heart,* by Breena Clarke

30. *Vinegar Hill,* by A. Manette Ansay
31. *A Map of the World,* by Jane Hamilton
32. *Gap Creek,* by Robert Morgan
33. *Daughter of Fortune,* by Isabel Allende
34. *Back Roads,* by Tawni O'Dell
35. *The Bluest Eye,* by Toni Morrison
36. *While I Was Gone,* by Sue Miller
37. *The Poisonwood Bible,* by Barbara Kingsolver
38. *Open House,* by Elizabeth Berg
39. *Drowning Ruth,* by Christina Schwarz
40. *House of Sand and Fog,* by Andre Dubus III
41. *We Were the Mulvaneys,* by Joyce Carol Oates
42. *Icy Sparks,* by Gwyn Hyman Rubio
43. *Stolen Lives: Twenty Years in a Desert Jail,* by Malika Oufkir
44. *Cane River,* by Lalita Tademy
45. *The Corrections,* by Jonathan Franzen
46. *A Fine Balance,* by Rohinton Mistry
47. *Fall on Your Knees,* by Ann-Marie MacDonald
48. *Sula,* by Toni Morrison

Within the first year, Oprah's Book Club had sold almost twelve million copies of contemporary fiction, a genre that typically sold no more than a few thousand copies per title per year, and according to *Publishing Trends,* an industry newsletter, she was responsible for $130 million in book sales. Consequently, she became known as "The Midas of the Midlist" for her ability to turn modestly successful novels into raging bestsellers. "This is a revolution," said Toni Morrison, the first black writer to win the Nobel Prize for Literature. Oprah introduced Morrison to her audience in 1996 as "the greatest living American writer, male or female, white or black." Over the next six years she selected Morrison for the book club four times, even hosting a master class so the erudite writer could instruct Oprah's audience on how to read a novel. Oprah began that show by reassuring viewers that she, too, had difficulty reading Toni Morrison, and revealed her conversation with the writer.

"Do people tell you they have to keep going over the words sometimes?" Oprah said.

"That, my dear," said Toni Morrison, "is called reading."

By the end of the first year of Oprah's Book Club, publishers were reeling. "It's like waking up in the morning and finding your husband has changed into Kevin Costner," said one female publisher. They turned themselves inside out to accommodate Oprah, signing confidentiality agreements to keep secret her selection until she announced it on her show. They agreed to contribute five hundred free copies of the book for her to distribute to her audience, and to donate ten thousand copies to libraries. They dispatched sales reps to sell blindly: "There will be an Oprah Book Club selection in two months. I don't know what it is. How many copies do you want to order?" In turn, booksellers had to sign confidentiality agreements not to open the boxes shipped with the Oprah stencil until the minute she announced her selection on the air. The anointed authors also signed affidavits swearing not to reveal their good fortune until Oprah had announced their books. They were permitted to tell their spouses but no one else, including parents, siblings, and children. In addition, publishers had to cede Oprah cover approval of the placement of the book club logo (a big yellow *O* with a white center) and agree to stop stamping books with the logo once the month was up. After that time, they could not even mention her book club in advertisements.

It's hard to believe that Oprah's crusade for literacy would trigger any criticism, but within months she had drilled into the raw nerves of literary elites. "Yes, her book club is a societal boon," stated *The New Republic*, "but her taste for the soap-operatically uplifting is not." The New York literary critic Alfred Kazin dismissed her book club as a "carpet bombing of the American mind." But culture critic Camille Paglia defended Oprah: "I think the reaction against her is sheer intellectual snobbery. The idea that a black woman with a devoted audience could have this kind of impact jeopardizes [her critics'] role as tastemakers." The carping reached a crescendo in 2001, when Oprah selected *The Corrections*, by Jonathan Franzen, for book club beatification. Franzen, whose first two novels combined sold a total of fifty thousand copies, seemed poised for gigantic commercial success as an Oprah pick, but he did not leap at the opportunity.

"The first weekend after I heard, I considered turning it down," he said later. "Yes, I was very serious. I see this as my book, my creation, and I didn't want that logo of corporate ownership on it. . . . It's not [just] a sticker. It's part of the cover. They redo the whole cover. You can't take it off. I know it says Oprah's Book Club, but it's an implied endorsement, both for me and for her. The reason I got into this business is because I'm an independent writer, and I didn't want that corporate logo on my book."

He went on to say that being selected for Oprah's Book Club did as much for her as it did for him. "[My book with three hundred thousand copies in print] was already on the best-seller list and the reviews were pretty much all in. What this means for us is that she's bumped the sales up to another level and gotten the book into Walmart and Costco and places like that. It means a lot more money for me and my publisher, [and] it gets that book—that kind of book into the hands of people who might like it."

Franzen defined his book—"that kind of book"—as in the "high-art literary tradition," whereas he said most of Oprah's books were merely "entertaining." He added, "She's picked some good books, but she's picked enough schmaltzy, one-dimensional ones that I cringe, myself, even though I think she's really smart and really fighting the good fight."

Franzen seemed to have publicly dismissed Oprah as a carnival barker, and she reacted by rescinding her invitation. She announced to her viewers, "Jonathan Franzen will not be on *The Oprah Winfrey Show* because he is seemingly uncomfortable and conflicted about being chosen as a book club selection. It is never my intention to make anyone uncomfortable or cause anyone conflict. . . . We're moving on to the next book."

Franzen told *USA Today* that he felt "awful" about what he had done. "To find myself being in the position of giving offense to someone who's a hero—not a hero of mine per se, but a hero in general—I feel bad in a public-spirited way."

Flabbergasted, *The Washington Post*'s literary critic, Jonathan Yardley, called Franzen's words "so stupid as to defy comprehension. He did everything he could to take Oprah Winfrey's money and then run as far away from her as possible." Chris Bohjalian, whose novel *Midwives* was the twenty-first book chosen by Oprah, said, "I was angry on behalf of the book club, and I was appalled as a reader who appreciates the incredible amount that Oprah Winfrey has done for books." He added that sales of *Midwives* jumped from 100,000 copies to 1.6 million after it became an Oprah pick.

Franzen was reviled from coast to coast. *Newsweek* called him "a pompous prick," *The Boston Globe* called him an "ego-blinded snob," and the *Chicago Tribune* called him "a spoiled, whiny little brat." Stepping in to defend him, David Remnick, editor in chief of *The New Yorker*, said, "I think the world of Jonathan. I think he's sorry about Oprah, but it's not a monumental issue. Everyone steps on someone's toes sometimes." E. Annie Proulx, the Pulitzer Prize–winning author of *The Shipping News*, also came to Franzen's defense. "Jon was so right," she said. "He objected because he didn't like a lot of Oprah's choices. And I can say this because I know none of my books will ever make Oprah's list. Some of the books she picks are a bit sentimental. I see where she's coming from, and she's done marvelous things for books and readers. But for someone to think that it's no kudo to be accepted on a list of sentimental books is understandable."

In November 2001, a month after his disinvitation by Oprah, Jonathan Franzen won a National Book Award for *The Corrections*, and a few months later she decided to discontinue her book club. Our Lady of Literacy had had it. "It has become harder and harder to find books on a monthly basis that I feel absolutely compelled to share," she said. "I will continue featuring books on *The Oprah Winfrey Show* when I feel they merit my heartfelt recommendation."

If she appeared overly sensitive to public criticism, it was because she had become accustomed to getting perpetual praise from the press—laudatory profiles, admiring interviews, adoring cover stories. With the exception of the tabloids, the U.S.S. *Oprah* sailed mostly smooth seas. Now she had hit a little turbulence over her lack of literary taste, and being derided as Our Lady of the Lowbrows had nicked her in a vulnerable spot. Never particularly proud of her education from the historic black college of Tennessee State University, she felt inferior around her Ivy League contemporaries. She knew her success and celebrity lifted her into most social circles, because, as she said many times, money opens every door in America. But the one marked "High-Art Literary" seemed to have slammed shut on her.

Oprah gave the publishing industry ten months to miss her book club before she announced that she was bringing it back. This time, though, she made herself immune to literary attacks by concentrating solely on the classics. For the next two years she rallied her viewers around some of literature's finest writers:

**2003–2005**

49. *East of Eden,* by John Steinbeck
50. *Cry, the Beloved Country,* by Alan Paton
51. *One Hundred Years of Solitude,* by Gabriel García Márquez
52. *The Heart Is a Lonely Hunter,* by Carson McCullers
53. *Anna Karenina,* by Leo Tolstoy
54. *The Good Earth,* by Pearl S. Buck
55. *As I Lay Dying,* by William Faulkner
56. *The Sound and the Fury,* by William Faulkner
57. *Light in August,* by William Faulkner

By 2005, America's literary community was starving. More than 150 writers, mostly female novelists such as Amy Tan, Louise Erdrich, and Jane Smiley, signed a petition to Oprah, saying "the landscape of literary fiction is now a gloomy place." They begged her to come back, and she agreed because she said she missed interviewing authors about their books. Interestingly, all of her next selections were books by men.

**2005–2008**

58. *A Million Little Pieces,* by James Frey
59. *Night,* by Elie Wiesel
60. *The Measure of a Man: A Spiritual Autobiography,* by Sidney Poitier
61. *The Road,* by Cormac McCarthy
62. *Middlesex,* by Jeffrey Eugenides
63. *Love in the Time of Cholera,* by Gabriel García Márquez
64. *The Pillars of the Earth,* by Ken Follett
65. *A New Earth,* by Eckhart Tolle
66. *The Story of Edgar Sawtelle,* by David Wroblewski

When she opened the 2005 season with her selection of *A Million Little Pieces,* by James Frey, she had no idea that she would become embroiled in a controversy that would trigger thirteen class-action lawsuits, a bruising clash with a prestigious publisher and a revered editor, plus a tirade from *The New York Times* that would make the Franzen fracas look like sweet potato pie. As Jonathan Franzen remarked a few years later, "Oprah should keep away from white guys with the initials J.F."

In the beginning, Oprah was bewitched by James Frey's harrowing memoir of addiction and recovery. For three months she gave him the full love treatment. "The book . . . kept me up for two nights straight," she told her audience on September 22, 2005, when she announced *A Million Little Pieces* as her next book club selection. "It's a wild ride through addiction and rehab that has been electrifying, intense, mesmerizing, and even gruesome."

On October 26, 2005, she introduced the thirty-six-year-old bearded writer as "the child you pray you never have to raise. At age ten he was drinking alcohol, by twelve he's doing drugs, and from there he spends almost every day the same: drunk and high on crack. . . . He does it all: freebases cocaine, drops acid, eats mushrooms, takes meth, smokes PCP, snorts glue, and inhales nitrous oxide."

Frey also wrote about boarding a plane drunk and bloodied

from a brawl, having two root canal operations without anesthesia, and finding his dead girlfriend hanging from a rope. He wrote graphically about the violence he had witnessed, suffered, and perpetuated at Hazelden during his rehabilitation, and about a crack-fueled confrontation with Ohio police that resulted in seven felony charges and eighty-seven days in jail. "I was a bad guy," he told Oprah.

Several book reviewers challenged his accounts as "lacking credibility," but they gave him high marks for vivid imagination. Others were not so forgiving. "Absolutely false," Dr. Scott Lingle, president of the Minnesota Dental Association, told Deborah Caulfield Rybak of the Minneapolis *StarTribune*. He said that no dentist in the state would perform surgery without Novocain: "No way. Nohow. Nowhere," said a former spokesman for Northwest Airlines about Frey's contention that he had boarded a plane wounded and inebriated. Counselors from Hazelden denied his claims of violence, and Ohio police laughed at his so-called criminal record, which consisted of a DUI when he was twenty-three years old. For that he had simply posted bond of $733, with no jail time. His "crimes" consisted of driving without a license and driving with an open container of beer, as opposed to being the chief target of an FBI narcotics probe, as he claimed. "He thinks he's a bit of a desperado," said David Baer, a former Ohio police officer amused by the bad-guy portrait Frey limned of himself.

Frey's publishers (Doubleday in hardcover and Anchor in paperback) gave Oprah's producers a copy of Rybak's damning article from the Minneapolis *StarTribune* when Oprah was considering the booking, but according to the reporter, she was never contacted by anyone at Harpo. "I was quite surprised by the lack of vetting done by her organization," Rybak recalled a few years later. At the time, Oprah didn't seem to care. She said she loved the book and wanted to make it her next selection.

During the narrated video segment that introduced Frey to her audience, seven of her employees extolled the book, bringing Oprah to tears. "I'm crying 'cause these are all my Harpo family and we all love the book so much." The book went on to sell two million copies in the next three months, impressing even Oprah. "Within hours of our book club announcement, readers across the country raced to get the book," she announced. "*A Million Little Pieces* hit number one on *USA Today, The New York Times,* and *Publishers Weekly,* the triple crown of books."

Then came the explosion from the website The Smoking Gun, which posted a story on January 8, 2006: "A Million Little Lies: The Man Who Conned Oprah." Citing a six-week investigation into Frey's so-called criminal record and his inability to explain the disparities between what he had written and what official records showed, the website stated, "[H]e has demonstrably fabricated key parts of the book, which could—and probably should—cause discerning readers . . . to wonder what is true." The next day Frey's publishers responded with a statement of support, which prompted Edward Wyatt's story in *The New York Times* to lead, "And on the second day Doubleday shrugged."

For the next seventeen days the James Frey story dominated the national news cycle, especially in *The New York Times,* which published thirty-one articles inside of a month questioning Frey's honesty, his publisher's credibility, and Oprah's complicity. Many at the publishing house felt the negative coverage was a way for the media to take on Oprah without doing so directly. "It was a veiled attack on her that kept the story going," said a vice president of Random House, Inc., the umbrella company of Doubleday and Anchor.

Oprah's producers, especially Ellen Rakieten, Sheri Salata, and Jill Adams, stayed in close touch with Frey, calling him every day and sending emails. "We love the book, James. We don't care what they say. It's irrelevant. Really." But the continual drubbing so unsettled Oprah that she finally insisted Frey go on *Larry King Live* to defend himself. She made the arrangements for his appearance herself and promised to call in at the end of the show with a statement. She had two prepared—one for him and one against him—and her decision of which she would read depended on how he did. "Go on with your mother," she told him. "You'll look more sympathetic."

So, on January 11, 2006, accompanied by his mom and two publicists from Anchor, James Frey appeared on CNN to discuss the controversy surrounding his book, now described as a "fraud" and "a scandal." Polite and low-key, he said he was a flawed person with a troubled past. He pleaded "a very subjective memory" due to his drug addiction and acknowledged that he had "changed some things" in the book but that it was "the essential truth" of his life. He would not admit to any lies or distortions. King pointed out that while Frey had the support of his publisher, he had yet to hear from Oprah. One of his callers asked, "Do you think [she] will support you?"

By the end of the hour there was still no call from Oprah, and Frey looked like a whipped dog, with his mother close to tears. Just as Larry was to turn the next hour over to Anderson Cooper, he announced, "I'm going to hold the show a little longer because I understand we have Oprah on the phone. Let's see what she has to say. Are you there, my friend?" The host leaned forward, straining his suspenders to hear whether Frey would live another day.

"I wanted to say because everyone's been asking me to release a statement," said Oprah. "I first wanted to hear what James had to say. . . . He's had many conversations with my producers, who do fully support him and obviously we support the book because we recognize that there have been thousands and hundreds of thousands of people whose lives have been changed by this book. . . . I feel about *A Million Little Pieces* that although some of the facts have been questioned . . . that the underlying message of redemption in James Frey's memoir still resonates with me. . . . Whether or not . . . he hit the police officer or didn't hit the police officer is irrelevant to me. . . ." She added, "To me, it seems to be much ado about nothing. . . . It's irrelevant discussing, you know, what happened or did not happen to the police."

"It's still an Oprah recommend, right?" said Larry King.

"Well, I certainly do recommend it for all."

The book remained number one on *The New York Times* bestseller list but not in the paper's newsroom, which was still reeling from the journalistic fraud of Jayson Blair, whose widespread fabrications and plagiarisms represented a profound betrayal of trust for the readers of the nation's most prestigious newspaper. Maureen Dowd struck first, with a column titled "Oprah! How Could Ya?" in which she compared the talk show host to George W. Bush's press secretary, Scott McClellan, who had told lies on behalf of the president about Iraq's weapons of mass destruction. "She should have said: 'Had I known that many parts were fake, I wouldn't have recommended the book to millions of loyal viewers. I wouldn't have made this liar a lot of money.'"

Three days later came a blast from *The Washington Post*, in a column by Richard Cohen titled "Oprah's Grand Delusion": "[F]ame and wealth has lulled her into believing that she possesses something akin to papal infallibility. She finds herself incapable of seeing that she has been twice fooled—once by Frey, a second time by herself."

The deathblow was delivered by Frank Rich's "Truthiness" column in *The New York Times*, in which he connected Frey's lies and Oprah's defense of him to the kind of propaganda that can lead a nation morally astray. "Ms. Winfrey's blithe reendorsement of the book is less laughable once you start to imagine some Holocaust denier using her imprimatur to discount Elie Wiesel's incarceration at Auschwitz in her next book club selection, *Night*."

This was too much for the woman who saw herself as the paragon of truth and honesty. Her producers stopped communicating with Frey and demanded the publishers defend their disputed book. Anchor and Doubleday quickly offered the *New York Times* interviews with two men from Hazelden to support Frey's accounts, which they basically did, but there was still no editorial support for Frey anywhere in the country, and Oprah, according to her producers, felt trapped. "They were getting too close," said one. "We started to get investigated, and Oprah said we had to put a stop to it."

The producers summoned Frey and his publisher, plus some of the columnists who had condemned Oprah's defense of the book, for a show on January 26, 2006, which they said was to be titled "Truth in America."

Nan Talese, publisher of Frey's hardback, and two of Doubleday's publicists accompanied Frey to Chicago. Seconds after they walked into Harpo they were separated: Frey was sent to one dressing room, the publishing representatives to another. Right before the show, Ellen Rakieten dashed into Frey's room and, in front of someone present, said, "Hey. We changed the show to 'James Frey and the *A Million Little Pieces* Controversy.' You are going to be on the entire hour. It's going to get pretty rough, but hang on. I promise you, there will be redemption for you at the end." Rakieten was right—about the rough part.

For the next hour Oprah gave her viewers a startling performance of fire-breathing indignation. She ran a statement from William Bastone of The Smoking Gun, who said, "Turns out he's a well-to-do frat boy who . . . isn't kind of this desperado that he'd like people to think he was. . . . He has been promoting the book for two and a half years and basically has lied continuously for two and a half years." She then ran Frey's response on *Larry King Live* that he had written "the essential truth" of his life. She also ran a portion of her call to the show defending Frey and his book. Then she dropped the hammer.

"I regret that phone call," she said. "I made a mistake and I left the impression that the truth does not matter. And I am deeply sorry about that, because that is not what I believe. I called in because I love the message of this book. . . ." She turned to face him. "It is difficult for me to talk to you, because I really feel duped. I feel duped. But more importantly I feel that you betrayed millions of readers."

She spent the rest of the show chastising Frey and then his publisher.

"Why did you lie?" she asked him. "Why do you have to lie about the time you spent in jail? Why do you have to do that?"

She wanted to know about the suicide death of his girlfriend. "So how did she do it?"

"She cut her wrists," said Frey.

"And so—hanging is more dramatic than cutting your wrists? Is that why you chose hanging? Why do you have to lie about that? Why didn't you just write a novel?"

Losing ground by the second, Frey stammered. "I think . . . I—I still think it's a memoir."

With barely controlled rage, Oprah continued: "I have been really embarrassed by this and, more importantly, feel that I acted in—in defense of you and, you know, as I said, my judgment was clouded because so many people . . . seemed to have gotten so much out of this book . . . but now I feel that you conned us all. Do you?"

Taking their cue from Oprah, the audience began booing. "Okay. Let him speak. Please. Let him speak," she said.

Frey tried to defend what he had done. "I've struggled with the idea of it, and—"

Oprah cut him off. "No, the lie of it. That's a lie. It's not an idea, James. That's a lie."

Before the next break she ran tape from three journalists, who functioned as her picadors:

"It's wrong and immoral to pass off a piece of fiction as a memoir," said Joel Stein of the *Los Angeles Times*. "I wouldn't do it."

"Oprah Winfrey is, number one, the queen of goodwill in the United States," said Stanley Crouch of the New York *Daily News*. "And she was had. It's that simple."

"James Frey very clearly lied to promote his book," said Maureen Dowd of *The New York Times*, "and I don't think that should get the Oprah seal of approval."

In the next segment Oprah lambasted Nan Talese as the publisher of the book.

"What responsibility do you take? What did you do as the publisher of this book to make sure that what you were printing was true?"

Talese said that she had read the manuscript and shared it with colleagues, and when they had no questions, she gave it to the editor, Sean McDonald, who, no longer with Doubleday, became the scapegoat.

"That book is so fantastical," said Oprah, "that . . . that's not washing with me. . . . What did you do legally to make sure?"

Talese said the book was vetted by lawyers, but that no one

questioned it because "this was James's memory of the hell he went through, and I believed it." She tried to explain the subjective thinking that goes into writing a memoir, but Oprah was having none of that, either, nor was her booing audience.

"I think this whole experience is very sad," said Talese. "It's very sad for you, it's very sad for us."

"It's not sad for me," snapped Oprah. "It's embarrassing and disappointing for me."

Talese said that Frey would be writing an author's note to address his made-up recollections in future editions of the book, but this drew more hisses from the audience, whom Talese later characterized as "hyenas."

During the break, James Frey said that if there was a gun backstage he might as well shoot himself. When Oprah came back on the air she said she appreciated him coming on the show. "I do believe that telling the truth can set you free. You know, you were joking, I hope—that if there's a gun backstage, whatever—but I know it's been difficult and I said to you, 'It's not worth all that. It's not worth all that. All you have to do is tell the truth.' "

With an understatement not shown in his writing, Frey said, "This hasn't been a great day for me . . . but I think I have come out of it better."

"Yeah, yeah," said Oprah.

"I mean, I feel like I came here and I have been honest with you. I have, you know, essentially admitted to . . ."

"Lying," said Oprah. "To lying."

Having been publicly flogged, Frey walked back to the green room as if in a coma. "Dude, I just got slaughtered by Oprah in front of twenty million people," he said to one of the publicists. They all sat down to watch Oprah tape *After the Show*, a segment for the Oxygen network. A methamphetamine addict stood up.

"Oprah, I don't care about the exaggerations in the book. I'm an addict and this is my story."

"I'm glad it helped you," said Oprah. "That's why we have the book club. James has apologized, so I'm okay with it." That comment was later edited out of the tape and deleted from the transcript that Harpo released.

As soon as Oprah finished the segment, she and Ellen Rakieten ran to the green room, where Frey and his publicists were sitting, still shell-shocked.

"Are you okay?" asked Oprah. "Are you okay?"

"This sucks," said Frey.

"Oh, James. I'm so sorry. I made a huge mistake. . . . If I hadn't said what I said on the Larry King show, none of this would've happened. We had two statements ready to go for me to read—one positive, one negative, depending on how you did on the show. If only I had said it correctly, none of this would've happened. But after that show *The New York Times* and *The Washington Post* wouldn't let it go. We had to stop it. I'm so sorry, but they were investigating us. And we just couldn't have that. If I had said correctly what was on the statement this would not have happened."

Sheri Salata and Jill Adams, the producers who had worked with Frey, felt awful. "I can't believe this happened," said one. "You went from the best book club ever to the worst. I can't believe it."

In the limousine taking everyone back to the airport Frey's cell phone rang, but he did not take the call. The message was from Larry King, who said to call him as soon as possible.

"I'm so sorry that happened to you, James," said King. "That was awful. Oprah should never have done that to you. Never."

The next day Liz Smith wrote in her syndicated column she was surprised "that Oprah didn't simply hand Mr. Frey a gun and make him shoot himself on her show to make up for his 'deception' of her." In an email years later she said she liked and admired Oprah, but "My only caveat is 'absolute power corrupts,' and in something like the matter . . . with James Frey . . . it was that kind of power. Very nerve wracking. I didn't really think it was a matter of defending the nation whether or not he was totally accurate in his so-called memoir. It was a wonderful book and I didn't feel his public humiliation was necessary. She originally recommended the book in good faith and nobody blamed her for that."

Two years later, when Jessica Seinfeld appeared on *Oprah* with her vegetables-for-kids cookbook and was sued for plagiarism, Liz Smith wrote another column: "[I]f Jessica loses her fight . . . does this mean that Oprah will sit her down in her studio some day and lambaste Ms. Seinfeld the way she devoured author James Frey for not telling the truth, the whole truth and nothing but in his 'memoir'? Maybe Jessica Seinfeld will win the lawsuit [she did], and that will make everything all right with Oprah. And these days, making everything all right with Oprah is practically the publishing world's 11th Commandment."

Harold Evans, who was president of Random House from 1990 to 1997 and just incidentally married to Oprah's nemesis Tina Brown, faulted Oprah as much as anyone. "I think [she] did harm to the concept of the book as a valuable artifact," he said. "It was irresponsible of her, before she blessed this piece of nonsense, not to do some checking."

The message boards at Oprah.com had lit up with hundreds of messages after the second show with James Frey, and most of them were against Oprah for being so harsh. Many acknowledged that while Frey had lied, she had been too hard on him simply because she had been embarrassed by the media. The next day she called Frey at home and, according to someone in the room at the time, she said: "I just want to make sure you're okay, James. You are not going to hurt yourself, are you? I'm really worried you're going to do something to yourself." She then shared her own personal history with drugs. "Listen, James, I, too, smoked crack when I was in Baltimore, and I did cocaine in Chicago. I, too, had a drug problem, but I finally achieved peace with my drug past and I'm hoping you can, too."

Oprah's phone call was of little consolation to Frey, who was fired by his agent at Brillstein-Grey and lost his movie deal with Warner Bros. Fox TV withdrew from the television drama they had signed to do, and Viking Penguin canceled his two-book publishing contract. In addition, a judge approved a settlement in which the publisher agreed to refund readers of *A*

*Million Little Pieces*, but of the millions of copies sold, Random House received only 1,729 requests for reimbursement. At the end of the debacle the one person left standing in James Frey's corner was his revered publisher, Nan Talese, who said Oprah had been "mean and self-serving," and that she should be the one apologizing for her "holier-than-thou" attitude and her "fiercely bad manners."

Having been accused in the past of lacking certain social graces, Oprah proved that she had at least mastered the niceties of thank-you note etiquette. The day after the show, Nan Talese received a one-page letter:

> *Dear Nan,*
> *Thanks for being on the show.*
> > *Sincerely,*
> > *Oprah*

"I got this tip from Bill Clinton," Oprah said later. "You know, Bill Clinton, former president of the United States, which is to write a note on one page so it can be framed. So that's what I do now."

# Sixteen

Phil Donahue hung up his microphone on May 2, 1996, and when television gathered to honor the talk show grandee at the Twenty-third Annual Daytime Emmy Awards in New York, Oprah presented him with a Lifetime Achievement Award. She probably owed him more than any of his other imitators because his show was the competition that whipped hers into the winner's circle. "I want to thank you for opening the door so wide, wide enough for me to walk through," she said. "I hope I can carry on the legacy that [you] began." Donahue blew her a kiss. His good friend Gloria Steinem later recalled, "He always said that if he did his job really well, that the next big talk show host would be a black woman."

For twenty-nine years Donahue had been jumping into his audiences with a microphone, asking for their opinions ("Help me out here") and taking questions from his viewers ("Is the caller there?"). He was the king of talk show television until Oprah arrived on the national scene in 1986 and immediately began trouncing him in the ratings. "She changed the ball game," said Penn State professor Vicki Abt. "She started the down-and-dirty exploitative show, the trailer trash, the unwashed parading of dysfunction. . . . He tried to compete but he couldn't do it as well or as badly. He was too smart."

From the beginning Donahue was controversial and sometimes outrageous. His shows provoked thought and discussion, starting with his first guest, Madalyn Murray O'Hair, the founder of American Atheists. Presenting a blunt denier of God to God-fearing America in 1967 was audacious, and it launched a new kind of talk show that all of his successors, including Oprah, would (try to) imitate. Consumer advocate Ralph Nader appeared on *Donahue* thirty-six times and personified the issue-oriented guest he most enjoyed interviewing. Unafraid to engage politicians, Donahue pressed the presidential candidate Bill Clinton in 1992 about his extramarital affairs. His audience booed him, and Clinton berated him, saying, "You are responsible for the cynicism in this country." But Donahue did not flinch.

Oprah, on the other hand, refused to have politicians on her show for many years because she was afraid of losing viewers. When Senator Bob Dole (R-Kans.) asked to appear during the 1996 presidential campaign, she turned him down. "I don't do politicians," she said, because their interviews "would lack genuineness and real dialogue." After rejecting Dole, Oprah polled her audience. "Those of you who've been watching *The Oprah Winfrey Show* over the last decade know that I don't interview politicians while they're campaigning. The question that's been causing such a big stir . . . is whether or not I should break my long-standing policy and invite President Bill Clinton and Senator Bob Dole to be guests on the show. It's [the issue] been making headlines. . . . I think one [newspaper] . . . even said 'Oprah Bounces Bob.' I did not—it's just a long-standing policy." The audience indicated they did not want her to go political.

"Maybe she realized I was too quick-witted and might steal the show," Dole joked years later. Known for his rapier wit, he once pointed to a photo of Presidents Carter, Ford, and Nixon standing side by side at a White House ceremony. "There they are," Dole said. "See no evil, hear no evil, and evil." After losing to Clinton in 1996, Dole went on *The Late Show with David Letterman,* where the host noted that Clinton was "fat" and probably weighed "three hundred pounds." Dole did not miss a beat. "I never tried to lift him. I just tried to beat him."

The senator again asked to go on Oprah's show in 2005, when he published his memoir *One Soldier's Story.* "It wasn't a political book but a story about growing up in Russell, Kansas, and serving in World War II. It's about my wartime injuries and overcoming adversity, which I thought would appeal to her audience. The book was already a best seller, but it would have been more of a best seller had I been able to get on her show. But she wouldn't take me because I am a Republican."

In contrast, Donahue once gave Senator Dole a full hour, and offered a platform to politicians of both parties, engaging in spirited debates with Gerry Ford, Jimmy Carter, Ronald Reagan, Ross Perot, and Bill Clinton. By the time his show was canceled in New York due to low ratings, talk show television had changed, becoming less thoughtful; the terrain had been invaded by men like Geraldo Rivera, Jerry Springer, Morton Downey, Jr., Montel Williams, and Maury Povich, who presided over screamers and chair-throwers. The goal was no longer to combine education with entertainment, but rather to pander to the lowest taste to get the highest ratings. "They're all my illegitimate children," Donahue said of his successors, "and I love them all equally." He never criticized his competitors, including Oprah, but he did acknowledge that she had muddied the turf. "After she hit . . . the talk show game took a significant turn toward the sensational and the bizarre," he said. His most frequent guest, Ralph Nader, was blunter in blaming her for plunging talk shows into the sewer, but Donahue said that daytime television was closer to the street, more irreverent than any other spot on the dial. "Does it mean that everything on daytime television is wonderful and deserves a Nobel Prize? No," he said. "There are sins. But I'm saying, let the wildflowers grow."

In that unruly garden with Oprah were Rosie O'Donnell, Ricki Lake, Sally Jessy Raphael, Jenny Jones, Joan Rivers, and Rolonda Watts. Each strained to do the kind of memorable television Donahue did at his best. He once lay in a satin-lined coffin to interview a funeral home director. Another time he and his cameras followed a couple as they gave birth. They showed the mother in labor, pushing as hard as she could, with her husband helping, while their three-year-old wandered around the living room. Just as the baby was born, the toddler came into view and shouted, "Mommy, it's a puppy!"

At the time, Oprah was getting high ratings with titillating shows on homosexuality, up to then a taboo subject for talk show television. Reflecting her interest in the subject, she continued to explore the topic of gay men and lesbians over the next two decades. Here is only a partial list:

| | |
|---|---|
| 11/13/86 | "Homophobia" |
| 1988 | "Women Who Turn to Lesbianism" |
| 2/88 | Lesbian separatists |
| 1990 | "Gay Adoption" |
| 1991 | "All the Family Is Gay" |
| 2/24/92 | "Straight Spouses and Gay Ex-Husbands" |
| 1993 | "Lesbian and Gay Baby Boom" |
| 5/4/94 | "School for Gay Teens" |
| 2/27/95 | Greg Louganis, Olympic diver, on revealing his homosexuality and AIDS |
| 7/11/96 | "Why I Married a Gay Man" |
| 4/30/97 | Ellen DeGeneres's coming-out episode |
| 5/5/97 | "Are You Born Gay?" |
| 1998 | Cher and Chastity Bono regarding Chastity being outed as lesbian |
| 4/16/04 | "Secret Sex World: Living on the Down Low" |
| 10/27/04 | "My Husband's Gay" |
| 10/20/05 | "Gay for 30 Days" |
| 11/9/05 | "Bestselling Author Terry McMillan Confronts Her Gay Ex-Husband" |
| 11/17/05 | "When I Knew I Was Gay" |
| 7/7/06 | "The Stars of *Brokeback Mountain* and Tyler Perry's Next Big Thing" |
| 9/19/06 | "Former Governor Jim McGreevey, His Gay Sex Scandal" |
| 10/2/06 | "Gay Wives Confess" |
| 1/29/07 | "Fascinating Families" (including a gay male couple in California who are foster parents) |
| 5/1/07 | "Dana McGreevey, Estranged Wife of the Gay Governor" |

| 6/6/07 | "Left for Dead: The Gay Man Who Befriended His Attacker" |
| 10/24/07 | "Gay Around the World" |
| 2/1/08 | "America's Toughest Matchmaker, Plus Katherine Heigl," including video of T. R. Knight after Isaiah Washington referred to him as "a faggot" on the set of *Grey's Anatomy* |
| 11/14/08 | "Oprah Fridays Live" (with Melissa Etheridge on Prop. 8, the anti–gay marriage amendment) |
| 1/28/09 | "Evangelist Ted Haggard, His Wife, and the Gay Sex Scandal" |
| 3/06/09 | "Women Leaving Men for Other Women" |
| 3/25/09 | Rerun of "Women Leaving Men for Other Women" |

In 1997, long before Ellen DeGeneres entered the talk show arena, she decided that she was going to make television history on her ABC sitcom by coming out as a lesbian. She called Oprah and asked her to appear on the show as the therapist to whom Ellen confides her sexual feelings for women. Oprah agreed, but Ellen was nervous because she had seen one of Oprah's shows on lesbians and thought the host had been quite judgmental. "I was so afraid you would find out I was gay and not like me," said Ellen.

Hers was to be the first prime-time series to feature an openly homosexual lead character, and for eight weeks the publicity leading up to the show saturated the media. Before her character came out on television, Ellen outed herself on the cover of *Time* under the headline "Yep. I'm Gay." General Motors, Chrysler, and Johnson & Johnson, which had aired commercials on previous episodes of *Ellen*, would not buy ads for the coming-out episode, and Oprah later told DeGeneres that she received more hate mail for doing that show than for anything she had done to date. But she frequently made this claim about her more controversial shows.

"I got more heat than I've ever gotten," Oprah said.

"And did you think you would get that?" Ellen asked.

"No, I really didn't, but it was okay because I did it for you and I did it because I believe I should have done it . . . so it didn't really bother me . . . but at the time it was really shocking to me why [anyone] would write hate mail for that."

Two days before Ellen's coming-out episode on April 30, 1997, Liz Smith ran a blind item in her gossip column:

> They do say that one of the biggest and longest-running TV stars is seriously contemplating making the same move that put Ellen DeGeneres on the cover of every magazine in the country and in the nation's newspapers.
>
> The star's sexual orientation has been hidden under a glare of publicity for years. But when—ok—if this announcement occurs, it will make the seismic tremors of Ellen's "Yep, I'm gay" statement look like small potatoes. It will be the furor to end all furors. (This celeb is an icon and role model to millions.) Remember, you heard it here first, even if we don't want to say the name. People should be allowed to "out" themselves.

The same day Oprah appeared on *Ellen* as the therapist, who said, "Good for you, you're gay," Ellen appeared on *The Oprah Winfrey Show*, where Oprah told her, "A lot of people said me being on your show was me promoting lesbianism. I simply wanted to support you in being what you believe was the truth for yourself."

"Everybody thinks I'm a freak," Ellen said, looking beleaguered.

Oprah's audience chastised her for guest-starring in the coming-out episode and then criticized Ellen for being a lesbian and making it public. Yet that night, when the "Ellen" character came out of the closet, she packed America's living rooms with thirty-six million viewers, and Oprah's show earlier that day, featuring Ellen and her then-girlfriend Anne Heche, also won high ratings. But Oprah's cameo appearance, plus the blind item, burned up the Internet for weeks with rumors about her sexuality, the most outlandish being that she was going to come out in *Newsweek* the way Ellen came out in *Time*. Oprah finally issued an official statement denying that she was a lesbian, thereby making her sexual orientation a public issue for years to come. Before her public denial she had denied the lesbian rumors to her audience after taping a show with Rosie O'Donnell, and she again addressed the subject in a keynote speech to a convention of seven thousand broadcasting executives in Chicago. Her words appeared under coy headlines around the country:

"Oprah Denies Rampant Gay Rumor" (*Variety*)
"Rumblings Behind the Oprah Rumor" (*New York Post*)
"Oprah Says She's Playing It Straight" (*Intelligencer Journal*)

The week before that speech, her ratings had slipped 9 percent. "Since my appearance on the 'Ellen' show, there have been rumors circulating that I'm gay," Oprah said in her press release. "I've addressed this on my show, but the rumor mill still churns. Several weeks ago, syndicated columnist Liz Smith wrote that 'one of the biggest and longest-running TV stars is contemplating coming out. . . .' Apparently, people assume that it's me. It's not.

"As I've said, I appeared on the Ellen show because I wanted to support her in her desire to free herself—and I thought it was a really good script. I am not in the closet. I am not coming out of the closet. I am not gay."

Unintentionally or not, Oprah issued her statement during Gay Pride Week, which Barney's downtown store in New York City celebrated with a window showing mannequins of Ellen DeGeneres and Anne Heche popping out of a volcano. The Ellen mannequin is reading a copy of the *New York Post*'s front page reporting that the Walt Disney Company, which owned ABC, was getting bashed by Baptists over its "gay-friendly" policies. Flying above the whole scene is Oprah Winfrey in an airplane trailing a banner that reads, "I Am Not Gay." In certain gay circles those words became as infamous as Richard Nixon's "I am not a crook."

Years later Rosie O'Donnell, who had come out as a lesbian, speculated on Oprah's relationship with her best friend: "I don't know that she and Gayle are necessarily doing each other, but I think they are the emotional equivalent of [a gay couple]. . . . When they did that road trip together ["Oprah and Gayle's Big Adventure," featured in five episodes on *The Oprah Winfrey Show* in 2006], that's as gay as it gets, and I don't mean it to be an insult, either. I'm just saying, listen, if you ask me, that's a [gay] couple."

Twelve years later, when Ellen DeGeneres married Portia de Rossi, Oprah presented their wedding video on what *The New York Times* called "the secular chapel" of her daytime talk show. She chose to make her pro-gay statement and celebrate Ellen's lesbian union less than a week after voters in Maine, like those in thirty other states, rejected same-sex marriage.

When Liz Smith was asked about the reaction to her blind item, she said, "I am sorry Oprah got what she considered grief because of this." Years later the columnist said that Mary Tyler Moore had phoned her the day the item ran and joked, " 'Liz, I'm *not* coming out.' So it has always amazed me that Oprah chose to assume I was talking about her [when I wrote that one of the biggest and longest-running TV stars is coming out]. . . . I came to sincerely regret this stupid blind item, and I have never done another one. [But] as a result, Oprah called a press conference to say she was not gay and would not be coming out. I hadn't even been thinking of her when I wrote it. But I always felt it created some hard feelings, which I had not intended. So this knee-jerk reaction [of hers] was peculiar, I felt. She should have just ignored it. But it caused enormous speculation, and maybe that's the kind of thing that keeps her front and center. She always seems to grasp the nettle."

The suggestion that Oprah purposely teased rumors about her sexuality seemed plausible in light of certain comments she made in interviews, in speeches, and on her show. Two months before appearing on Ellen's coming-out show, Oprah hosted a Valentine's Day segment entitled "Girlfriends" in which she mentioned the affectionate nicknames she and her best friend, Gayle King, called each other. Oprah was "Negro"; Gayle was "Blackie." Oprah joked on the air about rumors that Gayle was the reason Oprah avoided marrying Stedman, and Gayle joked that Oprah was the reason she got divorced. Their jokes led to lurid cover stories in the tabloids:

> "Oprah & Gayle Move In Together" (*Globe*)
> "Oprah's Secret Life: The Truth About Those Gay
>     Rumors" (*National Enquirer*)
> "Oprah & Gayle Like Lovers" (*Globe*)
> "Who's Gay & Who's Not in Hollywood" (*National
>     Examiner*)

It was not just the grocery store press that speculated on Oprah's sexuality, but also the mainstream media. Writing about her power as America's "talker-in-chief," the *National Review* said, "she may or may not be lesbian." In an essay about "the strange genius of Oprah," *The New Republic* proffered its analysis: "Though she claims to have been romantically involved for years with a man named Stedman Graham . . . the two have never married. Naturally, gossip has circulated for years that the relationship is a sham and that Oprah is actually gay. Provocatively enough, Oprah rarely refers to Graham on her show. Instead, her most frequent references are to Gayle King. . . . So, rather than refute rumors that she is homosexual, she seems to subtly encourage them. . . . Her detractors cry hypocrite. But there is nothing hypocritical about having a private life. If Oprah is in a fake romance, and if she is gay, neither reality would contradict her public advocacy of courage, fortitude and growth through suffering."

People wrote about Oprah and Gayle as if they were Gertrude Stein and Alice B. Toklas, although they did not live together, and they categorically denied they were lovers. There was no foundation for the rumors of a lesbian relationship, except for their constant togetherness and Oprah's bizarre teasing of the subject.

**Her cousin, Jo Baldwin, who once worked for Oprah, brushed off the subject of Oprah's attraction to women in an email: "Anything is possible but I wouldn't dare say it."**

**A prominent gossip columnist for the New York *Daily News* who has observed Oprah for years is convinced. "My**

gaydar first went up when I covered an event at Radio City Music Hall [April 14, 2000] and watched Oprah and Gayle walk the red carpet with their pinkie fingers linked and Stedman trailing behind them. Then came the huge, no-expense-spared launch of *O* magazine a couple nights later when Oprah installed Gayle as Editor-at-Large. If you get the text of Oprah's remarks, you'll see that she sounded like the husband who gives his trophy wife everything. . . . It was all in jest but . . ."

Onstage at Manhattan's Metropolitan Pavilion the night of April 17, 2000, Oprah introduced Gayle to a teeming crowd of alpha females (Barbara Walters, Diane Sawyer, Martha Stewart, Rosie O'Donnell, Maria Shriver, Diana Ross, Tina Turner), saying, "I'm known to be a good gift-giver. You've read rumors. It's true. . . . Over the years I've given Gayle a lot of great gifts." She then regaled the crowd in a Southern singsong voice. "I gave Gayle her nanny when she had her first chile, and then her second chile; we got extra hailp. I built the swimmin' pool for the children." The audience roared. "Paid for the children's private schools. Bought her a BMW for da birthday." The audience laughed as Oprah catalogued her largesse and her friend's indebtedness. Adopting a meek little voice to imitate Gayle, she continued, "Oh, I just don't know, I don't know what I can ever do to repay you. The children, we can never repay you. There's nothing we can do to repay you." The punch line came after Gayle quit her job in Hartford, started commuting to the Hearst offices in New York to help launch Oprah's magazine, and began working so hard that she finally said, "Bitch, I don't owe you nothing!" The audience screamed with laughter.

While Oprah had a live-in male partner, she seemed to spend more time with Gayle, and she talked about her best girlfriend at every turn, providing for her and her children in a way few men ever could. Oprah moved Gayle to New York City to take over *O* magazine, bought her a $7.5 million apartment in Manhattan in addition to her $3.6 million house in Greenwich, Connecticut, and traveled the world with her, sometimes with Stedman in tow, sometimes not.

Part of Oprah's strong fan base was in black churches, where traditional marriage between a man and a woman is honored. As one of their own, Oprah was a shining example to the world of African American achievement, and few would ever publicly criticize her, but there were murmurs among some black ministers that, despite her grand success, Oprah was not the best role model for young African American girls. For whatever reason, she was not prepared to make the commitment to marriage: "I can choose not to be married, if I want," she said, opting for the comfort and acceptance of being a couple in a coupled society. Yet her living situation with Stedman, her close friendship with Gayle, and her departure from the church in which she was raised made some in the black community wonder about her sexual moorings. While Oprah denied being a lesbian, she seemed to deliberately provoke discussion of her sexuality by issuing bizarre denials to questions no one asked, as if she wanted to stir publicity.

This became particularly noticeable in 2006, when *O, The Oprah Magazine,* devoted an issue to friendship and featured a Q&A titled "Oprah and Gayle Uncensored," which kicked off another furor of gay rumors:

> Q: Well, let's get right to it! Every time I tell somebody, "I'm interviewing Oprah and Gayle," the response is always the same: "Oh [long pause] are they . . . you know . . . together?"
>
> OPRAH: You're kidding. People are still saying that?
>
> Q: Every single person . . .
>
> OPRAH: I understand why people think we're gay. There isn't a definition in our culture for this kind of bond between women. So I get why people have to label it— how can you be this close without it being sexual? How else can you explain a level of intimacy where someone *always* loves you, *always* respects you, admires you?
>
> GAYLE: Wants the best for you.
>
> OPRAH: Wants the best for you in every single situation of your life.
>
> GAYLE: The truth is, if we were gay, we would so tell you, because there's nothing wrong with being gay.

OPRAH: Yeah. But for people to still be asking the
question when I've said it and said it and said it, that
means they think I'm a liar. And that bothers me. . . .
I've told *nearly* everything there is to tell.

It was the *nearly* in Oprah's response that jumped out,
drawing media attention and giving comedians a field day. In his
nightly monologue, David Letterman mentioned that Oprah
had denied she was gay. "I hear that and I go hmmmmm. . . ." At
the American Museum of the Moving Image tribute to Will
Smith, Jamie Foxx said, "I was talking about you the other day. I
was lying in bed with Oprah, and I turn over to Gayle and I say,
'You know what?'" When Kathy Griffin went on *Larry King
Live*, he asked, "Do you think we're ready for a gay president?"
She said, "I'd love it. By that, I assume you mean Oprah. I tease,
Larry. I know we're scared of her. Oprah, first lesbian president.
Gayle, lesbian vice president. Just a thought. I'm not outing
anybody."

The rumors that dogged Oprah probably said more about society's need to define people sexually and the discomfort many
feel about those who do not fit a prescribed definition of heterosexual or homosexual. The category of bisexual is too fraught for
most people, although Oprah introduced the subject with a
show on "sexual fluidity," showing women past the age of forty
who left their men for other women without necessarily defining
themselves as lesbians. She said she understood the resistance to
such labeling. After interviewing the evangelist Ted Haggard
about the gay sex scandal that forced him to resign as pastor of
the New Life Church, she told her audience, "I got [i.e., under-
stood] him as not wanting to be labeled—not wanting to be put
in a box." Throughout the Haggard interview, though, she
made a point of saying she did not agree with him that sexuality
is complex and complicated. "I am heterosexual," she stated. "I
don't know what it would be like to have that inclination [to the
same sex], but I have many friends who are gay." Even admitting
to having homosexual friends was a big step forward for the
young woman who once thought homosexuality was a sin and

who told her brother, who died of AIDS, that he would not go to Heaven because he was gay. Still, Oprah was so sensitive to the lesbian rumors surrounding her that she would not allow two women in her employ at Harpo to publicly declare their relationship, although they had been living together for several years. In other words, she seemed to say: It's okay to be gay, as long as I'm not tainted by it.

Perhaps Oprah's enthusiasm for her female friends was misinterpreted by those who made assumptions because they were looking through a prism of lesbian rumors and gave her comments far more weight than she intended. For instance, shortly after Liz Smith's blind item and Oprah's cameo as the therapist who gently urged Ellen to come out, Oprah and her camera crew went on tour with Tina Turner in 1997, to Houston, Las Vegas, and Los Angeles. "We followed her around the country because I wanted to be Tina," Oprah said. Instead, she became Tina's most famous groupie. Besotted with the rocker's personal story of survival, Oprah wore a blond-frosted Tina Turner wig, performed with her onstage, and gushed about her on the air the way she used to burble about Stedman when they first started dating. "Tina is our goddess of rock 'n' roll. . . . She is just the hottest. . . . I feel about Tina how men feel about football," Oprah said, giving rise to a rash of comments about a "girl crush." She told *Vibe* magazine that the most fun she has is "when me and Stedman and the dogs are in the Bentley and the top's down. And I'm wearing my Tina Turner wig, holding on to make sure it doesn't come off. That is a cool thing—the whole idea of it." Stedman finally told her to lose the wig. "Nobody's telling you that you are not Tina Turner, so I have to be the one to tell you. Take the wig off and stop pretending that you are Tina Turner." Oprah gave the wig to a cousin.

Shortly after the tour, Oprah sat down with Jamie Foster Brown of *Sister 2 Sister*, a black entertainment magazine. The article was titled "Everything Negroes Ever Wanted to Ask Oprah." During the interview Stedman telephoned, and Brown reported Oprah's side of the conversation: "Now Oprah starts talking about the Liz Smith column that said a prominent [television] person who is an icon is gay. Oprah had sent out a press release saying she wasn't gay," Brown wrote, before quoting what Oprah said to Stedman:

"No. Right. Okay, honey. So you're gonna tell them no? Whatever. I already sent out a press statement. Just say, 'I think she said it all.' Why can't you say that? You can say, 'I'm sick of this. We're so sick of this gay stuff.' Why does everybody want to think you're gay? Okay. Bye."

"So Oprah," asked Jamie Foster Brown. "Are you gay?"

Oprah laughed. "I think if you're gay, that's fine; it's your business and it's fine. But what offends me about anybody implying that I'm gay or Stedman is gay is this: that means that everything I've done or said is a sham. . . . It means it's a lie. The whole thing's a lie. It would mean that everything you've ever done or said, the whole thing is one great, big, faked-up lie."

Despite such denials, speculation persisted over Oprah's sexual preferences. She continued living with Stedman, but they maintained separate lives, which they said was necessary because of their careers. They came together for occasional weekends, holidays, and vacations. "This is what our life is like," Oprah explained to one writer. "I call it two ships passing." She made a loud tooting noise. "We just check at the beginning of the week:

" 'Where are you gonna be?' I say. 'Okay, I'm going to Maya's this weekend.'

"[He says:] 'Well, I'm gonna be in Colorado Springs.'

" 'When do you think you'll be home? Sunday? Okay. Could you take an early plane and get here Sunday afternoon? Maybe we can have dinner together.' That's what our life is like.

" 'Where are you gonna be?' 'I'm gonna be gone for the summer. . . . I'll try to get a house on the weekends so you can come up . . . and see me and the dogs.' "

To some, Stedman looked like Oprah's cover story—the presentable male partner she needed to be accepted by heterosexual society, nothing more than camouflage. Her close friends argued otherwise, saying he was the grounding force of her life. Others did not care one way or the other. "I would not be surprised if

Oprah is gay," said her friend Erica Jong. "If she is, she is. It certainly fits. Stedman is probably gay or neutral, but they have a bond because of where they come from. Her being gay would be the right reaction to the sexual abuse she says she's suffered and the mistrust she's always had of men. Remember, many people don't want to be outed, and I don't think everyone needs to declare themselves publicly. Besides, people, mostly women, can slide easily from one sexual preference to the other. If Oprah is gay, I can understand that she does not want that fact known in a society that is homophobic and might judge her negatively. As a businesswoman, to declare herself publicly as a lesbian might be detrimental."

During their interview Jamie Foster Brown asked Oprah, "How important is sex?"

Oprah said, "It's a natural part of the process. I mean I'm not one of those women who feels like I gotta have it all the time. . . . I wouldn't consider myself a very sexual being."

Some who knew Oprah well during her Baltimore years agreed with her assessment, speculating that her tormented four-year love affair with Tim Watts, who was married at the time, plus seriously involved with another woman when he was seeing Oprah, had so blindsided her that she was wrung out, emotionally and sexually, and never able to make herself vulnerable to any man again. Instead, she poured all her sexual energies into her career. Her conflict over submission and control found its resolution in her work, and soon the investment of time and energy in herself became its own reward, and her own survival.

With the retirement of Phil Donahue and the growing prestige of her book club, Oprah's show became the first stop for celebrities who wanted to promote their films, their albums, their tours, and themselves. She increased her star shows in 1996, but got off to a rocky start when she covered the red carpet for the Sixty-eighth Annual Academy Awards.

"The moment you realized it was going to be a long show [was] when a star-struck Oprah Winfrey acted as if she'd never handled a microphone or asked a question before in public," wrote the TV critic for the *Hartford Courant*.

"Hey, Brad [Pitt]! Oh, gosh. It's great to see you."

"Nicolas [Cage], hey! Great to see you!"

"Ron [Howard]! Hi, Ron. How are you? How are you? It's a long way from Mayberry."

"Hi, Jimmy [Smits]. We wanted to say, on behalf of all my friends, you're a babe, and we don't mean the pig. How cool is he? Oh!"

The critic from *The Buffalo News* said the first misstep of the evening was "the decision to have Oprah Winfrey fawn over celebrities as they entered the Dorothy Chandler Pavilion. 'Oh my God, Elisabeth [Shue]. What a year.' 'To die for [Nicole Kidman], that's what you look like.' Ohmygod, indeed. There hasn't been anything this embarrassing since, well, since Letterman opened last year's show with his 'Uma, Oprah' bit."

A British critic even took a whack at what Oprah wore. "The worst-dressed woman of the evening [was] Oprah Winfrey," wrote Stuart Jeffries in *The Guardian*, ". . . in a décolleté, backless dress that still contrived to have sleeves and shoulders." After viewing her role as the official greeter at the Oscars, Howard Rosenberg, TV critic of the *Los Angeles Times*, recommended, "Um, maybe she should keep her day job."

Oprah was more comfortable and in control in her own setting, with producers to prepare her, stylists to dress her, soft lights to frame her, and, most important, an audience to applaud her. What the critics did not appreciate was that she was not a journalist, she was a saleswoman, and like her twenty million viewers, she, too, was agog over celebrities. She brought them all to her stage with gushing introductions, conveyed with whoops and hollers, before she sat them down to wheedle out the most intimate details of their personal lives.

"We want to believe you are running Annette's bathwater on a regular basis and dropping rose petals along the side so she can . . . you know, whatever," she said to Warren Beatty.

"We have our moments," he said.

Oprah pressed. "You have your moments."

Beatty smiled. "We have our moments."

George Clooney told her, "I'm never going to get married";

Eddie Murphy said he preferred black women to white women; Kate Winslet said she was never going to have plastic surgery: "Why would I want to look like a wrapped testicle?" Britney Spears said she was "going to try" to remain a virgin until marriage; and Diane Keaton said shoes were her favorite accessory because "they're penis substitutes." Bicycling with Lance Armstrong around her estate in Montecito, Oprah asked, "How come your butt doesn't get sore?" She asked Jim Carrey, "Why do you think you are good at sex?" She asked Janet Jackson about her pierced nipples. "At any given moment of the day," said the singer, "a lot of it [body piercing] can be very sexual."

Oprah told Cybill Shepherd, "You can say *penis* and *vagina* on this show." So Shepherd proceeded to do so as she discussed her love affair with Elvis Presley. "A few things he had to be taught; he liked to get himself a big plate of chicken-fried steak, but there was one thing he wouldn't eat."

The audience gasped. "Did you teach him?" asked Oprah.

"I sure did."

When Lisa Marie Presley appeared on the show Oprah asked her why she had married Michael Jackson. "Was it a consummated marriage?" Again, the audience gasped, but Oprah admonished them. "You all damn well know you want to know."

"Yes," said Lisa Marie. "It was."

Oprah invited Patrick Swayze and Wesley Snipes to discuss their movie about drag queens (*To Wong Foo Thanks for Everything, Julie Newmar*). "I want to hear about the gender-benders," she said, "because how did you tuck in the penises? How did you keep them down—the peni? I mean—oh, God—is the gender-bender the same as a jock strap? Is it . . . sort of the same thing?"

"Sort of," said Swayze, "but it just yanks the other way."

"Yeah," said Snipes, "it's like a sock."

Despite her predilection for the risqué, Oprah dropped basketball's bad boy Dennis Rodman from her show because she said his book, *Walk on the Wild Side,* was too raunchy. "After reading the book, I did not feel that it was appropriate for my viewers," she said.

Over the years *The Oprah Winfrey Show* became a Mecca

for celebrities: Ben Affleck, Kirstie Alley, Jennifer Aniston, Drew Barrymore, Beyoncé, Mary J. Blige, Bono, Lynda Carter, Cher, Bill Cosby, Kevin Costner, Billy Crystal, Matt Damon, Johnny Depp, Cameron Diaz, P. Diddy, Robert Downey, Jr., Clint Eastwood, Michael J. Fox, Richard Gere, Robin Givens, Hugh Grant, Tom Hanks, Florence Henderson, Julio Iglesias, Michael Jordan, Ashton Kutcher, Jay Leno, David Letterman, Jennifer Lopez, Susan Lucci, Paul McCartney, Matthew McConaughey, George Michael, Bette Midler, Demi Moore, Mike Myers, Paul Newman, Gwyneth Paltrow, Brad Pitt, Sidney Poitier, Lionel and Nicole Richie, Chris Rock, Diana Ross, Meg Ryan, Brooke Shields, Jessica Simpson, Will Smith and Jada Pinkett Smith, Steven Spielberg, Jon Stewart, Barbra Streisand, Luther Vandross, Denzel Washington, Robin Williams, Stevie Wonder, Tiger Woods, and Renée Zellweger. They all understood that by appearing with Oprah they would be safe, secure, and swaddled—able to sell their shows, films, records, products, and, most important, themselves.

Wynonna Judd came to talk about her weight; Julia Roberts announced she was pregnant with twins; Madonna denied she'd adopted a baby from Malawi as a publicity stunt. Later, in reviewing all the celebrities she knew, Oprah told her audience, "Céline Dion, Halle Berry, and John Travolta really became friends of mine." She interviewed Tom Cruise nine times over the years and gave an entire hour to reuniting the cast of *The Mary Tyler Moore Show* because, as she said, "I wanted to be Mary Tyler Moore."

"My wife [Academy Award–winning actress Shirley Jones] and I did the *Oprah* show a couple of times," recalled Marty Ingels from his home in Beverly Hills. "Once was: 'Couples Who Have Some Secret to Hide.' We were on with Jayne Meadows and Steve Allen. She found him in bed [with another woman]. Blew us away . . . I made a big mistake by trying to kid around with Oprah. I said, 'C'mon, Oprah. You don't like Jews. You won't let me talk.' Whoa. Big mistake. Apparently, she's been accused of being anti-Jew—Anyway, we never got on again and here's the reason: we didn't get paid by Oprah."

Ingels explained that according to AFTRA (the American Federation of Television and Radio Artists), all performers are to be paid a minimum fee ($537 in 1997) for their appearances, whether or not they perform, but Oprah claimed to have a special arrangement with the local union and didn't pay anyone. Ingels demanded an investigation by AFTRA. "It's wrong that this billionaire lady should make her own rules different from any other talk show. . . . Why should she walk over her fellow performers? It's chicken feed to her, but some actors rely on that occasional check. For her to screw them is not right. . . . Is it a mortal sin? No. But it's small and nasty and told me something petty and mean about her. I remember her once saying control is ownership. . . . Despite her reputation as St. Oprah she's really all about money. . . . Yeah. Shirley finally got her check and so did all the other people who hadn't been paid, because I called *The Hollywood Reporter* and got publicity over the matter. And that's what Oprah didn't want. Publicity. That's a big disinfectant."

One of the biggest celebrity "gets" for *The Oprah Winfrey Show* was not a member of AFTRA but could have used the $537 check, after being shortchanged by the House of Windsor in her divorce. Sarah, Duchess of York, was better known as Fergie, a name inextricably linked to the phrase "toe sucking" because of photos taken of her with her lover, which led to the dissolution of her marriage to the queen's favorite son, Andrew, Duke of York.

"Oprah almost lost that interview because her producers insisted that Sarah appear on the show wearing a tiara," said an ABC executive involved in the negotiations. "Oprah's producers do Oprah-speak: 'Oprah wants,' 'Oprah says,' 'Oprah insists.' On this issue Oprah was *really* adamant.

" 'Oprah thinks it would be quite royal.'

" 'No way,' said Sarah's publicist.

" 'No tiara, no interview,' said Oprah's producers.

"This bubbled up into a real crisis," said the network executive. "Oprah's producers were dead serious about the tiara and pushed until Sarah's publicists almost canceled. There were two days and nights of high-level fits around here. . . . Finally

Oprah's side gave in and Sarah appeared on the show to promote her book—without a tiara."

The disgraced duchess was as close as Oprah ever came to interviewing British royalty. She had met Diana, Princess of Wales, in April 1994, when she lunched with her at Kensington Palace. "We had an honest and fun conversation when I came over for BAFTA," said Oprah. (The British Academy of Film and Television Awards had named *The Oprah Winfrey Show* "Best Foreign TV Program.") "I found her so charming, but she wasn't interested in doing an interview, so I didn't push it." After their lunch, the princess, still married to the Prince of Wales, sent Oprah a black-and-white photo of herself signed simply "Diana x" in a sterling-silver frame monogrammed with the initial *D.* She later gave her tell-all interview to the British broadcaster Martin Bashir.

"The Princess chose him over Oprah because she felt she'd make more impact in Britain with a flagship programme such as *Panorama,* and because it was the BBC," said Diana's former butler Paul Burrell in an email. "Martin Bashir also promised her full control. It was nothing to do with Oprah and everything to do with [Diana's] focus on the British market and sending out her deliberate message to the British people. It was a carefully managed event and the location/context was upper-most in her mind."

When Sarah Ferguson first appeared on *The Oprah Winfrey Show* she was promoting her book *My Story,* which touched on her conviction that Buckingham Palace had plotted to destroy her. She appeared a year later as a spokesperson for Weight Watchers and mentioned moving back in with Prince Andrew. She drew audible gasps from the audience when she discussed how she and her ex-husband shared the same house with their two daughters and accommodated each other's liaisons, a titillating revelation that gave Oprah the kind of news coverage she and her producers craved.

Oprah's producers were known to make outrageous demands of guests. "If she wants you on her show, her producers possess your life for weeks beforehand, and you and your family and your friends must be available twenty-four hours a day every day that they want you," said a publishing executive who has booked many authors on *The Oprah Winfrey Show*. "If it's three weeks, then you must be available morning, noon, and night for twenty-one days, but it's usually well over a month of your time. Her producers want the most intimate look at your life imaginable, and sometimes they go to places that can be considered exploitive, invasive, and quite painful. For example, Oprah's producers wanted Elizabeth Edwards [the wife of former senator John Edwards] to take them to the spot in the road where her son had been killed. Her publicists demurred. 'I don't think that will work,' they said, not even checking with Elizabeth. . . . Harpo producers root through everything, but the end result is not 'gotcha' television. Oprah is not about that. Rather, she wants to give her audience a personal experience they cannot get anywhere else, and of course most people agree to her demands because they want to get on her show."

There was one guest of whom absolutely nothing was demanded but his handsome presence. "I was really thrilled about John F. Kennedy, Jr.," said Oprah. "We had been asking and asking to have him on so many times, and this time he called us. I think he agreed to do it because it was convenient." Oprah cut short her vacation to fly back to Chicago in August 1996 to tape the interview when Kennedy was in town for the Democratic National Convention. She even ordered two new chairs for her set, but after the white upholstery got lint all over Kennedy's suit she had them re-covered in leather. Four years after he was killed piloting his plane, Oprah sold "the chairs that John F. Kennedy, Jr., sat in" in a charity auction on eBay for $64,000.

At the time of the interview Kennedy was considered the most eligible bachelor in the country, but Oprah, who asked intimate questions of everyone, would not ask him about his personal life. "I didn't ask him when he's getting married because it's the No. 1 question everyone asks me and it's nobody's business but his." Instead, she showed him the provocative video of Marilyn Monroe appearing in a low-cut flesh-colored sequined dress that looked sprayed on and singing "Happy Birthday, Mr.

President" to his father at Madison Square Garden. Young Kennedy smiled but did not take the bait. "Yes," he said. "I've seen that many times."

Although Oprah was unable to coax anything out of the dashing young man, his mere presence gave her record-breaking ratings, which were not topped until Barbra Streisand appeared two months later. Streisand returned in 2003 and topped her previous ratings by singing on daytime television for the first time in forty years. Still, Oprah was most ecstatic about the Kennedy interview. "I thought I loved him," she said after the taping. "Now I know I do."

Oprah was at the top of her game in 1996, making more than $97 million a year and stacking up Daytime Emmys like firewood. She ruled talk show television then because she gave her viewers compulsively watchable programming. It was not all celebrities all the time but a combination of pop culture and dramatic first-person stories of abuse and survival intermixed with books, movies, music videos, beauty makeovers, fad diets, and psychics, plus pressing issues of the day.

Shortly after the outbreak of mad cow disease (bovine spongiform encephalopathy) in Britain was linked to a neurological disease afflicting humans, Oprah presented a show on April 16, 1996, titled "Dangerous Foods" in which she asked if the fatal incurable disease that attacks the brain and leads to a slow excruciating death could spread to the United States. The first guest was a British woman who said that her dying eighteen-year-old granddaughter had fallen into a coma after eating hamburger tainted by a mad cow. Film footage showed stumbling, disease-ridden cattle in Britain. The second guest was a woman whose mother-in-law had died from the debilitating disease, which she felt was contracted from eating beef in England. The next two guests were Gary Weber from the National Cattlemen's Beef Association, who said government regulations ensured that U.S. beef is safe, and Howard Lyman from the U.S. Humane Society, who said the human form of the disease could make AIDS look like the common cold. The reason, he said, is that each year in the United States one hundred thousand sick cows are slaughtered, ground up, and used for feed.

"Howard, how do you know for sure that the cows are ground up and fed back to the other cows?" asked Oprah.

"Oh, I've seen it," said Lyman. "These are USDA [U.S. Department of Agriculture] statistics."

Looking sick, Oprah turned to her audience. "Now, doesn't that concern y'all a little bit right here, hearing that? It has just stopped me cold from eating another burger. I'm stuck. . . . Dr. Gary Weber says we don't have a reason to be concerned. But that in itself is disturbing to me. Cows should not be eating other cows. . . . They should be eating grass." The audience roared their approval.

The next day cattle prices dropped on the trading floor of the Chicago Mercantile Exchange, and the cattlemen blamed Oprah, although a livestock analyst with Alaron Trading Corporation said, "The program [only] exacerbated what was already a negative situation in the market." Oprah defended herself, saying, "I am speaking as one concerned consumer for millions of others. Cows eating cows is alarming. Americans needed and wanted to know that. I certainly did. We think we were fair. I asked questions that I think that the American people deserve to have answered in light of what is happening in Britain."

The National Cattlemen's Beef Association objected to the "unbalanced" editing of the show, pulled $600,000 in network advertising, and threatened to sue Oprah under a Texas statute that outlaws making bad and untruthful statements about perishable food products. Cowed, Oprah aired a second "Dangerous Foods" show the following week (April 23, 1996) and pointedly did not include Howard Lyman, who had said the U.S. livestock industry was feeding "roadkill" to cattle. An angry rancher later said the second show was "too little too late" because Oprah "didn't go on the program and eat a hamburger before the world."

Within six weeks, various cattle groups had banded together to sue her, King World Productions, Harpo, and Howard Lyman, seeking $12 million in damages. For the next year Oprah geared up to defend herself, spending hundreds of

thousands of dollars on lawyers and jury consultants, in addition
to the expense of moving her show to Amarillo, Texas, for a six-
week trial in federal court. In the past when she had skirted the
line between responsible and irresponsible comments, she had
not been called to account, except for her show on devil worship,
during which she introduced the suggestion of Jews sacrificing
their children. After meeting with Jewish leaders and apologizing, she was allowed to move on. This time was different: the
cattlemen, seeking revenge, wanted to go to court, despite efforts
made on Oprah's behalf to settle the case.

Phil McGraw (later known as Dr. Phil, when he became a
talk show host) was working as a trial consultant and had been
retained by Oprah's lawyers to help plan their courtroom strategy
and prepare the defendants for trial. He recalled meeting with
Oprah and her attorneys to discuss settling the case instead of
going to trial. When Oprah asked what he thought, McGraw
said, "If you fight this to the bitter end, the line at the Sue
Oprah window is going to get a lot shorter." Actually, that line
was never long, because Oprah's wealth had protected her from
serious litigation: few people wanted to go up against her bot-
tomless purse and crushing teams of lawyers. Other than a few
pesky lawsuits here and there, including one from former
Harpo photographers Paul Natkin and Stephen Green, who
sued Oprah (and settled) over a copyright infringement, she
had been fairly lucky. In a deposition during the photographers'
case, she said, "My intent always is to own myself and every part
of myself that I can, including photographs, a building, everything in the building. I have, you know, created a culture . . . at
Harpo of ownership." The attorneys representing the photographers recalled Tim Bennett testifying that Oprah did not know
the difference between a W2 form and a 1099, which they
found "totally unbelievable."

Hardly litigious, she had filed suit only once before, in
1992, when she and Stedman sued a Canadian tabloid that had
published an interview purporting to be with Stedman's male
cousin under the headline "I Had Gay Affair with Oprah's Fiancé." She and Stedman won that suit by default when the

publisher went out of business rather than defend the claim. She instigated one other lawsuit in 1995 by prompting her former decorator Bruce Gregga to sue the *National Enquirer* after the tabloid published color photos of her Chicago condominium, showing shiny gold-fringed chairs, satin damask couches strewn with velvet pillows, red silk wall coverings, and a marble bathtub with gold-plated faucets. "Her place was awful, so ornate and rococo, she should've sued the decorator for bad taste!" said one of the *Enquirer*'s attorneys from Williams and Connolly in Washington, D.C. Gregga was represented by Oprah's attorneys from Winston and Strawn, and Shearman and Sterling.

"I remember seeing her minutes after she had seen the pictures," said Bill Zwecker of the *Chicago Sun-Times*. "She had just flown back from Rancho La Puerta to attend Stedman's book party on the top floor of Michael Jordan's restaurant, and she was livid. 'I am so furious,' she said. 'I just got off the plane and saw a picture of my bathroom in the *National Enquirer*.' She fired Bruce, even though she knew he had nothing to do with publishing those pictures. He had a guy working for him who sold the photos for twenty-five thousand dollars to the tabs . . . but Oprah said they should have been locked in a safe. . . . She felt totally violated." In the end, Oprah and Gregga opted not to go to trial and settled with the tabloid.

She would say later that she never considered settling the "Dangerous Foods" lawsuit out of court, but her codefendant, Howard Lyman, claimed otherwise. "If they could have found a way to feed me to the cattlemen and gotten her out of the lawsuit, I would have been down in a heartbeat," he said. "I have the highest regard in the world for Oprah, but I can't say the same for her people at Harpo. . . . After the trial was over they contacted my attorney and told him they wanted me to pay Oprah's legal costs [approximately $5 million]." Lyman also said there was great fear resulting from the lawsuit. "The toughest thing for me was when my wife looked me in the eye and asked, 'If we lose, do we lose everything we have?' I had to tell her yes."

Oprah, too, was afraid. She told the *Amarillo Globe-News* that before the trial she sent a security team to the city to make sure she would be safe from a lunatic's bullet and her dogs would be safe from being poisoned. She later told Diane Sawyer, "I was afraid, physically afraid for myself. Before I went to Amarillo there were . . . 'Ban Oprah' buttons . . . and bumper stickers." She said she wasn't afraid of all the people in Amarillo, just a random fanatic who might get excited by all the controversy. Beyond concerns of bodily harm, Oprah realized that if she lost the case, she would lose more than money: she would forfeit the credibility that was the cornerstone of her career. Consequently, she spared no expense in defending herself.

A close reading of the depositions taken in the lawsuit indicates quite a bit of rancor and staff dissension within Harpo, underscoring what one of Oprah's former publicists described as "a snake pit." Employees testified to workplace problems of drugs, sexual addiction, and anger management. An anonymous letter sent to plaintiffs' attorneys on Harpo stationery was introduced as an exhibit at the deposition of a former employee. The letter directed the plaintiffs' counsel to look into the drinking problems of one of Oprah's senior producers, and race and sex discrimination throughout Harpo. The letter was signed "A Big Beef Fan."

In deposing one of Oprah's former senior producers, her attorney Charles ("Chip") Babcock discredited the producer by exposing his past police record, plus an outstanding arrest warrant, which may have been the reason why all future employees of Harpo began with a thirty-day probation period while they were investigated by Kroll Associates, the international detective agency, before being hired full-time.

Oprah gave her first deposition on June 14, 1997, and two days later she wrote that she was still "reeling" from what she felt was an indignity. "Crew cut. Southern, young snuff-spittin' lawyer, asking me if I'd just use my 'common sense.' Humiliating. They loved it. . . . First time I ever felt pinned down, my back against the wall. Looking into the eyes of those lawyers, I felt like when those mossy-toothed boys had Sethe [from *Beloved*] pinned down in the barn. . . . I can't shake the demeaning, gut-wrenching deposition."

Q: What reasonable scientific basis do you have for saying that cows should not eat other cows?

A: No scientific basis. Common sense. I've never seen a cow eat meat.

Q: That's the entire basis for the statement?

A: My common sense?

Q: Yes.

A: And knowledge that I've acquired over the years.

Q: What knowledge is that? That's what I'm trying to get at. . . . What's the basis for the statement that they shouldn't be eating other cows?

A: Because that's the way God created them, to eat grass and hay.

The attorney then asked about her professional credentials.

A: I'm the CEO of Harpo.

Q: You are also the host of *The Oprah Winfrey Show*?

A: Uh-huh.

Q: Are you an entertainer or a journalist?

A: I'm a communicator.

Q: Could you identify for me the awards that you have won?

A: Well, the award that means the most to me is being named one of the ten most admired women in the world, number three behind Mother Teresa.

He pressed her on the number of viewers she had, suggesting she did sensational shows like "Dangerous Foods" to draw more viewers, get higher ratings, and further enhance her business opportunities. She disagreed.

Q: So you don't care what your viewership is. . . .

A: That's not what I said.

Q: You do care?

A: I would like to have as many viewers as possible, but I don't do shows just to get viewers. I do not. This isn't Jerry Springer you're talking to . . . okay?

Oprah said there had been some shows that she had taped but then decided not to air:

A: One was a serial killer, Mercer, Ohio, who had allegedly killed 80 different people and he spoke about how he did it. Another one was a show on kidnapping. Another one was a stalker.

Q: What was the show on kidnapping, what was wrong with that?

A: Well, I thought that the way the show was presented it would encourage or present the idea of kidnapping to somebody who didn't have the idea. And since I'm a main target for kidnapping I thought it wouldn't be a good idea.

Six months later, on December 19, 1997, she gave the second part of her deposition and became a little testy when the plaintiffs' attorney suggested she did "sensationalist type of work."

A: I object to the word sensational. I object to the word sensational. I don't do sensational shows. Not from the beginning have I done sensational shows. My feeling is that life is sensational and if it exists in life and you can report it, tell about it, inform and make people more aware then so be it, but I object to the term sensational.

The day before the trial began (January 20, 1998), Oprah arrived in Amarillo on her Gulfstream jet accompanied by her two cocker spaniels, her trainer, her bodyguards, her hairdresser, her chef, and her makeup man. Prior to her arrival, the Amarillo Chamber of Commerce had issued a staff memo saying there would not be "any red carpet rollouts, key to the city [or] flowers" for her. Instead, she was welcomed to town (population 164,000) by bumper stickers that read, "The Only Mad Cow in America Is Oprah." She headed for the Adaberry Inn, a ten-suite bed-and-breakfast that she had taken over for herself and her personal entourage, which came to be known as Camp Oprah. The rest of the Harpo staff and production crew moved into the five-star Ambassador Hotel. She also rented the Amarillo Little Theatre to tape her shows in the evening after she attended the trial during the day. Oprah told the reporters gathered from around the country that she was in Amarillo to defend her "right to ask questions and hold a public debate on issues that impact the general public and my audience." She later said the trial was the worst experience of her life.

The judge, Mary Lou Robinson, issued a gag order, prohibiting both sides from discussing the case. "Can you imagine how hard it was for me NOT to talk about the trial?" Oprah said. "Can you imagine a gag order on a talk-show host? It was horrible." She came close, though, as she cleverly presented herself as pro-beef in Amarillo, where the feedlot/slaughterhouse is the single biggest employer. In her first taped show, she had steaks sizzling in the background as she said, "Of course, you're in Amarillo so there's beef, beef, and more beef." Interviewing Patrick Swayze, she said, "You had beef, did you? That's just fine by me." He presented her with a cowboy hat and a pair of black Lucchese boots. Then he taught her the Texas two-step. She adopted a countrified Texas accent, and at some point in every show (she taped twenty-nine) she mentioned the nice people of Amarillo. Within days she had the town wrapped around her little finger. The line for tickets to watch tapings of her show began forming at 4:00 A.M. every day and new bumper stickers sprouted up reading, "Amarillo Loves Oprah."

The female judge refused to allow women to wear pants in her courtroom, so Oprah wore a skirt every day. "I loved the fact no cameras were allowed in the courtroom," she said. "Those artist renderings made me look skinny." Even with her trainer and her chef in tow, she still battled her weight—at least for the first few days. Then she said she gave herself over to "Jesus and the comfort of pie." She gained twenty-two pounds during the six-week trial. "My trainer, Bob Greene, was very upset with me. He said, 'It's like you gained it, and you're very proud of it.' I'd say, 'Yes! I ate pie! I ate pie! And we had macaroni and cheese with seven different cheeses!'" Her codefendant, Howard Lyman, a cattle rancher turned vegetarian, was not allowed to mention weight or food to her. "Her attorneys told me I couldn't talk to her about her diet during the trial. . . . They felt she was under enough pressure." As director of the Humane Society's Eating with Conscience campaign, Lyman was covered by legal insurance, which also paid for half the fees of Phil McGraw.

After he was hired, McGraw flew to Chicago to meet with Oprah, but he was told by one of her assistants that she could give him only an hour of her time. "Excuse me," he said, "it isn't *my* ass getting sued. If that's all the time she's got, then I don't want to be part of this." Before he stomped out, Oprah agreed to give him as much time as he needed to help her drop her defensiveness. "She came across poorly," he said later, "in a state of disbelief that she was being sued." Midway into the trial he told her to "snap out of it" or she was going to lose. She had come to his door at 2:30 in the morning, sobbing hysterically and unable to cope with the frustration of being "unfairly" accused. "My advice to her was that 'right or wrong, Oprah, this is happening. They are well financed, dead serious, and deeply committed.' . . . I was a wake-up call that said deal with the fairness later, but right now you are in a fire-fight, and you'd better get in the game and get focused. . . . At that point she became a very different litigant."

Tall, balding, and broad-shouldered, McGraw walked behind her going in and out of the courthouse every day and never said a word to the news media. He did not even nod hello. Tim Jones of the *Chicago Tribune* said, "I thought he was one of her bodyguards."

"Phil met with us and all the lawyers after every day in court," said Lyman, "and he was worth every nickel he charged. His fee was $250,000—I know because I had to pay half of it—but I do not believe we would have won the lawsuit without the advice we got from him. . . . Phil said we could defend the case on the facts and march in all of our scientists to swear up and down that everything we said was true, and the other side would do the same thing. But the jury sitting there needed to know if they voted to take away our right of free speech, someone could come along and vote to take away theirs. That was what Phil came up with and that's why we won."

Midway through the third week of the trial, Oprah took the stand to testify. She ascended the steps of the courthouse clutching the hand of Maya Angelou, who whispered in her ear as she stood to walk to the witness stand. Stedman arrived a few days later to take over from Maya, who returned home and sent a group of preachers to church to pray around the clock for Oprah.

For three days Oprah was examined about her negligence in not double-checking Lyman's claims and not doing something about her producer's careless editing. At one point she lost her patience, sighed loudly, and tossed her hair over her shoulder. When asked about her huge viewership, she said, "My show has been built around people who are just regular people with a story to tell." Then she added, "I have talked to everybody I have ever wanted to, except for the pope." After repetitive questioning, she leaned in to the microphone and in a commanding voice said, "I provide a forum for people to express their opinions. . . . This is the United States of America. We are allowed to do this in the United States of America. . . . I come from a people who have struggled and died in order to have a voice in this country, and I refuse to be muzzled." She said if the guests on her show believe what they say is true and sign a statement to that effect, then truth is established for her, and accountability rests largely with the guests. "This is not the evening news," she said. "I'm a talk show where free expression is encouraged. . . . This is the United States and we are allowed to do that in the United States." When she was asked about her integrity, she said, "I am a black woman in America, having gotten here believing in a power greater than myself. I cannot be bought. I answer to the spirit of God that lives in us all." She said her influence was not enough to drive Americans away from beef. "If I had that kind of power, I'd go on the air and heal people."

Her attorney pleaded with the jury in his final argument. "You have an opportunity to silence one of the powerful voices of good in this country. She is here to validate our right to free speech." Describing Oprah as "a shining light" for millions of Americans, he said, "Her show reflects the right of the people in this country to have free speech . . . and robust debate."

After five and a half hours' deliberation over two days, the all-white jury of eight women and four men cleared Oprah, her production company, and Howard Lyman of knowingly making false and disparaging statements about beef. "We didn't like what we had to do," said the jury forewoman, "but we had to decide for the First Amendment." Hearing the verdict, Oprah lowered her head and wept. Moments later she appeared on the courthouse steps in sunglasses and flung her fists to the sky. "Free speech not only lives," she yelled, "it rocks."

# $S$ e v e n t e e n

O PRAH NEVER gave up her dream of becoming a marquee movie star, and by 1997 she felt she finally had the vehicle to put her name in lights. For nine years she had been trying to develop *Beloved,* Toni Morrison's novel about the effects of slavery. But even with a finished script, her own financing, and Disney as the distributor, she had been rejected by ten directors, including Jodie Foster (*Little Man Tate*), who said the book was too difficult to be filmed; Jane Campion (*The Piano*), who said she did not know enough about the black experience; and Peter Weir (*Witness, Dead Poets Society*), who said he did not want Oprah to play the lead of Sethe, the mother who kills her daughter rather than send her into enslavement.

"[He] couldn't quite see me in it," Oprah sarcastically told the writer Jonathan Van Meter. Mocking Weir's Australian accent, she said, "And would I please just trust him and if he felt that I could be in it he would certainly make every effort."

Although she had appeared in only two feature films and three made-for-television movies, Oprah insisted she was born to play the role of Sethe. So she dismissed Peter Weir without further consideration. "You want *me* to give you *my* script and *you* decide if *I* can be in it? Okay. Bye-bye."

In 1997 she found the Oscar-winning director Jonathan Demme (*The Silence of the Lambs*), who said he couldn't wait to see her play Sethe. Demme was hired on the spot, and Oprah became the producer and star.

"This is my *Schindler's List*," she said, referencing Steven Spielberg's masterpiece. She felt that she could do for descendants of slavery what Spielberg had done for Holocaust survivors—bring to the screen a story of heroism surrounded by heinous evil. This was to be her first feature film production, although she had been producing made-for-television films on ABC under the banner of "Oprah Winfrey Presents," and most had won their time slots with high ratings, if not rave reviews.

"Do you suppose anyone has ever had the nerve to tell Oprah Winfrey to go soak her head?" wrote *The Washington Post*'s TV critic, Tom Shales, about her production of *David and Lisa*, which was directed by Oprah's first Baltimore boyfriend, Lloyd Kramer. "[H]er evangelistic tendencies are beginning to spin way out of control. . . . She'll improve and nurture and inspire us even if it kills us." Shales objected to Oprah's on-camera introduction: "She tells us what the film is about, what the moral message is and how we should react to it. . . . She also spells out some of the plot, perhaps for people who move their lips when they watch TV. . . . Winfrey playing national nanny is getting to be a drag. 'It's a story I wanted to tell to a whole new generation,' she says grandly into the camera. Oh, Oprah. Give it a rest already."

She brought the same high moral fervor to the making of *Beloved*. "It's my history. It is my legacy. It is the capital WHO of who I am," she said of the three-hour film that cost $53 million to produce, plus another $30 million to promote. "It's wonderful to be in the position to finance the movie yourself," she said. "I don't care if two people come to see it or two million. This movie will be done and it will be incredible, one of the great statements in my life."

To prepare for her role she began collecting slave memorabilia, buying at auction ownership papers from various plantations, which listed the names and purchase prices of humans alongside those of mules and pigs under the designation of "property." She framed the wrenching documents and hung them in her home and in her trailer during filming. Five generations removed from slavery, she lit candles to "the spirits of the ancestors," said she heard the voices of slaves and prayed aloud to

them every day. She bought as her "first very serious art purchase from Sotheby's" a painting by Harry Roseland titled
*To the Highest Bidder,* which she hung over the fireplace in her
Indiana farm. The canvas shows a black slave and her young
daughter trembling with fear on the auction block.

Oprah also enrolled in "The Underground Railroad Immer-
sion Experience," to reenact the emotions of a runaway slave who
has been denied free will and independent thinking. For two days
she lived as a fugitive, blindfolded, chased by bloodhounds, and
spat upon by whiskeyed slave masters on horseback. "I knew I
was still Oprah Winfrey, and I could take off the blindfold anytime I wanted, but the reaction to being called a nigger was just
visceral for me. I wanted to quit. But I didn't. I wanted to feel it
all. I touched a dark, hollow place of hopelessness that I'll never
forget. It was a transforming experience for me. I came out fear-
less because I truly learned where I came from."

Oprah was determined to present a story that exposed how
slaves absorbed the abuse of their masters, turning it on their
own—physically, sexually, emotionally. The taboo theme of
sexual abuse, so frequently left out of slave narratives, drew her
because of her own personal experience, and she resolved to
show the horror of sexual molestation on-screen. She wanted audiences to experience slavery in a way they never had before: to
see a woman lynched, bound with tight leather cords, a metal
shiv jammed in her mouth; to hear the rope crack her neck; and
to smell her corpse as it is left to rot in the gallows. Oprah
wanted people to feel the lash of whips cutting across a bloody
black back, leaving a tree of scarred welts. She intended to produce something more memorable than the miniseries *Roots,*
Alex Haley's sweeping slave epic that transfixed 130 million television viewers in 1977. "While *Roots* was magnificent and
necessary for its time, it showed what slavery looked like, rather
than what it felt like," Oprah said. "You don't know what the
whippings really did to us."

With *Beloved,* she planned to recast the story of slavery in
America in all its hell and heroism. "We got it all wrong," she said
of the history books. "For years we've talked about the physicality

of slavery—who did what and who invented that. But the real legacy lies in the strength and courage to survive."

She wanted nothing less than to change America's consciousness with her film, and to heal racial wounds. "I understand a lot of what that conflict is about," she said. "It's about people truly not understanding one another. Once you understand, come to know people and have a knowledge of their hearts, the color of their skin means nothing to you."

During his second term in office, President Bill Clinton had called for a "national conversation on race," and Oprah felt the president would have done well to have chosen her to lead that conversation. "He should've," she told *USA Weekend.* "I know how to talk to people. . . . Everything is about imagery. We're people who respond to imagery. You need to see something different so you can feel something different."

She felt that her production of *Beloved* would provide the needed differential. "I just want this movie to be received in the way that I truly think it should be," she said. "I want people to be moved and disturbed by the power of Sethe. If that can happen, I'll be satisfied for a very long time."

When the film came out, the critics were moved but, disturbingly to Oprah, in the wrong direction. Most found her film too long, too confusing, and overwrought, and her acting less than star-making. *The New York Times*'s Janet Maslin said she was not "an intuitive actress"; *The New Republic*'s Stanley Kauffmann said she was merely "competent"; and *Commonweal*'s Richard Alleva dismissed her as "surprisingly dim." But her good friend Roger Ebert, the film critic, said she gave "a brave deep performance," and *Time*'s Richard Corliss agreed. "This isn't a gimmick performance; it is genuine acting." Even Toni Morrison, who worried about Oprah's ability to contain her oozing emotions, was impressed. "As soon as I saw her I smiled to myself, because I did not think of the brand name," said Morrison. "She looked like Sethe. She inhabited the role." But the public did not want to see Oprah as Sethe and watch her water breaking, or see her breast milk stolen by "mossy-toothed" white men, or her slitting the throat of her baby girl.

In a perceptive column for the *Chicago Sun-Times* Mary A. Mitchell, herself an African American, summed up why:

> Who are these kinds of movies supposed to appeal to anyway? Are black people supposed to enjoy being reminded that they were once chattel and treated like animals? Are whites supposed to empathize with such a fate and leave the theater more sensitive to its legacy? How many of us really, when swept into a sea of guilt, humiliation and anger, call it a good time? A documentary that guides us there is one thing. A star-studded cast is another. Unless you're a masochist, pain is not entertaining. If only these movies fostered a deeper understanding between the races, they would be worth the agony. But that is hardly the case.

*Beloved* was released on October 16, 1998, with one of the most expensive ($30 million), media-saturating publicity campaigns ever accorded a film—and perhaps that was part of the problem. To some people Oprah appeared to be promoting herself more than her movie, or the important message behind the movie, especially when she appeared on the cover of *Vogue,* the bible of fashion elites. The editor, Anna Wintour, who weighed barely one hundred pounds, had flown to Chicago to tell Oprah she had to lose weight before she could be considered for the cover. "It was a very gentle suggestion," recalled Wintour, who filled her pages with runway whippets. "She knew she had to lose weight. . . . I suggested that it might be an idea. . . . I said simply, 'You might feel more comfortable.'" Then she added, "She promised she would lose twenty pounds by our deadline."

Later, André Leon Talley, *Vogue's* editor at large, and quite sizable himself, told Oprah, "Most of the *Vogue* girls are so thin, tremendously thin, because Miss Anna don't like fat people."

Like a fashion slave hearing her master's voice, Oprah rushed off to a weight-loss boot camp and began sipping broth, climbing mountains, and running eight miles a day to get down to 150 pounds. Only then did Ms. Wintour allow her to pose for noted photographer Steven Meisel, a favorite of Diana,

Princess of Wales. Oprah's *Vogue* cover, in October 1998, sold 900,000 copies and became the top seller in the magazine's 110-year history. Oprah later told Sheila McLennan from BBC Radio 4's *Woman's Hour* that the idea of being on the cover of *Vogue* wasn't even a fantasy for a little girl who claimed to have been called "colored," "ugly," and "Buckwheat." Oprah devoted one of her shows to her *Vogue* makeover and flew to New York when Wintour hosted a cocktail party at Balthazar Restaurant during Fashion Week to unveil the cover.

"It's unbelievable," said Stedman Graham when he first saw the photo of Oprah lounging seductively in a black strapless Ralph Lauren gown. "It's like the culmination of all that she's worked for. . . . From being overweight to this point is one of the greatest victories a person can have."

It may have been this kind of thinking—putting the glamour of a weight-loss makeover on an equal footing with overcoming slavery—that caused the publicity and promotion surrounding *Beloved* to backfire.

In addition to *Vogue,* Oprah promoted her film by posing for the covers of *TV Guide, USA Weekend, InStyle, Good Housekeeping,* and *Time,* which heralded her with four articles and eleven pages as "The Beloved Oprah." Days after the film's release, she arranged a special showing for New Age guru Marianne Williamson's Church of Today in Detroit and told the congregation, which included Rosa Parks, sitting in the front row, "*Beloved* is my gift to you." On the day the film opened, *The Oprah Winfrey Show* presented the cast of *Beloved* and the making of the movie. "I'm having my baby," she told her audience. That same day launched publication of *Journey to Beloved,* by Oprah Winfrey, with photographs by Ken Regan—a forty-dollar coffee-table book of the daily diary Oprah kept during the three months of filming, in which she also recorded her shock over the murder of the designer Gianni Versace in Miami and the startling death of the Princess of Wales in a Paris tunnel. But most of her entries concerned filming *Beloved,* which Oprah said was the only time in her life, other than filming *The Color Purple,* when she was truly happy. A few excerpts:

Tuesday, June 17, 1997: The tree [prosthetic scars] went on my back. I wept. Could not but tried to stop myself. Couldn't. There's a tree on my back. Felt it. I pray to be able to trust to go all the way there. To feel the depth, power of what it all means.

Tuesday, July 1, 1997: The morning was abuzz with talk of a meeting in my trailer. Word was we needed a conference about me looking "too pretty." This is a first! In all my days I have never been called too pretty or expected this to be a subject of discussion. My teeth are too white. I'm too "luminescent." I need more sweat. . . . Lord, it is a new day.

Friday, September 12, 1997: It's a bittersweet time. My final day of shooting in the summer of my dreams. A dream bigger than anything my heart can ever hold. It will be a long time before I can take it all in. I can honestly say I embraced every moment, I did it my way. I have no regrets.

Oprah promoted her movie as medicine that is good for you whether or not you like it, and she sat for hours giving newspaper and television interviews. "The thing about this movie is . . . you really have to pay attention," she told one reporter. "And that's why this is probably my 135th interview. . . . Because I want people to know that there has not been a movie like this before, and you need to be prepared. . . . People need to know that this is a movie that requires your full attention, just as all art does. That it stimulates, is deep, goes down, down, down and comes back up again."

She gave these interviews under strict control: she could be quoted, but she would not be photographed unless the photographer agreed to sell her the rights to the images, an almost unheard-of request. Otherwise, all pictures of Oprah—airbrushed and stylized—had to be provided by Harpo. Each article had to run in the local newspaper and could not be put on the wire services, where other newspapers might pick it up. She set similar limitations on *The Today Show* and *Good Morning America*, stipulating one-time use of her words and images.

During a *20/20* segment on ABC with Diane Sawyer,

Oprah held forth on the subject of race, saying the country still shows the wounds of slavery. "It will be all right if [only] we're willing to have the courage to open up the wound, look at it. That's the only way it's going to get all right."

SAWYER: What do you see in white people today living with slavery?

WINFREY: Denial. Absolute denial.

SAWYER: But for everyone to go back and see it, it's probably white America saying, "Again? Go back again?"

WINFREY: That is so ridiculous.

SAWYER: What do we gain by going back to it again?

WINFREY: We haven't even gone there. Going back to it again? We have not even begun to peel back those layers. We haven't even ever gone there. This is the first time.

The public, black and white, did not want "to peel back those layers" and wallow in murder, rape, and racial mayhem. Despite efforts by Oprah and Disney Studios to sell the movie as a mother's love story, nobody was buying, not even Oprah's core audience of middle-aged women. Within six weeks of its release, *Beloved* was declared a box office flop, lagging behind the universally panned *Bride of Chucky*. It ultimately had a domestic box office gross of $22,843,047, after costing $83,000,000 to make and market.

People were astonished that the media Midas had produced and promoted something that had not turned to gold. Oprah, too, was shocked, although to the press she remained defiantly proud, and when promoting the film abroad, she blamed its failure on U.S. audiences. She told the *The Times* of London, "I think the reason why the film has not been received as well in America as I expected is because people in America are afraid of race and any discussion about race. I don't think it has anything to do with me in the role. I think for a lot of Americans the issue of race is so volatile that to bring it out front makes people embarrassed."

She told the *Sunday Express* that U.S. audiences stayed away because of their guilt over slavery. "The whole country was in denial," she said. Years later the comedian Jackie Mason rapped Oprah for saying that America was racist. "Please!" he said to Keith Olbermann on MSNBC. "There's very little bigotry against Jews in this country anymore or racism against blacks. Oprah Winfrey stands up and says, 'This is a racist society.' She's got billions. You've got a dollar and a quarter, but it's a racist society. She's a sick yenta."

The next day Liz Smith wrote in her syndicated column that she did not agree that there was no anti-Semitism or racism in America, "but you've got to hand it to Jackie Mason. There aren't too many people in showbiz who are brave enough to call Oprah a 'sick yenta.'"

At the time *Beloved* was dying at the box office, Oprah's friends ached for her. "That film was the dearest thing to her heart," said Gayle King. "She felt more passionate about it than anything I've ever seen her do." Acknowledging Oprah's distress, Maya Angelou said, "I don't know if *Beloved* is a commercial failure. It's not the commercial hit that Oprah and others wanted, but it's a majestic film and a great film. It will have its own life." The director, Jonathan Demme, said, "I'd love to make another movie with Oprah . . . I'd like to find her a comedy. And we wouldn't hype it as much as *Beloved*."

When Whoopi Goldberg appeared at Harvard for a campus event a few weeks after the film was released, she was asked whether Oprah represented all of black womanhood. Goldberg giggled, wrinkled her face, and joked that something "flew up my nose." The crowd in Sanders Theatre laughed.

"It's great to see that someone can create a frenzy the way Oprah has," Whoopi said, "but it's unfortunate it sort of backfired on the movie."

Sitting in the front row that day, Henry Louis ("Skip") Gates, Jr., asked Goldberg why she thought *Beloved* had failed at the box office.

"I don't think people are there yet. I believe you have to be very careful when you're as big as Oprah that your audience doesn't get lost." Then she said, "I know if I answer you truthfully I'll have to answer for it [later] and I don't want to get into that with her."

Unfortunately, Whoopi's remarks were reported in 1998, and seven years later Oprah was still so angry she would not invite Whoopi to the "Legends Weekend" she hosted in 2005 to celebrate the accomplishments of African American women. The rebuke was stunning, considering that few African American women had won more artistic awards than Whoopi Goldberg. She is one of only ten artists to receive the five major entertainment awards: an Academy Award (*Ghost*), two Golden Globes (*The Color Purple* and *Ghost*), an Emmy (*Beyond Tara: The Extraordinary Life of Hattie McDaniel*), a Tony for producer (*Thoroughly Modern Millie*), and a Grammy (*Whoopi Goldberg Direct from Broadway*). In addition, she has won a BAFTA award and four People's Choice Awards, and has been honored with a star on the Hollywood Walk of Fame. Her exclusion from Oprah's Legends Weekend seemed petty.

After the debacle of *Beloved* and the collapse of her dream to become a grand movie star, Oprah fell into a deep depression. "I was beyond hurt. I was stunned. I was devastated by the reaction. . . . I've been so in synch with the way people think and I've never been wrong. This was a first. The first time in my life . . . I felt rejected and it was a public rejection. . . ." She vowed: "I will never do another film about slavery. I won't try to touch race again in this form." She said she turned to food for comfort. "Like a heroin addict goes to heroin, I went to carbs," she said, explaining her macaroni and cheese binges. "I tried praying about it and I gave myself a 30-day limit: If I didn't feel better, I was heading to a psychiatrist. I asked God what this experience was supposed to teach me. Eventually I realized I was allowing myself to feel bad because of my attachment to an expectation that 60 million people would see the film. When I let go of that, I was healed."

Making matters worse at the time was losing her status as the country's number one talk show host. For twenty-five straight weeks Jerry Springer had beaten her in the ratings, and

Oprah was reeling. The previous summer she began hinting that she might give up her show, saying she was tired of the grind, but she always made this kind of feint right before contract negotiations.

"I'm not so much saddened by the way [my ratings are] going as stunned," she said at the time. "Unless you are going to kill people on the air—and not just hit them on the head with chairs—and unless you are going to have sexual intercourse—and not just, as I saw the other day [on Jerry Springer], a guy pulling down his pants and pulling out his penis—then there comes a time when you have oversaturated yourself." By then what she called Springer's "vulgarity circus" had beaten her in the ratings forty-six of the previous forty-seven weeks. "I can understand how you can get beaten in the ratings," she said. "I'm introducing books and they've got penises."

Oprah had come a long way from the days when she, too, loved to shock her audiences. But she no longer wanted to be seen as a vulgarian, hosting shows for nudists and shouting "penis, penis, penis." She believed that *Beloved* had transported her to a higher level. "It changed my life," she said. She told her producers that she felt she now had a moral obligation to change the lives of others. "I want to bring meaning to people's lives." She framed a huge photograph of herself as Sethe with "the tree" lashed across her back and hung it outside her Harpo office alongside a big leather whip as a reminder to her staff of her new vision for herself and her show. When Oprah's protégée Rachael Ray saw the photograph and the whip, she was reported to have said to friends, "Why is she wearing slave drag? She obviously has problems being black." Ray's publicist later denied that the TV chef had made the comment.

Oprah announced she would renew her contract with King World through the 1999/2000 and 2000/2001 seasons and begin a new kind of television. She received $130 million in cash advances and 450,000 King World stock options, in addition to the 1,395,000 options she already had from deals made in 1991, 1994, and 1995. By the time CBS took over King World in 1999, Oprah, whose fortune was then worth $725 million, had options on 4.4 million shares, worth $100 million.

Newly enriched and enlightened, she launched what she called "Change Your Life" television. She opened her 1998/1999 season with a new theme song based on an old spiritual, which she sang herself: "I believe I will run on and see what the end will be. . . . Come on and run with me. O-O-O-Oprah!" She introduced New Age guides such as the author John Gray (*Men Are from Mars, Women Are from Venus*) to instruct her audience "to determine for yourself your true soul's desire and to be on purpose with your life." He taught her viewers to meditate by saying, "O glorious future, my heart is open to you. Come into my life." Using colorful props in his presentations, he handed a big stick to one woman, who closed her eyes and sobbed when he said, "I'd like you to go back to your inner child. I want you to imagine Mommy and Daddy coming to you, and I want you to express your feelings to them."

Believing in spiritual empowerment, Oprah presented the Yoruba priestess and inspirational author Iyanla Vanzant (*Acts of Faith*) to counsel women on finding love and purpose in their lives. Vanzant advised viewers "to surrender to the god of your understanding." One audience member asked, "I want to know how do you find total and complete peace?"

"Get naked with yourself," said Iyanla Vanzant.

Oprah also introduced the financial author Suze Orman (*The 9 Steps to Financial Freedom*), who preached that "money is a living entity and responds to energy, including yours." Orman told Oprah's audience, "Your self-worth equals your net worth." She said they needed to get rid of their bad emotions and start believing they were destined for wealth in order to become wealthy.

Another regular "life coach" was Gary Zukav, who wrote *The Seat of the Soul,* which Oprah said was her second-favorite book, next to the Bible. She introduced him as a onetime Green Beret and former sex addict who lived on a mountain without television. His purpose was to help Oprah and her audience "delve into their souls" and resolve their fears. "Your feelings are the force field of your soul," he said, emphasizing that fear is the cause of everything from violence to meanness.

"So," Oprah said, "fear is the opposite of love?"

"Fear is the opposite of love," he said.

"And anything that isn't love is fear?"

"Correct," he said. "When you really look at your fears and you heal them, you can look at yourself and you'll be beautiful."

He and Oprah devoted one entire show to karma. "Energy is energy," he said, "and you cannot escape it."

Oprah also embraced Sarah Ban Breathnach, the author of *Simple Abundance*, a spiritual self-help book, from which she advised her viewers to keep gratitude journals. "Every night I write down five things in my journal I'm grateful for," Oprah said. "If you concentrate on what you have, you'll end up having more. If you constantly focus on what you don't have, you'll end up having less."

One of her most colorful "life strategy experts" was Dr. Phil, who had guided her through the cattlemen's lawsuit. She introduced him as "the deepest well of common sense I've ever encountered." At first the big, bald, blunt practitioner of tell-it-like-it-is therapy jolted her audience by telling them they were "way wrong," "full of crap," and "wimpin' out." He didn't spare Oprah, either. In a segment about weight, he said, "We don't use food, we abuse food. It's not what you eat, but why you eat that has you in the problem you're in."

"Well, there are some people who are just genetically disposed to being smaller," said Oprah.

"But the fact is that ain't you!"

He told one member of the audience, "You talked about flowers and cake and wedding and dress. You're preparing for the wedding but not for the marriage."

"Mercy," said Oprah. "That is a good statement. That is so good!"

Dr. Phil said, "People say, 'time heals all wounds.' Let me tell you, time heals nothing. You can do the wrong thing for ten years, and it doesn't equal the right thing for one day. And the fact that—"

"Whooo," yelled Oprah. "That's good, Phil! Whooo! That's a good Phil-ism."

Soon Dr. Phil owned Tuesdays on *The Oprah Winfrey Show,* where he appeared for three years before entering into negotiations with Harpo to have his own talk show, which started in 2002.

Oprah concluded her "Change Your Life" shows with a segment called "Remembering Your Spirit," which she introduced with soft lights and New Age music, saying, "I am defined by the world as a talk show host, but I know that I am much more. I am spirit connected to the greater spirit." She ended one segment sitting in a bubble bath, surrounded by candles. "The bathroom is my favorite room in the house," she told *Newsweek,* which reported her bathtub sits like a small pond with water pouring out of the rocks that surround it. "I had this structure added on," she explained, "and the tub was sculpted to fit my body. My favorite thing to do is take a bath." On the air she sat in her marble tub filled with bubbles and recited a mantra to the spirits; then she addressed the camera. She urged her viewers to sit in their bathtubs for fifteen minutes every day. "Your day will undoubtedly be more focused, more centered," she said. "Things tend to fall in line." She talked about her spirit in interviews, saying, "I think I'm just becoming more of myself, which is better than anybody can imagine. By 50, 52, I just can't wait to see me."

The bubble bath segment unleashed a torrent of "Deepak Oprah" criticism, comparing her to New Age guru Deepak Chopra. There was a severe media backlash, especially in Chicago. "[A]s I stand in the eye of this latest hurricane of national [self-] worship, may I point out one thing," wrote Richard Roeper in the *Chicago Sun-Times.* "She's getting really goofy with all the spiritual questing." Oprah had told *TV Guide* she was so happy she was "splendiferous," but Roeper disagreed. "It seems to me we're watching a woman go through an almost frantic search for spiritual bliss and higher consciousness."

The *Sun-Times* later reported that a seventy-three-year-old woman following Oprah's advice to light scented candles and "be reminded of the essential qualities of your light" had accidentally set fire to her retirement high-rise, sending a dozen people to the hospital.

The *Chicago Tribune*'s TV critic, Steve Johnson, advised Oprah-holics to draw a bubble bath for their guru. "Her spirit—battered of late by indifference, criticism and the befuddlement on the faces of all those devotees who don't even know what she means when she preaches 'remembering your spirit' on her show every day—just might need it." He pronounced Oprah's "Change Your Life" television "a fairly skin-crawling thing.

"Winfrey, by giving it a label, was not just saying 'I want to help you change your life,' but making a more aggressive suggestion: 'You need to change your life.' And coming from a woman who can snap her fingers and get what she wants, who just signed a $150 million contract to do her talk show through 2002 and whose personal fortune has been estimated at closer to $1 billion than $0, it rings a little patronizing."

He also took aim at her for presenting blatant medical quackery by endorsing a woman who described herself as a "medical intuitive," who Oprah said was genuine because the woman had intuited that Oprah was worried about joint pain. As if a medical psychic, this woman diagnosed members of Oprah's audience simply by having them stand and give their first names and ages. She told a man with chronic migraine headaches: "Life owes me an explanation. That thought is in your liver and so it's burning. And what happens from the liver is there's an energetic circuit and it goes right up to the brain channel. And that starts the fire neurologically and that's why you have migraines."

Oprah soon became a moving target for the mainstream media. *Psychology Today* lambasted her for contributing to lunacy. "It is apparently arrogant to think that psychiatrists, physicists, evolutionary scientists, and epidemiologists might know more about their areas of expertise than say, Oprah," wrote Gad Saad, PhD, in an article about narcissistic celebrities who play doctor. A decade later *Newsweek* put Oprah on the cover (June 8, 2009), with an eleven-page article that castigated her for "crazy talk" and "wacky cures." Like the Pardoner in *The Canterbury Tales* who sold fake relics and spurious indulgences, Oprah was blasted as irresponsible for not knowing the difference between useful medical information and New Age nonsense. This was a complete turnaround for the magazine that had lauded her eight years before with a breathless cover story proclaiming "The Age of Oprah," saying, "She's changing more lives than ever." During her "Change Your Life" phase the magazine nicked her with a "Periscope" item titled "Oprah-Di, Oprah Da," giving five takes on "The Big O":

1. Good Riddance. It's Springer time! Oprah's feel-good blab is passé. What we require now is fights and sluts. Jerry! Jerry!

2. She's a Ratings Martyr. She knew she'd lose fans with her self-help focus, and knew *Beloved* was a tough sell. But she needs to better us!

3. O Is for Get Over Yourself. Oprah gets preachier every year. She's a cult leader, a self-proclaimed guru. And besides . . .

4. She's Telling Us How to Live? Can't keep the fat off? Can't tie the knot? Girl, your life's a mess.

5. Don't You Say That About Oprah! Survived poverty and abuse, saved the book biz, uses TV for good, cares about her fans and looks fly! You go, Oprah.

It was not just the Chicago critics who came down on Oprah for presuming her viewers needed their lives changed. She took it on the chin from the *Orlando Sentinel*'s Hal Boedeker, who said her bubble-bath segment screamed for a parody on *Saturday Night Live*. He suggested an appropriate topic for her next show would be "Celebrity Run Amok" with a new theme song, "You're So Vain," which, he said, Oprah could sing to herself. "Her confident style has given way to arrogance."

Perhaps the cruelest blow came when Wiley A. Hall III compared Louis Farrakhan to Oprah in the *Afro-American Red Star*. Hall wrote that with his "feel-good" Million Man March on Washington in 2000, the Nation of Islam leader was "trying to position himself as another Oprah Winfrey. . . . [Like Oprah] he's become a master of the obvious, earnestly stated, passionately put. . . . With Oprah Winfrey and her new clone Louis Farrakhan, I have this strong sense that we're being manipulated. I just can't tell whether it's for good or ill." The kicker came the following week, when Hall reported that followers of Farrakhan, known for race-baiting and virulent anti-Semitism, felt he was being insulted to be compared to Oprah.

In *The New York Times,* the newspaper she cared most about, Jeff MacGregor dismissed Oprah's "Change Your Life" television as "host worship," filled with "mind numbing clichés of personal improvement." He said that "like many gurus and circuit riders before her, Oprah has found a way to shamelessly market the history of her own misery and confusion as a form of worship."

Yet what sounded loopy to critics resonated with many in Oprah's audience, who shared her hunger for greater meaning in their lives. "I was a rural mail carrier in Stem, North Carolina," said Susan Karns, who runs the beauty shop at Hillcrest Convalescent Center in Durham, "and if it wasn't for Oprah and her 'Change Your Life' television, I would never have gone to beauty school at night and gotten this great job. . . . It was scary to change my life but I'm so glad I did. I love what I do now because I make people feel good every day and they are so grateful."

While some questioned Oprah's common sense, none doubted her sincerity. "I want people to see things on our show that makes them think differently about their lives," she said. "To be a light for people. To make a difference . . . to open their minds and see things differently . . . how to get in touch with the spiritual part of their life." However, she disliked being called a "New Ager." She told one woman in her audience, "I am not New Age anything and I resent being called that. I am just trying to open a door so that people can see themselves more clearly and perhaps be the light to get them to God, whatever they may call that. I don't see spirits in the trees and I don't sit in the room with crystals."

"Oh, but she does invoke spirits," insisted Peter A. Colasante, owner of L'Enfant Gallery in Washington, D.C. He then added facetiously, "She probably speaks in tongues, too. . . . I do know she waves her hands above her head like a Pentecostal when she says she feels vibrations. At least that's been my personal experience with her."

After buying some oil paintings through her decorator Anthony Browne, Oprah wanted to purchase more by the same artist [John Kirthian Court], so she contacted the L'Enfant Gallery directly. "Her people from Harpo called endlessly to set up an appointment on the same day she was going to Deborah Gore Dean's shop, across the street from mine in Georgetown. We were both told to deliver photos of what Oprah wanted to see, and the photos were to be awaiting her arrival at the Four Seasons Hotel the night before. We were told to have our galleries ready for her arrival and her viewing because she did not have much time . . . We were told that Oprah is micromanaged to the minute, like the president of the United States. We received a partial schedule:

2:17 P.M.:  Oprah's limousine arrives at L'Enfant Gallery
2:20 P.M.:  Oprah walks into gallery
2:30 P.M.:  Oprah views paintings
3:00 P.M.:  Oprah leaves L'Enfant Gallery

"Well, you don't just consign a few paintings by John Kirthian Court for a viewing. He's the grand-nephew of James McNeill Whistler two times removed and is considered a great painter and portraitist in his own right. He lives in San Miguel. You must buy his paintings outright [$60,000–$80,000 average price] and then sell them after you've air-freighted them from Portugal and insured their transport for hundreds of thousands of dollars. That's what I did: I purchased three paintings for Oprah's two thirty viewing." The gallery owner admitted feeling tentative about the investment because he'd had "trouble getting paid for the first three paintings" he had sold to Oprah a year or so before. "But I went ahead and did it," he said.

"Because her secretaries told me she only had a few minutes and would be gone by three P.M., I made a three thirty P.M. appointment with another client. The day arrived and we waited and waited and waited for Oprah. Finally, we saw her two limousines pull up to Deborah's shop at two thirty-five P.M. Time was passing, so around two fifty-five P.M. I went across the street, where Oprah was bellowing at Deborah for not having had her photos delivered to the hotel the night before. Apparently, when she walked into the shop, she said to Deborah, 'Are you Anthony's girl?' Deborah, who owns her own store, naturally got a little huffy. 'No. I'm *not* Anthony's girl. I'm not anybody's girl.' Oprah berated her for not having anything ready and kept yelling about how precious her time was. That's when I interrupted.

" 'Hey. You've kept me waiting for over thirty minutes.' Her security guards moved in, and Deborah started laughing. 'C'mon,' I said to Oprah. 'I need to show you your paintings so I can get to my own appointment.' With that I started to walk her out of the shop.

" 'Oprah does not walk,' she said.

" 'Aw, c'mon. It's only a few yards,' I said with my hand on her shoulder, steering her across the street. She started screaming at her secretary.

" 'Who is this guy? I don't know this guy. Who is he? Tell me what's going on here.'

"I said, 'Your people made appointments for you, insisted on absolute times, and said that we all had to be ready for your arrival and let nothing interfere, so I'm doing exactly what your people told me to do.'

"The secretary was so frightened she couldn't speak and she started shaking so hard her notebook bobbed up and down. This only incensed Oprah more. I thought she was going to swat the secretary and then decapitate me. Just as this was happening, a busload of kids passed by. They immediately recognized Oprah and started screaming. Then the most amazing thing happened: Oprah stopped hissing and spitting, and her serpent eyes softened as she waved and beamed. 'Hi, y'all.' . . . She actually turned from screeching harridan to sweet goddess in less time than it takes to blink. I swear I thought I was in the middle of an alien attack. . . . Then I marched her into my gallery, trailed by her pilot, her secretary, her hairdresser, her makeup man, and two big security guards. She walked through the front door and started waving her hands over her head like she was doing a very slow St. Vitus' dance.

" 'I just don't feel it,' she said, shaking her head. 'I just don't feel it. The vibrations aren't right . . . they're not speaking to me. . . .'

" 'You'll feel 'em once you see the paintings we've assembled for you,' I said, pointing up the stairs where the Court oils had been hung.

" 'Oprah does not do stairs,' she said. Before I could even respond to this one, my assistant let her have it."

"Yes, I'm afraid I did," recalled Maureen Taylor. "She had been so impossible to deal with even before she arrived, and then after all the trouble she had put Peter to for that appointment, she came in here waving her hands like some kind of mumbo jumbo mystic, saying, 'I just don't feel it. . . . I just don't feel it.' When she said, 'Stairs? Stairs? Oprah does not do stairs,' I lost it. I said, 'Well, maybe you should try them, sister. You certainly could use the exercise.' "

"That did it," said Colasante. "Oprah flounced out of the gallery, and I followed her down the street to her limousines. She yelled at her pilot. 'Get the plane . . . Get the plane. We're leaving.' And that was the end of Oprah Winfrey and her spirits and her vibrations."

To reporters, Oprah tried to dismiss the avalanche of criticism about her "Change Your Life" shows by suggesting it might be a matter of overexposure. "Was it too much *Beloved* publicity? Was the so-called backlash because I did the [theme] song the same year I was on the *Vogue* cover?" Most of that "so-called backlash" came from white male critics, who had trouble understanding the increasing "Oprahfication" of female America. As the comic Jimmy Kimmel joked when introducing *The Man Show* on Comedy Central, "We're here because we have a serious problem in this country—and her name is Oprah. Millions and millions of women are under Oprah's spell. This woman has half of America brainwashed."

Several critics, some within her own family, took Oprah to

task when, in 2007, she promoted *The Secret*, a DVD and book by Rhonda Byrne, as the answer to living a good life. "I took God out of the box," Oprah told her viewers before pushing *The Secret*, which describes Jesus Christ not as divine or as the son of God, but merely as one of the "prosperity teachers" in the Bible.

"That is not the way I raised Oprah Gail," said Vernon Winfrey, who was so disgusted by his daughter's embrace of New Age beliefs that he no longer watched her show. "I need her show like a hog needs a holiday," he said. "Besides, the show is not that good anymore."

Oprah's "aunt" Katharine, who keeps a Bible by her bedside, was horrified by Oprah's embrace of "that New Age nonsense," as was Katharine's daughter, Jo Baldwin, Oprah's cousin, who was once vice president of Harpo. Baldwin now teaches English at Mississippi Valley State University and preaches in church on Sundays in Centobia, Mississippi. "I brought Katharine a copy of *The Secret*, and Jo wouldn't get near the book—wouldn't touch it," said Jewette Battles.

When Oprah introduced the self-help philosophy of *The Secret* to her viewers, she promised they would learn "the secret" to making more money, losing weight, finding the love of their life, and achieving job success, simply by visualizing. They could have it all, just like she had it all. She then introduced the author, who explained that *The Secret* espouses "the law of attraction": If you think positively, you attract good things to yourself; if you think negatively, you attract bad things. She later cited, as an outrageous example, the massacre in Rwanda, and said the victims' feelings of fear and powerlessness had led to the carnage.

"The message of *The Secret* is the message that I've been trying to share with the world on my show for the past twenty-one years," Oprah told Larry King on CNN. She presented two shows on *The Secret*, sending the book to the top of the bestseller list, where it sold more than three million copies and spawned "Secret" clubs around the world. She was promptly ridiculed for peddling what Peter Birkenhead described on Salon.com as "minty-fresh snake oil." Comedian/talk show host Bill Maher

declared the book "insane," and *The Washington Post* characterized it as "slimy." *Saturday Night Live* poked fun at Oprah's obsession with *The Secret* in a skit in which she interviewed a poor
starving man in Darfur. Putting on a deep Old Testament
voice, Oprah, played by Maya Rudolph, asked, "Why do you
think things are going so bad?" When the poor man couldn't answer, Oprah scolded him, saying the atrocities were the result of
his negative attitude. "When we come back, John Travolta!"

Shortly after, Oprah "clarified" her views on "the law of attraction." She did not apologize for endorsing *The Secret*, but she
now said it was not the answer to everything. "It is not the answer to atrocities or every tragedy. It is just one law. Not the only
law. And certainly, certainly, certainly not a get-rich-quick
scheme." Interestingly, in 2009, Oprah declared in court papers
that her "reputation depends, in part, on the quality of the
products she recommends, which she does only after careful
consideration and vetting to make sure such products meet her
standards and approval."

She certainly paid attention to her critics, especially when
they reported her viewers were complaining about her meddling with their religious beliefs. Stung by articles about "The
Church of Oprah" and "The Gospel According to Oprah," she
dropped "Change Your Life" television and renamed it "Live
Your Best Life" television. She changed "Remembering Your
Spirit" to "Remembering Your Joy."

WHILE SOME CRITICS were writing her obituary in 1999, she
was empire-building with a media move that would leave them
all speechless. Joining with Hearst in April 2000, she launched *O,
The Oprah Magazine*, which became the most successful start-up
in magazine history. She put herself on the cover of every issue
for the next nine years, which further inflamed her critics to produce long essays on her narcissism. They carped about "The Cult
of Oprah," because each issue of *O* carried "The O List" of things
Oprah liked (e.g., Burberry dog collars, Fendi sunglasses, Ralph
Lauren mules, Rocket e-books), plus two pages titled "Oprah:
Here We Go" and "Oprah: What I Know for Sure," in addition

to recipes by Oprah's personal chef, diet tips from Oprah's personal trainer, and advice from Oprah experts such as Dr. Phil and Suze Orman, plus ads for upcoming Oprah personal growth summits. In addition, there is an Oprah interview with a high-profile celebrity such as the Dalai Lama, Madeleine Albright, Jane Fonda, Phil Donahue, Laura Bush, Muhammad Ali, Meryl Streep, Martha Stewart, Ralph Lauren.

In her interview with Nelson Mandela, he talked about how he had changed himself in prison and learned to train his brain to dominate his emotions so that he could negotiate with South Africa's racist white leadership. That interview, published in April 2001, should have been hailed as a journalistic coup for Oprah, but one Chicago critic saw it only as Oprah crowing.

"Sometimes self-esteem can look a lot like pathological narcissism," wrote Carina Chocano in the *Chicago Sun-Times*. "The cover of this month's *O* reads: 'OPRAH talks to HER HERO, the awesome, inspiring, noble NELSON MANDELA.' (OPRAH and HER HERO are [in] noticeably larger [type] than NELSON MANDELA.) Other articles include 'O: What I Know for Sure,' 'Oprah on Setting Yourself Free,' and 'Five Things Oprah Thinks Are Great.' (These include faux apples and pears, $18 each; a set of Murano glasses, $40 each; and a book called 'Spiritual Literacy: Reading the Sacred Truth in Everyday Life,' which helps Oprah 'see the extraordinary in ordinary experiences.')"

Editorially, the magazine presented Oprah's commandments for Living Your Best Life:

Keeping It Off Forever: 10 Rules
12 Strategies for Getting the Best Health Care
9 Rules for Writing a Good Ad
12 Things a Stepmother Should Never Say
10 Easy Food Switches for an Extra 10 Good Years
9 Things Weight Loss Winners Know (that you don't)

Once again David Letterman took a poke at Oprah on his late-night show by announcing "The Top Ten Articles from Oprah's New Magazine":

No. 10.    P, R, A and H. The Four Runner-up Titles
           for This Magazine.

No. 9.     Do What I Say or I'll Make Another Movie.

No. 8.     Funerals and Meetings with the Pope:
           Occasions Not to Use "You Go, Girl."

No. 7.     While You're Reading This, I Made 50
           Million Dollars.

No. 6.     The Night I Nailed Deepak Chopra

No. 5.     The Million-Dollar Bill: A Convenience
           That's Long Overdue

No. 4.     My Love Affair with Oprah, by Oprah

No. 3.     You Suckers Will Never Know What It's
           Like to Live in a Solid Gold Mansion

No. 2.     Ricki Lake's Home Phone Number and
           How She Hates 3 A.M. Calls

No. 1.     The Time I Had to Wait 5 Minutes for a
           Skim Half-Decaf Latte

Oprah filled her "personal growth guide," as she called her beautifully produced magazine, with advice pages from some of her "Change Your Life" gurus, to give "confident, smart women the tools they need to reach for their dreams, to express their individual style and to make choices that will lead to a happier, more fulfilling life." She advertised *O, The Oprah Magazine,* on her website, Oprah.com:

> *O* offers compelling stories and empowering ideas stamped with Oprah's unique vision of everything from health and fitness, careers, relationships and self-discovery issues to beauty, fashion, home design, books and food.

Within a year she had a paid circulation of 2.5 million and had raked in more than $140 million in annual revenues. Her critics were dumbfounded by the spectacular success of her new venture, which enlarged her media conglomerate. But when Chicago reporters tried to interview her about her new magazine, she turned them down cold, still smarting from their negative coverage of her "Change Your Life" television. "I flew to New York for the magazine launch," said Tim Jones, the business reporter for the *Chicago Tribune*, "and I was desperately trying to get an interview with her. After all, we are her hometown newspaper. . . . She wouldn't talk to me, but she sure as hell talked to *The New York Times*." In fact, Oprah called the *Times*'s media reporter, Alex Kuczynski, at home to thank her for a story about the success of *O* magazine. "It was about seven A.M. and I said, 'Oprah. Wow. This is like getting a phone call from Jesus Christ or Santa Claus,'" joked Kuczynski.

Soon Oprah would put herself well beyond the reach of all her critics by becoming an international philanthropist whose giving would enshrine her as a global icon.

# *E*ighteen

W HEN OPRAH appeared on the *Forbes* list of the world's
476 billionaires in February 2003, she became what
she had set out to be: the richest black woman in the world.
"From the very beginning—as early as 1985," recalled her
friend Nancy Stoddart, "she always said she was going to be a
billionaire."

She reveled in her riches as a blessing from God. When she
returned to Kosciusko in 1998 to promote *Beloved* and to dedicate a house that she had financed through Habitat for Humanity, she quoted Psalms 37:4 to the hometown crowd:
"Delight thyself in the Lord and he shall give thee the desires of
thine heart." Her visit was trumpeted by *The Star-Herald* with a
front-page headline: "Oprah Comes Home." Wearing a brown
turtleneck sweater, a long tweed skirt, and high-heel boots, plus
a big gold Rolex watch and a pinkie ring, she stood in the rain to
address the crowd while her bodyguard held an umbrella over her
head. "I'm most proud of the fact that I'm one black woman
from Kosciusko, Mississippi, with my hand still in God's
hand," she said. During that visit she told reporters that being
one of the most powerful people in television and having great
wealth was no problem for her. "You receive in proportion to
how big your heart is and how willing you are to extend yourself
to other people."

Deconstructing that statement might lead some to conclude that Oprah believed she was a billionaire because she had

more humanity than most, but she softened the impression, if not clarifying it, by adding, "It is why you have to give that comes back to you."

Always generous, she began giving in earnest in 1997, donating $12 million to the Oprah Winfrey Foundation and forming Oprah's Angel Network to collect donations from her viewers. "I want you to open your hearts and see the world in a different way," she told them. "I promise this will change your life for the better." She started by asking for spare change to create "the world's largest piggy bank" to fund college scholarships for needy students. In less than six months her viewers had donated more than $3.5 million in coins and bills to send 150 students to college, 3 students from every state. Even the White House contributed, and First Lady Hillary Rodham Clinton flew to Chicago to appear on Oprah's show with a piggy bank full of coins she had collected from employees.

Deeply affected by the 1997 death of Diana, Princess of Wales, Oprah wanted to assume her humanitarian role. "We are . . . grieved by Princess Diana's death," she said on *The Today Show,* explaining Oprah's Angel Network, "and the world was talking about what she did charitably—and I wanted people to know, you can do that yourself in your own space where you are in your life. . . . You can be a princess . . . by taking what you have and extending it to other people."

Oprah partnered her Angel Network with 10,000 volunteers from Habitat for Humanity to build 205 houses, one in every city whose local television station broadcast *The Oprah Winfrey Show.* When Habitat for Humanity built a house for Oprah's Angel Network, they called the project Oprah's Angel House, and after the tsunami of 2004 and the 2005 hurricanes Katrina and Rita, Oprah Angel Houses sprang up like mushrooms. She took her show to New Orleans, pledging $10 million of her own money, and from 2005 to 2006 she raised $11 million more through her Angel Network for rebuilding. She paid the operating expenses of Oprah's Angel Network so that all donations went directly to the charities she selected. By 2008, her viewers had contributed more than $70 million to 172 projects around the world that focused on women, children, and families; education and literacy; relief and recovery; and youth and community development—all selected by Oprah and donated in her name. She fully understood the goodwill that accrues to those who give, and so when she gave, she did so very publicly. Her philanthropy was not quiet or anonymous.

"She certainly makes an effort to do good deeds," Steve Johnson wrote in the *Chicago Tribune*, "even if there is often an accompanying effort to make the effort known." It is true that most of Oprah's giving was followed by an Oprah press release, plus mentions on *The Oprah Winfrey Show*, but perhaps she was setting an example for others to follow and not just being self-aggrandizing.

**By 2010 viewer donations had fallen off by 50 percent, so without fanfare she posted an announcement on her Angel Network website that she would no longer be accepting donations. She also discontinued the network's grant-making program. A review of the tax returns of Oprah's Angel Network indicates that she has been donating more than one-half of her viewers' contributions to help the needy in sub-Saharan Africa ($2,821,611 in 2008) and non-U.S. regions in North America ($2,409,594). The total for non-U.S. grants and distributions: $5,231,205. The total for U.S. grants: $3,354,322.**

**Some might suggest that the 150,000 viewers who contributed to Oprah's Angel Network are contributing less because she donated more of their money outside the U.S. But Oprah's fans did not give their money with strings attached. Wherever she wanted to give was fine with them, and in the last few years she has decided to position herself more as a global philanthropist and concentrate more of her giving in Africa.**

**In March 2010, Oprah staged a ten-day online auction on eBay ("Oprah's Great Closet Cleanout"), selling 40 pairs of shoes and boots, 42 purses, and 101 items of clothing, including jackets, skirts, blouses, sweaters, and dresses. Each item was tagged as belonging to Oprah: "Oprah Winfrey Prada Red**

Suede Peep-Toe Heels" drew bids of over $573. "Oprah Winfrey Black Chanel Quilted Evening Bag" drew $2,025. "Oprah Winfrey Carolina Herrera Dress, Worn on Show!" drew $1,125.

Oprah did not reveal the total figure raised from her online auction, but she stated that all proceeds went to the Oprah Winfrey Leadership Academy in South Africa. Oprah's previous online auctions (1999, 2004, and 2005) benefited Oprah's Angel Network, which at the time gave most of their donations to U.S. charities.

In later years she tried to position her initial do-good efforts as unheralded. "Early on in my career, when I first came to Chicago, I had my own Big Sisters club where myself and the producers would go into the projects," she told *Television Week*. "Didn't tell anybody about it. It wasn't publicized." Actually, she mentioned the Big Sisters club in almost all of her interviews at the time.

That effort began with a 1985 show taped in Cabrini Green, a low-income housing project on Chicago's Near North Side, known as one of the most dangerous bullet-strewn ghettos in the country. Mary Kay Clinton, the associate producer of the show, was so moved by the young girls she met that she started a Little Sisters program in conjunction with a Cabrini Green counselor, and Oprah and her staff participated as Big Sisters. There was great enthusiasm at first as the Harpo group met with the youngsters, ten to thirteen years old, every two weeks. Arriving in her limousine, Oprah would gather the girls from their ghetto apartments to go shopping or to the movies or out to dinner. When Mike Wallace came to Chicago to do a *60 Minutes* segment on her, Oprah invited the Little Sisters for a slumber party at her condominium.

WALLACE: Oprah doesn't just make speeches to young people. She wanted to do more to help young black girls, so she and the women on her staff formed a "Little Sister" group with youngsters from one of Chicago's housing projects. In order to be able to stay in the group, there are two basic rules: You must do well in school and you can't get pregnant.

Camera shows Oprah with the group in pajamas, giggling and talking.

WALLACE: They get together several times a month. This night at a pajama party in Oprah's living room. . . . Along with the laughing, there is always something serious, something new to learn, some way for the kids to stretch their horizons. . . . And always there is mention of God.

Oprah tried to do with the Cabrini Green girls what Vernon had done with her: take them to the library and make them read books. She gave them dictionaries and ordered them to learn five new words a day. She lectured them: "I was like a lot of you. I was a hot little momma." She told *Ms.* magazine, "I shoot a very straight shot. 'Get pregnant and I'll break your face! Don't tell me you want to do great things in your life and still not be able to tell a boy no. You want something to love and to hug, tell me and I'll buy you a puppy.'

"When we talk about goals and they say they want Cadillacs, I say, 'If you cannot talk correctly, if you cannot read or do math, if you become pregnant, if you drop out of school, you will never have a Cadillac. I guarantee it! And if you get D's or F's on your report card, you're out of this group. Don't tell me you want to do great things in your life, if all you carry to school is a radio!'"

Even then Oprah was aware of the steep odds. "One girl on the Cabrini Green show said her goal was to have lots of babies, so she'd get more money from welfare. . . . We have twenty-four in our group. Maybe we'll save two."

The group did not last long. After Oprah's show went national, she said she no longer had the time, energy, or resources to shoulder a program that she felt needed more structure. "What happened was that when we took the girls out we would do nice things, good things, fun things . . . [but] what I realized was that those things were just activities. Good things to do but just activities. . . . I wasn't really able to deeply impact the way the girls thought about themselves. So I failed."

Oprah withdrew from personal involvement in her giving, but she continued writing checks and making fund-raising speeches and appearances for worthy causes. From what is available in the public record—Harpo press releases, plus Oprah's interviews with newspapers and magazines—one learns the following:

• In 1986 she earned $10 million and donated $13,000 to buy a mile in the four-thousand-mile chain of hand-holding across America to raise money to fight hunger and homelessness in what was promoted as "the largest number of celebrities ever assembled." Oprah told *Time,* "My mile will be for people who can't afford the $10 [standing fee]. No rich people in my mile."

• In 1987 she earned $31 million and donated $10,000 to the Marva Collins Preparatory School in Chicago and $50,000 to the Vernon Winfrey Scholarships at TSU, for which she would contribute $770,000 over eight years.

• In 1988 she earned $37 million and donated her Revlon fee of $100,000 to Chicago's Corporate/Community Schools of America. She wrote a check for $2,000 for the Special Olympics and one for $7,000 to provide hot meals for elderly citizens in Alexandra, South Africa, which she continued for three years. For this she received the National Conference of Christians and Jews Humanitarian Award for her "involvement in a college scholarship program and humanitarian aid to South Africa."

• In 1989 she earned $55 million and wrote a check for $1 million to Morehouse College for the Oprah Winfrey Scholars, to which she'd contributed $12 million by 2004. She also gave $25,000 to Chicago's House of the Good Shepherd, a shelter for battered and abused women; $10,000 to Glide Memorial Church in San Francisco, which provides services for the city's poor; $25,000 to the Corporate/Community Schools of America; $1,000 to the Purple Heart Cruise; $40,000 to the combined benefit of the Southern Christian Leadership Conference (SCLC) and the National Association for the Advancement of Colored People (NAACP); $100,000 to the Rape Treatment Center, Santa Monica, California. In addition, she raised $1 million for victims of Hurricane Hugo during her show from Charleston, South Carolina.

• In 1990 she earned $68 million and wrote checks for $20,000 to the B. Robert Lewis House in Eagan, Minnesota, to open a shelter for battered women; $25,000 to Art Against AIDS/Chicago. In addition, she generated more than $1 million in public donations for the World Summit for Children and UNICEF after a show devoted to the plight of starving children. She pledged $500,000 over two years to the Chicago Academy for the Arts and bought all the Broadway opening-night tickets (954 seats) for August Wilson's *The Piano Lesson* to benefit A Better Chance, or ABC, which provides scholarships to the best schools for students of color who are disadvantaged but academically able. She also flew Nelson Mandela's daughter and son-in-law from Boston to South Africa to witness her father's release from prison after twenty-seven years. Oprah's publicist told the *Chicago Sun-Times* that Mandela wanted to avoid "his children sitting around idle for three or four days while they waited for him to be released." In a prime-time television salute, Bob Hope presented Oprah with the America's Hope Award for "her career achievements and her humanitarian endeavors." She was so grateful for the celebrity tribute that she sent Hope a bouquet of roses every week until his death in 2003.

• In 1991 she earned $80 million and wrote checks for $100,000 to buy books for the Harold Washington Library in Chicago, $50,000 to the Rev. Cecil Williams's Glide Memorial United Methodist Church, and $1,000 to the Purple Heart Cruise.

• In 1992 she earned $88 million and wrote a check for $50,000 to the LaPorte County Child Abuse Prevention

Council in Indiana, near her farm, and $30,000 to Every Woman's Place, a women's shelter in Muskegon, Michigan. She also donated twenty Dakota adapters for deaf students for closed-caption TV shows.

• In 1993 she earned $98 million, and after filming *There Are No Children Here* in the Chicago projects, she donated her $500,000 salary to endow scholarships for low-income children in the Henry Horner Homes through a foundation she named "There Are No Children Here." She gave $50,000 to the Holy Family Preservation Society, one of Chicago's oldest churches, and $1 million to the city's predominantly African American Providence–St. Mel School. "The money will go towards setting up scholarships for disadvantaged children," she told reporters.

• In 1994 she earned $105 million and donated her $10,000 award from the Council on Women's Issues in Chicago to Providence–St. Mel. She held her first charity auction of her clothes and raised $150,000, which she divided between Hull House in Chicago and FamiliesFirst in Sacramento. More important, she felt financially secure enough to begin engaging again in her giving. This time she made a gesture that captured the country's attention: she would single-handedly stop the cycle of poverty in America. She held a press conference to say that she would start in Chicago by setting up a foundation called Families for a Better Life, with the intention of moving one hundred families out of the projects and into private housing, giving them job training, health care, financial counseling, educational assistance, and $30,000 in financial aid for two years. She pledged $6 million to her program. "I want to destroy the welfare mentality, the belief in victimization," she said.

Oprah had no sympathy for welfare recipients and frequently berated them. "I was a welfare daughter, just like you. . . . How did you let yourselves become welfare mothers? Why did you choose this? I didn't." The women looked ashamed that they were not good enough to be accepted by Oprah. "When Welfare Warriors, a Milwaukee group of activist moms in poverty, were invited to appear [on one of her welfare shows], we accepted . . . despite our anger at Oprah's betrayal of African American moms in poverty and her frequent attacks on all moms who receive welfare," wrote Pat Gowens, editor of *Mother Warriors Voice.* "Her contempt for impoverished mothers actually increased Welfare Warriors' membership when African American moms joined specifically to picket Oprah. (A typical Oprah assault on a welfare mom in her audience: 'But you sit home with your feet up collecting that monthly check.')."

Oprah promised there would be no government red tape involved in her Families for a Better Life program, to be run by Jane Addams Hull House Association, one of the oldest settlement houses in the nation. She also said she would use her considerable influence to get other corporations, institutions, and foundations to follow her example.

"It's a war zone," she told *Entertainment Weekly.* "We have to get them out. We're giving them bootstraps." Within months, Random House, Inc., and Capital Cities ABC each contributed $500,000 to Oprah's foundation.

"No one makes it alone," she said. "Everyone who has achieved any level of success in life was able to do so because something or someone served as a beacon to light the way. What seems to be an endless cycle of generational poverty and despair can be broken if each of us is willing to be a light to the other. When you learn, teach. When you get, give. That is how you change the world. One life, one family at a time."

She had arrived at this momentous decision after filming *There Are No Children Here,* based on the book by Alex Kotlowitz about a family who lived in one of Chicago's most violent housing projects. "Originally ABC wanted Diana Ross to play my part [but] Diana said she didn't want to do it because it didn't offer enough hope. I felt the book was reality," said Oprah, who canceled her vacation in the south of France to assume the role. "There's always hope," she said. "I didn't grow up in the projects, but I am the perfect example of someone who came up from zip. I mean zippola. Mrs. Outhouse herself here."

During filming she met a youngster named Calvin Mitchell, ten, who captured her heart. He lived in the projects with his four brothers and sisters and their mother, Eva, who was on welfare. After the movie, he visited Oprah at her office every week, and she took him to her farm on weekends, buying him clothes and shoes. Finally she asked her fiancé, "How would you feel about Calvin moving in?"

"If you are willing to move in the whole family," said Stedman, a board member of the Jane Addams Hull House Association. He explained that such a commitment had to be for the entire family, not just for one family member.

"Although I thought about it, Calvin did not move into my house," Oprah said. "We got his mother a job. We're teaching her life skills like opening a bank account, living on a budget and we moved them out of the project."

Together Oprah and Stedman worked on a plan for Families for a Better Life Foundation that they believed would eradicate the welfare dependency of the country's most impoverished families. "Stedman was the catalyst for this," Oprah told *People*. "He is a systems man and I was inspired by his guidance. And this project together, it's like we sing. We just really sing." Their approach relied on the tenets of self-improvement guru Stephen Covey, whose leadership center helped train the Hull House staff. Covey later wrote the foreword to Stedman's self-improvement book, *You Can Make It Happen*.

Having lifted one family out of the projects, Oprah now wanted to lift one hundred families out, but by calling so much media attention to her announcement she had conveyed the impression to Chicago's welfare recipients that she was going to buy their way out of poverty. Hull House received more than thirty thousand calls, which were winnowed to sixteen hundred applicants, but the misconception of a free house remained so prevalent that application forms had to be rewritten to specify, "We will not buy a home for you."

Having started at the same time the Clinton administration was trying to reform the welfare system, Oprah's experiment was watched closely and with great hope. She became actively involved in every aspect, helping to select the participating families and develop their eight-week curriculum. She participated in the counseling sessions and closely monitored their progress. But after spending $843,000 over eighteen months and seeing only paperwork, she abruptly folded the foundation and issued a terse public statement: "I felt myself turning into government. I spent nearly a million dollars on the program, most of it going to development and administrative costs. That was never my intention. I now want to figure out, with the help of people who understand this better than I, how to directly reach the families in a way that allows them to become self-reliant."

She refused to give any interviews about why she'd canceled the program and she demanded absolute silence from everyone associated with it, including personnel from Hull House and the participating families. There was never a report issued or a cost analysis published, and for this she was severely criticized by philanthropists who prize accountability as a curative force. "The problem with Families for a Better Life was not that it failed but that it was a wholly unconstructive failure that provided no systematic knowledge about the transition from welfare to work," wrote Peter J. Frumkin in *Strategic Giving: The Art and Science of Philanthropy*. Formerly with Harvard, the professor of public affairs at the Lyndon B. Johnson School of Public Affairs and director of the RGK Center for Philanthropy and Community Service faulted Oprah for being so secretive and protective of her image. He felt her welfare-to-work experiment was too important not to be shared with those who remained committed to making progress on the issue. "There should be no stigma attached to constructive failure that builds knowledge . . . [but] heavily funded initiatives that end in unconstructive failure like Winfrey's deserve all the criticism they presently receive and more. . . . There is no excuse for being both ineffective and unaccountable."

Oprah did not feel she owed anything to anybody. With the exception of the donations from Random House, Inc., and Capital Cities ABC, she had funded Families for a Better Life Foundation by herself, and she was not about to finance a public report on its failure. As she had earlier told the graduates of Miss Porter's School in Farmington, Connecticut, in her commencement address, "Know this—if you make a choice and come to realize that that choice is not the right one, you always have the right to change your mind, without guilt." She folded both her foundations, There Are No Children Here and Families for a Better Life. Then she started another one, named For a Better Life. She put Rufus Williams, a senior manager for Harpo, in charge of its operations. In the years between 1996 and 2000, she changed For a Better Life Foundation to the Oprah Winfrey Foundation, to encompass most of her charitable giving, and her largest contributions went to the Oprah Winfrey Scholars at Morehouse, the Oprah Winfrey Boys and Girls Club in Kosciusko, and Oprah's Angel Network, which she promoted on her show for viewer donations. She had no intention of throwing off the humanitarian mantle of Princess Diana, and despite Professor Frumkin, she was not about to acknowledge any mistakes that might diminish her role as an inspired leader.

In fact, Oprah considered herself and Stedman to be such enlightened leaders that they teamed up to teach a course at Northwestern University's Kellogg Graduate School of Management, titled Dynamics of Leadership. "It has been a dream of mine to teach," she told *Jet,* "and Stedman and I share the same beliefs in the importance of dynamic leadership in this country."

The university was thrilled by its new adjunct teacher. "The feedback we're getting from MBA students has been phenomenal," said Rich Honack, assistant dean and director of marketing and communications in 1999, "because she is truly admired, especially by the women and minority students, who see her as someone who has made it." Oprah insisted that no press be allowed on campus during her weekly Tuesday night classes, and each of the 110 students selected for the course had to present a special identification card and be checked by four security guards before he or she was admitted to the classroom. University officials warned that any student talking to reporters would be subject to disciplinary action, which could lead to expulsion.

The extreme security precautions prompted the student newspaper, also barred admission, to accuse the university of censorship. Oprah arrived on campus each week in her own black security van with bulletproof windows, accompanied by her own bodyguards.

She and Stedman taught their leadership course for two fall semesters, and Oprah sent her plane to bring in guest lecturers such as Coretta Scott King, Yahoo's Jerry Yang, Jeff Bezos of Amazon.com, and former secretary of state Henry Kissinger.

"I was Stedman's guest the evening Kissinger spoke to their class," recalled Fran Johns, a Chicago businesswoman. "Kissinger had come as a favor for Oprah. . . . We were sitting behind the students when Oprah came running up the steps. 'Wait. Wait,' she yelled to Kissinger. 'I can't see.' She sat down next to me and kept saying throughout his lecture, 'Isn't he great? Isn't he great?' I'm thinking to myself, 'Great? He's a murderer, a creep, Machiavellian . . . but he's an interesting speaker because he's got all these incredible inside stories about things.'"

Oprah was so grateful to Kissinger that she commissioned an oil painting of his Labrador and flew to Connecticut to personally present it. "The dog unveiling took place one weekend when Isaac and I were in the country [Connecticut] and the Kissingers invited us over," recalled Mrs. Isaac Stern, widow of the famed violinist. "Isaac went and met Oprah. I stayed home and took a nap."

Having steeped herself in the legacy of slavery to film *Beloved,* Oprah now became even more committed to helping African American children. Years later she explained her commitment: "The reason I spend so much of my money on educating young black children—$10 million to A Better Chance, which takes inner-city children out of the ghetto and puts them in private schools—is because I know that lives will then forever be changed." While heavily publicized, Oprah's giving in the early years of her career was minimal—less than 10 percent of her incredible income. In 1998 she began increasing her charitable contributions and making more sizable donations to her charitable foundation:

| Year | Estimated Net Worth (Forbes) (million $) | Estimated Income (Forbes) (million $) | Contributions to the Oprah Winfrey Foundation (IRS) ($) |
|---|---|---|---|
| 1998 | 675 | 125 | 11,323,201 |
| 1999 | 725 | 125 | 0 |
| 2000 | 800 | 150 | 15,020,932 |
| 2001 | 900 | 150 | 8,000,000 |
| 2002 | 975 | 150 | 28,038,583 |
| 2003 | 1,000 | 180 | 43,657,831 |
| 2004 | 1,100 | 210 | 45,000,000 |
| 2005 | 1,300 | 225 | 35,978,502 |
| 2006 | 1,400 | 225 | 0 |
| 2007 | 1,500 | 260 | 43,000,000 |
| | | Total | 230,019,049 |

Oprah's polestar for giving was Nelson Mandela, whom she had met through Stedman after he accompanied Mandela's daughter and son-in-law to South Africa for her father's release from prison on Robben Island. Although she had financed that trip in 1990, she did not meet Mandela until 2000. By then he had received the 1993 Nobel Peace Prize with Frederik Willem de Klerk for their efforts in uniting South Africa after years of apartheid. The following year, Mandela was elected the first black president of the country and served until 1999. When he left office he toured the United States to raise money for the Nelson Mandela Foundation, dedicated to educating his country's children. "It's not beyond our power to create a world in which all children have access to a good education," he said. "Those who do not believe this have small imaginations."

During his U.S. visit he appeared on Oprah's show, on November 27, 2000, and when he arrived for the taping, all three hundred employees lined the hallway at Harpo to shake his hand. "It was the interview of a lifetime," Oprah said later. When she visited South Africa she asked Mandela what gift she could give him and his country. He said, "Build me a school," and she agreed. His gift to her was a drawing of hands that he had done in prison. "She has lots of art in her home," recalled former Supreme Court justice Sandra Day O'Connor. "When I was visiting my friend Mary Dell Pritzlaff, her next-door neighbor in Montecito, Oprah heard I was there and insisted we both come for dinner. . . . It was a wonderful evening and Oprah was delightful. . . . What I loved most were the four hands she had framed and hanging on one wall. They were drawn by Nelson Mandela during his time on Robben Island."

Before Oprah embraced the project that would lead to the Oprah Winfrey Leadership Academy for Girls, she embarked on another project for Mandela and began planning "A Christmas Kindness" for fifty thousand South African children. She assembled a team of staff members from the Oprah Winfrey Foundation and Harpo, and a few personal friends, and they worked with the Nelson Mandela Foundation for a year to make Christmas 2002 memorable for youngsters who had never received presents. She said she did this because she remembered when she was a child and her mother, on welfare, could not afford to provide Christmas for her children.

"My sadness wasn't so much about not having toys as it was about facing my classmates," recalled Oprah. "What would I say when the other kids asked what I'd gotten? That Christmas, three nuns showed up at our house with a doll, fruit, and games for us. I felt such a relief that I'd been given something, that I wasn't forgotten. That somebody had thought enough of me to bring me a gift."

Oprah spoke with orphanage caretakers in South Africa about gifts that would be culturally appropriate. "I was told none of these children had ever seen a black doll—most were dragging around blond, naked Barbies. Wouldn't it be a wonder if each girl could see herself in the eyes of a doll that looked like her? It became my passion and mission to give a black doll to every girl I met."

She spent the summer of 2002 choosing presents for the children. "I got a thrill out of seeing 127 sample dolls filling my office. After I'd picked the one I would have wanted when I was a girl, I called up the manufacturer and asked that its barely brown dolls be double-dipped to darken them. We chose soccer balls for the boys, solar-powered radios for the teens and jeans and T-shirts for everyone. And I wanted every child to receive a pair of sneakers. In South Africa, where many of the children walk around barefoot in the blistering sun, shoes are gold."

Oprah financed the flights for herself, Stedman, Gayle, and thirty-seven employees, with all their technical equipment to film the events for future shows, plus three hundred thousand Christmas presents that her staff had spent months wrapping. Her first stop was Johannesburg, where she distributed presents to children in schools and orphanages. She traveled to Qunu, the rural village of Nelson Mandela, where he played the role of Father Christmas and helped her give gifts to sixty-five hundred children who had walked miles to meet the man they called Madiba, Mandela's tribal name. At each stop Oprah's staff set up party tents filled with bubbles, carnival music, jesters, and more food than these children had ever seen.

Oprah said her Christmas Kindness, which she filmed for her show, had transformed her life. "It cost me $7 million but it was the best Christmas I ever had." During those three weeks she was overwhelmed by the number of orphans she saw who had become parentless because of AIDS, and before she left South Africa she had adopted ten children, ages seven to fourteen, who had no one to care for them. "I knew I couldn't save all the children, but I could manage to stay personally engaged with these ten," she said. "I enrolled them in a private boarding school and hired caretakers to look after them."

Oprah justified her long-distance parenting because of her career. "I didn't bring these kids over here [because] my lifestyle is not such that I could devote all my time to them and that is what would need to happen." A continent away, she could hardly be a mother, but she became a generous benefactor. "Every Christmas I returned with gobs of presents," she said. In 2006 she bought her ten "children" a big house and hired a decorator to personalize each of their bedrooms. But when she returned the following year she was dismayed to find them riveted to their $500 RAZR cell phones and talking about their portable PlayStations, iPods, sneakers, and hair extensions. "I knew immediately that I'd given them too much," she said, "without instilling values to accompany the gifts." The following year she did not give them "gobs of presents." Instead she made them choose a family as impoverished as they had once been and spend their holiday doing something kind for others.

Before Oprah left South Africa in 2002, she broke ground on the site that would eventually become the Oprah Winfrey Leadership Academy for Girls. "This time I will not fail," she said. She returned home and started to do her homework on how to build the finest girls' prep school on the planet, for that's exactly what she had in mind. "This school will be an example to the world," she said.

Through her involvement with A Better Chance, Oprah sent her niece Chrishaunda Lee to Miss Porter's School, an elite, almost all-white girls' school in Farmington, Connecticut, that had graduated Gloria Vanderbilt, Jacqueline Bouvier Kennedy Onassis, and Barbara Hutton, the debutante dubbed America's "poor little rich girl." Oprah had been so impressed by the change in her niece after Chrishaunda attended Miss Porter's School that she established the Oprah Winfrey Prep School Scholars, and through the years contributed more than $2 million to scholarships.

To fund her own school she started the Oprah Winfrey Operating Foundation, later changed to the Oprah Winfrey Leadership Academy Foundation, which she financed herself. Initially she pledged $10 million, but by completion, the project would cost more than $40 million. Plans escalated from "a nice boarding school to a world-class boarding school for girls," said Dianne Hudson, who coordinated the effort.

| Year | Estimated Net Worth (Forbes) (million $) | Estimated Income (Forbes) (million $) | Contributions to the Oprah Winfrey Operating Foundation/ Oprah Winfrey Leadership Academy Foundation (IRS) ($) |
|------|------|------|------|
| 2002 | 975 | 150 | 18,000,000 |
| 2003 | 1,000 | 180 | 0 |
| 2004 | 1,100 | 210 | 5,000,000 |
| 2005 | 1,300 | 225 | 11,030,000 |
| 2006 | 1,400 | 225 | 50,200,737 |
| 2007 | 1,500 | 260 | 33,130,055 |
| | | Total | 117,360,792 |

Oprah continued researching other prep schools, including the Young Women's Leadership Charter School of Chicago and the SEED School of Washington, D.C. She also sought advice from Christel DeHaan, a philanthropist from Indianapolis who quietly built schools for poor children around the world.

By this time Oprah had developed very definite views on education, especially in U.S. public schools, which she was not shy about sharing. After doing two shows on the country's troubled educational system, one titled "Oprah's Special Report: American Schools in Crisis," she considered herself well versed in the subject. So much so that on a visit to Baltimore, she pronounced that city's school system an "atrocity."

In an interview with WBAL-TV, Oprah said, "What is going on [here] is a crime to the children of this city. It's a crime. It's a crime that people can't figure out." She added that she had considered making a charitable donation to Baltimore's public school system but decided it would be throwing good money after bad. "What I've learned from my philanthropic giving is that unless you can create sustainability, then it's a waste. You might as well pee it out." She also said she had discussed the city's "atrocity" with Nelson Mandela. "I was actually sitting in his house telling him about the black male situation here in Baltimore," she said, citing (inaccurately) a 76 percent high-school dropout rate among black males. "He did not believe me."

Neither did the Baltimore City School Board, which tried to set the record straight. "We need to be Dr. Phil and counter with the facts," said Anirban Basu, a school board member, who corrected the high-school dropout rate to 50 percent (not 76 percent) of Baltimore's black males.

Oprah's diatribe was met with a tepid response from city officials, who seemed afraid to tangle with someone of her wealth and high regard. "I think she's not aware of the progress that has been made here," said the mayor, Martin O'Malley. "I'm sure it was not malicious on her part."

*The Sun* was not so diplomatic. Stating that the problems of all inner-city schools are rooted in poverty, Dan Rodricks wrote, "High concentrations of poor children in schools is a formula for failure, and that's been studied and proved. Poor families have few choices, so they're stuck." He suggested that Oprah, who got her start in Baltimore, "hock a couple of rings or some shoes" and donate to the local chapter of the Children's Scholarship Fund, which provides partial scholarships for poor children. "I think you know about this. If not, ask Stedman . . . he sits on the organization's national board. . . . Think Baltimore children are being deprived of a good education, Oprah? Write a check."

But Oprah had already committed her millions to poor young girls in South Africa, where the high-school graduation rate was 76 percent in some places. She preferred to make a difference among high-achieving students there than to low-achieving students in America, where she said poor children did not appreciate education. "I became so frustrated with visiting inner-city schools that I just stopped going. The sense that you need to learn just isn't there. If you ask the kids what they want or need, they will say an iPod or some sneakers. In South

Africa, they don't ask for money or toys. They ask for uniforms so they can go to school."

Through Oprah's Angel Network she began directing more and more of the monies she collected from her viewers to South Africa. An analysis of IRS returns from 2003 through 2007 indicates that nearly 10 percent of the donations she generated from others went to that country:

| Year | Organization to Benefit South Africa | Oprah's Angel Network Contribution ($) |
|------|--------------------------------------|----------------------------------------|
| 2003 | Chris Hani Independent School, Cape Town | 30,000 |
| 2003 | Friends of South African Schools, Greenwich, Connecticut | 1,500 |
| 2003 | Kids Haven (orphanage), Guateng Province | 3,000 |
| 2005 | | 262,000 |
| 2006 | | 350,000 |
| 2003 | Place of Faith hospice, Hatfield | 3,000 |
| 2003 | READ Educational Trust, Johannesburg | 19,643 |
| 2003 | Salvation Army–Carl Silhole Social Centre, Johannesburg | 150,000 |
| 2007 | | 25 |
| 2003 | Thembalethu Home-based Care, Mpumalanga Province | 3,000 |
| 2004 | Seven Fountains Primary School, KwaZulu-Natal Province | 250,000 |
| 2005 | | 1,750,074 |
| 2006 | | 4,353 |
| 2007 | | 757,204 |
| 2004 | South Africa Fund (Gauteng, Cape Town, and the Sankonthshe Valley) | 30,975 |

| Year | Organization to Benefit South Africa | Oprah's Angel Network Contribution ($) |
|---|---|---|
| 2004 | South Africa Uniforms (seven provinces) | 1,000,000 |
| 2005 | Africa Gift Fund | 269 |
| 2005 | God's Golden Acre (orphanage), KwaZulu-Natal Province | 25,000 |
| 2005 | Ikageng Itireleng AIDS Ministry, Johannesburg | 180,000 |
| 2006 | | 35,308 |
| 2007 | | 250,000 |
| 2005 | Institute of Training and Education for Capacity-Building (ITEC) (scholarship), East London | 13,000 |
| 2005 | Saphela Care and Support, KwaZulu-Natal Province | 10,800 |
| 2006 | | 362 |
| 2005 | Centre for the Study of Violence and Reconciliation, Johannesburg | 25,000 |
| 2006 | Children in Distress Network (CINDI), KwaZulu-Natal Province | 5,000 |
| 2006 | CIDA (Community and Individual Development Association) City Campus, Johannesburg | 150,000 |
| 2006 | Ukukhula Project (for children of AIDS victims), Hatfield | 32,025 |
| 2006 | Western Cape Networking HIV/AIDS Community of South Africa (NACOSA) | 50 |
| 2007 | | 240,000 |
| 2007 | Mpilonhle (education and AIDS prevention), KwaZulu-Natal Province | 297,380 |
| 2007 | Teach South Africa Conference | 345 |
| | Total | 5,879,313 |

Oprah had fallen in love with Africa, and the continent became her new criteria for judging people. When she and Gayle attended the wedding of Scott Sanders and his partner, Gayle offered a toast to the couple. She said Oprah had given her the invitation list for the opening of the Oprah Winfrey Academy in South Africa and mentioned she was inviting Sanders, the producer of *The Color Purple—The Musical.* Gayle said that she had asked, "Is he Africa-worthy?" Oprah assured her that Sanders was indeed "Africa-worthy." Gayle's compliment, well-meant, seemed awkward and unkind in front of Alice Walker, who wrote *The Color Purple,* and was officiating as the minister marrying Sanders, because she had not been deemed worthy to be invited to the opening of Oprah's school.

Newly enthralled with her African roots, Oprah imagined herself a descendant of Zulu warriors. "I always wondered what it would be like if it turned out I am a South African," she told a crowd of thirty-two hundred people attending her "Live Your Best Life" seminar in Johannesburg. "I feel so at home here. Do you know that I actually am one? I went in search of my roots and had my DNA tested, and I am a Zulu." At that point she had not yet received the results from Henry Louis ("Skip") Gates, Jr., who was having her mitochondrial DNA tested for a PBS show titled *Finding Oprah's Roots.*

"If you tell me I'm not Zulu, I am going to be very upset," she warned him. "When I'm in Africa, I always feel that I look Zulu. I feel connected to the Zulu tribe." Gates looked nervous when he had to inform her that her ancestors were from Liberia, and Oprah looked crestfallen. She took no pride in being associated with a country colonized by freed U.S. slaves. Gates had to stop filming for a few minutes, because he said Oprah needed to compose herself.

"Her face fell when she found out she was descended from Liberians and not Zulus," said Badi Foster, president of the Phelps Stokes fund, which focuses on strengthening communities in Africa and the Americas. "She now needs to mend her fences with Liberia and not be so dismissive. . . . She flew Liberia's president, Ellen Johnson Sirleaf [first woman elected president of an African nation], to do her show but then she ignored her and spent all the time interviewing Queen Rania [of Jordan], the gorgeous young wife of King Abdullah."

From 2000 to 2006, Oprah battled South Africa's government to build her school on the twenty-two-acre site outside Johannesburg, on Henley-on-Klip, that had been recommended by the South African Department of Education. She did not like the initial designs because she said they looked like chicken coops or barracks. "Why would I build tin shacks for girls who come from tin shacks?" The government planners told her that African children sleep on dirt floors in huts with no water or electricity, or share mattresses with relatives, so even the simplest environment would be a luxury for them. Oprah rejected their attitude as well as their plans, and hired her own architects. "I am creating everything in this school that I would have wanted for myself so the girls will have the absolute best that my imagination can offer. . . . This school will be a reflection of me." And so would its students—all little Oprahs. "Every girl has some form of 'it,'" she said, "some form of light that says 'I want it.' 'I can be successful.' 'I'm not my circumstances.'"

Oprah was determined to make the Oprah Winfrey Leadership Academy for Girls her version of Miss Porter's School, wrapped up like the Ritz with a gymnasium, tennis courts, a beauty salon, a yoga studio, a wellness center, and a dining room with marble-topped tables, cloth napkins, and china, silver, and crystal, all of which she selected. She insisted on a six-hundred-seat amphitheater "for orators," because "in order to be a leader, you have to have a voice. To have a voice, you need oration." She demanded six labs, including two for science and one each for art, design, technology, and media. Each had to have the finest equipment, and her computer-filled classrooms had to have outdoor space, even "a reading tree." All the dormitories had kitchens, and each room had a balcony with a large closet. "People asked me why it was important to have closet space, and it's because [the girls] will have something," she said. "We plan to give them a chance to earn money to buy things. That's the only way to really teach them how to appreciate things." For the construction of the twenty-eight buildings on campus, Oprah chose bricks of soft gold sand and personally selected every tile, light fixture, and door handle. She stipulated a ten-thousand-volume library with a fireplace and little cubicles containing soft socks so the girls could curl up comfortably to read. She decorated all the living areas with scattered silk cushions and real orchids. She chose two-hundred-thread-count sheets, white pillowcases embroidered with *O*, and fluffy duvets, all of which she personally tested for luxury and comfort. She selected uniforms for the girls, five pairs of shoes, backpacks—even underwear. She designed a flag for her school and said she would teach leadership classes in person and by satellite. She commissioned artwork from five hundred South African artists and filled every building with baskets and paintings and beaded sculptures to reflect the country's rich tribal culture. Always concerned about security, she ordered double electric gates to be erected around the entrance of the school, with yards of electronic shock-effect fencing. A Venus Africa security van patrolled the grounds day and night, and no visitors were allowed inside, except families, and they were allowed only on specified weekends.

"Mum Oprah" vowed to build "the best school in the world" for the girls she now called "my daughters," and she promised to support them so they could attend any university of their choosing. She selected the first wave of 152 students (eleven, twelve, and thirteen years old) from 3,500 applicants, each of whom had superior grades and demonstrated leadership potential. None came from families that made more than $787 a month, and most had lives ravaged by AIDS, rape, and disease. Some were orphans, and many lived on only a bowl of rice a day. "I know their story," said Oprah, "because it is my story."

Seeing herself in each little girl, she said, "I want them to be surrounded by beauty because beauty does inspire. I want this to be a place of honor for them because these girls have never been treated with kindness. . . . This will be their safe place, a place to flourish free of violence, abuse and deprivation—a place of honor. . . . I want their parents to know they can trust me with their girls."

At that time, the girls' impoverished parents saw Oprah as the personification of goodness, for she was giving their daughters a chance for a better life—a gift they could never afford. Only later would some feel anger and bitter disappointment. Oprah would have her regrets as well, and be forced to admit that she had spent too much time prettying her school and not enough effort vetting the faculty entrusted with protecting the girls. "I had been paying attention to all of the wrong things," she said. "I built that school from the outside in when what really mattered was the inside out."

As part of that "outside" focus, Oprah orchestrated a worldwide publicity campaign for her school's opening that captured more attention than a moon launch, putting her on the cover of *People* and the front pages of newspapers around the globe. She was featured in a two-hour CNN special by Anderson Cooper and in special reports on all network newscasts, *The Today Show, Good Morning America, The Early Show* on CBS, CNN's *American Morning, ET,* and *Extra.* There were articles in *Time, Newsweek,* and, of course, *O* magazine and its spin-off *O at Home,* and a prime-time special on ABC titled *Building a Dream: The Oprah Winfrey Leadership Academy.* There was so much hoopla surrounding the opening of Oprah's sumptuous school that the state funeral of Gerald Ford, the thirty-eighth president of the United States, on the same day seemed merely a somber footnote.

A few weeks before Christmas, on HollywoodReporter .com, Ray Richmond was composing his 2006 gift list "for challenged media figures." For Oprah he wished "a conversation that isn't all about her and her uncompromising, sublime wonderfulness." At the same time, she was sending large, elaborate invitations to two hundred guests to celebrate New Year's Eve with her in Johannesburg. All received an itinerary of what was in store—elegant hotel suites, high teas, cocktail parties, candlelit dinners in the bush, a safari, and a five-course African feast of food, wine, and music on New Year's Eve at the Palace of the Lost City, in Sun City, with the Soweto Gospel Choir performing. She asked each guest to bring a personally inscribed book for her school's library.

Planes began arriving that weekend, disgorging movie stars, rock stars, and television stars: Tina Turner, Chris Rock, Mary J. Blige, Mariah Carey, Spike Lee, Sidney Poitier, Chris Tucker, Tyler Perry, Nick Ashford, Valerie Simpson, Kenneth ("Babyface") Edmonds, Star Jones, Patti LaBelle, Cicely Tyson, Quincy Jones, Reuben Cannon, Kimberly Elise, Anna Deavere Smith, BeBe Winans, Suzanne De Passe, Andrew Young, India.Arie, Holly Robinson Peete, Al Roker, Diane Sawyer, and Nobel laureate Wangari Maathai. All came to honor Oprah and her school.

In addition to the celebrities, Oprah invited her father, but not her mother. She paid tribute to Vernon during her opening-day speech by asking him to stand up. "What you have seen I have done, and what you have heard I have done. None of this could have been possible without my father." Vernon Winfrey was proud to be acknowledged in the presence of Nelson Mandela. "I stood up and turned around real slow, where they could see me well," he said later. "It brought tears to my eyes, her giving me credit for it. It was true. It wouldn't have been possible if she had not come back to me, and she gave me credit for that."

For the grand inauguration on January 2, 2007, Oprah wore a long pink silk taffeta ball gown with her hair softly curled and pulled back from her face to show gleaming dollops of big pink diamonds dangling from her ears. She stood in front of 152 little girls dressed in green uniforms, white blouses, white socks, and brown Mary Janes. They looked like flower girls flanking a bride.

["In my] pink dress with the pink diamonds and the girls I felt like people say they feel on their wedding day," Oprah recalled. "I really literally felt I got married 152 times."

Opening her arms to the girls' families, her celebrity guests, and reporters from around the world, she said, "Welcome to the proudest, greatest day of my life." With tears in her eyes, she spoke movingly. "I know what it feels like to grow up poor, to grow up feeling you are not loved. I want to be able to give back to people who were like I was when I was growing up. . . . The reason I wanted to build a school for girls is because I know that when you educate a girl you begin to change the face of a nation. Girls become women and they educate their girls and their boys. Girls who are educated are less likely to get diseases like HIV and AIDS—a pandemic in South Africa. . . . What I wanted to do is give an opportunity to girls who were like me—girls who were poor, who had come from disadvantaged circumstances, but girls who had a light so bright that not even poverty, disease, and life circumstances could dim that light."

Moved to tears, the audience applauded Oprah, grateful that she had opened her heart to these youngsters who she vowed would save their country and enrich the world. Yet some in Africa later criticized her for spending so much for so few, and others in America, aghast at the luxuries she had bestowed on her "daughters," berated her for not helping poor children in the United States. "Everybody is calling it lavish," said Oprah. "I call it comfortable."

The difference between "lavish" and "comfortable" could be attributed to the difference between ordinary people and a billionaire who paid $50 million for her mansion on forty-two acres in Montecito, California, which, according to the *Los Angeles Times*, was one of the highest prices ever paid for a private residence in the United States. She then poured $14 million into renovations, making her mansion, which she first named "Tara II" then changed to "The Promised Land," worth $64 million.

With commendable calm, Oprah explained to her critics that she was giving to South Africa because the country was young, only twelve years out of apartheid. She also said that with an entire generation decimated by AIDS, the country's children needed to be educated in order to save their nation. When South African reporters asked her why almost all her students were black, Oprah insisted the school was "open to everyone . . . to all girls who are disadvantaged." The reporters persisted, asking if there was an attempt to keep out white students. Oprah snapped: "I don't think I have to appease the white people [9.2 percent] of this country." Then a white reporter asked about the criticism she was receiving from whites. Again, she responded evenly: "I find it interesting that white people are concerned about me educating black girls." The chorus of carps continued, and after a few months Oprah spoke sharply in an interview with BET to all her critics: "To hell with your criticism," she said. "I don't care what you have to say about what I did. I did it."

Within nine months of opening the school, she was blindsided by a sex abuse scandal that resulted in a lawsuit against her for libel, assault, and slander by the former headmistress, **Nomvuyo Mzamane. After the judge refused Oprah's motion to dismiss, saying Mzamane had presented enough evidence to go to trial, Oprah settled the case days before the trial was to begin in Philadelphia.** Still, the sex abuse scandal resulted in several firings and a trial in South Africa of a dorm matron charged with fourteen counts of sexual assault and abasement of the students. A year later seven students were expelled for lesbian liaisons.

"This has been one of the most devastating, if not the most devastating experience of my life," Oprah said in a press conference with South African reporters. "When I first heard about it I spent about a half hour crying, moving from room to room in my house. I was so stunned, I couldn't even wrap my brain around it."

Some were taken aback by her comments, feeling that she was personalizing a tragedy in terms of how it might affect her image. "It was tasteless of her to talk about this experience as though it was about her," wrote Caille Millner in the *San Francisco Chronicle*. "It made her sound self-absorbed and a little clueless."

MSNBC's Keith Olbermann agreed. After running the video clip of Oprah at her press conference, he said, "Thank goodness, Ms. Winfrey is okay, since, after all, this was about her."

In a column titled "Oprah the Avenger," Eugene Robinson wrote in *The Washington Post*, "I did wince yesterday when she called allegations of sexual and physical abuse at the girls' school she founded in South Africa 'one of the most devastating, if not the most devastating experience of my life'—seeming to make it all about her, not the alleged victims. Still, my heart refused to harden."

Oprah said she had spent a month at the school before the scandal was reported, but knew nothing about it because the girls had not told her. They had been instructed to always put on happy faces around "Mum Oprah" and never complain to her about anything. It was not until they read an article in the *Sowetan* [September 27, 2007], a daily newspaper in South Africa, about one child being taken out of the school by her mother after suffering "emotional abuse," that fifteen students acknowledged the article's accuracy and stepped forward with their own charges of abuse.

Because of the international publicity surrounding her school, Oprah needed to address the scandal, which she did by satellite from her Harpo studios in Chicago. She then released the tape on November 5, 2007, to U.S. news outlets, with unusual usage rules:

> Please note the following per Harpo Productions for the use of Oprah News Conference footage:
>
> 1. Credit: Harpo Productions, Inc.
> 2. This footage may be used on our platforms only during the month of November 2007. No further use (including internet archiving) is authorized after November 30, 2007.

"She handled the matter of the sex scandal at her school with seeming transparency," said one network executive, "but she would not allow the footage to be played over and over again. She distributed the tape with instructions that we could only use it for the remainder of the month, and we could not archive it or show it in perpetuity. That is absolutely unheard-of."

The extreme control Oprah exercised over the press coverage of the sex abuse scandal stands in contrast to the unlimited press coverage she sought when opening her school. She spent months preparing for a ribbon-cutting that would showcase her dream to the world. She had talked about her school many times on her show, most recently before the official opening, when she introduced her audience to Muhammad Yunus, winner of the 2006 Nobel Peace Prize. They discussed the evils of moneylenders, and Oprah said she had learned about the practice "when I was in Africa the other day building a school." She wanted to be accepted by the Nobel laureate as a peer, perhaps because she herself was being put forward as a Nobel candidate.

"I started the Nobel movement after Oprah appeared at the Dream Academy Dinner [May 24, 2005] to raise money for at-risk children whose parents are in prison," said Washington, D.C., publicist Rocky Twyman. "When she stood up, praised God, opened her purse, and gave the Dream Academy a million dollars, I wanted to get her the Nobel Peace Prize . . . but the Nobel committee did not want to give it to a celebrity. So I formed a committee, and we talked to Dorothy Height [president emerita of the National Council of Negro Women], who was all for Oprah because Oprah had given Dr. Height two-point-five million in 2002 to pay off the mortgage on the NCNW headquarters. . . . Dr. Height contacted Nelson Mandela and Bishop Tutu, and we set out to get publicity to collect a hundred thousand signatures for Oprah's nomination to present to the Nobel committee. . . .

"Unfortunately, we only got forty thousand signatures . . . because a lot of men, black and white, refused to sign . . . and a lot of religious people would not sign because they said Oprah was not married to Stedman and she gave a bad example to our young people by her lifestyle. I believe we all sin and come short of the glory of God, but these folks, mostly from black churches, and all conservative and law-abiding, felt very strongly that Oprah had put herself above the laws of God. I was stunned, but I'm afraid there are strong feelings against her in our [African American] community. . . . Of the forty thousand signatures we were able to get, most were white, not black. We got a lot of publicity and raised awareness for her getting the prize, but in the end I guess God did not want it to happen."

# Nineteen

FIRST, LAST, and always was *The Oprah Winfrey Show.* Even during the years when she pursued a film career, she never let go of her television show. "It's the foundation for everything," Oprah said. When she finally stopped chasing her dream of becoming "a great movie star," she reclaimed her standing as America's number one talk show host. To stay on that pedestal, she allotted $50 million a year for her show's production costs and hired the best producers she could get, paying them top dollar to move to Chicago; then she supplemented their salaries with a system of bonuses to make sure they worked hard enough to give her the ratings she needed to stay on top.

A team of creative producers helped launch the new and improved Oprah as a beloved philanthropist. David Boul came up with the "World's Largest Piggy Bank," which enabled Oprah to collect coins from her audience to fund college scholarships for needy students. Kate Murphy Davis proposed Oprah's Angel Network, an ingenious way to raise millions from viewers and direct the monies in Oprah's name to Oprah's favorite charities. Alice McGee left her imprint by creating Oprah's Book Club, and Ellen Rakieten, who Oprah said was one of her best producers, thought up "Acts of Kindness," "Oprah's Favorite Things," "Thank You Day," and "The Big Give."

Oprah also solicited ideas on her website, urging visitors to "Call Harpo Productions Anonymous Confession Hotline":

Have you been keeping a secret that your family would
be shocked to learn? Have you cheated, stolen, or covered up a
secret that nobody knows about? Or have you uncovered a
family secret that completely shocked you or your family? Have
your parents, relatives, or ancestors tried to bury a shameful
family secret?

Call Us Now!

Most of "the girls" from the early days who had launched
Tabloid Oprah had burned out or been kicked out to make
room for the coronation crew, who carried the crown and the
ermine-trimmed robe. The *Oprah* shows on nudists, porn
stars, and prostitutes now shared the spotlight with "uplifting
shows" on God, giving, and giveaways. Some people marked
this as the start of Saint Oprah; others saw it as the Dawn of the
Diva. Whatever it was, it signaled a sharp departure from
Down-Home Oprah, especially in the newsrooms of Chicago.

"I saw it coming in 1994 when Colleen Raleigh [Oprah's
chief publicist for eight years] sued her," said Robert Feder, TV
critic for the *Chicago Sun-Times* from 1980 to 2008. "When I reported that lawsuit, and I had to report it because it was in the
public domain, Oprah froze me out. No more Christmas cards.
No calls returned. Nothing. Up to that point I had seen her at
least once a week and talked to her all the time. . . . But as she got
more powerful, she pulled back from the press and now she ig-
nores all Chicago media because she doesn't need us anymore."

The change from girlfriend to goddess became obvious to
those who covered television and noticed that Oprah no longer
spent time with her audience after every show. In her early,
eager days she shook hands with everyone as they left, hugged
them, gave autographs, and posed for pictures. Now she considered such personal interaction a waste of her time and energy,
and photographs were no longer permitted because she considered her image her brand. "No telling where those pictures
might turn up later," she said. "I don't want to wind up selling
Aunt Bessie's cookies somewhere in Minnesota."

Photojournalists also noted the change in Oprah. "I photographed her quite a few times—shot her first cover for *People*—but I like this one because I'd never seen a picture like that," said Harry Benson, describing a candid shot of Oprah in 1996, wearing workout togs and looking very slim. "You can't do pictures like this of her anymore. She lets herself be shot only by her own photographers. She was fine back then, but other people around her were closing in. . . . She wanted to buy my pictures so nobody would see them. Just a complete control freak. And this is not a mean picture! Now she's hiding all her fat."

Oprah was so adamant about protecting herself from enthusiastic fans that she insisted her studio audiences be searched by security guards before entering the building and give up their cameras, tape recorders, packages, and even pens and pencils before being seated.

In the old days it would never have occurred to her to put an *R* with a circle around it next to "You go, girl," the phrase most associated with her then, but once she became a brand, she began registering her utterances and applied for trademarks on "Aha! Moment" and "Give Big or Go Home." She also registered:

- Oprah
- *The Oprah Winfrey Show*
- Oprah Radio
- Make the Connection
- Oprah's Book Club
- Live Your Best Life
- Oprah's Favorite Things
- Oprah's Ambassadors
- Wildest Dreams with Oprah
- Oprah Boutique
- Harpo
- The Oprah Store
- Oprah.com
- Oprah's Big Give
- Expert Minutes
- The "Oprah" signature
- The "O" design
- Oprah's Angel Network
- Angel Network
- Oprah Winfrey Leadership Academy for Girls
- *O, The Oprah Magazine*
- *O at Home*
- Oprah Winfrey's Legends Ball
- Oprah and Friends

The Oprah who had been open and accessible now seemed aloof and slightly haughty, especially to the press. Having appeared on twenty covers of national magazines by 1995, she was accustomed to demanding (and getting) complete control over what was written about her in exchange for being on the cover. Frequently, she was allowed to choose the writer, and she always dictated the photographer. Most of the media accommodated her, except in Chicago, where reporters sought unfettered access.

"I wrote a piece on 'The 100 Most Powerful Women in Chicago,' and of course Oprah was named number one," said Cheryl L. Reed, former editorial page editor of the *Chicago Sun-Times*. "I called Harpo, but she wouldn't give us an interview. I tried everything—phone calls, letters, emails, even flowers—but her publicist said she was too busy. Finally I asked if I might send some questions for her to answer. What came back to me was a bunch of regurgitated junk that had been printed a million times before. So I called back and asked, 'Why did you send answers that are computer-generated and published in previous interviews?'

"'Well, Miss Winfrey says she is always asked the same questions and so she has put together answers that represent her thoughts on various subjects, and that's what she has to say in response to your questions.'

"'I thought you said that my questions would be put before her and she would answer them.'

"'I'm very sorry. That's how Miss Winfrey prefers to respond.'"

Reporters from the *Chicago Tribune* and *Chicago* magazine ran into the same stone wall at Harpo. Only the gossip columnists thrived, because they dutifully printed items fed to them by Oprah's publicists about Oprah's charitable good works, the celebrities coming to town for Oprah's shows, and Oprah's splendid trips for her employees. To their credit, the city's reporters did not allow personal pique to surface in their stories, and while gossip columnists such as Bill Zwecker of the *Chicago Sun-Times* and WBBM-TV acknowledged that Oprah had "become impossible to deal with," he said her continuing presence in the city was a boon to Chicago.

"It was after the Raleigh lawsuit that she slammed the door on everyone," said Robert Feder. "She felt her employees would sell her out and she became paranoid and even more controlling, forcing people to sign contracts that tied them in knots forever."

Feder did not exaggerate. Oprah made all her employees, even those on probation for the first thirty days, sign confidentiality agreements that bound them to the grave. The contracts read, in part:

> 1. During your employment or business relationship with Harpo, and thereafter, to the fullest extent permitted by law, you are obligated to keep confidential and never disclose, use, misappropriate, or confirm or deny the veracity of any statement or comment concerning Oprah Winfrey, Harpo (which, as used herein, included all entities related to Harpo, Inc., including Harpo Productions, Inc., Harpo Films, Inc.) or any of her/its Confidential Information. The phrase "Confidential Information" as used in this policy, includes but is not limited to, any and all information which is not generally known to the public, related to or concerning: (a) Ms. Winfrey and/or her business or private life; (b) the business activities, dealings or interests of Harpo and/or its officers, directors, affiliates, employees or contractors; and/or (c) Harpo's employment practices or policies applicable to its employees and/or contractors.
>
> 2. During your employment or business relationship with Harpo, and thereafter, you are obligated to refrain from giving or participating in any interview(s) regarding or related to Ms. Winfrey, Harpo, your employment or business relationship with Harpo and/or any matter which concerns, relates to or involves any Confidential Information.

Most former employees admit that fear enforces Oprah's contract, even for those who have been out of her employ for years. "All you need to know is her net worth [$2.7 billion in 2009], which can buy more lawyers than anyone can afford," said one former producer. "That, plus Elizabeth Coady."

The Coady case is known to all Harpo employees. "I was producing shows, conceiving shows, supervising a team of other assistant producers, coming up with guest ideas, doing research on guests and topics," said Coady, former senior associate producer who worked for Oprah for four years. She resigned in 1998 with the intention of writing a book about her experiences at Harpo. A trained journalist, Coady wrote an article in the *Providence Journal* titled "World-Class Phoney Oprah Winfrey and Her Sycophants," about what it was like to work for "the high priestess of hype, a living laminated product that loses luster once the bright lights and makeup are off." Because of the confidentiality agreement Coady had signed, Oprah threatened to sue her if she proceeded to write the book. Instead, Coady sued Oprah and took her to court to challenge the confidentiality agreement as an unenforceable restrictive covenant.

"I wanted people to be able to talk freely," Coady said. "No one will talk at Harpo. People are afraid for their careers. I didn't want them to fear Oprah coming after them." Coady characterized Harpo as "a very cynical and narcissistic place," and said that Oprah fed off the narcissism.

"Oprah doesn't believe what she says. Everything she says is intended to promote herself, not her female fans. She loves that they worship her and she believes they do so rightfully. . . . There's no sense of justice inside [Harpo], which is ironic in light of the public image of someone who touts herself as an advocate for business ethics and spirituality. This is not a spiritual place."

Describing Oprah as a master manipulator of the media, Coady said that her immense influence within ABC, Viacom (which owned CBS and King World), the Walt Disney Company, Hearst, and Oxygen immunized her against criticism and prevented anyone from stepping forward to reveal the "intrigue and deception" in her workplace. Oprah realized that a book such as Coady's threatened to strip the bark off her carefully constructed public image while making her words during the "mad cow" trial look hypocritical when she said: "This is America. People are allowed to say things we don't like."

"There is an audience for a book [like mine]," said Coady, "but [Oprah] has a stranglehold on the publishing industry because of the popularity of her book club." The writer did acknowledge the good that Oprah had done and said she saw people whose lives had been positively affected by her. "She gives a lot of people the belief that there's some magic in the world." Yet, overall, Coady felt that Oprah held sway over her gullible audience because of her "constant references to a higher power and her pandering to stay-at-home moms."

Elizabeth Coady never got the chance to write her book because the Illinois Appellate Court ruled against her and upheld Oprah's confidentiality agreement as "reasonable and enforceable." The court made its decision based on contract law, which left Coady, a free speech advocate, asking, "Why does a woman with unprecedented influence over so many communication companies have to silence her employees? Why does a woman who has made her millions telling people's stories deserve this level of protection from the courts?"

Scores of producers flocked to Harpo to work for Oprah, leaving network jobs in New York City to relocate to Chicago because, as one former employee said, "Her salaries are terrific." In a confidential interview another said, "As much as the money, I signed on because I believed in her message—to do uplifting television. I thought I would be working for the warm and fuzzy person I saw on television. But, God, was I conned. . . . It's a cult at Harpo. So oppressive it's frightening . . . Oprah is ruthless about protecting her brand and she's so concerned— obsessed, really—about who she hires that she has Kroll Associates [worldwide detective agency] vet every potential employee, including a review of their financials. She's worried about moles in her company who might talk to the press about what goes on, and that would definitely damage her image. If you pass Kroll, you are put on one month's probation and in that thirty-day period you are watched by the Harpo elders—the ones who long ago drank the Kool-Aid. If you disagree with a proposed show or express doubt about production values or story ideas, you're viewed as a possible troublemaker. . . . I got so spooked that even after I was on staff, I began to believe the stories about our phones being tapped and our emails being read. . . . If America really knew how this woman operated behind the scenes, they'd be shocked, but no one inside will tell you, because they'd be canned, and those who've escaped to the outside don't want to risk being sued. Oprah has lawyers straining at the leash like pit bulls to go after anyone who might diminish her brand."

The confidentiality agreements gave Oprah a sense of security about anyone stepping forward to sully the image she had created. Not that the image was totally fraudulent, but it was fragile to exposure, because as open as she appeared to be, Oprah shared herself only in the most measured ways, doling out dollops of what she called "the bad stuff" in settings that she controlled totally. Having been "sold out for $19,000" by her sister, Patricia, who had been paid by the tabloids to talk about Oprah's promiscuous childhood, her truancy, her teenage pregnancy, and the death of her baby boy, Oprah feared further tell-alls. Unable to put her trust in her Harpo "family," she assumed the worst of everyone and threw up the strongest defense she could devise. Realistically, there was no way for her to pursue every former employee who might talk, but the prospect that she could kept most of them in line. Fear directed traffic on both sides of the street: she was as terrified of their revelations as they were of her lawsuits.

In addition to her five hundred employees at Harpo, Oprah required everyone at O, The Oprah Magazine, to sign confidentiality agreements and swear never to reveal anything about her, something few other publications required of their employees. When Oprah was asked why she imposed such imperial restrictions on those who worked for her, she again said it was all about "trust," but this time Chicago Tribune journalists Ellen Warren and Terry Armour called her on it. "Actually, that's precisely what it's not about," they wrote. "It's about mistrust."

Oprah made the headhunters who helped recruit teachers for her leadership academy, and every member of the faculty and all the dorm matrons, sign nondisclosure agreements. Her visits to the school were always shrouded in secrecy, and she insisted that guests at functions she attended in South Africa sign agreements banning cameras and tape recorders. People who purchased her real estate also had to sign covenants not to reveal details about her ownership. Her caterers, florists, party planners, interior decorators, upholsterers, painters, electricians, plumbers, gardeners, pilots, security guards, and even the veterinarians who treated her dogs had to sign. She once sent a cease-and-desist order during the taping of a VH1 reality show about dating because one of Gayle King's ex-boyfriends was a contestant, and he had signed a confidentiality agreement not to talk about Oprah and Gayle.

"Everyone who works at Atlantic Aviation, the hangar where Oprah keeps her plane [the $47 million Bombardier BD-700 Global Express high-speed jet she purchased in 2006] has been signed to secrecy," said Laura Aye, a former airfield safety officer. "They are not allowed to discuss her. If you ask about her, they say, 'We can't talk or we'll lose our jobs.' The girls there are very nervous. Before Oprah got her Global, she had a Gulfstream, and I had dealings with her at Midway. . . . I saw her about twenty times in the years I worked there and I never once saw her with a man. She always traveled with women. . . . She was cold, standoffish, and very difficult. . . . She's not nice to the employees, except at Christmas, when she distributes gifts to everyone. I once had to yell at her when she took her dog out on the AOA [air operations area] to pee. No one is ever supposed to be there, because planes come in and out, and the jet blast could be fatal. I got a call from the tower that some woman was walking her dog and I had to get her out of there fast. I ran out and saw it was Oprah.

"'Please, get out of the area right away, ma'am,' I said.

"She roared back, 'I beg your pardon? . . .'

"'Right now, ma'am. That dog will get sucked up. We can't have you out here. It's regulations.' She was furious. . . . I had to report the incident."

The sense of entitlement that accompanies the life of a billionaire celebrity seemed to surface shortly after Oprah purchased her first plane (a $40 million Gulfstream GIV). "She was going in and out of Signature then, a field-based operation for private jets, which is separate from the commercial airport," said Laura Aye, "and she did not want the fuelers around because she didn't like the smell of gas and grease. Her pilot would radio her arrival, and the fuelers would all be banned from the hangar. The guys inside quickly whipped up a batch of popcorn to cover the fumes. That way she wouldn't have to smell anything for the thirty feet she had to walk from her plane to her security van."

During her Gulfstream days she gave an interview to Harry Allen of *Vibe*, who asked how much her plane had cost. Oprah said, "I'm not going to discuss that. Jet etiquette means you never discuss how much the plane costs. . . . But sometimes, and I get a kick out of this—there's all black people on the plane. Just the other day the flight attendant was passing out some lobster and I said, 'We still black! It's not like we turned white! We still black, y'all. Oprah's still black.' It's like, who knew?"

The *Vibe* writer said, "Do you understand the effect of stories like these? You're the richest black person in the universe."

Sounding disingenuous, Oprah said, "Am I? Let me think. . . . I always think of other people as being rich. It's not a concept that I'm attuned to."

**Always particular about her food, Oprah retained three chefs for her private plane. She instructed the flight attendants on the menus she preferred, saying, according to Corinne Gehrls, "White folks don't know what southern food should taste like."**

When Oprah upgraded from her $40 million Gulfstream to her $47 million Global Express, she moved hangars and secured a new space near the Sara Lee jets. "It was an old, dilapidated warehouse with sliding doors—imagine a garage for an airplane," said one airport employee. "She poured a million dollars into it, completely refurbishing the place. She carpeted the concrete floor, redid the walls and cuttings and doors. She even built offices upstairs with elaborate fittings and got the City of Chicago to put in a parking lot, and then she redid the parking lot. . . . She tapes her shows in Chicago on Tuesday, Wednesday, and Thursday, and flies to Santa Barbara every Thursday night, arriving back in Chicago on Sunday at nine P.M." If Oprah is asleep on either leg of the flight, her pilots are under orders not to disturb her until she's slept eight hours. . . . They must sit and wait until she wakes up.

Oprah could not force celebrities to sign her confidentiality agreements, so she frequently isolated herself at galas and benefits. "When we performed *The Vagina Monologues* at Madison Square Garden [February 2001], the one person with a private entrance and a private dressing room was Oprah," recalled Erica Jong. "The rest of us—me, Jane Fonda, Glenn Close, Rita Wilson, Calista Flockhart, Shirley Knight, Amy Irving, all the rest—were girls together in our panty hose getting dressed and made up gratis by Bobbi Brown. No one was paid. No one had star privileges, except Oprah. She was separate and apart from all of us, and I think it was because she was afraid and not confident, but why, I don't know."

That evening Oprah had used the Garden's rock star entrance—with an elevator big enough to accommodate limousines—so that she could bypass fans and be driven from the street to her dressing room. A friend later suggested she might have removed herself from the rest of the cast because she felt self-conscious about her size. "Maybe she was uncomfortable being the only heavy black woman among all those skinny white girls."

Race was definitely the reason Oprah cited when she was barred from Hermès in Paris. She and Gayle arrived at the luxury retail store fifteen minutes after closing and expected to be admitted because they saw shoppers inside. Oprah said she wanted to buy a particular watch for Tina Turner, with whom she was having dinner that evening, but the salesclerk at the door would not let her in, and neither would the store manager. Later Hermès said the store was preparing for a special event that evening.

"I saw it," said Gayle King, "and it was really, really very bad. Oprah describes it herself as one of the most humiliating moments of her life.... We are calling it her *Crash* moment [referring to the film detailing racism]." She added, "If it had been Céline Dion or Britney Spears or Barbra Streisand, there is no way they would not be let in that store."

Some news reports said the Hermès salesclerk did not recognize Oprah (*The Oprah Winfrey Show* is not seen in France), and the store had been "having a problem with North Africans." Oprah called the U.S. president of Hermès and said she had been publicly humiliated, and although she had recently bought twelve Hermès handbags ($6,500 apiece), she would no longer be spending her money on the firm's luxury goods. The company immediately issued a statement of regret for "not having been able to welcome Madame Winfrey" to the store, saying that "a private public relations event was being prepared inside."

*Je suis désolée, monsieur.* Oprah issued her own statement, saying she would address the matter on her season's opening show in the fall, giving people weeks to weigh in on the international furor.

"Had Winfrey been turned away in regular hours, the racism charge might have traction," wrote Anne Kingston in Canada's *National Post.* "But she wasn't, which suggests other 'isms' might be at play. Maybe it was celebrity-ism."

An editorial in the Montreal *Gazette* accused Oprah of being quick to "play the race card," saying, "Everyone has endured something like this. Fortunately few of us fly into 'don't you know who I am?' mode. This is Paris, Madame Winfrey, not Chicago. Even if they know who you are, they just don't care."

The conservative *National Review* said, "What she should have done, in our opinion, is buy Hermès on the spot." The comic strip *The Boondocks* showed the ten-year-old black radical Huey Freeman watching television news and hearing:

> Oprah Winfrey is so convinced that her denial into the Paris Hermès store was race-related that she will be discussing it on her show.
>
> In other news, Hermès has announced a huge "Going Out of Business" sale.

The comedian Rosie O'Donnell wrote in her blog:

> I cannot wait to hear
> all the details—
> one of the most humiliating moments of her life . . .
> oprah

      a poor overweight
     sexually abused
    troubled black female child
     from a broken home—
      that oprah
suffered ONE of the most HUMILIATING moments of
HER life
     at hermès in paris.
     hmmmmm.

Orlando Patterson, Harvard's eminent professor of sociology, later asked in *The New York Times*, "Oprah may have been denied a prerogative of elite status in our new gilded age—being waited on in luxury stores after hours—but had she been the victim of racism?"

Richard Thompson Ford, a law professor at Stanford, answered the question in his provocative book *The Race Card: How Bluffing About Bias Makes Race Relations Worse:* "If the reason for Oprah's humiliation was that the incident at Hermès triggered memories of her past experiences with racism, then Oprah's race was the reason she felt humiliated. In that sense, Oprah was humiliated because of her race."

In the early part of her career Oprah maintained she had never experienced racism. "I transcend race, really," she said in 1986. Yet the following year she told *People* she had been refused entrance to a Manhattan boutique. In 1995 she told *The Times Magazine* (London) that she had been barred from "one of Chicago's ritziest department stores." She laughed as she told the writer, "They didn't recognize me because I was wearing my hair all kind of [bouffant]. I was with my hairdresser, a black man. They hummed and they hummed and then they said that they'd been robbed the week before by two black transvestites. 'And we thought they'd come back.' 'Oh, thank you very much,' I said. 'I'm changing my hair-do.' Then I turned to my hairdresser and said, 'I think we are experiencing a racial moment. . . . So this is what it's like. Oh, man!' "

Six years later she retold a similar version of that same story, but by 2001 it was a Madison Avenue boutique that had kept her out. She said she had seen a sweater in the window and rang to be buzzed in, but the door was not opened. Then she saw two white women entering the store. So she rang again, but still was not admitted. "I certainly didn't think, 'This is a racial moment!'" she said. She called from a pay phone to make sure the store was open. "We started banging on the windows." Nothing. Back in Chicago she called the store. "This is Oprah Winfrey. I was trying to get in your store the other day and . . ." She quoted the manager as saying, "I know you're going to find this hard to believe, but we were robbed last week by two black transsexuals—and we thought they'd come back."

Whether these stories were real or rhetorical, Oprah certainly was accustomed to celebrity treatment from stores that opened their doors after hours so she could shop. In Chicago, Bloomingdale's had extended this courtesy and even accommodated her insistence that all nonessential employees be kept off the floor so they would not gawk or report what she had purchased. (She was irate when the *National Enquirer* revealed the Christmas presents she had bought for her employees at the studio and the magazine—fourteen-karat gold and diamond *O* initial pendants.)

A few days before her season's opening show in September 2005, billed as "Oprah's 20th Anniversary Season Premiere," her publicist announced that Robert B. Chavez, the president and CEO of Hermès USA, would be Oprah's guest, stirring speculation about a monumental slapdown on national television.

Oprah opened the show by joking about what she did on her summer vacation and later launched into her version of what had happened in Paris. She claimed that most of the press reports were "flat-out wrong," although her best friend had been the source of those reports. She scolded her audience for thinking she might have been upset for not being able to get into a closed store to shop. "Please," she said. "I didn't get to be this old to be that stupid. I was not upset about not getting to buy a bag—I was upset because one person at the store was so rude, not the whole company."

Mr. Chavez looked at Oprah as she continued to berate his company. "There were reports that I was turned away because the store was closed. The store was in the process of being closed—the store was very active. . . . The doors were not locked. My friends and I were standing inside the doorway and there was much discussion among the staff about whether or not to let me in. That's what was embarrassing. . . . I know the difference between a store being closed and a store being closed to me.

"Everybody who has ever been snubbed because you were not chic enough or thin enough or the right class or the right color or whatever . . . you know that it is very humiliating, and that is exactly what happened to me."

The whipping boy from Hermès sounded contrite: "I would like to say to you we're really sorry for all of those unfortunate circumstances that you encountered when you tried to visit our store in Paris," he said. "We really try to service all of our clients all over the world." Then he stubbed his toe. "The woman who turned you away did it because, honest to God, she didn't know who you were."

"This wasn't even about, 'Do you know who I am?'" Oprah snapped. "I wasn't trying to play that celebrity card."

Chavez quickly apologized. "You did meet up with one very, very rigid staff person."

"Rigid or rude?" asked Oprah.

"Rigid and rude, I'm sure," he said.

Having pilloried the firm's president, Oprah now pardoned him and commended his company for instituting sensitivity training for its employees. She concluded the segment by hugging Chavez and urging her viewers to shop at the luxury goods emporium, where alligator Kelly bags cost $18,000 to $25,000. Oprah, too, resumed shopping there, and when she gave a "girlfriend" party for twelve at her Montecito estate in honor of Maria Shriver, she had the invitation stitched on twelve Hermès scarves ($375 apiece).

Mr. Chavez was one of the few guests to get out of Harpo without having to sign a confidentiality agreement. Most who appear on Oprah's show are sworn to secrecy, but they are so grateful to be there that they willingly sign away their rights. "My publisher told me the difference between *Oprah* and other shows is the difference between a lightning bug and the sun," said a member of the American Society of Journalists and Authors, too scared to be quoted by name. "So, of course, I want to be in the sun."

Swallowing professional reservations, most writers sign Oprah's binding agreements, but one man objected on principle. "I just couldn't do it," said Chris Rose, a prizewinning columnist for New Orleans's *Times-Picayune*. "It struck me as wrong and ran counter to everything that I believe as a writer and a journalist and a human being."

Rose had written moving columns about the harrowing depression he suffered in the wake of Hurricane Katrina. His columns were nominated for a Pulitzer Prize and later published in a book titled *1 Dead in Attic*. On the second anniversary of the hurricane, he was contacted by Oprah's show to discuss post-traumatic stress disorders among Katrina survivors. "They wanted my expertise, not as a book writer or even a newspaper columnist, but as the city's most famously depressed resident, by virtue of my columns about battling the disease," he said. "Yet they would not allow me to mention my book or even show a copy of it on the air, although the subject of their show and my book was the mental health crisis in New Orleans. At the end of a long and excruciating day—ten hours—revisiting the emotional wreckage of the hurricane, Oprah's producer pulled out a sheet of paper and said I had to sign it. . . . Now, I was willing to give her the right to use my name, my image, my story, even footage of my youngest child, but I could not give her the right to void my experience for the last ten hours. . . . I explained that writing is my life and writing about my experience is what I do for a living.

"'If you don't sign, we don't run the segment,'" the producer said.

"They had just sucked out of me my inner darkness and were exposing my personal struggles to the entire country," Rose recalled. "As exhausted as I was I was not going to cave in to this kind of brinksmanship." The producer panicked, and for the next three hours Rose was peppered with calls from various producers up the chain of Oprah's command, insisting that he sign the confidentiality agreement, and threatening to cut his segment if he didn't.

"Trust us," they said. Rose held firm. That night he wrote a column about the experience of dealing with Oprah and her producers, which was posted on the newspaper's website.

"The next morning I found out what it meant to 'go viral,'" he said. "I had stuck my hand into a hornet's nest of anti-Oprah sentiment on the Internet that pushed my book from number eleven thousand on Amazon to number eighteen by the end of the day and then on to *The New York Times* bestseller list. I was stunned because I had always considered Oprah to be an engine for good.... I had no idea there were negative feelings about her and her confidentiality agreements out there, but I received calls and emails from writers all over the country saying they were going to buy my book that day to send her a message.... The irony is that my segment did run on *Oprah* ["Special Report: Katrina—What Will It Take to Recover?"] and my book was posted on her website—at least for a while. But I guess I go down as the guy whose book became a bestseller for not having been seen on *The Oprah Winfrey Show*."

Harpo producers consistently presented shows with quality production values—arresting visuals, fast-paced segments, and exclusive interviews tailored to a female audience looking for entertainment, diversion, and self-improvement. Because of Oprah's big-money bonuses for those who gave her high ratings, there was fierce competition among her producers to get their stories on the air. Consequently, they took no prisoners in their negotiations.

"They are bullies," said Rachel Grady, who with her partner, Heidi Ewing, runs Loki Films, which produced *The Boys of Bakara* and *Jesus Camp*, the latter of which was nominated for an Academy Award. "Oprah and her producers feel like everyone owes them for the privilege of being on their show, and they expect you to work for free for the honor." Loki Films was called in the summer of 2006 to produce the ABC prime-time special on Oprah's school in South Africa. "We were to do the job but not be given credit for our work," said Grady. "So we asked for double the money. They [Harriet Seitler and Kate Murphy Davis] gave us a contract that said they could fire us without cause at any time. They also refused to speak with our lawyer because they said it was better for their budget that way. 'Besides,' they said, 'we usually end up firing everybody anyway and having to do it ourselves.' That's the way they put it. . . .

"I think Oprah's school is a wonderful idea, but having worked in that poor country I think it's crazy to spend $40 million on one school when $75 million could probably eradicate poverty throughout all of South Africa. But Oprah lives in such a gilded cage she no longer has a grip on reality. We had to fly to Chicago three times at her request. . . .

"When we realized that we would have to give up six months of our lives for her, get little money and no acknowledgement for our work, plus we had to sign a nondisclosure contract swearing that Oprah's name would never pass our lips—please! That's when we said we could not accept the job on those terms. Harriet Seitler went off on us. 'You are just two little girls in a room in New York City,' she said. 'We are Oprah Winfrey. We are Harpo. You need us. We don't need you.' "

Liz Garbus, another documentary filmmaker and daughter of famous First Amendment attorney Martin Garbus, also encountered problems when her film *Girlhood* was featured on an Oprah show titled "Inside Prison: Why Women Murder." The two young women featured in the documentary—Shanae and Megan—agreed to appear on condition that Oprah not mention the drug addiction of Megan's mother. Promises were made and then mauled. When Oprah asked Megan on-camera about her mother's addiction to drugs, Megan walked off the set, providing what one producer later called "good television"—the show's first priority.

"I'll say what I want to say," said Oprah in an unguarded on-camera moment, and with the exception of her celebrity friends like John Travolta and Tom Cruise—neither of whom she ever questioned about Scientology—she spared few others. She drilled Liberace about his palimony suit and how much he was worth, how many houses he owned, how many cars he drove, how many furs he bought, and how much he spent on jewelry. She quizzed Robin Givens about getting beaten up by her former husband, boxing heavyweight champion Mike Tyson: "Is it true that he would hit you until you would vomit?" She asked Kim Cattrall of *Sex and the City,* "Are you dating? Is it hard because people expect you to put out?" Looking askance at Boy George, the cross-dressing British pop star, she asked, "What does your mother say when you leave the house, honey?" To Jean Harris, who murdered her lover, Dr. Herman Tarnower, the creator of the Scarsdale Diet, Oprah asked, "Do you think that one of the things that hurt you [in the trial] was that you were perceived on the witness stand as being this cold bitch?" To Richard Gere, she said, "I . . . read that you live like a monk, except for the celibacy part." She interrogated Billy Joel about the drinking problem that had landed him in rehab: "What's with all the car crashes?" After Lance Armstrong had radiation therapy for testicular cancer, she asked, "You want more children? Got extra sperm?" When Oscar de la Renta appeared on her show and introduced his adopted son, who was seated in the audience, Oprah looked at the young boy and then asked the designer, "How did you get a black son?"

Behind-the-scenes competition became fierce when the talk show titans battled for exclusive "gets." In 2003, Oprah and Katie Couric went to the mat over Elizabeth Smart, the fourteen-year-old girl who was snatched from her bed in Salt Lake City, hidden in a hole, chained to a tree, and not allowed to bathe for nine months. Upon Smart's rescue by police, her parents asked the media for privacy so that she might recover. Seven months later, Ed and Lois Smart had written a book, *Bringing Elizabeth Home: A Journey of Faith and Hope,* and sold television rights to CBS for a movie. Publication was set for October, to be followed by the movie in November. The promotion campaign set by the publisher (Doubleday) gave Katie Couric, then with NBC, the prime-time interview for *Dateline,* to be followed by Oprah for daytime. The ground rules, set by the Smarts for their interviews, prohibited any on-camera interview with their daughter, although silent footage of Elizabeth was allowed.

The book's publication created such a media frenzy that CBS decided to air the interview with the Smarts that was to accompany the movie as a network special before Katie or Oprah had aired their interviews. Oprah's producers flew to Utah to get footage of Elizabeth's bedroom, zooming in on the white patchwork quilt, ruffled pillows, and Raggedy Ann dolls, and also filmed the filthy hole where she was chained for nine months. Katie Couric accompanied her producers to Utah, and after interviewing the Smarts, she persuaded them to allow her verbal exchange with Elizabeth to be shown on the air, which gave NBC an exclusive no one else had. Couric tried to circle the subject of sexual abuse with the youngster without getting explicit:

> COURIC: How do your friends treat you, Elizabeth?
>     I mean, obviously, you know . . .
> ELIZABETH: Regular.
> COURIC: Do they ever ask you anything or . . .
> ELIZABETH: No.
> COURIC: You must have been frightened . . .
> ELIZABETH: Yeah . . .
> COURIC: Do you think you have changed?
> ELIZABETH: No.

Oprah was enraged when she found out about the interview, but instead of calling Katie Couric to scream, she telephoned Suzanne Herz, then head of publicity for Doubleday. "Oprah reamed her," recalled a Doubleday employee. "Just laid her out . . . It was quite traumatic for Suzanne to be treated that way by Oprah Winfrey." Herz later said, "It was more bad behavior on the part of Katie Couric, not Oprah. Katie was the one who broke the rules to get the exclusive. Oprah was angry because she followed the rules and then got screwed. . . . I don't blame her. . . . In the end, both of them got huge ratings."

Couric's interview with Elizabeth Smart and her parents

won the hour for NBC, with 12.3 million viewers, handily beating Barbara Walters's ABC *20/20* interview with Princess Diana's butler. Oprah retaliated by releasing footage from her show before it aired, for two segments on ABC's *Good Morning America*, the show that competed directly with Katie Couric and *The Today Show*. "It wasn't vengeance," said Oprah's publicist. "Just promotion."

Not everybody enjoyed being on *The Oprah Winfrey Show*. "I represented Anne Robinson, who wrote *Memoir of an Unfit Mother* in 2001, when she got a call from Oprah's producers four years later to go on the show," recalled literary agent Ed Victor. "Anne asked me if she should do it, and I told her yes, because as soon as her publisher [Pocket Books] heard that Oprah wanted her and her daughter to appear, they offered to publish her book in paperback. So I said she should do the show, sell some books, and get her message out." Robinson, the curt British host of the weekly game show *The Weakest Link,* had a certain visibility in the United States at the time, but according to her agent, her experience with Oprah was "hellacious."

"Anne yelled at me after the show," said Victor. "She hated Oprah and felt she had not been treated right by the Oprah people." Robinson refused to discuss the matter, but Ed Victor recalled it as "a nightmare all around," adding, "As a consequence, I no longer represent her."

Marian Fontana, whose husband, Dave, a firefighter, died at the World Trade Center on 9/11, was hounded by Oprah's producers, who had booked her for an upcoming show. "It was right after Dave's funeral . . . and they were calling every ten minutes wanting something else. They wanted wedding videotapes and they wanted family photos and they wanted close-up shots." When they heard she was holding a service for her husband on the beach where he had been a lifeguard for sixteen years, they insisted on coming. "They were very pushy," she said, and when she declined, they canceled the booking.

In the spring of 2008, Oprah's producers began booking for May sweeps and called James Frey to come on the show to talk about the paperback publication of his novel *Bright Shiny*

*Morning.* They knew a rematch between Oprah and the author of *A Million Little Pieces* was a guaranteed ratings geyser, but the writer was not so eager to return to the scene of his reaming. Since getting bludgeoned on *The Oprah Winfrey Show* in 2006, Frey and his wife had lost their newborn son, Leo, who died eleven days after birth from spinal muscular atrophy, and the writer was not going to put himself through another one of Her Majesty's muggings, even to promote his novel, unless there were certain stipulations in place. Oprah's producers explained the situation to her, and in the end, Frey was not booked, but Oprah did call him to apologize for how she had treated him two years before. She did not use her show to publicly say she was sorry, but Frey told reporters he appreciated her private apology. Oprah's remorse may have been triggered by reading about a character in Frey's novel who is embroiled in a scandal and, feeling people turn on him, begins to tape-record his conversations with the producers and host of a television talk show, including confessions the host made when she called him at home.

In their scramble to give Oprah ratings her producers can be rambunctious. "I found them to be . . . exceedingly difficult," said Daniel J. Bagdade, the attorney who represented the first child in the United States to be sentenced as an adult for murder. His client, Nathaniel (Nate) Abraham, shot and killed Ronald Greene in Pontiac, Michigan. At the age of eleven Nate was sent to a maximum-security juvenile detention facility until he was twenty-one. Upon his release, Oprah's producers were waiting to sign him to do a show, featuring his on-air apology to the family of his victim. His lawyer was not sanguine about putting him in the intense media spotlight of *The Oprah Winfrey Show,* but Nate was enthralled with the celebrity allure of Oprah. "She's the person he admires most," said the attorney. "So I agreed. . . . But once we got to Chicago, well . . ."

Seeing that what the producers had in mind for the show would put his client in legal jeopardy, Bagdade revoked Nate's signed release. "Then it was two days and nights with Oprah and her attorney, a tough older gentleman [William Becker heads

Harpo's legal staff of twenty-five], and her hard-charging producers, who were aggressive and really backed us into a corner. They threatened to sue us for breaking the contract. . . . 'We are not going to leave it here,' they said. Oprah and I were back and forth on cell phones at midnight as she tried to get the show on the air. When I explained the legal complications to her, she called a lawyer in Michigan to make sure I was telling her the truth. She was reasonable and professional throughout, but I can't say the same about her staff."

In the end the show never aired. Instead, Oprah mediated Nate's apology to his victim's family privately, and Bagdade accompanied him and his mother and Ronald Greene's relatives into Oprah's office, which, he said, "was the size of a large house. Directly off her office is a wardrobe room, which is the size of another large house. . . . The shoe area alone seems to cover half a block." Bagdade did not see Oprah's huge office bathroom with its pond-sized tub of rose-colored marble.

With Harpo's lawyer sitting in the corner, Oprah stood at her big desk and proceeded to bring the two families together. "A true apology had never been given before, so this was a very moving experience for all of us," said Nate's lawyer. "It's a good thing it was not on-camera. It would've been too exploitive. The two mothers—Nate's and Mrs. Greene—hugged and kissed. Both are churchgoing ladies, so they talked about God and his forgiveness."

Once Oprah realized she was not going to get the gripping television show she wanted, she could easily have sent the Abrahams and the Greenes back to Pontiac, Michigan. But to her credit she chose to complete the stated purpose of the show: to give a young killer the chance to express remorse for his crime by apologizing to his victim's family, which gave everyone a measure of peace. "Oprah really went out of her way with Nate," said his attorney. "She gave him lots of advice and took a special interest in him during those couple of days."

Not all scrapped shows brought out Oprah's magnanimity, however, particularly if money was involved. When she got a chance to interview Monica Lewinsky, she said she was thrilled

to land the young intern's first interview about her sexual relationship with President Clinton, which eventually led to his
impeachment. Lewinsky, too, was excited, especially when told
that Oprah was going to embrace her in front of her studio audience. But when the former White House aide insisted on
keeping the foreign distribution rights to that interview after it
aired in the United States, Oprah balked. At issue were world licensing fees in excess of $1 million, which Lewinsky said she
needed to pay her mounting legal fees. Being one of the world's
most sought-after interviewees then, she was of immense international interest, because no one had ever heard her voice or her
side of the story that nearly toppled a president. Oprah insisted
on keeping the foreign rights to the interview; Monica said she
could not afford to give them up. The next day on her talk
show, Oprah announced, "I did have the interview with Monica
Lewinsky, and then the conversation moved in a direction that I
did not want to go. I don't pay for interviews, no matter how it's
couched. I've taken myself out of the running. I don't even want
the interview now. Whoever gets the interview, God help you in
your struggle."

The two-hour interview went to Barbara Walters, for a special edition of *20/20* on ABC, and drew forty-five million viewers in the United States, with Lewinsky retaining world rights.
Later, in a story titled "How Oprah Dumped Monica," *George*
magazine recounted that Oprah had "trashed" the former intern
when she refused to sign an agreement with Harpo. "[I]n
Lewinsky's eyes, Winfrey proved to be . . . heartless, treacherous,
and disloyal."

None of that would be believed by any of Oprah's adoring
fans or the studio audiences, who wait months, sometimes
years, for tickets to her show and then stand in line for hours to be
admitted. "Everything about *The Oprah Winfrey Show* is orchestrated right down to the last squeal of the studio audience," said a
publishing executive who has escorted many authors to
Chicago over the years. "The drill goes something like this: Once
you get through security and get seated, four or five producers—
not just one—warm up the audience for about forty-five minutes.

We are all given directions on how to act. We're told to jump and scream. When Oprah says something funny, we're supposed to laugh and clap. Then we are rehearsed. 'Now let's try it. If Oprah is shocked, you are shocked. C'mon. Act horrified. Show it. Let's do it again. The more you react, the better chance you'll have to be shown on television. This is important. You are Oprah's audience. You are her portal to the world. So you must respond.' These producers are trained to work everyone into a frenzy so the audience is hysterical by the time Oprah comes out of the tunnel. The minute she appears, everyone jumps up and begins cheering and weeping and screaming and stomping."

Oprah became so accustomed to rapturous audiences that she reacted negatively if she saw someone not standing to applaud her. "One time she spotted a young black man who just sat there," said the publishing executive. "She began heckling him. 'I see someone here who is very brave.' She began shuckin' and jivin': 'Oh no. I don't have to stand up and cheer for Oprah. No, sir. Not me. I'm the man. I won't bow to Oprah.' She did her whole ghetto shtick. It was ugly, very ugly for about four or five minutes while the poor guy just sat there as she mocked him. She wouldn't let up. . . . She was pissed that he was not giving her the adoring routine that the rest of the audience was. . . . Turned out the young man was mentally challenged and severely disabled."

Part of the excitement in attending one of Oprah's shows is the possibility of walking away with a fabulous giveaway—TiVos, iPods, Kindles, cakes, clothes, even cars. The most anticipated gift show of every year—"Oprah's Favorite Things"—started in 1999 as an outgrowth of Oprah's passion for shopping. For years she had shared her spending orgies with her viewers—her towels, her pajamas, her cashmere sweaters, her diamond earrings—and they enjoyed her unbridled enthusiasm over her newfound wealth. Excited about becoming a millionaire, she constantly asked her celebrity guests, "When did you know you were rich?" "How does it feel to be able to buy anything you want?" "What did you do when you first got real money?" "Has being a millionaire changed your life?"

When she started "Oprah's Favorite Things" she called the

manufacturer of each item she picked and asked them to send her three hundred freebies to give to her studio audience. The publicity they received in exchange launched many into new levels of profitability because they were then flooded with orders from her viewers. Small businesses such as Spanx, Inc., Thermage beauty treatment, Philosophy skin care, Carol's Daughter beauty products, and Lafco fragrances became behemoths as a result of making something that Oprah liked; thus few companies ever denied her free merchandise. "My deal is only this: If I'm going to say it's my favorite thing because it is my favorite thing, all you have to do is give me three hundred of them, okay? [T]here was this book that somebody had given me—a book called *The Way We Live*. It was a great coffee table book, and it had pictures from all over the world of different homes and how people live in these different homes. Do you know we called the publisher [Crown] and they said no? They said they didn't have that many books to give away for free because I think the book is expensive [$75], if you buy it in stores. Can you believe that? So you know what I said, 'Well, it's not going to be my favorite thing no more!' But how dumb is that [publisher]? That's pretty dumb. It's a book. How many books could they have sold?"

Oprah referred to her "Favorite Things" show as "the hottest ticket in television" and kept the airdate secret until the day of the show. Then she devoted an hour to giving away her favorite things of that year, which have included organic cheesecakes, candied popcorn, Ugg boots, CDs, books, coats, laptops, digital cameras, custom-designed Nike shoes, diamond watches, BlackBerrys, and flat-screen TVs. Each year she announced the items with great fanfare and always included the retail price. In 2007 she presented her most outrageously exorbitant item at the end of the show, when she hollered, "This is my most expensive favorite thing ever, ever, ever." Nearly spent with orgasmic delight over what they had already received, her studio audience trembled as the drums rolled and the velvet curtains opened to reveal an LG refrigerator with a high-definition TV built into the door, a DVD hookup, and a radio, plus technology for a slide show, a five-day forecast, and a laptop holding one hundred recipes. "It [retails for] $3,789.00," Oprah screamed. The grand total for that year's Favorite Things was $7,200. Conan O'Brien joked on late-night television, "*Forbes* magazine released its list of the twenty richest women. . . . Oprah is number one. The rest are in her audience."

The list of "Oprah's Favorite Things" seemed to get longer and more expensive over the years, making her, as one writer noted, "The countess of ka-ching, the monarch of materialism." When she was criticized for crass commercialism, Oprah announced that, going forward, the audiences for her "Favorite Things" shows would be deserving recipients such as underpaid teachers or Katrina volunteers.

Her most ballyhooed giveaway occurred on September 13, 2004. "That was the best year I've ever experienced in television with the exception of the first year," she told the writer P. J. Bednarski. She opened the season by giving away 276 brand-new Pontiac G6s, worth more than $28,000 apiece, for a collective total of $7.8 million.

"It was not a stunt and I resent the word *stunt*," she said, explaining that when a General Motors executive offered to give the cars as part of her "Favorite Things" show, she said no. "I can't do that because that's not my favorite car and I'm not going to say it is." Then she remembered Jane Pauley's new talk show was launching in September as a strong alternative to her own. Oprah's producers pushed, saying she could not turn down the opportunity to give away cars, so they set about finding worthy souls who needed wheels. Jane Pauley's launch show was buried under Oprah's free cars show, which became one of the most talked-about giveaways in television history.

"My heart was palpitating [that day]," she recalled. "We had real emergency medical personnel standing by because sometimes people really do pass out in the audience."

Revving herself and her audience into a paroxysm of ecstasy, she passed out small boxes to everyone and said that one box contained the keys to a free car. The audience opened their boxes and each found a set of keys. Oprah started yelling and jumping and pumping her arms: "You win a car! You win a car! Everybody gets the car. Everybody gets the car! Everybody gets the car!" She led her delirious audience out to the Harpo parking lot, where 276 gleaming blue Pontiac G6s had been wrapped in huge red bows. "This car is so cool," said Oprah. "It has one of the most powerful engines on the road."

Teachers and ministers and nurses and caregivers who had been walking to work for years or taking buses and having to transfer three times were thrilled by their life-changing gifts. However, almost immediately they learned they would have to pay taxes (approximately $7,000) on the cars, because they were considered prizes rather than gifts. Many turned to Oprah for help, and her publicist said they had three options: They could keep the car and pay the tax, sell the car and pay the tax with the profit, or forfeit the car. There was no other option from Oprah, and Pontiac already had donated the cars and paid the sales tax and licensing fees.

"Was this really a do-good event Winfrey pulled off," asked Lewis Lazare in the *Chicago Sun-Times,* "or a cold-blooded publicity stunt carefully designed to make the talk show diva really look good at the expense of Pontiac, which gladly provided cars in exchange for some of Winfrey's promotional plugging?" He added: "It's increasingly apparent she's . . . become an unabashed shill for a slew of marketing-savvy companies salivating at the prospect of getting her to back their products in the hope big sales will ensue."

Oprah was incensed. "For all the people who say, 'Oh, you didn't personally pay for the cars yourself,' which I heard, I say, 'Well, I could have, and what difference does it make, if they get the cars? And why should I have paid for them if Pontiac was willing to do so?'"

By then she was surfing on high waves of spending, and sounding a trifle cavalier as she discussed her $500 mink eyelashes, her one-thousand-thread-count sheets, and FedEx-ing her horses from her farm in Indiana to her house in Hawaii. She frequently name-dropped when talking of the celebrity gifts she had received, such as the twenty-one pairs of Christian

Louboutin shoes ($1,600 a pair) from Jessica Seinfeld; the
Rolls-Royce Corniche II convertible ($100,000) from John
Travolta; the roomful of Casa Blanca lilies from *American Idol*
judge Simon Cowell, which she said "looked like a Mafia funeral"; and the white Bentleys ($250,000 each) that she and
Gayle received from Tyler Perry. "I call him my rich Negro
man," Oprah told viewers.

Speaking at a fund-raiser for a community school in Baltimore, she said, "I have lots of things like all these Manolo Blah-
niks. I have all that and I think it's great. I'm not one of these
people, like, 'Well, we must renounce ourselves.' No. I have a
closet full of shoes, and it's a good thing." She told the well-
heeled crowd she enjoyed her money without guilt or apology. "I
was coming back from Africa on one of my trips. I had taken one
of my wealthy friends with me. She said, 'Don't you just feel
guilty? Don't you feel terrible?' I said, 'No, I don't. I do not
know how my being destitute is going to help them.' Then I said
when we got home, 'I'm going home to sleep on my Pratesi
sheets right now and I'll feel good about it.'"

She recalled for her magazine readers that on her forty-
second birthday she and Gayle were in Miami, where she decided to buy herself a big Cartier watch as a present. En route,
she spotted a black Bentley Azure in a dealership window. "Oh,
my God," she said. "That is the most beautiful car." She bought
the Bentley on the spot. "It's a convertible. The top is down and
guess what? It starts to rain. It's pouring." Oprah did not put the
top up on her $365,000 car. "Because I want[ed] to ride in a
convertible on my birthday." Next stop: the Cartier boutique
for the Diabolo small model watch in yellow gold with all-
diamond bezel, case, dial, and bracelet for $117,000.

She told viewers after attending her first couture show in
Paris, "I could have bought a home for what I bought the
Chanel outfits for." She entertained at the same apex of luxury,
spending millions to host parties. "Eyes have not seen, nor ears
heard," said Vernon Winfrey as he tried to describe the sumptuous events his daughter staged for Maya Angelou's birthday
every five years. Many guests recalled Maya's seventieth, in

April 1998, as Oprah's most opulent. She rented the *Seabourn Pride* for a week's cruise in the Caribbean, invited two hundred people, and gave each a suite with a balcony on the luxury ship. "She even had two thousand yellow rubber duckies dropped into the ship's pool so we could play like children in a bathtub," recalled one guest. Their invitations arrived four months before the Easter event asking everyone for shirt size; pant size; shoe size; champagne preference; favorite liquors, foods, cosmetics, fragrances, and body lotions—all of which were stocked in their suites, along with terry-cloth robes stitched with their names. "I think she spent four million dollars on that party," said Vernon, shaking his head as he recalled the many stops the ship made for lavish lunches on white beaches, the silk-lined tents for dinners, and the moonlit concerts with Nancy Wilson singing under the stars. Oprah threw a similar bash for Maya when she turned seventy-five; on Angelou's eightieth birthday, Oprah rented Donald Trump's Mar-a-Lago Club in Palm Beach for a weekend and arranged special performances by Michael Feinstein, Natalie Cole, Jessye Norman, and Tony Bennett.

In 2005, at her Montecito mansion, Oprah hosted her most lavish event, which she billed as "A Bridge to Now—A Celebration for Remarkable Women During Remarkable Times," with cameras filming every moment for a special on ABC titled *Oprah Winfrey's Legends Ball.* A year and a half in the planning, the event honoring black women gave the network its biggest non-sports ratings in three years. The year before, 2004, Oprah had devoted two shows to celebrating her fiftieth birthday, the first of which was said to be a "surprise" hosted by "my best friend" (Gayle King) and "my favorite white man" (John Travolta). That show, called a "modest little Super Bowl of Love" by the *Chicago Sun-Times,* was followed by an after-party at Harpo for 500 employees and then 5 days of celebration, beginning with a dinner, hosted by Stedman at Chicago's Metropolitan Club for 75 people, including Oprah's father and mother.

The next day they boarded Oprah's jet and flew to California, where she was guest of honor at a ladies' luncheon for 50 at the Bel-Air Hotel, her favorite LA retreat. The guests there included

Salma Hayek, Diane Sawyer, Maria Shriver, Toni Morrison, Ellen DeGeneres, and Céline Dion. The following night there was a dinner dance for 200 at a neighbor's estate in Montecito, and the next morning a Sunday brunch for 175 people at the San Ysidro Ranch, all of which was filmed for a second Oprah show. In addition, Oprah invited *People* to cover the dinner dance staged by her party planner, Colin Cowie, full of what he called JDMs (jaw-dropping moments): 50 violinists, 200 waiters (one per guest), a chocolate-and-raspberry pound cake gilded with twenty-three-karat gold, music by Stevie Wonder, and wall-to-wall celebrities, including the Bel-Air luncheon ladies and their husbands and partners, Tom Hanks and Rita Wilson, John Travolta and Kelly Preston, Robin and Dr. Phil McGraw, Tina Turner, and Brad Pitt and Jennifer Aniston.

For "The Legends Weekend," Oprah selected twenty-five black women she considered to be legends:

Maya Angelou (author/poet/actor/producer/director)
Shirley Caesar (singer)
Diahann Carroll (actor/singer)
Elizabeth Catlett (sculptor)
Ruby Dee (actor/playwright)
Katherine Dunham (dancer/choreographer)
Roberta Flack (singer)
Aretha Franklin (singer)
Nikki Giovanni (poet)
Dorothy Height (activist)
Lena Horne (singer/actor)
Coretta Scott King (activist)
Gladys Knight (singer)
Patti LaBelle (singer)
Toni Morrison (author)
Rosa Parks (activist)
Leontyne Price (opera singer)
Della Reese (singer/actor)
Diana Ross (singer/actor)
Naomi Sims (model)

Tina Turner (singer)
Cicely Tyson (actor)
Alice Walker (author/poet)
Dionne Warwick (singer)
Nancy Wilson (singer)

Inexplicably missing from Oprah's list were her onetime friend Whoopi Goldberg, the singer Eartha Kitt, acclaimed opera star Jessye Norman, respected broadcaster Gwen Ifill, and Secretary of State Dr. Condoleezza Rice. Of the twenty-five women Oprah selected as legends, seven did not attend: Katherine Dunham, Aretha Franklin, Nikki Giovanni, Lena Horne, Toni Morrison, Rosa Parks, and Alice Walker. "Just too many television cameras," said one who did not participate. "Too much Oprah."

The "young 'uns," as Oprah called those following in the footsteps of the "legends," included:

Yolanda Adams (singer)
Debbie Allen (actor/dancer)
Ashanti (singer)
Tyra Banks (model/talk show host)
Angela Bassett (actor)
Kathleen Battle (opera singer)
Halle Berry (actor)
Mary J. Blige (singer)
Naomi Campbell (model)
Mariah Carey (singer)
Pearl Cleage (poet/playwright)
Natalie Cole (singer)
Suzanne De Passe (producer/writer)
Kimberly Elise (actor)
Missy Elliot (rap artist)
Pam Grier (actor)
Iman (model)
Janet Jackson (singer)

Judith Jamison (dancer/choreographer)
Beverly Johnson (model)
Chaka Khan (singer)
Gayle King (editor, *O* magazine)
Alicia Keys (singer)
Audra McDonald (actor/singer)
Terry McMillan (author)
Darnell Martin (director/screenwriter)
Melba Moore (actor/singer)
Brandy Norwood (singer)
Michelle Obama (community affairs executive)
Suzan-Lori Parks (playwright)
Phylicia Rashad (actor)
Valerie Simpson (singer/composer)
Anna Deavere Smith (actor/playwright)
Susan L. Taylor (editorial director of *Essence*)
Alfre Woodard (actor)

Oprah began the weekend with a luncheon at her estate on Friday (May 13, 2005), during which she gave six-carat diamond teardrop earrings to "the legends" and ten-carat black-and-white diamond hoop earrings to "the young 'uns," all presented in red alligator boxes inside of which were engraved silver cases. "I'm a girl who loves a good diamond earring, you know?" Oprah told her astounded guests.

"Are they real?" asked author Terry McMillan.

"They are black diamonds, crazy love! Of course they're real!"

During the "Legends" weekend, even the wealthiest stars were dumbfounded, especially when they saw the trolley Oprah had installed on the grounds for guests to tour "The Promised Land," as Oprah called her rolling estate with its various promenades, pools, ponds, rose arbors, romantic bridges, and winding trails, all bordered by five thousand white hydrangeas and two thousand white flowering trees. She called her equally luxurious home in Hawaii "Kingdom Come." As she told reporters, "I'm very biblical, you know. I got two roads to my [Hawaii] house . . . Glory and Hallelujah."

But it was her home in Montecito that left guests breathless. "The driveway is five miles long, and every stone was cut by hand," said one. "Her bathtub is a solid piece of jade, and her bathroom overlooks the entire forty-two-acre estate and gives her an eighty-degree view of the ocean. Her closet is three thousand square feet and she has a thousand drawers for everything—yes, one thousand—sweaters and T-shirts and one hundred hats. Each drawer has a glass front so nothing gets dusty and she can see what's inside. . . . Gayle has her own room in the main house with rose wallpaper, and Stedman's study overlooks the Montecito Mountains. . . . The views throughout are magnificent. . . . I think it's the most beautiful house I've ever seen."

The following night (Saturday, May 14, 2005), Oprah invited 362 people to a white-tie dinner dance at the Bacara Resort and Spa in Santa Barbara. She ordered 80 cases of champagne flown in from France, 120 pounds of tuna flown in from Japan, and 20,000 white peonies flown in from Ecuador. Entertainment was provided by Michael McDonald and a twenty-six-piece orchestra. Her party planner had sent his two hundred servers to waiter boot camp for three days to properly serve Oprah's A-list celebrity guests. As everyone sat for dinner, a drum rolled and the black-tied waiters laid down 362 plates at the same moment. It was another JDM. Oprah expected no less.

That night, after a sumptuous meal and dancing, guests returned to their hotel rooms to find on their pillows a gift-wrapped souvenir photograph of the evening in a sterling-silver frame from Asprey, the jeweler who carries royal warrants from Queen Elizabeth II and the Prince of Wales. Oprah had instructed the women to wear black or white gowns for the ball, while she appeared in flaming red, just like Norma Shearer did at a black-and-white ball she threw—so everyone would look *only* at her. The following morning (Sunday, May 15, 2005), Oprah wore a tall feathered hat to host a gospel brunch at "The Promised Land," where Senator Barack Obama, wearing sunglasses, stood under a tree a few feet away from Oprah, who had her arm draped around Barbra Streisand, swaying to the music.

Later Oprah approached Obama, who had been sworn in as a U.S. senator four months earlier. "If someone were to announce one of these days that he was going to run for president," she said, "don't you think this would be a sweet place to hold a fund-raiser?"

Senator Obama grinned.

# Twenty

B Y THE twenty-first century, Oprah was omnipresent, if not omnipotent. She appeared on television five days a week, claimed 44 million viewers in the United States, and was broadcast in 145 countries, from Saudi Arabia to South Africa. She was a daily presence on satellite radio (Sirius XM) with her own twenty-four-hour channel, Oprah and Friends. Her monthly magazine, with her picture on every cover, had a paid circulation of 2.4 million in the United States and was published also in South Africa. Through her investment in Oxygen she was seen on cable television with segments entitled *Oprah After the Show*. When Oxygen was sold to NBC Universal, she recouped her $20 million investment and announced plans to start her own television network in 2011, to be called OWN (Oprah Winfrey Network). She produced made-for-television movies under the banner "Oprah Winfrey Presents," and prime-time network specials. Her website, Oprah.com, attracted 6.7 million visitors a month, and her Twitter following numbered more than 2 million. A Google search of her name generated more than 8 million results, and there were 529 websites devoted solely to her.

By the millennium she was known and recognized throughout the country, even by those who never watched daytime television. She entered the vocabulary as a noun, a verb, and an adjective. Even disgruntled media critics acknowledged they had entered the Oprahsphere. "She puts the cult in pop culture,"

Mark Jurkowitz sniped in *The Boston Phoenix,* prompting Oprahettes to howl about the *jerk* in "Jurkowitz." Oprahholics worshipped her, and Oprahphiles studied her, making her the subject of more than three dozen PhD dissertations listed in the Library of Congress. The object of a case study on corporate success by the Harvard Business School, she was also studied at the University of Illinois at Urbana-Champaign in a course titled History 298: Oprah Winfrey, the Tycoon: Contextualizing the Economics of Race, Gender, Class in Black Business in Post–Civil Rights America. *Newsweek* declared the new century's touchy-feely era to be the "Age of Oprah," and *The Wall Street Journal* defined "Oprahfication" to mean "public confession as a form of therapy." *Jet* magazine used *Oprah* as a verb: "I didn't want to tell her . . . but she Oprah'd it out of me." Politicians everywhere began "to go Oprah," holding town meetings to let constituents vent their feelings. Companies lucky enough to have their products featured on "Oprah's Favorite Things" experienced an avalanche of orders known as the "Oprah Effect." By 2001, the nation had become so Oprahfied that New York's mayor, Rudolph Giuliani, chose Oprah along with James Earl Jones to lead the memorial service at Yankee Stadium in honor of the victims of 9/11.

With the country in her thrall, Oprah finally felt secure enough to break her "no politicians" rule and wade into their divisive waters. For years she had avoided politics because she did not want to alienate her audience. "If I support one person or another, I will piss a lot of people off," she said. "And I have not met the politician that was worth going to the mat for. When I do, I certainly will." By staying above the political fray, she felt she retained more affection from her viewers than her highly partisan predecessor, Phil Donahue. "Oprah would not even attend a Gridiron dinner," said former Hearst columnist Marianne Means, a past president of The Gridiron Club, whose annual dinner in Washington, D.C., is attended by the president, the vice president, and members of Congress, the Senate, and the Supreme Court. Members of the media perform skits and songs poking fun at both political parties. "We invited her many times, but she always turned us down, saying she did not get involved with politics."

After fifteen years on the air Oprah finally decided to enter the political arena. "She waited until she was rich enough so it wouldn't affect her bottom line," said her cousin Katharine Carr Esters. "And that was very smart of her. . . . But then when it comes to money, no one is smarter than Oprah."

Once she became a fixture on the *Forbes* "400 Richest Americans" list, Oprah became part of the nation's political conversation by extending an invitation in 2000 to the two presidential candidates to appear on her show. "I hope to create the kind of environment and ask the questions that will allow us to break the political wall and see who each one is as a person," she said through her publicist. The next day's news was more about Oprah going political than it was about Vice President Al Gore and Governor George W. Bush. The headline on Salon .com read, "The Road to the White House Goes Through Oprah."

Politically, she appeared to be a Democrat, having contributed $1,000 in 1992 to Chicago's Carol Moseley Braun, a Democrat and the first African American woman to be elected to the U.S. Senate. Oprah also donated $10,000 to the Democratic Senatorial Campaign Committee in 1996, and $5,000 to the Democratic National Committee in 1997. Yet she claimed to have voted "for as many Democrats as I have Republicans." However, federal election records do not show any Republican votes, only that she voted in four Democratic primaries between 1987 and 1994. She skipped voting in the 1996, 1998, and 2000 primaries, but did cast a ballot in the general elections for president.

She once boasted to a British writer, "I think I could have a great influence in politics, and I think I could get elected." But, she added, "I think a politician would want to be me [instead]. If you really want to change people's lives, have an hour platform every day to go into their homes." To *The Times* of London she said, "Having this big voice on television is what every politician wants. They all try and get on the show and I don't do politics on the show."

Careful at the time not to get partisan, Oprah invited First Lady Barbara Bush to be her guest in 1989, and she later extended several invitations to First Lady Hillary Rodham Clinton, who appeared four times during her husband's eight years in the White House. Hillary celebrated her fiftieth birthday on Oprah's show, and Oprah asked Hillary to present her with her Lifetime Achievement Award from the International Emmys. During that ceremony, Oprah, clutching Hillary's hand, said, "I hope you do us the privilege of running for . . . president of the United States."

Oprah had considered breaking her "no politicians" rule back in 1992 by inviting Texas billionaire H. Ross Perot, Sr., to be her guest, because, as she said at the time, "He's become larger than politics," but she backed off. Still skittish four years later, she turned down a request from Senator Robert Dole, the 1996 GOP presidential candidate, who was running against Bill Clinton.

"I was very torn [about Dole's request to come on the show]," she told her viewers. "I went to my producers and said, 'Maybe this isn't the right decision.' But in the end I decided to stay out of politics, maintaining my long-standing policy: I don't do politicians." At the time, her studio audience gave her a resounding ovation. "I've tried to stay out of politics for my entire tenure on the air," she said that day. "Basically, it's a no-win situation. Over the years, I have not found that interviewing politicians about the issues worked for my viewing audience. I try to bring issues that people understand through their hearts and their feelings so they can make decisions."

Senator Dole laughed at Oprah's explanation. "Riiight," he jibed years later. "She doesn't do politicians—if they run against Democrats."

Oprah admitted she had been "asked to do everything" at the 1996 Democratic National Convention in Chicago, but she insisted she would not participate in any way, except for attending the parties thrown by "my friends Ethel Kennedy and John

Kennedy, Jr." Since meeting Maria Shriver in Baltimore, where they both worked for WJZ-TV, Oprah had been besotted by the Kennedys. She boosted them at every turn, contributing to Ethel Kennedy's online charity, promoting the books of Caroline Kennedy and Maria Shriver, attending fund-raisers for Kathleen Kennedy Townsend, hosting a show titled "The Kennedy Cousins," and inviting any and all Kennedys to appear with her throughout the years. In 2009, Victoria Kennedy gave Oprah her first interview after the death of her husband, Senator Edward Kennedy.

Although Oprah had not publicly declared herself a Democrat, her close friends—Maya Angelou, Henry Louis Gates, Jr., Quincy Jones, Coretta Scott King, Toni Morrison, Andrew Young—were all Democrats committed to Clinton, and Oprah herself had been invited to the Clintons' first white-tie state dinner in 1994, for Japan's emperor, Akihito, and empress, Michiko. (She admitted later she had been tongue-tied in the presence of Japanese royalty. "I didn't know what to say, and it was one of the few times.") Oprah had attended her first White House state dinner in 1989, during the George Herbert Walker Bush administration, with Stedman Graham, a conservative Republican, who would not accompany her to the Clinton White House five years later. So she took Quincy Jones.

"I met her that evening," recalled the art dealer Christopher Addison, who, with his wife, owns the Addison/Ripley Fine Art gallery in Washington, D.C. "I did not recognize her as anybody famous then because I don't watch daytime television, but the eighty-year-old woman who was my guest that evening told me who she was. . . . Oprah had brought a little instamatic camera with her and asked me to take her photograph. I thought it was endearing of her to want her picture taken in the White House, almost like a tourist. Very sweet."

Oprah had charmed them downstairs at the Bush White House by visiting the kitchen staff after the state dinner, but upstairs was another matter: the social staff found her to be overbearing and unreasonable. "She was rude and demanding, impossible to deal with," Lea Berman, a former White House social secretary, told the Colonial Dames of America. "She insisted she be allowed to bring her own security into the president's mansion. This is so against White House policy, but Ms. Winfrey became so adamant and shrill that we finally relented and allowed her to be accompanied by her own bodyguards."

When Oprah issued her invitations to Vice President Al Gore and Governor George W. Bush in 2000 to appear on her show, both accepted because the presidential race was close, and each man wanted to reach her large female audience. A Gallup/CNN/*USA Today* poll had Bush trailing Gore by ten percentage points before the visit with Oprah; days later the same poll showed Bush in a statistical tie. News reports called it the "Oprah Bounce." The *Chicago Sun-Times* editorial page saluted her for getting involved in the presidential race, and she hyped her first political foray before her season's opening show, prompting the comedian Chris Rock to joke, "Both Gore and Bush are going to appear on Oprah, but for different reasons. Gore is trying to appeal to women voters. Bush wants to find out how in the world did this black woman get all that money."

Oprah welcomed the vice president on September 11, 2000, and he strode onstage, greeting her with a handshake and a one-armed half-hug.

"No kiss? I was hoping for something," she teased, referring to the exceedingly long on-camera kiss Gore had planted on his wife at the Democratic Convention. "Until today I've stayed away from politicians, but after fifteen years I need to try to penetrate that wall," she told her viewers as she put Gore on notice that she was going to be more grill than gush. Despite twenty-four years in public office, he demurred, "I am a little bit more of a private person than a lot of the people in the profession." Oprah was having none of it.

"Let's get to that kiss," she said. "What was that all about? What did you say to your wife? Was it scripted? Were you trying to send a message?"

"I was trying to send a message to Tipper," Gore quipped, prompting a huge laugh from the studio audience.

"No, really," Oprah persisted. To her credit, she interrupted whenever he lapsed into his stump speech, and tried to get something more truthful and heartfelt.

"Well . . . I . . . It was an overwhelming surge of emotion. This was a great moment in our lives. I mean, it's not as if I got there by myself. This has been a partnership, and she is my soul mate."

The studio audience, mostly female, erupted in wild applause for the romantic robot, usually stiff and awkward, who seemed so in love with his wife after thirty years of marriage.

For an hour Oprah huffed and puffed and tried to blow "that wall" down, but all she got was Gore's favorite movie (*Local Hero*), Gore's favorite music (The Beatles), and Gore's favorite cereal (Wheaties). "The woman who has persuaded hundreds of people to reveal things about themselves that might better have been kept private couldn't get Gore out of his comfort zone," wrote Mark Brown in the *Chicago Sun-Times*. "Best of all for Gore, he handled her so smoothly that Oprah never seemed to realize it."

The following week (September 18, 2000) she welcomed Governor Bush of Texas, who arrived with coconut macaroons from Texas-based Neiman Marcus for her studio audience and greeted her with a huge kiss. The photo of Bush bussing Oprah on the cheek as she smiled gleefully made the front page of *The New York Times*.

"Thanks for the kiss," she said, sitting down next to him.

"My pleasure." He grinned.

"There were people on the street yesterday who told me that they were going to make their decision [about whom to vote for] after today's show," she told him. The cocky governor nodded as the cocky host dug right in and asked if he was running to restore his father's defeat by Bill Clinton. "To get revenge?"

"Not even in the teeniest, tiniest part," Bush insisted, saying he felt "a calling" to be president. "I see America as a land of dreams, hopes, and opportunities. . . ."

"I wanna go behind the wall now," snapped Oprah. "Tell us about a time when you needed forgiveness."

"Right now," said Bush as the studio audience erupted with laughter.

"I'm looking for specifics," Oprah said sternly.

"I know you are, but I'm running for president." Even she had to laugh at that, and her studio audience clapped with delight. When she asked him his "favorite dream," he raised his right hand as if to be sworn in as president, and the studio audience again rocked with laughter. Bush later got teary-eyed as he discussed his wife's difficult pregnancy and the birth of their twin daughters. He admitted that he finally stopped drinking at the age of forty because alcohol had taken over his life.

"Ever mindful of her status as the Most Powerful Woman on the Planet, Winfrey approached the Gore and Bush interviews as if they were a sacred duty," Joyce Millman wrote on Salon.com. "You could tell she was serious, because she interrupted Gore and Bush even more than she usually interrupts guests who have ceased to interest her. . . . I don't understand why Bush was so reluctant to debate his opponent; facing Al Gore for 90 minutes has got to be easier than keeping She Who Must Be Obeyed amused for an hour."

Oprah did not endorse either candidate, but by the end of his hour, George W. Bush had hit a home run straight out of her ballpark. When Chris Rock appeared a few months later he blamed Oprah for handing the White House to the Republicans.

"You made Bush win. He came here and sat in the chair and you gave the man a win. You know you did."

"I did not," she said with an unconvincing laugh.

Gloria Steinem sided with the comedian. In her profile of Oprah for *Time,* she wrote, "Only when she leaves her authentic self behind does she lose trust, as when she aided the election of George W. Bush."

A few weeks after Bush became president, Oprah asked for an interview with Laura Bush for *O* magazine, and while she and the First Lady were talking in the family quarters at the White House, the president poked his head in, saying he wanted to greet the next president of the United States. "Thank you for coming to see Laura," he said, "and letting her show her stuff."

Days after 9/11 shattered the country, the White House called Oprah and asked if the First Lady might appear on her show to address teachers and parents on how they could help their children through the trauma. Oprah welcomed Mrs. Bush on September 18, 2001, and they walked onstage hand in hand to try to reassure a nation that had been profoundly shaken by the horrific attacks. Reflecting the mood of the country at the time—a desire and need to come together to try to understand what had happened—Oprah presented shows on "Islam 101," "Is War the Only Answer?" and "What Really Matters Now?"

She also did a show featuring Afghani women titled "Inside the Taliban," which prompted another call from the White House, asking her to join Mrs. Bush, Communications Director Karen Hughes, and National Security Advisor Condoleezza Rice as part of an official U.S. delegation to visit Afghani girls returning to school after the fall of the Taliban. Oprah declined, saying she was too busy, when in fact she, like many, was too scared to travel in the wake of the terrorist attacks. She canceled a trip to launch O, The Oprah Magazine, in South Africa in April 2002, saying, "I started feeling uncomfortable about traveling. My instinct says things aren't right in parts of the world. All parts."

The White House leaked the story to the press on March 29, 2002, that Oprah had said no to the president and, as a consequence, the trip, designed to dampen images of global violence, had to be postponed. A controversy ensued over Oprah's rejection after her publicist told the *Chicago Tribune*, "Given her responsibility to the show, she isn't adding anything to her calendar. She was invited, but she respectfully declined."

The headlines kicked up a media storm:

"Winfrey Won't Tour for Bush" (*New York Times*)
"Envoy Oprah a No-Go: Talk Queen Declines Bush
       Invite to Tour Afghanistan Schools" (*New York Post*)
"No Oprah, No Afghan Trip" (*Washington Post*)
"Winfrey Declines Bush Invite to Afghan Trip; US
       Hoped to Show Its Help for Women" (*Chicago
       Tribune*)
"Oprah Balks; Talk Show Diva Refuses Afghanistan
       Invitation" (*Daily News* [Los Angeles])

A columnist from the *Chicago Tribune* wrote: "It's great to live in a country in which a black woman finally has the power and the self-esteem to say no to the man in charge."

That triggered a letter to the editor about what looked like a blatant snub:

> I lost a lot of respect for Oprah when she declined our president's invitation to join the U.S. delegation to tour Afghanistan's schools. What a wonderful opportunity she had to spread good will around the world on behalf of America.
>
> I'm sure she could have worked around her "busy schedule" as payback for all the opportunities and good fortune she has been given in our land of the free. Has she forgotten where she came from? Shame on her!

In a swivet over the negative publicity, Oprah called her friend Star Jones, then appearing on *The View,* to say the White House story was untrue. Jones went on the air moments later to share Oprah's call:

> [S]he had some fund-raisers that she had committed to and anybody knows when you do these things . . . people sell tickets expecting you to be there. So she couldn't get out of doing [them] and she didn't want to because she had made the commitment.
>
> She said the White House told her they were going anyway. Then she said, "So imagine my surprise, I wake up and read in the newspaper that I'm being cavalier, I'm too busy." She said it didn't happen that way and it really wasn't fair. We all know what kinds of philanthropic things that Oprah does across the country and across the world so that wasn't fair.
>
> She did say, "Star, I felt extremely used by the Bush administration."

Yet within six months Oprah appeared to be helping the president in his lead-up to the invasion of Iraq. On October 9, 2002, she presented a show to "help you decide if you think we should attack Iraq." Although she featured speakers on both sides of the issue, she gave more time and weight to those who supported going to war. At one point a member of the studio audience stood to question the existence of weapons of mass destruction, and Oprah cut her off, saying the weapons were "just a fact," not something up for debate. "We're not trying to propaganda—show you propaganda—we're just showing you what is," Oprah said.

Immediately after the show, the antiwar website Educate yourself.org published a letter to Oprah, saying:

> A talk show host and idol to many, you usually present an open exchange of opinions. How could you allow such an unbalanced show like that to air, when the future of the entire planet is at stake?

The Swedish Broadcasting Commission also pounced, saying Oprah's show, one of Sweden's most popular daytime programs, betrayed bias toward a U.S. attack on Iraq. "Different views were expressed, but all longer remarks gave voice to the opinion that Saddam Hussein was a threat to the United States and should be the target of attack," stated the commission. The Swedish government strongly opposed the invasion, saying it lacked a UN Security Council mandate.

Neither objection fazed Oprah. Needing the approval and good opinion of others, she preferred joining the establishment to jabbing it, and the establishment view then was in support of invading Iraq. Temperamentally, Oprah would have been uncomfortable putting herself in the minority by questioning the president's policies, especially in the wake of 9/11, when any kind of dissent was looked upon as unpatriotic. Fox News's Bill O'Reilly had announced, "I will call those who publicly criticize their country in a time of military crisis . . . bad Americans." Later Oprah presented a two-part program, "Should the U.S. Attack Iraq?" on February 6 and 7, 2003, and claimed she received hate mail, calling her "the *N* word" and telling her "to go back to Africa" because she was not pro-war enough. That was her last show on the subject. The United States invaded Iraq on March 30, 2003.

Four years later, *Bill Moyers Journal* produced a compelling ninety-minute program on PBS titled "Buying the War," which showed how the mainstream media had abandoned their role as watchdogs and became lapdogs for a failed policy that cost thousands of American and Iraqi lives. Moyers, who received an Emmy for his documentary, included Oprah in his condemnation of the media.

At the time she seemed to be cheerleading for the Bush administration, Oprah had attracted numerous complaints to the Federal Communications Commission for airing explicit sexual material during hours when children watched television. Particularly at issue was a show titled "Is Your Child Living a Double Life?" in which Oprah and her guests spoke graphically about the sexual slang and sexual acts of teenagers. "If your child said they had their salad tossed . . . would you know what they meant?" she asked viewers. She then provided the graphic and salacious definitions of "tossed salad," "outercourse," "booty call," and "rainbow parties," which prompted a barrage of complaints to the FCC. Shock jock Howard Stern tried to air her remarks on his radio show the next day, but his New York station manager bleeped them for obscene and indecent language. "But it's Oprah," protested Stern, who had been fined almost $2 million by the FCC for using similar language. Without friends in high places, he felt that he was being held to a double standard.

One of the FCC complainants against Oprah agreed. "The very day that Howard Stern was fined, Oprah broadcast sexual and excretory material that was even more explicit," wrote Jeff Jarvis, the former television critic of *TV Guide.* "I've complained and so have many others. But you can bet she won't be fined. . . ." Claiming that Oprah had done her show on teen sex just to get the subject of sex on the air, Jarvis called her a hypocrite. "Oprah: You can't act as if you don't bear considerable responsibility for this. You brought sex to afternoon TV. Now I don't think you should be fined for that and I don't think you should be taken off the air for that: I just don't watch you. But you're doing nothing different from Howard Stern—except getting away with it. So cut your holier-than-thou disapproval of sex on the rest of TV. You are the Queen of Trash."

The *Santa Barbara News-Press*, which served the area where Oprah's mansion in Montecito was located, also noted the hypocrisy. "What parents want their kids to come home from school, run to turn on Oprah and be subjected to that stuff?" wrote Scott Steepleton, assistant metro editor. "The time has come for the FCC to stop applying the law in such an arbitrary fashion. If it's crude, it's crude—no matter whose show it's on." Yet the FCC ruled in 2006 that Oprah's show on teenage sex was not indecent because the explicit language was not used to shock.

One can only wonder if the FCC was out of order during the February sweeps of 2006 when Oprah did a show titled "Women Who Use Sex to Find Love." She interviewed a woman, given the fictitious name of Jennifer, who claimed to have had sex with ninety men, keeping an ongoing list and video diary of her one-night stands. Oprah stunned the blogosphere when she said to Jennifer, "So you've had men ejaculate in your face who you don't even know who they are." The mainstream media did not comment on the Jennifer show, but Robert Paul Reyes, on AmericanChronicle.com, accused Oprah of trolling the gutter to rack up ratings.

"Millions of women tune in to you for inspirational and educational programming and you interview a nymphomaniac who's had unprotected sex with almost 100 guys?"

Unfazed, Oprah may have felt immunized from FCC pressure because of her relationship with the Bush White House, so she continued presenting tabloidy sex shows intermixed with feel-good and do-good shows. A partial list of 2004–2009 shows:

"Is Your Sex Life Normal?" (2/19/04)
"Is Your Child Living a Double Life?" (3/18/04)
"Secret Sex in the Suburbs" (11/19/04)
"Wife Swapping" (12/27/04)
"Venus, Serena and Jada Pinkett Smith on Dating, Sex and Weight" (3/30/05)
"Releasing Your Inner Sexpot" (5/31/05)
"Women Who Use Sex to Find Love" (2/23/06)

"Female Teachers, Young Boys, Secret Sex at School"
(4/27/06)

"Why Do Men Go to Strip Clubs, and Other Burning
Questions" (1/1/07)

"237 Reasons to Have Sex" (9/25/07)

"How They Revved Up Their Sex Life" (8/27/08)

"Behind Closed Doors: Sex Therapy" (10/2/08)

"Sex Therapy 2: Fears, Fantasies and Faking It"
(11/21/08)

"Best Life Week: Relationships, Intimacy and Sex"
(1/9/09)

"Sex: Women Reveal What They Really Want" (4/03/09)

"How to Talk to Your Kids About Sex, with Dr. Laura
Berman" (4/09/09)

"14 Years Old: They Say They're Ready for Sex"
(4/16/09)

"How to Get Your Sexy Back Makeovers" (6/15/09)

"Former Child Star Mackenzie Phillips' Startling
Revelations" (9/23/09)

"Mackenzie and Chynna Phillips, Jay Leno and Harry
Connick Jr." (9/25/09)

As much as she may have helped George W. Bush get
elected president, Oprah did even more for Arnold Schwarzenegger's 2003 race for governor of California. "Both of those candidates had real difficulty on policy issues and had issues with
women voters," said Mark Sawyer, director of UCLA's Center
for the Study of Race, Ethnicity and Politics. "The 'are-you-a-
nice-guy-to-talk-to' aspect of [going on] *Oprah*" made both
Bush and Schwarzenegger more approachable candidates.

When Schwarzenegger appeared on the show, he was being
investigated by the *Los Angeles Times* for numerous incidents of
sexual harassment over three decades. By the time the newspaper
ran its series, there were sixteen women who claimed to have
been groped and mauled by him against their will. Most did not
come forward voluntarily because they were afraid of reprisals in
Hollywood. Some said Schwarzenegger had attacked them in

elevators or on movie sets. One said he wrestled her from behind, shoving his hands up her skirt. Another said he grabbed her breasts, threw her up against the wall, and demanded sex. All described his language as lewd and demeaning.

That evening David Letterman joked, "Today the *L.A. Times* accused Schwarzenegger of groping . . . women. I'm telling you. This guy is presidential material."

Schwarzenegger admitted to telling coarse and bawdy jokes in front of women, but he denied all charges of sexual harassment. Still, his sudden decision to enter California's recall election had exposed his personal behavior to public scrutiny, and so his first interview after announcing his candidacy on *The Tonight Show* was on *The Oprah Winfrey Show*.

"Everyone wanted that interview," Oprah said of her exclusive booking. "But I played the friendship card." She also bathed Schwarzenegger in the warm glow of her acceptance: "Arnold is a mentor to a lot of men, but the thing that they're mentoring is the macho, the muscles. But what makes Arnold Arnold is the balance. He knows and practices sensitivity." She extolled him as a father and lauded the Schwarzeneggers' four children as a tribute to both parents. Such praise from Oprah enabled him to overcome the resistance of women who remembered the boasts of "Arnold the Barbarian" to *Oui* magazine in 1977 about his drug exploits, gymnasium gang-bang orgies, and demands for oral sex during bodybuilding tournaments.

Weeks before he announced his candidacy he had given an interview to *Esquire* comparing himself to a beautiful woman whose looks cause people to underestimate her intelligence:

> When you see a blonde with great tits and a great ass, you say to yourself, hey, she must be stupid or must have nothing else to offer. . . . But then again there is the one that is as smart as her breasts look, great as her face looks, beautiful as her whole body looks, gorgeous, you know, so people are shocked.

His crude and galloping arrogance sparked Molly Ivins to write, "Is it just me, or doesn't he look like a condom filled with walnuts?"

Oprah promoted her new season's premiere, on September 15, 2003, as "my exclusive with Arnold and Maria—the campaign, the rumors, their first interview together, *ever!*" She opened with Maria Shriver, who was familiar to Oprah's viewers from her past appearances, from the many references Oprah made to their friendship, and from the pages she devoted to Maria on her website. They began with girlfriend memories of working together in Baltimore, and Oprah showed pictures of herself at Maria's wedding at the Kennedy compound in Hyannisport. Then she asked about her husband's reputation as a womanizer.

"I know the man I'm married to," said Maria. "I've been with him for twenty-six years. I make up my mind on him based on him. Not based on what people say."

"Do you think Kennedy women are bred to look the other way when it comes to marital infidelity?"

"That ticks me off. I have not been quote 'bred' to look the other way. I accept him with all his strengths and all his weaknesses. I'm not perfect either."

Oprah brought up the stories depicting Arnold as a misogynist, and Maria said he was "the exact opposite" of a woman-hater. "He makes me coffee every morning, tells me I'm wonderful, and has been supportive of my career."

Arnold joined his wife in the next segment. Sitting down, he reached over and grabbed Maria's hand. "This woman here has been the most incredible friend, the most incredible wife and mother," he said. Oprah beamed happily, and her studio audience clapped. "They love celebrities," she said later, knowing her show was Celebrity Central for her viewers.

She asked Schwarzenegger about his infamous *Oui* interview, but he said he didn't remember it. "The idea [then] was to say things that were so over the top you could get headlines."

"But did you remember the parties, Arnold?"

"I really don't. These were the times I was saying things like 'a pump is better than coming.'"

Maria's hand shot to his face, clamping his mouth shut. "My mother is watching this show. My God!"

*The New York Times* later chided Oprah for doing such "a big favor" for Schwarzenegger by having him on her show. Citing the federal equal-time rule, the newspaper said, "Now she needs to do the voters a favor, and extend an invitation to the other top candidates in the California governor's race. . . . [E]ven if Ms. Winfrey has the right to invite only one candidate, it is a poor use of her franchise."

Oprah ignored the editorial advice because the Kennedy franchise was far more important to her. She also dismissed the *Nation* article titled "Governor Groper," which accused her of caring more about "celebrity . . . than sisterhood," saying that the people who really needed her platform were "women who think humiliating, insulting and harassing women is something worth talking about." Schwarzenegger won the recall election in 2003 and was reelected in 2006. Oprah contributed $5,000 to his campaign that year, the only political contribution she made.

Having flexed her muscle, she now became a political celebrity herself, and members of the Reform Party set up a website to entice her to run for president, while the documentary filmmaker Michael Moore started an online petition:

> We, the undersigned, call on you to declare yourself a candidate for the Presidency of the United States of America. We want to hear your ideas on how to straighten this country out and we think you can force the other candidates to stand by their hearts and consciences. At the very least, you can shake things up, but more likely, you can destroy the field and blow through the elections to become our first black President, our first woman President and our first President in recent memory who represents the interests of the American People.

Others took up the call, including the author Robert Fulghum (*All I Really Need to Know I Learned in Kindergarten*), who also endorsed Oprah for president on his website. This prompted David Letterman to read as one of his "Top Ten Things Overheard at the Republican Weekend": "We've all had it—Oprah just announced her candidacy!" Aaron McGruder's TV series *The Boondocks* ran an episode titled "Return of the

King," about Martin Luther King, Jr., that ended with a news-paper headline: "Oprah Elected President." The biggest effort to make Oprah commander in chief came in 2003, when Patrick Crowe, a former schoolteacher and owner of Wonderful Waldo Car Wash in Kansas City, Missouri, set up a website selling "Oprah for President" mugs, T-shirts, and bumper stickers. He reaped tons of publicity after publishing the book *Oprah for President: Run, Oprah, Run!* Immediately, the sixty-nine-year-old fan got slapped with a three-page cease-and-desist letter from Oprah's lawyers, citing nineteen copyright violations, plus the unauthorized use of her name, image, and likeness. They gave him five days to respond.

"They should not have sent that letter," Oprah told Larry King. "I didn't appreciate that my attorneys did that."

Mr. Crowe was not intimidated. When Oprah called him to suggest he put his time and energy into supporting Barack Obama, who was not a presidential candidate at the time, Crowe suggested that Oprah give the new Illinois senator a seat in her cabinet. He then explained to reporters why she would make a great president: "The business genius. The heart of gold. Her ability to get folks to work together . . . her fierce de-termination—she's just not a girl you'd wanna mess with."

Although Oprah never ran for public office and said she never would, she possessed immense charisma and represented credibility to millions. In addition, she took stands on issues that alternated between pleasing both Democrats and Republicans. She was for a woman's right to choose. She was against the death penalty, and she opposed guns, legalized drugs, and welfare. She supported the war in Iraq (and then she opposed it). On crime, she recommended hanging drunk drivers, but keeping them alive so they would be continuously tortured "in their privates." A little squishy on religion, she quoted the Bible but did not attend church. She preached self-improvement (makeovers and cleansing fasts) and self-empowerment (believe it and achieve it) sprinkled with the New Agey piffle of *The Secret.* On family val-ues she covered all the bases: she applauded motherhood but for herself she had chosen a career over children; she lived with a man outside of marriage but traveled constantly with her best female friend.

Contradictions aside, Oprah became a towering presence in America, a one-woman cathedral collecting alms for the poor, hearing confessions, and issuing edicts: "Don't chew gum in my presence." "Always bring a hostess gift." "Soak in your tub fifteen minutes a day." "Shop, shop, shop." Dispensing judgments from on high, she chastised Lionel Richie for being an absentee father, thumped Olympic track-and-field star Marion Jones for lying about taking performance-enhancing drugs, and upbraided Toni Braxton for going bankrupt after spending $1,000 for Gucci silverware.

Occasionally Oprah bestowed forgiveness ex cathedra. In a satellite interview with twenty-two-year-old Jessica Coleman, serving a six-year sentence in the Ohio Reformatory for Women for killing her newborn baby when she was fifteen, Oprah was as tough as a hanging judge throughout most of the show. She directed Coleman to tell the story of hiding her pregnancy; having the baby, which appeared to be stillborn; stabbing the infant; and then stuffing its body into a duffel bag, which her boyfriend ended up tossing into a quarry. When the baby was found, the community of Columbia Station, Ohio, named him Baby Boy Hope and gave him a proper funeral. For six years police searched for the infant's killer and found her only after Coleman was overheard in a bar sobbing out her sad story.

"Did you know that at the age of fourteen, I hid a pregnancy?" Oprah asked her. "I was raped at nine and sexually abused from the time I was ten to fourteen. At fourteen years old I became pregnant. . . . The stress of [having to confess my pregnancy to my father] caused me to go into labor, and the baby died [thirty-six days later]. . . . There are a lot of teenagers out there right now who are hiding their secret, just as I hid mine, because . . . like you, I didn't feel there was anybody I could tell. Your speaking out today is going to give a lot of girls the courage to do that. . . . You are not your past. You are what is possible for you. Own this truth and move forward in your life. Forgive yourself, and others will be able to forgive you."

Oprah's show had become the place where miscreants begged for mercy or, as in the case of NBC's anchorman Brian Williams and news president Steve Capus, defended controversial actions. After airing photos and parts of videos sent by the maniacal killer who shot thirty-two people on the Virginia Tech campus in 2007, NBC was severely criticized for broadcasting the shooter's final hate-filled words before he killed himself. Many felt the network had been exploitive in giving the mass murderer national attention without considering the feelings of the bereaved. So a week after the broadcast, Williams and Capus appeared on *The Oprah Winfrey Show*.

"We were . . . very careful as to how many pictures we were showing," Brian Williams told Oprah, "and I think . . . now, it has all but disappeared."

Oprah set him straight. "It disappeared, Brian, because the people said, because the public said, 'We don't want to see it.'"

Williams looked so chastened that one old-fashioned Catholic watching the show wondered half-humorously if Oprah was going to give him absolution: "For your penance say five Our Fathers and five Hail Marys. Now make a good Act of Contrition and go in peace."

Like the village vicar, she tended her flock, helping them atone for past sins. She mediated the public apology of heavyweight champion Mike Tyson when he said he wanted to make amends to Evander Holyfield for biting off a piece of his ear during their 1997 title bout. Twelve years later the two men came together on her show and shook hands, hoping their reconciliation might set an example to warring gangs of young men. Although many viewers criticized Oprah for having Tyson, a convicted rapist, on her show, others saluted her. The two Tyson shows, not incidentally, garnered huge ratings at a time when her ratings were slipping.

Oprah continued to be unbending in her condemnation of child abusers, knowing all too well the trauma to victims. Interviewing a man in prison for sexual molestation, she referred to him as "slime." Still, her contradictions could be confounding. While she gave her friend Arnold Schwarzenegger a pass on sexual harassment, she condemned rappers because their lyrics debased women. She was unforgiving of racism but pardoned the president of Hermès after his Paris store barred her entry because of alleged "problems with North Africans." Yet she was barely civil to Hazel Bryan Massery, who as a young white student had yelled at Elizabeth Eckford, one of the Little Rock Nine, who integrated Central High School in 1957 after President Eisenhower sent federal troops into Arkansas. In the intervening years, Massery had apologized to Eckford for her hateful rants, and the two became close. Oprah invited both women on her show but was highly skeptical of their friendship and would not accept that Hazel's remorse had led to reconciliation. "They are friends," Oprah told her audience in disbelief. "They . . . are . . . friends," she repeated with obvious distaste. She then showed a massive blowup of the photograph taken that historic day, showing Elizabeth, silent and dignified, carrying her books into school as a crowd of screaming white students taunted her, the most menacing being Hazel. Oprah was icy as she asked Eckford why that photo still upset her so many years later.

"She [Oprah] was as cold as she could be," Eckford told David Margolick of *Vanity Fair*. "She went out of her way to be hateful."

Margolick, who spent time with Eckford and Massery to write their story, added, "Characteristically, though, Elizabeth felt sorrier for Hazel. She was treated even more brusquely [by Oprah]."

Still, people flocked to the Church of Oprah. Online there were twenty-eight thousand websites devoted to getting on *The Oprah Winfrey Show*, and late-night television's David Letterman, who had been excommunicated for years, began an "Oprah Log," begging to be invited. Oprah ignored him, but he persisted. "It ain't Oprah til it's Oprah," he told his audiences night after night. Soon his fans began holding up signs in front of the Ed Sullivan Theater, in airports, and at football games: "Oprah, Please Call Dave."

After eighty-two nights, Phil Rosenthal advised Oprah in the

First Lady Barbara Bush on *The Oprah Winfrey Show,* October 23, 1989, discussing her life in politics. Oprah had asked Mrs. Bush to appear on her show after she attended her first White House state dinner in June 1989.

President Bill Clinton greets Oprah and Quincy Jones on June 13, 1994, at the White House state dinner for Emperor Akihito and Empress Michiko of Japan. Stedman, a confirmed Republican, would not attend, so Oprah invited her good friend.

Former South African president Nelson Mandela with Oprah in 2002 when she asked what she could do for him. "Build me a school," he said. Five years and $40 million later, she opened the Oprah Winfrey Leadership Academy for Girls in South Africa.

Michelle Obama, Caroline Kennedy, Maria Shriver, and Oprah campaigning for Barack Obama on February 3, 2008, at UCLA's Pauley Pavilion. After the rally, Oprah, who believed in the tenets of *The Secret,* returned home and created a vision board (see it, believe it, achieve it). She put Obama's picture in the middle of the board alongside a picture of the dress she wanted to wear to his inauguration.

The front page of the conservative *New York Post* interprets Oprah's political endorsement of Barack Obama for president, December 9, 2007.

The satirical cover of *The New Republic* following Oprah's trip to
Auschwitz with Elie Wiesel announcing his book *Night* as her
book club selection for May 24, 2006. She sells the DVD of that
trip to the concentration camp at the Oprah Store for $30.

Maya Angelou

Tom Cruise

Michael Jackson

Diane Sawyer

Julia Roberts

John F. Kennedy, Jr.

Toni Morrison

John Travolta

Five days after Oprah apologized on her show for defending James Frey's book *A Million Little Pieces* and then shredded him and his publisher, Pulitzer Prize winner Mike Luckovich drew this cartoon in *The Atlanta Journal-Constitution,* January 31, 2006, characterizing President George W. Bush's State of the Union address.

After Oprah called into *Larry King Live* on January 11, 2006, to defend Frey's book, saying the factual truth was not important given its emotional truth, she was criticized by *The New York Times.* Two weeks later she backtracked, apologized to her viewers, and called Frey a liar.

1985

1986

1987

1988

1989

1990

1991

1992

1993

1994

1995

1996

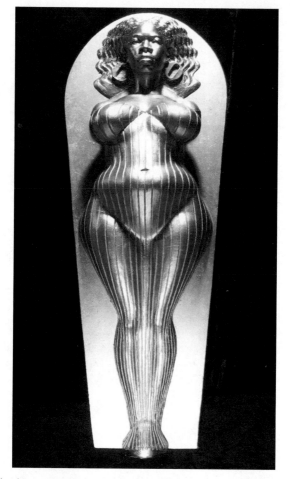

The ultimate icon of popular culture is Daniel Edwards's golden resin image of Oprah. "Of all the celebrity pieces I've done, this was the first time I had considered sending a complimentary cast to the subject," said the sculptor, "[but] many people interpreted [this] sculpture as unflattering [and] I just kind of figured Oprah might not find favor with my depiction."

*Chicago Sun-Times,* "This is a call you have to make.... Every night ... he is making you look like a humorless, self-important diva who spouts all kinds of New Age platitudes about forgiveness and positive thought but stubbornly clings to grudges. He's not the one who looks bad in this. It's a funny bit, and so long as you refuse to play, you're the butt of it.... You're simply digging in your heels, being stubborn, petty and stupid."

Oprah was still steamed about Letterman's jokes over the years:

Top Ten Disturbing Examples of Violence on TV:
No. 6:      Unknowing guest gets between Oprah and the buffet

Top Ten Least Popular Tourist Attractions:
No. 3:      The Grand Ole Oprah

Top Ten Death-Defying Stunts Robbie Knievel Won't Perform:
No. 8:      Screwing up Oprah Winfrey's lunch order

Top Ten Things You Don't Want to Hear from a Guy in a Sports Bar:
No. 1:      "Oops—time for Oprah."

Top Ten Things Columbus Would Say About America If He Were Alive Today:
No. 6:      "How did you come to choose the leader you call Oprah?"

Top Ten Dr. Phil Tips for Interviewing Oprah:
No. 4:      Grovel

Rapprochement came on December 1, 2005, when Oprah finally agreed to appear on Letterman's show and then allowed him to escort her to the Broadway premiere of *The Color Purple,* prompting *People* to surmise:

And now, ladies and gentlemen, the Top Ten Most Likely Reasons Why Oprah Winfrey Ended Her 16-Year Rift with

David Letterman and Agreed to Appear on His CBS Late
Show December 1, 2005:

No. 10:        She is producing a Broadway musical, *The
               Color Purple,* across the street.

Nos. 9–1:     See No. 10.

"At last our long national nightmare is over," said *The
Kansas City Star.*

Letterman behaved like a starstruck schoolboy. "It means a
great deal to me, and I'm just very happy you're here," he gushed
to Oprah. "You have meant something to the lives of people."

An estimated 13.5 million people stayed up to watch that
night, giving Letterman his biggest audience in more than a
decade. The next day *Washington Post* TV writer Lisa de
Moraes observed: "Letterman had become that which he once
mocked. An Opraholic."

It wasn't simply a late-night comic who wanted to bathe in
the reflected glory of Oprah Winfrey. To promote his 1,008-
page memoir, *My Life,* former president Bill Clinton appeared
on her show (June 22, 2004), sat with her for her Oxygen segment *Oprah After the Show,* and, hugging her and holding
hands, took her on an extended tour of his home in Chap-
paqua, New York, to accompany a long interview in *O* magazine. On the show, Oprah made a point of saying that "nothing
was off-limits," as she directed the former president to read all
the pages dealing with his sexual indiscretions.

"What were your feelings toward Hillary during those
many times you betrayed her?" she asked.

"I always loved her a lot," he said, "but not always well."

"Weren't you afraid of getting caught?"

Clinton dodged the question, saying he was in a "titanic
struggle" with a Republican Congress, but Oprah pressed.

"You didn't expect you'd be caught?"

"No, I did not," he finally admitted.

She had packed the audience with young, pretty women,
whom Jeff Simon described in *The Buffalo News* as looking at
Clinton at certain moments "the way they'd look at a chocolate

sundae; at others, the way they'd look at an infant's first steps to the couch."

Oprah's ties to Clinton were strong. She attended his inauguration in 1993 and his first state dinner in 1994. In December 1993 she stood by his side in the White House as he signed the National Child Protection Act to establish a database network for all indictments and convictions on child abuse and sexual molestation. This law was known informally as the "Oprah Bill."

Both Southerners from broken homes, Bill Clinton and Oprah Winfrey had a great deal in common. Each had risen from roots of meager expectations to achieve worldwide success based on a superlative ability to communicate. Both had well-publicized weight problems and were, in the words of Clinton, "secret keepers," who knew how to live parallel lives—one in public, the other in private. Appearing together, they were mesmerizing. He gave her the second-highest overnight rating of the season, and she gave him a boost in book sales. It was a mutually admiring and advantageous relationship until July 27, 2004, when a young man running for the U.S. Senate gave the speech of his life at the Democratic National Convention. That evening Barack Obama's soaring rhetoric and inspiring message rocked the convention and swept him into the hot strobes of national recognition. Among those leaping with joy was Oprah, deeply moved by his magical delivery. "It was one of the most extraordinary speeches I've ever heard," she told him later. "There's a line in *The Autobiography of Miss Jane Pittman* [a 1974 TV movie based on Ernest J. Gaines's novel] when Jane is holding a baby and asking, 'Will you be the one?' While you were speaking, I was alone in my sitting room cheering and saying, 'I think this is the one.'"

After that speech, Oprah, who barely knew the Obamas, asked to interview them for the November issue of *O*, which strategically hit the stands days before the election that sent him to Washington as only the third African American to sit in the U.S. Senate since Reconstruction. By then Oprah had embraced the young senator as "my favorite guy." She introduced him to her viewers in January 2005 as part of a show titled "Living the

American Dream." She honored his wife, Michelle, a few months later by including her as a "young 'un" during "The Legends Weekend," and the following year she publicly endorsed him for president, months before he had endorsed himself.

During his Senate campaign, Obama had opposed the Iraq War as unnecessary, and by then Oprah, too, had changed her stance. Subsequently, she invited the esteemed *New York Times* columnist Frank Rich on her show (October 12, 2006) to discuss his book *The Greatest Story Ever Sold: The Decline and Fall of Truth from 9/11 to Katrina,* which indicted the Bush administration for selling the war to the country on false premises. Entitled "Truth in America," the show included an appearance by Roy Peter Clark, senior scholar of the Poynter Institute, to discuss looking at the world from different points of view. He later reported in his online column that Oprah was dynamic, intelligent, funny, charismatic, and beloved by the women in her audience. "She walked out onto the stage, before the cameras started rolling, holding her shoes in her hand, a very down-to-earth image, but when she sat down, her shoe person rushed onstage, knelt down, and put them on for her. A coronation of sorts, if you can crown someone's feet."

At Fox News, Bill O'Reilly was going postal over Oprah devoting her entire show to Frank Rich. "She has declined to interview me, even though I had four number one bestselling books," O'Reilly fumed. He went on the air four nights later with a segment "Is Oprah Fair and Balanced?" during which he claimed that Oprah was "leaning left," with her liberal guests far outnumbering her conservative guests. He said Oprah was being dishonest with her viewers about her politics. "Wouldn't it be better if she looked everyone in the eye . . . ?" A few days later Oprah invited Obama on her show (October 18, 2006) to talk about his book *The Audacity of Hope.*

"I know I don't just speak for myself," she said. "There are a lot of people who want to feel the audacity of hope, who want to feel that America can be a better place for everybody. There are a lot of people who would want you to run for the presidency of the United States. Would you consider that?"

Obama danced around the question to talk about the importance of the midterm elections. Then Oprah returned to the subject.

"So, if you ever would decide to run within the next five years—I'm going to have this show for five more years—would you announce on this show?"

"I don't think I could say no to you."

"Okay. Okay. So if you ever, ever decided that you would."

"Oprah, you're my girl."

"Okay. That's all I ask."

"Fair enough."

Bill O'Reilly was nearly apoplectic. He, too, had a book (*Culture Warrior*) to promote, and Oprah had "declined" to have him on her show. "He was so mad that he picked up the phone, called Oprah himself, told her she had no right to be so one-sided by having 'a Bush hater like Frank Rich' on to trash the president of the United States," recalled a Doubleday publicist. "O'Reilly demanded that she be fair and let him come on her show with his book. . . . He absolutely browbeat her and Oprah was so cowed that she agreed to have him on."

The show (October 27, 2006), titled "Oprah's Town Hall with Bill O'Reilly," with a mostly male audience, allowed O'Reilly to rail against the "secular progressive movement," or "SPs," as he called them, which he said consisted of Frank Rich, the American Civil Liberties Union, George Clooney, Hollywood, Holland, mall zombies, the Democratic Party, the FBI, the Clintons, and *The New York Times*. Traditionalists, on the other hand, included "good folks" like him, President Bush, blue-collar towns, the working class, the little man, people who call Christmas Christmas, and Oprah. At the end of the hour, O'Reilly said, "This is the best show I've been on."

In researching this book, I emailed Bill O'Reilly October 10, 2009, to confirm that he had called Oprah to have him on her show. He did not respond to the email, but upon publication of the book he had me on his show, April 14, 2010. He denied making the call to Oprah but acknowledged that pressure was brought to bear. Two sources within his publishing house

**recollect the call being made by O'Reilly, who said: "She was fair to me once I got her attention."**

Having proven to Bill O'Reilly she was fair and balanced, Oprah now made a decision that would put her at odds with Fox News as well as the Clinton wing of the Democratic Party. Feeling she had found "the One," she decided to publicly embrace Barack Obama to the exclusion of all other presidential candidates. She had not been happy with those who suggested her show in 2000 had given George W. Bush a winning edge, so this time around she decided to give her powerful platform to only her "favorite guy."

"If everybody knows I'm for Barack, it would be really disingenuous of me to be sitting up there interviewing other people as though . . . pretending to be objective," she said. "So I won't be doing anybody, because of that, on my show."

As a talent scout without peer, Oprah recognized telegenic magic when she saw it. After all, she had introduced Dr. Phil, Rachael Ray, and Dr. Oz to America, and their talk shows, all of which she launched, had succeeded beyond industry expectations. The same instincts now drove her to put all her political cards on the table. It was a daring gamble, because Hillary Clinton was expected to be the Democratic nominee, and in going against the first woman with impressive credentials and immense backing who actually had a chance of winning, Oprah stood to alienate many of her female viewers. In supporting Obama, she was criticized for backing her race over her gender, while most of her African American friends supported Hillary Clinton.

Maya Angelou, Henry Louis Gates, Jr., Quincy Jones, and Andrew Young felt they owed their allegiance to Senator Clinton because, in the words of Gates, it was Bill Clinton "who brought us to the table." Standing with Oprah, though, were Gayle King and Stedman Graham, a conservative Republican; plus her father, Vernon Winfrey, who pointed to the Obama poster on his barbershop wall. "I'm supporting him on the issues. . . . Oprah might be supporting him for something else." He chuckled about his daughter's obvious crush on the Illinois senator, an inference that sprang from her flirtatious body language whenever she was around him—what her father called "her adoring eyes and all . . . I can tell you that Stedman isn't getting any of that."

Oprah's best friend from high school agreed. "Obama is everything she ever wanted," said Luvenia Harrison Butler. "Light-skinned and Ivy-Leagued."

Late-night comics chimed in as well. "Over the weekend, Obama celebrated his wedding anniversary," noted Conan O'Brien. "He went out for a romantic candlelit dinner with just his wife and Oprah."

Obama's influence on Oprah was not lost on anyone in Chicago, either. "When Paula Crown needed a star to appear at the Children's Circle of Care benefit, she went to Barack, and he persuaded Oprah to speak," said one of the city's philanthropists. "Otherwise, we would never have gotten her, and she made the evening a smashing success."

By endorsing Barack Obama for president, Oprah staked out a position that would subject her to criticism and partisan rebuke. "It was awful for her at one point," recalled Alice Walker. "I remember when she and Gayle came to a wedding at the Bel-Air hotel. . . . It was shortly after Oprah had refused to have Sarah Palin on her show, and the Republican women in Florida decided to boycott Oprah. . . . She had tears in her eyes when she told us how they called her the *N* word."

Oprah later mentioned the backlash. "I got some hate calls [that were] 'Go back to Africa,' 'We gonna lynch you bad,'" she said. "I wasn't snubbing Sarah Palin. I was just holding true to the policy that I had set for myself [not to invite other candidates on the show]." Two days after the election she invited Tina Fey, the comedienne who had filleted Sarah Palin with her dead-on imitation of the Alaska governor on *Saturday Night Live*. "I was in Denver—I had just attended the big speech Barack Obama gave—and the next day was when Senator John McCain announced Sarah Palin," Oprah recalled. "I said, 'Oh, my god. She's Tina Fey.'"

To appease Republicans after the election, Oprah said she would be happy to ask Sarah Palin to be on the show. "I went and tried to talk to Sarah Palin, and instead she talked to Greta Van Susteren. She talked to Matt Lauer. She talked to Larry King, but she didn't talk to me," said Oprah. "But maybe she'll talk to me [when] she has a book deal." Sure enough, Palin launched publication of her memoir with Oprah on November 16, 2009, leading to Oprah's highest ratings in two years.

"Oprah was all about wooing back conservative viewers she'd lost when she endorsed Barack Obama for president," wrote Lisa de Moraes in *The Washington Post,* so she veered away from controversial subjects. The next day she interviewed porn superstar Jenna Jameson, who wrote *How to Make Love Like a Porn Star,* but then the media was more interested in politics than pornography. Two days after the Sarah Palin show, Tina Brown pounded Oprah in *The Daily Beast:* "She opened up with whether Palin thought she had snubbed her during the '08 campaign by not asking her on the show. You could see Palin thinking as we in the audience were, 'Huh? Why the eff are we wasting time talking about you?'"

**Behind the scenes Oprah made no pretense about her partisan preferences. She strongly supported Cory Booker, the Democratic mayor of Newark, New Jersey, who, like Oprah, was an early and ardent supporter of Barack Obama. The forty-year-old mayor was dating Gayle King, who introduced him to Oprah, and she contributed more than $1.5 million to various nonprofits that Booker had championed in his district, including $500,000 to the foundation of a Booker foe who threatened to split the Democratic Party. Thus appeased by Oprah's contribution, the foe became a friend and Booker was easily reelected. Four months later, *O, The Oprah Magazine,* for which Gayle is the editor-at-large, ran an eight-page story titled "Cory Booker . . . Greatest Mayor in America." When the Obamas invited Cory Booker to attend the White House state dinner for the president of Mexico, the mayor of Newark brought Gayle King as his guest.**

Before the 2008 presidential election, Oprah was so determined to preserve her platform for Obama that when Bill Clinton returned to her show on September 4, 2007, to promote his second book, *Giving,* she made a point of telling viewers that he had called her himself, asking to appear. Months later the former president shrugged off Oprah's lack of support for his wife. "Oprah is from Chicago," Clinton said. "She was never going to be for anybody but Obama."

The timing of Clinton's second appearance on Oprah's show was politically sensitive, because everyone knew that four days later she was hosting a huge fund-raiser for Obama at "The Promised Land," her forty-two-acre estate in Montecito. The event, planned to accommodate at least sixteen hundred people paying $2,300 apiece, was trumpeted as one of the largest political fund-raisers in history. One late-night comic joked, "Oprah's fund-raiser is projected to raise three million dollars; two million of which is to come from the 'Dunk Stedman' booth."

Oprah's fund-raiser had been announced in July, and people across the country scrambled to buy tickets as much to support Obama as to see Oprah's $50 million mansion, with its man-made lake and rolling meadows. The event received wide coverage around the world and, according to Oprah, it "was no small thing for me [to open the gates of my estate].... I really do feel that this place is God's gift to me. It is a very, very special place.... There are going to be some serious restrictions and requirements to get in there."

She insisted that no one be allowed inside the twenty-three-thousand-square-foot mansion, so the event was staged outside on a sunny Saturday afternoon with Stevie Wonder (an Obama favorite) performing. More than sixteen hundred people attended, sitting on apple green blankets that Oprah had commissioned with "Obama 08" woven in the corner. Tents filled with tables of food and drink (mini hamburgers and "electric" lemonade spiked with vodka) dotted the landscaped lawns, where squadrons of waiters scampered about with silver trays. No press was allowed, and all guests were wanded by security guards after being relieved of cameras and recording devices. With the exception of a few VIPs, no one was allowed to drive into the premises, so everyone had to assemble ten miles away and be transported by shuttle buses. Celebrities in the majority

African American crowd included Whoopi Goldberg, Sidney Poitier, Ernie Banks, Bill Russell, Jimmy Connors, Linda Evans, Lou Gossett, Jr., Cicely Tyson, Forest Whitaker, Tyler Perry, Chris Rock, Cindy Crawford, George Lucas, and Kenneth "Babyface" Edmonds.

After the picnic, Oprah hosted a dinner party for two hundred in a huge tent with crystal chandeliers. "It was a magical night that I will never forget," said Valerie Jarrett, a close Chicago friend of the Obamas and now senior advisor to the president.

"Marred only by one diva moment," recalled another Chicago guest. "When Cindy Moelis and her husband, Bob Rivkin, arrived with the Obamas—Cindy is one of Michelle Obama's best friends—Oprah was very ungracious. She invited the Obamas inside, but directed Cindy and Bob to wait outside, where they sat on one of the unreserved green blankets. The meadow soon filled up. . . . Oprah and Stedman came out and sat on a reserved blanket in front of Cindy and Bob, an arm's length away. One of Oprah's bodyguards came over and told Cindy they had to move. Cindy asked why, pointing out there was no room, and Stevie Wonder was about to perform. Another guard came over and told Bob they had to move or leave. Bob said they had come with the Obamas and they were not moving or leaving. This all happened within earshot of everyone on adjacent blankets, who were watching, except for Oprah and Stedman, who sat with their backs to Cindy and Bob as if they didn't know what was going on. One would think a hostess would have her security guards stand down to avoid escalating an unpleasant situation. But no. The guards then took out notebooks and wrote down their names, repeatedly asking for the spelling of *Moelis* as if to loudly embarrass them into leaving. They stayed for the performance. . . . The event was fantastic, except for Oprah making two people feel very unwelcome."

Such moments become indelible because some people expected Oprah to be at all times what she appeared to be on the air—a woman of enveloping warmth, charm, and affability.

"She was fabulous when she took the microphone and introduced Barack," said another guest. "She was passionate, gracious, and intoxicating in her remarks."

She began by saying that her home in Montecito was sacred to her, explaining that she called it "The Promised Land" because she was living Martin Luther King's dream. For that reason she said she would not open it for just any event. "This is where Stedman and I lead our private life," she said. "I haven't participated in politics because no one inspired me until now.... After all of my years in business I don't trust many people, but I have learned to trust my own instincts.... I believe we have a man here who can make a difference and bring dignity back to the people of the United States.... I believe in destiny. If someone has a calling, there is nothing that can stop that destiny." For that reason she said she had committed herself totally to Obama and was willing to take whatever the media hurled at her for doing so. She also mentioned the $2,300 price tag for the event and said that no one, "not even my best friend, Gayle," got in without paying.

Oprah understood her worth to Obama. When she talked about her endorsement on *Larry King Live*, she said, "I think my value to him, my support of him, is probably worth more than any check that I could write." Federal Election Commission records show that she wrote only one—for $2,300. Yet she raised more than $3 million for him in California, and in Chicago some of her employees provided additional funds:

| | |
|---|---:|
| Jill Adams, Harpo producer | $ 250 |
| Judith Banks-Johnson, Harpo producer | 500 |
| William L. Becker, Harpo, Inc., general counsel | 300 |
| Timothy Bennett, Harpo, Inc., president | 2,300 |
| Tracey Carter, Harpo associate producer | 250 |
| Amy Coleman, Harpo supervising producer | 2,000 |
| Lisa Erspamer, Harpo co-executive producer | 2,300 |
| John Gehron, Harpo Radio general manager | 250 |
| Aaron Heeter, Harpo Studios freelance production | 250 |
| Dianne A. Hudson, Harpo Studios special advisor | 2,300 |
| John Keith, Harpo Radio producer | 250 |
| Lindsey Kotler, Harpo executive assistant | 250 |

| | |
|---|---|
| Joseph Lecz, Harpo production manager | 250 |
| Elizabeth E. Moore, Harpo chief of staff | 2,300 |
| Irma Norris, Harpo production manager | 3,300 |
| Ellen S. Rakieten, Harpo executive vice president | 2,300 |
| Davida Rice, Harpo attorney | 4,500 |
| Hilary Robe, Harpo senior associate producer | 500 |
| Sheri Salata, Harpo co-executive producer | 2,300 |
| Harriet Seitler, Harpo executive vice president | 4,600 |
| James Slanger, Harpo Studios audio engineer | 500 |
| Erin Dailey Smith, Harpo researcher | 250 |
| Stacy Strazis, Harpo producer | 500 |
| Oprah Winfrey, self-employed, Harpo | 2,300 |
| Andrea Wishom Young, Harpo producer | 2,000 |
| **TOTAL:** | **$36,800** |

After endorsing Obama, Oprah experienced repercussions from viewers, who lashed out on her message boards:

"Oprah is a traitor!!!!"

"In bad taste."

"I will never watch your show again."

In 2008 the Harris poll announced that Ellen DeGeneres had beaten Oprah as America's Favorite TV Personality, a position Oprah had held for the previous five years.

Twelve weeks after her California fund-raiser, Oprah hit the road for Obama, flying with Gayle to Iowa to speak in Des Moines (attendance 18,500) and Cedar Rapids (attendance 10,000) before being whisked off to Columbia, South Carolina (attendance 30,000), and Manchester, New Hampshire (attendance 8,500). In each city, the media stands were crammed with television cameras from around the world waiting to record her first campaign utterances.

Initially she seemed awkward, saying she felt she had stepped out of her pew, as she again referenced *The Autobiography of Miss Jane Pittman* and how the enslaved woman was searching for "the one" who would lead her people to freedom. "Well, I do believe in '08 I have found the answer to Miss

Pittman's question. I have fooo-uu-nd the answer! It is the same question that our nation is asking, 'Are you the one? Are you the one?' I'm here to tell y'all, he is the one. He is the one. . . . Barack Obama!"

By the fall, Hillary and Obama had sprinted ahead of the six other Democratic candidates, with Hillary enjoying the overwhelming support of women, while Obama captured the enthusiasm of the highly educated and the antiwar activists. He won the Iowa caucuses; she won the New Hampshire primary. On Super Tuesday she won 836 delegates; he won 845. Their neck-and-neck race continued until June 7, 2008, when Hillary officially ended her campaign and eloquently endorsed him.

During the early months of the campaign, Oprah had been alone in carrying the high-wattage celebrity torch for Obama, but on January 27, 2008, Caroline Kennedy stepped forward to announce her endorsement. In a *New York Times* op-ed titled "A President Like My Father," the daughter of John F. Kennedy wrote, "I have never had a president who inspired me the way people tell me that my father inspired them. But for the first time, I believe I have found the man who could be that president—not just for me, but for a new generation of Americans." With Caroline Kennedy came her cousin Maria Shriver, and their uncle Senator Ted Kennedy, whose endorsement galvanized the campaign and shook the timbers of support for Hillary Clinton, especially among African Americans, who began to see that Barack Obama might actually have a fighting chance.

By the time Oprah appeared at UCLA's Pauley Pavilion flanked by Caroline Kennedy, Maria Shriver, and Michelle Obama, she felt emboldened enough to address her critics:

"After Iowa, there were some women who had the nerve to say to me, 'How could you, Oprah, how could you?' " she said, imitating a nasal twang. " 'You're a traitor to your gender.' The truth is, I'm a free woman. I am a free woman." She repeated this three times. "Being free means you get to think for yourself and you get to decide for yourself what to do. So I say I am not a traitor. I am just following my own truth, and that truth has led me to

Barack Obama." She mocked women who declared, "I'm a woman; I have to vote for a woman." She fired up the crowd. "As free women, you have the right to change your mind. You're not a traitor because you believe and see a better way."

At the end of that rally Michelle Obama told the rapt crowd, "I want you to leave here and envision Barack Obama taking the oath of office."

So Oprah, who believed in the tenets of *The Secret*, a book she had pressed on Obama, returned home and created a vision board (see it, believe it, achieve it). She put Obama's picture in the middle of the board, alongside a picture of the dress she wanted to wear to his inauguration. Then she began visualizing the success she wanted. By the time Obama secured the Democratic nomination in August, she was fully convinced that he was destiny's child and would be elected president.

"I'm very happy that I made the decision early last year to come out for him. . . . I decided early on that even if I lost every sponsor on the show—there's a wonderful Bible passage [Matthew 16:26] that says, 'What does it do for a man to gain the world and lose his soul?' If I had not come out for Barack Obama when I did, I know I would have lost a piece of my soul."

On election night, Oprah, in a bright green dress with a suggestion of cleavage, joined the joyous throng of 125,000 people in Grant Park to cheer Chicago's favorite son as the first man of color to be elected president of the United States. With tears streaming down her face she rejoiced, standing on the right side of history and knowing that she just may have had a role in shaping it.

"My job was to make people, or allow people, to be introduced to Obama who might not have been at the time," she said. "I wanted him elected, and I think I did that."

# Afterword

I REMEMBER Oprah standing in the control room watching Phil Donahue toward the end of his run and shaking her head," recalled a former Harpo employee. "She said, 'If I ever stay that long, kick my ass out of here.' Of course, that'll never happen because she'll never give up her show. She can't . . . she needs to be on television. It's her oxygen."

Most people assumed that it would take a wrecking crew with tasers and stun guns to get Oprah to retire, but on November 20, 2009, she announced she was stopping her show after twenty-five years—when her contract expired in September 2011.

"This show has been my life," she told her viewers with trembling lips, "and I love it enough to know when it's time to say goodbye."

Those words sent an "Oh, my God" shudder across the country and triggered Code Orange distress throughout the television industry. Oprah's departure from four o'clock in the afternoon would crater a hole in daytime broadcasting and deprive local stations, especially those owned and operated by ABC, of a gigantic ratings lead-in to their evening news hours. The financial ramifications were potentially enormous.

From the next day's headlines it seemed as if Chicken Little was right: the sky had fallen. Oprah's announcement made the front pages of most newspapers, the cover of *People,* and the evening news broadcasts, and prompted a tidal wave of commentary, most of which praised her for hanging up her gloves before she risked getting knocked out by dwindling network audiences and flaccid ratings.

Alessandra Stanley applauded her in *The New York Times* for practicing "The Fine Art of Quitting While She's Ahead," and Gail Collins wrote a column about "Putting the Fond in Farewell." The *Los Angeles Times* mourned "Afternoons Without Oprah," and *The Wall Street Journal* wondered what her departure would mean for the economic future of Chicago.

Oprah said she planned to concentrate on OWN (Oprah Winfrey Network) in partnership with Discovery Communications. The debut of OWN, announced in 2008, was originally scheduled for 2009. Now it will be sometime in 2011. Once launched, Oprah's network will replace the Discovery Health Channel, which is available in 74 million homes. *The Oprah Winfrey Show,* in 2008–2009, before the nation switched to a digital system, reached approximately 110 million homes. In its current incarnation, the show is watched by around 7 million people each day. There is little doubt that switching to OWN will dramatically lower her viewership.

OWN is based in Los Angeles, and soon after her announcement, Oprah was quoted as saying she wanted to divest her real estate in Chicago "as soon as possible," adding, "Why would anyone stay in Chicago? It's freezing here, and I have a mansion in Montecito that I haven't been able to enjoy."

While the national media mourned the departure of daytime's Goliath, the Davids of Chicago grabbed their slingshots. "[H]er announcement spurs a question: Does it matter?" asked the *Tribune's* Rick Kogan. "Over the years she has become, with some justification, increasingly isolated, distrustful of all but a close circle of friends and associates, and remote . . ." With tongue in cheek, the *Trib's* media critic, Phil Rosenthal, told readers: "Deal with it however you see fit. Maybe ask yourself: What would Oprah do? Then call your best friend Gayle to commiserate."

Chicago's mayor, Richard Daley, was furious at the tone taken by the city's media and blamed them for driving Oprah out of town. At her request, he had closed part of Michigan Avenue for her season's opening show in September 2009, which lured twenty thousand fans, snarling traffic in the middle of the city's busiest street. The havoc did not go unnoticed by reporters, some of whom saw it as just one more example of Oprah's hubris.

"That became a big rhubarb in the Chicago press—beat up Oprah," said Mayor Daley. "So you keep kicking people, people will leave, simple as that."

She returned the mayor's favor and support by flying to

Copenhagen to join him and the president and First Lady to lobby the International Olympic Committee to bring the 2016 games to Chicago, which had spent $60 million on its presentation. When the IOC knocked Chicago out of the competition almost immediately and gave the nod to Rio de Janeiro instead, Oprah, Mayor Daley, and the Obamas were made to look like losers in the Chicago press.

**Months later Stedman Graham told Fox News in Chicago that the city took Oprah for granted. "I really don't think they appreciate her," he said. "I don't think they understand the value of who she is, as a human being, what she's done, because a prophet has no honor in his hometown and, uh, you know, first of all, she's brought a lot of national attention to Chicago. . . . From an insider's point of view, I don't think she gets the just due based on who she is and what she's done for the Chicago area . . . it's natural for people to take her for granted, until you leave and you don't have a show anymore."**

Critics and columnists from Chicago's newspapers pilloried Graham, with one writing: "Wow. That is one big heaping, steaming pile of . . . questionable opinion."

The media maelstrom over Oprah's retirement continued for days. "Why is she quitting?" "What will she do next?" "Who will replace her?" Then dire predictions about her health flooded the Internet, along with photos suggesting her weight would lead to debilitating diabetes and an inevitable heart attack. The *National Enquirer* ran a cover of her looking haggard and bloated with a headline that blared: "Oprah's Booze & Drug Binges! Fed Up Stedman Walks Out—for Good! She'll Pay $150 Million to Buy His Silence." This prompted the always cheeky David Letterman to announce: "Top Ten Signs Oprah Doesn't Care Anymore." The number one sign: "Her last three guests were Johnnie Walker, Jim Beam, and José Cuervo."

It began to look as if her withdrawal from network television and her perceived loss of influence was turning her into a target, after years of reverential treatment. However, as she was being depicted as a dipsomaniac and dismissed by polls that (supposedly) showed her dwindling popularity, Oprah showed she

should never be underestimated, pulling off a coup that bur-
nished her luster on the world stage. She took her cameras to the
White House for an intimate conversation with the Obamas as
they prepared to spend their first Christmas as president and
First Lady. Her hourlong prime-time special gave ABC the
evening's most watched entertainment program (11.8 million)
and showed that at the age of fifty-five, Oprah Winfrey is not
about to relinquish her crown as the queen of talk show television. **In the spring of 2010, Oprah made the *Time* 100 list of
people who have changed the world for better or for worse. As
the only person to appear on the list eight times in eight years,
she was duly saluted by Phil Donahue, who wrote: "There is no
match for you in media history. You are not only hot, you are
cool: the Dream Girl for millions of ambitious young women
whom you've inspired all over the world."**

Determined to reinvent herself with her own network ("All
Oprah all the time," said one critic), she was going to present on
cable what she presented so effectively in her magazine: her
philosophy of life with its perplexing mix of crass materialism
and uplifting spirituality.

Some critics tut-tutted that her fans will not follow her to
cable. Others speculated that OWN will never get off the
ground, citing its start-up problems with scheduling, the fact
that three CEOs have already been hired and fired, and the
head of programming deposed, all of which has delayed the
launch date several times. But Oprah had already embarked
upon her next career, and *The New Yorker*'s media critic predicted unbounded success. "Oprah is going to a growing enter-
prise," said Ken Auletta. "She's leaving a listing ship and
getting on a rocket ship."

She was also taking her halo to Hollywood, where she
would reign supreme among the celebrities she adored. The town
had first fired her fantasies as a young girl when she toured the
Walk of Fame in front of Grauman's Chinese Theatre. After that
trip she returned to her father's house in Nashville and told him
she was going to be a star.

"Daddy, I got down on my knees there and ran my hand

along all those stars on the street, and I said to myself, 'One day I'm going to put my own star among those stars,'" recalled Vernon Winfrey. He knew then there was no stopping his daughter.

After the Hollywood Walk of Fame had been expanded to include stars of the small screen, as filmdom once dismissed television, Oprah got her star. On June 17, 2010, her name was included with other TV personalities: Neil Patrick Harris, Tina Fey, Danny DeVito, Ed O'Neill, and John Langley, plus movie stars Penelope Cruz, Bruce Dern, Laura Dern, Diane Ladd, Ed Harris, Gwyneth Paltrow, Sissy Spacek, Donald Sutherland, and Reese Witherspoon.

Now, as Oprah retires from broadcast television, the pilot light that fired her ambitions since childhood still flames, and her work and the applause that come from it continue to fill her soul, giving her her greatest pleasure in life. Consequently, she will never retire. Without children and grandchildren, it seems as if she will fill her later years with the rewards of work. Yes, she has slowed down a bit and often seems fatigued, occasionally appearing listless on her show, the one hour a day when she had sparkled in the past. During the last year her producers began booking more segments to move it along at a faster pace so everyone, including the host, would stay engaged.

As Oprah embarked on her final year in broadcast television her friends showered her with honors. Anna Wintour, editor-in-chief of *Vogue*, asked her to cochair the Metropolitan Museum of Arts Costume Institute Gala Benefit in New York City, the fashion event of the year at which the top table costs $250,000. The evening in May 2010 celebrated American fashion, which is why Wintour said she chose Oprah to be her cochair: "[S]he is the American woman." Escorted by Oscar de la Renta, Oprah wore a gown he designed for her, which took four people working 150 hours to make.

A few months later, Henry Louis "Skip" Gates chaired the jury that selected Oprah to receive Cleveland's Anisfield-Wolf Lifetime Achievement Award, usually given to literary figures like Langston Hughes, Toni Morrison, and Martin Luther King Jr. Then Maria Shriver announced she would present

Oprah with the Minerva Medal, which she created as First Lady of California to honor women "who serve on the front lines of humanity."

As Oprah gets older, she no longer expends the energy necessary to stay in shape, and she remains seventy-five pounds overweight, sagging into her mother's genes after years of swearing to fight heredity. **In January 2005, Oprah posed for the cover of her magazine looking toned, glowing, and glamorous. Five years later, she had gained forty pounds. This time she posed for the cover looking like a blown-up version of her formerly trim self. "How did I let this happen again?" she asked. "I'm mad at myself. I'm embarrassed. I can't believe that after all these years, all the things I know how to do, I'm still talking about my weight." She blamed a faulty thyroid.**

The responsibility of her $40 million school in South Africa has also weighed on her, especially as the sex scandals involving a dorm matron and several students dragged through the courts. The publicity surrounding the sordid case was demoralizing, and prompted some to question how anyone, even with Oprah's vast resources, could take care of three hundred children eighty-seven hundred miles away. Still, she remains committed to her "girls" and flies to South Africa at least once a year. But even in her own private jet the seventeen-hour trip takes its toll.

Despite a setback in her show's ratings, a dip in her magazine's circulation, and a couple of chinks in the armor of her public image, Oprah remains the most influential woman of her generation. She has always lived on the ascent, and even as she ages, she continues aiming upward.

She has dominated her era by reaching uncommon and unexpected heights, and in doing so, she has become an icon, especially to women. For she has broken through all the barriers that once held them back, and her life story inspires others because she has never stopped pushing ahead. She has remained driven, and in all likelihood will continue to remain so to the end of her days because she has always embraced the poetry of Robert Browning, who wrote that "a man's reach should exceed his grasp, or what's a heaven for?"

# Some Oprah Credits, 1984–2009

## OPRAH AS ACTOR/PERFORMER/INTERVIEWER/ NARRATOR/HOST, TV AND MOVIES, 1984–2009

*A.M. Chicago* (1984–1985, Chicago WLS-TV, local daytime talk show, premiered 1/2/84), host

*Survival: Everything to Live For* (according to *McCall's* in August 1987, Oprah had in her office an Emmy for this special on teenage suicide)

*When the School Bell Rings* (1984, Chicago WLS-TV, children's program), host

*The Oprah Winfrey Show* (1985–1986, Chicago WLS-TV, local daytime talk show, successor to *A.M. Chicago*, premiered 9/30/85), host

*The Color Purple* (1985, theatrical release; available on DVD), Sofia

*Saturday Night Live* (1986, NBC, comedy, episode originally aired 4/12/86), guest host

*Native Son* (1986, theatrical release), Mrs. Thomas

*Throw Momma from the Train* (1987, theatrical release, comedy, available on DVD), herself

*Chicago Grapevine* (1987, ABC, pilot for sitcom taped in April 1987, rejected in June 1987, never seen publicly), starring role as talk show host

*Star-Spangled Celebration* (1987, ABC, prime-time special, originally aired 7/4/87), cohost with Robert Urich

*Dolly* (1987, ABC, first episode of Dolly Parton's second variety TV show, originally aired 9/27/87), singing

*Pee-Wee's Playhouse Christmas Special* (1988, CBS, prime-time special, originally aired 12/21/88; available on DVD), herself

*America's All-Star Tribute to Oprah Winfrey* (1990, ABC, prime-time special, originally aired 9/18/90), recipient of America's Hope Award from Bob Hope

*Gabriel's Fire* (1990, ABC, "'Tis the Season" episode of James Earl Jones's dramatic series, originally aired 12/20/90), talk show host

*Scared Silent* (1992, NBC, CBS, PBS, documentary, originally aired 9/4/92; aired on ABC 9/6/92), host

*The Fresh Prince of Bel-Air* (1992, NBC, "A Night at the Oprah"
     episode of Quincy Jones–produced comedy series, originally aired
     11/9/92), herself

*Lincoln* (1992, ABC, documentary, originally aired 12/26 and
     12/27/92), voice of Elizabeth Keckley

*Learning Not to Hurt* (1993, ABC, Afterschool Special, discussion,
     originally aired 5/27/93), introduction

*All-American Girl* (1995, ABC, "A Night at the Oprah" episode of
     Margaret Cho comedy series, originally aired 2/14/95), herself

*America's Top Story* (1995, Hearst Broadcasting, town
     meeting/discussion, originally aired 10/1/95), host

*The 68th Annual Academy Awards* (ABC, producer Quincy Jones, aired
     3/25/96), official greeter on the red carpet

*About Us: The Dignity of Children* (1997, ABC, prime-time documen-
     tary, co–executive producer Jeff Jacobs, Children's Dignity Project),
     host

*Ellen* (1997, ABC, parts 1 and 2 of "The Puppy Episode" of comedy
     series, originally aired 4/30/97; available on DVD, *Ellen Season 4*),
     Ellen's therapist

*Our Friend Martin* (1999, Starz!, animated educational film; available
     on DVD), voice of Coretta Scott King

*Home Improvement* (1999, ABC, "Home Alone" episode of comedy
     series, originally aired 1/19/99), herself

*The Hughleys* (1999, ABC, "Milsap Moves Up" episode of comedy
     series, originally aired 10/1/99), herself

*Bette* (2000, CBS, "Two Days at a Time" episode of Bette Midler
     comedy series, originally aired 11/8/2000), herself

*Chicago Matters* (2001, Chicago WTTW-11, "Teaching Readers"
     episode of public television documentary series, originally aired
     4/19/01), narrator

*Unchained Memories: Readings from the Slave Narratives* (2003,
     HBO, documentary, originally aired 2/10/03; available on DVD),
     reader

*Brothers of the Borderland* (2004, continuing film exhibit at National
     Underground Railroad Freedom Center, Cincinnati), narrator

*Emmanuel's Gift* (2004, documentary, limited theatrical release;
     available on DVD), narrator

*Kennedy Center Honors* (2005, CBS, prime-time special, originally aired
     12/26/05), giving tribute to Tina Turner

*Charlotte's Web* (2006, animated theatrical release; available on DVD),
     voice of Gussy Goose

*African American Lives* (2007, special episode "Oprah's Roots" in PBS
    documentary series, originally aired 1/24/07), interviewed by Henry
    Louis Gates, Jr.

*Ocean's 13* (2007, theatrical release; available on DVD), herself

*Bee Movie* (2007, animated theatrical release; available on DVD), voice
    of Judge Bumbleden

*60th Annual Emmy Awards* (2008, ABC, originally aired 9/21/08),
    opening statement

*30 Rock* (2008, NBC, episode of Tina Fey comedy series, originally
    aired 11/6/08), herself

*The Princess and the Frog* (2009, animated theatrical release), voice of
    Eudora

## Oprah as Producer and Performer/Interviewer/ Narrator/Host, TV and Movies, 1984–2009

*The Oprah Winfrey Show* (1986–present, nationally syndicated daytime
    talk show, premiered 9/8/86; produced by Harpo since 1988), host;
    Harpo Productions

*No One Dies Alone* (1988, ABC, prime-time special documentary,
    directed by Lloyd Kramer, cowritten by Juan Williams; originally
    aired 12/88), narrator; Harpo Productions

*The Women of Brewster Place* (1989, ABC, prime-time miniseries;
    originally aired 3/19 and 3/20/89; available on DVD), starring role
    as Mattie; Harpo Productions

*Just Between Friends* (1989, ABC, prime-time special, originally aired
    6/10/89), host; Harpo Productions

*Brewster Place* (1990, ABC, prime-time weekly series, half-hour drama,
    eleven episodes aired, premiered 5/1/90; available on DVD)
    starring role as Mattie; Harpo Productions

*In the Name of Self-Esteem* (1990, ABC, prime-time special, originally
    aired 1990), host; Harpo Productions

*Oprah Behind the Scenes* (1992, ABC, prime-time special, with Michael
    Bolton, Goldie Hawn, Meryl Streep, and Dustin Hoffman,
    originally aired 5/19/92), host; Harpo Productions

*Surviving a Break-up* (1992, ABC, Afterschool Special, discussion,
    originally aired 10/1/92), host/moderator; Harpo Productions

*Oprah Behind the Scenes* (1992, ABC, prime-time special with Jodie
    Foster, Richard Gere, Vanessa Williams, and the Simpsons,
    originally aired 11/4/92), host; Harpo Productions

*Shades of a Single Protein* (1993, ABC, Afterschool Special, discussion,
    originally aired 1/28/93), host/moderator; Harpo Productions

*Michael Jackson Talks . . . to Oprah* (1993, ABC, prime-time special, originally aired 2/10/93), interviewer; Harpo Productions

*I Hate the Way I Look* (1993, ABC, Afterschool Special, discussion, originally aired 3/18/93), host/moderator; Harpo Productions

*Girlfriend* (1993, ABC, Afterschool Special, drama, originally aired 4/15/93), host; Harpo Productions

*There Are No Children Here* (1993, ABC, prime-time drama special, originally aired 11/28/93), starring role as Lajoe Rivers; Harpo Productions

*Oprah Winfrey Presents: Before Women Had Wings* (1997, ABC, prime-time drama special, originally aired 11/2/97; available on DVD), starring role as Zora; Harpo Films

*Beloved* (1998, theatrical release; available on DVD), starring role as Sethe; Harpo Films

*Oprah Goes Online* (2000, Oxygen Network, series of twelve weekly episodes, premiered 2/6/00), cohost with Gayle King; Oxygen Media, Oprah Winfrey executive producer

*Use Your Life* (2001, Oxygen Network, series of twelve weekly episodes, premiered 9/10/01), host; Oxygen Media, Oprah Winfrey executive producer

*Oprah After the Show* (2002–2007, Oxygen Network, weekday series 2002–2004, weekly series 2005–2007, premiered 9/16/02), host; Harpo Productions

*Oprah Winfrey's Legends Ball* (2006, ABC, prime-time special, originally aired 5/22/06), host/narrator; Harpo Productions

*Building a Dream: The Oprah Winfrey Leadership Academy* (2007, ABC, prime-time special, originally aired 2/26/07; available on DVD), host/narrator; Harpo Productions

*The Oprah Winfrey Oscar Special* (2007, ABC, prime-time special, originally aired 5/27/07), host; Harpo Productions

*Oprah's Big Give* (2008, ABC, prime-time reality show, eight weekly episodes, premiered 3/2/08), Oprah made appearances in each episode; Harpo Productions

## Oprah as Producer, TV/Movies, 1984–2009

*Nine* (1992, TV documentary, originally aired 4/4/92, directed by Lloyd Kramer), Harpo Productions

*Overexposed* (1992, ABC, prime-time drama special, originally aired 10/11/92), Harpo Productions

*Oprah Winfrey Presents: The Wedding* (1998, ABC, prime-time drama special, originally aired 2/22 and 2/23/98), Harpo Films

*Oprah Winfrey Presents: David and Lisa* (1998, ABC, prime-time drama special, originally aired 11/1/98), Harpo Productions

*Oprah Winfrey Presents: Tuesdays with Morrie* (1999, ABC prime-time drama special, originally aired 12/5/99; available on DVD), Harpo Productions

*Oprah Winfrey Presents: Amy and Isabelle* (2001, ABC, prime-time drama special, originally aired 3/4/01), Harpo Films

*Dr. Phil* (2002–present, syndicated weekday talk show, premiered 9/16/02), Harpo Productions until 2005 (when Dr. Phil McGraw's company took over production)

*Oprah Winfrey Presents: Their Eyes Were Watching God* (2005, ABC, prime-time drama special, originally aired 3/5/05; available on DVD), Harpo Films

*Rachael Ray* (2006–present, syndicated weekday talk/cooking show, premiered 9/18/06), Harpo Productions

*Oprah Winfrey Presents: Mitch Albom's For One More Day* (2007, ABC, prime-time drama special, directed by Lloyd Kramer, originally aired 12/9/07; available on DVD), Harpo Films

*The Great Debaters* (2007, theatrical release; available on DVD), Harpo Films

*Dr. Oz* (2009–present, syndicated weekday talk show, premiered 9/14/09), Harpo Productions

*Precious: Based on the Novel Push by Sapphire* (2009, theatrical release, originally *Push: Based on the Novel by Sapphire*), credited as executive producer, with Tyler Perry and others

## OPRAH AS PRODUCER, THEATER, 1984–2009

*From the Mississippi Delta* (1991–1992, Circle in the Square Theatre, New York), with Susan Quint Gallin, Calvin Skaggs, Susan Wexler, and Judith Resnick

*The Song of Jacob Zulu* (1992, Steppenwolf Theatre, Chicago), with others

*The Color Purple* (2005–2008, Broadway Theatre, New York; 2007–present, national tours), with Scott Sanders, Roy Furman, Quincy Jones, and others

# Notes

### FOREWORD

ARTICLES: Amy Argetsinger and Roxanne Roberts, "The Reliable Source," *Washington Post,* Dec. 14, 2006; George Rush and Joanna Molloy, "Dad's Book Is No Oprah Pick," New York *Daily News,* May 22, 2007; transcript, *"A New Earth* Online Class, Chapter 7," www.oprah.com, Apr. 14, 2008; **Michael Starr, "Barbara Won't Get O's Spot,"** *New York Post,* **June 4, 2010.**

TV: *The View,* aired April 12, 2010.

INTERVIEWS: Judy Stone, Apr. 2, 2007; **Jo Baldwin, July 14, 2010, and correspondence with Jo Baldwin, July 15, 16, 20, and 27, Aug. 17, and Sept. 14, 2010.** Jonathan Van Meter, Dec. 2, 2007; Jura Konscius, Mar. 3, 2008; correspondence with Erin Moriarty, June 16, 2007; Tim Watts, May 23, 2007, and correspondence with Tim Watts, June 30, 2007.

### ONE

RECORDS: Transcript, "Oprah" segment, *60 Minutes,* CBS, Dec. 14, 1986; Oprah Winfrey testimony in "Hearing Before the Committee on the Judiciary, United States Senate, 102nd Congress, Second Session, on The National Child Protection Act of 1991, Nov. 12, 1991."

BOOKS: Robert Waldron, *Oprah!* (St. Martin's Press, 1987); Bill Adler, ed., *The Uncommon Wisdom of Oprah Winfrey* (Citadel Press, 1997); Eva Illouz, *Oprah Winfrey and the Glamour of Misery* (Columbia University Press, 2003); Henry Louis Gates, Jr., *Finding Oprah's Roots* (Crown Publishers, 2007).

ARTICLES: Bill Zehme, "It Came from Chicago," *Spy,* Dec. 1986; Richard Sanders and Barbara Kleban Mills, "TV Host Oprah Winfrey Boots Up for Star-Making Role," *People Weekly,* Dec. 16, 1985; "INC.lings . . . ," *Chicago Tribune,* Jan. 2, 1984; Judy Flander, "TV Highlights," *Chicago Tribune,* Jan. 2, 1984; P. J. Bednarski, "The Talk Show Diva Named Oprah," *Channels of Communication,* Jan./Feb. 1986; "Chicago's Grand New Oprah," *Newsweek,* Dec. 31, 1984; "Oprah Talks Up Her Show," New York *Daily News,* Aug. 19, 1986; Bruce Cook, "Oprah Enjoying Sweet Success," *L.A. Life/Daily News,* Mar. 17, 1986; Joanna Powell, "I Was Trying to Fill Something Deeper," *Good Housekeeping,* Oct.

1996; Lee Winfrey, "Talking Her Way to TV Stardom," *Philadelphia Inquirer TV Magazine,* Sept. 7, 1986; Anne Chambers, "She's Been Fat and Thin," *Woman,* Dec. 1989; Pamela Noel, "Lights! Camera! Oprah!" *Ebony,* Apr. 1985; Jonathan Van Meter, "Oprah's Moment," *Vogue,* Oct. 1998; Bill Zwecker, "Color Purple Nostalgic," *Chicago Sun-Times,* May 4, 2007; Edward Wyatt, "Oprah Winfrey to Back 'Purple,'" *New York Times,* Sept. 26, 2005; John C. Shelton, "Ex-Local TV Anchor Enjoys Her Success," *Nashville Banner,* Dec. 26, 1985; P. J. Bednarski, "Winfrey's Dream Hits High Gear," *Chicago Sun-Times,* May 22, 1984; Academy of Achievement, "Oprah Winfrey Interview," Feb. 21, 1991, www.achievement.org; Vyvyan Mackeson, "A Day in the Life of Oprah Winfrey," London *Sunday Times,* Sept. 8, 1991; Alan Richman, "Oprah," *People Weekly,* Jan. 12, 1987; Eirik Knutzen, "Oprah Kicks Past for Bright Future," *Boston Herald,* Jan. 13, 1987; "In Time of Trouble, Oprah Looks for Help from Above," *Newsday,* July 14, 1987; Mary H. J. Farrell, et al., "Oprah's Crusade," *People Weekly,* Dec. 2, 1991; Ken Potter, "Oprah Winfrey: How I Changed My Life—and How You Can Too," *National Enquirer,* Jan. 26, 1988; Jim Nelson and Roger Capettini, "Oprah in Tears," *National Enquirer,* Nov. 19, 1991; Honie Stevens, "From Rags to Riches," *Saga,* May 2002; Cheryl Lavin, "It's All Going Oprah's Way," *Chicago Tribune,* Dec. 19, 1985; Morgan Thomas, "Troubled Girl's Evolution into an Oscar Nominee," *New York Times,* Mar. 4, 1986; Maralyn Lois Polak, "Oprah Winfrey, So Much to Reveal," *Philadelphia Inquirer Magazine,* Oct. 12, 1986; P. J. Bednarski, "Pandering Her Way to No. 1," *Chicago Sun-Times,* Feb. 28, 1985; P. J. Bednarski, "When Nothing's Off Limits," *Chicago Sun-Times,* Aug. 2, 1984; Joan Barthel, "Here Comes Oprah," *Ms.,* Aug. 1986; P. J. Bednarski, "All About Oprah Inc.," *Broadcasting and Cable,* June 24, 2005; "Oprah Winfrey Is Hotter Than Hot," *Afro-American,* Sept. 20, 1986; Jon Anderson, "Wingin' It with Ch. 7's Oprah Winfrey," *Chicago Tribune,* Mar. 13, 1984; P. J. Bednarski, "Oprah Exposes Nudity," *Chicago Sun-Times,* Feb. 6, 1985; Judy Markey, "Brassy, Sassy Oprah Winfrey," *Cosmopolitan,* Sept. 1986; Alan Artner, "Oprah Winfrey: A Cutup Becomes a Slice of Life," *Chicago Tribune,* Jan. 10, 1988; Howard Rosenberg, "Winfrey Zeroing in on Donahue," *Los Angeles Times,* Sept. 12, 1986; Stephanie Mansfield, "And Now, Heeeeeeere's Oprah," *Washington Post,* Oct. 21, 1986; Richard Zoglin, "'People Sense the Realness,'" *Time,* Sept. 15, 1986; Lloyd Sachs, "Does Oprah Still Make the Grade?" *Chicago Sun-Times,* July 29, 1985; Chrissy Iley, "The Power of Oprah," *Daily Mail,* Oct. 14, 1989; Peter Conrad, "The Divine Oprah," *The Observer,* June 3, 1990; Robert Feder, "Ch. 7 Taps Winfrey as Anchor," *Chicago Sun-Times,* Mar. 24, 1984; P. J. Bednarski, "Oprah Winfrey

Rides the Whirlwind," *Chicago Sun-Times,* Feb. 17, 1985; Audrey Andrews, "Stealing the Show," *Essence,* Oct. 1986; Bill Brashler, "Next on Oprah . . . ," *Ladies' Home Journal,* Aug. 1991; Sujata Moorti, "Cathartic Confessions or Emancipatory Texts? Rape Narratives on *The Oprah Winfrey Show,*" *Social Text 57* 16, no. 4 (Winter 1998); "On Abuse," *USA Today,* Sept. 3, 1992; Jennifer Mangan, "Facing Abuse," *Chicago Tribune,* May 25, 1994; "America's Shame," www.oprah.com, Oct. 4, 2005; "Court Rejects Appeal by Convicted Molester," *Indianapolis Star,* May 9, 2007; Karen S. Peterson, "The Toast of Chicago TV Goes National," *USA Today,* Sept. 18, 1986; Richard Zoglin, "Lady with a Calling," *Time,* Aug. 8, 1988; Jackie Roberts, "Understanding Oprah," *Redbook,* Sept. 1993; Laura B. Randolph, "Oprah Opens Up About Her Weight, Her Wedding, and Why She Withheld the Book," *Ebony,* Oct. 1993; P. J. Bednarski, " 'Blue Thunder' Boundless in Its Brutality and Telefascism," *Chicago Sun-Times,* Jan. 6, 1984; Ian Woodward, "The World of Oprah," *OK!,* June 29, 1994; Nancy Griffin, "Oprah (Lite)," *Us,* Mar. 20, 1989; Sharon Ring, title unknown, *News of the World,* Oct. 1998; Lyn Tornabene, "Here's Oprah," *Woman's Day,* Oct. 1, 1986; Pat Colander, "Oprah Winfrey's Odyssey: Talk Show Host to Mogul," *New York Times,* Mar. 12, 1989.

TV/DVDS: *The Oprah Winfrey Show 20th Anniversary Collection* (DVD set); *The Oprah Winfrey Show,* WLS-TV Chicago, "Second Anniversary," aired Jan. 2, 1986 (viewed at www.museum.tv); *The Barbara Walters Special,* ABC, aired Apr. 11, 1988 (viewed at The Paley Center for Media, New York); *Scared Silent,* PBS, NBC, and CBS, aired Sept. 4, 1992, and ABC, aired Sept. 6, 1992 (viewed at www.museum.tv).

INTERVIEWS: Bill Zwecker, Oct. 11, 2007; Ed Kosowski, Jan. 18, 2008.

## Two

RECORDS: Transcript, Oprah Winfrey speech to American Women's Economic Development Corporation conference, New York City, Feb. 25, 1989; death certificates, Patricia Lloyd (died Feb. 18 or 19, 2003, New Berlin, Wisc.) and Jeffrey Lee (died Dec. 22, 1989, Milwaukee, Wisc.), Wisconsin Department of Health and Family Services; Vernon Winfrey, with Craig Marberry, sample pages for *Things Unspoken: A Memoir by Oprah's Father,* 2007; verification of birth facts and verification of death facts, Vincent Miquelle Lee (born Feb. 8, 1969, and died Mar. 16, 1969, Nashville, Tenn.), Tennessee Department of Health, Office of Vital Records; transcript, interview of Oprah Winfrey by Diane Sawyer, *20/20,* ABC, Oct. 25, 1998.

BOOKS: Henry Louis Gates, Jr., *Finding Oprah's Roots* (Crown Publishers, 2007); Merrell Noden, *People Profiles: Oprah Winfrey* (Time Life, 1999); Katharine Carr Esters, *Jay Bird Creek and My Recollections: A Memoir* (Solid Earth, 2005); Norman King, *Everybody Loves Oprah* (Bill Adler Books, 1987); Vince Staten, *Do Bald Men Get Half-Price Haircuts?* (Touchstone, 2001); Bill Adler, ed., *The Uncommon Wisdom of Oprah Winfrey* (Citadel Press, 1997).

ARTICLES: Lyn Tornabene, "Here's Oprah," *Woman's Day,* Oct. 1, 1986; Laura B. Randolph, "Oprah Opens Up About Her Weight, Her Wedding, and Why She Withheld the Book," *Ebony,* Oct. 1993; Leslie Rubenstein, "Oprah! Thriving on Faith," *McCall's,* Aug. 1987; "Chicago's Grand New Oprah," *Newsweek,* Dec. 31, 1984; Kathleen Fury, "Oprah! Why She's Got America Talking," *TV Guide,* Mar. 5, 1988; Gretchen Reynolds, "Oprah, a One-Woman Show," *Options,* May 1994; Edna Gundersen, "Wildest Dreams Do Come True," *USA Today,* May 15, 1997; Adam Richman, "Oprah," *People Weekly,* Jan. 12, 1987; Patricia King, "Move Over, Phil Donahue—Here Comes Oprah," *Family Circle,* Oct. 21, 1986; Jim Nelson and Barbara Sternig, "Talk Show Star's Wild and Wicked Childhood—Sister Reveals the Shocking Truth at Last," *National Enquirer,* Mar. 20, 1990; Marilyn Johnson, "Oprah Between the Covers," *Life,* Sept. 1997; Bob Michals, "The Uncle Oprah Accuses of Sexually Abusing Her," *Globe,* Sept. 8, 1992; Jonathan Van Meter, "Looking for Oprah," *The Oxford American,* Apr./May 1999; "Living Legend Barbra Streisand," www.oprah.com, Sept. 24, 2009; Barbara Grizzuti Harrison, "The Importance of Being Oprah," *New York Times Magazine,* June 11, 1989; Stephanie Mansfield, "And Now Heeeeeeere's Oprah," *Washington Post,* Oct. 21, 1986; Lee Winfrey, "Talking Her Way to TV Stardom," *Philadelphia Inquirer,* Sept. 7, 1986; "Thursday Rites Set for Zelma Winfrey, Oprah's Stepmother," *Nashville Banner,* Nov. 5, 1996; Tony Brown, "Even Without Scissors, Elder Winfrey a Cutup," Newhouse News Service, Feb. 12, 2007; Susan Goldfarb, "I Drove the Devil Out of Oprah Winfrey—Says Her Dad," *Globe,* Mar. 3, 1987; Joanna Molloy, "Dad's Book Is No Oprah Pick," New York *Daily News,* May 22, 2007; LaTonya Taylor, "The Church of O," *Christianity Today,* Apr. 1, 2002; Jill Nelson, "The Man Who Saved Oprah Winfrey," *Washington Post Magazine,* Dec. 14, 1986; "Oprah Winfrey's Commencement Address, Wellesley College, May 30, 1997," www.wellesley.edu; Jaap Kooijman, "From Elegance to Extravaganza: The Supremes on *The Ed Sullivan Show* as a Presentation of Beauty," *Velvet Light Trap* (Spring 2002); Diahann Carroll, "From 'Julia' to 'Cosby' to 'Oprah,'" *Ebony,* Nov. 2005; Barney

Brantingham, "Oprah: 'This Is My Montecito Coming Out Party,'" *Santa Barbara News-Press,* Apr. 25, 2003; "Eugene H. Abrams," *Chicago Sun-Times,* Sept. 5, 1991; Irene Hoe, "I Went to School with Oprah Winfrey," *Straits Times,* Sept. 17, 1993; Marilyn Jackson, "Oprah Between the Covers," *Life,* Sept. 1997; Judy Markey, "Brassy, Sassy Oprah Winfrey," *Cosmopolitan,* Sept. 1986; Barbara Sternig and Jim Nelson, "Oprah's Shameful Secret Past—the Sister Who Saw It All," *National Enquirer,* Mar. 27, 1990; Ian Woodward, "The World of Oprah," *OK!,* June 29, 1994; Jill Brook Coiner, "Oprah Sets the Record Straight," *McCall's,* Nov. 1993; Ginny Holbert, "Oprah Winfrey Breaks Silence on Child Abuse," *Chicago Sun-Times,* Aug. 30, 1992; Bob Michals and Bob Hartlein, "Oprah's Torment," *Star,* Mar. 23, 2003; Eirik Knutzen, "Oprah Star," Toronto *Starweek,* Jan. 10, 1987; Barbara Reynolds, "Because of Others I Can Live the Dream," *USA Today,* Aug. 6, 1986; Honie Stevens, "From Rags to Riches," *Saga,* May 2002; Rod Gibson, "How Oprah's Baby Died," *Globe,* Feb. 8, 2000; Oprah Winfrey, "What I Know for Sure," *O, The Oprah Magazine,* Feb. 2007.

TV/DVDS/PODCASTS: "Oprah Winfrey: Heart of the Matter," A&E *Biography* special, aired Jan. 16, 2000; *The Barbara Walters Special,* ABC, aired Apr. 11, 1988 (viewed at The Paley Center for Media, New York); Oprah Winfrey speech at the Women's Business Development Center luncheon, Chicago, Ill., Sept. 27, 2006 (mp3 downloaded from www.odeo.com/audio/2003955/play on Nov. 13, 2006); *The Oprah Winfrey Show 20th Anniversary Collection* (DVD set).

INTERVIEWS: Katharine Carr Esters, July 30, 2007 (along with Jewette Battles), Aug. 1, 2007, Sept. 11, 2007, Feb. 5, 2008; **Jo Baldwin, July 14, 2010, and correspondence with Jo Baldwin, July 15, 16, 20, and 27, Aug. 17, and Sept. 14, 2010;** Vernon Winfrey, Apr. 22, 2008, and Apr. 24, 2008; correspondence with Jewette Battles, Mar. 4, 2008; Larry Carpenter, Apr. 21, 2008.

# THREE

RECORDS: East Nashville High *Grey Eagle,* 1971; Oprah Gail Winfrey application for Miss Black Nashville of the Miss Black America Beauty Pageant; Vernon Winfrey with Craig Marberry, sample pages for *Things Unspoken: A Memoir by Oprah's Father,* 2007; *Listening to Youth Voices,* U.S. Government Printing Office pamphlet on White House Conference on Youth, 1971.

BOOKS: Henry Louis Gates, Jr., *Finding Oprah's Roots* (Crown Publishers,

2007); Robert Waldron, *Oprah!* (St. Martin's Press, 1987); Merrell Noden, *People Profiles: Oprah Winfrey* (Time Life, 1999); Norman King, *Everybody Loves Oprah* (Bill Adler Books, 1987).

ARTICLES: Ken Harrell, "My 2½-Year Romance with Oprah," *Globe,* Oct. 26, 1993; Honie Stevens, "From Rags to Riches," *Saga,* May 2002; Academy of Achievement, "Oprah Winfrey Interview," Feb. 21, 1991, www.achievement.org; Pat Embry, "Oprah Winfrey's Father Says Her Success Is No Surprise," *Nashville Banner,* Jan. 20, 1986; Sandy Smith, "Oprah Reunites with First Love," *Tennessean,* Feb. 12, 1992; "Oprah Heads for Forensic Nationals," East Nashville High *East Eagle,* Apr. 1970; Gary Ballard, "Oprah Winfrey," *Drama-Logue,* Mar. 20–26, 1986; "Mayor Evers to Receive Award," *New York Amsterdam News,* June 20, 1970; Louis Martin, "White Elks Show: How to Inspire Racial Violence," *Chicago Daily Defender,* Aug. 1, 1970; Marilyn Johnson, "Oprah Between the Covers," *Life,* Sept. 1997; Leslie Rubenstein, "Oprah!" *McCall's,* Aug. 1987; Joan Barthel, "Here Comes Oprah," *Ms.,* Aug. 1986; "Miss Wool Contest," East Nashville High *East Eagle,* Dec. 1970; Lucia Monet, "Estes Park Conference on Youth," *Christian Science Monitor,* Apr. 16, 1971; "The Voice of Youth," *New York Times,* Apr. 23, 1971; John Mathews, "Game Plan for a Youth Conference," *Nation,* May 17, 1971; "Discontent of the Straights," *Time,* May 3, 1971; "Snow Country," *Newsweek,* May 3, 1971; "U.S. Youth Chooses Radical Path," *Christian Science Monitor,* Apr. 26, 1971; Nan Robertson, "White House Youth Conference Proves to be Anti-Establishment," *New York Times,* Apr. 22, 1971; R. C. Smith, "She Once Trashed Her Apartment to Make a Point," *TV Guide,* Aug. 30, 1986.

TV/DVDS: *The Oprah Winfrey Show 20th Anniversary Collection* (DVD set); *The Oprah Winfrey Show,* "Is There Life After High School?" aired 1994 (viewed at East Nashville High Alumni Association, East Alumni House, Nashville).

INTERVIEWS: Andrea Haynes, Sept. 1, 2008; Luvenia Harrison Butler, Apr. 22, 2008, and Apr. 24, 2008; Larry Carpenter, Apr. 21, 2008, and correspondence with Larry Carpenter, July 29, 2008, and July 30, 2009; Cynthia Connor Shelton, Aug. 26, 2008; Gary Holt, Apr. 23, 2008, and correspondence with Gary Holt, Aug. 22, 2008; correspondence with Jackie Oates, National Forensic League, Feb. 11, 2008, and Aug. 1, 2008; correspondence with Jeannine Kunz, National Elks Foundation, Mar. 19, 2008; correspondence with Sylvia Watts Blann, July 30, 2008; Sheryl Harris Atkinson, June 25, 2008; Nancy Solinski, Apr. 25, 2008; correspondence with Patsy R. Cline, Apr. 12, 2008, and May 7, 2008.

**Four**

RECORDS: East Nashville High *Grey Eagle,* 1971; *Tennessee State University Bulletin,* 1971–1973; *Fisk University Catalog,* 1971–1972; transcript, "Oprah" segment, *60 Minutes,* CBS, Dec. 14, 1986; Oprah Gail Winfrey application for Miss Black Nashville of the Miss Black America Beauty Pageant.

BOOKS: Vince Staten, *Do Bald Men Get Half-Price Haircuts?* (Touchstone, 2001); Robert Waldron, *Oprah!* (St. Martin's Press, 1987); Merrell Noden, *People Profiles: Oprah Winfrey* (Time Life, 1999).

ARTICLES: Transcript, *Larry King Live,* May 1, 2007, www.transcripts.cnn.com; Richard Severo, "Kenneth Clark, Who Fought Segregation, Dies," *New York Times,* May 2, 2005; Sugar Rautbord, "Oprah Winfrey," *Interview,* Mar. 1986; Alan Richman, "Oprah," *People Weekly,* Jan. 12, 1987; transcript, *"A New Earth* Online Class, Chapter 7," www.oprah.com, Apr. 14, 2008; J. Zamgba Browne, "Angela, 'Free at Last,'" *New York Amsterdam News,* June 10, 1972; Mary Ann Bendel, "Oprah Winfrey," *Ladies' Home Journal,* Mar. 1988; Oprah Winfrey, "Oprah Talks to Charlize Theron," *O, The Oprah Magazine,* Nov. 2005; Joanna Powell, "Oprah's Awakening," *Good Housekeeping,* Dec. 1998; Leslie Marshall, "The Intentional Oprah," *InStyle,* Nov. 1998; Lee Siegel, "Thank You for Sharing," *New Republic,* June 5 and 12, 2006; Arline Ambrose, "Martin Luther King Murdered Twice," *Tennessee State University Meter,* May 14, 1973; Academy of Achievement, "Oprah Winfrey Interview," Feb. 21, 1991, www.achievement.org; "Oprah Returns to Mississippi Birth Place," www.foxnews.com, Sept. 5, 2006; Francine Knowles, "Becoming Oprah," *Chicago Sun-Times,* Sept. 29, 2006; "Transcript of Oprah Winfrey's Commencement Address," *Stanford Report,* June 15, 2008; Judy Markey, "Brassy, Sassy Oprah Winfrey," *Cosmopolitan,* Sept. 1986; Patricia Towle and Roger Capettini, "Oprah Stole Beauty Contest Crown," *National Enquirer,* Oct 20, 1992; "Miss Black Nashville TSU Student," *Tennessean,* Mar. 12, 1972; "Oprah Faked a Robbery," *Globe,* Mar. 8, 2004; Luther Young, "She's Found Success by Just Being Oprah," *Baltimore Sun,* Jan. 27, 1985; "Miss Black America Rejects Title," *New York Times,* Aug. 28, 1972; "Beauty Refuses 'America' Crown," *Chicago Daily Defender,* Aug. 28, 1972; Ken Beck, "50 Years of Channel 5," *Tennessean,* Aug. 4, 2004; Ruth Ann Leach, "Outrageous Racism Still Alive in Every State," *Nashville Banner,* July 25, 1995; "The Price of Fame," *Celebrity,* Oct. 1987; John C. Shelton, "Ex-Local TV Anchor Enjoys Her Success," *Nashville Banner,* Dec. 26, 1985; Patricia King, "Move Over, Phil Donahue—Here Comes Oprah," *Family Circle,* Oct. 21, 1986; Richard Sanders and Barbara Kleban

Mills, "TV Host Oprah Winfrey Boots Up for Star-Making Role," *People Weekly,* Dec. 16, 1985; Jamie Foster Brown, "Everything Negroes Ever Wanted to Ask Oprah, Part 2," *Sister 2 Sister,* Dec. 1997; Ken Beck, "Nashville TV Icon Chris Clark Signs Off the Air," *Tennessean,* May 1, 2007; Margaret D. Pagan, "Oprah," *Metropolitan,* Oct. 1979; Eirik Knutzen, "Close to the Hart," *Toronto Star,* Aug, 22, 1989; **"Former *ET* Host Confirms He Dated Oprah Winfrey," www.etonline.com, April 12, 2010;** Bill Zwecker, "It's True, Prince Will Take a Bride," *Chicago Sun-Times,* Feb. 1, 1996; MacKenzie Carpenter, "Former WPXI News Director Knew Young Oprah Was a Keeper," *Pittsburgh Post-Gazette,* Sept. 8, 2006; Eve Zibart, "Baltimore Position Only 'Stopover' for Oprah Winfrey," *Tennessean,* May 4, 1976.

TV/DVDS: *The Oprah Winfrey Show 20th Anniversary Collection* (DVD set); "Oprah Winfrey: Heart of the Matter," A&E *Biography* special, aired Jan. 16, 2000; Oprah video tribute to Chris Clark at the time of his retirement, WTVF-TV, aired May 23, 2007 (viewed at www.newschannel5 .com May 25, 2007); *The Oprah Winfrey Show,* "Oprah Anchors the 5 O'Clock News: Celebs Go Back to Their First Jobs," aired Nov. 3, 2009.

INTERVIEWS: Luvenia Harrison Butler, Apr. 22, 2008, and Apr. 24, 2008; Sheryl Harris Atkinson, June 25, 2008; Katie Rawls, Apr. 21, 2008; **Andrea Haynes, Sept. 1, 2008; Jo Baldwin, July 14, 2010, and correspondence with Jo Baldwin, July 15, 16, 20, and 27, Aug. 17, and Sept. 14, 2010;** Barbara Wright, July 2, 2008; confidential source, Oct. 30, 2007; confidential source, May 24, 2007; Bonnie Goldstein, June 2007; Gordon El Greco Brown, Apr. 24, 2008; Patrice Patton-Price, Sept. 17, 2008; Chris Clark, Apr. 23, 2008; Joseph Davis, Apr. 25, 2008; Patty Outlaw, Apr. 21, 2008, and correspondence with Patty Outlaw, Apr. 27, 2008; Jimmy Norton, May 9, 2008; Joyce Daniel Hill, Apr. 25, 2008; Elaine Garnick, June 30, 2008; confidential source, Jan. 23, 2007; Janet Wassom, Apr. 24, 2008.

FIVE

RECORDS: Transcript, "Oprah" segment, *60 Minutes,* CBS, Dec. 14, 1986; transcript, Oprah Winfrey speech to American Women's Economic Development Corporation conference, New York City, Feb. 25, 1989.

BOOKS: Countee Cullen, "Incident," from *Color* (Harper and Brothers, 1925); Bob Greene and Oprah Winfrey, *Make the Connection* (Hyperion, 1996); Robert Waldron, *Oprah!* (St. Martin's Press, 1987); Michael Olesker, *Tonight at Six* (Apprentice House, 2008); Merrell Noden, *People Profiles: Oprah Winfrey* (Time Life, 1999); Norman King, *Everybody*

*Loves Oprah* (Bill Adler Books, 1987); Katrina Bell McDonald, *Embracing Sisterhood* (Rowman and Littlefield, 2007).

ARTICLES: "Chaos in Charm City," *Time,* July 22, 1974; Mark Kamine, "Walk This Way," *New York Times Book Review,* Dec. 16, 2007; Laura Charles, "'Defector' Oprah Gets Sweet Send-Off," *Baltimore Sun,* Dec. 14, 1983; "Off-Camera: The Living's Convenient in Cross Keys," *Baltimore News-American,* June 1, 1980; Rod Gibson, "Secrets of the Mortician Oprah Was Dying to Wed," *Globe,* Feb. 16, 1999; Peter Williams, "Oprah and Her Men," *Star,* July 6, 1993; Peter Williams, "The Untold Story of Oprah's Heartbreak," *Star,* Dec. 13, 1988; Patricia King, "Move Over, Phil Donahue—Here Comes Oprah," *Family Circle,* Oct. 21, 1986; Bill Carter, "Baltimore's First Hour News," *Baltimore Sun,* Aug. 13, 1976; Bill Carter, "Look for Hour-Long Baltimore News Programs," *Baltimore Sun,* May 14, 1976; Bill Carter, (title unknown), *Baltimore Sun,* June 18, 1976; Bill Carter, (title unknown), *Baltimore Sun,* May 11, 1976; Larry Carson, "Area TV Series Was City Hall Brainchild," Baltimore *Evening Sun,* Sept. 1, 1976; Grant Pick, "Oprah!" *Republic,* Jan. 1986; Oprah Winfrey, "This Month's Mission," *O, The Oprah Magazine,* Dec. 2003; Bill Carter, "The WJZ Weeknight News Is Looking Better and Al Sanders Is Why," *Baltimore Sun,* Apr. 27, 1977; Academy of Achievement, "Oprah Winfrey Interview," Feb. 21, 1991, www.achievement.org; "Transcript of Oprah Winfrey's Commencement Address," *Stanford Report,* June 15, 2008; "Oprah Winfrey's Commencement Address, Wellesley College, May 30, 1997," www.wellesley.edu; Bill Carter, "Hour News Is Smooth and Professional, But Why Is Tom Boyd So Cute?" *Baltimore Sun,* Sept. 9, 1976; "Baltimore TV Reporter Dies at 58," *Washington Post,* Jan. 1, 1988; Alan Richman, "Oprah," *People Weekly,* Jan. 12, 1987; Oprah Winfrey, "It's Not Over Till It's Over," *O, The Oprah Magazine,* Jan. 2004; Lisa Kogan, "Oprah and Gayle Uncensored," *O, The Oprah Magazine,* Aug. 2006; Bill Carter, "WJZ Announces News Shake-Up," *Baltimore Sun,* Apr. 2, 1977; Eve Zibart, "Baltimore Position Only 'Stopover' for Oprah Winfrey," *Tennessean,* May 4, 1976; Jon Anderson, "Wingin' It with Ch. 7's Oprah Winfrey," *Chicago Tribune,* Mar. 13, 1984; Margaret D. Pagan, "Oprah," *Metropolitan,* Oct. 1979; transcript, "*A New Earth* Online Class, Chapter 9," www.oprah.com, Apr. 28, 2008; Jeffrey Strickler, "Winfrey, Having Achieved Quite a Bit, Expects 'Great Things from Myself,'" Minneapolis *StarTribune,* Apr. 18, 1986; Elizabeth Colt, "Oprah Winfrey Goes National," *Boston Globe,* Sept. 2, 1986; Linda Robinson, "Over 1000 Turn Out for Turner Funeral," *Baltimore Sun,* Jan. 4, 1988; Lyn Tornabene, "Here's Oprah," *Woman's Day,* Oct. 1, 1986; Ian Woodward,

"The World of Oprah," *OK!*, June 29, 1994; Fred Hines, "News Man Reports on S. African Horrors," *Afro-American*, Sept. 10, 1977; LaTonya Taylor, "The Church of O," *Christianity Today*, Apr. 1, 2002; Ann Kolson, "Sassy Oprah Has Her Say," *Providence Journal*, Feb. 6, 2007; Cheryl Lavin, "It's All Going Oprah's Way," *Chicago Tribune*, Dec. 19, 1985; "Carter Foundation Presents Oprah Winfrey in a One-Woman Show," *Afro-American*, May 28, 1983; Stephanie Chetas, "One Woman Show," Goucher College *Goucher*, Feb. 11, 1982; Kathleen Fury, "Oprah! Why She's Got America Talking," *TV Guide*, Mar. 5, 1988; Pat Gregor, "Oprah Hides Lover," *Star*, July 18, 2000; Judy Markey, "Brassy, Sassy Oprah Winfrey," *Cosmopolitan*, Sept. 1986; Joe Mullins, "Touching Last Interview with Oprah's AIDS-Stricken Brother," *National Enquirer*, Jan. 16, 1990; Jamie Foster Brown, "Everything Negroes Ever Wanted to Ask Oprah," *Sister 2 Sister*, Nov. 1997; Gerri Kobren, "Co-Hosts Love Their Work," *Baltimore Sun*, Sept. 17, 1978; Oprah Winfrey, "This Is the Body You've Been Given—Love What You've Got," *O, The Oprah Magazine*, Aug. 2002; Francine Knowles, "Becoming Oprah," *Chicago Sun-Times*, Sept. 29, 2006; "Oprah: The Story of My Life," *National Enquirer*, May 14, 1996; Leslie Rubenstein, "Oprah! Thriving on Faith," *McCall's*, Aug. 1987; Bill Carter, "Winfrey's Show Goes On," *Baltimore Sun*, Aug. 19, 1986; Bill Carter, "Sher, Winfrey to Host 13's Talk Show," *Baltimore Sun*, Aug. 2; 1978; Bill Carter, "Channel 13 Getting Over Its Morning Jitters," *Baltimore Sun*, Aug. 23, 1978.

INTERVIEWS: Barbara L. Hamm, July 23, 2007, and Aug. 2, 2007; Dr. William F. Baker, Mar. 12, 2008, and Oct. 28, 2008; Bob Turk, Mar. 3, 2008, and correspondence with Bob Turk, Mar. 4, 2008; Gary Elion, May 27, 2007; Hilda Ford, Nov. 6, 2008; Frank Miller, June 11, 2008; Cynthia Todd, Sept. 21, 2007; correspondence with Bernice Johnson Reagon, Feb. 10, 2007; Jane McClary, Nov. 6, 2009; Katrina Bell McDonald, Jan. 6, 2008; correspondence with Peter Gethers, Nov. 11, 2008; Dr. Frank M. Reid, Sept. 21, 2007; Adam Shapiro, June 16, 2008; Larry Singer, June 19, 2007.

## Six

RECORDS: Documents in the case of *Donna P. Watts v. Timothy C. Watts*, case no. 88CSP133, Circuit Court for Baltimore County, Maryland State Archives; transcript, "Oprah" segment, *60 Minutes*, CBS, Dec. 14, 1986.

BOOKS: Robert Waldron, *Oprah!* (St. Martin's Press, 1987); Michael

Olesker, *Tonight at Six* (Apprentice House, 2008); Bill Adler, ed., *The Uncommon Wisdom of Oprah Winfrey* (Citadel Press, 1997).

ARTICLES: David Folkenflik, "WJZ's Sher Marks 25 Storied Years in TV," *Baltimore Sun,* Oct. 18, 2000; Bill Carter, " 'People Are Talking': A Breath of Hot, Stale Air," *Baltimore Sun,* Aug. 15, 1978; Michael Hill, " 'People Are Talking' Off to a Rough Start," Baltimore *Evening Sun,* Aug. 15, 1978; Gerri Kobren, "Co-Hosts Love Their Work," *Baltimore Sun,* Sept. 17, 1978; Richard Zoglin, "Lady with a Calling," *Time,* Aug. 8, 1988; David Rensin, "The Prime Time of Ms. Oprah Winfrey," *TV Guide,* May 16, 1992; Chris Anderson, "Meet Oprah Winfrey," *Good Housekeeping,* Aug. 1986; Academy of Achievement, "Oprah Winfrey Interview," Feb. 21, 1991, www.achievement.org; Bill Carter, "Channel 13 Getting Over Its Morning Jitters," *Baltimore Sun,* Aug. 23, 1978; Michael Hill, "Richard Sher: Life After Oprah," Baltimore *Evening Sun,* Mar. 20, 1987; Margaret D. Pagan, "Oprah," *Metropolitan,* Oct. 1979; Dave Koppel, "Newscaster Took Her Cue from Romance," Fort Lauderdale *Sun-Sentinel,* Oct. 10, 1997; Gary Ballard, "Oprah Winfrey," *Drama-Logue,* Mar. 20–26, 1986; Liz Smith, "Oprah Debunks 'Em," *Newsday,* July 28, 1997; P. J. Bednarski, "Oprah Winfrey Rides the Whirlwind," *Chicago Sun-Times,* Feb. 17, 1985; Patricia King, "Move Over, Phil Donahue—Here Comes Oprah," *Family Circle,* Oct. 21, 1986; Jim Nelson and Barbara Sternig, "Talk Show Star's Wild and Wicked Childhood—Sister Reveals the Shocking Truth at Last," *National Enquirer,* Mar. 20, 1990; Joan Barthel, "Here Comes Oprah," *Ms.,* Aug. 1986; Lisa DePaulo, "Oprah's Private Life," *TV Guide,* June 3, 1989; Julia Lawlor, "The Other Oprah," *USA Weekend,* June 2–4, 1989; Jan Herman, "Sly Stallone Will Match Rocky Against Russkies," *Chicago Sun-Times,* June 17, 1984; Cheryl Lavin, "Vital Statistics: Oprah Winfrey," *Chicago Tribune* Sept. 7, 1986; Laura B. Randolph, "Networks Help Celebrities Deal with Fame and Pain," *Ebony,* July 1990; Stephanie Mansfield, "And Now, Heeeeeeere's Oprah," *Washington Post,* Oct. 21, 1986; Judy Markey, "Brassy, Sassy Oprah Winfrey," *Cosmopolitan,* Sept. 1986; Dana Kennedy, "Oprah Act Two," *Entertainment Weekly,* Sept. 9, 1994; Kwaku Alston and Oprah Winfrey, "Oprah Talks to Tina Turner," *O, The Oprah Magazine,* May 2005; Chrissy Iley, "The Power of Oprah," *Daily Mail,* Oct. 14, 1989; "In Time of Trouble, Oprah Looks for Help from Above," *Newsday,* July 14, 1987; Karen S. Peterson, "The Toast of Chicago TV Goes National," *USA Today,* Sept. 18, 1986; "Off-Camera: The Living's Convenient in Cross Keys," *Baltimore News-American,* June 1, 1980; Bill Carter, " 'People Are

Talking' Flops as Syndicated Show," *Baltimore Sun,* Sept. 7, 1981; P. J. Bednarski, "All About Oprah Inc.," *Broadcasting and Cable,* June 24, 2005; Michael Hill, " 'People Are Talking' Gains Some Limited Syndication," Baltimore *Evening Sun,* Mar. 26, 1981; Bill Carter, "Can Oprah and Richard Hack It in Boise?" *Baltimore Sun,* Mar. 15, 1981; Chrissy Iley, "Grand Oprah," *Daily Mail,* Feb. 18, 2006; Bob Burns, "Oprah's Suicide Note Revealed," *Globe,* Nov. 16, 1999; Barbara Grizzuti Harrison, "The Importance of Being Oprah," *New York Times Magazine,* June 11, 1989; Transcript, Oprah Winfrey Commencement Speech at Goucher College, May 24, 1981, www.goucher.edu; Bill Carter, (title unknown), *Baltimore Sun,* Feb. 24, 1982; Jon Anderson, "No Dog Days of August for Ch. 7's New Chief," *Chicago Tribune,* Aug. 16, 1983; Gretchen Reynolds, "Oprah Unbound," *Chicago,* Nov. 1993; Peter Conrad, "The Divine Oprah," London *Observer,* June 3, 1990; Kathleen Fury, "Oprah! Why She's Got America Talking," *TV Guide,* Mar. 5, 1988; Luther Young, "She's Found Success by Just Being Oprah," *Baltimore Sun,* Jan. 27, 1985; Bill Carter, "Oprah Leaving Soon for Chicago," *Baltimore Sun,* Oct. 19, 1983; Oprah Winfrey, "I Created This Happiness by Choice," *O, The Oprah Magazine,* Mar. 2004; Oprah Winfrey, "Wind Beneath My Wings," *Essence,* June 1989; "Tribute: A Salute to Dr. William F. Baker," *Broadcasting and Cable* advertising supplement, May 28, 2007; Michael Olesker, "Today They Grieve for a Guy Who Made Folks Laugh," *Baltimore Sun,* July 25, 1993; Sylvia Badger, "Local Stars Turn Out for Oprah's Signing-Off Party," *Baltimore News-American,* Dec. 14, 1983; Laura Charles, " 'Defector' Oprah Gets Sweet Send-Off," *Baltimore Sun,* Dec. 14, 1983.

DVD: *The Oprah Winfrey Show 20th Anniversary Collection* (DVD set).

INTERVIEWS: Barbara L. Hamm, July 23, 2007, and Aug. 2, 2007; Jane McClary, Nov. 6, 2009; Bob Leffler, Nov. 6, 2008; Dr. William F. Baker, Mar. 17, 2008, and Oct. 28, 2008; Dave Gosey, June 2007; Michael Fox, Jan. 17, 2007, and correspondence with Michael Fox, Dec. 10, 2007, Oct. 31, 2008, and Nov. 7, 2008; Judy Colteryahn, Mar. 16, 2008, and correspondence with Judy Colteryahn Mar. 17, 2008, Aug. 5, 2008, Aug. 6, 2008, Sept. 30, 2008; Eileen Solomon, Mar. 28, 2007; Susan Rome, Nov. 21, 2008; Ellen Lightman, Nov. 21, 2008; Paul Dickson, Jan. 17, 2007; Beverly Burke, July 25, 2007; correspondence with Wayne Kabak, Dec. 18, 2008; Ron Shapiro, Aug. 6, 2007.

## SEVEN

RECORDS: Documents in the case of *Randolph L. Cook v. Oprah Winfrey,* case no. 1:97-cv-00322, United States District Court, Northern District of

Illinois; sample chapters from *The Wizard of O,* by Randolph Cook; transcript, testimony of Paul Natkin, on Aug. 15, 2000, in the case of *Paul Natkin and Stephen Green v. Oprah Winfrey* et al., case no. 1:99-cv-05367, United States District Court, Northern District of Illinois.

BOOKS: James "Quick" Tillis, as told to J. Engleman Price, *Thinking Big* (The LPG Group, 2000); Robert Waldron, *Oprah!* (St. Martin's Press, 1987).

ARTICLES: Michael Sneed et al., "The Parking Plot," *Chicago Tribune,* Mar. 20, 1985; Luther Young, "She's Found Success by Just Being Oprah," *Baltimore Sun,* Jan. 27, 1985; Richard Roeper, "New Age Oprah Forgets Those Tacky Old Shows," *Chicago Sun-Times,* Oct. 1, 1997; Mel Novit, "Oprah Winfrey," *Boston Herald,* Sept. 4, 1986; Grant Pick, "Oprah!" *Republic,* Jan. 1986; Patricia Sellers, "The Business of Being Oprah," *Fortune,* Apr. 1, 2002; Robert Feder, "A Slimmer Winfrey Feasts on the Glory of Her Rich TV Deal," *Chicago Sun-Times,* Aug. 22, 1988; Kathy O'Malley and Dorothy Collin, "INC." *Chicago Tribune,* Dec. 4, 1990; Fred Goodman, "The Companies They Keep," *Working Woman,* Dec. 1, 1991; Barbara Grizzuti Harrison, "The Importance of Being Oprah," *New York Times Magazine,* June 11, 1989; Lyn Tornabene, "Here's Oprah," *Woman's Day,* Oct. 1, 1986; Jan Herman, "Sly Stallone Will Match Rocky Against Russkies," *Chicago Sun-Times,* June 17, 1984; Stephen Hunter, "Oprah!" *Baltimore Sun,* Dec. 17, 1985; Judy Markey, "Brassy, Sassy Oprah Winfrey," *Cosmopolitan,* Sept. 1986; JoAnn Harris, "'Della' Premiers Monday," *Washington Post,* June 8, 1967; Robert Kurson, "The Silent Treatment," *Chicago,* July 2001; Clarence Peterson, "Very Illuminated People," *Chicago Tribune,* Dec. 26, 1985; Robert Feder, "An Eyewitness Guide to Sprucing Up Channel 7," *Chicago Sun-Times,* Dec. 26, 1985; Maralyn Lois Polak, "Oprah Winfrey: So Much to Reveal," *Philadelphia Inquirer Magazine,* Oct. 12, 1986; Bill Zehme, "It Came from Chicago," *Spy,* Dec. 1986; "Chicago's Grand New Oprah," *Newsweek,* Dec. 31, 1984; Michael Sneed and Cheryl Lavin, "A Superstadium?" *Chicago Tribune,* Jan. 27, 1985; Jon Anderson, "Oprah Winfrey Conquers Tonight Show Challenge," *Chicago Tribune,* Jan. 31, 1985; P. J. Bednarski, "The Talk Show Diva Named Oprah," *Channels of Communication,* Jan./Feb. 1986; Luther Young, "Oprah and Joan Square Off," *Baltimore Sun,* Jan. 31, 1985; Marla Donato, "One Last Food Fling with Oprah," *Chicago Tribune,* Feb. 6, 1985; book chapters and introduction, www.thewizardofo.com; Sarah Gallick, "Keep Quiet!" *Star,* Feb. 18, 1997; "Oprah and Coke," *Atlanta Daily World,* Feb. 12, 1995; Ann Witheridge, "Oprah Drug Nightmare," *Star,* Jan. 31, 1995; Laura B. Randolph

"Networks Help Celebrities Deal with Fame and Pain," *Ebony,* July 1990; "What She Did for Love," *People Weekly,* Jan. 30, 1995; Patrice Gains, "How Oprah's Confession Tumbled Out," *Washington Post,* Jan. 13, 1995; Ellen Edwards, "Oprah Winfrey Admits Drug Use," *Washington Post,* Jan. 13, 1995; Bill Zwecker, "Oprah Drug Revelation Could Backfire," *Chicago Sun-Times,* Jan. 15, 1995; Robert Feder, "Oprah Agonized Over Drug Story," *Chicago Sun-Times,* Jan. 19, 1995; Chris Kaltenbach, "As Fans Applaud Honesty, Others Wonder If Ratings Prompted Admission," *Baltimore Sun,* Jan. 14, 1995; Jeffrey Rodack, "Oprah Erupts in Sex and Drug Shocker," *National Enquirer,* Feb. 18, 1997; Cindy Adams, "He May Try to Bond with NYC," *New York Post,* Oct. 1, 2007; Lucinda Hahn, "New Mom Samantha Harris; Expectant Mom Jennifer Lopez," *Chicago Tribune,* Oct. 17, 2007.

TV/DVD/PODCAST: Oprah Winfrey interviewed by Fred Griffith, *The Morning Exchange,* fifteenth anniversary, WEWS-TV, aired Jan. 1987; Oprah Winfrey speech at the Women's Business Development Center luncheon, Chicago, Ill., Sept. 27, 2006 (mp3 downloaded from www .odeo.com/audio/2003955/play on Nov. 13, 2006); *Oprah Winfrey Show 20th Anniversary Collection* (DVD set).

INTERVIEWS: Margo Howard, July 25, 2008, and correspondence with Margo Howard, Dec. 13, 2006; Dori Wilson, Sept. 8, 2008; **Jo Baldwin, July 14, 2010, and correspondence with Jo Baldwin, July 15, 16, 20, and 27, Aug. 17, and Sept. 14, 2010;** Robert Waldron, Sept. 4, 2008; Robert Feder, Oct. 11, 2007; Randolph Cook, July 25, 2007, and Aug. 15, 2007; Diane Dimond, Apr. 29, 2007, and correspondence with Diane Dimond, Dec. 14, 2006; confidential source, Oct. 8, 2009; Jerry Oppenheimer, Nov. 2, 2007; Patty O'Toole, Nov. 20, 2008; confidential source, Jan. 2, 2008, Mar. 19, 2008, Mar. 21, 2008, and June 3, 2008.

## EIGHT

BOOKS: Alice Walker, *The Same River Twice* (Scribner, 1996); Quincy Jones, *Q: The Autobiography of Quincy Jones* (Harlem Books, 2001); Robert Waldron, *Oprah!* (St. Martin's Press, 1987); Evelyn C. White, *Alice Walker* (W.W. Norton and Co., 2004); Lawrence Leamer, *Fantastic: The Life of Arnold Schwarzenegger* (St. Martin's Press, 2005).

ARTICLES: Louis B. Parks, "'Purple' Actresses Make Most of Meaty Roles," *Houston Chronicle,* Mar. 21, 1986; Susan Dworkin, "The Strange and Wonderful Story of the Making of *The Color Purple,*" *Ms.,* Dec. 1985; Elena Featherstone, "The Making of *The Color Purple,*" *San Francisco Focus,* Dec. 1985; Jack Mathews, "3 'Color Purple' Actresses Talk About

Its Impact," *Los Angeles Times*, Jan. 31, 1986; Philip Wuntch, "Best Known as Comedian, Whoopi Goldberg Uneasy with Movie Stardom," *Ottawa Citizen*, Dec. 23, 1985; Gene Siskel, " 'Color Purple': Powerful, Daring, Sweetly Uplifting," *Chicago Tribune*, Dec. 20, 1985; Denise Abbott, "The Price of Fame," *Celebrity*, Oct. 1987; Richard Zoglin, "Lady with a Calling," *Time*, Aug. 8, 1988; Alessandra Stanley, "Morning TV Veers from News to Frills," *New York Times*, Dec. 4, 2007; Amy Wallace, "War of Words," *Los Angeles Times*, Sept. 25, 1998; Ann Kolson, "Oprah a Name to be Reckoned With," *Philadelphia Inquirer*, Jan. 14, 1986; Delores Brooks, "The Phenomenal Oprah Winfrey," *Dollars and Sense* (date unknown); Bruce Cook, "Oprah Enjoying Sweet Success," *L.A. Life/Daily News*, Mar. 17, 1986; Jonathan Van Meter, "Oprah's Moment," *Vogue*, Oct. 1998; Gary Ballard, "Oprah Winfrey," *DramaLogue*, Mar. 20–26, 1986; Fred Goodman, "The Companies They Keep," *Working Women*, Dec. 1, 1991; Grant Pick, "Oprah!" *Republic*, Jan. 1986; "Oprah: Tom Cruise's Couch Jumping Was Wilder Than It Seemed," www.ABCNews.go.com, Nov. 11, 2005; "Loving Life," www.oprah.com, May 23, 2005; Janet Charlton, "In Happier Times," www.janetcharltonshollywood.com, Aug. 20, 2006; Michael Sneed et al., "Oprah Goes Hollywood," *Chicago Tribune*, June 4, 1985; "Names and Faces," *Los Angeles Herald Examiner*, Sept. 19, 1998; Ann Marie Lipinski, "Oprah Winfrey Buying West Side Studios," *Chicago Tribune*, Sept. 18, 1988; Pat Colander, "Oprah Winfrey's Odyssey: Talk Show Host to Mogul," *New York Times*, Mar. 12, 1989; Veronica Chambers and Allison Samuels, "The Women of 'Beloved,' " *Newsweek*, Oct. 19, 1998; Mary Gillespie, "The Women of 'Brewster Place,' " *Chicago Sun-Times*, Mar. 12, 1989; Gene Wyatt, "Oprah Winfrey Learns How to Get Mad for 'Color Purple,' " *Tennessean*, Dec. 15, 1985; Roger Ebert, "In Film Debut, Oprah Proves She's Born to the 'Purple,' " *Chicago Sun-Times*, Dec. 15, 1985; Gene Siskel, "With 'Purple' Spielberg Finally Grows Up and Gets Serious," *Chicago Tribune*, Dec. 15, 1985; Sheila Benson, "Two Women of Substance in Unlikely Settings: 'The Color Purple,' " *Los Angeles Times*, Dec. 18, 1985; David Ansen, "The Color Purple," *Newsweek*, Dec. 30, 1985; Rita Kempley, " 'Purple' Making Whoopi a Star," *Washington Post*, Dec. 20, 1985; Stephen Hunter, "Oprah," *Baltimore Sun*, Dec. 17, 1985; Lou Cedrone, "The Color Purple," *Baltimore Evening Sun*, Dec. 20, 1985; Diane Bartley, "An Oscar for Oprah," *Tennessean*, Feb. 7, 1986; Robert Feder, "Nice Guy Newman Cancelled by Channel 5," *Chicago Sun-Times*, July 25, 1985; Michael Sneed et al., "City Ditties," *Chicago Tribune*, Aug. 29, 1985; "Oprah Returns to Nashville as Millionaire," *Tennessean*, Aug. 8, 1985; Lou Cedrone, "Winfrey Story Only Beginning," *Baltimore*

*Evening Sun,* Mar. 18, 1986; Luther Young, "Oprah," *Baltimore Sun,* Feb. 21, 1986; Jeffrey Strickler, "Winfrey, Having Achieved Quite a Bit, Expects 'Great Things from Myself,'" Minneapolis *StarTribune,* Apr. 18, 1986; R. C. Smith, "She Once Trashed Her Apartment to Make a Point," *TV Guide,* Aug. 30, 1986; E. R. Shipp, "Blacks in Heated Debate Over 'The Color Purple,'" *New York Times,* Jan. 27, 1986; Josephine Trescott, "Passions Over 'Purple,'" *Washington Post,* Feb. 5, 1986; Roger Ebert, "The Top Ten Films of 1985," *Chicago Sun-Times,* Dec. 29, 1985; Roger Ebert, "Hope Lives in a Character's Truth," *Chicago Sun-Times,* Mar. 28, 2004; Rose P. B. Venditti and Sylvia Badger, "Coming Home," *Baltimore News American,* Feb. 21, 1986; Lyn Tornabene, "Here's Oprah," *Woman's Day,* Oct. 1, 1986; Bill Zehme, "It Came from Chicago," *Spy,* Dec. 1986; Stephanie Mansfield, "And Now, Heeeeeeere's Oprah," *Washington Post,* Oct. 21, 1986; Robert Kurson, "The Silent Treatment," *Chicago,* July 2001; Barbara Grizzuti Harrison, "The Importance of Being Oprah," *New York Times Magazine,* June 11, 1989; Tina Brown, "My New Mantra for 2009," www.thedailybeast.com, Jan. 2, 2009; Tina Brown, "Is Michelle the New Oprah?" www.thedailybeast.com, Apr. 2, 2009; "Bad Press," www.thedailybeast.com, Aug. 21, 2009; Lloyd Grove, "Oprah and the Sweat Lodge Guru," www.thedailybeast.com, Oct. 23, 2009.

TV: Oprah Winfrey episode, *E! The True Hollywood Story,* aired Oct. 17, 2004.

INTERVIEWS: Alice Walker, Oct. 7, 2008; correspondence with confidential source, Dec. 5, 2007, and Dec. 12, 2007; Erica Jong, Dec. 17, 2006; confidential source, Nov. 9, 2007; Sandi Mendelson, Jan. 7, 2008; correspondence with Tina Brown's assistant, Jan. 7, 2008.

## NINE

RECORDS: Transcript, Oprah Winfrey speech to American Women's Economic Development Corporation conference, New York City, Feb. 25, 1989; Stedman Graham marriage records details, Tarrant County public access; verification of birth of Wendy Graham, Texas Department of State Health Services; documents in the case of *Stedman Graham and Oprah Winfrey v. Extra Media, Inc.,* case no. 1:92-CV-02087, United States District Court, Northern District of Illinois; "Join the Team" form for Member Athletes, www.joinaad.com; IRS forms 990 for Athletes Against Drugs, 2002–2007, EIN 36-3463119.

BOOKS: Bill Adler, ed., *The Uncommon Wisdom of Oprah Winfrey* (Citadel Press, 1997); Robert Waldron, *Oprah!* (St. Martin's Press, 1987); Stedman

Graham, *You Can Make It Happen* (Fireside, 1998) and *Build Your Own Life Brand* (Free Press, 2001); Stedman Graham, "Whitesboro: A Hometown Remembered," in Wendel A. White, *Small Towns, Black Lives* (The Noyes Museum of Art, 2003).

ARTICLES: Timothy McDarrah, "Talk's Not Cheap," *New York Post,* Jan. 1, 1987; Lloyd Shearer, "Oprah Winfrey—How Rich?" *Parade,* Feb. 15, 1987; Stephen Viens, "Secret Ways That Oprah Windfall Enjoys Her Millions," *Star,* Aug. 23, 1988; Alan Richman, "Oprah," *People Weekly,* Jan. 12, 1987; "And Another," *Boston Globe,* Mar. 1, 1988; Charles Whitaker, "The Most Talked-About TV Show Host," *Ebony,* Mar. 1987; Aljean Harmetz, "Learning to Live with Runaway Fame," *New York Times,* May 18, 1986; Alan G. Artner, "Oprah Winfrey," *Chicago Tribune,* Jan. 10, 1988; Marla Donato, "One Last Food Fling with Oprah," *Chicago Tribune,* Feb. 6, 1985; Leslie Rubenstein, "Oprah! Thriving on Faith," *McCall's,* Aug. 1987; Elizabeth Sporkin et al., "Her Man Stedman," *People Weekly,* Nov. 23, 1992; Barbara Grizzuti Harrison, "The Importance of Being Oprah," *New York Times Magazine,* June 11, 1989; "Oprah Winfrey," *Chicago Sun-Times,* Dec. 13, 1987; "Will Opulence Spoil Oprah?" *Chicago Sun-Times,* Mar. 1, 1988; "Oprah's Best Friend, Gayle King, Lists 10,433-Square-Foot House in Greenwich, CT for $7.45M," www.bergproperties.com/blog, July 7, 2008; Robert Feder, "Five More Reasons You Gotta Love Outrageous Oprah," *Chicago Sun-Times,* Dec. 1, 1987; Nicole Sweeney, "When I Was 30: Vernita Lee," www.mkeonline.com, May 19, 2005; Joan Barthel, "Here Comes Oprah," *Ms.,* Aug. 1986; Steve Sonsky, "Oprah Winfrey!" *Miami Herald,* Sept. 7, 1986; Lyn Tornabene, "Here's Oprah," *Woman's Day,* Oct. 1, 1986; Jill Brook Coiner, "Oprah Sets the Record Straight," *McCall's,* Nov. 1993; R. C. Smith, "She Once Trashed Her Apartment to Make a Point," *TV Guide,* Aug. 30, 1986; Marilyn Johnson, "Oprah Between the Covers," *Life,* Sept. 1997; Kwaku Alston and Oprah Winfrey, "Oprah Talks to Tina Turner," *O, The Oprah Magazine,* May 2005; Alan Bash, "Viewers Can Get a Dose of Reality in Syndication," *USA Today,* May 30, 1995; **Zondra Hughes, "Family Secrets: Oprah's Mother Speaks Out," *N'Digo,* May 6–12, 2010;** Judy Markey, "Opinionated Oprah!" *Woman's Day,* Oct. 4, 1988; **"Oprah Talks to You," *O, The Oprah Magazine,* May 2010;** Jim Nelson and Barbara Sternig, "Talk Show Star's Wild and Wicked Childhood— Sister Reveals the Shocking Truth at Last," *National Enquirer,* Mar. 20, 1990; Jamie Foster Brown, "Everything Negroes Ever Wanted to Ask Oprah, Part 2," *Sister 2 Sister,* Dec. 1997; Lisa DePaulo, "Oprah's Private Life," *TV Guide,* June 3, 1989; Mary Gillespie, "Oprah's Main Squeeze,"

*Chicago Sun-Times,* Apr. 14, 1987; Eric Sherman, "Oprah Winfrey's Success Story," *Ladies' Home Journal,* Mar. 1987; Nancy Griffin, "Oprah (Lite)," *Us,* Mar. 20, 1989; David Rensin, "The Prime Time of Ms. Oprah Winfrey," *TV Guide,* May 16, 1992; Mary Ann Bendel, "Oprah Winfrey," *Ladies' Home Journal,* Mar. 1988; "Stedman Stole Oprah from Rich Doc's Arms," *Globe,* Feb. 16, 1993; Debra Pickett, "Boring, Cool, Silly, Sublime," *Chicago Sun-Times,* Dec. 29, 2002; George Rush and Joanna Molloy, "When a Rumor Is Dead Wrong," New York *Daily News,* Apr. 18, 2002; Mike Kiley, "His Own Man," *Chicago Tribune,* May 24, 1995; Michel Marriott, "They Used to Call Me Oprah's Boyfriend," *New York Times,* Feb. 26, 1997; JaNae' Bates, "Stedman Defines Himself and Tells Students to Do the Same," Cleveland *Call and Post,* Aug. 3–9, 2006; Gretchen Reynolds, "The Man She's Marrying," *Chicago,* Dec. 1993; Jack Anderson and Dale Van Atta, "Winnie Mandela's U.S. Promoter," *Washington Post,* Mar. 8, 1989; "Lunch on Oprah in South African Town," *Boston Herald,* July 23, 1988; Brian Williams and David Barritt, "Oprah's Mission of Mercy," *National Enquirer,* Apr. 3, 1990; Richard Schweid, "Oprah Takes a Risk with TV Special," *Tennessean,* Nov. 20, 1988; Julia Lawlor, "The Other Oprah," *USA Weekend,* June 2–4, 1989; LaTonya Taylor, "The Church of O," *Christianity Today,* Apr. 1, 2002; Ken Harrell, "Shocking Secrets Stedman Hides from Oprah," *Globe,* May 7, 1991; "One on One with Oprah," www.etonline.com, Jan. 3, 2007; "And Oprah's No Mike Tyson," *New York Post,* Nov. 11, 1988; "I Want a Baby—A Little Heir," *Star,* Sept. 12, 1989; Joanna Powell, "Oprah's Awakening," *Good Housekeeping,* Dec. 1998; "New Oprah Shocker! Fiancé Stedman Had Sex with a Gay Cousin," *News Extra,* Mar. 24, 1992; Laura B. Randolph, "Oprah Opens Up About Her Weight, Her Wedding, and Why She Withheld the Book," *Ebony,* Oct. 1993; Rosalind Rossi, "New Oprah 'Shocker' Spurs $300 Million Defamation Suit," *Chicago Sun-Times,* Mar. 27, 1992; Ann McLaughlin, "Oprah Wins Suit Against Montreal Tab," Montreal *Gazette,* May 3, 1992; Rosalind Rossi, "Winfrey, Friend Win Lawsuit by Default," *Chicago Sun-Times,* May 2, 1992; "Oprah Winfrey Wins Suit by Default," *Chicago Tribune,* May 2, 1992; Mark Steyn, "Comic Oprah," *National Review,* Mar. 23, 1998; Barbara Reynolds, "Because of Others I Can Live the Dream," *USA Today,* Aug. 8, 1986; Bill Zehme, "It Came from Chicago," *Spy,* Dec. 1986; Leslie Marshall, "The Intentional Oprah," *InStyle,* Nov. 1998; "Oprah to Offer Eccentric Dining," *USA Today,* Nov. 21, 1988; Irv Kupcinet, "Kup's Column," *Chicago Sun-Times,* Apr. 26, 1988; "Oprah Winfrey," *People Weekly,* Dec. 28, 1987; "Grapevine Squashed," *Newsday,* Sept. 10, 1987; Tony Castro, "Threat to Top Talk Show," *Globe,* Sept. 1, 1987; Bill Carter, "Oprah!" *Baltimore Sun,* Sept. 24, 1987;

Robert Feder, "WMAQ Sale Will Leave Big Talkers Speechless," *Chicago Sun-Times,* June 29, 1987.

TV/DVD/OTHER: *The Oprah Winfrey Show 20th Anniversary Collection* (DVD set); "Oprah Winfrey: Heart of the Matter," A&E *Biography* special, aired Jan. 16, 2000; Kathy Griffin at Constitution Hall in Washington, D.C., Sept. 15, 2008; *Sit Down Comedy with David Steinberg,* TV Land, aired Feb. 28, 2007.

INTERVIEWS: Correspondence with Michael Fox, Dec. 10, 2007; Ed Kosowski, Nov. 8, 2008; Nancy Stoddart, July 8, 2009; Katharine Carr Esters, Aug. 1, 2007; Joanna Molloy, July 7, 2008; E. Faye Butler, Apr. 3, 2009; Fran Johns, Sept. 2007; correspondence with Dorothy H. Kiser, Hardin-Simmons University, Feb. 4, 2009; correspondence with investigator Dale Lee Hinz, Fort Worth Police, Mar. 13, 2009; correspondence with Richard W. Schott, Federal Bureau of Prisons, Feb. 20, 2007; Armstrong Williams, Nov. 19, 2008; correspondence with Henry Fulmer, University of North Carolina; confidential source, June 11, 2007; confidential source, Oct. 8, 2009; Vernon Winfrey, Apr. 24, 2008; Paxton Quigley, Mar. 10, 2008, and Mar. 12, 2008; Bill Zwecker, Oct. 11, 2007.

## TEN

RECORDS: Transcript, Oprah Winfrey speech to American Women's Economic Development Corporation conference, New York City, Feb. 25, 1989.

BOOKS: Merrell Noden, *People Profiles: Oprah Winfrey* (Time Life, 1999).

ARTICLES: Alan Richman, "Oprah," *People Weekly,* Jan. 12, 1987; "Oprah: The Best Is Yet to Come," www.msnbc.msn.com, May 19, 2006; Renard A. Hirsch, Sr., " 'Anger' Oprah Recalls Not Apparent to All," *Tennessean,* Mar. 17, 1987; Roderick McDavis, "Oprah Winfrey's Credibility," Tennessee State University *Meter,* Mar. 26, 1987; Amy Gutman and David Graham, "TSU Commencement to Feature Winfrey," *Tennessean,* Mar. 28, 1987; Patricia Templeton, "Oprah Gets Her College Degree," *Nashville Banner,* May 4, 1987; Sue Thomas, "Oprah Returns to TSU in Triumph," *Sunday Tennessean,* May 3, 1987; "Transcript of Oprah Winfrey's Commencement Address," *Stanford Report,* June 15, 2008; Dwight Lewis, "Oprah Winfrey Funding 10 Full Scholarships," *Tennessean,* Aug. 3, 1987; Marcia Ann Gillespie, "Winfrey Takes All," *Ms.,* Nov. 1988; Roger Hitts, "New Oprah Anguish as Dad Is Named in Sex Complaint," *Star,* Feb. 14, 1995; Dani Cestaro et al., "Oprah Fights to Save Her Dad in Sex Scandal," *National Enquirer,* Feb. 19, 1995; Karen

Thomas, "Oprah Stands by Her Dad," *USA Today,* Feb. 3, 1995; "Oprah Winfrey Responds to Allegations That Her Father Harrassed College Student," *Jet,* Feb. 20, 1995; Rod Gibson, "Oprah to the Rescue," *Globe,* Feb. 1995 (exact date unknown); Peter Burt and Dani Cestaro, "Oprah in Tears as Dad's Accuser in Sex Scandal Passes Lie Test," *National Enquirer,* Feb. 31, 1995; Kirk Loggins, "Bribe Solicited from Winfrey, Prosecutors Say," *Tennessean,* Apr. 1, 1995; Toni Drew, "Winfrey Accuser's Attorney Pleads Guilty," *Nashville Banner,* Aug. 25, 1995; "Lawyer Loses Again in Oprah's Dad's Case," *Chicago Tribune,* Dec. 1, 1995; Laura B. Randolph, "Oprah!" *Ebony,* July 1995; **Jonathan Pinkerton, "Dolly Parton's Personal Message Urging Nashville Flood Relief; Donates Weekend Admissions Proceeds," www.examiner.com, May 22, 2010;** Delores Brooks, "The Phenomenal Oprah Winfrey," *Dollars and Sense* (date unknown); "Oprah Gives $1 Million to Morehouse College," *Baltimore Evening Sun,* May 22, 1989; "Oprah Winfrey Makes Second $5 Million [Donation]," www.morehouse.edu, Feb. 24, 2004; Kim Cunningham "Behind Closed Doors," *People Weekly,* Apr. 29, 1996; Lisa Kogan, "Oprah and Gayle Uncensored," *O, The Oprah Magazine,* Aug. 2006; Jennifer Hunter, "Even Well-Intended Celebs Adopt Aloof Attitudes," *Chicago Sun-Times,* Nov. 1, 2006; Debbie Schlussel, "Oprah Discovers the Holocaust," www.frontpagemag.com, May 29, 2009; "Putting Down Rover, and the Year's Other Disasters," *Chicago Sun-Times,* Dec. 29, 2006; Bob Monk, "Oprah Event Nets $5000," *Kosciusko Star-Herald,* June 9, 1988; "Newsmakers," *Houston Chronicle,* June 6, 1988; Kevin Pilley, "Grand Ol' Oprah," *Express,* Aug. 8, 1998; Barbara Grizzuti Harrison, "The Importance of Being Oprah," *New York Times Magazine,* June 11, 1989; transcript, *CNN Newsroom,* May 12, 2007, www.transcipts.cnn.com; "Oprah Winfrey's commencement address, Wellesley College, May 30, 1997," www.wellesley.edu; Mark Thornton, "Grand Oprah-ning," *Kosciusko Star-Herald,* Sept. 4, 2006; "Oprah Comes Home," *Kosciusko Star-Herald,* Nov. 19, 1998; Jonathan Van Meter, "Looking for Oprah," *Oxford American,* Apr./May 1999; "Kosciusko Prepares for Oprah's Nov. 14 Visit," *Kosciusko Star-Herald,* July 30, 2007; Bob Michals and Bob Hartlein, "Oprah's Torment," *Star,* Mar. 25, 2003; **Molly Parker, "Relative: Winfrey Book Untrue," *Clarion-Ledger,* April 20, 2010; Alex Heard, "Oprah's Cousin Bashes Book," *The Daily Beast,* April 22, 2010; Danny Shea, "Oprah Dismisses Kitty Kelley Book: 'So-Called Biography,'" *Huffington Post,* April 19, 2010; Zondra Hughes, "Family Secrets: Oprah's Mother Speaks Out," *N'Digo,* May 6–12, 2010;** Bob Michals, "The Uncle Oprah Accuses of Sexually Abusing Her," *National Enquirer,* Sept. 9, 1992; Julia Lawlor, "The Other Oprah," *USA Weekend,* June 2–4,

1989; Pearl Cleage, "Walking in the Light," *Essence,* June 1991; Oprah's Steady to Be Her Hubby," *USA Today,* Nov. 9, 1992; *People Weekly,* Nov. 23, 1992; Elizabeth Sporkin et al., "Her Man Stedman," *People Weekly,* Nov. 23, 1992; Robert Feder, "Jones Turns Misery into Ratings Circus," *Chicago Sun-Times,* Feb. 24, 1992.

TV/PODCAST: Alan Frio interview with Vernon and Barbara Winfrey, WMSV-TV, aired Feb. 12, 2007 (viewed at www.wmsv.com); *The Oprah Winfrey Show,* "Oprah at Auschwitz," aired May 24, 2006; Oprah Winfrey speech at the Women's Business Development Center luncheon, Chicago, Ill., Sept. 27, 2006 (mp3 downloaded from www.odeo.com/audio/2003955/play on Nov. 13, 2006).

INTERVIEWS: Brooks Parker, Apr. 29, 2008; Chris Clark, Apr. 23, 2008; Vernon Winfrey, Apr. 22, 2008; Paul Moore, Apr. 21, 2008; Katie Rawls, Apr. 21, 2008; correspondence with confidential source, Feb. 18, 2009; Jewette Battles, July 31, 2007, Aug. 14, 2007, and correspondence with Jewette Battles, Apr. 29, 2008, and Oct. 8, 2008; Katharine Carr Esters, July 30, 2007 (along with Jewette Battles), Aug. 1, 2007, Sept. 11, 2007, and Feb. 5, 2008; **Jo Baldwin, July 14, 2010, and correspondence with Jo Baldwin, July 15, 16, 20, and 27, Aug. 17, and Sept. 14, 2010;** Nancy Green, July 30, 2007; James van Sweden, Dec. 12, 2007, and Dec. 27, 2007.

## Eleven

RECORDS: "The Oprah Winfrey Show," King World press release, 1987; documents in the case of *Colleen M. Raleigh v. Harpo, Inc. and Oprah Winfrey,* case no. 94L-13511, Circuit Court of Cook County; death certificate, Jeffrey Lee, Wisconsin Department of Health and Family Services; transcript, testimony of Paul Natkin, on Aug. 15, 2000, in the case of *Paul Natkin and Stephen Green v. Oprah Winfrey* et al., case no. 1:99-cv-05367, United States District Court, Northern District of Illinois; transcript, "Headlines That Shocked the Nation: Mexican Satanic Cult Murders," *The Oprah Winfrey Show,* aired May 1, 1989; documents from the files of the Anti-Defamation League of B'nai B'rith, Greater Chicago Regional Office, concerning reaction to *The Oprah Winfrey Show,* May 1, 1989, and the meeting with Jewish leaders, May 9, 1989.

BOOKS: Mark Mathabane, *Kaffir Boy in America* (Free Press, 1990); Jecquin D. Irwin, *My Life After Oprah* (self-published, 2006, Kindle ed.); Paul Natkin and Stephen Green, *To Oprah with Love* (New Millennium Press, 2002); Robert Waldron, *Oprah!* (St. Martin's Press, 1987).

ARTICLES: Joan Barthel, "Here Comes Oprah," *Ms.*, Aug. 1986; Richard Zoglin, "Lady with a Calling," *Time*, Aug. 8, 1988; Cheryl Lavin, "It's All Going Oprah's Way," *Chicago Tribune*, Dec. 19, 1985; Yardena Arar, "Winfrey's Talk Show Makes National Debut," Fort Lauderdale *Sun-Sentinel*, Sept. 8, 1986; John Carmody, "The TV Column," *Washington Post*, Aug. 26, 1986; Mel Novit, "The Women Behind Oprah," *Baltimore Sun*, Mar. 22, 1987; P. J. Bednarski, "All About Oprah Inc.," *Broadcasting and Cable*, June 24, 2005; John Dempsey, "Winfrey Agrees to Produce Her Own Show," *Variety*, Aug. 14, 1988; Marla Donato, "One Last Food Fling with Oprah," *Chicago Tribune*, Feb. 6, 1985; Barbara Grizzuti Harrison, "The Importance of Being Oprah," *New York Times Magazine*, June 11, 1989; Bill Zehme, "It Came from Chicago," *Spy*, Dec. 1986; Marcia Ann Gillespie, "Winfrey Takes All," *Ms.*, Nov. 1988; Lisa DePaulo, "Oprah's Private Life," *TV Guide*, June 3, 1989; "William Rizzo," *Chicago Sun-Times*, Apr. 4, 1990; Bill Zwecker, "United Front Ousted Oprah Aide," *Chicago Sun-Times*, June 29, 1994; Gretchen Reynolds, "The Oprah Myth," *TV Guide*, July 23, 1994; Charles Whitaker, "The Most Talked About TV Show Host," *Ebony*, Mar. 1987; Dana Kennedy, "A New Soap Oprah," *Entertainment Weekly*, Nov. 11, 1994; Nancy F. Koehn and Erica Helms, "Oprah Winfrey," Harvard Business School Publication 9-803-190, May 8, 2003, revised June 1, 2005; Patrick Goldstein, "The Influences on Our Taste," *Los Angeles Times*, Dec. 20, 1987; Larry Finley, "A Look at Liberty," *Chicago Sun-Times*, July 20, 1987; "Whitney Houston: Eight American Music Awards Make Her Top Female Singer," *Jet*, Feb. 28, 1994; Eric Sherman, "Oprah's Wonder Year," *Ladies' Home Journal*, May 1990; Cynthia McGee, "Oprah's Mag Set to Debut," New York *Daily News*, Apr. 10, 2000; "He Sure Looks Like Oprah," *People Weekly*, Apr. 29, 1991; "Oprah Look-Alike Winner a Man, at Least for Now," *Chicago Tribune*, Apr. 13, 1991; Tim Jones, "Attorneys Take Cuts at Editing of 'Oprah' Show," *Chicago Tribune*, Feb. 3, 1998; David Treadwell and Barry Bearak, "20,000 March Against Klan Attack in Georgia," *Los Angeles Times*, Jan. 25, 1987; "Williams Will Picket Oprah Winfrey Show," *Orlando Sentinel*, Feb. 9, 1987; "Oprah's Show on Ga. March Bars Blacks, Protest Called," *Chicago Sun-Times*, Feb. 9, 1987; "Civil Rights Group to Picket Winfrey Episode," *Tennessean*, Feb. 7, 1987; Robert Feder, "White-Hot Georgians Cut Loose on 'Oprah,'" *Chicago Sun-Times*, Feb. 10, 1987; "Vintage Oprah: Racial Tensions in Georgia, Feb. 9, 1987," www.oprah.com, Aug. 31, 2001; Clarence Page, "The Forsyth Saga Comes to TV," *Chicago Tribune*, Feb. 15, 1987; Howard Rosenberg, "Oprah's Sweep Through Georgia," *Los Angeles Times*, Feb. 16, 1987; Robert Feder, "Winfrey to Hit the Road in Talk Show Ratings War,"

*Chicago Sun-Times,* Feb. 5, 1987; Jeff Jarvis, "Top Ten Oprahs," *People Weekly,* Sept. 5, 1988; "Vintage Oprah: AIDS in West Virginia, Nov. 16, 1987," www.oprah.com, July 27, 2001; Lynn Rosellini and Erica E. Goode, "AIDS: When Fear Takes Charge," *US News & World Report,* Oct. 12, 1987; David Friedman, "In Praise of Oprah," *Newsday,* Nov. 25, 1987; Joe Mullins et al., "Oprah's Gay Brother: 'I'm Dying of AIDS,'" *National Enquirer,* Mar. 14, 1989; "Oprah's Christmas Heartbreak as AIDS Kills Kid Brother," *Star,* Jan. 9, 1990; "Oprah's Brother Dies of AIDS," *USA Today,* Jan. 4, 1990; "Memorable Moments," www.oprah.com, Nov. 14, 2005; Liz Smith, "Liz Taylor and Oprah Didn't Hit It Off," *San Francisco Chronicle,* Feb. 12, 1988; Robert Feder, "Oprah Regrets Airing Racial Confrontation," *Chicago Sun-Times,* Feb. 9, 1988; Irv Kupcinet, "Kup's Column," *Chicago Sun-Times,* Feb. 5, 1988; John Carmody, "The TV Column," *Washington Post,* Feb. 5, 1988; Dennis Kneale, "Titillating Channels," *Wall Street Journal,* May 18, 1988; Nan Robertson, "Donahue vs. Winfrey," *New York Times,* Feb. 1, 1988; Howard Rosenberg, "Sweeps Time on TV: All the Swill That's Unfit to Screen," *Los Angeles Times,* Nov. 16, 1988; Jim Bawden, "Oprah Winfrey Steps Away from the Microphone," *Toronto Star,* Mar. 18, 1989; Daniel Golden, "Oprah, Phil, Sally Jessy," *Boston Globe,* July 10, 1988; Myra Mensh Patner, "The Tragic Legacy of a Sexual Deviation," *Washington Post,* May 9, 1989; Richard C. Miller, "Oprah Bombshell—She's Blamed in 2 Bizarre Deaths," *National Enquirer,* Nov. 28, 1999; "Oprah Blasts Critics Who Blame Her Show for Triggering Sex Deaths," *Star,* Jan. 2, 1990; Jerome George and Denny Johnson, "Oprah Show Leaves Guest So Ashamed He Hung Himself," *National Enquirer,* Aug. 21, 1990; "Oprah Crucified My Son," *Star,* Aug. 21, 1990; Janet Langhart, "It's Not All Talk with Oprah," *Boston Herald,* Oct. 18, 1986; Jeremy Gerard, "Winfrey Show Evokes Protests," *New York Times,* May 6, 1989; Steve Dale, "'Letterman' Camera's Capturing City Sights," *Chicago Tribune,* Apr. 28, 1989; Rick Kogan, "Letterman, City Hit It Off," *Chicago Tribune,* May 8, 1989; Jason Gay, "Dave at Peace," *Rolling Stone,* Feb. 18, 2008; Irv Kupcinet, "Kup's Column," *Chicago Sun-Times,* May 9, 1989; Andrew Duncan, "Grand Oprah," London *Sunday Express,* Dec. 10, 1989; Jeremy Gerard, "TV Notes," *New York Times,* May 15, 1989; Neil Steinberg, "City's Elite Remember Marovitz as True Friend," *Chicago Sun-Times,* Apr. 4, 2001; Ann Gerber, "Sondra Wants a Fistful of Clint's Dollars," *Chicago Sun-Times,* May 14, 1989; Barbara Sternig and Jim Nelson, "Oprah's Shameful Secret Past—the Sister Who Saw It All," *National Enquirer,* Mar. 27, 1990; Ann Gerber, "Animal Rights Folks Bark Up Wrong Tree," *Chicago Sun-Times,* May 17, 1990; Kathy O'Malley and Hanke Gratteau, "O'Malley and Gratteau INC.," *Chicago Tribune,* May 19, 1989; Jesse Walker, *"Sun-Times* Fires Columnist on Oprah Rumors," *New York Amsterdam News,* June 10, 1989; Mike Royko, "Gossip's Credibility Is Only a Bad Rumor," Mike Royko, *Chicago Tribune,* May 22, 2009; "Gerber's Column Is Discontinued," *Chicago Sun-Times,* May 24, 1989; Delores Brooks, "The Phenomenal Oprah Winfrey," *Dollars and Sense* (date unknown).

DVD: *The Oprah Winfrey Show 20th Anniversary Collection* (DVD set).

INTERVIEWS: Confidential source, Mar. 3, 2009, and Apr. 24, 2009; confidential source, June 8, 2007; Robert Waldron, Sept. 4, 2008; confidential source, Apr. 24, 2009; **Jo Baldwin, July 14, 2010, and correspondence with Jo Baldwin, July 15, 16, 20, and 27, Aug. 17, and Sept. 14, 2010;** Andy Behrman, Aug. 24, 2007, Sept. 8, 2007, Sept. 24, 2007, Feb. 5, 2008, and correspondence with Andy Behrman, Mar. 15, 2009; Katharine Carr Esters, Oct. 4, 2007; Jewette Battles, July 28, 2008; Fran Johns, Sept. 2007; Michael Brooks, Sept. 20, 2007; Blair Sabol, July 28, 2007; Paxton Quigley, Mar. 12, 2008; Eileen Solomon, Mar. 28, 2007; Peggy Furth, Mar. 16, 1007; Suzy Prudden, Feb. 5, 2008; confidential source, Oct. 31, 2007; correspondence with Kevin McShane, Mar. 13, 2009; Margo Howard, Jan. 23, 2008, and July 25, 2008, and correspondence with Margo Howard, Mar. 31, 2009; confidential source, Sept. 7, 2007; Sugar Rautbord, June 19, 2008; Myrna Blyth, May 29, 2007, and correspondence with Myrna Blyth, Mar. 27, 2009; Roger Hitts, Apr. 14, 2008; correspondence with Peter Cherukuri, May 4, 2007; Dr. Harvey Resnik, July 20, 2007, and Apr. 6, 2009; Robert Holm, Mar. 27, 2009; Bill Zwecker, Oct. 11, 2007, and June 25, 2008; Ann Gerber, June 24, 2008; Wayne Kabak, Apr. 25, 2007.

## TWELVE

RECORDS: IRS forms 990 for Oprah's Angel Network, 2002–2007, EIN 36-4231488; IRS forms 990 for Angel Network Support Foundation, 2002–2004, EIN 74-2962189; IRS forms 990-PF for The Oprah Winfrey Foundation, 2001–2007, and For A Better Life Foundation, 1998–2000, EIN 36-3976230; Illinois Secretary of State Corporation File Detail Reports for Harpo Productions, Inc., File no. 55194122, Harpo, Inc., File no. 54254253; Harpo Films, Inc., File no. 55895309, Harpo Video, Inc., File no. 59052705, Harpo Studios, Inc., File no. 55281467, and Studio Merchandise, Inc., File no. 5738876; documents in the case of *Lerato Numvuyo Mzamane v. Oprah Winfrey* et al., case no. 2:08-CV-4884 (BWK), U.S. District Court, Eastern District of Pennsylvania; documents in the case of *Dr. Mehmet Oz* et al. *v. FWM Labratories, Inc.,* et al., case no. 1:09-CV-07297-DAB, U.S. District Court, Southern District of New York; State of Delaware Division of Corporations, Entity Details for Harpo Print LLC, File no. 3052257, and Harpo Radio, Inc., File no. 4097492; *Oprah Make the Connection,* Buena Vista Home Video and Harpo Productions Press Release, Sept. 11, 1997.

BOOKS: George Mair, *Oprah Winfrey: The Real Story* (Birch Lane Press, 1994); Robert Waldron, *Oprah!* (St. Martin's Press, 1987).

ARTICLES: Matt Roush, "Return to Brewster," *USA Today,* May 1, 1990; Barbara Grizzuti Harrison, "The Importance of Being Oprah," *New York Times Magazine,* June 11, 1989; Janet Langhart, "It's Not All Talk with Oprah," *Boston Herald,* Oct. 18, 1986; Marty Daniels, "Oprah the Collector," *Chicago Tribune,* Sept. 30, 1990; Marge Colburn, "With Clients Like Oprah, This Designer's Favorite Color Is Green," *Detroit News,* Feb. 22, 1992; Linda Gross, "Oprah Winfrey, Wonder Woman," *Ladies' Home Journal,* Dec. 1988; Mary Ann Bendel, "Oprah Winfrey," *Ladies' Home Journal,* Mar. 1988; Mark Caro, "The Mogul Shows Off Her Studio, Her 'Control,' " *Chicago Tribune,* Mar. 18, 1990; Chris Anderson, "Meet Oprah Winfrey," *Good Housekeeping,* Aug. 1986; transcript, *Larry King Live,* Sept. 4, 2001, www.transcripts.cnn.com; Irv Kupcinet, "Kup's Column," *Chicago Sun-Times,* Feb. 7, 1986; Julie Salamon, "On Film: Richard Wright Minus the Rage," *Wall Street Journal,* Jan. 8, 1987; Hal Ericson, All Movie Guide, www.allmovie.com (undated); Vincent Canby, "Screen: 'Native Son,' Based on Wright's Novel," *New York Times,* Dec. 24, 1986; Richard Zoglin, "Lady with a Calling," *Time,* Aug. 8, 1988; Rick Kogan, " 'Brewster' Is One of Many Stories Oprah Has to Tell," *Chicago Tribune,* Mar. 19, 1989; "Oprah Winfrey Plans Production Company," *Atlanta Daily World,* Feb. 15, 1987; Pat Colander, "Oprah Winfrey's Odyssey: Talk Show Host to Mogul," *New York Times,* Mar. 12, 1989; James Warren, "King World Sounds Confident of Keeping 'Ambitious' Oprah," *Chicago Tribune,* Dec. 14, 1989; "Winfrey Options 'Beloved' Rights," *Hollywood Reporter,* Jan. 12, 1988; Pearl Cleage, "The Courage to Dream," *Essence,* Dec. 1998; Steven R. Strahler, "Oprah Buys Studio in Chicago," *Electronic Media,* Sept. 26, 1988; "Oprah's Show Is Honored by British Academy as Best Foreign TV Program," *Jet,* Mar. 2, 1994; Timothy McDarrah, "Talk's Not Cheap," *New York Post,* Jan. 1, 1987; Lloyd Shearer, "Oprah Winfrey—How Rich?" *Parade,* Feb. 15, 1987; "Rich Get Richer," *Chicago Tribune,* Sept. 17, 1989; Calvin Trillin, "Half an Oaf," *New York Times,* Apr. 12, 2009; Marla Hart, "Chicago Is No. 1 When It Comes to Talk Show Audiences," *Chicago Tribune,* Apr. 18, 1993; Jennifer Shaw, "Oprah Strikes Gold," *New York Post,* Aug. 2, 1988; Mel Tapley,

"Oprah Signs $500M 5-Year Contract," *New York Amsterdam News,*
Aug. 6, 1988; Matt Roush, "Oprah Gains More Than Money in New
Contract," *USA Today,* Aug. 4, 1988; Robert Feder, "A Slimmer Oprah
Feasts on the Glory of Her Rich TV Deal," *Chicago Sun-Times,* Aug. 22,
1988; Daniel Ruth, "Has the New Winfrey Diet Made Oprah Light-
Headed?" *Chicago Sun-Times,* Sept. 1, 1988; Lois McAloon, "The Birth of
the West Side," *Chicago Sun-Times,* Jan. 2, 1998; Ann Marie Lipinski,
"Oprah Winfrey Buying West Side TV Studios," *Chicago Tribune,*
Sept. 18, 1988; Marcia Ann Gillespie, "Winfrey Takes All," *Ms.,* Nov.
1988; Robert Feder, "Oprah Buys Studio on W. Side," *Chicago Sun-
Times,* Sept. 17, 1988; Delores Brooks, "The Phenomenal Oprah Winfrey,"
*Dollars and Sense* (date unknown); Robert Feder, "Five More Reasons You
Just Gotta Love Outrageous Oprah," *Chicago Sun-Times,* Dec. 1, 1987;
Robert Feder, "America's TV Reporters Get Their Minutes with Oprah,"
*Chicago Sun-Times,* Mar. 15, 1990; Shelly Levitt, "Flush Femmes," *People
Weekly,* Aug. 30, 1993; "About Harpo," www.oprah.com, June 7, 2006;
"Jeffrey Jacobs," www.luc.edu, Jan. 19, 2007; "Harpo Films Feature Films
and TV Movies," www.oprah .com, July 1, 2008; Stephen Galloway,
"Winfrey Leads with a Mighty Heart," *Hollywood Reporter,* Nov. 26, 2007;
Jerry C. Davis, "Winfrey's Studio Should Invigorate Near West Side,"
*Chicago Sun-Times,* July 30, 1990; Bob Goldsborough, "Oprah's Empire,"
*Chicago Tribune,* Dec. 11, 2006; Marcia Froelke Coburn, "Oprah Un-
bound," *Chicago,* Dec. 2008; "Dogs Are Children, Too," *People Weekly,*
May 23, 2005; Nancy Mills, "Hard Times, Brave Women Reside on
'Brewster Place,'" *Los Angeles Times,* Jan. 27, 1989; "Oprah Goes Holly-
wood," *People Weekly,* June 13, 1988; Solomon Herbert, "The Women of
Brewster Place," *Essence,* Nov. 1988; Michael Hill, "Oprah Feels Fame Has
Given Her Responsibilities," *Baltimore Evening Sun,* Jan. 16, 1989; "The
Women of Brewster Place," *Ebony,* Mar. 1989; Michele Kort, "Lights,
Camera, Affirmative Action," *Ms.,* Nov. 1988; Bill Carter, "Oprah Dons
Actress, Producer Hat, Promotes ABC Miniseries," *Baltimore Sun,* Jan. 16,
1989; Mary Gillespie, "The Women of Brewster Place," *Chicago Sun-
Times,* Mar. 12, 1989; Robert Feder, "Ch. 5 Wants to Take Joan Esposito
from Ch. 7 News," *Chicago Sun-Times,* Mar. 22, 1989; "Oprah Beats 'The
Wiz,'" New York *Daily News,* Mar. 21, 1989; Daniel Ruth, "Despite Its
Sexism, 'Brewster Place' Tells Poignant Tale," *Chicago Sun-Times,* Mar. 17,
1989; Robert Feder, "ABC Pleases Oprah with 'Brewster' Slot," *Chicago
Sun-Times,* Apr. 17, 1990; John Martin, "A Palace for Talk Show Queen,"
*Providence Journal,* Mar. 15, 1990; Bill Brashler, "Next on Oprah . . . ,"
*Ladies' Home Journal,* Aug. 1991; Pearl Cleage, "Walking in the Light,"
*Essence,* June 1991; Barbara Grizzuti Harrison, "The Importance of

Being Oprah," *New York Times Magazine,* June 11, 1989; Tim Appelo and Frank Spotnitz, "Love Prophet," *Entertainment Weekly,* Mar. 6, 1992; Gretchen Reynolds, "Oprah Unbound," *Chicago,* Nov. 1993; Elizabeth Payne, "The Word According to Winfrey," *Ottawa Citizen,* June 24, 2000; "Joy," *O, The Oprah Magazine,* May 2001; "Oprah Hosts Live Your Best Life Tour 2003," *Business Wire,* Mar. 18, 2003.

TV/DVD: Oprah Winfrey interviewed by Fred Griffith, *The Morning Exchange,* fifteenth anniversary, WEWS-TV, aired Jan. 1987; *The Barbara Walters Special,* ABC, aired Apr. 11, 1988 (viewed at The Paley Center for Media, New York); *The Oprah Winfrey Show 20th Anniversary Collection* (DVD set); "A Special Presentation: Oprah and Elie Wiesel at the Auschwitz Death Camp," *The Oprah Winfrey Show,* aired May 24, 2006.

INTERVIEWS: Cheryl Reed, Oct. 11, 2007; confidential source, Apr. 15, 2009; confidential source, Nov. 9, 2007; Blair Sabol, July 28, 2007; confidential source, Jan. 28, 2008; confidential source, Mar. 13, 2009, and Apr. 24, 2009; correspondence with Daniel Ruth, Apr. 13, 2009.

REAL ESTATE HOLDINGS: In addition to her Harpo properties cited in this chapter, Oprah also owns real estate in:

- *California:* Oprah purchased her forty-two-acre estate in Montecito in July 2001 through The Promised Land LLC for a reported $50 million. The *Santa Barbara News-Press* (5/10/2006) estimated that improvements to the property raised its value to $64.2 million.
- *Connecticut:* Oprah's Overground Railroad LLC bought Gayle King's house at 37 Richmond Road, Greenwich, in 2000 for $3.6 million. The assessed value in 2008 was $4.8 million. In 2009 the house went on the market for $7.45 million, and later the price was dropped to $6.95 million.
- *Georgia:* Oprah's Overground Railroad LLC bought a five-bedroom house in Douglasville, in 2005 for $825,000. She had purchased a penthouse condo for Coretta Scott King in Atlanta's Buckhead area for $1,515,000 in 2003. After Mrs. King's death, Oprah sold the property for $1,800,000 in 2008.
- *Hawaii:* Oprah's Yellow Brick Road LLC, Kingdom Come LLC, and O.W. Ranch LLC paid a total of approximately $23 million in 2002 and 2003 for properties on the island of Maui, including a vacation home in Hana and a twelve-bedroom vacation rental in Kula.
- *Illinois:* Her Chicago residence consists of three condominiums in the Water Tower, 180 E. Pearson Street, purchased through Restoration LLC. According to Cook County assessment documents of 2008, the market value is between $2.7 million and $3.5 million.

Oprah's Overground Railroad LLC also purchased a house in the Chicago suburb of Elmwood Park in 2001 for $298,000.

- *Indiana:* Oprah's Overground Railroad LLC purchased a house at 5585 Jackson Street, Merrillville, appraised at $133,500. The occupant is Joni Jacques, the woman who appeared on *The Oprah Winfrey Show* in 1997 after buying a pair of Oprah's shoes that were too big for her, saying it gave her hope just to stand in them.
- *New York:* Oprah bought Penthouse 36 at 270 East Fifty-seventh Street, New York City, through Sophie's Penthouse LLC in 2008 for $7.1 million.
- *Tennessee:* The Oprah Winfrey Trust bought Vernon Winfrey a home in Franklin, in 2000, including an empty lot next door, for $1.5 million. Overground Railroad purchased a house at 9219 Sawyer Brown Road, Nashville, for $191,500 for Calvin and Roslind Eddins, whom Oprah calls her godparents.
- *Wisconsin:* Oprah bought her mother, Vernita Lee, a condo in Milwaukee, at 1522 N. Prospect Avenue, through Overground Railroad LLC. In 2004, the condo was valued at $450,600.

## Thirteen

RECORDS: Transcript, testimony of Paul Natkin, on Aug. 15, 2000, in the case of *Paul Natkin and Stephen Green v. Oprah Winfrey* et al., case no. 1:99-cv-05367, United States District Court, Northern District of Illinois; death certificate, Patricia Lloyd, Wisconsin Department of Health and Family Services.

BOOKS: Robert Waldron, *Oprah!* (St. Martin's Press, 1987); Bob Greene and Oprah Winfrey, *Make the Connection* (Hyperion, 1996); Bill Adler, ed., *The Uncommon Wisdom of Oprah Winfrey* (Citadel Press, 1997).

ARTICLES: John Stratford, "Sex: The Three-Letter Word That Kept Oprah on Her Diet," *Star,* Nov. 22, 1988; Judy Markey, "Opinionated Oprah!" *Woman's Day,* Oct. 4, 1988; "Is That You, Oprah?" *Tennessean,* Nov. 16, 1988; Irene Sax, "The Once Fat Lady Sings," *Newsday,* Nov. 16, 1988; Oprah Winfrey, "The Wind Beneath My Wings," *Essence,* June 1989; "Oprah to Wait, Relate Weight's Fate," *Nashville Banner,* Nov. 16, 1988; Robin Abcarian, "Oh-Oh Oprah, Let's Get a Little Perspective," *Chicago Tribune,* Dec. 7, 1988; Janet Sutter, "Oprah Pulls a Fast One, Tells How," *San Diego Union,* Nov. 16, 1988; Bob Kerr, "Oprah Unveils Herself Free of Former Fat," *Providence Journal,* Nov. 16, 1988; Dan Sperling and Lorrie Lynch, "Oprah's Diet Rings Up Calls," *USA Today,* Nov. 17, 1988; Clarissa Cruz, "Worth the Weight," *Entertainment Weekly,* Nov. 17,

2000; "Big Gain, No Pain," *People Weekly*, Jan. 14, 1991; Betsy A. Lehman, "Oprah Winfrey Shed Pounds but Fed a Weight-Loss Myth," *Boston Globe*, Nov. 28, 1988; "Winfrey Wants Kids," *Baltimore Evening Sun*, June 2, 1989; "An Oprah Show with Her Beau," *USA Today*, Jan. 26, 1989; John Carmody, "The TV Column," *Washington Post*, Nov. 17, 1988; Pat Colander, "Oprah Winfrey's Odyssey: Talk Show Host to Mogul," *New York Times*, Mar. 12, 1989; "Shedding Pounds with Liquids," *San Francisco Chronicle*, Feb. 15, 1989; Lorenzo Benet, "Sure Oprah Slimmed Down Fast, but Liquid Diets Aren't Right for Everyone," *Los Angeles Daily News*, Dec. 28, 1988; Stephanie Young, "Liquid Diets," *Glamour*, Apr. 1989; Marcia Ann Gillespie, "Winfrey Takes All," *Ms.*, Nov. 1988; Princess Simmons, "Oprah Loses Weight but Causes Concern," *Tennessean*, Dec. 1, 1988; "New Woman," *Boston Herald*, Dec. 19, 1988; Allan Johnson, "Oprah, Watch Out," *Chicago Tribune*, May 12, 1989; "Phlabe Phobia," *New York Post*, Nov. 12, 1988; Liz Smith, "Ackroyd Advises Bush on B-1," *San Francisco Chronicle*, Dec. 14, 1988; Karen G. Jackovich, "Take One," *People Weekly*, Dec. 12, 1988; Irv Kupcinet, "Kup's Column," *Chicago Sun-Times*, Nov. 14, 1989; "Conventional Wisdom Watch," *Newsweek*, Apr. 2, 1990; "Oprah! The Richest Woman on TV? How She Amassed Her $250 Million Fortune," cover, *TV Guide*, Aug. 26–Sept. 1, 1989; Mark Shwed, "Where's the Rest of Me?" *Los Angeles Herald Examiner*, Aug. 29, 1989; Leslie Marshall, "The Intentional Oprah," *InStyle*, Nov. 1998; "Oprah Splurges $10G in 2 Hours on Oversize Outfits," *Star*, July 16, 1991; "Ask the Insider," *Star*, Nov. 21, 1989; Ann Trebbe and Linda Stahl, "Despite Gains, Oprah Won't End Flab Fight," *USA Today*, Nov. 16, 1989; Monica Collins, " 'Real' Is Oprah's Appeal," *Boston Herald*, Nov. 21, 1989; Richard Phillips, "Oprah's Optifade," *Chicago Tribune*, Nov. 16, 1989; Irv Kupcinet, "Kup's Column," *Chicago Sun-Times*, Nov. 7, 1990; Robert Feder, " 'If You Believe,' Oprah Can Help," *Chicago Sun-Times*, Sept. 29, 1997; "Oprah Proves It's Not Funny When You're Fat," *National Enquirer*, Mar. 8, 1994; Catherine McEvily Harris, "Ultimate Success Story," *Shape*, Dec. 1996; Audrey Edwards, "Stealing the Show," *Essence*, Oct. 1986; Charles Whitaker, "The Most Talked About TV Show Host," *Ebony*, Mar. 1987; Julia Lawlor, "The Other Oprah," *USA Weekend*, June 2–4, 1989; Abiola Sinclair, "The New Women of Brewster Place," *New York Amsterdam News*, May 12, 1990; Norma Langly, "Oprah: I've Done It," *Star*, Nov. 6, 1988; Luchina Fisher et al., "In Full Stride," *People Weekly*, Sept. 14, 1994; Jim Nelson and Barbara Sternig, "Talk Show Star's Wild and Wicked Childhood—Sister Reveals the Shocking Truth at Last," *National Enquirer*, Mar. 20, 1990; Joe Mullins and Brian Williams, "Oprah Saves Cocaine Addicted Sister,"

*National Enquirer,* Dec. 12, 1989; Oprah Winfrey, "What I Know for Sure," *O, The Oprah Magazine,* Feb. 2007; Honie Stevens, "From Rags to Riches," *Saga,* May 2002; Nancy Griffin, "Oprah (Lite)," *Us,* Mar. 20, 1989; Barbara Sternig and Jim Nelson, "Oprah's Shameful Secret Past—the Sister Who Saw It All," *National Enquirer,* Mar. 27, 1990; Jacquelyn Mitchard, "Maybe We Know Now What Makes Oprah Run," *Milwaukee Journal,* May 20, 1990; "Walter Scott's Personality Parade," *Parade,* May 6, 1990; Karen Ridgeway, "Winfrey Says She Had a Baby at 14," *USA Today,* May 4, 1990; Peter Kent, "How I Blew Oprah's $1M and Lost Her Love Forever," *Globe,* Oct. 28, 1997; Ian Woodward, "The World of Oprah," *OK!,* June 29, 1994; Laura B. Randolph, "Oprah Opens Up About Her Weight, Her Wedding, and Why She Withheld the Book," *Ebony,* Oct. 1993; "Oprah Gave Me $1 Million and I Blew It," *Now,* Nov. 20, 1997; Andrew Duncan, "The Andrew Duncan Interview," *Radio Times,* Feb. 27–Mar. 5, 1999; Jacqueline Siebel, "Overdose Killed Winfrey's Half Sister," *Milwaukee Journal Sentinel,* Sept. 25, 2003; Chrissy Iley, "The Power of Oprah," *Daily Mail,* Oct. 14, 1989; Dana Skrebneski, "Oprah Act Two," *Entertainment Weekly,* Sept. 9, 1994; Tom Shales, "Talk Is Cheap," *Washington Post,* Nov. 18, 1988; Erma Bombeck, "Digging Up the Deviants," *Chicago Sun-Times,* Jan. 23, 1991; Diana Maychick, "Oprah, Inc.," *New York Post,* Oct. 30, 1989; Andrew Duncan, "Grand Oprah," London *Sunday Express,* Dec. 10, 1989; Martha Bayles, "Oprah vs. Phil," *Wall Street Journal,* Jan. 26, 1987; Paige Albiniak, "Syndication Ratings: Pregnant Man Sends Oprah Back to the Stratosphere," *Broadcasting and Cable,* Apr. 15, 2008; David Rensin, "The Prime Time of Ms. Oprah Winfrey," *TV Guide,* May 16, 1992; Katherine Seigenthaler, "Oprah, Judges Aim at Drunk Drivers," *Chicago Tribune,* Dec. 13, 1989; "Dot's All," New York *Daily News,* Oct. 5, 1989; Trudy S. Moore, "How 'The Oprah Winfrey Show' Helps People Live Better Lives," *Jet,* Apr. 18, 1994; "Memorable Guests Followup," www.oprah.com, May 2, 2007; Janice Peck, "Talk About Racism," *Cultural Critique,* Spring 1994; Howard Rosenberg, "It's Time for More Heart, Less Heat on TV," *Los Angeles Times,* May 6, 1992; Richard Corliss, "Peter Pan Speaks," *Time,* Feb. 22, 1993; Tom Shales, "A Night in Neverland with the President and the King of Pop," *Washington Post,* Feb. 11, 1993; transcript, "Michael Jackson Talks to Oprah," www.allmichaeljackson.com; John Carmody, "The TV Column," *Washington Post,* Feb. 12, 1993.

TV/DVDS: *The Oprah Winfrey Show 20th Anniversary Collection* (DVD set); "Oprah on Eating," *In Living Color,* Fox, aired 1990 (viewed at www.blackbottom.com).

INTERVIEWS: Candy Miles Cocker, Apr. 20, 2007; James van Sweden, Dec. 12, 2007, and Dec. 27, 2007; Bob Jones, May 2, 2007.

## Fourteen

RECORDS: State of Connecticut Judicial Branch, *Gayle King Bumpus v. William G. Bumpus,* docket no. HHD-FA-92-0518354-S; documents in the case of *Colleen M. Raleigh v. Harpo, Inc., and Oprah Winfrey,* case no. 94L-13511, Circuit Court of Cook County; decision in the case of *Elizabeth Coady v. Harpo, Inc.,* case no. 1-99-0481, 1st District, Illinois Appellate Court; documents in the case of *Lerato Numvuyo Mzamane v. Oprah Winfrey* et al., case no. 2:08-CV-4884 (BWK), U.S. District Court, Eastern District of Pennsylvania.

BOOKS: Henry Louis Gates, Jr., *Finding Oprah's Roots* (Crown Publishers, 2007); Eva Illouz, *Oprah Winfrey and the Glamour of Misery* (Columbia University Press, 2003); Vicki and Leonard Mustazza, *Coming After Oprah: Cultural Fallout in the Age of the TV Talk Show* (Bowling Green State University Popular Press, 1997).

ARTICLES: Paul D. Colford, "American Booksellers Convention," *Newsday,* June 1, 1993; Tim Warren, "By the Book?" *Baltimore Sun,* May 31, 1993; Jocelyn McClurg, "Booksellers Sold on Oprah Winfrey's Story," *Hartford Courant,* June 1, 1993; Deidre Donahue, "Oprah's Life to Be Open Book," *USA Today,* June 2, 1993; David Streitfeld, "Oprah Pulls Bio from Publication," *Washington Post,* May 16, 1993; "Why Oprah's Banning Her Sexy Tell-All Book," *Star,* July 6, 1993; Paul D. Colford, "Book Pull-out a Case of Cold Feet," *Newsday,* June 24, 1993; "Backing Off from the Book," *People Weekly,* July 5, 1993; John Blades, "They're Celebrities of Few Words," *Chicago Tribune,* June 25, 1993; Laura B. Randolph, "Oprah Opens Up About Her Weight, Her Wedding, and Why She Withheld the Book," *Ebony,* Oct. 1993; Robert Feder, "Oprah Wanted Book to Be More Than 'Recitation,'" *Chicago Sun-Times,* June 18, 1993; "Rumors Still Swirl as Oprah Remains Silent," *Los Angeles Sentinel,* June 24, 1993; Deidre Donahue and Ann Trebbe, "Oprah's Book Delay Leaves World Guessing," *USA Today,* June 17, 1993; Sarah Lyall, "Book Notes," *New York Times,* June 9, 1993; transcript, *Larry King Live,* Sept. 4, 2001, www.transcripts.cnn.com; Sarah Lyall, "More Lessons to Learn Before Oprah Tells All," *New York Times,* June 16, 1993; Karen Freifeld, "Oprah Pulls Plug on Autobiography," *Newsday,* June 17, 1993; Linda Kramer, "Marathon Woman," *People Weekly,* Nov. 7, 1994; Gretchen Reynolds, "Oprah Unbound," *Chicago,* Nov. 1993; Jill Brook Coiner, "Oprah Sets the Record Straight," *McCall's,* Nov. 1993; Miriam Kanner,

"Oprah at 40," *Ladies' Home Journal,* Feb. 1994; Jonathan Van Meter, "Oprah's Moment," *Vogue,* Oct. 1998; Chrissy Iley, "The Power of Oprah," *Daily Mail,* Oct. 14, 1989; Maya Jaggi, "The Power of One," *Guardian Weekend,* Feb. 11, 1999; Ian Woodward, "The World of Oprah," *OK!,* June 29, 1994; Dana Kennedy, "Oprah Act Two," *Entertainment Weekly,* Sept. 9, 1994; Ginny Dougary, "Soul Queen," London *Times Magazine,* Mar. 4, 1995; Academy of Achievement, "Oprah Winfrey Interview," Feb. 21, 1991, www.achievement.org; Richard Zoglin, "Lady with a Calling," *Time,* Aug. 8, 1988; Jeff Jarvis, "Top Ten Oprahs," *People Weekly,* Sept. 5, 1988; Robert Feder, "Oprah Opens Road Show in Search of Big Ratings," *Chicago Sun-Times,* Oct. 29, 1987; "Oprah Off-Broadway, *Chicago Reader,* Nov. 1, 1991; Jeff Strickler, "How Success Changes Attitudes Irks Actress," Minneapolis *StarTribune,* Apr. 25, 1986; Judy Markey, "Brassy, Sassy Oprah Winfrey," *Cosmopolitan,* Sept. 1986; William Sullivan, "Div Grad Bares All in Callgirl Biography," *Yale Daily News,* Sept. 3, 2004; "Oprah Glad She Booked from Autobiography," *New York Post,* Dec. 26, 1997; Steven Pratt, "Oprah's Favorites," *Chicago Tribune,* Apr. 21, 1994; Janet Kidd Stewart, "Oh, Rosie," *Chicago Sun-Times,* May 9, 1994; Daisy Maryles, "Behind the Bestsellers," *Publishers Weekly,* May 15, 1995; "Ready for Prime Time," *People Weekly,* Feb. 14, 1994; Gayle King, "What I Learned from Dad," *Good Housekeeping,* June 2005; Aaron Barnhart, "KCTV Goes to Hartford for New Anchor," www.blogs.kansascity.com/tvbarn, Mar. 24, 2001; Samantha Miller, "Gayle Force," *People Weekly,* Feb. 23, 1998; Lisa Kogan, "Oprah and Gayle Uncensored," *O, The Oprah Magazine,* Aug. 2006; George Rush and Joanna Molloy, "Gayle Airs Her Story: Ex-Hubby a 'Cheater,'" New York *Daily News,* Nov. 14, 2006; "Oprah Winfrey Tribute: Gayle King," *TelevisionWeek,* Apr. 19, 2004; Ed Susman and Jeffrey Rodack, "Oprah Wrecks Best Friend's Marriage," *National Enquirer,* Dec. 29, 1992; Jim Calio, "If You Knew Oprah Like I Know Oprah . . . ," *Redbook,* Feb. 1998; Bill Zwecker, "Oprah's Hitting 40 with Flair," *Chicago Sun-Times,* Jan. 26, 1994; "40th Birthday Slumber Party," *Star,* Feb. 15, 1994; Eric Munoz et al., "Wow! Super-Sexy Oprah Turns 40," *National Enquirer,* Feb. 15, 1994; "Are You There, God? It's Me, Oprah," *Esquire,* Apr. 1994; Martin Townsend, "Oprah Winfrey," *Sunday Mail,* July 2, 1995; Gretchen Reynolds, "A Year to Remember: Oprah Grows Up," *TV Guide,* Jan. 7, 1995; Oprah Winfrey, "What We Can All Do to Change TV," *TV Guide,* Nov. 11, 1995; Howard Kurtz, "Morality Guru Takes on Talk TV," *Washington Post,* Oct. 26, 1995; Joshua Green, "The Bookie of Virtue," *Washington Monthly,* June 2003; Jim Kirk, "Putting Talk Shows on Notice," *Chicago Sun-Times,* Nov. 15, 1995; Jae-Ha Kim, "Behind the

Scenes at 'Oprah,' " *Chicago Sun-Times*, Dec. 4, 1994; "Rack Race," July 4, 1994; Dana Kennedy, "A New Soap Oprah," *Entertainment Weekly*, Nov. 11, 1994; Gretchen Reynolds, "The Oprah Myth," *TV Guide*, July 23, 1994; Robert Feder, "Oprah's Ex-Producer Lands NBC Online Gig," *Chicago Sun-Times*, May 2, 2000; Bill Zwecker, "United Front Ousted Oprah Aide," *Chicago Sun-Times*, June 29, 1994; "Oprah Wins Two Emmys," *Chicago Tribune*, May 20, 1995; "Oprah's Secretary Quits," *National Enquirer*, Sept. 20, 1994; Mike Kerrigan, "Oprah Studio 'Big Happy Family' Is a Sham," *Globe*, Nov. 15, 1994; Robert Feder, "Publicist Claims Oprah in 'Chaos,'" *Chicago Sun-Times*, Oct. 26, 1994; Irv Kupcinet, "Kup's Column," *Chicago Sun-Times*, Oct. 30, 1994; Ellen Warren and Terry Armour, "Oh, No: Oprah Faces Tribulation of Another Trial," *Chicago Tribune*, Apr. 20, 2000; Susan Crabtree, "Trash TV Pulls America Down the Tubes," *Insight*, Dec. 4, 1995; Dan Santow, "Christmas at Oprah's," *Redbook*, Dec. 1994.

TV/DVDS: "Living a Secret Life," *Oprah After the Show*, Oxygen, aired Sept. 21, 2004 (viewed at www.oprah.com); *The Oprah Winfrey Show 20th Anniversary Collection* (DVD set).

INTERVIEWS: Confidential source, Nov. 9, 2007; confidential source, May 24, 2007; correspondence with Jeanette Angell, May 3, 2007; correspondence with Gloria Steinem, Nov. 29, 2007; Nancy Stoddart, July 8, 2009; confidential source, June 8, 2007; Andy Behrman, Aug. 24, 2007; confidential source, Jan. 2, 2008; confidential source, Nov. 28, 2007; Patty O'Toole, Nov. 20, 2008; confidential source, June 24, 2008; correspondence with Adam Shapiro, Mar. 6, 2009; Dianne Laughlin, Aug. 7, 2007; confidential source, Sept. 7, 2007.

## Fifteen

RECORDS: Documents in the case of *Paul Natkin and Stephen Green v. Oprah Winfrey* et al., case no. 1:99-cv-05367, United States District Court, Northern District of Illinois; "Oprah: Make the Connection," Buena Vista Home Video and Harpo Productions press release, Sept. 11, 1997; "Oprah's Book Club Fact Sheet," *The Oprah Winfrey Show* press release, Sept. 1999; transcript, "The Man Who Kept Oprah Awake at Night," *The Oprah Winfrey Show*, Oct. 26, 2005; transcript, "James Frey and the *A Million Little Pieces* Controversy," *The Oprah Winfrey Show*, Jan. 26, 2006.

BOOKS: Neil Steinberg, *The Alphabet of Modern Annoyances* (Doubleday, 1996); Cecilia Konchar Farr, *Reading Oprah* (SUNY Press, 2005); Bob Greene and Oprah Winfrey, *Make the Connection* (Hyperion, 1996);

Kathleen Rooney, *Reading with Oprah,* Second Edition (University of Arkansas Press, 2008); Eva Illouz, *Oprah Winfrey and the Glamour of Misery* (Columbia University Press, 2003); James Frey, *A Million Little Pieces* (Anchor, 2004).

ARTICLES: Kevin Williams, "Oprah Steps out of the Gutter," *Chicago Sun-Times,* Nov. 8, 1995; Julie A. Johnson, "Oprah Captures the Prize in '96," *Advertising Age,* Jan. 13, 1997; Eric Zorn, "Trying to Keep Up with O.J.?" *Chicago Tribune,* Oct. 12, 1995; Steve Johnson, "Ratings Slide, Winfrey's Happy She Took the High Road," *Chicago Tribune,* May 1, 1995; Robert Feder, "Oprah Still Reigning as Talk-Show Queen," *Chicago Sun-Times,* July 3, 1995; John J. O'Connor, "Yes, More on the Trial That Won't Go Away," *New York Times,* June 12, 1996; Daryl Fears, "Black Opinion on Simpson Shifts," *Washington Post,* Sept. 27, 2007; Ruth Ann Leach, "Oprah Told the Truth About How Many Blacks Feel About Whites," *Nashville Banner,* Oct. 5, 1995; "Oprah: I'll Help You Fight Back," *Now,* Oct. 24, 1996; Laura B. Randolph, "Oprah!" *Ebony,* July 1995; John Carmody, "The TV Column," *Washington Post,* Feb. 14, 1997; Chinta Strausberg, "Pincher Rips Oprah for Having Fuhrman on Show," *Chicago Defender,* Feb. 13, 1997; Ed Fishbein, "Fuhrman Scores First," *Sacramento Bee,* Feb. 26, 1997; Robert Feder, "Cynics' Shots at Oprah 'Come with the Territory,'" *Chicago Sun-Times,* Sept. 30, 1997; Richard Roeper, "New Age Oprah Forgets Those Tacky Old Shows," *Chicago Sun-Times,* Oct. 1, 1997; Robert Feder, "Oprah Does an About-Face on Program About Race," *Chicago Sun-Times,* Oct. 21, 1997; Sidney Blumenthal, "Base Instincts," www.Salon.com, Nov. 23, 2006; Neely Tucker, "Throwing the Book at O. J. Simpson," *Washington Post,* Sept. 13, 2007; "Goldmans Discuss O.J. Book on Oprah," *San Francisco Chronicle,* Sept. 13, 2007; **"Oprah Talks to You,"** *O, The Oprah Magazine,* **May 2010;** Lynette Clemetson, "Oprah on Oprah," *Newsweek,* Jan. 8, 2001; D. T. Max, "The Oprah Effect," *New York Times Magazine,* Dec. 26, 1999; Annette Chavez, "Thanks Oprah," *Los Angeles Times,* Nov. 15, 1996; Jackie Rogers, "Outstanding Oprah," *Redbook,* Sept. 1993; Sherri Winston, "Thin's Within," Fort Lauderdale *Sun-Sentinel,* Oct. 9, 1996; "'Oprah' Begins Campaign of Exercise, Nutrition," *St. Louis Post-Dispatch,* May 6, 1995; Robert Schaltz, "Oprah Draws Even When She's Online," *Newsday,* May 8, 1995; "Oprah Winfrey Is Only Entertainer and Only Black on Forbes List of 400 Richest Americans," *Jet,* Oct. 16, 1995; Hal Boedeker, "Too Much Oprah, Too Much Vanity," *Orlando Sentinel,* Sept. 18, 1998; "Oprah Secedes from U.S., Forms Independent Nation of Cheesecake-Eating Housewives," *Onion,* May 26, 1996; "Prose & Cons," New York

*Daily News,* June 18, 1996; John Marshall, "Bookseller Blues," *Seattle Post-Intelligencer,* June 20, 1996; Paul D. Colford, "A Mario-Beaters Book," *Newsday,* June 13, 1996; Renee James, "Empowerment Won't Help Oprah's Ratings Slipping," Allentown *Morning Call,* June 1, 2008; Paul D. Colford, "Hype Covers Oprah's 'Body,'" *Newsday,* Sept. 5, 1996; Lisbeth Levine, "It's Not Who You Know . . . It's Who You Train," *Chicago Tribune,* Sept. 12, 1996; Alex Tresniowski, "Oprah's Buff," *People Weekly,* Sept. 9, 1996; M. Eileen Brown, "Oprah: Make the Connection," *Chicago Sun-Times,* Sept. 27, 1997; Susan Berfield, "The Making of *The Color Purple,*" *BusinessWeek,* Nov. 21, 2005; David Mehegan, "Oprah's Book Club Is Back and Reading," *Chicago Tribune,* July 4, 2003; Julia Keller and Mark Caro, "Author's Rejection of Winfrey Book Logo Stirs Literary Tempest," *Chicago Tribune,* Oct. 25, 2001; Stephen Braun, "The Oprah Seal of Approval," *Los Angeles Times,* Mar. 9, 1997; Kelley Blewster, "Oprah Winfrey: Testifying to the Power of Books," *Biblio,* Jan. 1998; David Roeder, "Winfrey Recommendation Fuels Demand for Novel," *Chicago Sun-Times,* Sept. 27, 1996; Caryn James, "The Book Club," *Chicago Tribune,* Nov. 25, 1996; Jeane Wolf, "Have Faith in Something Big," *Parade,* Oct. 25, 2009; Tom Shone, "Poets in Love," *New York Times,* Apr. 22, 2001; Keith J. Kelley, "Oprah Makes Book on Author's Tome," New York *Daily News,* Oct. 20, 1997; David Streitfeld, "Queen of All the Media," *Mirabella,* July/Aug. 1997; Martha Bayles, "Imus, Oprah and the Literary Elite," *New York Times,* Aug. 29, 1999; Marilyn Johnson, "Oprah Between the Covers," *Life,* Sept. 1997; Suzy Schultz, "It's Simple, If She Reads It They Will Buy," *Chicago Sun-Times,* Feb. 24, 1997; Craig Offman, "Oprah Pick Sends Publisher Scrambling," www.Salon.com, Feb. 9, 2000; Steven Barrie-Anthony, "A Nod from Winfrey Lifts Author," *Los Angeles Times,* Sept. 30, 2005; "The Battle of the Book," *New Republic,* Dec. 10, 2007; "Novel Approach," *People Weekly,* Nov. 12, 2001; Jeff Baker, "Oprah's Stamp of Approval Rubs Writer in Conflicted Ways," *Oregonian,* Oct. 12, 2001; David Kirkpatrick, "Winfrey Rescinds Offer to Author for Guest Appearance," *New York Times,* Oct. 24, 2001; Ann Oldenburg, "Franzen Says He Feels 'Awful' About Feud," *USA Today,* Oct. 25, 2001; Jonathan Yardley, "The Story of O," *Washington Post,* Oct. 29, 2001; Jeff Giles, "Books: Errors and Corrections," *Newsweek,* Nov. 5, 2001; Jeff Jacoby, "Too Good for Oprah," *Boston Globe,* Nov. 1, 2001; David Pesci, "Poor Little Johnny," *Chicago Tribune,* Oct. 28, 2001; Richard Johnson, "Correction by Oprah-Basher," *New York Post,* Oct. 31, 2001; Cindy Pearlman, "Sinise Eager to Unleash Steppenwolf for Documentary," *Chicago Sun-Times,* Dec. 11, 2001; Hillel Italie, "Winfrey Cuts Back on Book Club Picks," *Chicago Sun-Times,* Apr. 6, 2002; Richard Lacayo, "Oprah Turns the Page," *Time,* Apr. 15, 2002; "Insecure Oprah Picks the Right Road," *Rocky Mountain News,* Apr. 6, 2007; Marja Mills, "Oprah to Bard, 'You Go, Will,'" *Chicago Tribune,* Mar. 5, 2003; Patrick J. Reardon, "Lessons in Civility," *Chicago Tribune,* Apr. 25, 2005; Edward Wyatt, "Oprah's Book Club Reopening to Writers Who'll Sit and Chat," *New York Times,* Sept. 23, 2005; Janelle Nanos, "Franzen Meets Palestinian Flutist," *New York,* Feb. 27, 2006; Deborah Caulfield Ryback, "Taking Liberties," Minneapolis *StarTribune,* July 27, 2003; Edward Wyatt, "Treatment Description in Memoir Is Disputed," *New York Times,* Jan. 24, 2006; "A Million Little Lies: The Man Who Conned Oprah," www .TheSmokingGun.com, Jan. 8, 2006; Edward Wyatt, "Fact or Fiction, It's His Story," *New York Times,* Jan. 11, 2006; transcript, *Larry King Live,* Jan. 11, 2006, www.transcripts.cnn.com; Maureen Dowd, "Oprah! How Could Ya?" *New York Times,* Jan. 14, 2006; Richard Cohen, "Oprah's Grand Delusion," *Washington Post,* Jan. 17, 2006; Frank Rich, "Truthiness 101: From Frey to Alito," *New York Times,* Jan. 22, 2006; Edward Wyatt, "Publisher Offers Witnesses to Disputed Addiction Book," *New York Times,* Jan. 25, 1996; Michael Mershel, "Publisher Blasts Oprah at Grapevine Conference," *Dallas Morning News,* July 30, 2007; Liz Smith, "Mel's Career Hurt? Not Likely," *New York Post,* Aug. 9, 2006; Liz Smith, "New Editor for O Magazine," *Buffalo News,* July 8, 2008; Sara Nelson, "Stir Frey," *Publishers Weekly,* Sept. 17, 2007; Claudia Eller, "Film of 'A Million Little Pieces' Up in Air," *Los Angeles Times,* Jan. 28, 2006; "Riverhead Books Pulls Out of James Frey Deal," *New York Times,* Feb. 24, 2006; "Judge Approves 'A Million Little Pieces' Refund for Disgruntled Readers," www.foxnews.com, Nov. 2, 2007; Samantha Conti and Jeff Bercovici, "Memo Pad," *WWD,* Feb. 9, 2006.

TV/DVDS: *The Oprah Winfrey Show 20th Anniversary Collection* (DVD set); "The O.J. Book Controversy: The Goldmans and Denise Brown Speak Out," *The Oprah Winfrey Show,* aired Sept. 13, 2007.

INTERVIEWS: Confidential source, June 3, 2008; confidential source, May 25, 2009; confidential source, Aug. 28, 2008; Katharine Carr Esters, July 30, 2007, and Aug. 1, 2007; James van Sweden, Dec. 12, 2007, and Dec. 27, 2007; Alice Walker, Oct. 10, 2008; Michael Anderson, Nov. 4, 2007; correspondence with Deborah Caulfield Ryback, June 8, 2008; confidential source, Mar. 22, 2007; confidential source, Nov. 9, 2007, and Aug. 22, 2008, and correspondence with confidential source, Nov. 27, 2007, Nov. 28, 2007, Dec. 10, 2008, May 11, 2009, and June 4, 2009; Nan Talese, Mar. 23, 2007; correspondence with Liz Smith, Sept. 25, 2007.

Sixteen

RECORDS: Deed, 207 East Fifty-seventh Street, 36PH, Mar. 10, 2008, New York City Department of Finance, Office of the City Register, Document ID 2008031700333001; transcript, "Dangerous Food," *The Oprah Winfrey Show*, Apr. 16, 1996; transcript, Oprah Winfrey with Phil McGraw, *Dr. Phil*, aired Feb. 11, 2008; documents in the case of *Bruce Gregga v.* National Enquirer et al., case no. 1:95-cv-01671, U.S. District Court, Northern District of Illinois; transcripts of depositions of Rayford Dotch (June 16, 1997), LeGrande Green (Dec. 19, 1997, with exhibit Green 5), Dianne Hudson (June 18, 1997), James Kelley (June 18, 1997, and Dec. 19, 1997), Alice McGee (June 19, 1997), Oprah Winfrey (June 14, 1997, and Dec. 12, 1997), and Andrea Wishom (June 17, 1997) in the case of *Texas Beef Group* et al. *v. Winfrey* et al., case no. 2:96-cv-00208, U.S. District Court, Northern District of Texas.

BOOKS: Howard F. Lyman with Glen Merzer, *Mad Cowboy* (Touchstone, 1998); Oprah Winfrey, *Journey to Beloved* (Hyperion, 1998); Phillip McGraw, *Life Strategies* (Hyperion, 1999).

ARTICLES: "Oprah Winfrey, Montel Williams and Kevin Mambo Among Winners at Daytime Emmy Awards," *Jet*, June 10, 1996; Meredith Moss, "Donahue Tapes Last of 7000 Shows," *Cleveland Plain Dealer*, May 1, 1996; John Carmody, "Donahue to End Trail-Blazing Show," *Washington Post*, Jan. 18, 1996; Ed Bark, "Phil Donahue Bids Us Adieu," *St. Louis Post-Dispatch*, Sept. 11, 1996; Thomas Galvin, "Oprah Tells Bob to Take a Hike," *New York Post*, Oct. 8, 1996; Michael Kranish, "Oprah on Dole Chat: I Just Won't Do It," *Boston Globe*, Oct. 11, 1996; Michael Starr, "Oprah Denies Bouncing Dole," *New York Post*, Oct. 11, 1996; Scott McKay, "Droll Dole Stumps for State GOP," *Providence Journal*, Oct. 1, 1998; Katharine Q. Seelye, "Dole Gets a Few Laughs and $200 on Talk Show," *New York Times*, Nov. 9, 1996; Jane Hall, "Donahue: Nothing Left to Say but Goodbye," *Oregonian*, May 4, 1996; Marvin Kitman, "Phil, the Founding Talker," *Newsday*, Nov. 12, 1992; David Zurawik, "'Ellen' Breaks with the Past," *Baltimore Sun*, Apr. 27, 1997; Brian Lowry, "'Ellen' Gets Ready to Open the Closet Door," *Los Angeles Times*, Mar. 1, 1997; W. Speers, "DeGeneres Outs Herself Before Her Character Does," *Philadelphia Inquirer*, Apr. 7, 1997; "Yep. I'm Gay," cover, *Time*, Apr. 14, 1997; Alan Bash, "Three Big Sponsors to Bypass 'Ellen,'" *USA Today*, Mar. 27, 1997; "Oprah's Visit to 'Ellen' Airs Today," www.eurweb.com, Feb. 22, 2007; transcripts, "The Puppy Episode," Parts 1 and 2, *Ellen*, Apr. 30, 1997, www.twiz.tv.com/scripts; Liz Smith, "It's Rolonda Time," *Newsday*, Apr. 28, 1997; Claire Bickley, "Oprah

Audience Generally Unsympathetic to Ellen," www.canoe.ca, May 1, 1997; Brian Lowry, "A Closet Door Opens and 36 Million Watch," *Los Angeles Times*, May 2, 1997; George Rush and Joanna Malloy, "Oprah Gives Straight Dope About Gay Rumors," New York *Daily News*, June 5, 1997; Jenny Hortz, "Oprah Denies Rampant Gay Rumor," *Variety*, June 5, 1997; Judy Hevrdejs and Mike Conklin, "Oprah Leaves No Doubt About What's In, Out of Her Closet," *Chicago Tribune*, June 5, 1997; "Nope, She's Not Gay," *People Weekly*, June 23, 1997; "The Rumblings Behind the Oprah Rumor," *New York Post*, June 18, 1997; "Oprah Says She's Playing It Straight," Lancaster *Intelligencer-Journal*, June 6, 1997; John Carmody, "The TV Column," *Washington Post*, June 9, 1997; "Hot Lava," *New York Post*, June 20, 1997; "Rosie O'Donnel [*sic*] on Oprah Gay Rumors," posted by Runteldat at www.blogs.bet.com/entertainment, Oct. 28, 2009; Frank Bruni, "A Sapphic Victory, but Pyrrhic," *New York Times*, Nov. 15, 2009; "Oprah and Gayle Move In Together," cover, *Globe*, July 31, 2006; "Oprah's Secret Life: The Truth About Those Gay Rumors," *National Enquirer* (date unknown); "Oprah & Gayle Like Lovers," *Globe*, Mar. 16, 2009; "Who's Gay and Who's Not in Hollywood," *National Review*, July 14, 2008; Mark Steyn, "Comic Oprah," *National Review*, Mar. 23, 1998; Lee Siegel, "Thank You for Sharing," *New Republic*, June 5 and 12, 2006; "Celebrities Gather for Magazine's 30th Birthday," *Orlando Sentinel*, Apr. 15, 2000; Andre Goldman, "The Night of the Big O," Ontario *National Post*, Apr. 22, 2000; Lillian Ross, "Oprah's Understudy," *New Yorker*, Apr. 24 and May 1, 2000; Branden Keil, "Gimme Shelter," *New York Post*, Jan. 17, 2008; Max Abelson, "Did Oprah's Dead Dog Sophie Inspire Gayle King's New Penthouse?" *New York Observer*, Mar. 24, 2008; Lisa Kogan, "Oprah and Gayle Uncensored," *O, The Oprah Magazine*, Aug. 2006; "For Mel B, a Case of Murphy's Law," New York *Daily News*, Dec. 5, 2006; transcript, *Larry King Live*, Dec. 5, 2006, www.transcripts.cnn.com; "Oprah Winfrey's Commencement Address, Wellesley College, May 30, 1997," www.wellesley.edu; Edna Gunderson, "Wildest Dreams Do Come True," *USA Today*, May 15, 1997; Lucio Guerrero and Bill Zwecker, "Tina's Last Turn," *Chicago Sun-Times*, Oct. 5, 2000; "Tina Turner Returns to 'Wildest Dreams' World Tour," *Jet*, Mar. 17, 1997; Neal Travis, "Good Vibes for Oprah and Beau," *New York Post*, Aug. 3, 1997; Jamie Foster Brown, "Everything Negroes Ever Wanted to Ask Oprah," *Sister 2 Sister*, Nov. 1997; James Endrst, "To Endure Academy Awards Show, You Have to Seize the Moments," *Hartford Courant*, Mar. 27, 1996; Richard Roeper, "Oprah's Real Talent? Playing the Role of Fan, Not Celebrity," *Chicago Sun-Times*, Jan. 12, 1997; Alan Pergament, "Oscar Telecast Is a Tearful Evening of Some Nonsense and

Understated Sensibility," *Buffalo News*, Mar. 26, 1996; Stuart Jeffries, "The Oscars: 'I Have a List . . . Quite a Long List,'" *Guardian*, Mar. 27, 1996; Howard Rosenberg, "A Night to Kilt For," *Los Angeles Times*, Mar. 26, 1996; "If Body Piercing Is So Hazardous, Why Is It Popular?" *Jet*, Apr. 19, 1999; "Rodman Book Too Risqué; Oprah Nixes Appearance," *Chicago Sun-Times*, Apr. 29, 1997; "Winfrey Says No to Worm," *Chicago Sun-Times*, Apr. 30, 1997; Lisa Adams, "The Oprah Show and Tell," *Daily Record*, Oct. 27, 2006; "Love Is All Around," www.oprah.com, May 19, 2008; David Robb, "Free Speech on 'Oprah' May Be AFTRA Breach," *Hollywood Reporter*, Jan. 31, 1997; Shauna Snow, "Arts and Entertainment Reports," *Los Angeles Times*, Feb. 1, 1997; "On Book Signing Tour, Fergie Confesses Sins and Bares Her Soul," *Chicago Tribune*, Nov. 14, 1996; Martin Townsend, "Oprah Winfrey," *Sunday Mail*, July 2, 1995; John James, "My Sex Pact with Andy," *Mirror*, Nov. 21, 1997; Robert Feder, "Oprah Opens Season Looking for More Fun," *Chicago Sun-Times*, Sept. 3, 1996; "Oprah Awed," *USA Today*, Aug. 28, 1996; "Oprah Winfrey Kicks Off 11th Season with New Format and Theme Song, 'Get with the Program,'" *Jet*, Sept. 30, 1996; "Oprah's Charity Auction," www.oprah.com, Oct. 2003; "Quotes of the Day," *Chicago Tribune*, Aug. 28, 1996; Irv Kupcinet, "Kup's Column," *Chicago Sun-Times*, Aug. 28, 1996; Richard Huff, "Streisand's 'Oprah' Visit Brings Big Nielsen Bounce," *New York Daily News*, Nov. 13, 1996; Bill Zwecker, "Babs Talks Politics with a 'Smile' on *Oprah*," *Chicago Sun-Times*, Sept. 12, 2003; "Money Madness," *People Weekly*, Nov. 4, 1996; Eric Markus, "Where's the Beef?" www.Salon.com, Jan. 20, 1998; Adam Cohen, "Trial of the Savory," *Time*, Feb. 2, 1998; "Oprah Says She's Eaten Her Last Burger," *Seattle Post-Intelligencer*, Apr. 18, 1996; "Oprah Moves Markets," *Omaha World-Herald*, Apr. 17, 1996; George Gunset, "Oprah Airs Beef Fears, Draws Ire," *Chicago Tribune*, Apr. 17, 1996; Ken Herman, "Perry Pursues Action Against Talk Show Guest's Cattle Remarks," *Austin American Statesman*; Sheldon Rampton and John Stauber, "One Hundred Percent Pure Baloney: Lessons from the Oprah Trial," *PR Watch*, First Quarter 1998; "Oprah: Home on the Range," *Newsweek*, Feb. 2, 1998; Rick Hepp, "Winfrey's Lawyers to Defend Ownership of Photos in Book," *Chicago Tribune*, Dec. 10, 1999; Tim Jones, "Jubilant Winfrey: 'I Refuse to Be Muzzled,'" *Chicago Tribune*, Feb. 27, 1998; "Oprah 1, Beef 0," *People Weekly*, Mar. 16, 1998; "Talk Show Host Transformed," *Los Angeles Sentinel*, Mar. 25, 1998; "Oprah Says She Felt Redeemed After Victory Over Texas Cattlemen," *Jet*, Mar. 23, 1998; Tom Gliatto, "So Where's the Beef?" *People Weekly*, Feb. 16, 1998; "Oprah: Home on the Range," *Newsweek*, Feb. 2, 1998; Mark Donald, "Analyze This," *Dallas Observer*,

Apr. 13, 2000; Lynn Allison, "Oprah's Real Beef," *Globe*, Mar. 17, 1998; Mark Babineck, "Oprah Charms Amarillo Audience," *Chicago Sun-Times*, Jan. 24, 1998; Richard Roeper, "Oprah Unfurled Charm, Lassoed Heart of Texas," *Chicago Sun-Times*, Mar. 2, 1998; "Oprah Charms Amarillo Jury at Texas Beef Defamation Trial," *Los Angeles Sentinel*, Feb. 18, 1998; Joanna Powell, "Oprah's Awakening," *Good Housekeeping*, Dec. 1998; Skip Hollandsworth, "Phillip McGraw," *Texas Monthly*, Sept. 1999; John W. Gonzales, "Winfrey Has a Cow as Beef Trial Drags On," New Orleans *Times-Picayune*, Feb. 6, 1998; Skip Hollandsworth and Pamela Colloff, "How the West Was Won," *Texas Monthly*, Mar. 1998; Tim Jones, "Muzzling Employees Host's Prerogative but Winfrey's Restriction Makes Some Howl," *Chicago Tribune*, Apr. 16, 2000; Tim Jones, "Trial Offers Revealing Look Behind the Talk," *Chicago Tribune*, Feb. 8, 1998; Tim Jones, "A Bit Agitated but Uncowed, TV Star Calls Lawsuit 'The Most Painful Thing' She Has Ever Endured," *Chicago Tribune*, Feb. 5, 1998; Alex Rodriguez, "No Beef with Oprah," *Chicago Sun-Times*, Feb. 27, 1998; Leslie Baldacci, "Land of the Winfrey," *Chicago Sun-Times*, Mar. 1, 1998; Tim Jones, "Attorneys Square Off in Closing Arguments," *Chicago Tribune*, Feb. 26, 1998.

TV/DVDS/VIDEOS: Archive of American Television interview with Phil Donahue, May 9, 2001 (nine parts, viewed on YouTube); *The Oprah Winfrey Show 20th Anniversary Collection* (DVD set); *Late Show with David Letterman*, aired July 19, 2006; "Women Leaving Men for Other Women," *The Oprah Winfrey Show*, aired Mar. 6, 2009; "Evangelist Ted Haggard, His Wife and the Gay Sex Scandal," *The Oprah Winfrey Show*, aired Jan. 28, 2009; "Oprah Winfrey: Heart of the Matter," A&E *Biography* special, aired Jan. 16, 2000.

INTERVIEWS: Gloria Steinem, June 5, 2007; Senator Robert Dole, May 23, 2008; Phil Donahue, Aug. 9, 2007; correspondence with Liz Smith, Sept. 25 and Sept. 26, 2007; **Jo Baldwin, July 14, 2010, and correspondence with Jo Baldwin, July 15, 16, 20, and 27, Aug. 17, and Sept. 14, 2010;** confidential source, July 7, 2008; confidential source, Aug. 22, 2008; Rocky Twyman, May 20, 2008; Erica Jong, Dec. 17, 2006; Marty Ingels, Dec. 21, 2006; confidential source, Nov. 9, 2007; confidential source, Mar. 22, 2007; correspondence with Paul Burrell, Aug. 24, 2007; Howard Lyman, Mar. 24, 2008; Elliott Zinger and Patrick Walsh, Oct. 9, 2007, and correspondence with Elliott Zinger, June 22, 2009; confidential source, Oct. 1, 2008; Bill Zwecker, Oct. 11, 2007; confidential source, Nov. 26, 2007; Tim Jones, Apr. 5, 2007.

Seventeen

records: Transcript, interview of Oprah Winfrey by Diane Sawyer, *20/20*, ABC, Oct. 25, 1998; King World Productions, Inc., General Statement of Beneficial Ownership (SEC Schedule SC 13D), filed Oct. 27, 1997; King World Productions, Inc., General Statement of Beneficial Ownership (SEC Schedule SC 13G), filed Oct. 13, 1998; transcript, Oprah Winfrey with Phil McGraw, *Dr. Phil,* aired Feb. 11, 2008; documents in the case of *Dr. Mehmet Oz* et al. *v. FWM Labratories, Inc.,* et al., case no. 1:09-CV-07297-DAB, U.S. District Court, Southern District of New York.

books: Oprah Winfrey, *Journey to Beloved* (Hyperion, 1998); Natalie Zemon Davis, *Slaves on Screen* (Harvard University Press, 2000); Rhonda Byrne, *The Secret* (Atria Books/Beyond Words, 2006); *Live Your Best Life: A Treasury of Wisdom, Wit, Advice, Interviews and Inspiration from* O, The Oprah Magazine (Oxmoor House, 2005); *O's Guide to Life: The Best of* O, The Oprah Magazine (Oxmoor House, 2007); *O's Big Book of Happiness: The Best of* O, The Oprah Magazine (Oxmoor House, 2008).

articles: "Winfrey's Company Buys Rights to 'Beloved,' 'Boy,' " *Variety,* Jan. 12, 1988; Jonathan Van Meter, "Oprah's Moment," *Vogue,* Oct. 1998; Gretchen Reynolds, "A Year to Remember: Oprah Grows Up," *TV Guide,* Jan. 7, 1995; "Dumbing Up," *Economist,* Oct. 17, 1998; Tom Shales, " 'David and Lisa' and a Little Too Much Oprah," *Washington Post,* Oct. 31, 1989; Roger Ebert, "Oprah Meets Her Match," *Chicago Sun-Times,* Oct. 11, 1998; Ron Stodghill, "Daring to Go There," *Time,* Oct. 5, 1998; Laura B. Randolph, "Oprah and Danny Sizzle in Their First Love Scene in the Powerful Film 'Beloved,' " *Ebony,* Nov. 1998; Honie Stevens, "From Rags to Riches," *Saga,* May 2002; Clarence Page, "Taking Off Blinders About Slavery," *Chicago Tribune,* Oct. 21, 1998; Lorrie Lynch, "Oprah's New Mission," *USA Weekend,* Oct. 9–11, 1998; John Millar, "Oprah Winfrey and Thandie Newton," *OK!,* Mar. 12, 1999; Janet Maslin, "No Peace from a Brutal Legacy," *New York Times,* Oct. 16, 1998; Stanley Kauffmann, "Of Human Bondages," *New Republic,* Nov. 16, 1998; Richard Alleva, "Beloved," *Commonweal,* Nov. 20, 1998; Roger Ebert, "Grand Oprah," *Chicago Sun-Times,* Oct. 16, 1998; Richard Corliss, "Bewitching Beloved," *Time,* Oct. 5, 1998; Mary A. Mitchell, "Nothing Entertaining About Films on Slavery," *Chicago Sun-Times,* Oct. 18, 1998; Anita Creamer, "Beautiful Pictures Reveal Ugly Truth," *Sacramento Bee,* Oct. 12, 1998; Marisa Meltzer, "The Fat Wars," www.thedailybeast .com, May 19, 2009; Marilyn Gardner, "*Vogue*'s Oprah Sends Mixed Message," *Christian Science Monitor,* Oct. 18, 1998; Lloyd Grove, "*Vogue*

Editor Rouses the Fat and the Furious," New York *Daily News*, Sept. 19, 2005; Cynthia Grenier, "*Vogue* Scores in Big Fashion Getting First Lady for Cover," *Washington Times*, Dec. 12, 1998; "Oscar Fashions/More Maria Shriver," www.oprah.com, Mar. 5, 1999; "Oprah Winfrey and *Beloved*," www.news.bbc.co.uk, Mar. 5, 1999; Jeannie Williams, "Cover Girl Oprah a Model of Makeover," *USA Today*, Sept. 18, 1998; Veronica Chambers and Allison Samuels, "The Women of 'Beloved,'" *Newsweek*, Oct. 19, 1998; Jill Vejnuska, "It's Oprah's World," *Palm Beach Post*, Oct. 16, 1998; Steve Holsey, "Oprah Winfrey, Talk Show Queen, Has Complex Movie She Believes In," *Michigan Chronicle*, Oct. 14, 1998; Mary McNamara, "O to a Higher Power," *Los Angeles Times*, Dec. 11, 2005; Sharon Waxman, "Beloved Gets the Cold Shoulder," Montreal *Gazette*, Nov. 12, 1998; "Autumn Flops," *Economist*, Nov. 21, 1998; Martyn Palmer, "Unloved but Unbowed," London *Times*, Feb. 25, 1999; John Millar, "Grand Oprah," *Sunday Express*, Feb. 21, 1999; Liz Smith, "Jackie Mason on Mel," *New York Post*, Aug. 3, 2006; "Oprah Winfrey: For a Beloved TV Icon, a Year of Grit, Glamour—and Jeers," *People Weekly*, Dec. 28, 1998; Cindy Pearlman, "Poet Angelou Has Few Kind Words for Clinton," *Chicago Sun-Times*, Dec. 3, 1998; Liz Smith, "Still an Open Fan of Andre's," *New York Post*, June 10, 1999; Scott A. Resnick, "Whoopi Goldberg Fields Questions, Holds Back Little," *Harvard Crimson*, Nov. 10, 1998; "It's War," *National Enquirer*, Dec. 31, 1998; Maya Jaggi, "The Power of One," *Guardian Weekend*, Feb. 11, 1999; Lynette Clemetson, "It's Constant Work," *Newsweek*, Oct. 8, 2001; Phil Rosenthal, "Soul Second," *Chicago Sun-Times*, June 28, 2000; Jill Smolowe and Sonja Steptoe, "O on the Go," *People Weekly*, July 16, 2001; Richard Huff, "Happy Days Here Again for Top-Rated 'Oprah,'" New York *Daily News*, Oct. 1, 1998; Robert Feder, "Why Oprah Keeps Faith with Her Faithful Followers," *Chicago Sun-Times*, Sept. 16, 1997; Robert Feder, "Springer Isn't Stung by Winfrey's Remarks," *Chicago Sun-Times*, Feb. 10, 1999; "Rachael Ray?" www.tmz.com, Jan. 24, 2007; "Business and Finance," *Wall Street Journal*, Sept. 16, 1998; Lisa de Moraes, "In CBS Deal, Oprah Gets a Wheel Fortune: $100 Million," *Washington Post*, Apr. 2, 1999; Tim Jones, "In a Blink, CBS Changes Its Make-Up," *Chicago Tribune*, Apr. 2, 1999; Forbes 400 list 1999, www.Forbes.com; Amy Wellborn, "The Feel-Good Spirituality of Oprah," *Our Sunday Visitor*, Jan. 13, 2002; Lyn Garrett, "Oprah Gets Spiritual," *Publishers Weekly*, Sept. 14, 1998; Bob Longino, "Oprah Exhorting Fans to 'Change Your Life,'" *Atlanta Constitution*, Sept. 10, 1998; Christopher John Farley, "Queen of All Media," *Time*, Oct. 5, 1998; Richard Roeper, "'Deepak Oprah's' Inner Journey Is an Ego Trip," *Chicago Sun-Times*, Oct. 12, 1998; Libby Copeland, "Our Lady of Perpetual Help," *Washington Post*, June 26, 2000; Skip Hollandsworth, "Phillip McGraw," *Texas Monthly*, Sept. 1999; Cheryl Lavine, "Dr. Tell It Like It Is," *Chicago Tribune*, June 12, 2001; "Oprah Winfrey Reinvents Her Show," *Atlanta Daily World*, Sept. 13, 1998; Ann Oldenburg, "Oprah: 'These Are the Glory Days for Me,'" *USA Today*, Oct. 8, 1998; Shu Shin Lu, "Oprah Fan's Tragedy," *Chicago Sun-Times*, Dec. 24, 1999; Steve Johnson, "Oh, No, Oprah! Enough!" *Chicago Tribune*, Nov. 23, 1998; Weston Kosova and Pat Wingert, "Live Your Best Life Ever," *Newsweek*, June 8, 2009; Lucy Howard et al., "The Buzz," *Newsweek*, Feb. 22, 1999; Hal Boedeker, "Too Much Oprah, Too Much Vanity," *Orlando Sentinel*, Sept. 18, 1998; Wiley A. Hall III, "Urban Rhythms: The Marches," *Afro-American Red Star*, Oct. 27, 2000; Jeff MacGregor, "Inner Peace, Empowerment, and Host Worship," *New York Times*, Oct. 25, 1998; "The Gospel According to Oprah," *Vantage Point*, July 1998; Phil Rosenthal, "What a 'Man,'" *Chicago Sun-Times*, June 16, 1999; Jerry Adler, "'The Secret': Does Self-Help Book Really Help?" *Newsweek*, Mar. 5, 2007; transcript, *Larry King Live*, May 1, 2007, www.transcripts.cnn.com; Steve Rabey, "Oprah's 'Gospel,'" *Christian Examiner*, May 2008; Marco R. della Cava, "Secret History of 'The Secret,'" *USA Today*, Mar. 28, 2007; Peter Birkenhead, "Oprah's Ugly Secret," www.Salon.com, Mar. 5, 2007; transcript, *Real Time with Bill Maher*, Mar. 9, 2007, www.safesearching.com; Tim Watkin, "Self-Help's Slimy 'Secret,'" *Washington Post*, Apr. 8, 2007; "Letters to Oprah," www.oprah.com, Mar. 26, 2007; Lynn Clemetson, "Oprah on Oprah," *Newsweek*, Jan. 8, 2008; Robert Feder, "Oprah Set to Launch Magazine Next Year," *Chicago Sun-Times*, July 9, 1999; Robert Feder, "Give Her an O—Oprah Names New Magazine," *Chicago Sun-Times*, Jan. 13, 2000; Keith Kelly, "Oprah Magazine Goes with O," *New York Post*, Jan. 13, 2000; Lillian Ross, "Oprah's Understudy," *New Yorker*, Apr. 24 and May 1, 2000; April Peterson, "Combining Mass and Class: The Story of *O, The Oprah Magazine*," *Journal of Magazine and New Media Research*, Fall 2003; Marina Benjamin, "O is for Oprah and Over-the-Top," *Evening Standard*, Apr. 26, 2000; "Oprah Talks to Nelson Mandela," *O, The Oprah Magazine*, Apr. 2001; Carina Chocano, "Look Out O: Twins Go Glossy," *Chicago Sun-Times*, Apr. 11, 2001; "Top Ten Articles in Oprah's New Magazine," *Late Show with David Letterman*, Apr. 10, 2000, www.cbs.com/latenight/lateshow.

TV/DVDS: *Beloved*, 1998 (DVD); "Oprah Winfrey: Heart of the Matter," A&E *Biography* special, aired Jan. 16, 2000; *The Oprah Winfrey Show 20th Anniversary Collection* (DVD set); "What Happened to the Mom Who Shopped Her Family Broke?" *The Oprah Winfrey Show*, aired Jan. 18, 2008.

INTERVIEWS: Confidential source, Nov. 26, 2007; Susan Karns, July 29, 2009; Peter Colasante, Dec. 17, 2007; Maureen Taylor, Dec. 17, 2007; Vernon Winfrey, Apr. 24, 2008; Nan Talese, Mar. 23, 2007; Tim Jones, Apr. 5, 2007; correspondence with Alex Kuczynski, Apr. 13, 2008.

## Eighteen

RECORDS: "Oprah's Angel Network Fact Sheet," *The Oprah Winfrey Show* press release, Sept. 1999; IRS forms 990 for Oprah's Angel Network, 2002–2008, EIN 36-4231488; IRS forms 990 for Angel Network Support Foundation, 2002–2004, EIN 74-2962189; transcript, "Oprah" segment, *60 Minutes*, CBS, Dec. 14, 1986; transcript, Oprah Winfrey speech at Miss Porter's School, June 12, 1994; Illinois Secretary of State Corporation File Detail Report for The Oprah Winfrey Foundation, File no. 57496614; IRS forms 990-PF for The Oprah Winfrey Foundation, 2001–2007, and For A Better Life Foundation, 1998–2000, EIN 36-3976230; "Oprah Winfrey Leadership Academy for Girls—South Africa Celebrates Its Official Opening," TOWLAG press release, Jan. 2, 2007; IRS forms 990-PF for The Oprah Winfrey Operating Foundation, 2002–2005, and The Oprah Winfrey Leadership Academy Foundation, 2006, 2007, EIN 74-3048315; documents in the case of *Lerato Nomvuyo Mzamane v. Oprah Winfrey* et al., case no. 2:08-CV-4884 in the U.S. District Court for the Eastern District of Pennsylvania.

BOOKS: Robert Waldron, *Oprah!* (St. Martin's Press, 1987); George Mair, *Oprah Winfrey: The Real Story* (Birch Lane Press, 1994); Peter Frumkin, *Strategic Giving: The Art and Science of Philanthropy* (University of Chicago Press, 2006); Henry Louis Gates, Jr., *Finding Oprah's Roots* (Crown Publishers, 2007).

ARTICLES: Andrew Gumbel, "Oprah Becomes First Black Woman to Join Billionaires' Club," *Los Angeles Times*, Mar. 1, 2003; "Oprah Comes Home," Kosciusko *Star-Herald*, Nov. 15, 1998; "Oprah Winfrey Reveals the Real Reason Why She Stayed on TV," *Jet*, Nov. 24, 1997; "FAMU Habitat for Humanity Chapter Selected to Build Oprah House," *Tennessee Tribune*, Apr. 16, 1998; Shawn Reeves, "The House That Oprah Built," *Habitat World*, Oct./Nov. 1999; "Habitat Plans Six Houses in '98," *Atlanta Journal-Constitution*, Jan. 22, 1998; Jennifer Wulff and Mike Lipton, "These Are My Dream Girls," *People Weekly*, Jan. 15, 2007; "Building Oprah Katrina Homes," www.oprah.com; Mary Perez, "With Little Fanfare, Oprah's Angel Network Is Quietly Helping Coast People and Communities Recover," Biloxi-Gulfport *Sun-Herald*; Steve Johnson, "Oh, No, Oprah! Enough," *Chicago Tribune*, Nov. 23, 1998; Alex Ben Block,

"Oprah on the Record," *TelevisionWeek,* Apr. 19, 2004; "How Big Sister Oprah Opened Her Arms and Her Heart to Save 24 Ghetto Kids," *Star,* Sept. 5, 1989; Bill Brashler, "Next on Oprah . . . ," *Ladies' Home Journal,* Aug. 1991; Joan Barthel, "Here Comes Oprah," *Ms.,* Aug. 1986; "Bill Cosby Leads the Millionaire Entertainers," *San Francisco Chronicle,* Sept. 7, 1987; Marilynn Marchione, "Coast-to-Coast: U.S. Reaches Out," *Chicago Sun-Times,* May 25, 1986; Charles Krauthammer, "Celebrities in Politics," *Time,* Apr. 21, 1986; Timothy McDarragh, "Talk's Not Cheap," *New York Post,* Jan. 1, 1987; Irv Kupcinet, "Kup on Sunday," *Chicago Sun-Times,* Mar. 8, 1987; "$25,000 Kiss," *Nashville Banner,* Aug. 4, 1987; Robert Feder, "Oprah Buys Studio on West Side," *Chicago Sun-Times,* Sept. 17, 1988; "Oprah, Revlon Give School $100,000," *New York Amsterdam News,* Feb. 4, 1989; "Generous Oprah," New York *Daily News,* Dec. 27, 1988; "Lunch on Oprah in South African Town," *Boston Herald,* July 23, 1988; Brian Williams and David Barritt, "Oprah's Mission of Mercy," *National Enquirer,* Apr. 3, 1990; Brian Lowry, "NCCJ Humanitarian Award Presented to Oprah Winfrey," *Variety,* Oct. 24, 1988; "Oprah Gives Donation," Fort Lauderdale *Sun-Sentinel,* Apr. 30, 1988; "Rich Get Richer," *Chicago Tribune,* Sept. 17, 1989; "Oprah Winfrey Establishes Morehouse College Fund," *Atlanta Daily World,* May 25, 1989; "Oprah Makes Her Second $5 Mil Donation to Morehouse College," *Chicago Defender,* Feb. 26, 2004; Lisbeth Levine, "Show Supports Shelter," *Chicago Sun-Times,* Aug. 23, 1989; "Check Oprah—She Saves the Day," *Chicago Sun-Times,* Mar. 28, 1989; Irv Kupcinet, "Kup's Column," *Chicago Sun-Times,* June 22, 1989; "Star Watch," *USA Today,* Sept. 26, 1989; "Oprah Winfrey Helps," *Atlanta Daily World,* Mar. 12, 1989; "Cosby Tops List of Money-Makers," *Los Angeles Times,* Sept. 17, 1990; "Oprah, Church Make Way for Dakota Shelter," Minneapolis *StarTribune,* Aug. 16, 1990; Mary Cameron Frey, "Chicago Opens Its Heart for Art Against AIDS," *Chicago Sun-Times,* Apr. 22, 1990; ". . . And Winfrey Deserves Salute," *Chicago Sun-Times,* Oct. 2, 1990; Irv Kupcinet, "Kup's Column," *Chicago Sun-Times,* Jan. 25, 1990; Susan Heller Anderson, "Chronicle," *New York Times,* Jan. 26, 1990; "Standing Room Only," *Atlanta Daily World,* May 11, 1990; "Oprah Flying Mandela Kin to South Africa," *Chicago Sun-Times,* Feb. 2, 1990; Robert Feder, "Bob Hope Leads Stars in Salute to Winfrey," *Chicago Sun-Times,* Sept. 12, 1990; "The Dish!" *Globe,* Jan. 21, 2003; Edward R. Silverman, "Big Bucks on the Block," *Newsday,* Sept. 16, 1991; Eric Siegel, "Talk Show Host Winfrey Gives Money for Books," *Baltimore Sun,* Sept. 18, 1991; Edward R. Silverman, "Big Bucks," *Newsday,* Sept. 14, 1992; "Oprah Gives $50,000 to Fight Abuse," *Chicago Sun-Times,* Jan. 15, 1992; "People,"

*Orange County Sentinel,* Aug. 1, 1992; Irv Kupcinet, "Kup's Column," *Chicago Sun-Times,* Jan. 16, 1992; David E. Kalish, "Oprah Tops Forbes' List of Entertainers," *San Francisco Chronicle,* Sept. 13, 1993; Ginny Holbert, "Winfrey Thinks Show Can Help," *Chicago Sun-Times,* Nov. 23, 1993; M. W. Newman, "Restoration Brings Out Best in Holy Family," *Chicago Sun-Times,* July 12, 1993; Mary Cameron Frey, "Oprah Looks Like a Million to West Side School," *Chicago Sun-Times,* Oct. 27, 1993; Bill Zwecker, "The Top Earners," *Chicago Sun-Times,* Sept. 12, 1994; "Oprah Winfrey Donates Prize Money to School," *New York Amsterdam News,* Feb. 12, 1994; "Rack Race," *People Weekly,* July 4, 1994; Luchina Fisher et al., "In Full Stride," *People Weekly,* Sept. 12, 1994; " 'Taking on Welfare'—Next on Oprah," *Chicago Tribune,* Sept. 16, 1994; Gary Wisby, "Oprah Picks Up the Tab," *Chicago Sun-Times,* Sept. 14, 1994; Barbara Grizzuti Harrison, "The Importance of Being Oprah," *New York Times Magazine,* June 11, 1989; Pat Gowens, "A Woman's Response to the 'Oprah Effect,'" www.blackagendareport.com, Nov. 1, 2006; Dana Kennedy, "Oprah Act Two," *Entertainment Weekly,* Sept. 9, 1994; Maudlyne Ihejirika, "7 Star in Oprah's Pilot," *Chicago Sun-Times,* Sept. 15, 1995; Allyson C. Ward, "Oprah, Hull House Help 100 Needy Families with Housing," *Chicago Defender,* Sept. 14, 1994; Christopher John Farley, "Oprah Springs Eternal," *Time,* Aug. 30, 1993; Melissa Key, "Secret Heartache Behind Oprah's $6M Giveaway," *Star,* Sept. 17, 1994; Jamie Foster Brown, "Everything Negroes Ever Wanted to Ask Oprah," *Sister 2 Sister,* Nov. 1997; Louise Kiernan, "Oprah's Poverty Program Stalls," *Chicago Tribune,* Aug. 27, 1996; Clarence Page, "Oprah Asking the Right Questions," *Chicago Tribune,* Sept. 4, 1996; Richard Thomas, "Queen of the Dream," *Guardian,* May 10, 1997; "Oprah Winfrey and Beau Stedman Graham to Teach Class at Northwestern University," *Jet,* June 7, 1999; Cliff Edwards, "Professor Oprah to Teach Leadership at N'western," *Commercial Appeal,* May 20, 1999; "Oprah on Oprah," *Newsweek,* Jan. 8, 1999; Bill Hoffman, "On Guard! Here Comes Oprah," *New York Post,* Nov. 15, 2000; Mike Thomas, "Class Dismissed," *Chicago Sun-Times,* Jan. 3, 2001; Michael Sneed, "Sneed," *Chicago Sun-Times,* Nov. 12, 1999; Forbes 400 list 1998, 1999, 2000, and 2002, www.Forbes.com; "O, No! Oprah Talks of Retiring," *New York Post,* Mar. 12, 2002; "World's Richest People" list 2003 and 2004, www.Forbes.com; "Billionaires" list, 2006 and 2007, www.Forbes.com; "Oprah, Master P and Puff Daddy Among Forbes' List of 40 Highest Paid Entertainers," *Jet,* Sept. 28, 1998; "Oprah and Michael Jordan Among Forbes' List of Top 50 Highest Paid Performers," *Jet,* Mar. 22, 1999; "Who Are the Highest-Paid Black Celebrities," *Jet,* Mar. 27, 2000; "100 Top Celebrities" list, 2001, 2002,

2003, 2004, 2005, 2006, and 2007, www.Forbes.com; "Mandela's Passion for Education," *Mercury,* July 15, 2008; "Newsmakers," *Houston Chronicle,* Nov. 5, 2000; Belinda Robinson, "Oprah's African Dream Realized," London *Voice,* Dec. 7, 2006; Oprah Winfrey, "O Happy," *O, The Oprah Magazine,* Apr. 2003; Darren Scheuttler, "Crowding Mars Mandela Holiday Party," *Chicago Tribune,* Dec. 23, 2002; P. J. Bednarski, "All About Oprah Inc.," *Broadcasting and Cable,* June 24, 2005; Oprah Winfrey, "What I Know for Sure," *O, The Oprah Magazine,* Dec. 2006; Patricia Edmonds, "This Time I Won't Fail," *USA Weekend,* Dec. 17, 2006; Pamela Gien, "Building the Dream," *O, The Oprah Magazine,* Jan. 2007; Rosalind Rossi, "Oprah Visits Local Charter School to Get Tips for Her South African," *Chicago Sun-Times,* Nov. 15, 2003; transcript, *Anderson Cooper 360 Degrees,* www.cnn.transcripts.com, Jan. 8, 2007; Debby Knox, "The Christel Touch," www.wishtv.com, Feb. 12, 2007; "Talk Show Host Reinvigorates Attention on City's Failing Schools," www.thewbalchannel.com, Apr. 12, 2006; Dan Rodricks, "Listen Up, Oprah: There Are Other Ways to Help City Kids," *Baltimore Sun,* Apr. 13, 2006; Lynn Anderson, "Baltimore Turns the Other Cheek for Oprah," *Baltimore Sun,* Apr. 12, 2006; Daphne Merkin, "Soap Oprah," *Radar,* Feb. 2008; Allison Samuels, "Oprah Winfrey's Lavish South African School," *Newsweek,* Jan. 8, 2007; "Oprah Reveals She Is a Descendant of Zulus," *Jet,* July 4, 2005; "One on One with Oprah," www.etonline.com, Jan. 3, 2007; "Oprah Opens Her Dream School for Poor South African Students," Yahoo News (AFP), Jan. 2, 2007; Rebecca Traister, "What Oprah Can't Forget," www.Salon.com, Jan. 13, 2007; Janet Silvera, "Mixed Feelings for New 'Oprah' School," *Jamaica Gleaner,* May 29, 2007; "Oprah Admits Having Nearly Given Up South African School Project," Yahoo News (AFP), Jan. 3, 2007; Suzanne Slesin, "Live and Learn," *O at Home,* Summer 2007; "KZN Girls Head for Oprah's School," Durban *Daily News,* Nov. 20, 2006; Chrisena Coleman, "Oprah's Schooled," New York *Daily News,* Jan. 2, 2007; "Statement from Oprah Winfrey," *Boston Globe,* Jan. 20, 2007; "Oprah: Their Story Is My Story," www.ABCNews.go.com, Jan. 2, 2007; "Oprah Winfrey Press Conference," www.oprah.com, Nov. 5, 2007; "Transcript of Oprah Winfrey's Commencement Address," *Stanford Report,* June 15, 2008; Lumka Oliphant, "Stars at Oprah's S. A. Bash," *Pretoria News,* Dec. 23, 2006; Ray Richmond, "Gift List for Challenged Media Figures," www.hollywoodreporter.com, Dec. 19, 2006; Beverly Keel, "Oprah's School for Girls in Africa Impresses Dad," *Tennessean,* Jan. 12, 2007; "Oprah Winfrey Talks About 'Her Girls,'" www.ABC7Chicago.com, Feb. 26, 2007; Jodi Poirier, "Building a Dream," *New York Amsterdam News,* Mar. 1–7, 2007; Ruben Navarette, "The Truth

According to Oprah," *San Diego Union-Tribune,* Jan. 14, 2007; Maulina Karenga, "Oprah in Africa," *Los Angeles Sentinel,* Jan. 17, 2007; Gill Guilford and Bothos Molosanka, "Accused Pleads Not Guilty in Oprah Case," Johannesburg *Star,* July 29, 2008; Solly Maphumulo, "Oprah Sex Scandal," Johannesburg *Star,* Mar. 31, 2009; Caille Millner, "Oprah's Opportunity," *San Francisco Chronicle,* Nov. 12, 2007; transcript, *Countdown with Keith Olbermann,* www.msnbc.msn.com, Nov. 5, 2007; Eugene Robinson, "Oprah the Avenger," *Washington Post,* Nov. 6, 2007; Canaan Mdletshe, "Girl Quits Winfrey Academy," *Sowetan,* Sept. 27, 2007; Andrew Leonard, "Live on Oprah: Microfinance!" www.Salon.com, Dec. 5, 2006.

TV/DVDS: *The Oprah Winfrey Show 20th Anniversary Collection* (DVD set); *The Oprah Winfrey Show,* WLS-TV Chicago, "Second Anniversary," aired Jan. 2, 1986 (viewed at www.museum.tv); Oprah Winfrey interviewed on *Meet the Faith,* BET, aired July 29, 2007; "Oprah's Roots" special episode of *African American Lives,* PBS, aired 1/24/2007; *Building a Dream,* ABC special, aired Feb. 26, 2007; "Inside Oprah's Holiday Trip," *The Oprah Winfrey Show,* aired Jan. 17, 2007.

INTERVIEWS: Nancy Stoddart, July 8, 2009; Fran Johns, Sept. 2007; Linda Reynolds Stern, Dec. 2008; Sandra Day O'Connor, Nov. 2008; Alice Walker, Oct. 7, 2008; Badi Foster, Feb. 27, 2007; Vernon Winfrey, Apr. 24, 2008; confidential source, Nov. 9, 2007; Rocky Twyman, May 20, 2008.

## NINETEEN

RECORDS: Transcripts of depositions of Rayford Dotch (June 16, 1997), LeGrande Green (Dec. 19, 1997), Dianne Hudson (June 18, 1997), James Kelley (June 18, 1997, and Dec. 19, 1997), Alice McGee (June 19, 1997), Oprah Winfrey (June 14, 1997, and Dec. 12, 1997), and Andrea Wishom (June 17, 1997) in the case of *Texas Beef Group* et al. *v. Winfrey* et al., case no. 2:96-cv-00208, U.S. District Court, Northern District of Texas; documents in the case of *Mutual of Omaha Insurance Company v. Winfrey* et al., case no. 8:09-cv-00145-JFB-TDT, U.S. District Court, District of Nebraska; results of searches "Harpo" and "Oprah," U.S. Patent and Trademark Office, Trademark Electronic Search System; decision in the case of *Elizabeth Coady v. Harpo, Inc.,* case no. 1-99-0481, 1st District, Illinois Appellate Court; documents in the case of *Lerato Nomvuyo Mzamane v. Oprah Winfrey* et al., case no. 2:08-CV-4884 in the U.S. District Court for the Eastern District of Pennsylvania; **documents in the case of *Corrine Gehrls v. Myron Gooch* et al., case no. 1:09-CV-06338 in the**

**U.S. District Court for the Northern District of Illinois, Eastern Division;** transcript, Jean Harris on *The Oprah Winfrey Show*, Aug. 22, 1988.

BOOKS: Bill Adler, ed., *The Uncommon Wisdom of Oprah Winfrey* (Citadel Press, 1997); Susan Faludi, *The Terror Dream* (Metropolitan Books, 2007).

ARTICLES: Patricia Sellars, "The Business of Being Oprah," *Fortune,* Apr. 1, 2000; Robert Feder, "Cynics' Shots at Oprah 'Come with the Territory,'" *Chicago Sun-Times,* Sept. 30, 1997; "Happy Anniversary! The Oprah Show Turns 20," *O, The Oprah Magazine,* Oct. 2005; P. J. Bednarski, "All About Oprah Inc.," *Broadcasting and Cable,* June 24, 2005; Robert Kurson, "The Silent Treatment," *Chicago,* July 2001; "Call Harpo Productions Anonymous Confession Hot Line," www.oprah.com (downloaded Nov. 2, 2006); "Listing of Full Trademarks," www.oprah.com (downloaded Sept. 9, 2009); Mary McNamara, "The Life of Hollywood," *Los Angeles Times,* Dec. 11, 2005; Logan Hill, "Harry Benson Gets Shots You Just Don't See Anymore," *New York,* Dec. 7, 2009; Kandace Raymond, "Oprah Fan Awaits Big Day," Nov. 14, 2007, www.13wmaz .com; Elizabeth Coady, "World Class Phoney Oprah Winfrey and Her Sycophants," *Providence Journal,* Knight-Ridder/Tribune News Service, Sept. 28, 2000; Michael Milner, "Free Speech Rocks! (When Oprah Calls the Tune)," *Chicago Reader,* Dec. 10, 1999; Tim Jones, "Muzzling Employees Host's Prerogative but Winfrey's Restriction Makes Some Howl," *Chicago Tribune,* Apr. 16, 2000; Eric Deggans, "Oprah Fans Get into the Spirit," *St. Petersburg Times,* June 21, 2003; Emily Farache, "Oprah to Underlings: Shut Your Mouth," www.eonline.com, Apr. 17, 2000; Libby Copeland, "Our Lady of Perpetual Help," *Washington Post,* June 26, 2000; Keith J. Kelly, "Oprah Defends Her Gag Rule for Staffers," *New York Post,* Apr. 18, 2000; Ellen Warren and Terry Armour, "Oh, No: Oprah Faces Tribulation of Another Trial," *Chicago Tribune,* Apr. 20, 2000; Grant McArthur, "Oprah Winfrey's Search for Aussie Leader," *Sydney Daily Telegraph,* Mar. 23, 2008; Ian Evans, "Trial to Lift Veil of Secrecy Over Oprah's African Academy," *Independent,* July 27, 2008; Sonia Murray, "Peach Fuzz," *Atlanta Journal-Constitution,* Feb. 4, 2004; "Rumor: Oprah Shuts Down Filming of VH1 Reality Show . . . ," www .mediatakeout.com, Dec. 24, 2008; "Oprah to Take Delivery of Canadian Jet," *Toronto Star,* June 4, 2006; Ben Bradley, "Winfrey's Jet Grounded After Striking Bird in CA," www.ABC7Chicago.com, Dec. 27, 2005; Harry Allen, "Owned by Nobody," *Vibe,* Sept. 1997; Bill Zwecker, "Paris Store's Hard Lesson: Don't Mess with Oprah," *Chicago Sun-Times,* June 23, 2005; George Rush and Joanna Molloy, "Snub a Pocketbook Issue to

Oprah," New York *Daily News,* June 22, 2005; "Store Sorry for Closed Door Policy," *Chicago Tribune,* June 24, 2005; Gersh Kuntzman, "Pal: Oprah Humiliated by Hermès," *New York Post,* June 24, 2005; "Ted and Sally's Hot Buggy Ride," *New York Post,* June 20, 2005; Pete Samson, "Noprah," *Daily Mirror,* June 25, 2005; "French Diss?" *People Weekly,* July 11, 2005; Anna Kingston, "Rosa Parks She's Not," *National Post,* June 28, 2005; "Oprah's Woes," Montreal *Gazette,* June 30, 2005; Mary Mitchell, "In Paris, Not Even Oprah Winfrey Can Escape the Reality of Being Black," *Chicago Sun-Times,* July 3, 2005; "Oprah Winfrey Was Denied Entry in Paris Because, as One Employee Said, They Had Been 'Having a Problem with North Africans,'" *National Review,* July 18, 2005; Aaron McGruder, *The Boondocks,* July 11, 2005, www.gocomics.com; Rosie O'Donnell, "oprah hermès," www.rosie.com, June 25, 2005; Orlando Patterson, "The Blind Pig," *New York Times,* Feb. 10, 2008; William Grimes, "Colorblind Conclusions on Racism," *New York Times,* Feb. 6, 2008; "Oprah Winfrey," *People Weekly,* Dec. 28, 1987; Ginny Dougary, "Soul Queen," London *Times Magazine,* Mar. 4, 1995; "Oprah Mistaken for Gender-Bending Bandit," *National Enquirer,* Oct. 23, 2001; "Oprah After-Hours Shopping Spree," *National Enquirer,* Dec. 20, 2001; "Anything Can Happen," www.oprah.com, Sept. 19, 2005; Don Kaplan, "Oprah: Hermès Embarrassed Me," *New York Post,* Sept. 20, 2005; "Oprah Gets On-Air Apology for Hermès Snub," *Chicago Sun-Times,* Sept. 21, 2005; Chris Rose, "As Not Read by Oprah," New Orleans *Times-Picayune,* Aug. 29, 2007; "Inside Prison," www.oprah.com, Dec. 12, 2003; Marieke Haredy, "Spare Me That Oprah Ego," www.theage.com.au, Dec. 21, 2006; Grant Pick, "Oprah!" *Republic,* Jan. 1986; "Dot's All . . . ," New York *Daily News,* Oct. 20, 1997; Elliott Harris, "St. Valentine Had a Cannon Out There," *Chicago Sun-Times,* Feb. 24, 2005; "Fashion Scoop: Oprah's Playbill," *WWD,* Apr. 18, 2006; Richard Roeper, "Apparently the Right Thing Isn't the Smart Thing," *Chicago Sun-Times,* Nov. 4, 2003; Margery Eagan, "Ethics Go Out the Window with Titillating Smart Story," *Boston Herald,* Oct. 28, 2003; Lisa de Moraes, "3 Weeks at No. 1: Fox Leads the League," *Washington Post,* Oct. 29, 2003; Peter Johnson, "Personal Tragedy or Media Event?" *USA Today,* Oct. 27, 2003; "Elizabeth Smart TV Crossfire," www.cnn.com, Oct. 27, 2003; Evgenia Peretz, "James Frey Gets a Bright, Shiny Apology from Oprah," www.VanityFair.com, May 11, 2009; Jennifer Armstrong, "New James Frey Paperback Implies He Has Scandalous Recordings of Oprah . . . Or Not," www.ew.com, May 5, 2009; Keith Bradsher, "Boy Who Killed Gets 7 Years; Judge Says Law Is Too Harsh," *New York Times,* Jan. 14, 2000; Jennifer Chambers, "Oprah Gets Abraham to Apologize to Family,"

*Detroit News,* Feb. 1, 2007; Marilyn Johnson, "Oprah Between the Covers," *Life,* Sept. 1997; Josh Young, "How Oprah Dumped Monica," *George,* Mar. 1999; Howard Kurtz and Lisa de Moraes, "Oprah Drops Monica Exclusive Over Money Issues," *Washington Post,* Dec. 30, 1998; Barbara McMahon, "Why Oprah Rejected Lewinsky Interview," *Evening Standard,* Sept. 30, 1998; Mike McDaniel, "ABC Catapults to Top of Weekly Ratings with Lewinsky and 'Friends,'" *Houston Chronicle,* Mar. 10, 1999; Lawrie Mifflin with Stuart Elliott, "Lewinsky Proves to Be Popular with Both Viewers and Sponsors," *New York Times,* Mar. 5, 1999; "Queen Oprah Speaks: Talk Show Is Becoming Guide to Winfrey Ways," *Boston Herald,* Dec. 19, 1996; Natasha Singer, "The Oprah Treatment," *New York Times,* May 11, 2006; Sarah Fiedelholtz, "These Are a Few of Oprah's Favorite Things," *Chicago Sun-Times,* Nov. 23, 2004; "Favorite Things" lists, www.oprah.com, 1999, 2000, 2002, 2003, 2004, 2005, 2007, 2008; "Late Night Jokes," Jan. 19, 2007, www.newsmax.com; "7000 Reasons to Love Oprah," *Chicago Tribune,* Nov. 22, 2005; Lewis Lazare, "Oprah Carried Away with Giveaways," *Chicago Sun-Times,* Sept. 16, 2004; Kelly Williams, "Drive, She Said," *People Weekly,* Sept. 27, 2004; Richard Roeper, "Oprah-mercial Turns Her into Hawk Show Host," *Chicago Sun-Times,* Sept. 16, 2004; Richard Roeper, "Car Winners Finding Out There Is No Free Lunch," *Chicago Sun-Times,* Sept. 20, 2004; Lucio Guerro, "Oprah's Car Giveaway Not Totally Free," *Chicago Sun-Times,* Sept. 22, 2004; "Oprah Car Winners Hit with Hefty Tax," www.CNNMoney.com, Sept. 22, 2004; Howard Gensler, "Yale Classroom Takes Two Days to Play Jax," *Philadelphia Daily News,* Sept. 27, 2004; "Vanity Fair 100," *Vanity Fair,* Oct. 2006; Katherine Thomson, "The Billionaire Thank-You Note," www.HuffingtonPost.com, Oct. 15, 2007; "More from Monterey: Would You Buy a Used Car from Oprah Winfrey?" www.latimesblogs.latimes.com/uptospeed, July 28, 2008; "From Fat to Fabulous," www.oprah.com, Sept. 15, 2005; "Madea Is Tyler Perry's Other Half," www.oprah.com, Mar. 6, 2009; Stephen M. Silverman, "Oprah Winfrey: Wealth Is a Good Thing," www.people.com, Apr. 11, 2006; Leslie Marshall, "The Intentional Oprah," *InStyle,* Nov. 1998; Lisa Kogan, "Oprah and Gayle Uncensored," *O, The Oprah Magazine,* Aug. 2006; Susan Yerkes, "Out to Sea with Oprah," *San Antonio News Express,* May 19, 1998; Mike O'Neill, "Key West Agog Over Oprah," *Tampa Tribune,* Apr. 18, 1998; Nancy Wilson, "Maya's Birthday," *Life,* July 1998; "Oprah Gives Maya Big Birthday Bash," *Jet,* May 19, 2003; "Oprah for Maya," *St. Louis Post-Dispatch,* May 2, 2008; Aldore D. Collier, "Oprah Honors Her Heroes in Three-Day Bash in Santa Barbara, CA," *Jet,* June 6, 2005; Laurie Winer, "The Legends Who Lunch," *O, The Oprah*

*Magazine,* Aug. 2005; Lisa de Moraes, "Fox Crushes the Competition," *Washington Post,* June 1, 2006; Bill Zwecker, "For Oprah, a Night Full of Friends," *Chicago Sun-Times,* Mar. 1, 2005; Michelle Tauber and J. D. Heyman, "What a Party!" *People Weekly,* Feb. 16, 2004; "Oprah Turns 50," *Us,* Feb. 16, 2004; Phil Rosenthal, "What Are You Looking At?" *Chicago Sun-Times,* Feb. 6, 2004; "Oprah's Big Birthday Plans," *Us,* Feb. 16, 2004; Tom Gliatto, "A Party from the Heart," *People Weekly,* May 30, 2005; Bill Zwecker, "Kate Minogue Postpones Tour to Battle Breast Cancer," *Chicago Sun-Times,* May 18, 2005; André Leon Talley, "Thick and Thin," *Vogue,* July 2005; "Oprah Talks About 'Legends Ball,'" www .ABCNews.go.com, May 22, 2006; Stephanie A. Frederic, "Inside Oprah's Bash for Obama," *Los Angeles Sentinel,* Sept. 13–19, 2007; John McCormick and Christi Parsons, "Winfrey Draws Rich, Famous to Obama Bash," *Chicago Tribune,* Sept. 9, 2007; Logan Hill, "Harry Benson Got Shots You Just Don't See Anymore," *New York,* Dec. 7, 2009.

TV/DVD: *The Oprah Winfrey Show 20th Anniversary Collection* (DVD set); "The Oprah Effect," *CNBC Originals,* CNBC, aired May 8, 2009; "Oprah's Favorite Things," *The Oprah Winfrey Show,* aired Nov. 20, 2007; "Oprah's Song of Maya, Parts 1 and 2," *The Gayle King Show,* aired May 20, 1998, and May 21, 1998.

INTERVIEWS: Confidential source, Mar. 21, 2008; Robert Feder, Oct. 11, 2007; Cheryl Reed, Oct. 11, 2007, and June 25, 2007; Bill Zwecker, Oct. 11, 2007, and June 25, 2008; confidential source, Nov. 26, 2007; Laura Aye, June 24, 2008; confidential source, Nov. 28, 2007; Erica Jong, Dec. 17, 2006; confidential source, Oct. 17, 2007; Chris Rose, Aug. 20, 2009; Rachel Grady, Dec. 15, 2006, and Apr. 27, 2007; Suzanne Herz, June 15, 2007; confidential source, Mar. 22, 2007; Ed Victor, Nov. 9, 2007; confidential source, Aug. 22, 2008; Daniel J. Bagdade, May 7, 2008; Peggy Furth, Mar. 16, 2007; correspondence with Wayne Kabak, Sept. 29, 2009; correspondence with Cameron Smith, Apr. 25, 2007; Blair Sabol, July 28, 2007; Miyuki Williams, Jan. 20, 2007; correspondence with Joe Armstrong, Mar. 6, 2009; Alice Walker, Oct. 7, 2008; David McFadden, M.D., Dec. 24, 2008.

## TWENTY

RECORDS: Search results for "Winfrey" at www.opensecrets.org; Federal Communications Commission file of complaints against *The Oprah Winfrey Show,* 2004–2007; Federal Communication Commission, "Notices of Apparent Liability and Memorandum Opinion and Order, Mar. 2006," released Mar. 15, 2006; letter, Jerry Glover, The Entertainment and

Intellectual Property Group LLC, to Patrick Crowe, Oprah for President, Aug. 22, 2006; Public Law 103-209, 103rd Congress, National Child Protection Act of 1993; transcript, "Keeping Hope Alive," *The Oprah Winfrey Show,* Oct. 18, 2006; search results for "Oprah Winfrey," "Stedman Graham," and "Harpo," Federal Election Commission, Individual Contributions Search, Disclosure Data Search.

BOOKS: Patrick H. Crowe, *Oprah for President: Run, Oprah, Run!* (Crowe Enterprises, 2005); Richard Wolffe, *Renegade* (Crown Publishers, 2009).

ARTICLES: "Oprah Winfrey's Biography," www.oprah.com (downloaded Feb. 20, 2009); *"The Oprah Winfrey Show* Global Distribution List," www.oprah.com, May 2009; Stephanie D. Smith, "The Circulation Gauge," *WWD,* Aug. 27, 2009; Patricia Sellars, "The Business of Being Oprah," *Fortune,* Apr. 1, 2000; Peter Lauria, "NBC Breathes In," *New York Post,* Oct. 10, 2007; Meg James, "Oprah Teams with Discovery on New Cable Channel," *Los Angeles Times,* Jan. 15, 2008; "Oprah.com Facts," www.oprah.com, May 2008; "Oprah Most Requested Stop in PR Campaigns," www.PR-inside.com, Jan. 12, 2008; Mark Jurkowitz, "Attack of the 50-Foot Oprah," *Boston Phoenix,* Feb. 9, 2006; Nancy F. Koehn and Erica Helms, "Oprah Winfrey," Harvard Business School Publication 9-803-190, May 8, 2003, revised June 1, 2005; "A Class Act: Oprah Hosts Students of History 298," *Inside Illinois,* May 17, 2001; "The Age of Oprah," cover, *Newsweek,* Jan. 18, 2001; "Queen Oprah," *Wall Street Journal,* Sept. 17, 1997; LaTonya Taylor, "The Church of O," *Christianity Today,* Apr. 1, 2002; Mary McNamara, "The Life of Hollywood," *Los Angeles Times,* Dec. 11, 2005; Lynn Sweet, "Bush, Gore in Hot Seat with Oprah," *Chicago Sun-Times,* Sept. 10, 2000; Robert Feder, "Gore to Help Kick Off New Season of Oprah," *Chicago Sun-Times,* Sept. 1, 2000; "Oprah Lines Up Gore as Guest for Sept. 11," *Chicago Tribune,* Sept. 1, 2000; Joyce Millman, "The Road to the White House Goes Through Oprah," www.Salon.com, Sept. 25, 2000; transcript, "Bill Moyers Talks with Dr. Ronald Walters," *Bill Moyers Journal,* Dec. 14, 2007, www.pbs.org; Lynn Sweet, "Oprah Backs Obama but Will She Vote for Him?" *Chicago Sun-Times,* Sept. 7, 2007; Brad Ritzer, "I Would Have Done This Job for Free," *Woman,* Dec. 14, 1998; Ginny Dougary, "Soul Queen," London *Times Magazine,* Mar. 4, 1995; Martyn Palmer, "Unloved but Unbowed," London *Times,* Feb. 25, 1999; Joshua Green, "Take Two," *Atlantic Monthly,* Nov. 2006; "Obama and the Oprah Factor," *Newsmax,* May 2008; Larry King, "Hannibal Lecter Turns Up in Italy," *USA Today,* June 15, 1992; Michael Kranish, "Oprah on Dole Chat: I Just Won't Do It," *Boston Globe,* Oct. 11, 1996; Michael Starr,

"Oprah Denies Bouncing Dole," *New York Post*, Oct. 11, 1996; Thomas Galvin, "Oprah Tells Bob to Take a Hike," *New York Post*, Oct. 8, 1996; Robert Feder, "Oprah Lets Political Parade Pass Her By," *Chicago Sun-Times*, Aug. 26, 1996; Phil Kloer, "Beatles and 'Soul Train' Make Music for Sweeps," *Atlanta Constitution*, Nov. 1, 1995; Irv Kupcinet, "Kup's Column," *Chicago Sun-Times*, Nov. 7, 1997; Louis Lague, "The White-Tie House," *People Weekly*, June 27, 1994; Donnie Radcliffe and Jacqueline Trescott, "Politics and Putters," *Washington Post*, June 28, 1989; Will Lesher, "Bush, Gore Hope Oprah Will Be the Way to Gain Crucial Female Votes," *Chicago Tribune*, Sept. 8, 2000; David Skinner, "Gore's Softsell on 'Oprah,'" www.Salon.com, Sept. 12, 2000; Phil Rosenthal, "Selling Obama May Be Beyond Oprah's Reach," *Chicago Tribune*, Sept. 7, 2007; "Getting Off the Couch," *Chicago Sun-Times*, Sept. 21, 2000; Gary Wisby, "Punch Card, Punch Line," *Chicago Sun-Times*, Sept. 17, 2000; "Gore Gets a Laugh on Oprah's Show," *Chicago Sun-Times*, Sept. 11, 2000; Naftali Bendavid, "Gore Wins Battle of Wills on 'Oprah' Show," *Chicago Tribune*, Sept. 12, 2000; Mark Brown, "Gore Had Nothing to Fear with Oprah," *Chicago Sun-Times*, Sept. 22, 2000; Michael Sneed, "Sneed," *Chicago Sun-Times*, Sept. 22, 2000; "Bush Has His Turn to Woo Women Voters on 'Oprah,'" *Chicago Tribune*, Sept. 18, 2000; Richard Roeper, "Preppies Bush, Gore Are Hard Not to Heckle," *Chicago Sun-Times*, Sept. 20, 2000; "Texas Governor George W. Bush Has Revealing Talk with Oprah," *Jet*, Sept. 19, 2000; Matthew Mosk, "The Magic Touch?" *Washington Post*, Sept. 5, 2007; Gloria Steinem, "Oprah Winfrey: How America Got with the Program," *Time*, Apr. 18, 2005; Ellen Warren and Terry Farmer, "Bush Has Idea for Oprah's Next Lifestyle Makeover," *Chicago Tribune*, Apr. 16, 2001; "Oprah Talks to Laura Bush," *O, The Oprah Magazine*, May 2001; Tara Copp, "First Lady Working Hard on Home Front," *Chicago Sun-Times*, Sept. 19, 2001; "Oprah Fears Trip, Skips O Premiere in South Africa," *Chicago Sun-Times*, Apr. 11, 2002; "Oprah Skips South African Launch of 'O' Magazine," *National Enquirer*, Apr. 11, 2002; Jeff, Zeleny, "Oprah Declines Bush Invite to Afghan Trip," *Chicago Tribune*, Mar. 29, 2002; "Winfrey Won't Tour for Bush," *New York Times*, Mar. 30, 2002; Andy Geller, "Envoy Oprah a No-Go," *New York Post*, Mar. 30, 2002; Barbara E. Martinez, "No Oprah, No Afghan Trip," *Washington Post*, Mar. 30, 2002; Joseph Honig, "Oprah Balks," *Los Angeles Daily News*, Apr. 8, 2002; "Oprah Just Says No," *People Weekly*, Apr. 15, 2002; Sally A. Tully, "Oprah's Decline," *Chicago Tribune*, Apr. 16, 2002; Michael Starr and Adam Buckman, "Oprah Complains to Pals on 'The View,' White House Set Me Up," *New York Post*, Apr. 3, 2002; Anne Basile, "My Letter to Oprah," www.educate-yourself.org, Oct. 9, 2002; Sacha Zimmerman, "Saint Oprah," www.thenewrepublic.com, May 21, 2007; transcript, "Buying the War," *Bill Moyers Journal*, Apr. 25, 2007, www.pbs.org; Laurence van Gelder, "Arts Briefing," *New York Times*, Sept. 18, 2003; "Sweden Censures Oprah for Pro-War Bias," *Circom Report*, Oct. 2003; Bill O'Reilly, "I Made a Mistake . . . ," www.foxnews.com, Mar. 3, 2003; Larry Elder, "You've Got Mail," www.worldnetdaily.com, Dec. 29, 2006; Tom Shales, "A Media Role in Setting the War? No Question," *Washington Post*, Apr. 25, 2007; "Howard vs. Oprah," *Star*, Mar. 27, 2004; Greg Gatlin, "Stern Drags Oprah into Indecency Battle," *Boston Herald*, Mar. 20, 2004; "Is Oprah Next in FCC Crosshairs?" *Newsweek*, Apr. 12, 2004; Richard Roeper, "By FCC Standards, Oprah More Dangerous Than Stern," *Chicago Sun-Times*, Mar. 24, 2004; Brian Hutchinson, "Stern Rebuke by FCC," New York *Daily News*, Mar. 19, 2004; Jeff Jarvis, "Oprah, Pontificating Panderer," www .buzzmachine.com, Mar. 26, 2004; Scott Steepleton, "FCC Should Gauge All by the Same Rules," *Santa Barbara News-Press*, Apr. 12, 2004; Robert Paul Reyes, "Oprah Winfrey Goes the Jerry Springer Route to Garner High Ratings," www .americanchronicle.com, Feb. 24, 2006; Nitya Venkataraman, "Oprah Winfrey Presents: Barack Obama," www.ABCNews.go.com, Dec. 7, 2007; Gary Cohen et al., "Women Say Schwarzenegger Groped, Humiliated Them," *Los Angeles Times*, Oct. 2, 2003; Tracy Weber et al., "3 More Women Allege Misconduct," *Los Angeles Times*, Oct. 4, 2003; Gary Cohen et al., "4 More Women Go Public Against Schwarzenegger," *Los Angeles Times*, Oct. 5, 2003; Carla Hall, "Another Alleged Victim Comes Forward," *Los Angeles Times*, Oct. 7, 2003; Maltea Gold and George Rubin, "Critics See Story as Hatchet Job," *Los Angeles Times*, Oct. 4, 2003; Bill Carter and Brian Stelter, "Letterman Extortion Question Raises Questions for CBS," *New York Times*, Oct. 3, 2009; Mark Steyn, "Comic Oprah," *National Review*, Mar. 23, 2008; Tim Griere, "Would You Let Your Sister Vote for This Man?" www.Salon.com, Aug. 30, 2003; Hank Steuver, "Is This Any Way to Make a Movie?" *Washington Post*, Sept. 7, 2003; Molly Ivins, "So Whose Mess Is California Anyway?" *Tulsa World*, Aug. 27, 2003; "Season Premiere," www.oprah.com, Sept. 15, 2003; Scott Martelle, "Schwarzenegger Plays Up Family in 'Oprah' Talk," *Los Angeles Times*, Sept. 16, 2003; David K. Li, "Maria Defends Her Husband on *Oprah*," *New York Post*, Sept. 16, 2003; "The Arnold Show," *Chicago Tribune*, Sept. 16, 2003; Mary McNamara, "O to a Higher Power," *Los Angeles Times*, Dec. 11, 2005; "Oprah, Arnold and Equal Time," *New York Times*, Sept. 17, 2003; Katha Pollitt, "Governor Groper?" *Nation*, Oct. 6, 2003; "President

Oprah Hits the Web," www.news.bbc.co.uk, Oct. 6, 1999; Michael Moore, "Draft Oprah for President," www.michaelmoore.com (downloaded June 28, 2006); Robert Fulghum, "Journal," www.robertfulghum .com, Aug. 14, 2006; "Top Ten Things Overheard at the Republican Weekend," *Late Show with David Letterman,* Feb. 21, 1995, www.cbs .com/latenight/lateshow; Kelli Bamforth, "One Man's Idea for President Turns National Sensation," *Wednesday Sun,* Dec. 26, 2007; transcript, *Larry King Live,* Sept. 25, 2006; Don Kaplan, "Please Hold for Oprah," *New York Post,* Oct. 14, 2006; Judy Markey, "Opinionated Oprah!" *Woman's Day,* Oct. 4, 1988; Nell Scovell, "Dressing Room Dropout," *New York Times Style Magazine,* Holiday 2006; "Former Olympic Medalist Marion Jones' First Interview After Prison," www.oprah.com, Oct. 24, 2008; Allison Samuels, "Toni Tells Her Troubles," *Newsweek,* May 1, 2000; Howard Kurtz, "For NBC President, a Week in the Hot Seat," *Washington Post,* Apr. 30, 2007; "The Virginia Tech Videotape Debate," www.oprah.com, Apr. 24, 2007; Richard Zoglin, "Lady with a Calling," *Time,* Aug. 8, 1988; Daniel Margolick, "Through a Lens Darkly," www.vanityfair.com, Sept. 24, 2007; "Fun with Oprah," www.ddy.com ("Oprah Log" downloaded Oct. 9, 2009); Alyson Ward, "Oprah, Dave, Dave, Oprah," *Fort Worth Star-Telegram,* Nov. 30, 2005; Phil Rosenthal, "What Are You Looking At?" *Chicago Sun-Times,* Feb. 1, 2002; Phil Rosenthal, "Oprah, Please Call Dave," *Chicago Sun-Times,* Jan. 7, 2002; Top Ten Lists, *Late Show with David Letterman,* Nov. 11, 1993, June 29, 1994, May 3, 1999, Mar. 29, 2004, Oct. 10, 2005, and Nov. 22, 2005, www.cbs.com/latenight/lateshow; "Scoop," *People Weekly,* Dec. 5, 2005; Aaron Barnhart, "Back on Speaking Terms: Dave and Oprah Chat Tonight," *Kansas City Star,* Dec. 1, 2005; David Bauder, "Oprah's Appearance Triples Letterman's Audiences," *Chicago Sun-Times,* Dec. 3, 2005; Lisa de Moraes, "Oprah Gives Peace—and Letterman—a Chance," *Washington Post,* Dec. 2, 2005; "Oprah Talks to Bill Clinton," *O, The Oprah Magazine,* Aug. 2004; Tom McNamee and Mike Thomas, "Clinton Book Tour Gets Around to Oprah's Set," *Chicago Sun-Times,* June 23, 2004; Jeff Simon, "A Long 'Life,' " *Buffalo News,* June 26, 2004; "Glitz Meets Grits," *Chicago Sun-Times,* Jan. 19, 1993; "President Clinton Signs 'Oprah Bill,' New Law to Protect Children," *Jet,* Jan. 10, 1994; Mark Jurkowitz, "Clinton's Charm and Confessions Play Well on TV," *Boston Globe,* June 24, 2004; "Presidential Performance," *Broadcasting and Cable,* June 28, 2004; "Performance of the Week," *Time,* July 5, 2004; "Oprah Talks to Barack Obama," *O, The Oprah Magazine,* Nov. 2004; "Living the American Dream," www.oprah.com, Jan. 19, 2005; Dr. Ink, "A Look Behind the Scenes," *Poynter Online* (www.poynter.org),

Oct. 17, 2006; Noel Sheppard, "Bill O'Reilly and Michelle Malkin Take on Oprah," www.newsbusters.org, Oct. 17, 2006; Matthew Mosk, "Oprah's Couch for Obama Only," www.blogs.washingtonpost .com, Sept. 5, 2007; "Late Night Jokes," Oct. 5, 2009, www.newsmax.com; "Oprah's Statement Regarding Gov. Sarah Palin on *The Oprah Winfrey Show*," www.oprah.com, Sept. 5, 2008; Alex Leary, "Florida Republicans Say No to Oprah," *The Buzz* (www .blogs.tampabay.com), Sept. 6, 2008; "Oprah on the Palin Rumors," www.extratv.warnerbrothers.com, Dec. 4, 2008; Garance Franke-Ruta, "Oprah and Obama, Together Again," www.voices.washingtonpost.com, Nov. 25, 2009; Lisa de Moraes, "Who's Unwilling to Pull Punches with Sarah?" *Washington Post*, Nov. 18, 2009; Tina Brown, "Sarah Drops the Act," www.thedailybeast.com, Nov. 18, 2009; **"Oprah Winfrey Donates to Newark Nonprofits,"** *Newsday*, **Feb. 1, 2009; Max Pizarro, "The Guru, the Star and Oprah," www .politickernj.com, Feb. 9, 2009;** Sharon Cotlier, "15 Questions with Bill Clinton," www.people.com, May 22, 2008; "Late Night Jokes," Sept. 5, 2009, www.newsmax.com; Dan Frederick, "Oprah to Host Obama Fundraiser," *Top of the Ticket* (www.latimesblogs.latimes.com), July 7, 2007; Lynn Sweet, "Oprah's Obama Fundraiser Sold Out?" *Chicago Sun-Times*, July 30, 2007; Soo Youn and Michael Saul, "Oprah Winfrey Raises $3 Million for Barack Obama," New York *Daily News*, Sept. 9, 2007; John McCormick and Christi Parsons, "Winfrey Draws Rich and Famous to Obama Bash," *Chicago Tribune*, Sept. 9, 2007; Jonathan King, "The Oprah/Barack Affair," *Montecito Journal*, Sept. 13, 2007; Richard Mineards, "From the First Canape to the Very Last Cocktail," *Santa Barbara News-Press*, Sept. 11, 2007; "Oprah Rolls Out the Red Carpet for Obama," *USA Today*, Sept. 9, 2007; Tina Daunt, "Obama Finds Lots of Green in Oprah's Meadow," *Los Angeles Times*, Sept. 9, 2007; transcript, *Larry King Live*, May 1, 2007; Colleen Mastory, "Oprah's Gamble," *Chicago Tribune*, Dec. 13, 2007; "Ellen DeGeneres Is New Favorite TV Personality as Oprah Slips to Number Two," *The Harris Poll*, #6, Jan. 14, 2008; John McCormick, "First Oprah, Next Gayle King," *Swamp* (www .weblogs.baltimoresun.com), Dec. 12, 2007; "How He Did It," *Newsweek*, Nov. 5, 2008; Caroline Kennedy, "A President Like My Father," *New York Times*, Jan. 27, 2008; Joan Walsh, "Don't Call Oprah a 'Traitor,'" www.Salon.com, Feb. 4, 2008; "The Secret Behind the Secret," www .oprah.com, Feb. 6, 2008; Edward McClellan, "More Than 125,000 Witness History in Chicago," www.Salon.com, Nov. 26, 2008; "Madonna, Oprah, Other Celebrities React to Obama's Win," AP, Nov. 5, 2008; Craig Garthwaite and Timothy J. Moore, "The Role of Celebrity Endorsements in Politics: Oprah, Obama, and the 2008 Democratic

Primary," unpublished, Sept. 2008; John Carlucci, "Winfrey on Politics: I Did My Part for Change," AP, Sept. 14, 2009.

TV/DVDS/AUDIO/OTHER: "Remembering Ted Kennedy: Vicki Kennedy's First TV Interview," *The Oprah Winfrey Show*, Nov. 25, 2009; *The Oprah Winfrey Show 20th Anniversary Collection* (DVD set); "Return of the King," *The Boondocks* (viewed at www.vidilife.com); "All American Tragedy," *The Oprah Winfrey Show*, Nov. 3, 2006; "Oprah Fridays Live: Mike Tyson Returns, Plus Evander Holyfield," *The Oprah Winfrey Show*, Oct. 16, 2009; "Truth in America," *The Oprah Winfrey Show*, Oct. 12, 2006; "Oprah's Town Hall with Bill O'Reilly," *The Oprah Winfrey Show*, Oct. 27, 2006; *The O'Reilly Factor*, **aired April 14, 2010;** Henry Louis Gates, Jr., Alma and Joseph Gildenhorn Talk, Aspen Institute, Washington, D.C., Feb. 27, 2007; Oprah Winfrey call in to *The Ed Lover Show*, WWPR-FM, Nov. 4, 2008 (audio heard at www.power1051fm.com); "Will Smith and Tina Fey," *The Oprah Winfrey Show*, Nov. 6, 2008; Oprah speech, Columbia, S.C., Dec. 9, 2007.

INTERVIEWS: Correspondence with Mary Ann Gilbert, ProQuest, Sept. 14, 2009; Marianne Means, Feb. 9, 2007; Katharine Carr Esters, Aug. 1, 2007; Senator Robert Dole, May 23, 2008; correspondence with Eileen Wood, Sept. 19, 2009; Christopher Addison, Nov. 20, 2007; Trudie Munson, 2007; correspondence with Patrick Crowe, June 3, 2008; confidential source, Aug. 10, 2007; confidential source, Oct. 26, 2006; Vernon Winfrey, Apr. 24, 2008; Luvenia Harrison Butler, Apr. 24, 2008; confidential source, June 23, 2008; Alice Walker, Oct. 10, 2008.

## AFTERWORD

ARTICLES: Alessandra Stanley, "The Fine Art of Quitting While She's Ahead," *New York Times*, Nov. 20, 2009; Gail Collins, "Putting the Fond in Farewell," *New York Times*, Nov. 21, 2009; Joe Flint and Meg James, "Afternoons Without Oprah," *Los Angeles Times*, Nov. 21, 2009; Julia Viatullo-Martin, "What Oprah's Departure Means for the Windy City," *Wall Street Journal*, Nov. 28, 2009; Nikki Finke, "The End of 'Oprah' as We Know Her," www.deadline.com/hollywood, Nov. 5, 2009; Daniel Frankel, "Oprah's Network Sets Yet Another Launch Date," www.thewrap.com, Nov. 20, 2009; Nikki Finke, "Oprah Promises Cable Show 'Smaller and Different,'" www.deadline.com/hollywood, Nov. 20, 2009; Rick Kogan, "City of 1000 Stars: Should Chicago Be Defined by Its Celebrities?" *Chicago Tribune*, Nov. 29, 2009; Phil Rosenthal, "Say It Ain't So, O," *Chicago Tribune*, Nov. 6, 2009; "Why Is She Ending the Show? Daley Blames the Media," *Chicago Sun-Times*, Nov. 19, 2009;

Richard Roeper, "Oprah Doesn't Feel Chicagoans' Love? Oh, Please!" *Chicago Sun-Times,* June 7, 2010; Patricia Shipp, "Oprah's Booze and Drug Binges," *National Enquirer,* Nov. 9, 2009; "Late Show Top Ten," www.newsmax.com/jokes, Nov. 23, 2009; Bill Gorman, "'Christmas Special at the White House: An Oprah Primetime Special' Draws ABC's 2nd-Biggest Audience in the Hour This Season," tvbythenumbers .com, Dec. 14, 2009; Jason Links, "The *Time* 100 in 2010," *Huffington Post,* April 29, 2010; Phil Donahue, "Oprah Winfrey," www.time.com, April 29, 2010; Claire Atkinson, "Maria Grasso and Nina Wass Exit Cable Channel Before Launch," *Broadcasting and Cable,* Aug. 25, 2009; Ken Auletta, "Why Oprah Needs Cable," www.newyorker.com, Nov. 20, 2009; Pat Embry, "'Oprah Winfrey's Father' Says Her Success Is No Surprise," *Nashville Banner,* Jan. 20, 1986; Cathy Horyn, "Elegance Is the Norm at Costume Institute Gala," *New York Times,* May 3, 2010; Anahita Moussavian and Serena French, "Oversexed in the City," *New York Post,* May 4, 2010; Amy Diluna, "Stars Come Out to Shine at the 2010 Metropolitan Museum of Art's Costume Institute Gala," New York *Daily News,* May 4, 2010; Kaitlin Knoll, "Oprah Winfrey to Receive Minerva Award," *Hollywood Reporter,* June 2, 2010; Karen R. Long, "Oprah Winfrey Is a Surprise Winner of Cleveland's Anisfield-Wolf Award," *Plain Dealer,* April 22, 2010; "We Hear You," *O, The Oprah Magazine,* May 2010.

TV: "Oprah's Fridays Live," *The Oprah Winfrey Show,* aired Nov. 20, 2009; "Oprah's Season 24 Kickoff Party," *The Oprah Winfrey Show,* aired Sept. 10, 2009.

INTERVIEW: Confidential source, Jan. 2, 2008.

# Bibliography

Abt, Vicki, and Leonard Mustazza. *Coming After Oprah: Cultural Fallout in the Age of the TV Talk Show.* Bowling Green, Oh.: Bowling Green State University Popular Press, 1997.

Adler, Bill, ed. *The Uncommon Wisdom of Oprah Winfrey.* Secaucus, N.J.: Citadel Press, 1997.

Almond, Steve. *(Not That You Asked).* New York: Random House, 2007.

Angelou, Maya. *Letter to My Daughter.* New York: Random House, 2008.

Black, Cathie. *Basic Black.* New York: Crown, 2007.

Bly, Nellie. *Oprah! Up Close and Down Home.* New York: Zebra Books, 1993.

Bonvillain, Keifer. *Ruthless.* Atlanta: Keifer Enterprises, 2007.

Burrell, Paul. *A Royal Duty.* New York: Putnam, 2003.

Crowe, Patrick H. *Oprah for President.* Self-published, 2005.

Davis, Natalie Zemon. *Slaves on Screen.* Cambridge, Mass.: Harvard University Press, 2000.

Dougherty, Jack. *More Than One Struggle: The Evolution of Black School Reform in Milwaukee.* Chapel Hill: University of North Carolina Press, 2004.

Elliot, Jeffrey M., ed. *Conversations with Maya Angelou.* Jackson: University Press of Mississippi, 1989.

Esters, Katharine Carr. *Jay Bird Creek.* Kosciusko, Miss.: Solid Earth LLC, 2005.

Farr, Cecilia Konchar. *Reading Oprah.* Albany, N.Y.: SUNY Press, 2005.

Frey, James. *A Million Little Pieces.* New York: Anchor, 2003.

Frumkin, Peter. *Strategic Giving: The Art and Science of Philanthropy.* Chicago: University of Chicago Press, 2006.

Funderburg, Lise, and Jennifer S. Altman. (Foreword by Oprah Winfrey.) *The Color Purple: A Memory Book of the Broadway Musical.* New York: Carroll and Graf, 2006.

Gamson, Joshua. *Freaks Talk Back.* Chicago: University of Chicago Press, 1998.

Garson, Helen S. *Oprah Winfrey: A Biography.* Westport, Conn.: Greenwood Books, 2004.

Gates, Henry Louis, Jr. *Finding Oprah's Roots*. New York: Crown, 2007.

Gillespie, Marcia Ann, Rosa Johnson Butler, and Richard A. Long. (Foreword by Oprah Winfrey.) *Maya Angelou: A Glorious Celebration*. New York: Doubleday, 2008.

Graham, Stedman. *Build Your Own Life Brand*. New York: Free Press, 2001.

———. *Diversity: Leaders Not Labels*. New York: Free Press, 2006.

———. *Move Without the Ball*. New York: Fireside, 2004.

———. *Teens Can Make It Happen*. New York: Fireside, 2000.

———. *Who Are You?* Carlsbad, Calif.: Hay House, 2005.

———. *You Can Make It Happen*. New York: Fireside, 1998.

Graham, Stedman, Lisa Delpy Neirotti, and Joe Jeff Goldblatt. *The Ultimate Guide to Sport Event Management and Marketing*. Chicago: Irwin Professional Publishing, 1995.

———. *The Ultimate Guide to Sports Marketing* (2nd ed.). New York: McGraw-Hill, 2001.

Greene, Bob, and Oprah Winfrey. *A Journal of Daily Renewal: The Companion to Make the Connection*. New York: Hyperion, 1996

———. *Make the Connection*. New York: Hyperion, 1996.

Griffin, Kathy. *Official Book Club Selection: A Memoir According to Kathy Griffin*. New York: Ballantine Books, 2009.

Harris, Jennifer, and Elwood Watson, eds. *The Oprah Phenomenon*. Lexington: University of Kentucky Press, 2007.

Illouz, Eva. *Oprah Winfrey and the Glamour of Misery*. New York: Columbia University Press, 2003.

Irwin, Jecquin D. *My Life After Oprah*. Self-published, 2006 (Kindle ed.).

Jalloh, Alusine, and Toyin Fabola, eds. *Black Business and Economic Power*. Rochester, N.Y.: University of Rochester Press, 2002.

Jones, Quincy. *Q: The Autobiography of Quincy Jones*. New York: Harlem Moon, 2001.

Kaminer, Wendy. *I'm Dysfunctional, You're Dysfunctional*. New York: Vintage Books, 1993.

King, Norman. *Everybody Loves Oprah*. New York: William Morrow and Co., 1987.

Kogan, Rick. *America's Mom: The Life, Lessons, and Legacy of Ann Landers*. New York: William Morrow, 2003.

Krohn, Katherine. *Oprah Winfrey*. Minneapolis: 21st Century Books, 2002.

Kurtz, Howard. *Hot Air: All Talk All the Time*. New York: Basic Books, 1997.

Lawrence, Ken. *The World According to Oprah*. Kansas City, Mo.: Andrews McMeel Publishing, 2005.

Leamer, Lawrence. *Fantastic: The Life of Arnold Schwarzenegger*. New York: St. Martin's Press, 2005.

*Live Your Best Life: A Treasury of Wisdom, Wit, Advice, Interviews, and Inspiration from* O, The Oprah Magazine. Birmingham, Ala.: Oxmoor House, 2005.

Lowe, Janet. *Oprah Winfrey Speaks*. New York: John Wiley and Sons, 1998.

Lyman, Howard F., with Glen Merzer. *Mad Cowboy*. New York: Touchstone, 1998.

Mair, George. *Oprah Winfrey: The Real Story*. New York: Birch Lane Press, 1994.

Marberry, Craig. *Cuttin' Up: Wit and Wisdom from Black Barbershops*. New York: Doubleday, 2005.

Marshall, P. David. *Celebrity and Power*. Minneapolis: University of Minnesota Press, 1997.

Mathabane, Mark. *Kaffir Boy in America*. New York: Free Press, 1990.

McDonald, Katrina Bell. *Embracing Sisterhood*. New York: Rowman and Littlefield, 2007.

McDowell, Josh, and Dave Sterrett. *"O" God: A Dialogue on Truth and Oprah's Spirituality*. Los Angeles: WND Books, 2009.

McGraw, Philip. *Life Strategies*. New York: Hyperion, 1999.

Natkin, Paul, and Stephen Green. *To Oprah with Love*. Beverly Hills, Calif.: New Millennium Press, 2002.

Nelson, Marcia Z. *The Gospel According to Oprah*. Louisville, Ky.: Westminster John Knox Press, 2005.

Nicholson, Louis P. (Introduction by Coretta Scott King.) *Oprah Winfrey, Entertainer*. Danbury, Conn.: Grolier Inc., 1994.

Noden, Merrell. *People Profiles: Oprah Winfrey*. New York: Time Inc., 1999.

*O's Big Book of Happiness: The Best of* O, The Oprah Magazine. Birmingham, Ala.: Oxmoor House, 2008.

*O's Guide to Life: The Best of* O, The Oprah Magazine. Birmingham, Ala.: Oxmoor House, 2007.

Olesker, Michael. *Michael Olesker's Baltimore*. Baltimore: Johns Hopkins University Press, 1995.

———. *Tonight at Six*. Baltimore: Apprentice House, 2008.

Oppenheimer, Jerry. *Front Row.* New York: St. Martin's Griffin, 2005.

Peck, Janice. *The Age of Oprah.* Boulder, Colo.: Paradigm Publishers, 2008.

Roberts, Gene, and Hank Klibanoff. *The Race Beat.* New York: Alfred A. Knopf, 2006.

Rooney, Kathleen. *Reading with Oprah* (2nd ed.). Fayetteville: University of Arkansas Press, 2008.

Shattuc, Jane M. *The Talking Cure.* New York: Routledge, 1997.

Sloan, Bill. *I Watched a Wild Hog Eat My Baby.* Amherst, N.Y.: Prometheus Books, 2001.

Smith-Shomade, Beretta E. *Shaded Lives: African-American Women and Television.* New Brunswick, N.J.: Rutgers University Press, 2002.

Staten, Vince. *Do Bald Men Get Half-Price Haircuts?* New York: Touchstone, 2001.

Steele, Carrington. *Don't Drink the Kool-Aid.* Self-published, 2008.

Steinberg, Neil. *The Alphabet of Modern Annoyances.* New York: Doubleday, 1996.

Tillis, James "Quick," as told to J. Engleman Price. *Thinking Big.* Chicago: The LPG Group, 2000.

Tolle, Eckhart. *A New Earth.* New York: Plume, 2005.

Waldron, Robert. *Oprah!* New York: St. Martin's, 1987.

Walker, Alice. *The Same River Twice.* New York: Scribner, 1996.

Walker, Andre. (Foreword by Oprah Winfrey.) *Andre Talks Hair!* New York: Simon and Schuster, 1997.

Walker, Margaret. *Jubilee.* New York: Mariner Books, 1999 (originally published 1966).

White, Evelyn C. *Alice Walker.* New York: W.W. Norton and Co., 2004.

White, Wendel A. *Small Towns, Black Lives.* Oceanville, N.J.: The Noyes Museum of Art, 2003.

Wilson, Melba. *Crossing the Boundary: Black Women Survive Incest.* Seattle: Seal Press, 1994.

Winfrey, Oprah. *The Best of Oprah's What I Know for Sure.* Supplement to *O, the Oprah Magazine,* undated.

———. *Journey to Beloved.* New York: Hyperion, 1998.

Winfrey, Shakeeta. *The Other Winfrey: Life in the Shadow of O.* Decatur, Ga.: Marketing Communications Group, 2007.

Wolffe, Richard. *Renegade: The Making of a President.* New York: Crown, 2009.

# Acknowledgments

A BOOK ABOUT someone as complex and fascinating as Oprah Winfrey could not have a better home than Random House, Inc., and the Crown Publishing Group. The support of Peter Olson, former CEO, and Jenny Frost, former president of Crown, to present a full, comprehensive biography of one of the most powerful public figures of our time gave me the opportunity to write about the American dream with all its rags and riches, ravages and rewards.

Throughout four years of research and reporting I was guided—superbly—by the exacting voice of my editor Peter Gethers and assisted at every turn by his extraordinary assistant Christina Malach and the supremely talented editor Claudia Herr. Under the leadership of Markus Dohle, CEO of Random House, Crown's president Maya Mavjee, publisher Tina Constable, and marketing director Philip Patrick, I began to live the dream of all authors: a fabulous publishing experience, which included the wonderful organizational skills of Amy Boorstein, the artistic eye of Mary Choteborsky, the copyediting genius of Jenna Dolan, David Tran's sophisticated cover design, and the silken talents of David Drake, head of publicity, in conjunction with Marina Ein, Jeff Ingram, and Rebecca Kelley of Ein Communications. In addition, I was blessed during the lawyering process with outstanding counsel from Kathy Trager and Matthew Martin.

I'm grateful to all of the Crown Publishing Group, most particularly Robert Siek, production editorial; Linnea Knollmueller, production; Barbara Sturman, design; Amanda D'Acierno, publisher of audio; Jill Flaxman, sales marketing; Linda Kaplan, subrights; and Jacob Bronstein, who introduced me to the twenty-first-century wonders of Twitter and Facebook.

I owe immense thanks to my longtime agent, Wayne S. Kabak, who has held my hand through many books, and to Larry Kirshbaum, who joined us in this publishing venture.

The research for this book began with my assistant Stephanie K. Eller, who organized 2,732 files on the life of Oprah Winfrey, divided into names, dates, and subjects. In addition, Stephanie pored over the 990 tax returns of Oprah's various foundations to design the financial graphs in Chapter 18. She spent days fact-checking every chapter and compiling the documentation for the end notes. Along the way we were assisted by excellent research and reporting from Liz Rich, Leon Wagener, Carolyn Hardnett Robinson, Monika Blackwell, Alexander Hilhorst, Shilpa Nadhan, Wendy Lyons Sunshine, and Patti Pancoe.

Most of the sources in this book are named with the exception of past and present Harpo employees, who could speak only on condition of absolute confidentiality. I appreciate the trust they put in me.

Journalists, as always, were exceedingly generous, and I'm grateful to all of them, especially Margaret Engel, director of the Alicia Patterson Foundation; her twin Alison Engel, director of University Communications, University of Southern California; Linda Cashdan, who walked me through every chapter on the C & O Canal; and the late John Mashek, who did not live long enough to celebrate what he called "The Continuing Saga of St. Oprah."

In alphabetical order I thank the following for all they did for this book and/or its author: Christopher Addison, Kurt Anderson, Michael Anderson, Jeanette Angell, Alexandra Armstrong, Joe Armstrong, Sheryl Harris Atkinson, Lissa August, Laura Aye, Daniel Bagdade, Barry Baird, William F. Baker, Bob Barnes, Ysaye M. Barnwell, Alexa Bartel, Jewette Battles, Andy Behrman, Phoebe Beasley, Kathy Berlin, Ellen Bennett, Jenna Bett, Rob Birkhead, Alexandra Mayes Birnbaum, Sylvia Watts Blann, Mervin Block, Myrna Blyth, Anne Borchardt, David and Amanda Bowker, Richard Brase, Richard Brenneman, Michael Brooks, Gordon El Greco Brown, Beverly Burke, Bonnie Burlbaw, Deborah Bush, E. Faye Butler, Paul Burrell, Kenneth Burrows, David Bushman, Dale Buss, Luvenia Harrison Butler, Maria Calcagni, William Chaput at the Lotos

Club, Trace Chapman, Larry Carpenter, Kathryn Carrick, Peter Cherukuri, Chris Clark, Steve Clark, Winnie Clark, Elizabeth Clauhsen, Patsy Cline, Peter Colasante, Judy Colteryahn, David Patrick Columbia, Mike Conway, Randolph Cook, Krysten Coppoletta, Paul Costello, Margo Cozell, Thomas Craft, Todd Cranford, Lynn Crawford, Candy Miles-Crocker, Nancy Cronk, David Crossland, Page Crossland, Patrick Crowe, Renee Crown, Barbara Dale, Mike Dalton, Peggy Datillo, Gwen Davis, Joseph Davis, Virginia Davis, Spider Dean, Tatiana de Fidler, Charles DeFanti, Steve Dennis, Sally Denton, Paul Dickson, Grace Diekhaus, Maria di Martini, Diane Dimond, Barbara Dixon, Sen. Robert Dole, Pier Dominguez, Phil Donahue, Todd Doughty, Kathleen Drew, Helen and Richard Dudman, Robert Duffy, Bill East, Daniel Edwards, Bonnie Eldon, Gary Elion, Katharine Carr Esters, Don Everett, Penny Farthing, Nancy Fax, David Fechheimer, Robert Feder, Carol Felsenthal, Kathleen Fennell, Hilda Ford, Badi Foster, Michael Fox, Drew Friedman, Rick Frishman, Tony Frost, Peter Frumkin, Harry G. Fulmer, Peggy Furth, Keri L. Gaither, Tony and Marsha Gallo, Elaine Ganick, Ray Garcia, Patricia A. Garrett-Oluade, Ann Gerber, Robin Gerber, Mary Ann Gilbert, Mary Gilliat, Michelle Gillion, Jean and Tom Gilpin, Mishelle Gilson, Vivian and Bob Glick, Bonnie Goldstein, Alex Goode, Nina Goodman, Sarah Gorman, Rachel Grady, Diedre Stoelze Graves, Don and Judy Green, Nancy Green, Kevin Grogan, Michael Gross, Patricia Gurne, Barbara L. Hamm, Joy Handler, Joyce Saenz Harris, Judith L. Harris, Stacy Harris, Anna Harrison, Fruzsina Harsanyi, Darlene Hayes, Andrea Haynes, J. C. Hayward, James Henderson, Suzanne Herz, Stephen Hess, Joyce Daniel Hill, Michael Hill, Dale Lee Hinz, Roger Hitts, Robert Holm, Gary Holt, Jay Houston, Glenn Horowitz, Sandy Horwitt, Margo Howard, Beth Howse, Charlotte Huff, Bobbie Huffmister, Bob Hughes, Janis Ian, Gail Ifshin, Marty Ingels, Mark Itkin, Paula K. Jacobs, Jeremy Jacobs, Beverly Jackson, Tracey Jackson, James Jenkins, Ken Jennings, Fran Johns, Keith Johnson, Peter Johnston, Doug Joiner, Bob Jones, Tim Jones, Erica Jong,

Carol Joynt, David Jozwiak, Andre Julian, Blair Kamin, Susan Karns, Beverly Keel, John Keller, Susie Kelly, Karen Kennedy, Kathy Kiely, Dorothy H. Kiser, Rick Kogan, Arnold Koonin, Jesse Kornbluth, Ed Kosowski, Bill Kovach, Alex Kuczynski, Jeanine Kunz, Ris La Coste, Melissa Lakey, Lynne Lamberg, Norma and Roger Langley, Kitty Lansdale, Janine Latus, Diane Laughlin, Bob Leffler, A. J. Lehter, Pat and Randy Lewis, Beatrice Liebenberg, Ellen Lightman, Lisa Lucke, Mike Luckovich, Howard Lyman, Sharon Malone, Mary Jo Manning, Cecily Marcus, Alice Masemer, Darlene Mathis, Jane McClary, Jerry McCoy, Katrina Bell McDonald, David McFadden, M.D., Marvin McIntyre, Pat McNees, Grace McQuade, Kevin McShane, Marianne Means, Sandi Mendelson, Caroline Michel, Zoe Mikva, Frank Miller, Marc E. Miller, Mark Crispan Miller, Richard Mineards, Rachel Mirsky, Dan E. Moldea, Joanna Molloy, John Moran, James McGrath Morris, Susan Morrison, Barbara and David Morowitz, Dan Moore, Paul Moore, Luther T. Munford, Trudie Munson, Alanna Nash, Tracy Noble, Jimmy Norton, Janette Nunez, Jackie Oakes, Patricia O'Brien, Justice Sandra Day O'Connor, Mike Olesker, Jerry Oppenheimer, Patty O'Toole, Patty Outlaw, Marc Pachter and the Washington Biography Group, Margaret Pagan, Jack Panczak, Brooks Parker, Bob Parr, Patrice Patton-Price, Topher Payne, Scott Peacock, Pamela Peeke, M.D., Alexandra Penney, JoAnn Pinkerton, Diane M. Praet, Suzy Prudden, Paxton Quigley, Sugar Rautbord, Katie Rawls, Sonny Rawls, Bernice Johnson Reagon, Cheryl Reed, Judith Regan, Dr. Frank M. Reid, Bonnie Remsberg, Bev Reppert, Harvey Resnick, M.D., Barry Ribock, Carol Ribock, Allen Rice, Jewell Robinson, Patsy Rogers, Richard Redpants Rogers, Carl Rollyson, Louisa Romano, Paula Rome, Susan Rome, Chris Rose, George Rush, Daniel Ruth, Colleen Ryan, Deborah Caulfield Ryback, Robert Rynasiewicz, Blair Sabol, Jeff Samuels, Conrad Sanford, Bob Sector, Richard W. Schott, Pat Shakow, Adam Shapiro, Amy Shapiro, Ron Shapiro, Claudia Shear, Riki Sheehan, Barbara Shellhorn, Cynthia Connor Shelton, Anne Boone Simanski, Larry Singer, Cameron Smith, Esther Smith, Lisa Smith, Liz

Smith, Sharon Hull Smith, Eileen Solomon, Nancy Solinski, Brenda Billips Square, Julie Johnson Staples, Neil Steinberg, Linda Reynolds Stern, Ann Stock, Nancy Stoddart, John B. Straw, Gloria Steinem, Nancy Harvey Steorts, Andrew Stephen, Allen J. Streiker, Kimba Stroud, Michael Sullivan, Richard Swartz, Nan Talese, Deborah Tannen, Maureen Taylor, Rose Thomas, Patricia Thompson, Cynthia Todd, Sue Tolchin, Jeffrey Toobin, Darlene Tracy, Bob Turk, Rocky Twyman, James van Sweden, Ed Victor, Robert Waldron, Alice Walker, Patrick Walsh, Jeanette Walls, Mike Walter, Ellen Warren, Eddie Washington, Janet Wassom, Susan Weaving, Steve Weisman, Gregg A. Wilhelm, Armstrong Williams, Miyuki Williams, Dori Wilson, Vernon Winfrey, Judy Wise, Jeanette Witter, Eileen Wood, Barbara Wright, Irene Wurtzel, Catherine Wyler, Elliot Zinger, Jeremy and Gretchen Zucker, Bill Zwecker.

Thanks, also, to Sheila and Dobli Srinivasan and their pals at PGA West in La Quinta, who provided their warmth during the winter in addition to the California sun: Jim and Connie Alderson; Stephanie Arthur; Jon Caruana; Howard and Monique Culver; George and Geraldine Harmina; Jim and Gail Hawkins; Jim and Barbara Lambert; Bill and Sandi Phillips; Terry and Patricia Pracht; Debra Schwanke; Jesse and Ellen Sprecher; David and Lorraine Stearns.

My deepest thanks to my husband, Jonathan Zucker, who continues to make the sun shine.

*January 27, 2010*

# Photograph Credits

# Index

## A

*A&E Biography,* 165
ABC entertainment network,
239, 322, 349, 408, 473, 476
A Better Chance (ABC), 296,
379, 385, 389
Abraham, Nathaniel (Nate), 424
Abrams, Dan, 285
Abrams, Eugene H., 34
Abt, Vicki, 282, 316
Academy Awards (1996), 331
Adams, Jill, 313
Adams, Yolanda, 434
Addison, Christopher, 442
affirmative action, 52–53, 54, 72,
73, 124
African American women
bond among, 135
and racism, 117
and slave mentality, 108, 112,
231
and success, 122, 124, 223, 231
*Afro-American Red Star,* 363
AFTRA, 334
AIDS, 209–210, 328
Akihito, Emperor of Japan, 442
Albright, Madeleine, 370
Alfred A. Knopf, publishers, 262,
264–266, 275
Ali, Muhammad, 111, 370
Allen, Debbie, 434
Allen, Harry, 412
Allen, Steve, 333
Alleva, Richard, 351
*All My Children,* 100–101
Amarillo, Texas, 340–344

Amblin Entertainment, 139
*A.M. Chicago,* 1, 115, 201
in Ethiopia, 10
ratings, 6–7, 10, 14, 25, 120
sexual content on, 3–18, 120
American Atheists, 317
American Booksellers Association
(ABA), 262–265, 270, 295
American Double-Dutch League
World Invitational Champi-
onship, 281
American Dream, 224
American Jewish Congress, 220
American Red Cross, 257
American Women's Economic
Development Corporation,
180
*Amos and Andy,* 32
Anchor Press, 306, 307
Anderson, Loni, 288
Anderson, Marian, 67
Andrew, Duke of York, 334, 335
Angell, Jeannette, 273–274
Angelou, Maya, 52, 111, 262, 277
on *Beloved,* 356
*The Heart of a Woman,* 296
*I Know Why the Caged Bird
Sings,* 11
as legend, 433
as mentor, 150, 153, 171, 270–
271, 272, 346
Oprah's gifts to, 150, 180, 277,
431–432
"Phenomenal Women," 114
and politics, 442, 464
Aniston, Jennifer, 433

Ann-Margret, 247, 262
Anouilh, Jean, 294
Armour, Terry, 410
Armstrong, Lance, 332, 421
Art Against AIDS/Chicago, 379
Artner, Alan G., 8
Ashanti, 434
Aspen, Marvin E., 167
Associated Press, 243
Association of Black Media
    Workers, 90
Atchison, Calvin O., 175
Athletes Against Drugs (AAD),
    159, 169, 281
Atkinson, Sheryl Harris, 62–63,
    64, 66, 69
Atlantic Aviation, 411
Aubrey, Jennifer, 122
Auletta, Ken, 476
Avedon, Richard, 247
Avery, Margaret, 136, 139, 140,
    142–143, 144
Aye, Laura, 411–412

B

Babcock, Charles "Chip," 341
Baer, David, 306
Bagdade, Daniel J., 424
Bailey, Pearl, 111
Baker, William F.:
    and Oprah in Baltimore, 92,
        96–99, 117, 118
    and People Are Talking, 96–99,
        98, 104, 111
    and WJZ staff, 84, 88, 96
Bakker, Jim and Tammy Faye,
    213
Baldwin, Jo, 150, 195, 368
Ball, Lucille, 231
Ball, Skip, 119
Baltimore, 81–82, 91

Oprah's departure from, 116–
    119
Oprah's move to, 81–82
Oprah's star status in, 113
politics in, 91
school system of, 390–391
Baltimore Evening News, 141
Baltimore Sun, The, 141, 172, 391
Banks, Ernie, 468
Banks, Tyra, 434
Barbieri, Paula, 290
Barnes & Noble, 264
Barthel, Joan, 263
Bashir, Martin, 335
Bass, Marty, 104, 119
Bassett, Angela, 434
Bastone, William, 310
Basu, Anirban, 391
Battle, Kathleen, 434
Battles, Jewette, 21, 182, 186, 368
Baum, Phil, 220
Beatles, 32
Beatty, Warren, 331
Becker, William, 424–425
Bednarski, P. J., 6, 8, 429
Behrman, Andy, 196, 197, 199,
    201
Beloved (film), 137, 227, 348, 357
    as box office failure, 355, 356
    critical reviews of, 352
    director for, 348, 356
    publicity for, 186, 352–355,
        367, 373
    and slave memorabilia collec-
        tion, 349
    and slavery experience, 349,
        355
Bennett, Tim, 132, 286, 339
Bennett, Tony, 432
Bennett, William, 279
Benson, Harry, 405

Berger, Stuart, 197

Berman, Lea, 442–443

Berry, Halle, 333, 434

BET (Black Entertainment Television), 400

Bethel A.M.E. church, 90, 91, 93

Betty Jean (childhood friend), 28

Bezos, Jeff, 385

Big Sisters, 376

*Bill Moyers Journal,* 448–449

Birkenhead, Peter, 368

Black Elks Club, Nashville, 48–49, 67–68

Black History Month, 6, 290

Blair, Jayson, 308

Blann, Sylvia Watts, 50

Blige, Mary J., 434

Blue, Linda Bell, 130

Blyth, Myrna, 204, 205, 206

B'nai B'rith, 219

Boedeker, Hal, 363

Bohjalian, Chris, *Midwives,* 303

Bombeck, Erma, 255–256

Boul, David, 403

Boy George, 421

Bradley, Ed, 60

Brady, Harriet Bookey, 219, 220, 221

Braun, Carol Moseley, 440

Braxton, Toni, 456

Breathnach, Sarah Ban, *Simple Abundance,* 289, 360

*Brewster Place* (TV), 238–239

Briley, Clifton Beverly, 72

Brinkley, Christie, 9

B. Robert Lewis House, Eagan, Minnesota, 379

Brock, David, 161

Brooks, Michael, 198

Broom, Maria, 84, 90, 92

Brown, Bobbi, 413

Brown, Denise, 291–292, 292–293

Brown, Glenda Ann, 159

Brown, Jamie Foster, 328, 329

Brown, Mark, 444

Brown, Robert J., 159, 161, 244–245

Brown, Tina, 145, 147, 149, 314, 466

*Brown v. Board of Education,* 60

Browne, Anthony, 190, 225, 365

Browning, Robert, 478

Bryant, Rev. John Richard, 93

Bumpus, Kirby, 179

Bumpus, William G., 151, 243, 276–277

Burch, Janet, 71

Burke, Beverly, 118, 119

Burnett, Carol, 206

Burns, Sherry, 103

Burrell, Paul, 335

Bush, Barbara, 206, 441

Bush, George Herbert Walker, 159, 258, 442

Bush, George W., 161, 440, 443, 444, 449, 450, 462

Bush, Laura, 370, 445

Busia, Akosua, 137, 139

Butler, E. Faye, 158

Butler, Luvenia Harrison, 45, 57, 59–60, 66, 79, 465

Byrne, Rhonda, *The Secret,* 368, 472

## C

Caesar, Shirley, 433

Cage, Nicolas, 331

Campbell, Naomi, 434

Campion, Jane, 348

Canby, Vincent, 227

Cannon, Reuben, 138, 237

Capital Cities/ABC, 229, 381, 383
Capote, Truman, "A Day's Work," 227
Capus, Steve, 457
Caray, Harry, 121
Carey, Mariah, 434
Carl, Jann, 164
Carpenter, Larry, 41, 45, 50, 56
Carr, Greg, 174
Carr, Ida Presley, 24
Carrey, Jim, 332
Carroll, Diahann, 33, 175, 433
Carson, Johnny, 127, 150
Carter, Bill, 85, 94, 96, 100, 100–101, 117, 172
Carter, Jimmy, 317, 318
Cartwright, Roosevelt, 183, 199
Catchings, Harvey, 158–159
Catlett, Elizabeth, 433
Cattrall, Kim, 421
Cavett, Dick, 111
CBS, 408
Cedrone, Lou, 141
Chapman, Harry, 76
Chavez, Robert B., 416–417
Cher, 206
*Chicago*, 406
Chicago:
    Corporate/Community Schools of America, 378–379
    Holy Family Preservation Society, 380
    House of the Good Shepherd, 378
    Marva Collins Preparatory School, 378
    Near West Side, 237
    Oprah's move to, 116–119, 120–123, 125
    Oprah's philanthropy in, 228–229, 376–378
    Oprah's popularity in, 123, 138, 228
    tourism in, 228–229
    Young Women's Leadership Charter School, 390
*Chicago Defender*, 290
*Chicago Sun-Times*, 121, 208, 212, 221, 229, 239, 296, 352, 361, 370, 406, 430
*Chicago Tribune*, 8, 120, 223, 362, 372, 406
Child, Julia, 275
Childers, Mary Ann, 10
Chocano, Carina, 370
Choice, Gail, 78
Chopra, Deepak, 361
Christmas Kindness, 387–388
Churchill, Winston, 96
Churchwell, Andre, 58
Civil Rights Act (1964), 32, 50
Clark, Chris, 72, 73, 74–75, 77, 80, 177
Clark, Kenneth, 60
Clark, Leroy, 143
Clark, Marcia, 286, 290, 292
Clark, Roy Peter, 462
Cleage, Pearl, 434
Cline, Patsy Rainey, 56
Clinton, Bill, 315, 351, 426, 464
    appearances on Donahue's show, 317
    appearances on Oprah's show, 317, 318, 460, 466–467
    and elections, 441, 444
    similarities to Oprah, 461
Clinton, Hillary Rodham, 374, 441, 460, 464, 471
Clinton, Mary Kay, 194, 376
Clooney, George, 331, 463
Close, Glenn, 413
Coady, Elizabeth, 407–409

Coalition Against Black Exploitation, 143

Cochrane, Johnnie, 286

Cohen, Janet Langhart, 225

Cohen, Richard, 309

Colasante, Peter A., 364–365

Cole, Natalie, 432, 434

Cole, Olivia, 237

Coleman, Beverly, 183, 280, 284

Coleman, Jessica, 456

Collins, Gail, 473

Collins, Jackie, 127

Collins, Joan, 206

Color Purple, The (film), 2, 60, 134, 135–146, 146, 178, 190, 237, 279, 353
  casting of, 136–137, 139
  critical reviews of, 140, 143, 227
  Oprah's acting in, 2, 140, 226
  and Oscar nominations, 136, 140, 142
  promotion of, 79, 459
  and race, 143, 144

Color Purple, The (Walker), 11, 17, 135–136, 297, 394

Color Purple—The Musical (Broadway), 139, 141, 297

Colteryahn, Judy Lee, 106–107, 115

Committee to Keep Forsyth White, 208

Commonweal, 351

Connors, Jimmy, 468

Conrad, Peter, 116

Cook, Randy, 129–130, 133, 270

Cooney, Joan Ganz, 119

Cooper, Alice, 27, 150

Corliss, Richard, 351

Cosby, Bill, 124, 157, 171, 225, 231, 239, 296

Cosmopolitan, 109, 124, 141

Couric, Katie, 421

Court, John Kirthian, 365

Covey, Stephen, 382

Cowell, Simon, 431

Cowie, Colin, 433

Cox, W. D., 65

Craig, Kelly, 102–103

Crawford, Cindy, 468

Cronkite, Walter, 83

Crosby, Mary, 127

Crouch, Stanley, 311

Crowe, Patrick, 455

Crown, Paula, 465

Cruise, Tom, 138–139, 235, 333, 420

Cullen, Countee, "Incident," 81

D

Daily Beast, The, 149, 466

Dalai Lama, 370

Daley, Richard, 220–221, 474

Daley, Rosie, 251, 275

Dallas (TV), 261

Darden, Christopher, 286, 290, 292

David and Lisa (TV), 349

Davidson, Dana, 55

Davis, Angela, 62, 124

Davis, Joseph, 72

Davis, Katy Murphy, 403, 420

Day After, The (TV), 261

Dean, Deborah Gore, 365

Dean, Dizzy, 126

Dee, Ruby, 433

DeGeneres, Ellen, 229, 320–323, 328, 433, 470

DeHaan, Christel, 390

de la Renta, Oscar, 192, 267, 421

Demme, Jonathan, 348, 356

Denny, Reginald, 258

De Passe, Suzanne, 434

Dershowitz, Alan, 289
Diana, Princess of Wales, 173, 261, 335, 352–353, 374, 384, 423
Dickinson, Angie, 127
Dickson, Paul, 111
Dietz, Park, 214
Dillon, Matt, 226
DiMaio, Debra, 115, 124, 128, 228
    career with Oprah, 193–194, 195, 198, 281, 282
    and Oprah's birthday party, 275, 277
    Oprah's friendship with, 248
    Oprah's gifts to, 150–151
    resignation of, 195–196, 280, 281
    and TV show content, 6–7, 7–8, 211, 212, 214, 219, 259
Dimond, Diane, 130, 260
Dion, Céline, 333, 413, 433
Discovery Health Channel, 474
Disney Studios, 348, 355
Dole, Bob, 317, 441
Dolgen, Jonathan, 130
Donahue, Phil, 101, 151, 279, 285, 439
    cerebral style of, 120, 121, 196, 212, 256, 317
    competition with, 1–2, 98, 110, 117, 120, 121, 126, 140, 194, 212, 252
    Donahue, 2, 110, 211
    leaving Chicago, 2, 121
    media stories about, 370
    politicians on show of, 317
    ratings of, 98, 121, 126, 317
    retirement of, 316–317, 317, 330, 473
    and talk show TV, 316–317, 318

Doubleday Book Club, 264, 266
Doubleday Publishers, 306, 307, 309–310, 311–312, 421, 422
Dougary, Ginny, 270
Dowd, Maureen, 309, 311
Downey, Morton, Jr., 213, 318
Dream Academy, 402
Dunham, Katherine, 433, 434
Dunne, Dominick, 287, 291

E

East Nashville High School, 41, 44, 51, 56, 59
Ebert, Roger, 143, 351
Ebony, 16, 42, 141, 167, 168, 177, 249, 267, 289
Eckford, Elizabeth, 458
Economic Opportunity Act (1964), 34
Eddins, Mrs. (honorary godmother), 251
Edmonds, Kenneth "Babyface," 468
Ed Sullivan Show, The, 32–33
Educate-yourself.org, 448
Edwards, Elizabeth, 336
Eisenhower, Dwight D., 458
El Greco Brown, Gordon, 67, 68, 69
Elion, Gary, 84, 90, 91, 96
Elise, Kimberly, 434
Elizabeth II, Queen of England, 278
Elle, 141
Elliot, Missy, 434
Entertainment Weekly, 109
Epstein, Jeffrey, 227
Erdrich, Louise, 304
Erickson, Hal, 227
Ernsberger, Gail, 202
Esquire, 452

*Essence*, 239
Esters, Katharine Carr:
   *Jay Bird Creek* by, 296
   and Oprah's charitable dona-
     tions, 186, 186–187
   and Oprah's family, 155, 184,
     186–187
   and Oprah's stories, 21–23, 26,
     27, 83, 95, 186–187
   and Oprah's teen years, 39, 56
   and Oprah's work, 368, 440
*E.T.: The Extra-Terrestrial* (film),
   137
Evans, Harold, 314
Evans, Linda, 468
Evers, Charles, 49
"Everybody Loves Oprah," 10
Every Woman's Place, 380
Ewing, Heidi, 419

**F**

Families for a Better Life, 380,
   381–384
FamiliesFirst, Sacramento, 380
Farrakhan, Louis, 363–364
Federal Communications Com-
   mission (FCC), 449–450
Feder, Robert, 125, 132, 182, 208,
   229, 404, 406–407
Feinstein, Michael, 432
Ferguson, Sarah "Fergie," 334–
   335
Fey, Tina, 465
Field, Sally, 9
*Finding Oprah's Roots* (TV), 394
Fisk University, 61, 62–63, 64
Flack, Roberta, 433
Fleiss, Heidi, 130
Flockhart, Calista, 413
Follett, Ken, 262
Fonda, Jane, 370, 413

Fontana, Marian, 423
For a Better Life Foundation, 384
*Forbes*, 228, 294, 373, 440
Forbes, Malcolm, 211
Ford, Gerald R., 318, 397
Ford, Hilda, 94
Ford, Richard Thompson, 415
Foster, Badi, 394
Foster, Jodie, 348
Fox, Jim and Roberta, 106
Fox, Michael, 106
Fox News, 462
Foxx, Jamie, 327
Frank, Alan, 98
Franklin, Aretha, 38, 433, 434
Franzen, Jonathan, 305
   *The Corrections*, 301–302
Frey, James:
   *Bright Shiny Morning*, 423–424
   *A Million Little Pieces*, 305–315
Frieda, John, 206
Friedman, Arlene, 266
*From the Mississippi Delta*
   (drama), 273
Frumkin, Peter J., 383, 384
Fuhrman, Mark, 286, 288, 290
Fulghum, Robert, 454
Furth, Peggy, 201

**G**

Ganick, Elaine, 76
Garbus, Liz, 420
Garbus, Martin, 420
Gates, Henry Louis, Jr., 44, 282,
   356, 394, 442, 464
Gay Pride Week, 322
Geary, Tony, 16
Geller, Uri, 111
*George*, 426
Gerber, Ann, 221–222
Gere, Richard, 421

Gethers, Peter, 92
Gifford, Kathie Lee, 213
Giovanni, Nikki, 433, 434
Givens, Robin, 237, 421
Glass, Nancy, 192
Glide Memorial Church, San Francisco, 378, 379
*Globe*, 161
Glover, Danny, 143
*Godfather, The* (film), 143
Goldberg, Whoopi, 137, 206, 434, 468
  awards and honors to, 356
  and *Color Purple*, 136, 140, 142–143, 144
Goldman, Fred, 291–292
Goldman, Kim, 291–292
Goldman, Ron, 285, 289, 290
Goldstein, Bonnie, 64
Gonzalez, Jorge, 119
*Good Housekeeping*, 226, 353
*Good Morning America*, 89, 97, 141, 354, 423
Gordon, Ed, 153
Gore, Al, 440, 443, 445
Gore, Tipper, 178
Gossett, Lou, Jr., 468
Goucher College, 113–115
Gowens, Pat, 381
Grady, Rachel, 419
Graham, Darras, 163
Graham, James, 163
Graham, Stedman Sardar, 107, 109, 129, 152, 183, 277, 346, 436
  and American Double-Dutch League, 281
  and Athletes Against Drugs, 159, 169, 281
  and charities, 382, 391
  and Harpo staff, 281

and leadership course, 384
and Mandela, 385
and Oprah's birthdays, 432
and Oprah's book, 267–270, 272
Oprah's relationship with, 156–171, 190–191, 192, 202, 204, 221, 225–226, 231, 242–243, 244–245, 323–324, 325, 328, 339, 353, 468
and politics, 442, 464, 468
Graham, Wendy, 159, 165
Graham Williams Group (GWG), 160
Gray, John, 359
Great Migration, 25
Green, Stephen, 339
Greene, Bob, 251, 279, 294, 296, 344
Greene, Ronald, 424
Gregga, Bruce, 340
Grier, Pam, 434
Griffin, Kathy, 166, 327
Griffith, Fred, 224, 228
Gumbel, Bryant, 124, 171

*H*

Habitat for Humanity, 185, 186, 373, 374
Haggard, Ted, 327
Halberstam, David, 212
Haley, Alex, *Roots*, 350
Hall, Wiley A. III, 363
Halliday, Lisa, xiii
Halprin, Stacey, 257
Hamer, Fannie Lou, 52, 230
Hamilton, George, 211
Hamm, Barbara, 102, 103, 104, 110
Hanks, Tom, 233, 433
*Hard Copy*, 130

Harpo Entertainment Group, 232
Harpo Films, Inc., 233, 407
Harpo, Inc., 232, 241, 386, 387
  control exercised by, 354, 407
  establishment of, 122
  and lawsuits, 337–347, 369, 410
Harpo Print LLC, 233
Harpo Productions, 132, 195, 231, 232, 286, 407
Harpo Radio Inc., 233
Harpo staff, 279, 341
  and Big Sisters, 376
  bonuses to, 403, 419
  confidentiality agreements of, 69, 195–196, 280, 281, 281–282, 407–413
  and Mandela, 387, 388
  and Oprah's birthday party, 277
  Oprah's gifts to, 150–152, 283–284, 411
  Oprah's relationship with, 194–197, 407–408
  political contributions of, 469–470
  probation periods of, 341, 409
Harpo Studios, Inc., 233, 234, 234–237
Harpo Video Inc., 233
Harris, Jean, 421
Harrison, Barbara Grizzuti, 112, 147–148, 224, 240–241
Harry, Jackée, 237
Hart, Mary, 77
Hasey, Candace, 116
Hayek, Salma, 433
Haynes, Andrea, 44, 46, 47, 48, 49, 53, 57, 61
Head Start, 34
Heche, Anne, 321, 322
Heidelberg, John, 54–55, 56

Height, Dorothy, 402, 433
Hermès, Paris, 413–417
Herz, Suzanne, 422
Hess, Stephen, 53
Hill, Joyce Daniel, 74
Hirsch, Renard A., Sr., 174
Hitts, Roger, 205
Hoe, Irene, 34
Holland, Endesha Ida Mae, 273
Hollywood Reporter, The, 334
Hollywood Wives, 127
Holm, John, 214–215
Holm, Robert, 214–215
Holmes, Katie, 138
Holocaust Memorial Museum, 180–181
Holt, Gary, 47, 51, 52, 57
Holyfield, Evander, 457
Honack, Rich, 384
Hope, Bob, 379
Horne, Lena, 433, 434
Houston, Whitney, 171, 204
Howard, Margo, 203
Howard, Ron, 331
Hudson, Dianne, 194–195, 280, 389
Hughes, Karen, 446
Hughes, Langston, 52
Hull House, Chicago, 381
Hurricane Hugo, 257, 379
Hurricane Katrina, 374, 418
Hurricane Rita, 374
Hussein, Saddam, 448
Huston, Anjelica, 144
Hutton, Barbara, 389
Hyperion Press, 295

I
Ifill, Gwen, 434
Iger, Robert, 239
Iman, 434

"I'm Every Woman," 204, 284
Ingels, Marty, 333
Ingram, Jerry, 174
*Inside Edition*, 192
*InStyle*, 353
*Interview*, 141, 145, 203
Iraq, U.S. invasion of, 448–449, 462
Irving, Amy, 413
Irving, Julius "Dr. J.," 277
Isaiah 54:17, 223
Ito, Lance, 286
Ivins, Molly, 452

J

Jackson, Janet, 206, 332, 435
Jackson, Michael, 34, 130, 173, 199, 243, 259–261, 332
Jackson, Rev. Jesse, 90–91, 111, 171
Jacobs, Jeffrey D.:
    and movies, 238
    as Oprah's lawyer/agent, 121–122, 127, 139, 141, 162, 183, 223, 229, 231, 280, 281
    and Oprah's media empire, 231
    photographs controlled by, 69
    and TV show content, 218
    and TV show ownership, 226, 230–231
James, Renee A., 295
Jameson, Jenna, 466
Jamison, Judith, 435
Jarrett, Valerie, 468
Jarvis, Jeff, 209, 294, 449
Jeffries, Stuart, 331
*Jet*, 168, 384
Joe Colter Agency, 74
Joel, Billy, 9, 421
Johns, Deborah, 132
Johns, Fran, 158, 385

Johnson, Beverly, 104, 435
Johnson, Dick, 10
Johnson, James Weldon, *God's Trombones: Eight Negro Sermons in Verse*, 47
Johnson, Lyndon B., 32
Johnson, Steve, 362, 375
Jones, Bob, 260
Jones, Carlton, 163, 167
Jones, Jenny, 213, 279, 285, 318
Jones, Marion, 456
Jones, Quincy
    and *Color Purple*, 2, 136–138, 143, 144
    Oprah's friendship with, 138, 154, 172, 231, 277
    and politics, 442, 464
Jones, Shirley, 333–334
Jones, Star, 447
Jones, Tim, 345, 372
Jong, Erica, 111, 147, 148, 330, 413
Jordan, Michael, 168, 169, 340
Judd, Wynonna, 333
*Julia*, 33
Jurkowitz, Mark, 439

K

Kabak, Wayne S., 116
Kaelin, Kato, 286
Karns, Susan, 364
Kauffmann, Stanley, 351
Kazin, Alfred, 301
Keaton, Diane, 332
Kelly, Paula, 237
Kennedy, Caroline, 471
Kennedy, Ethel, 146
Kennedy family, 146, 441–442, 453, 454, 471
Kennedy, Jacqueline (Onassis), 146, 172, 389

Kennedy, Jayne, 175
Kennedy, John F., x, xiv
Kennedy, John F., Jr., 336–337
Kennedy, Pamela D., 176
Kennedy, Ted, 146, 471
Kern, Art, 111
Keys, Alicia, 435
Khan, Chaka, 435
Kidman, Nicole, 331
Kilcrease, Clarence, 82
Kimatian, Steve, 88
Kimmel, Jimmy, 367
King, Coretta Scott, 65, 385, 433, 442
King, Gayle:
  family of, 180
  and Hermès, 413
  marriage and divorce of, 276–277
  and O magazine, 325, 326, 435
  and Oprah's birthdays, 432
  and Oprah's book, 272
  Oprah's friendship with, 134, 154, 155, 166, 191–192, 231, 243, 276–277, 322–323, 435
  Oprah's gifts to, 151, 276–277, 325
  and Oprah's movies, 356
  and Oprah's relationships, 60, 107, 112, 192, 268
  and politics, 465, 470
  and Vernon's book proposal, 30–31
  and WJZ, 87–88, 90, 110
King, Larry, 226, 290–291, 308, 310, 313, 327, 368, 455, 466, 469
King, Martin Luther, Jr., 29, 178, 179, 207, 455, 469
King, Rodney, 258
Kingston, Anne, 414

King World, 116, 141, 227, 229, 230–231, 245, 338, 358, 408
Kinski, Nastassja, 277
Kissinger, Henry A., 385
Kitt, Eartha, 434
Klein, Calvin, 9, 172, 244
Knight, Gladys, 433
Knight, Shirley, 413
Knight Ridder, 243
Kobren, Gerri, 94
Kogan, Rick, 474
Kolson, Ann, 141–142
Koncius, Jura, xvi
Koppel, Ted, 111
Kosciusko, Mississippi, 182–189, 373
Kosowski, Ed, 10
Kotlowitz, Alex, 203, 381
Kotzin, Michael, 219
Kramer, Lloyd, 92, 349
Kroll Associates, 341, 409
Kropp, Arthur J., 218
Krueger, James, 257
Kuczynski, Alex, 372
Ku Klux Klan, 6, 77, 207
Kunen, James S., 54

L

LaBelle, Patti, 433
LaCalamita, Michael, Sr., 216
Ladies' Home Journal, 156, 204, 206, 226, 267
Lake, Ricki, 213, 279, 285, 318
Lamb, Wally, She's Come Undone, 298
Landers, Ann, 121, 193, 202
LaPorte County Child Abuse Prevention Council, Indiana, 379
Larry King Live, 307, 310, 313, 327, 469
Latifah, Queen, 200

Lauer, Matt, 291, 466

Lauren, Ralph, 353, 370

Laurie (sexual abuse victim), 3–4

Lazare, Lewis, 430

Leach, Ruth Ann, 72, 73–74, 79, 288

Lederer, Eppie (Ann Landers), 121, 202

Lee, Alisha, 253

Lee, Chrishaunda La'ttice, 179, 253, 389

Lee, Earlist (grandfather), 23, 26, 184
    death of, 25

Lee, Hattie Mae Presley (grand-mother), 183, 184
    family background of, 23
    and Oprah's childhood, 21, 22, 23, 24, 269

Lee, Jeffrey (brother), 27, 36, 93, 108, 119, 154, 210, 328

Lee, Patricia (sister). *see* Lloyd, Patricia Lee

Lee, Suzie Mae, 184

Lee, Vernita (mother):
    children of, 25, 27
    and Oprah's birth, 24, 187–188
    and Oprah's career, 119
    and Oprah's childhood, 21, 22, 25, 31–32, 269
    Oprah's gifts to, 151–153, 155, 188
    and Oprah's teen years, 35, 39
    and Oprah's visits, 184

Lee, Vincent Miquelle (son), 43

Leffler, Bob, 104, 113

Leiber, Judith, 121, 203

Leonard family, 22–23

Letterman, David, 141, 218, 317, 326, 370–371, 452, 454, 458, 475

Lettuce Entertain You Enter-prises, 171

Levine, Jonathan, 219

Levinson, Barry, 111

Lewinsky, Monica, 425–426

Liberace, 421

Lieberman, Joseph, 279

*Life*, 21, 261, 294

Lightman, Ellen, 111

Lilly (childhood friend), 28

Limbaugh, Rush, 262

Lingle, Scott, 306

Literary Guild, 264

*Little Rascals*, 32

Little Rock Nine, 458

Live Your Best Life, 241, 369, 394

Lloyd, Patricia Lee:
    death of, 254
    drug use of, 154, 253–254
    and Oprah's childhood, 20, 25
    and Oprah's gifts, 154
    and Oprah's relationships, 105
    and Oprah's teen years, 35–36, 38, 39, 43, 272
    and publicity, 221
    tabloid story sold by, 43, 45, 251, 272, 410

Loki Films, 419

London *Daily Mail*, 109, 268

*Los Angeles Times*, 8, 140, 208, 451

Lott, Lana, 48

Loverd, William T., 266

Lucas, George, 468

Lunden, Joan, 89, 145

Lyman, Howard, 337, 338, 340, 344, 345, 347


M

MacGregor, Jeff, 364

Mackie, Bob, 247

MacLaine, Shirley, 245

Madonna, 206, 333

Maher, Bill, 368

*Make the Connection* (Winfrey and Greene), 295, 296

Mandela, Nelson, 159, 370, 379, 386–388, 387, 391, 402

Mandela, Winnie, 160

Marberry, Craig, 29

Margolick, David, 458

Marine Corps Marathon, 279

Markey, Judy, 93

Marovitz, Abraham Lincoln, 219–221

Martin, Darnell, 435

*M\*A\*S\*H*, 261

Maslin, Janet, 351

Mason, Jackie, 356

Mason, Vic, 75, 77

Massery, Hazel Bryan, 458

Mathabane, Mark, 202

Maurice, Dick, 101

McCain, John, 465

McClary, Jane, 91, 94, 96, 103

McClellan, Scott, 309

McDavis, Roderick, 174

McDonald, Audra, 435

McDonald, Erroll, 264, 266

McDonald, Katrina Bell, *Embracing Sisterhood*, 92

McDonald, Michael, 436

McDonald, Sean, 311

McGee, Alice, 125, 195, 293, 403

McGovern, Elizabeth, 226

McGraw, Phil, 339, 345, 433

McGruder, Aaron, 454

McKee, Lonette, 237

McLennan, Sheila, 353

McMillan, Terry, 435

Meadows, Jayne, 333

Means, Marianne, 439

Mehta, Sonny, 266, 275

Meisel, Steven, 352

Meltzer, Adrienne, 93

*Merv Griffin Show*, 141

Mfume, Kweisi, 91

Michiko, Empress (Japan), 442

Middle Tennessee Business Association, 74

Miles-Crocker, Candy, 251

Millay, Edna St. Vincent, 180

Miller, Dan, 76

Millman, Joyce, 445

Millner, Caille, 400

Minneapolis *Star Tribune*, 142

Minnelli, Liza, 206

Minow, Newton, 119

Miss Black America, 71

Miss Black Nashville, 46, 67–70, 73

Miss Black Tennessee, 70–71

Miss Fire Prevention, 55, 67, 70, 73, 150

Miss Porter's School, Farmington, Connecticut, 384, 389

Mitchard, Jacquelyn, 252

 *The Deep End of the Ocean*, 298

Mitchell, Calvin, 382

Mitchell, Eva, 382

Mitchell, Mary A., 352

Mobley, Maude, 68

Moelis, Cindy, 468

Molloy, Joanna, 157–158

Monroe, Marilyn, 336–337

Montreal *Gazette*, 414

Moore, Dudley, 9

Moore, Mary Tyler, 323, 333

Moore, Melba, 435

Moore, Michael, 454

Moore, Paul, 178

Moraes, Lisa de, 460, 466

Moran, Terry, 285

Morehouse College, Atlanta, 178, 378, 384
Moriarty, Erin, xvii
Morrison, Barry, 219, 220
Morrison, Toni, 108, 403, 442
   *Beloved,* 227, 348, 351
   *The Bluest Eye,* 11
   as legend, 433, 434
   *A Mercy,* 108
   and Oprah's Book Club, 299
Moyers, Bill, 119, 449
*Ms.,* 245, 377
Murdoch, Rupert, 291
Murphy, Eddie, 171, 172, 332

*N*

NAACP, 72, 144, 157, 237, 250, 379
Nader, Ralph, 255, 317, 318
Nashville:
   affirmative action in, 53, 55, 72, 74
   interracial dating in, 76–77
   the *N* word in, 73
*Nation,* 454
National Association of Women Executives, 74
National Child Protection Act "Oprah Bill" (1993), 14–18, 461
National Council of Negro Women, 402
*National Enquirer,* 69, 130–131, 161, 210, 251, 255, 271, 340, 475
*National Review,* 168, 324, 414
*Native Son* (film), 178, 226
Natkin, Paul, 210, 339
NATPE convention (1981), 110
Naylor, Gloria, 237, 297–298
NBC Universal, 438

Nelson Mandela Foundation, 386
*New Republic, The,* 301, 324, 351
*News Extra,* 167
*Newsweek,* 126, 141, 293, 361, 362–363, 439
New York *Daily News,* 157, 324
*New Yorker, The,* 147, 303
*New York Times, The,* 293, 305, 307, 308, 313, 351, 364, 372, 419, 454
*New York Times Magazine, The,* 147, 240
Nicolet High School, 34–35, 41, 48
Nixon, Richard M., 54, 159, 317, 322
No Child Left Behind Act, 161
Noe, Alfonso, 206
Norman, Jessye, 432, 434
Northwestern University, 384
Norton, Jimmy, 73, 75, 76, 77, 79–80
Norwood, Brandy, 435
*N* word, 73, 208, 290, 465

*O*

Obama, Barack, 437, 455, 462, 476
Obama, Michelle, 435, 462, 468, 472, 476
O'Brien, Conan, 429, 465
O'Connor, Sandra Day, 387
O'Donnell, Rosie, 246, 318, 322, 325, 414–415
O'Hair, Madalyn Murray, 316–317
Olbermann, Keith, 356, 400
Olesker, Michael, 84, 86, 89, 93, 104
*O* magazine, 325, 326, 370, 397, 410, 438, 446, 460, 461

O'Malley, Martin, 391
Onion, The, 294
Operation PUSH (People United to Serve Humanity), 91
Oppenheimer, Jerry, 130
Oprah After the Show, 438, 460
Oprah and Friends, 438
Oprah.com, 371, 439
Oprah's Angel Network, 185, 236, 374, 384, 392, 403
Oprah's Book Club, 263, 293–315, 330, 409
  beginning of, 293, 296, 403
  book lists, 299–300, 304–305
  confidentiality agreements signed for, 301
  temporary discontinuance of, 297–298, 303, 304
Oprah's Child Predator Watch List, 15
Oprah's Studio Merchandise Inc., 233
Oprah Store, 236
Oprah! (Waldron), 125
Oprah Winfrey Boys and Girls Club, 186, 384
Oprah Winfrey Endowed Scholarship Fund, 179
Oprah Winfrey Foundation, 374, 384, 386, 387
Oprah Winfrey Leadership Academy for Girls, South Africa, 281, 387, 389, 391, 394, 395, 420
Oprah Winfrey Leadership Academy Foundation, 236, 389
Oprah Winfrey Network (OWN), 232, 438, 474, 476
Oprah Winfrey Prep School Scholars, 389
Oprah Winfrey Presents, 349, 438

Oprah Winfrey Show, The, 403, 474
  "Change Your Life" on, 359–365, 359–365, 372
  changing content of, 196, 197
  and free speech, 346
  giveaways on, 427–430
  guests on, 196, 197–198, 255–256, 273, 275, 279, 332–333, 413, 418–426, 439–447
  lawsuits against, 337–347, 369, 404, 406–407, 408
  "live your best life" on, 241, 369, 394
  and merchandise, 236, 333
  "no politicians" rule on, 439–440, 439–440
  and Oprah's charities, 375–380, 403
  "Oprah's Favorite Things," 427–430, 439
  ownership of, 226, 229, 230–231
  ratings, 126, 132, 194, 207, 210, 212, 213, 255, 256, 286–287, 293, 318, 322, 341, 357, 424, 458
  rehearsals of, 426–427
  staff of. see Harpo staff
  success of, 227, 229, 258
  syndication of, 2, 141
  topics covered in, 209, 214–223, 241, 243, 255, 273, 282, 319–320, 319–320, 323, 327, 331, 342, 353, 404, 420, 450–451, 456
Optifast powder, 244, 246
O'Reilly, Bill, 448, 462
Orman, Suze, 359, 370
Otey, Anthony, 44, 47, 54
Our Gang, 32

Outlaw, Patty, 73, 75, 77
Overeaters Anonymous, 94
OW Licensing Co., 233
OWN (Oprah Winfrey Network), 232, 438, 474, 476
Oxygen, 408, 438
Oz, Dr. Mehmet, 464

**P**

Page, Geraldine, 226
Paglia, Camille, 301
Palin, Sarah, 465
Palley, Stephen W., 245
*Parade,* 5
Parker, Brooks, 177
Parks, Rosa, 229, 353, 433, 434
Parks, Suzan-Lori, 435
Patterson, Orlando, 203, 415
Patton, Patrice, 68, 70
Pauley, Jane, 429
Peale, Norman Vincent, 278
Peeler, Susie Mae, 24
*People,* 141, 166, 173, 174, 191–192, 209, 246, 249, 296, 382, 397, 405, 415, 433, 459
*People Are Talking,* 97–98, 98–99, 110, 118, 200
People for the American Way, 218
Perdue, Frank, 103–104
Perkins, Bill, 72
Perot, Ross, 318, 441
Perry, Tyler, 298, 431, 468
Petersen, Clarence, 125
Phil, Doctor (McGraw), 339, 360, 370, 433, 464
*Philadelphia Inquirer, The,* 141
*Philadelphia Inquirer Magazine, The,* 8, 125
Philbin, Regis, 213
Pickett, Debra, 157
Pickford, Mary, 231

Pincham, Eugene, 290
Pitt, Brad, 331, 433
Poitier, Joanna, 277
Poitier, Sidney, 33, 154, 277, 468
Pontiac G6s, as "giveaways," 429–430
Povich, Maury, 213, 318
*Precious* (film), 233, 298
Presley, Elvis, 32, 101, 213, 286, 332
Presley, Lisa Marie, 22, 332
Presley, Rebecca, 24
Preston, Kelly, 433
Price, Leontyne, 229, 433
Pritzlaff, Mary Dell, 387
Procter & Gamble, 279
Proulx, E. Annie, 303
Prudden, Suzy, 197, 201
Pryor, Richard, 269–270
Psalms 37:4, 373
*Psychology Today,* 362
Pugh, Willard, 138
Purple Heart Cruise, 379

**Q**

Quigley, Paxton, 200

**R**

"Rachel," on devil worship, 216–217
Rakieten, Ellen, 194, 197, 198, 219, 307, 310, 313, 330, 403
Raleigh, Colleen, 216, 266, 280, 404
Randolph, Laura, 42, 167, 289
Random House, Inc., 263, 296, 307, 314, 381, 383
Rania, Queen of Jordan, 395
Rankin, Donna, 216
Rape Treatment Center, Santa Monica, 379

Raphael, Sally Jessy, 197, 213, 279, 285, 318
Rashad, Phylicia, 435
Rautbord, Sugar, 145, 203
Ray, Rachael, 358, 464
Reagan, Nancy, xiv
Reagan, Ronald, 111, 132, 159, 318
Reagon, Bernice Johnson, 91
*Redbook,* 282–284
Reed, Cheryl L., 228, 406
Reed, Donna, 114
Reese, Della, 124, 433
Regan, Ken, 353
ReganBooks, 291
Remnick, David, 303
Resnik, Harvey, 213, 214–215
Revlon, 247
Reyes, Robert Paul, 450
Reynolds, Burt, 9, 288
Reynolds, Frank, 103
Reynolds, Gretchen, 241, 274
Rice, Condoleezza, 434, 446
Rice, Linda Johnson, 168
Rich, Frank, 309, 462–463
Richie, Lionel, 144, 456
Richmond, Ray, 397
Rivera, Geraldo, 213, 279, 285, 318
Rivers, Joan, 10, 127, 138, 206, 213, 318
Rivkin, Bob, 468
Rizzo, Bill, 150, 194, 195
Roberts, Julia, 64, 173, 235, 333
Robinson, Anne, 423
Robinson, Eugene, 400
Robinson, Mary Lou, 344
Robinson, Max, 157
Robinson, Robin, 159, 168
Rock, Chris, 333, 445
Rodgers, Carolyn, 114
Rodgers, Nile, 152

Rodman, Dennis, 332
Rodricks, Dan, 391
Roeper, Richard, 120, 291, 361
Rome, Susan, 111
*Roots* (TV), 350
Rose, Charlie, 119
Rose, Chris, 418
Roseland, Harry, *To the Highest Bidder,* 350
Rosenberg, Howard, 8, 208, 258, 331
Rosenthal, Phil, 458–459, 474
Ross, Diana, 32, 101, 113, 260, 263, 325, 381, 433
Rossi, Portia de, 323
Royko, Mike, 223
Rudolph, Maya, 369
Rush, George, 157
Russell, Bill, 468
Ruth, Daniel, 230, 239
Ruth, Doctor, 262
Rybak, Deborah Caulfield, 306

S

Saad, Gad, 362
Sabol, Blair, 197, 199, 200
Sajak, Pat, 76
Salamon, Julie, 226–227
Salata, Sheri, 313
Salon.com, 368
Sanders, Al, 85, 88, 90, 119
Sanders, Scott, 297, 394
*Santa Barbara News-Press,* 450
Santow, Dan, 282–283
Saperstein, Rabbi David, 218
Sapphire, *Push,* 298
Sarah, Duchess of York "Fergie," 334–335
*Saturday Night Live,* 141, 369
Sawyer, Diane, 64, 290–291, 325, 341, 354–355, 433

Sawyer, Mark, 451
*Scared Silent: Exposing and Ending Child Abuse* (documentary), 14
Scavullo, Francesco, 206
Schaalman, Rabbi Herman, 219
Schaefer, William D., 85
Schmoke, Kurt, 91
Schwarzenegger, Arnold, 111, 127, 146, 278, 451, 457
SCLC, 379
Scott, Don, 119
Sears, Roebuck and Co., 279
Sears Roebuck Charm School, 60
Seinfeld, Jessica, 314, 431
Seitler, Harriet, 420
Senate Judiciary Committee, 14
September 11 attacks, 445–446
Shales, Tom, 255, 349
Shapiro, Ron, 110, 113, 116
Shearer, Norma, 436
Shearman and Sterling, 340
Shelton, Cynthia Connor, 45, 51
Shepherd, Cybill, 332
Sher, Annabelle, 106
Sher, Richard, 91, 98, 106, 119
    and *People Are Talking*, 98, 101, 110, 118
Shields, Brooke, 9, 260
Shirley, Frank, 208
Shone, Tom, 299
Shriver, Eunice Kennedy, 146
Shriver, Maria, 146, 325, 433, 471
    and Arnold, 127, 146, 453
    Oprah's friendship with, ix, 146, 278
    and WJZ, 96, 110, 442
Shue, Elisabeth, 331
Simmons, Richard, 102, 200
Simmons, Sue, 85

Simon, Jeff, 460
Simpson, Nicole Brown, 285, 286, 291, 293
Simpson, O. J., 130, 285
Simpson, Valerie, 435
Sims, Naomi, 434
Sinatra, Frank, xiv
Sinbad, 157
Sinclair, Abiola, 250
Singer, Larry, 95
Sirius XM radio, 438
Sirleaf, Ellen Johnson, 394
*Sister 2 Sister*, 328
*60 Minutes*, 62, 105, 141, 376
Skerbneski, Victor, 203
Smart, Elizabeth, 421
Smiley, Jane, 304
Smith, Anna Deavere, 435
Smith, Liz, 246, 313–314, 321, 323, 328, 356
Smith, Maggie, 194
Smith, R. C., 142
Smith, Will, 327
Smith, William Kennedy, 130
Smits, Jimmy, 331
Smoking Gun, The, 307, 310
Snipes, Wesley, 332
Solinski, Nancy, 55–56
Solomon (dog), 235
Solomon, Eileen, 113, 115, 117, 200
"Sometimes I Feel Like a Motherless Child," 71
Sophie (dog), 235
South Africa:
    charities in, 392–393, 397, 420, 478
    Oprah's school in, 281, 387, 389, 391, 394, 395, 420
Spaulding, Benjamin, 163
Spears, Britney, 332, 413

Special Olympics, 378

Spielberg, Steven, 2, 135, 136–140, 143, 146, 190, 277, 297, 349

Springer, Jerry, 213, 279, 285, 318, 342, 357–358

*Spy,* 147, 148

Stanley, Alessandra, 473

*Star, The,* 130, 161

Steepleton, Scott, 450

Stein, Gertrude, 324

Stein, Joel, 311

Steinberg, David, 221

Steinberg, Neil, 221

Steinem, Gloria, 273, 316, 445

Stern, Howard, 449

Stern, Isaac, 385

Stern, Robert A. M., 234

Stewart, Martha, 325, 370

Stewart, Paula, 48

Stitt, Jecquin, 205–206

Stoddard, Brandon, 171, 237

Stoddart, Nancy, 152, 156, 158, 276, 373

Streep, Meryl, 370

Streisand, Barbra, 24, 337, 413, 437

Stricklen, Frank, 25

Strickler, Jeff, 142

Styron, William, 262

Sullivan, Ed, 32

Sundance Film Festival, 233

*Sunday Express* (London), 356

Sundquist, Donald K., 177

Supremes, The, 32–33

Swanson, Dennis, 5–6, 10, 116

Swayze, Patrick, 332, 344

Sweden, James van, 189, 251

Swedish Broadcasting Commission, 448

Sweet Honey in the Rock, 91

*T*

Talese, Nan, 310, 311–312, 315

*Talk,* 149

Talley, André Leon, 352

Tan, Amy, 304

Tardio, Christine, 194

Taylor, Elizabeth, 127, 173, 210–211, 260

Taylor, Maureen, 367

Taylor, Susan L., 435

Taylor, William "Bubba," 60, 82–83, 105

*Tennessean, The,* 174

Tennessee State Players Guild, 65

Tennessee State University (TSU), 61–66, 74, 174, 304
    scholarships, 175, 176, 378

Teresa, Mother, 278

Tesh, John, 76, 77

*There Are No Children Here* (ABC-TV), 203, 380, 381

Theron, Charlize, 63

Thompson-McLeod, Frank, 177

Tillis, James "Quick," 121

*Time,* 261, 294, 321, 351, 353, 378

*Times, The* (London), 355, 415

Tiven, Kenneth, 77

*Today Show, The,* 124, 354, 423

Toklas, Alice B., 324

Tolle, Eckhart, 62

*Tonight Show, The,* 2, 10, 127, 138, 150, 206, 452

Tornabene, Lyn, 19, 123

Towers, Kenneth, 223

Travolta, John, 42, 154, 235, 333, 431, 433

Trillin, Calvin, 228

Trinity United Church, Chicago, 163

Trump, Donald, 432

Truth, Sojourner, 52, 114, 230

Tubman, Harriet, 52, 230
Turk, Bob, 83, 87, 119
Turner, Jerry, 83, 90, 101, 119
Turner, Tina, 109, 136, 153, 277, 325, 328, 413, 434
Tutu, Bishop Desmond, 402
*TV Guide,* 40, 122, 142, 155, 165, 247, 279, 294, 353, 361
*20/20,* 354, 423, 426
Twyman, Rocky, 402
Tyson, Cicely, 237, 434, 468
Tyson, Mike, 248, 421, 457

### U

UNICEF, 379
Updike, John, xiii
Upward Bound, 34
*USA Weekend,* 353

### V

Vanderbilt, Gloria, 389
*Vanity Fair,* 146–147, 246, 458
Van Meter, Jonathan, 348, xiii
Van Susteren, Greta, 285, 466
Vanzant, Iyanla, 359
*Variety,* 150
Versace, Gianni, 353
Viacom, 408
*Vibe,* 328, 412
Victor, Ed, 423
Viking Penguin, 298
Virginia Tech massacre, 457
*Vogue,* 2, 268, 352
Volvo Tennis Tournament, 281

### W

Waldheim, Kurt, 146
Waldron, Robert, 71, 125, 126, 227
Walker, Alice, 434, 465
    *The Color Purple,* 11, 17, 136, 237, 297, 394

    and the movie, 136, 137, 140, 143
Walker, Andre, 183, 199, 206
Walker, Madame C. J., 170
Walker, Margaret, *Jubilee,* 49, 91
Walker, Thomas, 178
Wallace, Mike, 62, 83, 105, 141, 376
*Wall Street Journal, The,* 141, 212, 439
Walt Disney Company, 322, 355, 408
Walters, Barbara, 20, 55, 78, 89, 100, 141, 224, 325, 423, 426
Wang, Vera, 206
Warhol, Andy, 145, 203
Warner, John, 127
Warner Books, 289
War on Poverty, 34
Warren, Ellen, 410
Warwick, Dionne, 434
Washington, D.C., SEED School, 390
Washington, Dinah, 227
Washington, Harold, 25, 117
*Washington Post, The,* 140, 255, 303, 309, 313, 349, 369
Wassom, Janet, 78
Watts, Donna, 115
Watts, Rolonda, 318
Watts, Tim, 105–109, 112, 115, 119, 330
Wayans, Keenan and Damon, 249–250
Wayans, Kim, 250
WBAL-TV, 390
WBBM-TV, 406
WDCN, 72
Weber, Gary, 337
Weiner, Arleen, 96, 105, 110–111, 119

Weir, Peter, 348
Welfare Warriors, 380–381
Weller, Robb, 115
Wenner, Jann, 125
Wheeler, Pat, 94
Whitaker, Forest, 468
White House Conference on Children and Youth (1971), 53
Whitfield, Lynn, 237
Wiesel, Elie, 181, 240, 309
Wietrak, Robert, 264
Wilkin, Abra Prentice Anderson, 145
Williams, Armstrong, 160–161, 169
Williams, Barbara, 165
Williams, Brian, 457
Williams, Rev. Hosea, 207, 208
Williams, Montel, 213, 279, 318
Williams, Robin, 166
Williams, Rufus, 384
Williams, Ted, xiii
Williams and Connolly, 340
Williamson, Marianne, 199, 278–279, 353
Wilson, August, 379
Wilson, Dori, 121
Wilson, Flip, 59
Wilson, Nancy, 432, 434
Wilson, Rita, 413, 433
Winfrey, Barbara, 178, 183, 205
Winfrey, Elmore and Ella, 31
Winfrey family:
    and Oprah's childhood, 19–43
    and Oprah's control issues, 205
    and Oprah's gifts, 153, 154
    and Oprah's public image, 155, 173–174, 264
    and Oprah's sexual abuse, 5, 14–15, 17–18, 42, 173–174, 269

Winfrey, Oprah:
    airplanes of, 411–412
    ambition of, 48, 75, 78, 142, 145, 170–171, 203–204, 225, 239, 252, 476–477
    assassination fears of, 235, 340–341
    awards and honors to, 2, 51, 70, 74, 151, 178, 226, 245, 250, 294, 337, 342, 378, 380, 441
    birthday party for, 275, 277
    birth of, 20, 24, 187
    and books, 198–199, 255, 262–266, 268–271, 275, 292–293, 293–315, 330–331, 369–370, 409
    childhood of, 19–43, 32, 124, 252, 253, 254, 263, 269, 272
    college years of, 60–71, 174
    confidence of, 142
    control exercised by, 149, 204, 229, 231, 237, 272, 280–281, 331, 334, 335, 339–340, 349, 354, 384, 402, 404
    as cultural icon, 3, 11, 173
    DNA of, 394
    drug use of, 45, 75, 129, 131–132, 169, 254, 269–270, 270, 314
    fan art to, 236
    generosity of, 150–152, 175, 185, 228, 296, 325, 372, 374, 403
    influence of, 148, 174, 223, 224–225, 253–254, 258, 404, 408, 439, 441, 455, 471, 472, 475–476, 478
    media empire of, 231
    and movies, 2, 137, 178, 226, 237, 348–358, 358
    name of, 24, 43, 47, 96

Winfrey, Oprah *(continued)*:
Nobel candidacy of, 402
pregnancy of, 42–43, 44, 45–
46, 166, 251, 253, 254, 269,
272, 456
properties and homes of, 145,
189–191, 234–235, 239,
399, 435–436, 467–469,
474–475
public image of, 106, 132, 149,
155, 199, 204, 263–264, 272,
289, 295, 364, 369–370, 384,
404, 408–409, 410, 426–427,
439, 455, 469, 478
as public speaker, 47, 48–51, 67,
91, 113–115, 180, 263, 384
and race, 123, 211–212, 229,
250, 257, 288, 289, 349–351,
355–356, 413, 465
registered trademarks of, 405
and retirement, 473–474, 477
self-promotion of, 124, 141,
145, 162, 172, 186, 204, 229,
230, 375–377, 406
and sexual abuse, 3–5, 8–10,
14–15, 36–37, 65, 173, 253,
257, 269, 272, 330
and sexual identity, 320–332
and skin color, 25–26, 41, 60–
61, 107, 124, 163, 199
spending spree, 264
spirituality of, 193, 236, 239,
278, 282, 359–365, 368–369,
404
and Stedman. *see* Graham,
Stedman Sardar
success of, 74–75, 123, 139,
140, 141–142, 150, 193–194,
224, 250
talent of, 124, 140

as teenager, 31, 34–36, 44–58,
166, 251, 253, 254, 268–271,
269, 456
television debut (1974), 74–75
wealth of, 6, 224, 225, 227–228,
295, 296, 310, 334, 337, 339–
340, 358–359, 373, 385,
412–413, 440
and weight, 10, 93–94, 118,
121, 128, 131, 138, 173–174,
197, 200, 200–201, 242–243,
245, 257, 263, 275, 279, 294–
296, 344, 352, 357, 361, 475,
478
Winfrey's Barber Shop, 31, 48, 61,
78, 151, 164
Winfrey, Trenton, 37, 42, 269
Winfrey, Vernon, 154, 175, 176,
205, 464
book proposal of, 29–31, 39–40
and Oprah's birth, 24, 187
and Oprah's celebrity, 175
and Oprah's charities, 398
and Oprah's childhood, 28, 269,
377
and Oprah's gifts, 151, 155,
431–432
and Oprah's move to Baltimore,
78
and Oprah's teen years, 31, 37–
38, 39, 45, 47, 52, 61, 66, 269,
272
and Oprah's visits, 177, 183,
184
and Oprah's work, 140, 368,
477
and Stedman, 163
wedding to Zelma, 192
Winfrey, Zelma Myers, 28, 32, 39,
43, 52, 67, 151, 165, 192, 205

Winslet, Kate, 332
Winston and Strawn, 340
Wintour, Anna, 352
Wishner, Maynard, 219
WJZ-TV:
  Oprah's contract with, 77–78,
    115, 116–117
  Oprah's demotion at, 87–88,
    94–95
  Oprah's departure from, 116–
    117, 119
  Oprah's early work with, 90,
    442
  *People Are Talking* on, ix, 96–99,
    100–103, 110, 118
  Turner's position on, 83–88
WLAC, 72
WLS-TV, 1, 5–18, 226. *see also*
  *A.M. Chicago*
  Oprah's audition with, 115
*Woman's Day*, 141
women:
  African American, 117, 118,
    123–124, 135–136, 224,
    231
  film studios owned by, 231
  lipstick lesbians, 166
  subordination of, 108, 112, 114,
    231

*Women of Brewster Place, The* (TV
  film), 237–238
Wonder, Stevie, 433, 468
Woodard, Alfre, 435
World Summit for Children, 379
Wright, Barbara, 62, 69
Wright, Bob, 119
Wright, Rev. Jeremiah, 163
Wright, Willie, 27
WSB Atlanta, 77
WSMV, 76
WTVF-TV, 72, 79
WVOL, 54, 65, 72
Wyatt, Edward, 307

Y

Yang, Jerry, 385
Yardley, Jonathan, 303
Yates, Paul, 106, 117, 119
Young, Andrew, 442, 464
Young, Luther, 141
Yunus, Muhammad, 402

Z

Zehme, Bill, 126, 145, 146–147
Zorn, Eric, 286
Zukav, Gary, 359
Zwecker, Bill, 1, 132, 221, 340,
  406

# About the Author

KITTY KELLEY is the internationally acclaimed bestselling author of *Jackie Oh!*; *Elizabeth Taylor: The Last Star*; *His Way: The Unauthorized Biography of Frank Sinatra*; *Nancy Reagan: The Unauthorized Biography*; *The Royals*; and *The Family: The Real Story of the Bush Dynasty*. The last four titles were all #1 on the *New York Times* bestseller list. Kelley has been honored by her peers with such awards as the Outstanding Author Award from the American Society of Journalists and Authors for her "courageous writing on popular culture," the Philip M. Stern Award for her "outstanding service to writers and the writing profession," the Medal of Merit from the Lotos Club in New York City, and the 2005 PEN Oakland Literary Censorship Award. Her articles have appeared in *The New York Times*, *The Washington Post*, *The Wall Street Journal*, *Newsweek*, *People*, *Ladies' Home Journal*, *McCall's*, the *Los Angeles Times*, and the *Chicago Tribune*. She lives in Washington, D.C., with her physician husband, Jonathan Zucker.